Classic Virginia Rivers

A Paddler's Guide to Premier Whitewater
and Scenic Float Trips in the Old Dominion

by Ed Grove

Eddy Out Press

Second Printing, 1995

Printed and bound in the United States of America
by the George Banta Company

CIP 92-085570
ISBN 0-9634575-1-9

*Cover photo of world champion C-1 paddler Davey Hearn running
The Spout of Great Falls on the Potomac. Photo by Don Watkins.*

Eddy Out Press
Arlington, Virginia

Dedication

This book is dedicated to Whitney Shields, who sought excellence in everything he did. That commitment clearly showed in his incredible craftsmanship at woodworking and boundless enthusiasm for whitewater. Whitney especially loved the Great Falls of the Potomac and freely shared his knowledge of this very difficult rapids—which is now part of his legacy in this book. We will deeply miss him, but the spirit of his friendship and his pursuit of excellence will always be with us on the river.

C-2 team of Joe Jacobi (stern) and Scott Strausbaugh (bow) training on the foggy new Dickerson Powerplant slalom course before they won their 1992 Olympic Gold Medal at Seu d'Urgill, Spain.

Contents

Acknowledgments

This is not Ed Grove's book. It is a book of the paddling community. Without the help of the strong network of paddlers in the Canoe Cruisers Association, the Blue Ridge Voyagers, the Coastal Canoeists, and other clubs and individuals, this book of classic Virginia streams would not have been possible. Indeed, the book has been vastly enriched by committed paddlers who have unselfishly taken time to write about and review drafts of rivers special to them.

First, and most importantly, I must thank my wife Carol for her continued saintly patience while I worked on this book. Next, I would like to thank numerous fellow paddlers for drafting portions of the book. I am deeply indebted to Bill Kirby for parts of the South Fork of the Shenandoah, Passage Creek, Aquia Creek, Potomac, Rappahannock, Tye, Maury, and James. In addition, the following paddlers drafted other portions of the book: parts of the Rapidan—Bill Micks; Laurel Fork of the Potomac and Ogle—Ollie Fordham; Johns Creek—Tim "Catfish" Vermillion and Frank Miles; parts of the James—Hank Dial, Johnny Eanes, Jim Lowenthal, and Lou and Mike Hannon; parts of the Jackson—Bill Kirby and Dan Elasky; Gooney Run—Bob Walsh and Ed Evangelidi; Bull Run, Cub Run, and Potomac (Violettes Lock and Needles)—Ed Evangelidi; Whitetop Laurel and Little River (New tributary)—Doug Howell; Smith—Charles Ware; Big Reed Island Creek—Mac Whitaker and Ed Gertler; Elk and Chestnut Creeks—Tom Peddy; Russell Fork and Guest—Dale Adams; Upper Passage Creek—Ron Knipling; Little River (North Anna tributary) and Pamunkey—Chris Leonard; middle part of the Tye—Bob Taylor; middle part of the Rivanna—Larry Gross; South Anna—Greg Doggett; Moormans—Paul Marshall; Slate—Ben Johnson; Buffalo Creek—Glenn Rose; upper Rappahannock and lower Broad Run—Doug White; Great Dismal Swamp, Northwest, West Neck Creek, Blackwater, and Merchants Millpond—Lillie Gilbert; Assateague Island—John Williams; Roanoke/Staunton—Bo Tucker; Big Stony—Ron Mullet and Dave Brown; Rock Creek—Steve Ettinger and Ron Knipling; New—Tom Peddy, Mac Whitaker, and Bob Benner; Clinch—Terry Dougherty and John Butcher; Holston, Big Moccasin, and Copper Creek—Terry Dougherty; Rucker Run—Tom Saxton; Powell—Bill Reynolds and Dale Adams; upper Appomattox—Bob Taylor and Tom Saxton; Catawba, and Dunlap Creeks—Ed Gertler; Eastern Shore—Curtis Badger; Tearcoat Creek—Ron Knipling.

I would also like to thank the following individuals for their help in reviewing drafts and other aspects of this book: John Adamson, David B. Arbogest, Lee Baihly, Frank Baker, Gordon Bare, Rich Bowers, John Cantwell, JEB and Vinnie Carney, Sam Chambliss, Clark Childers, Roger Corbett, Stephen Ensign, Frank Fico, Greg Fischer, Les Fry, Scott and Glenn Gravatt, Tom Gray, Neil and Beth Groundwater, Grant Grove, Grayson Grove, Greg Grove, Mike Harvey, Jane Hitt, John Heerwald, Butch Hogan, Howard Kirkland, the Library of Congress (Patrick E. Dempsey and James A. Flatness), Bob List, Hunter Marrow, Louis Matacia, Millard Mathews, Tim McDonald, Ronnie Meadows, Holt Messerly, Denise Micks, Buddy Murray of the Sportsman's Inn, The Nature Conservancy, Eric Nelson, Bill Opengari, Brian Rigglemans, Nick Evans, Tom Rogers, Jeff and Christie Schmick, Dave Schmidt, Shenandoah River Outfitters (Nancy Goebel and Joe Sottosanti), Whitney Shields, Dallas Sizemore, Jim Snow, the Taylorstown General Store (Ralph Stanley and Elizabeth Callaham), Steve Thomas, Al and Esther Thompson, the United States Geological Survey (Bruce Hubbard, Merry Richardson, and Beatrice Beander), the Virginia Canals and Navigations Society (Bill Trout and Lynn and Myles Howlett), Bob Whaley, Jennie Wiley, Floyd Williams, and Jon Wright. For their help with the overview map of Virginia, I especially want to thank John McComb, Pope Barrow and Bill Millard. For the geomorphology and geology portion of the section on Virginia's Natural Landscape, I am indebted to Richard Dietrich and his book *Geology and Virginia*, published by the University Press of Virginia. Furthermore, I am grateful for the work done by Jessica Letteney of Menasha Ridge Press who put the manuscript on computer disk.

Finally, I am deeply indebted to Keith Fletcher, Chuck Hoffman, and Arlene Allegretto for working many long hours and nights to get this book ready for printing. Without their help, infinite patience, and understanding this book would not have been possible.

Hope you will enjoy some of these special rivers soon!

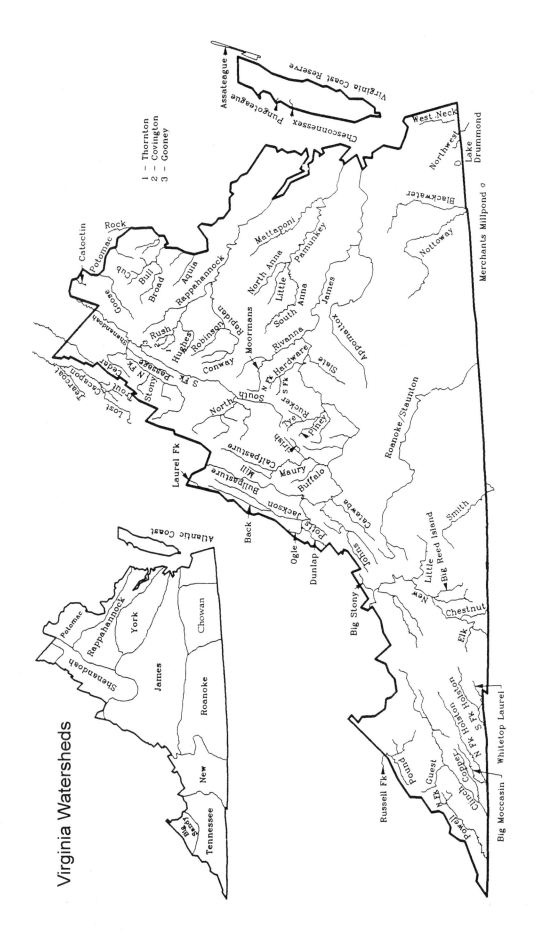

Virginia Watersheds

1 – Thornton
2 – Covington
3 – Gooney

How to Use This Guide

For each stream or other body of water in this guide you will find a general narrative description and at least one data list and map. (A Stream is flowing water and may be a river, a creek, or a branch or fork of a river.)

Narrative Stream Descriptions

These are intended to give you a feel for the stream and its surroundings, and are presented in general, nontechnical terms. Each narrative was written from the standpoint of the individual most likely to paddle it. For example, for beginner and float trips, minor gentle rapids and hazards are often described in detail so nervous novices can anticipate what is in store for them. Conversely, for expert runs, only the most prominent rapids are described since these paddlers do not need information on lesser rapids. Also, I must emphasize that the specifics of these narratives are not meant to be blindly followed by paddlers. River conditions can change tremendously because of high water levels or other natural phenomena. Consequently, nothing must take the place of each paddler's good judgement on the river. Not only are you responsible for your own safety, but you should extend this concern to fellow paddlers.

Stream Data

Each stream data list provides the necessary technical and quantitative information for each of the streams featured, as well as some additional descriptive data. Occasionally, certain facts will be covered in both the general description and in the data list for added emphasis. Below are fuller explanations of the categories found on the data lists.

Each list begins with the specific stream **Section** to which the data apply and the **Counties** in which the stream is located.

USGS Quads—The names of the 7.5 minute and 15 minute topographical maps are included here to give the paddler a reference for the contours of the land and river

involved. To order these maps, see the address list in "Where to Buy Maps" in the appendices.

Suitable for—While most streams described in this book are best suited to day cruising, some provide the opportunity for canoe camping.

Skill Level—For definitional purposes, *families* connote adults of various skill levels who want to take nonswimming adults or children in the canoe with them. We always assume that personal flotation devices (PFDs), e.g., life jackets, will be worn by all parties on moving water. We also assume that no passengers will be carried in whitewater.

Beginners and *novices* have a knowledge of strokes and self-rescue and can maneuver their boats more or less intuitively on still water (lakes and ponds). True *intermediates* meet all beginner qualifications, have a working knowledge of river dynamics, have some ability in rescuing others, and (for our purposes) are competent and at home on Class II-III whitewater. *Advanced paddlers* possess all the foregoing qualifications in addition to specialized rescue skills, and are competent and at home on Class III and IV whitewater. *Experts* are paddlers who easily exceed all the foregoing qualifications. Needless to say, these definitions could be refined or elaborated ad infinitum. They are not intended to be all-inclusive but rather to give you a reasonable idea of how to classify yourself and how experienced practitioners of the sport may tend to class you.

Months Runnable—The months given are based on the average rainfall for a year. Different sections of rivers may be runnable at different times. Some rivers are not necessarily runnable at a given time of year but are only runnable after a heavy rainfall or when a dam or powerhouse is releasing enough water.

Interest Highlights—This category includes special *scenery*, *wildlife*, *whitewater*, *local culture* and *industry*, *historical locations*, and unusual *geology*.

Scenery—Taste is relative, and I have given my best opinions.

Difficulty—The level of difficulty of a stream is given according to the Class I-VI International Scale of River Difficulty described at the end of this chapter. Such ratings are relative and pertain to the stream described under more or less ideal water levels and weather conditions. For streams with two International Scale ratings, the first represents the average level of difficulty of the entire run and the second (expressed parenthetically) represents the level of difficulty of the most difficult section or rapids on the run. Paddlers are cautioned that changes in water levels or weather conditions can alter the stated average difficulty rating appreciably.

Average Width—Rivers tend to start small and enlarge as they go toward their confluence with another river. Pools form in some places, and in other places the channel may constrict, accelerating the current. All of these factors affect the width and make the average width an approximate measure.

Velocity—This represents the average speed of the current in nonflood conditions. Velocity can vary incredibly from section to section on a given stream depending on the stream's width, volume, and gradient at any point along its length. Velocity is a partial indicator of how much reaction time you might have on a certain river. Paddlers are known to describe a high velocity stream as "coming at them pretty fast," meaning that the speed of the current does not allow them much time for decision and action. Rivers are described here as *slow*, *moderate*, and *fast*. *Slow* rivers have velocities of less than 2 miles per hour. *Moderate* velocities range between 2 and 4 miles per hour, and *fast* rivers are those that exceed 4 miles per hour.

Gradient—Gradient is expressed in feet per mile and refers to the steepness of the streambed over a certain distance. It is important to remember that gradient (or "drop" as paddlers refer to it) is an average figure and does not tell the paddler when or how the drop occurs. A stream that has a listed gradient of 25 feet per mile may drop gradually in 1- or 2-inch increments (like a long, rocky slide) for the course of a mile, or it may drop only slightly over the first nine-tenths of a mile and then suddenly drop 24 feet at one waterfall. As a general rule, gradient can be used as a rough indicator of level of difficulty for a given stream (i.e., the greater the gradient, the more difficult the stream). In practice, gradient is almost always considered in conjunction with other information.

Runnable Water Level (Minimum)—Minimum means the lowest possible level to paddle the rivers in this book. However, certain groups using these rivers may require a higher water level. Specifically, the minimum level for whitewater rivers generally applies to experienced solo canoeists in boats with no keel. Other types of paddlers in other craft would probably need higher levels, which would be acceptable minimums for them. Specifically, tandem novices in aluminum canoes with keels, folks paddling fiberglass decked boats (kayaks and C-1s), and rafters would often want these rivers 3 to 6 inches higher than the minimum in this book to have an enjoyable river experience.

On occasion, water levels are expressed in terms of volume as cubic feet per second (cfs). The use of cfs is doubly informative in that knowledge of volume at a gauge on one stream is often a prime indicator of the water levels of ungauged runnable streams in the same watershed, or for other sections of the gauged stream, either up- or downstream.

Runnable Water Level (Maximum)—In this book, "runnable" does not mean the same thing as "possible." The maximum runnable water level refers to the highest water level at which the stream can be safely run (this may vary for open and decked boats). With few exceptions (which can only be run when flooded), this categorically excludes rivers in flood.

Hazards—Hazards are dangers to navigation. Because of the continuous action of the water, many of these hazards may change and new ones might appear. Low-hanging trees, which can be a nuisance, may become deadfalls, blowdowns, and strainers. Human intervention creates hazards such as dams, low-water bridges, powerboat traffic, and fences (an especially dangerous "strainer"). Some watersheds have soils that cannot retain much water and the streams in that watershed may have a flash flood potential. Additionally, geologically young rivers, usually whitewater rivers, may have undercut rocks, keeper hydraulics, difficult rapids, and a scarcity of eddies.

Scouting—This guidebook attempts to list spots on specific rivers where scouting is required, i.e., recommended for the continuation of life and good health. Because many hazards may change in a short period of time, this guidebook also subscribes to the rule of thumb that you should scout any time you cannot see what is ahead (whitewater or flatwater and even on familiar rivers). That small, turning drop that you have run a thousand times may have a big log wedged across it today.

Portages—This book generally adheres to the rule that dams should be portaged. Additionally, portages are recommended for certain rapids and other dangers. The fact, however, that a portage is not specified at a certain spot or rapid does not necessarily mean that you should not portage. It is the mark of good paddlers to be able to make safe and independent decisions about their own ability for a given river or rapid.

Rescue Index—Many of the streams in this book run through wild areas. A sudden serious illness or injury could become an urgent problem if you can't get medical attention quickly. To give you an idea of how far you may be from help, a brief description is given of what may be expected. *Accessible* means that you might need up to an hour to secure assistance, but evacuation is not difficult. *Accessible but difficult* means that it might take up to 3 hours to get help, and evacuation may be difficult. *Remote* indicates it might take 3 to 6 hours to get help; and *extremely remote* means that you could expect to be 6 hours from help and would need expert assistance to get the party out.

Source of Additional Information—Various sources of additional information on water conditions are listed.

Access Points—River and shuttle miles are shown and access points rated.

Maps

The county and other maps in this guide are not intended to replace topographical quadrangles for terrain features. Rather, they are intended to illustrate the general configuration of the stream, its access points, and surrounding shuttle networks. **River sections are shown with a solid line and shuttle routes with a dotted line.**

Some of the maps are congested to the point that access letters may not be exactly where they should, but are only in the general vicinity. You may have to scout the area before launching. Approximate river miles and car shuttle miles from one access point to the next are provided with the maps. Additionally, the names of the 7.5 minute topographic quadrangles on which the streams appear are provided under Stream Data. To order these maps, see the address list in "Where to Buy Maps" in the appendices.

AWA Safety Code

All paddlers should read and follow the American Whitewater Affiliation's (AWA) safety code. It is perhaps the most useful overall safety guideline available.

I. Personal Preparedness and Responsibility
 1. **Be a competent swimmer** with the ability to handle yourself underwater.
 2. **Wear a lifejacket.** A snugly-fitting vest-type life preserver offers back and shoulder protection as well as the flotation needed to swim safely in whitewater.
 3. **Wear a solid, correctly-fitting helmet** when upsets are likely. This is essential in kayaks or covered canoes, and recommended for open canoeists using thigh straps and rafters running steep drops.
 4. **Do not boat out of control.** Your skills should be sufficient to stop or reach shore before reaching danger. Do not enter a rapid unless you are

reasonably sure that you can run it safely or swim it without injury.

 5. **Whitewater rivers contain many hazards** which are not always easily recognized. The following are the most frequent killers:

    A. **High Water.** The river's speed and power increase tremendously as the flow increases, raising the difficulty of most rapids. Rescue becomes progressively harder as the water rises, adding to the danger. Floating debris and strainers make even an easy rapid quite hazardous. It is often misleading to judge the river level at the put-in since a small rise in a wide, shallow place will be multiplied many times where the river narrows. Use reliable gauge information whenever possible, and be aware that sun on snowpack, hard rain, and upstream dam releases may greatly increase the flow.

    B. **Cold.** Cold drains your strength and robs you of the ability to make sound decisions on matters affecting your survival. Cold water immersion, because of the initial shock and the rapid heat loss which follows, is especially dangerous. Dress appropriately for bad weather or sudden immersion in the water. When the water temperature is less than 50°F, a wetsuit or drysuit is essential for protection if you swim. Next best is wool or pile clothing under a waterproof shell. In this case, you should also carry waterproof matches and a change of clothing in a waterproof bag. If, after prolonged exposure, a person experiences uncontrollable shaking, loss of coordination, or difficulty speaking, he or she is hypothermic and needs your assistance.

    C. **Strainers.** Brush, fallen trees, bridge pilings, undercut rocks or anything else which allows river current to sweep through can pin boats and boaters against the obstacle. Water pressure on anything trapped this way can be overwhelming. Rescue is often extremely difficult. Pinning may occur in fast current with little or no whitewater to warn of the danger.

    D. **Dams, Weirs, Ledges, Reversals, Holes, and Hydraulics.** When water drops over an obstacle, it curls back on itself forming a strong upstream current which may be capable of holding a boat or swimmer. Some holes make for excellent sport; others are proven killers. Paddlers who cannot recognize the differences should avoid all but the smallest holes. Hydraulics around man-made dams must be treated with utmost respect regardless of their height or the level of the river. Despite their seemingly benign appearance, they can create an almost escape-proof trap. The swimmer's only exit from the "drowning machine" is to dive beneath the surface when the downstream current is flowing beneath the reversal.

E. **Broaching.** When a boat is pushed sideways against a rock by strong current it may collapse and wrap. This is especially dangerous to kayak and decked canoe paddlers; these boats will collapse and the combination of indestructible hulls and tight outfitting may create a deadly trap. Even without entrapment, releasing pinned boats can be extremely time-consuming and dangerous. To avoid pinning, throw your weight downstream towards the rock. This allows the current to slide harmlessly underneath the hull.

6. **Boating alone is discouraged.** The minimum party is three people and two craft.

7. **Have a frank knowledge of your boating ability** and don't attempt rivers or rapids which lie beyond that ability.

A. **Develop the paddling skills and teamwork required to match the river you plan to boat.** Most good paddlers develop skills gradually, and attempts to advance too quickly will compromise your safety and enjoyment.

B. **Be in good physical and mental condition**, consistent with the difficulties which may be expected. Make adjustments for loss of skills due to age, health, and fitness. Any health limitations must be explained to your fellow paddlers prior to starting the trip.

8. **Be practiced in self-rescue**, including escape from an overturned craft. The Eskimo Roll is strongly recommended for decked boaters who run rapids of Class IV or greater, or who paddle in cold environmental conditions.

9. **Be trained in rescue skills, CPR, and first aid with special emphasis on recognizing and treating hypothermia.** It may save your friend's life.

10. **Carry equipment needed for unexpected emergencies**, including footwear which will protect your feet when walking out, a throw rope, knife, whistle and waterproof matches. If you wear eyeglasses, tie them on and carry a spare pair on long trips. Bring cloth repair tape on short runs and a full repair kit on isolated rivers. Do not wear bulky jackets, ponchos, heavy boots, or anything else which could reduce your ability to survive a swim.

11. Despite the mutually supportive group structure described in this code, **individual paddlers are ultimately responsible for their own safety and must assume sole responsibility for the following decisions:**

A. **The decision to participate on any trip.** This includes an evaluation of the expected difficulty of the rapids under the conditions existing at the time of the put in.

B. **The selection of appropriate equipment,** including a boat design suited to their skills and the appropriate rescue and survival gear.

C. **The decision to scout any rapid and to run or portage according to their best judgement.** Other members of the group may offer advice, but paddlers should resist pressure from anyone to paddle beyond their skills. It is also their responsibility to decide whether to pass up any walk out or take out opportunity.

D. **All trip participants should constantly evaluate their own and their group's safety,** voicing their concerns when appropriate and following what they believe to be the best course of action. Paddlers are encouraged to speak with anyone whose actions on the water are dangerous, whether they are a part of your group or not.

II. Boat and Equipment Preparedness

1. **Test new and different equipment** under familiar conditions before relying on it for difficult runs. This is especially true when adopting a new boat design or outfitting system. Low volume craft may present additional hazards to inexperienced or poorly conditioned paddlers.

2. **Be sure your boat and gear are in good repair** before starting any trip. The more isolated and difficult the run, the more rigorous this inspection should be.

3. **Install flotation bags** in non-inflatable craft, securely fixed in each end, designed to displace as much water as possible. Inflatable boats should have multiple air chambers and be test inflated before launching.

4. **Have strong, properly sized paddles or oars for controlling your craft.** Carry sufficient spares for the length and difficulty of the trip.

5. **Outfit your boat safely.** The ability to exit your boat quickly is an essential component of safety in rapids. It is your responsibility to see that there is absolutely nothing to cause entrapment when coming free of an upset craft. This includes:

A. Spray covers which won't release reliably or which release prematurely.

B. Boat outfitting too tight to allow a fast exit, especially in low volume kayaks or decked canoes. This includes low hung thwarts in canoes lacking adequate clearance for your feet and kayak footbraces which fail or allow your feet to become wedged under them.

C. Inadequately supported decks which collapse on a paddler's legs when a decked boat is pinned by water pressure. Inadequate clearance with the deck because of your size or build.

D. Loose ropes which cause entanglement. Beware of any length of loose line attached to a whitewater boat. All items must be tied tightly and excess line eliminated; painters, throw lines, and safety rope systems must be completely and effectively stored. Do not tow the end of a rope, as it can get caught in cracks between rocks.

6. Provide ropes which permit you to hold on to your craft so that it may be rescued. The following methods are recommended.

A. Kayaks and covered canoes should have grab loops of 1/4" plus rope or equivalent webbing sized to admit a normal sized hand. Stern painters are permissible if properly secured.

B. Open canoes should have securely anchored bow and stern painters consisting of 8–10 feet of one-quarter-inch-plus line. These must be secured in such a way that they are readily accessible but cannot come loose accidentally. Grab loops are acceptable but are more difficult to reach after an upset.

C. Rafts and dories may have taut perimeter lines threaded through the loops provided. Footholds should be designed so that a paddler's feet cannot be forced through them causing entrapment. Flip lines should be carefully and reliably stowed.

7. Know your craft's carrying capacity and how added loads affect boat handling in whitewater. Most rafts have a minimum crew size which can be added to on day trips or in easy rapids. Carrying more than two paddlers in an open canoe when running rapids is not recommended.

8. Car top racks must be strong and attach positively to the vehicle. Lash your boat to each crossbar, then tie the ends of the boats directly to the bumpers for added security. This arrangement should survive all but the most violent vehicle accidents.

III.Group Preparedness and Responsibility

1. Organization. A river trip should be regarded as a common adventure by all participants, except on instructional or commercially guided trips as defined below. Participants share the responsibility for the conduct of the trip, and each participant is individually responsible for judging his or her own capabilities and for his or her own safety as the trip progresses. Participants are encouraged (but are not obligated) to offer advice and guidance for the independent consideration and judgement of others.

2. River Conditions. The group should have a reasonable knowledge of the difficulty of the run. Participants should evaluate this information and adjust their plans accordingly. If the run is exploratory or no one is familiar with the river, maps and guidebooks, if available, should be examined. The group should secure accurate flow information; the more difficult the run, the more important this will be. Be aware of possible changes in river level and how this will affect the difficulty of the run. If the trip involves tidal stretches, secure appropriate information on tides.

3. Group equipment should be suited to the difficulty of the river. The group should always have a throw line available, and one line per boat is recommended on difficult runs. The list may include carabineers, prussick loops, first aid kit, flashlight, folding saw, fire starter, guidebooks, maps, food, extra clothing, and any other rescue or survival items suggested by conditions. Each item is not required on every run, and this list is not meant to be a substitute for good judgement.

4. Keep the group compact, but maintain sufficient spacing to avoid collisions. If the group is large, consider dividing into smaller groups or using the "Buddy System" as an additional safeguard. Space yourselves closely enough to permit good communication, but not so close as to interfere with one another in rapids.

A. The lead paddler sets the pace. When in front, do not get in over your head. Never run drops when you cannot see a clear route to the bottom or, for advanced paddlers, a sure route to the next eddy. When in doubt, stop and scout.

B. Keep track of all group members. Each boat keeps the one behind it in sight, stopping if necessary. Know how many people are in your group and take head counts regularly. No one should paddle ahead or walk out without first informing the group. Weak paddlers should stay at the center of a group and not allow themselves to lag behind. If the group is large and contains a wide range of abilities, a designated "Sweep Boat" should bring up the rear.

C. **Courtesy.** On heavily used rivers, do not cut in front of a boater running a drop. Always look upstream before leaving eddies to run or play. Never enter a crowded drop or eddy when no room for you exists. Passing other groups in a rapid may be hazardous; it's often safer to wait upstream until the group ahead has passed.

5. **Float plan. If the trip is into a wilderness area or for an extended period, plans should be filed with a responsible person who will contact the authorities if you are overdue.** It may be wise to establish checkpoints along the way where civilization could be contacted if necessary. Knowing the location of possible help and preplanning escape routes can speed rescue.

6. **Drugs. The use of alcohol or mind altering drugs before or during river trips is not recommended.** It dulls reflexes, reduces decision making ability, and may interfere with important survival reflexes.

7. **Instructional or Commercially Guided Trips.** In contrast to the common adventure trip format, in these trip formats a boating instructor or commercial guide assumes some of the responsibilities normally exercised by the group as a whole, as appropriate under the circumstances. These formats recognize that instructional or commercially guided trips may involve participants who lack significant experience in whitewater. However, as a participant acquires experience in whitewater, he or she takes on increasing responsibility for his or her own safety, in accordance with what he or she knows or should know as a result of that increased experience. Also, as in all trip formats, every participant must realize and assume the risks associated with the serious hazards of whitewater rivers. It is advisable for instructors and commercial guides to acquire trip or personal liability insurance.

A. An "instructional trip" is characterized by a clear teacher/pupil relationship, where the primary purpose of the trip is to teach boating skills, and which is conducted for a fee.

B. A "commercially guided trip" is characterized by a licensed professional guide conducting trips for a fee.

IV. Guidelines for River Rescue

1. **Recover from an upset with an eskimo roll whenever possible.** Evacuate your boat immediately if there is imminent danger of being trapped against rocks, brush, or any other kind of strainer.

2. **If you swim, hold on to your boat.** It has much flotation and is easy for rescuers to spot. Get to the upstream end so that you cannot be crushed between a rock and your boat by the force of the current. Persons with good balance may be able to climb on top of a swamped kayak or flipped raft and paddle to shore.

3. **Release your craft if this will improve your chances, especially if the water is cold or dangerous rapids lie ahead.** Actively attempt self-rescue whenever possible by swimming for safety. Be prepared to assist others who may come to your aid.

A. **When swimming in shallow or obstructed rapids, lie on your back with feet held high and pointed downstream. Do not attempt to stand in fast moving water;** if your foot wedges on the bottom, fast water will push you under and keep you there. Get to slow or very shallow water before attempting to stand or walk. Look ahead! Avoid possible pinning situations including undercut rocks, strainers, downed trees, holes, and other dangers by swimming away from them.

B. **If the rapids are deep and powerful, roll over onto your stomach and swim aggressively for shore.** Watch for eddies and slackwater and use them to get out of the current. Strong swimmers can effect a powerful upstream ferry and get to shore fast. If the shores are obstructed with strainers or undercut rocks, however, it is safer to "ride the rapid out" until a safer escape can be found.

4. **If others spill and swim, go after the boaters first.** Rescue boats and equipment only if this can be done safely. While participants are encouraged (but not obliged) to assist one another to the best of their ability, they should do so only if they can, in their judgement, do so safely. The first duty of a rescuer is not to compound the problem by becoming another victim.

5. **The use of rescue lines requires training; uninformed use may cause injury.** Never tie yourself into either end of a line without a reliable quick-release system. Have a knife handy to deal with unexpected entanglement. Learn to place set lines effectively, to throw accurately, to belay effectively, and to properly handle a rope thrown to you.

6. **When reviving or rescuing a drowning victim, be aware that cold water may greatly extend survival time underwater.** Victims of hypothermia may have depressed vital signs so they look and feel dead. Don't give up; continue CPR for as long as possible without compromising safety.

V. Universal River Signals

Stop: Potential hazard ahead. Wait for "all clear" signal before proceeding, or scout ahead. Form a horizontal bar with your outstretched arms. Those seeing the signal should pass it back to others in the party.

Help/Emergency: Assist the signaller as quickly as possible. Give three long blasts on a police whistle while waving a paddle, helmet, or life vest over your head. If a whistle is not available, use the visual signal alone. A whistle is best carried on a lanyard attached to your life vest.

All Clear: Come ahead (in the absence of other directions, proceed down the center). Form a vertical bar with your paddle or one arm held high above your head. Paddle blade should be turned flat for maximum visibility. To signal direction or a preferred course through a rapid around an obstruction, lower the previously vertical "all clear" by 45 degrees toward the side of the river with the preferred route. Never point toward the obstacle you wish to avoid.

VI. International Scale of River Difficulty

This is the American version of a rating system used to compare river difficulty throughout the world. This system is not exact; rivers do not always fit easily into one category, and regional or individual interpretations may cause misunderstanding. It is no substitute for a guidebook or accurate first-hand descriptions of a run. Paddlers attempting difficult runs in an unfamiliar area should act cautiously until they get a feel for the way the scale is interpreted locally. River difficulty may change each year due to fluctuations in water level, downed trees, geological disturbances, or bad weather. Stay alert for unexpected problems!

As river difficulty increases, the danger to swimming paddlers becomes more severe. As rapids become longer and more continuous, the challenge increases. There is a difference between running an occasional Class IV rapid and dealing with an entire river of this category. Allow an extra margin of safety between skills and river ratings when the water is cold or if the river itself is remote and inaccessible.

The Six Classes of Whitewater:

Class I: Easy. Fast moving water with riffles and small waves. Few obstructions, all obvious and easily missed with little training. Risk to swimmers is slight; self-rescue is easy.

Universal River Signals

Stop

Help/Emergency

All Clear

Class II: Novice. Straightforward rapids with wide, clear channels which are evident without scouting. Occasional maneuvering may be required, but rocks and medium sized waves are easily missed by trained paddlers. Swimmers are seldom injured and group assistance, while helpful, is seldom needed.

Class III: Intermediate. Rapids with moderate, irregular waves which may be difficult to avoid and which can swamp an open canoe. Complex maneuvers in fast current and good boat control in tight passages or around ledges are often required;

large waves or strainers may be present but are easily avoided. Strong eddies and powerful current effects can be found, particularly on large volume rivers. Scouting is advisable for inexperienced parties. Injuries while swimming are rare; self-rescue is usually easy but group assistance may be required to avoid long swims.

Class IV: Advanced. Intense, powerful but predictable rapids requiring precise boat handling in turbulent water. Depending on the character of the river, it may feature large, unavoidable waves and holes or constricted passages demanding fast maneuvers under pressure. A fast, reliable eddy turn may be needed to initiate maneuvers, scout rapids, or rest. Rapids may require "must" moves above dangerous hazards. Scouting is necessary the first time down. Risk of injury to swimmers is moderate to high, and water conditions may make self-rescue difficult. Group assistance for rescue is often essential but requires practiced skills. A strong eskimo roll is highly recommended.

Class V: Expert. Extremely long, obstructed, or very violent rapids which expose a paddler to above average endangerment. Drops may contain large, unavoidable waves and holes or steep, congested chutes with complex, demanding routes. Rapids may continue for long distances between pools, demanding a high level of fitness. What eddies exist may be small, turbulent, or difficult to reach. At the high end of the scale, several of these factors may be combined. Scouting is mandatory but often difficult. Swims are dangerous, and rescue is difficult even for experts. A very reliable eskimo roll, proper equipment, extensive experience, and practiced rescue skills are essential for survival.

Class VI: Extreme. One grade more difficult than Class V. These runs often exemplify the extremes of difficulty, unpredictability and danger. The consequences of errors are very severe and rescue may be impossible. For teams of experts only, at favorable water levels, after close personal inspection, and taking all precautions. This class does not represent drops thought to be unrunnable but may include rapids which are only occasionally run.

The Three Classes of Flatwater

Class A: Pools, lakes, or rivers with water velocity of less than 2 miles per hour.

Class B: Streams or rivers with water velocity of 2 to 4 miles per hour.

Class C: Streams or rivers with water velocity of over 4 miles per hour.

A Word About Gauges

There are two types of gauges used for paddling. The first is a scale (in feet) developed by whitewater pioneer Randy Carter in Virginia, and other boaters, which is painted on bridge abutments or prominent rocks in rivers. The minimum for these paddling gauges is 0, which means that the water is 3 to 4 inches deep at the most shallow and scrapey parts of the river or just enough to float the tender bottom of your boat at these places. The 0 has been determined by hard paddler experience on each river.

The second type of gauge is made by the U.S. Geologic Survey and placed at numerous bridge abutments and gauging stations throughout the state. This is a professional gauge in tenths of feet with different levels for different gauging points. Paddlers have also had to interpret these gauges by hard experience to determine paddling 0.

Often you can find a paddler's gauge and a USGS gauge very close together. The correlation between these two gauges gives a better idea how they are used. For example, for the Rappahannock River above Fredericksburg, 2.4 feet on the USGS Fredericksburg gauge is equal to 0 on the paddler's gauge painted on the Route 1 bridge crossing the Rappahannock in Fredericksburg.

Disclaimer

I want to conclude this introduction first by stating again that this guide cannot get you safely down the river. You alone are responsible for your safety, and nothing can take the place of your good judgement. If you follow practices outlined by the AWA Safety Code and look after fellow companions on the river, you should have a safe and enjoyable trip on these classic Virginia rivers.

Virginia's Natural Landscape

Virginia is an incredibly beautiful state. Its rivers and streams are special wilderness highways from which one can view the rich variety of this beauty, which extends from the mountains in the far west to the swamps in the southeast.

In the far western part of Virginia, near Elkhorn City, Kentucky, lies Breaks Interstate Park. Here the Russell Fork River (a tributary of the Levisa Fork of the Big Sandy River) has carved a gorge nearly 5 miles long and 1,000 feet deep. This is a section of expert whitewater that offers the bonus of outstanding scenery.

In the west one also finds the scenic Blue Ridge Mountains, a part of which are in Shenandoah National Park. Numerous streams tumble out of these mountains as incredible waterfalls and cascades to be viewed by hikers and change to outstanding whitewater rivers when the gradient slackens so that mortal paddlers can attempt them. An example is Crabtree Falls in western Nelson County. This series of cascades and falls drops about 1,000 feet to the South Fork of the Tye River. Soon below these falls, the South Fork and the North Fork of the Tye combine to form one of the premier whitewater runs in Virginia.

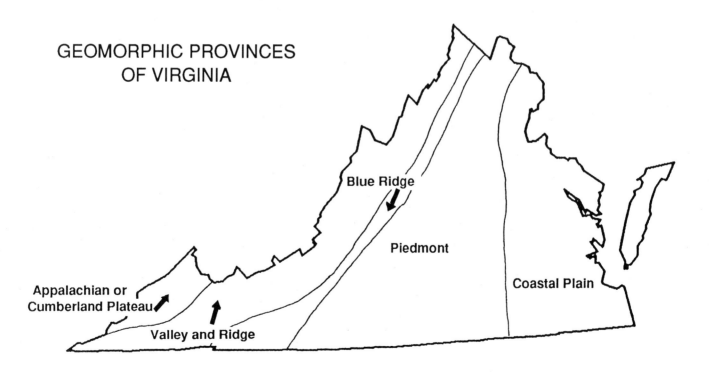

GEOMORPHIC PROVINCES
OF VIRGINIA

Blue Ridge

Piedmont

Coastal Plain

Appalachian or
Cumberland Plateau

Valley and Ridge

There are numerous caves in western Virginia, and rivers often flow close to them. For example, gentle Cedar Creek in northern Virginia has banks and islands of travertine near the end of one section; just a few miles downstream is historic Panther Cave and a nearby cavelike arch you can paddle a boat under. Much farther southwest (near the town of Covington), Potts Creek and Dunlap Creek also pass through several interesting limestone formations. For those interested in side trips to classic commercial caverns, the North Fork of the Shenandoah flows close to Shenandoah Caverns, the South Fork of the Shenandoah flows near Luray Caverns, and the South River north of Waynesboro passes Grand Caverns.

Virginia streams highlight other geologic wonders. Southwest of Lexington is Natural Bridge—an internationally famous limestone arch 150 feet high and 90 feet wide. Route 11 runs on top of Natural Bridge and a creek flows beneath it. The Natural Chimneys, 15 miles north of Staunton, are striking 100-foot-high rock towers rising perpendicularly from the floodplain of the North River just below its beautiful and challenging gorge. Similarly spectacular rock towers are also found on the New River near Eggleston and on the North Fork of the Shenandoah at Brocks Gap (Chimney Rock).

A quite different example of geomorphic beauty is shown on the North and South Forks of the Shenandoah. These rivers display some of the finest meanders in the world. In particular, the North Fork between the towns of Edinburg and Strasburg meanders 50 miles over a straight line distance of only 15 miles!

The eastern swamps also have interesting geomorphic features. For example, Lake Drummond in the Great Dismal Swamp is one of only two natural lakes in Virginia (the other is Mountain Lake in Giles County). Though it covers 3,000 acres and is 3 miles across, Lake Drummond is only 6 feet at its deepest point. Dark, acidic water and beds of peat make this an unusual ecosystem (one that is rare and threatened by coastal development) in the mid-Atlantic states.

Geomorphology and Geology

The landscape can be divided into geomorphic or physiographic provinces, each having its own set of landforms (or surface relief) and vegetation. The United States contains about 30 such provinces. The five in Virginia are, from east to west, the Coastal Plain, the Piedmont, the Blue Ridge, the Valley and Ridge, and the Appalachian or Cumberland Plateau.

Coastal Plain

The Coastal Plain province of Virginia has low topographic relief and a maximum elevation of 300 feet above sea level. The land slopes east and continues beneath the Atlantic Ocean to form the continental shelf, which extends 200 miles offshore.

The bedrock of the Coastal Plain is partially consolidated sedimentary rocks. These rocks are composed primarily of Cretaceous, Eocene, and Miocene marine sand, gravels, and clays. In some places the rocks are overlain by Pleistocene, Recent, and even Pliocene sand and gravel, which formed marine terraces when the ocean level was higher.

The onshore part of the Coastal Plain shows characteristics of emergence (such as shell beds) and submergence (drowned valleys). There are swamps, of which the Great Dismal Swamp is the largest. Finally, the coastline is cut deeply by branching bays and estuaries. Natural harbors, sandy beaches, and barrier beaches are common and 100-foot-high bluffs border the estuaries in places.

Many Coastal Plain streams are tidal as far west as the fall line. This line is so named because it is where many Virginia streams develop rapids or falls as they drop off the relatively harder metamorphic rocks of the Piedmont onto the softer sedimentary rocks of the Coastal Plain. Prime examples are the 77-foot Great Falls of the Potomac River (just above the District of Columbia); the rapids (and dam) dropping 40- to 50-feet on the Rappahannock River (near Fredericksburg); and the rapids descending a good 80 feet on the James River (in the heart of Richmond).

Piedmont

Just west of the Coastal Plain is the Piedmont province—a rolling landscape of gentle slopes where valleys and hills merge with relatively little break in slope. The province is often characterized as a peneplain—a low plateau that resulted from erosion. In Virginia this province is 30 miles wide at the Maryland border and 160 miles wide at the North Carolina border. It slopes eastward from an elevation of just over 1,000 feet in the west to 300 feet in the east at the fall line.

The Piedmont is mostly underlain by older Precambrian and Paleozoic metamorphic and igneous rocks as well as by relatively large areas of younger Mesozoic sedimentary and igneous rocks. Prolonged weathering has created soils 150 feet deep in places. Because much of the Piedmont is covered by deep soil, the major streams show little control by the underlying bedrock and generally flow southeast. However, there are important exceptions that reflect the underlying geology. For example, the James River between

Lynchburg and Scottsville flows northeast for 45 miles in a belt underlain by soft marble. The Blue Ridge foothills mark the transition between the Piedmont province and the Blue Ridge province to the west.

Blue Ridge

The Blue Ridge province is long and narrow in Virginia and consists of two parts—one northeast and the other southwest of the Roanoke River. Northeast of the Roanoke River this province is an irregular mountain chain, ranging from a single ridge less than 2 miles wide to a complex group of closely spaced ridges a dozen miles wide. This area is rugged with many rock exposures and slopes covered with rubble (talus). Southwest of the Roanoke River, the Blue Ridge province is a mature eroded surface up to 70 miles wide.

Elevations in the Blue Ridge province generally range between 2,300 and 3,200 feet. Virginia's highest mountain, Mount Rogers (5,719 feet), is in this province. Streams draining this upland are being rejuvenated today—perhaps from a recent geologic uplift.

The two parts of the Blue Ridge province drain differently. The ridges northeast of the Roanoke River are drained by high gradient streams ultimately reaching the Atlantic. The area southwest of the Roanoke River is drained by low-gradient streams flowing to the Gulf of Mexico—mainly from the New and Holston Rivers.

The Blue Ridge bedrock varies. In the east, late Precambrian volcanics dominate in some places, while diverse Precambrian and Paleozoic metamorphic and intrusive igneous rocks occur elsewhere. The western boundary of the Blue Ridge province consists of ancient Precambrian and Cambrian rocks—conglomerate, sandstone, siltstone, and orthoquartzite—which form steep ridges covered with talus. Directly west of these ridges, younger Cambrian shale and dolomite underlie a broad, low-relief area used for farmland. The base of the steep ridges marks the boundary between the Blue Ridge province and the Valley and Ridge province to the west.

Valley and Ridge

The aptly named Valley and Ridge province is also divided in two: a northeastern part draining into the Atlantic and a southwestern part draining into the Gulf of Mexico. The Atlantic portion consists of a large valley on the east (including the historic Shenandoah Valley) and a series of parallel, narrower valleys and ridges in the west. The Gulf of Mexico portion has a broad, nearly ridgeless area near its eastern boundary and several narrower valleys and ridges to the west. However, the southwestern valleys are more than 1,000 feet higher than the northeastern valleys of this province. Rocks in the Valley and Ridge province are of Cambrian through Mississippian age. "Folded Appalachians" is the structural term describing this province. Many of the ridges are composed of Silurian sandstone, while a few are Mississippian sandstone, siltstone, and shale. Most valleys are less resistant shales and carbonate (limestone) rocks.

Only a few master streams cut across the rocks in the Valley and Ridge province. Most streams flow either in the main valleys or perpendicular to them. This forms a rectilinear pattern called trellis drainage. The boundary between the Valley and Ridge province and the Appalachian province to the west is quite distinct. Folded rocks and linear ridges in the east give way to flat-lying strata and irregularly shaped hills and valleys in the west.

Appalachian Province or Cumberland Plateau

In Virginia the Appalachian province (or Cumberland Plateau) occurs mainly in the southwestern counties of Buchanan, Dickenson, and Wise. This province is flat-lying Mississippian and Pennsylvanian sedimentary rocks and is drained by the Tennessee River which flows into the Gulf of Mexico. The overall drainage pattern is highly irregular and dendritic (like tree branches).

Watersheds

Crossing these five geomorphic (or physiographic) provinces are 11 watersheds. This book describes the classic rivers in each watershed. From east to west these watersheds are: the Atlantic Coast and Great Dismal Swamp, the Chowan River, the York River, the Rappahannock River, the Potomac River, the Shenandoah River, the James River, the Roanoke River, the New River, the Big Sandy River, and the Tennessee River. Eight of these watersheds drain into the Atlantic. The Roanoke and Chowan Rivers (as well as most of the Great Dismal Swamp) drain into Albemarle Sound in northern North Carolina. Of the other five Atlantic watersheds, the Shenandoah flows into the Potomac while the Potomac, Rappahannock, York, and James successively empty into the central and southern reaches of Chesapeake Bay. The last three watersheds (New, Big Sandy, and Tennessee) ultimately empty into the Gulf of Mexico. The map showing these watersheds and their classic rivers is on page viii earlier in this book.

Canals and Batteaux

Virginia is rich in the history of canals and river navigation systems. The most important 19th century inland waterways of Virginia are the 184-mile Chesapeake and Ohio Canal on the Potomac; the Shenandoah and the Goose Creek navigation systems which fed the Potomac; the Rappahannock navigation system; the 197-mile James River and Kanawha Canal; the North (Maury) River, Rivanna River, Slate River, and Appomattox navigation systems which fed the James; the Roanoke/Staunton River navigation system; the Smith and Dan River navigation system, which fed the Roanoke; the Dismal Swamp Canal; and the New River navigation system, which fed the Kanawha and Ohio Rivers.

To carry cargo on most of these inland waterways, a unique boat was developed. This was the batteau (plural batteaux) from the French word for boat, *bateau*. These river boats were 60 feet long by 8 feet wide and had a shallow draft enabling them to navigate the Virginia river systems. In recognition of the historic importance of these craft, a Second Batteau Era has begun on Virginia's rivers. The Virginia Canals and Navigations Society has spearheaded this effort.

Actually, the exploration of Virginia's rivers and streams for signs of batteau navigation has just begun. Indeed, most of Virginia's rivers and streams have not been carefully investigated at low water for wing dams and sluices used by batteaux, to say nothing of early boat wrecks. Paddlers who find new evidence of batteau navigation are encouraged to contact Dr. William E. Trout, III, President of the American Canal Society, at 35 Towana Road, Richmond, VA 23226 (phone 804-288-1334), or Mrs. Lynn Howlett, of the Virginia Canals and Navigations Society, at 6826 Rosemont Drive, McLean, VA 22101 (phone 703-356-4027).

The batteau Minnie Lee built and captained by Joe Ayers running Balcony Falls on the upper James River.

Atlantic Coast and Great Dismal Swamp

Assateague Island and Chincoteague Bay

Assateague Island is a barrier reef island built by sand on the Atlantic Coast. This 33-mile-long island straddles the Maryland-Virginia border and provides a unique opportunity for canoeing, backpacking, and camping. On the ocean side is a magnificent wide beach where waves of the Atlantic strike the shore and shift its sands. Behind the beach are the dunes, shaped more by wind than water, which form the backbone of the barrier reef. Here one finds grasses and even butterflies clinging to existence. West of the dunes are swamplands of marsh grasses and scrubby trees broken only by hummocks supporting loblolly pine groves.

Separating Assateague Island from the mainland is Chincoteague Bay, a shallow and beautiful body of water which is protected from the ocean's wildness and provides habitat for waterfowl and shellfish. Chincoteague Island is in the southern part of Chincoteague Bay between Assateague Island and the mainland.

Incidentally, the name Assateague means "a running stream between." It comes from the Gingoteague Indians who lived in this area until the late 1600s when they were displaced by Europeans. The name Chincoteague originated with this tribe and means "beautiful land across the waters."

All 19,000 acres of Assateague Island are parkland used for recreation and wildlife refuge purposes. A 2-mile-long northern strip of the island is Assateague State Park, managed by the Maryland Department of Natural Resources. The long middle part of the island is Assateague Island National Seashore, under the jurisdiction of the National Park Service (NPS). The southern remainder of the island is Chincoteague National Wildlife Refuge, managed by the U.S. Fish and Wildlife Service. These three different government agencies work together to protect this special island.

As a magnificent barrier reef system, Assateague Island is a place of wonder and joy for all—especially children. In recognition of this reality, the National Park Service has opened a canoe trail in the protected shallow waters of Chincoteague Bay behind the island. The 28-mile trail extends from Old Ferry Landing on the northern Maryland end of the island to Toms Cove Visitor Center at the southern Virginia end.

There are six campsites on the northern Maryland half of Assateague Island. Four are bayside campsites for both canoe and backpack campers; the remaining two are oceanside campsites for backpackers only. The four bay canoe/backpack campsites are open between February 1 and November 1, while the two ocean backpack campsites are open the entire year. Camping and canoeing are free, and there currently is no limit to the number of persons allowed to camp at the four bay campsites. However, camping is by permit only and several restrictions apply. Most importantly, canoeists can only camp at the four sites on the 13 miles of the canoe trail in Maryland; canoe camping is prohibited elsewhere, especially on the remaining 15 miles of the canoe trail in Virginia, which runs through a wildlife preserve. Also, no pets are allowed. It is

Chincoteague ponies on Assateague Island.

recommended that your trip start from Old Ferry Landing on the Maryland side. From here the colorful names (distances in parentheses) of the four bay campsites to the south are: Tingles Island (2 miles), Pine Tree (5 miles), Jims Gut (7 miles), and Pope Bay (13 miles). Most people who use the canoe trail will put in and take out at Old Ferry Landing, canoeing as far down the bay as their inclinations take them. Families with young children and carefully supervised scout troops will probably want to use the two closest sites—Tingles Island and Pine Tree.

The four campsites are marked with NPS signs. The three most northern sites are located in loblolly pine groves on hillocks above the swamp. The trees on the northern three sites not only provide shade from the sun but also give some measure of protection to tents from strong winds driven by storms that strike the island. Pope Bay, the southernmost site, is in a more open setting.

You will have to carry your gear about 100 yards from your canoe to these campsites which are provided with picnic tables, fire rings, and chemical toilets. However, they do not have water. Accordingly, all canoeists must bring an ample supply of potable water. Also, pull your canoes well up on shore—tides and storms could set them aimlessly adrift.

If you leave from Virginia, you must launch from Toms Cove and face a long 15-mile paddle north to reach the nearest campsite at Pope Bay. This is not recommended unless you are an experienced hard core flatwater paddler and there is no wind. Also, Virginia and Maryland paddlers must leave for Pope Bay by noon, and Maryland paddlers must leave for the other three sites by 5 p.m. During early spring and late fall, you may have to get your permit in mainland Maryland from the NPS Visitor Center for Assateague Island National Seashore on Route 611 before crossing Chincoteague Bay to Assateague Island. Between early spring and late fall you should cross over to Assateague Island, drive south 2 miles through Assateague State Park, and get your permit at the Ranger Station just after entering Assateague Island National Seashore. In Virginia, you can get your permit at the NPS Toms Cove Visitor Center on Assateague Island after crossing Chincoteague Island via Route 175. Besides issuing a camping permit, park rangers at these places will provide other useful information and an overnight parking permit for your car.

Probably the best time to take a trip is in April or the last half of October. During these periods the beaches are less heavily populated by dune buggies as well as people. More importantly, the mosquitoes at the bayside campsites are less numerous, and you do not have oppressive heat or humidity.

Enough of these logistical preliminaries. Old Ferry Landing is a good launch point with its ample parking, good beach, and a small dock for unloading canoes. The canoe trail is somewhat well marked for the 13 miles from Old Ferry Landing to the Pope Bay campsite, and there are signs numbered 1 through 19 that mark the canoe trail and campsites. Tingles Island is between canoe markers 4 and 5; Pine Tree is between markers 8 and 9; Jims Gut is just before you get to marker 13; and Pope Bay is after you pass marker 19 and paddle up an inlet. You should get a detailed map that shows the location of these sites from the ranger station. As a contingency in case the ranger station is out of detailed maps, it might be wise to get the USGS Tingle Island 7.5 minute series topographical map beforehand and plot the Tingles Island camp on it at the ranger station before you start.

Be sure to allow plenty of time to get to your campsite. First, unless you are used to navigating among islands and inlets that are indistinct low shapes on the horizon, you could get disoriented. A compass will help. Also, the canoe trail markers are spaced rather far apart, and it is sometimes hard to see them. Further, one or more of these markers may be knocked over, which could add to your difficulty.

However, the most important reason for planning conservatively and earmarking extra time is summed up in one word—wind! Carefully check the weather forecast and call the park headquarters at Assateague Island National Seashore just before you leave on your trip. The National Park Service will cancel paddling if there are small craft advisories. It also helps to have boats with keels. You need to exercise particular care if the wind is blowing toward the west—away from the island and out into Chincoteague Bay. If the wind is especially heavy and you have novice or young boaters, you may have to walk your boats along the shallows near the shore and inlets of Assateague Island to reach your destination. I speak from personal experience, having had to shepherd some novice scouts along the shore on a very windy day—it took us 4 hours to go 2 miles! For safety's sake, please abide by the specific camping plans you make with the park rangers when you get your permit, and don't hesitate to sit tight at your campsite if the water or wind conditions are really adverse. There are widely spaced emergency phones along the sandy road on the ocean side of Assateague, and you can use this road to walk back to the ranger station if necessary.

The geographic landmarks as you go south indicate the colorful history of this area. First you pass Little Egging Beach, Great Egging Beach, and Lumber Marsh on the way to Tingles Island campsite. Between Pine Tree and Jims Gut campsites there is Sugar Point and Fox Hill Point.

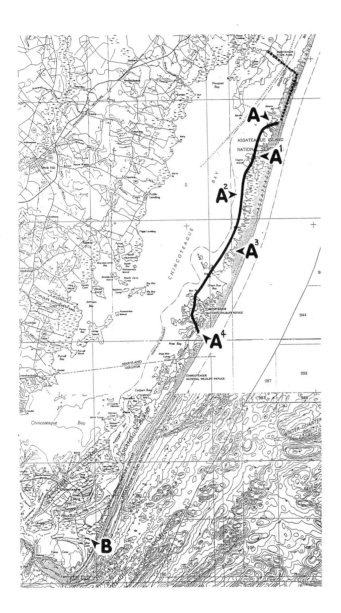

Beyond Jims Gut you pass Lone Pond, Pirates Island, and Rum Harbor Marsh before reaching the Pope Bay campsite.

Once launched you will find this to be an incredible place. As you head out into Chincoteague Bay the industrial world fades into insignificance. Here is wide open sky and water. The signs marking the canoe trail every mile or so are very small amidst all this spaciousness. Soon you are far from shore, perhaps concerned about being in a frail canoe in the midst of the enormous bay. On some days, if the atmospheric conditions are right, the sound of surf from the beach a mile or 2 away to the east may sound ominously loud. But, dip your paddle into the water, and you may find it to be only a few inches deep. In fact, getting stuck in the shallows at low tide may be more of a concern than waves or depths. Note that the times for tides on the ocean differ from those in the bay and that the ranger station only posts ocean tides. For example, on one trip we found Atlantic high tides posted in the ranger station and had low tide on the bay.

This is a great trip for prepared families with children, particularly those with beachcomber instincts. The observant child may notice shells in the shallow bay waters under the canoe. The bay is brackish water, generally unpolluted, sandy bottomed, and protected from commercial fishermen. In the vicinity of the campsites, some parts of the bottom are almost paved with clams. Armed with a clam rake and an instruction pamphlet from park headquarters, you may try clamming. If the rake scrapes anything, it is a clam; there are no rocks at Assateague. You can also try crabbing at the Old Ferry Landing in Maryland or near the Toms Cove NPS Visitor Center in Virginia. Finally, remember that the famous Chincoteague oysters come from this area.

The wildlife is also compelling. It is rare to go more than a mile without seeing the famous Chincoteague ponies that make their homes on Assateague Island. Their origins are somewhat unclear. One theory is that they descended from ponies that came ashore following the wreck of a Spanish galleon in the 16th century. Other historians believe these ponies are the feral descendants of domesticated stock that grazed on Assateague in the 17th century. Regardless of their origin, these small sturdy ponies are handsome animals—solid-colored bays, blacks, and sorrels with long shaggy hair. Well adapted to their harsh environment, they feed on marsh grasses, bayberry leaves, and occasionally poison ivy while drinking water from natural freshwater ponds. However, these ponies are wild and should be viewed from a safe distance as there have been instances of their biting and kicking. The Park

Service instructs that under no circumstances should you feed or pet the ponies.

There are two herds of these ponies on Assateague Island. They are separated by a fence at the Maryland-Virginia boundary. The Maryland herd is managed by the National Park Service while the Virginia herd is owned by The Chincoteague Volunteer Fire Company. To raise money, this volunteer fire company has established a unique tradition that will delight children. During the last Wednesday and Thursday of July, the Virginia ponies are rounded up on the southern end of Assateague Island and made to swim the channel to Chincoteague Island. Then the ponies run through the streets of Chincoteague and are penned up for auction. Foals and yearlings primarily are sold at this auction, and the proceeds support the fire company. Children (and adults) who love horses should read *Misty of Chincoteague* by Marguerite Henry—an enchanting story about these ponies.

Other wild animals live on Assateague Island, too. Most impressive are the white-tail deer and small Sika deer (which were imported from the Orient in 1923). There are also resident raccoons, foxes, and other small mammals. Another inhabitant is the hog-nosed snake. This harmless, nonpoisonous reptile is quite an actor. It first tries to scare you by huffing and puffing like one of its venomous relatives. However, if unsuccessful with this ruse, it rolls over on its back and plays dead. There are no poisonous snakes on Assateague; the only other snakes encountered are black snakes.

Another major attraction is bird life. Over 300 species of birds have been identified on Assateague Island, particularly the Virginia portion. In 1943, the Chincoteague National Wildlife Refuge was established as a bird resting and feeding area, primarily for the imperiled greater snow goose. To see (and hear) the V-shaped formation of these big white birds with distinctive black wing tips in flight is truly memorable.

Indeed, this refuge is one of the finest places in the United States to add sightings to a birdwatcher's life list. October and March are the best months because the refuge is on the Atlantic flyway for migratory birds, especially waterfowl. In addition to snow geese, Canada geese, swans, and cormorants, you can see numerous duck species such as teal, shovelers, scooters, oldsquaws, black ducks, wigeons, mallards, mergansers, gadwalls, pintails, loons, grebes, and buffleheads. Then, there are a host of wading birds, such as great blue herons, little blue herons, tricolored herons, greenbacked herons, black-crowned night herons, snowy egrets, great egrets, cattle egrets, and even glossy ibises. On the seashore you can see various types of terns, gulls, dunlins, plovers, yellowlegs,

dowitchers, willets, whimbrels, and the ever-present sandpipers working the beaches. In the pine forests and thickets inland from the sea are mainland birds. Most common of the raptors are osprey and northern harriers, although you might see an endangered peregrine falcon. Other common mainland birds are bobwhite quail, clapper rails, mourning doves, belted kingfishers, horned larks, brown thrashers, eastern meadowlarks, cardinals, northern flickers, cuckoos, owls, towhees, blackbirds, goldfinches, wrens, pewees, flycatchers, kinglets, kingbirds, thrushes, vireos, and numerous species of warblers and sparrows. Serious birders can get a birdlist from the Chincoteague National Wildlife Refuge.

The flora is surprisingly varied, too. The interior woods contain loblolly pine, Virginia pine, post oak, black oak, white oak, black cherry, sweet gum, red cedar, holly, and red maple. Typical ground cover is myrtle bushes, greenbriar, sumac, ivy, grape, blackberry, bayberry, broom sedge, and prickly pear cactus. In autumn, this shrubbery becomes remarkably colorful.

Upon reaching the bay campsites, there is much for families to do: tents to set up, walks to take, and beaches to explore. Once your campsite is set, take time to trek east to the Atlantic beach, roughly a mile away. On a typical trip to the Atlantic from the Tingles Island camp you will probably see deer, ponies, and egrets. Also, high in the dunes near the Tingles Island camp are the remains of an ancient shipwreck. During the brief walk, you will experience a certain exhilaration hearing the increasing crescendo to the sea, and its salty fragrance becomes stronger until you step through the dunes and see the ocean. The surging Atlantic surf is a striking contrast to the usually placid waters of the bay. Unfortunately, the beach can be covered with the heavy tracings of numerous four-wheel drive vehicles, which careen up and down the beach every weekend.

In spring or fall the beach can be warm or cold. Even if the sun is shining, a northeast breeze may make the water's edge feel positively wintry. However, if you back up into the shelter of the first row of dunes, you may be as warm as summer. In situations like this, you can pick your spot and choose your temperature.

The children will spread out. Some will build sand castles; others will want to go for a walk and look for such treasures as huge horseshoe crab shells and skate egg cases. Others may just play tag with the surf. These special beach experiences are a source of wonder and sustenance long after one returns to the routines of everyday life.

After several hours on the beach and upon returning to the campsite, the adventure continues. Sunsets are often magnificent. If the night is clear, the stars are brilliant for those who come from the city. You can see the magnificent canopy of the Milky Way, and traditional constellations like the Big Dipper are so close you can almost touch them.

However, in addition to the aforementioned possibility of heavy winds, you must consider several other possible perils in planning this trip. Thunderstorms are the most dangerous. To avoid lightning, get canoes off the bay and stay off the beach. Do not take shelter or erect tents near or under large trees. Next, in warm weather you should periodically check for ticks which can carry Lyme Disease or Rocky Mountain Spotted Fever. Poison ivy is also abundant, and between May and October mosquitoes can make your camping miserable without proper protection. Take sun screen and be prepared for long periods without shade. The National Park Service notes that other dangers may occur from the breaking surf on the beach, abandoned fishing lures with nasty hooks, glass on the beach, and hot coals left in the sand by thoughtless campers.

However, if you prepare for these problems, carefully check the weather, and set a leisurely pace, a canoe trip along Assateague Island will refresh your spirits and captivate your children.

Section: Chincoteague Bay— northern MD end of Assateague Island (Old Ferry Landing off Rt. 611) to southern VA end of Assateague Island (Toms Cove off Rt. 175)

Counties: Worcester (MD) and Accomack (VA)

USGS Quads: Tingles Island, Whittington Point, Boxiron, Chincoteague East, Chincoteague West

Suitable for: 2- to 4-night camping trips; extended day-trips

Skill Level: Beginners and families if wind and weather are favorable

Months Runnable: February 1 to November 1 by permit only; closed November 1 to February 1; mosquitoes may discourage use from May to September

Interest Highlights: Chincoteague ponies, exotic waterfowl, clamming, combining beachcombing with canoe camping

Scenery: Beautiful in backcountry marsh on Chincoteague Bay; Atlantic Beach marred by occasional to numerous 4-wheel drive vehicles in the northern MD part of Assateague Island

Difficulty: Class A; no whitewater

Average Width: Shallow bay several miles wide

Velocity: Slow

Gradient: 0 feet per mile

Runnable Water Levels:
  Minimum: At very low tides, canoeists may get stuck in shallows; current is negligible except when surface of water is driven by winds
  Maximum: N/A

Hazards: Heavy winds, storms, and lightning will make canoeing hazardous; get off the bay and off the beach under those conditions! The National Park Service will not issue canoeing permits if winds/storms are too adverse.

Scouting: None

Portages: None

Rescue Index: Accessible to remote (the further you go toward the middle of Assateague Island); the 2 most northern campsites, Tingles Island (2 miles) and Pine Tree (5 miles), may be reached by 4-wheel drive vehicle from NPS Assateague Island National Seashore Ranger Station.

Source of Additional Information: 3 jurisdictions on Assateague Island: Assateague State Park, Route 2, Box 293, Berlin, MD 21822 (410) 641-2120; Assateague Island National Seashore, Route 2, Box 294, Berlin, MD 21811 (410) 641-3030; Chincoteague National Wildlife Refuge, Chincoteague, VA 23336 (804) 336-6122 and Toms Cove Visitor Center (804) 336-6577. Also, please see the official park guide, *Assateague Island Handbook*, by marine biologist William H. Amos.

Access Points	River Miles	Shuttle Miles
A–A	4–26*	N/A – circuit
B–B	30	N/A – circuit
A–B	28	60

*River miles assume round trips of 4 miles to Tingles Island (A1), 10 miles to Pine Tree (A2), 14 miles to Jims Gut (A3), and 26 miles to Pope Bay (A4).

Access Point Ratings:
  A–at Old Ferry Landing (from Rt. 611) on northern Assateague Island just south of the ranger station for Assateague Island National Seashore, excellent
  B–at Toms Cove Visitor Center (from Rt. 175) in Chincoteague National Wildlife Refuge on southern end of Assateague Island, excellent

Eastern Shore of Virginia

A canoeing guide to Virginia waters would be incomplete without a section on the creeks and bays of Virginia's Eastern Shore, that narrow peninsula which separates the Chesapeake Bay from the Atlantic Ocean. Canoeing here is a contemplative experience, one of quiet discovery. Among the remote headwaters of the dozens of creeks, one can still find the illusion of wilderness and can share an afternoon with black ducks, herons, and an occasional family of otters.

On the Eastern Shore a canoeing thrill is to paddle, just before sunset, out to the Chesapeake and watch the sun as it glides beneath the horizon. If the breeze is calm the water will be like a giant mirror, and as you paddle along you will get a feeling of weightlessness, of floating effortlessly through space. You look up and the sky is washed in a purple and gold afterglow; you look down and the scene is repeated. Only a rippled wake reminds you that half your world is water.

The Eastern Shore has two shorelines, each of which has its own personality. The western side of the peninsula, which fronts the Chesapeake, is called the bayside. The eastern margin separates the mainland from the Atlantic and is called the seaside. Both the seaside and bayside offer great opportunities for canoeists, especially for those who enjoy watching wildlife. We'll talk about the bayside first.

The Bayside

The bayside has some 30 creeks along its 70-odd miles of shoreline, beginning with Old Plantation near Cape Charles and extending northward to the Pocomoke River which runs along the Virginia-Maryland state line. On the lower part of the peninsula, in Northampton County, the creeks have high banks and wooded shorelines. As you go northward, the creeks have a widening margin of salt marsh which separates the navigable water from the upland.

Pungoteague Creek

One of Curtis Badger's favorite bayside creeks is Pungoteague, which, like many of the Eastern Shore waterways, retains its rhythmic, polysyllabic Indian name. Pungoteague, again like most bayside creeks, once was a great avenue of commerce. Before the days of railroads and highways, sailing schooners would cruise the creeks, stopping at plantations and harbors to take on loads of farm produce destined for markets in Baltimore and Norfolk.

One such harbor, appropriately named Harborton, is on the south side of Pungoteague Creek on Route 180 and has a boat launch facility operated by the state. It's a good put-in spot, and is the only public access on the creek.

From Harborton you can paddle west toward the Chesapeake, or you can head east toward the headwaters and explore the shallow, protected coves and side creeks. I would suggest the latter.

Along the creek you'll see several graceful old plantation homes as well as the ubiquitous new houses and housing developments which, unfortunately, are spreading like a virus now that land developers have discovered the Eastern Shore. Paddle past the developments, though, and you can explore the more remote headwaters of the watershed. In these areas you can turn back the clock and imagine what the creek must have been like when the Indians lived here. The water is too shallow for motorboat traffic and the marshes are too mucky for foot traffic, so you'll have the headwaters to yourself. Depending upon the season, you should be able to see numerous herons (especially great blues), black ducks, mergansers, buffleheads, egrets, and hawks. Beginning in March, ospreys will be nesting on channel markers and in the tops of dead pine trees.

Pungoteague, like all the bayside creeks, is tidal, and it will make for easier paddling if you plan your trip to coincide with the tides. That is, paddle upstream on an incoming tide, and paddle downstream when the tide is ebbing. At the headwaters the water will be brackish and the current fairly weak. The division between salt marsh and brackish marsh is most accurately designated by the plant species; as you paddle up the creek you'll notice that salt marsh species such as Spartina gradually give way to needlerush, pickerelweed, arum, and cattails. One of the stream heads, Warehouse Prong, has a beautiful stand of pickerelweed which is worth visiting when it blossoms in July.

Chesconnessex Creek

Chesconnessex is another fairly typical bayside creek. It has a state boat ramp on the southern side (at the terminus of Route 655), making access easy. A nice day-trip is to paddle out the creek and head south along the bay shore and visit Parkers Marsh, a state-owned natural area which offers a beautiful, and very remote, sandy beach. Parkers Marsh separates Chesconnessex and Onancock Creeks and is a great area for marsh exploration and wildlife photography. Many bird species, especially wading birds, use the marsh and deer, fox, raccoon, and other mammals can often be sighted.

Be aware that the beach directly fronts the Chesapeake, so the water can often be rough, especially when the wind is from the west. If you go, get an updated weather forecast before putting in, and keep an eye out for approaching storms during the summer.

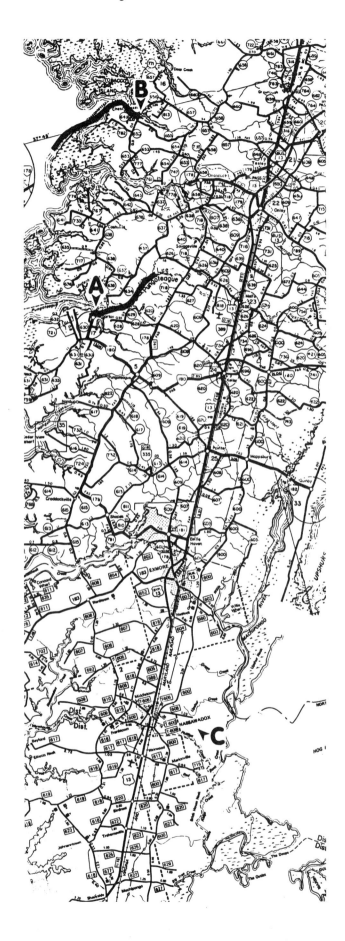

Section: Fisherman Island to the Virginia-Maryland state line

Counties: Accomack and Northampton

USGS Quads: Pungoteague, Nassawadox

Suitable for: Day use

Skill Level: Beginners

Months Runnable: Entire year

Interest Highlights: Wildlife, fishing, solitude, barrier island wilderness area

Scenery: A few waterfront developments, but most areas are pretty to spectacular, especially if you like remote islands and salt marshes

Difficulty: No whitewater, but strong currents, especially on seaside; strong winds sometimes in open water

Average Width: Canoe width at headwaters to bays several miles wide

Velocity: Tidal

Gradient: None

Runnable Water Levels: N/A

Hazards: Winds and rough water in open bays, strong currents, summer storms, hypothermia in winter

Scouting: None

Portages: None

Rescue Index: Accessible on most of bayside; remote on seaside

Sources of Additional Information: Navigational charts, topo maps (see Virginia list published by Division of Mineral Resources, Box 3667, Charlottesville, VA 22903 for specific areas), saltwater boating atlas

Access: Numerous public launch facilities on both seaside and bayside; contact Department of Game and Inland Fisheries for listing. Access over private land is usually granted if you ask permission.

Access Points	River Miles	Shuttle Miles
A–A	5–7 (round trip)	0
B–B	6–8 (round trip)	0
C–C	2–10 (round trip)	0

Access Point Rating:
A–Bayside: Pungoteague Creek (Harborton, Rt. 180), excellent
B–Bayside: Chesconnessex Creek (Rt. 655), excellent
C–Seaside: Virginia Coast Reserve (many access points; please write Virginia Coast Reserve, Brownsville, Nassawadox, VA 23413 for specifics), excellent

The Seaside

The ocean side of the peninsula is protected from the Atlantic by a series of long, narrow barrier islands. Behind the islands are thousands of acres of low, flat salt marsh, interrupted by a maze of tidal creeks and shallow bays. This island-estuary system is one of the most productive in the world; a large percentage of the commercial and recreational catch of shellfish and finfish is dependent upon the marshes and bays.

Most of the barrier beaches along the Atlantic Coast have been highly developed: Atlantic City in New Jersey, the Rehobeth-Fenwick area in Delaware, Ocean City in Maryland, and the Carolina Outer Banks. It is our good fortune that The Nature Conservancy came along some 20 years ago to assemble the Virginia Coast Reserve, a 45,000-acre preserve that includes all or most of 13 barrier islands, leeward marshes, and some continuous upland. As development has spread along the coast, this island preserve stands alone as a coastal wilderness, offering the same delights as the wilderness areas of the west and equally as important to future generations of Americans.

The islands are good places to canoe, but they must be taken on their own terms. Currents are strong and the seaside bays can become very rough. The area is expansive, and there are few shelters. When the wind is out of the east or northeast, it blows unimpeded across the bays and marshes. Still, the seaside is a wonderful wild place where you can pick up a few clams for dinner or catch a mess of flounder to fillet.

The state operates a dozen or so boat ramps on the seaside, so access is easy. Be sure to peruse the navigational charts before you go. It's a good idea to pick areas where you can paddle in the creeks rather than in open bays, which can become very disagreeable in a blow. During the summer, bring sun screen and bug repellent.

The Virginia Coast Reserve allows day use on most of the islands. Overnight camping is not permitted, pets are asked to remain at home, and some parts of the islands may be closed when the colonial nesting birds raise their young in May and June. For information, write to the Virginia Coast Reserve, Brownsville, Nassawadox, VA 23413. When you write, please consider sending $25.00 for a 1-year membership and help this organization preserve the last great wilderness barrier island system on the Atlantic.

A great blue heron stalking lunch on quiet Pungoteague Creek. Photo by Curtis Badger.

Lake Drummond and Great Dismal Swamp

Lake Drummond is truly unique! It is the only lake in Virginia that is higher than most of the land surrounding it. Also, it is one of only two natural lakes in Virginia (the other is Mountain Lake, at an elevation of about 3,000 feet, in western Virginia about 20 miles northwest of Blacksburg). Finally, Lake Drummond is very shallow. Although it covers 3,000 acres and is 3 miles across, it is only 6 feet deep at its deepest point.

This scenic, oval lake forms the center of the Great Dismal Swamp. Formed 6,000 years ago, the Great Dismal covered over 2,000 square miles in colonial times. The swamp now covers only 750 square miles, primarily because of human efforts to drain parts of it and cut canals through it. Even the water in Lake Drummond is special: it has a very distinctive dark color and is unusually pure because of its low pH. Indeed, the water was pure enough in the early 1800s to be barreled and drunk by sailors on ships that sailed the Atlantic and Pacific. It is even said that Commodore Perry took casks of this water with him when he opened the doors to Japan in 1853. However, because some of the water entering the lake now comes from developed areas, I cannot recommend drinking it.

The water's acidity comes from the tannic acid leached from the forest of black gum, cypress, and cedar trees that surrounds the lake. These tannins make the water both dark and effervescent—adding to its mystique. Because the acidity makes it difficult for bacteria to grow, the water is not stagnant and debris accumulates on the lake bottom and in the surrounding swamp from year to year. Consequently, Lake Drummond is one of the few places in North America where peat (in beds 2 to 9 feet deep) is being formed.

The lake has no real shoreline; its water just disappears into the dense forest encircling the lake. This, combined with shallow water, results in a lot of jagged roots and stumps poking up or lying just beneath the surface of the dark water, making it difficult to get boats ashore in many spots.

These unique conditions make Lake Drummond and the surrounding Great Dismal Swamp a special community for many plants and animals, some of which are at the northern edge of their range. Two swamp forest types predominate: black gum (tupelo) and cypress. The water in black gum forests is much darker than that in cypress forests. The gnarled trunks of black gum trees and bottlelike bases and knobby "knees" of the cypresses are impressive sights. In some places you will also see the last survivors of a great white cedar (sometimes called juniper) forest. These ghostly evergreens are covered with mistletoe and Spanish moss.

One of the striking dead cypress trees in Lake Drummond in the early morning mist. Photo by Patty DiRienzo.

Perhaps the oddest vegetation found here is the dense thicket of "pocosin"— an evergreen shrub-dominated bog that is basically impenetrable by humans. But this and other parts of the Great Dismal Swamp create excellent habitat for black bear, otter, muskrat, weasel, mink, raccoon, opossum, rabbit, squirrel, gray fox, bobcat (called wildcat by locals), and white-tailed deer. (Only deer hunting is allowed, and this is during daylight hours on October and November weekends.) There are also numerous species of game fish in the lake: perch, catfish, bream, pickerel, pike, sunfish, and bass.

The Great Dismal Swamp is a great place for birds; over 200 species have been seen there. Larger birds inhabiting the swamp are great blue herons, egrets, double-crested cormorants, turkey vultures, turkeys, and an occasional bald eagle. More abundant are quail, barred owls, and red-shouldered hawks. Migrating swans, ducks, and geese stop on Lake Drummond in spring and fall. Important smaller birds are the hermit thrush, the veery, towhee,

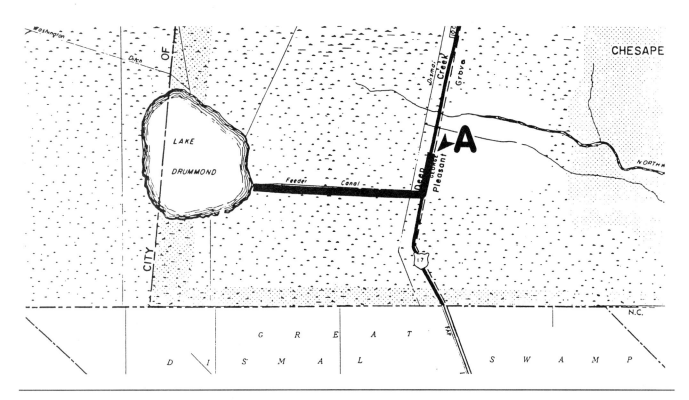

Section: Dismal Swamp Canal to Feeder Canal to Lake Drummond and return

Counties: Norfolk, Nansemond, and Suffolk City (VA); Camden (NC)

USGS Quads: Suffolk, Lake Drummond Northwest, Corapeake, Lake Drummond spillway

Suitable for: Day cruising or camping

Skill Level: Beginners

Months Runnable: Entire year

Interest Highlights: Unique shallow lake surrounded by cypress and tupelo swamp; bird life; wildlife; fishing

Scenery: Beautiful to spectacular in spots

Difficulty: Class A; must paddle 3.25 miles on Feeder Canal upstream to Lake Drummond spillway

Average Width: Dismal Swamp Canal 100 feet; Lake Drummond Feeder Canal 50 feet; Lake Drummond 2 by 3 miles

Velocity: Slow

Gradient: 0 feet per mile

Runnable Water Levels: N/A

Hazards: None, except occasional poisonous snakes (mainly copperheads)

Scouting: None

Portages: From Feeder Canal over spillway that leads to Lake Drummond

Rescue Index: Somewhat remote once you leave the campground

Source of Additional Information: Dismal Swamp National Wildlife Refuge, P.O. Box 349, Suffolk, VA 23434 (804) 986-3705; Lake Drummond Campground (owned by the U.S. Army Corps of Engineers) (804) 421-7401; Wild River Outfitters, Virginia Beach (804) 431 8566.

Access Points	River Miles	Shuttle Miles
A–A	8.5*	0

*This is the circuit to Lake Drummond and return; paddling on 3-by-2-mile Lake Drummond is additional

Access Point Ratings:
A–U.S. 17 and West Ballahack Road at Chesapeake Boat Landing on Dismal Swamp Canal, excellent

ruby-throated hummingbird, northern pharalope, and prothonotory and hooded warblers.

There are over a dozen species of snakes in the Great Dismal Swamp. Three of them are poisonous: water moccasin, canebrake rattlesnake, and copperhead. Fortunately, only the copperhead is occasionally seen; sightings of water moccasins and canebrake rattlesnakes are rare. Other crawling denizens of the swamp are the milk snake, hog-nosed snake, various species of water snakes (southern, red-bellied, and common), pilot black snake, king snake, black rat snake, and green snake.

Bugs are also prevelent in the Great Dismal Swamp. May through September is usually bad for mosquitoes and ticks, while June and July is the worst time for yellow flies.

Having given such a heady introduction, it is now necessary to guide you to Lake Drummond. Park on U.S. 17 (directly east of the lake) near the intersection of West Ballahack Road at the Chesapeake Boat Landing. There is a generous-sized parking area and easy put-in for canoes here. Paddle south one-half mile on the 100-foot-wide Dismal Swamp Canal (which is part of the Intracoastal Waterway) to the Feeder Canal which leads to Lake Drummond. Turn right (west) on the 50-foot-wide Feeder Canal. Now you have a 3.75-mile paddle to the banks of Lake Drummond. Depending on the amount of water released into the Feeder Canal, you may have to paddle against a current of up to 2 miles an hour for 3.25 miles. Then you will reach a spillway (from Lake Drummond) and campground maintained by the U.S. Army Corps of Engineers. Portage around the spillway and through the campground to put in again on the Feeder Canal, which continues the remaining half mile to Lake Drummond.

The Corps has certain rules for paddlers. Most importantly, check to see if canoeing on Lake Drummond is allowed only during daylight hours. No open fires are allowed. The campground is open the entire year, but most water is shut off for the winter. The campground has bathrooms, grills, outdoor picnic tables, and screened houses with tables.

Once you put in on Lake Drummond, I suggest paddling south (clockwise) around the banks of the lake. Somewhere southwest of the Feeder Canal and on the shore of Lake Drummond you should find the "Deer Tree"—a striking old cypress. According to local legend, this tree represents the lonely vigil of an ever watchful Indian lover turned into a deer by an evil witch. Lightning and storms have taken their toll on this old tree. With perseverance you should be able to find it.

Continuing around the lake, you will notice numerous gnarled, windblown cypress sentinels on its banks and along several ditches. Exploring the ditches is not recommended by the staff of Dismal Swamp National Wildlife Refuge; they are often blocked by fallen trees and are nesting areas for resident birds, particularly wood ducks. When you reach the northern end of the lake you should find Washington Ditch and Jericho Canal which join at the lake. Here there is some high ground and an opportunity for a short hike. Incidentally, the elliptical shape of the lake and the trees encircling it make a perfect echo chamber for those who like to talk to the woods.

The history of Lake Drummond and the Great Dismal Swamp is fascinating. The lake was discovered in 1650 by William Drummond, the first governor of North Carolina, when he returned as the sole survivor of a hunting expedition in the swamp. He was hung 10 years later for taking part in Bacon's Rebellion. Then, in 1728, Colonel William Byrd surveyed this swamp and gave it the appropriate name of Great Dismal. George Washington first visited the swamp in 1763 and later organized a lumber company, which dug many drainage ditches and two major canals. The Washington Ditch was the most important and runs from the northern end of Lake Drummond west for 7.5 miles. Then, in the early 1800s, the Dismal Swamp Canal was dug. This 22-mile-long canal runs south from Deep Creek, Virginia, to South Mills, North Carolina, and parallels Route 17. It currently is the oldest working canal in the United States and is part of the Intracoastal Waterway. Numerous yachts and large commercial boats use this waterway, so be alert for these craft when on it.

While paddling on Lake Drummond, contemplate the Indian legend that describes its genesis. Originally, the lake was the nest of a horrible Fire Bird that terrorized the local Indians and ate their children. A pair of Indian lovers, Big Bear and White Swan, were given the task of driving the terrible Fire Bird from the swamp with the help of a friendly Swamp Spirit. This they did by killing the seven offspring of the Fire Bird. When this happened, the Fire Bird left. Then the Swamp Spirit filled the nest of the Fire Bird with water, and the water overflowed from the nest in seven rivers. These seven rivers washed away the remains of the seven young Fire Birds. However, the lake and these seven rivers are still tainted with the blood of the slain Fire Birds. To thank the Swamp Spirit for its help, Big Bear and White Swan gave their first child to the Spirit. This child is now the white-tailed deer in the swamp.

Merchants Millpond

Merchants Millpond in North Carolina is a pocket-sized version of Lake Drummond, which is just over the Virginia border to the northeast. However, while Lake Drummond is large, open, and expansive, Merchants Millpond is small, close, intimate, and has many trees in its water. The pond itself is only 750 acres compared to the 3,000 acres of Lake Drummond. Similarly, Merchants Millpond State Park is only 2,500 acres compared to the 750 square miles of the Great Dismal Swamp which contains Lake Drummond.

Still, there is much similarity between the two parks. First, the kidney-shaped millpond is a rare combination of coastal pond and southern swamp forest. Huge cypress trees and black gum (tupelo) trees surround and intrude into the pond. Resurrection ferns and Spanish moss cover these trees with ghostly shrouds. At the upper end of Merchants Millpond is Lassiter Swamp which has the remains of an ancient cypress swamp and an eerie enchanted forest of tupelo trees that have been twisted into bizarre shapes by mistletoe. The water is also black— the result of tannic acid from cypress and tupelo trees. Prominent undergrowth on the banks of the pond are wild roses and blueberries. Surrounding the aquatic plant communities of the millpond and nearby swamp are a mixture of pine and hardwood forests, including impressive stands of beech trees.

There is quite a diversity of wildlife, beginning with large numbers of reptiles and amphibians: 12 species of frogs, 9 kinds of turtles, 6 varieties of lizards, and 17 types of snakes. A variety of mammals live here, such as beaver, mink, otter, raccoon, fox, bobcat, rabbit, bats, deer, and black bear. Bird life is also rampant. Over 160 species have been seen in the park. The most striking common year-round residents are pileated and red-bellied woodpeckers, northern flickers, belted kingfishers, bobwhite quail, wood ducks, tufted titmice, whitebreasted nuthatches, Eastern bluebirds, Carolina wrens and chickadees, pine warblers, goldfinches and rufous-sided towhees. In spring and fall you have the migrations of warblers and other birds, while in winter large numbers of waterfowl remain here. Fishing is great, too. However, you need a North Carolina fishing license to catch the largemouth bass, bluegill sunfish, black crappie, and chain pickerel that live in the millpond.

The main state park entrance is west of Elizabeth City on US 158 between Gatesville and Sunbury, North Carolina. The park is open the entire year, and you can park and camp overnight within its boundaries. If you want fancy camping, use the campground just south of the park entrance. Each site contains a picnic table and grill. Although drinking water and washhouse facilities are

Lillie Gilbert (stern) and Nancy Shelhorse (bow) enjoying the Spanish moss and mystery of Merchants Mill Pond.
Photo by Patty DiRienzo.

available, there are no water or electrical hookups for trailers. There are also backpacking trails and a backpacking campsite in the state park north of the millpond.

However, for canoe rentals, canoe camping, and the put-in, you need to go just west of the main entrance and take Route 1403 south for nearly a mile to the upper west side of the pond. For those not bringing their own boats, canoes can be rented from 8 a.m. until 5 or 6 p.m. for day-trips (until 8 p.m. in summer) and also can be used for canoe campsites. You must be at least 15 years old to rent a canoe, and the rates are currently $2.50 an hour and $10.00 a day. For further information call Merchants Millpond State Park at (919) 357-1191. The primitive camping is on the banks of the pond. There is a choice of family and group canoe camping sites on a first-come, first-served basis. Just follow the buoys around a peninsula from where you launch and then head east to the campgrounds.

Around the first bend after the put-in is a treat: all the trees are suddenly draped in Spanish moss. Cypress and tupelo trees are everywhere, and you start paddling between them like a slalom course. Some of the cypress are gathered into little islands. Indeed, there are so many islands you can paddle the whole day and never take the same path twice. The family canoe camp path is marked by orange buoys, and the group canoe camp path is marked by yellow buoys. The family site is less than a mile, and the group site is just over a mile of paddling from the put-in. Both are on the northern bank of Merchants Millpond.

After setting up camp, explore the pond and Lassiter Swamp which forms its northeast corner. Lassiter Swamp is roughly a 4 mile round-trip from the canoe campsites. Take your compass to help find the way.

Traveling due east from the semi-cleared peninsula just south of the primitive group camping area will lead you into the most interesting and wild part of the millpond where there are hundreds of cypress and tupelo trees draped with Spanish moss. Roughly a half mile from the group canoe camp, if you stay close to the center of the millpond, you will come upon the largest beaver lodge (5 feet high) in the park. From this lodge, travel northeast until you are near the edge of Lassiter Swamp.

Finding Lassiter Creek in order to explore the interior of this swamp is tricky. Look for a distinctive current bending the river grass and follow the strongest current against you. You may find yourself at a dead end or two, but keep traveling against the current. If you do this right, you will find the entrance to the "Enchanted Forest"—a wonderland of gnarled tupelo trees. Here the water closes in to a 8-foot-wide channel. It's very green and very dark. In some places you can only see from tree to tree. The black gum trees are twisted into fantastic shapes. If you were a troll or a gnome, this is where you'd live.

Keep working your way up Lassiter Creek, crossing several beaver dams as you go. In less than a mile you will be in the Cathedral. This is an untimbered cypress area with 18 ancient trees estimated to be between 700 and 1,000 years old. On the way upstream to the Cathedral, there are a couple of great lunch stops on high ground to your left.

The only negative aspects of Merchants Millpond are those found in other nearby coastal swamps and rivers—snakes and insects. Primarily in spring and summer, you need to watch for occasional water moccasins in the swamp and copperheads on the high ground. Mosquitoes, yellow flies, and ticks can be bothersome during this time also.

If you want additional adventure, try Bennetts Creek, which begins below the dam at the west end of Merchants Millpond. A more detailed description of Bennetts Creek, which winds it way south for 20 miles across a freshwater swamp to the Chowan River, is found in Bob Benner's *A Paddler's Guide to Eastern North Carolina.*

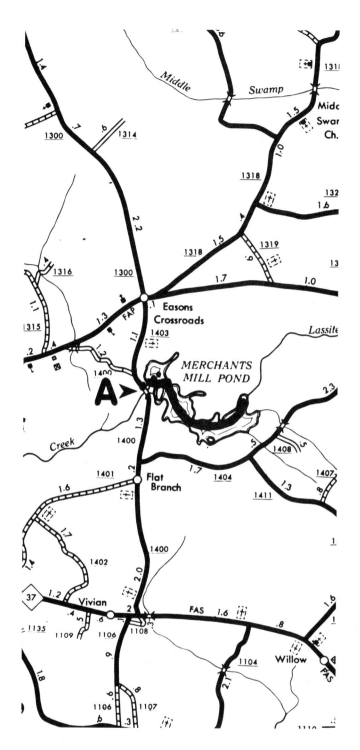

Section: Rt. 1403 to campsite to Lassiter Swamp and return

Counties: Gates (NC)

USGS Quads: Beckford

Suitable for: Day cruising or camping

Skill Level: Beginners

Months Runnable: Entire year

Interest Highlights: Unique small pond surrounded and intruded by cypress/tupelo swamp; bird life; wildlife; fishing

Scenery: Beautiful to spectacular in spots

Difficulty: Class A

Average Width: 30 to 40 feet in Lassiter Swamp, to 200 feet in Merchants Millpond because of many trees in water

Velocity: Slow

Gradient: 0 feet per mile

Runnable Water Levels: N/A

Hazards: None, except disorientation and occasional poisonous snakes

Scouting: None

Portages: Perhaps a couple of beaver dams in Lassiter Swamp

Rescue Index: Somewhat remote once you leave the campground

Source of Additional Information: Merchants Millpond State Park, Rt. 1, Box 141A, Gatesville, NC 27938 (919) 357-1191; Wild River Outfitters, Virginia Beach (804) 431-8566

Access Points	River Miles	Shuttle Miles
A–A	2–6*	0

*2-mile circuit to campground and return; 4-mile circuit from campground to Lassiter Swamp and return

Access Point Ratings:
A–Rt. 1403 on west end of Merchants Millpond, excellent

Northwest River

An ironic twist to the Northwest river is that it is in the southeast corner of Virginia—southwest of Virginia Beach. Nevertheless, it is a great placid trip for beginners. The Northwest begins as a tiny intimate stream near the Great Dismal Swamp, widens substantially as it reaches Northwest River Park, and then turns south before it enters North Carolina.

The best section is the 6.5-mile stretch from Bunch Walnuts Road to Battlefield Boulevard (Route 168). Here the Northwest has no discernible current, but is very narrow and twisty. Like other rivers near the Great Dismal Swamp, it is tea-colored—stained by tannic acid from vegetation. This stretch is completely forested except for one place—the Triple R Ranch, a children's camp located at the put-in on Bunch Walnuts Road. The bridge near Triple R Ranch is a safe place to leave your vehicle. Because there is virtually no current, you can make this a back and forth trip from Bunch Walnuts Road, eliminating the extra time and logistics of a shuttle. For those using a shuttle, the Battlefield Boulevard take-out is at Northwest River Campground. They charge a small fee to use their boat landing area, but the safety of your vehicle is worth this small cost. Also, be sure you don't confuse this campground with the Northwest River Park campground further downstream which is discussed below.

If you put in at Battlefield Boulevard, there are two options in addition to paddling upstream. First, you can take a finger of the Northwest that goes (where else?) northwest for 2 miles or so. This back and forth finger trip is very scenic, and the river gets narrower and more wooded as you go north. If you paddle downstream instead, the river becomes much wider and passes several islands. After about 2.5 miles, Indian Creek enters from the left, and you reach Northwest River Park. This park of 763 wooded acres is on the left (north) bank of the Northwest River. There is a pier here for your boat, picnic tables for lunch, and bathrooms for other needs.

Should you wish to stay the night, you could explore the Northwest from the campground at this park, which has 100 campsites, bathhouses, laundry, and a general store. The camp is open April 1 to December 1, and the rates are currently $12.00 to $15.00 a night. However, there is one serious catch to doing this. If you camp here, you cannot use your own boat to fish for largemouth bass, bream, crappie, and channel catfish in the lake of this park or to launch on the Northwest River (100 yards south of the lake). You must rent a boat from the park to put in or take out from the park—even for day-tripping. Call the campground at (804) 421-3145 for further information.

On the other hand, the park managers do not object to two reasonable alternatives for launching or taking out your own canoe near the park. First, there is a put-in on Indian Creek, which is by aptly named Indian Creek Road at the northwest corner of Northwest River Park. You put in at the bridge here and paddle south. Northwest River Park forms the left bank for 1.25 miles until Indian Creek joins the Northwest River. Nearby is the free picnic area the park provides for private and other boaters. Alternatively, you can go just over 2 miles further east on Indian Creek Road, turn right on Baum Road for one-quarter mile, and put in on Smith Creek just east of Northwest River Park. In this case, you paddle 1.5 miles west to join the Northwest River, with the park and picnic pier being on the right bank.

Section: Bunch Walnuts Road to Battlefield Blvd. (Rt. 168)

Counties: City of Chesapeake

USGS Quads: Lake Drummond Southeast and Moyock

Suitable for: Day cruising

Skill Level: Beginners

Months Runnable: Entire year

Interest Highlights: Intimate wooded stream at beginning, tea colored water, fishing

Scenery: Pretty to beautiful in spots

Difficulty: Class A

Average Width: 10 to 20 feet at beginning; quite wide at Northwest River Park at end

Velocity: Slow

Gradient: 0 feet per mile

Runnable Water Levels: N/A

Hazards: Occasional trees in river

Scouting: None

Portages: None

Rescue Index: Generally accessible

Source of Additional Information: Northwest River Park (804) 421-3145

Access Points	River Miles	Shuttle Miles
A–B	6.5	7
B–C	4.0	3
B–D	5.0	5

Access Point Ratings:
A—Chesapeake (Bunch Walnuts Road), good
B—Battlefield Blvd. (Rt. 168), fair
C—Indian Creek Road, good
D—Smith Creek, good

Note: All access points can be used for circuit trips. Also, you cannot put in or take out private canoes in Northwest River Park; you must rent canoes from the park to do this.

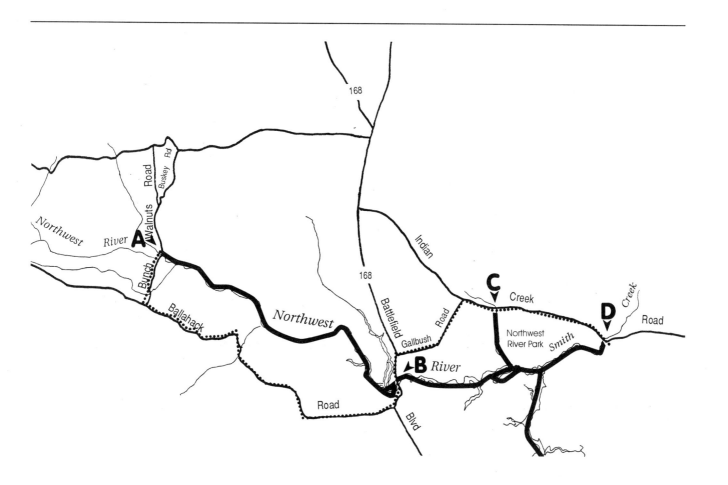

West Neck Creek

West Neck Creek is an incredible success story! It proves that paddlers and others concerned with the environment can make a difference. In 1980, a 28-mile waterway bisecting Virginia Beach and running from North Landing River in the south to Lynnhaven Bay in the north was blocked in many places by fallen trees and man-made objects ranging from washing machines to shopping carts. Then Lillie Gilbert and Nancy Shelhorse (co-owners of Wild River Outfitters in Virginia Beach) decided to see if they could paddle this stretch. Armed with hedge clippers and insect repellent, they hacked their way through the narrow and overgrown waterway. Their success led them to ask Virginia Beach officials to clean up the trail and to preserve it from encroaching development. As a result, the city sent teams with chain saws by boat to clear the debris. Meanwhile, Boy Scouts, the Sierra Club, and canoeists cleared out other litter along the way. As a result, in September 1986, the first segment of this 28-mile Virginia Beach Scenic Waterway System was dedicated—8.6 miles of West Neck Creek from West Neck Road to Shipps Corner Road.

West Neck Creek is the ecological heart of this waterway, and the 5-mile section from West Neck Marina north to Princess Anne Road is the prettiest part of the creek. It is incredible to realize that this creek has not been developed even though it is centered in one of the East's fastest growing metropolitan areas. Because there is virtually no current, you can put in at either place. However, if you plan to put in at West Neck Marina, there is a small fee to park your vehicle. Traveling north from West Neck Marina you can see Virginia Beach as it used to be when Atlantic coastal marshes were untouched by humans. Here the creek is narrow, pristine, and most scenic. The brackish "blackwater" of the creek is stained by tannins from cypress, cedar, gum, oak, maple, and pine. Dense woods line the banks and overhang the waters. Wildlife abounds, particularly deer, otter, squirrels, rabbits, opossum, raccoon, and washtub-sized turtles. There are also numerous large birds—egrets, herons, ducks, owls, kingfishers, and ospreys. Occasionally there are sightings of bald eagles and falcons. Smaller birds are abundant, too. Lillie Gilbert

Section: West Neck Creek—West Neck Road to Princess Anne Road; Virginia Beach Scenic Waterway—Munden Point Park to Shore Drive

Counties: City of Virginia Beach

USGS Quads: Pleasant Ridge, Princess Anne, Cape Henry, and Creeds

Suitable for: Day cruising

Skill Level: Alert beginners

Months Runnable: Entire year; however, snakes, insects, and poison ivy may make summer trips uncomfortable

Interest Highlights: West Neck Creek—tea-colored water, fishing, wildlife, huge ancient cypress tree

Scenery: West Neck Creek—Pretty to beautiful in spots; Virginia Beach Scenic Waterway—fair to pretty in spots

Difficulty: Class A

Average Width: West Neck Creek—10 to 30 feet; Virginia Beach Scenic Waterway—100 to 2,500 feet

Velocity: Slow

Gradient: 0 to 1 foot per mile

Runnable Water Levels: N/A

Hazards: Occasional downed trees; occasional poisonous snakes, insects, and poison ivy in spring/summer

Scouting: None

Portages: Maybe a fallen tree or so

Rescue Index: Accessible

Source of Additional Information: Wild River Outfitters (804) 431-8566

Access Points	River Miles	Shuttle Miles
A–B	3.5	5
A–C	10.5	11
C–D*	5.0	6
D–E	7.5	8
E–F	5.5	8

Access Point Ratings:
A—Munden Point Park, excellent
B—Pungo Ferry Bridge, excellent
C—West Neck Marina*, very good
D—Princess Anne Road*, very good
E—Virginia Beach Blvd., very good
F—Shore Drive (before Lesner Bridge), excellent

*Best section of West Neck Creek. West Neck Marina is just southeast of where West Neck Road crosses the creek.

remembers one trip when she came around a bend and saw hundreds of little warblers fly up in a yellow wave. Anglers can try their luck for bass, bream, perch, and crappies.

Headed north you will go under Indian River Road Bridge 2 miles beyond West Neck Marina. Soon you will come to the most important landmark on this section: a cypress tree once thought to be the largest and oldest in the state. You will find it on the east side of the river halfway between the Indian River Road Bridge and the Princess Anne Bridge. This ancient giant is estimated to be 300 years old, and it takes four people to link hands around its huge trunk. Despite a bolt of lightning that shattered its top several years ago, the tree still towers above the surrounding forest. If the 5.25-mile trip is enough, you can take out at Princess Anne Road near the intersection of Route 149 and Hotland Road. There is off-road parking for shuttle cars at the southwest corner of the Princess Anne Road Bridge.

Grittier paddlers can travel the entire 28.5-mile north south length of the Virginia Beach Scenic Waterway System. This route gives a variety of scenery to supplement beautiful West Neck Creek—from coastal marshlands to suburban sprawl to the salt water estuary of Chesapeake Bay. If you wish to paddle the entire waterway, begin at Munden Point Park at its south end near the mouth of the North Landing River. You reach this park by going to the south end of Princess Anne Road, turning right (west) on Munden Point Road, and following the signs. This put-in is a canoe/motorboat launch site. Although there is a large lovely park here with covered picnic areas, you cannot camp overnight.

As you start north on the North Landing River, you must realize that it is part of the Intracoastal Waterway which is used by boats to travel between Virginia and North Carolina. Accordingly, you need to be alert for water-skiers (in summer), large yachts, cargo barges, and other large boats. Be cautious of boat wakes and avoid collisions with these faster craft. After 9 miles, turn right (east) on West Neck Creek. The scenery here is wooded swamps and agricultural areas. Having paddled 1.5 miles on this creek, you will reach West Neck Marina—the put-in for the section described above.

Going north of Princess Anne Road (the take-out for the section described above), West Neck Creek leads to a canal dug during World War II to allow small boats to move undetected in the event of an invasion. Civilization soon intrudes as the canal cuts through industrial and residential areas. The canal then empties into London Bridge Creek, which subsequently joins the Lynnhaven River in a neighborhood of well-tended lawns and huge yachts. You need to start watching out for big boats and

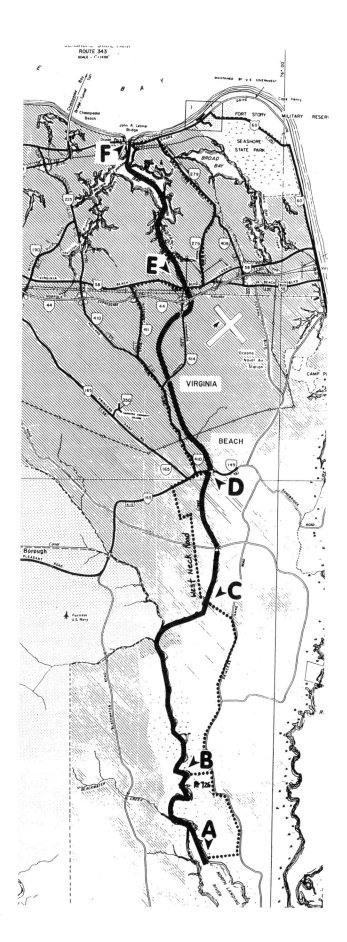

their wakes again. The river subsequently widens into Lynnhaven Bay, and the waterway ends at Lesner Bridge. Do not take out at Lesner Bridge: dangerous currents here have killed people in recent years. Instead, the final take-out must be from Shore Drive (Route 60), at the Virginia Beach sand storage area near Chesapeake Bay. Park in the free public lot at the southwest corner (river left) of the Lynnhaven River Bridge. Headed north from Munden Point, the best access points on the 28-mile waterway are at Pungo Ferry Bridge (3.5 miles), the aforementioned West Neck Marina (10.5 miles), the aforementioned Princess Anne Road (15.75 miles), and Virginia Beach Boulevard (23 miles).

There are three main concerns while paddling the Virginia Beach Scenic Waterway System. First, and most importantly, you should be alert for snakes, especially in the spring. Water moccasins and copperheads as well as nonpoisonous water snakes should be watched for, particularly on overhanging branches. Second, insects can be bad in the warmer months. Prepare for mosquitoes, deer flies, may flies, and ticks with appropriate clothing, netting, and insect repellent. Finally, stay away from the poison ivy, oak, and sumac which are common along the sunny banks of this stream system, primarily in wooded swampy areas.

Better yet, why not paddle this stretch in the late fall, winter, or early spring when your favorite rivers are too low or too iced up to navigate? This way you can avoid snakes, bugs, and poison ivy during a day that is probably warmer than if you were in western and northern Virginia.

David Price enjoying the tranquility of Lake Drummond in the Great Dismal Swamp. Photo by Patty DiRienzo.

Chowan

Blackwater River

The Blackwater is aptly named. The tannins produced by the huge amount of organic matter in surrounding swamps have stained its water a coffee color. This is your first indication that the Blackwater is a unique river that can provide a rich experience. Basically, you have 30 miles of this river to float between Route 620 north of Zuni to Franklin. The Blackwater above Route 620 is virtually impassable, and below Franklin heavy barge and motorboat traffic make canoe travel unappealing.

Between Route 620 and Franklin, however, the Blackwater is runnable most of the year. The only caveat is that the City of Norfolk draws water from this stream, so call the Blackwater River Pumping Station at (804) 539-4621 in Suffolk, Virginia, to see if the river has enough water to paddle. This pumping station is manned 24 hours a day.

Day-trippers and campers can divide the Blackwater into manageable sections depending on their interest and time available. Between Route 620 and Franklin there is access at Route 614 in Zuni (5.5 miles), Route 603 (14.5 miles), Route 619 (18 miles), and Route 611 (23 miles). The best midway access points are the Commission of Game and Inland Fisheries parking areas and boat ramps

at Route 603 and Route 611. There are few houses along the river and many places for camping. However, most of the Blackwater is on private land, so get permission first.

In general, much of the Blackwater has a sandy bottom and low sand bluff banks. However, this 30 mile stretch can be broken into three distinct sections. The 14.5 mile upper section from Route 620 to Route 603 is a classic lowland swamp of cypress and hardwood trees. Contrasting with this, the middle 8.5 mile section from Route 603 to Route 611 has a wider, clearly defined, gently winding channel with steep, heavily wooded hillsides of hickory and white oak. In the final 7 mile section from Route 611 to Franklin the Blackwater becomes a swamp again.

If you start your trip at either Route 620 or Zuni, it is the swamp which rivets your attention. Here you have cypress and dense stands of huge hardwoods creating a high canopy above. In certain places black gum trees predominate. Meanwhile, the narrow, winding channel of the Blackwater and the heavy vegetation give the paddler a real feeling of solitude. The continual oxbows and braided channels require patience as you work along this river, particularly since many of them dead end into swampy

Paddlers floating the quiet Blackwater. Photo courtesy of Peter Money.

tangles. At any level, there are at least a few fallen trees to get over, under, or around.

A real treat awaits you 6 miles below Zuni. Here you come to the Zuni Pine Barrens. Unfortunately, you can't see these stately trees from the river. The approximately 100 trees here comprise the last stand of longleaf pine forest in Virginia. These trees used to be part of a huge pine savanna, which originally extended from New Jersey through southeastern Virginia and along the Coastal Plain to Texas. Not only do longleaf pines have needles up to 1.5 feet long, but their bark is 2 to 3 inches thick. This makes them very fire resistant, and, indeed, dependent on periodic fires to maintain the pine barrens savanna in which they live.

The longleaf pine has played an important part in U.S. history. The most resinous of southern pines, this tree resists rot and thus, for 200 years was prized for building and boat construction. During the colonial period, these 100 foot tall pines were used for ship masts, and tar and pitch distilled from the trees caulked ships. A 318 acre portion of the Zuni Pine Barrens, called the Blackwater Ecological Preserve, was given to Old Dominion University by the Union Camp Corporation in 1984.

Besides longleaf pines, the Blackwater has other enchanting plant life. One plant is the rare emerald colored pyxie moss which glows pink with delicate dime sized flowers in April. Another rare plant is the October flower. Its tiny white flowers, which bloom in the fall, resemble baby's breath and turn pink as they age. Two more intriguing plants are the ghostly white Indian pipe plant and British soldier's lichen, the latter so called because of its red tips. In spring and early summer, the beautiful mosses and lichens along the route are particularly striking. Other flora are turkey oak, teaberry, the evergreen shiny leaved galax, blueberries, and huckleberries.

Wildlife abounds along the Blackwater. In addition to large deer, squirrel, raccoon, and rabbit populations, there are river otter, beaver, and oodles of turtles. Concerning birds, most impressive and prevalent are the owls. Screech, barred, and great horned owls who make the Blackwater their hunting preserve will certainly entertain you at night. Other large birds of note in the area are the red-shouldered hawk and, possibly, the very rare red-cockaded woodpecker. Finally, numerous species of ducks delight hunters in the fall.

The Blackwater is a real angler's river too. The dark, slow waters of the river and its innumerable snags are great for largemouth bass. Also, there are panfish and catfish, particularly channel and white catfish. In swampier areas of the river intrepid anglers can even do battle with the aggressive chain pickerel.

Your experience on the Blackwater can vary radically, depending on the season. Clearly the worst season to try the Blackwater is summer. Not only do you have heat and humidity to contend with, but the mosquitoes and other insects are murderous. Long shirts, long pants, netting, and vats of insect repellent are de rigueur at this time. Also, this is when you may have to deal with an occasional water moccasin or copperhead, as well as various nonpoisonous snakes. Finally, summertime is when the water is the lowest. The amount of inconvenience caused by downed trees, dead-end channels, and shallow sandbars increases geometrically as the water level drops. In winter and early spring, the level of the Blackwater is much higher. Consequently, there are more channels around deadfalls and other obstacles. However, the increased choices still occasionally lead to dead-end tangles. You have better views of the nearby hills and wildlife since the leaves are off the trees. In fall, the trip is a riot of color with the changing foliage, particularly the orange fire of turkey oak and the scarlet leaves of shrubs.

Another interesting feature of the Blackwater is its wet sandy soil, which farmers used to call quicksand. This is caused by a high water table created by a layer of sand overlying an impervious clay formation. With no drainage, each rainfall simply fills the porous sands on top of the clay.

Remember that the Blackwater was an historic artery of commerce. Early colonists used this river to transport their possessions from settlements on the James to new settlements in southern Virginia and eastern North Carolina. Later, large plantations near Zuni sent tobacco, lumber, and grain to Franklin for transshipment to markets in tidewater North Carolina and Virginia. Boaters planning to paddle the Blackwater should be aware of a very recent development. The three middle sections of this river (from access points B to E) now have many more fallen trees to deal with. Call the Blackwater River Pumping Station to be sure most of the trees from B to E are covered by water. About 5 feet on the pumping station gauge should be sufficient to do this.

Section: Rt.620 to Franklin (Rt.58)

Counties: Isle of Wight, Southampton

USGS Quads: Raynor, Zuni, Sedley, Franklin

Suitable for: Day cruising and camping

Skill level: Beginners

Months Runnable: Virtually the entire year except for late summer and periods of drought; call Blackwater River Pumping Station to ensure enough water; low water, insects, and snakes may make summer trips uncomfortable

Interest Highlights: Tea-colored water, fishing, wildlife, Zuni Pine Barrens, intimate cypress/hardwood swamp at beginning and end, heavily wooded hilly banks in middle

Scenery: Pretty to beautiful and even spectacular in spots

Difficulty: Class A

Average Width: 10 to 30 feet

Velocity Slow

Gradient: 0 to 1 foot per mile

Runnable Water Levels:
  Minimum:: Call Blackwater Pumping Station; 5 feet on the gauge there should be sufficient to cover most of the fallen trees between access points B and E
  Maximum:: N/A

Hazards: Trees and tangled dead ends in river; occasional poisonous snakes in summer

Scouting: None

Portages: At least a few fallen trees and tangles; many fallen trees recently in the 3 sections between access points B and E

Rescue Index: remote

Source of Additional Information: Blackwater River Pumping Station (804) 539-4621; Old Dominion University Biology Department manages the Zuni Pine Barrens and knows about periodic burns and trails to the Barrens (804) 683-3595; Virginia Living Museum in Newport News schedules trips to the Blackwater and other nearby rivers, (804) 595-1900.

Access Points	River Miles	Shuttle Miles
A-B	5.5	6
B-C	9.0	6
C-D	3.5	5
D-E	5.0	6
E-F	7.0	6 or 8

Access Point Ratings:
A-Rt.620, good
B-Zuni (Rt.614), very good
C-Rt.603, excellent
D-Rt.619, very good
E-Rt.611, excellent
F-Franklin (US 58), very good

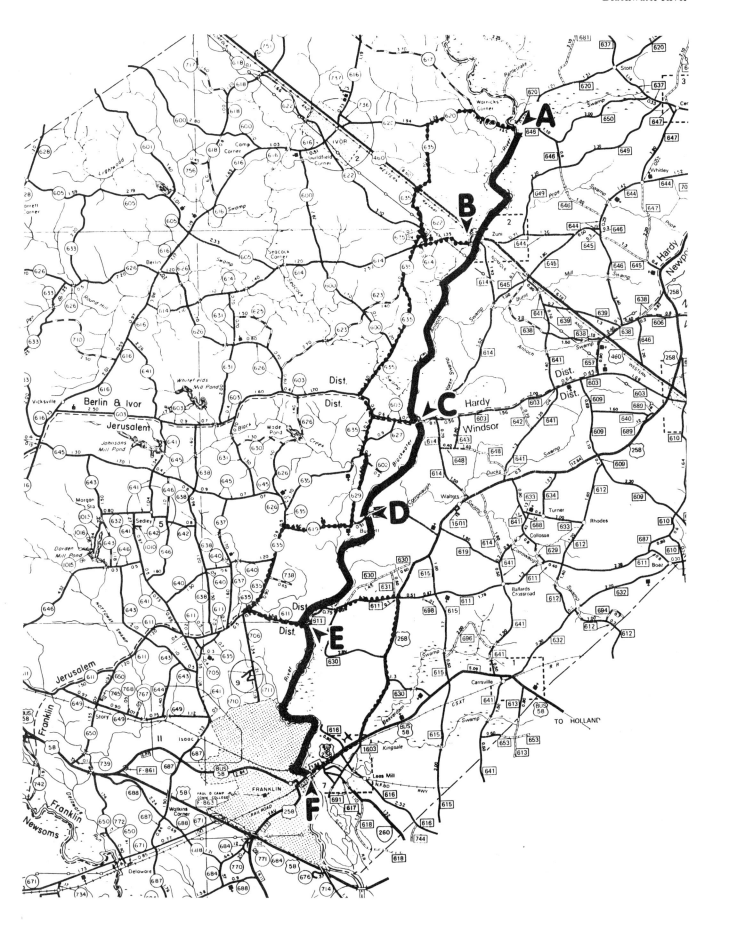

Nottoway River

Driving toward the Nottoway, one encounters scenery similar to that of the upper Coastal Plain of North Carolina: tall pines and scrub oaks growing in sandy soil. Unfortunately, one also sees much clear cutting, some of it the result of lumber company activity and the rest new farmland. However, you will experience a change for the better when you reach the Nottoway.

The 10-mile stretch of the Nottoway from Cutbank Bridge to Double Bridge is a delight for shepherded novices, whether on a day-trip or a really laid back camping trip. Campers will be glad to hear that there are only a couple of rapids until the halfway point; this is a good insurance for dry gear. Then, having camped and arisen, hopefully refreshed, you will find an increasing number of rapids in the second half of the trip. At first these are Class I–II—small ledges and boulder gardens. However, the rapids suddenly become solid Class II–III drops in the last mile of the trip when the river cuts separate invigorating channels as it weaves around several interesting islands. It is here that novices (particularly with boats full of camping gear) need to be especially careful.

This river is surprisingly remote. For most of the trip you will only see 5- to 10-foot-high sandy or clay banks topped with forests of beech, river birch, loblolly pine, and cedar. The main sign of human presence is numerous platforms for deer hunters which are built part way up the trunks of trees along the river bank. This is deer country, and you are advised not to paddle here during hunting season, unless you want to find hunters perched on deer platforms around every bend. Incidentally, these stands are quite varied. Some are merely tiny platforms; others are full-fledged tree houses. One even has a window.

You will also see many signs of beaver. On one trip I saw 100 chewed branches in 50 yards. All their bark was gnawed off, and they were neatly snipped at both ends. There is also much bird life, particularly during the spring and fall migrations. For example, on one May day, a couple of paddling bird watchers saw eight species of migrating birds, including 100 red and yellow scarlet tanagers. On the same trip, 60 ducklings, 2 beaver, 5 otters (including 2 babies), and numerous deer were seen.

Put in on river right of the narrow one-lane Route 609 bridge. The banks are sandy and moss covered. Be careful parking cars here because certain places are posted, in part because careless individuals have abused this beautiful spot.

After putting in, you drift peacefully along for nearly 2 miles before coming to the first significant riffles. Take note of this spot, because 100 yards below is the main rapid for the first half of the trip—a short Class I–II rock garden. The easiest way to run it is by a separate channel on the far left. However, first make sure the channel is not blocked by a tree. The next best alternative is in the center, but novices with camping gear should look this drop over before running it. Just below the far left channel is a delightful place for lunch. There is a problem when it rains,

Tom Bary on the Nottoway River. Photo by Holt Messerly.

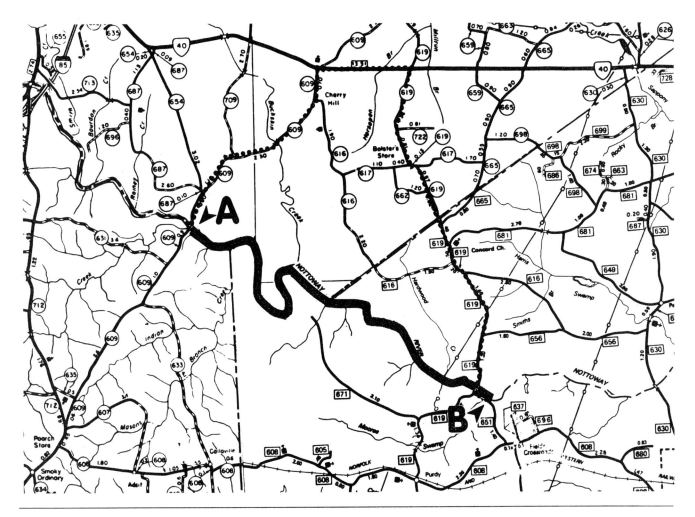

Section: Cutbank Bridge (Rt.609) to Double Bridge (Rt.619)

Counties: Greensville, Brunswick, Dinwiddle, and Sussex

USGS Quads: McKenney, Smoky Ordinary, Cherry Hill, and Purdy

Suitable for: Day cruising or camping

Skill Level: Intermediates or carefully shepherded novices

Months Runnable: Winter, spring, and early summer

Interest Highlights: Remote Piedmont river; deer and beaver country

Scenery: Pretty to beautiful in spots

Difficulty: Class I-II with 3 Class II-III options in last mile on river left

Average Width: 75 to 100 feet

Velocity: Generally moderate

Gradient: 3 feet per mile for 9 miles; 10 feet per mile for last mile

Runnable Water Levels:
  Minimum: Rt.619 gauge 0 feet
  Maximum: Rt.619 gauge 4 feet

Hazards: Occasional trees in river; tight maneuvering in optional Class II-III rapids on left at end of trip

Portages: None

Rescue Index: Accessible to remote

Source of Additional Information: Call the Jones residence for the river level at (804) 634-9719

Access Points	River Miles	Shuttle Miles
A-B	10	12

Access Point Ratings:
  A-Rt.609, very good
  B-Rt.651 (just off Rt.619), excellent

however. The banks are now clay instead of sand, and they are really slippery when wet.

After another mile you pass a quaint, low bridge over a small creek on the right. Another mile and a half later you come to some riffles. Note that there are occasional rope swings interspersed with hunter's deer stands along here. Buckskin Creek enters on the left a mile beyond these riffles. The banks of this creek are sandy, and the flat ground just above makes this an excellent camping spot after 5.5 miles of paddling.

A mile below Buckskin Creek the river goes over two small Class I–II ledges as it bends right. Along this stretch you will notice that the woods have been clear cut almost to the river in spots. Also, you will see pine groves of various ages. The river then bends left, and you reach an island. Take the right channel with its two mini-rock gardens. Soon below is an interesting little ledge. Here, on a recent trip, there were two rusty signs on a tree on the left riverbank. The upstream sign said Sussex County and the downstream sign said Dinwiddie County. It must be comforting to know you have crossed a county line in the wilderness.

A half mile later is another island; go right. Shortly after the island ends you encounter several pleasant Class I–II rock gardens and ledges. After this, the river is calm for nearly a mile as you pass numerous loblolly pines 60 to 70 feet tall. You then reach another island. Left is more intimate; right has more water. Soon comes a nice little drop followed a quarter mile later by another drop with a rocky washboard on the left and a clear channel on the right.

Less than half a mile beyond you reach a power line that crackles as you pass underneath. This landmark signals that things are going to get more interesting soon. For the last mile of the trip you are going to be playing hide and seek as the river threads its way around several islands over ancient igneous rock. The river is hiding the rapids, and you are seeking them out. While you work your way through these channels, be alert for downed trees. In this last mile, the left channels are the most exciting; right channels are more conservative for nervous novices, particularly those with camping gear.

About 300 yards below the power line is an island. Most of the river goes right. But if there is enough water you can go to the far left and squeeze through two narrow slots the width of your boat. Soon, this island ends and another island quickly follows. Go far left for the most challenging action. Here the river goes over three ledges, dropping a total of 4 feet. Novices should look at these ledges first.

Just 200 yards downstream is a more challenging rapid in the left channel. The center of this channel is a tricky Class II–III drop over a couple of padded boulders, while the right is a Class II–III chute going very close to a headache threatening boulder on the left. Novices should definitely scout these two alternatives before running this drop or taking the easier (but bumpy) channels to the right.

In a quarter mile, you reach another rock garden, followed a couple of hundred yards later by another Class II–III drop if you stay far left. Novices should also look at this drop before attempting it because there is a pinning snaggletooth rock to avoid after entry. The center and right channels are easier but still bumpy. After the left and center channels join, you reach the Route 619 one-lane Double Bridge. The main bridge supports are on an island, and if you are still in the left channel, look for a crude canoeing gauge on the upstream edge of the left abutment.

About 100 yards below the bridge the right channel rejoins, and then you run a Class I drop. The take-out is immediately below this drop on the river right sandy bank where a small stream enters.

You will enjoy the take-out off Route 651; it is a first class Public Landing built by the Virginia Game Commission. You can get the river level from the Jones family by calling (804) 634-9719. From 0 to 2 feet, this is a trip for shepherded novices. From 2 to 4 feet it is a strong intermediate trip.

York

Little River

The best section of the Little River is the 6-mile stretch from Route 685 to Route 689. Above here the 9 miles starting at Route 601 have only a 3-foot-per-mile gradient, slow current, and trees across the stream.

However, the Little River makes up for its dawdling with a bang as it drops over a Class IV–V falls just below Route 685. Indeed, if novice paddlers want to avoid crowds and love to carry boats, they can walk in about one-half mile from Route 685 on river right and admire the falls as they muscle their boats to the more quiet water below.

Little River Falls is a good example of a heavy duty fall line rapid. This is the same fall line which parallels Interstate 95 and features rapids at the Gunpowder near Baltimore, the Potomac in Washington, D.C., the Rappahannock at Fredericksburg, and the nearby North Anna and South Anna. These fall line rapids vary from Class II rock gardens to Class VI maelstroms. The Little River is closer to the maelstrom category.

After placidly flowing down to the Route 685 bridge, the Little River suddenly goes wild. Just below this bridge the river quickly changes to steady Class II–III action, which gets progressively more difficult (including one juicy 3-foot drop) until it drops 15 feet in 50 yards over a two-section falls. The entry to the Class IV-V falls begins with a 3-foot chute in the center of the river; a quick, tough, hard right turn at the bottom of this chute; and then a bumpy ride down a 5-foot washboard. After going through the turbulent water below the washboard for about 20 yards, you line up for the final 5-foot drop, which is in river center just right of an exposed rock. Complicating this last drop is a jet of water that comes in from the left. Scout this double falls on the left and carry on the right.

The Little River flattens out quickly below its falls and becomes a Class I–II novice stream again. However, it is more interesting than the section above Route 685. The gradient is still 12 feet per mile, so there is some whitewater action. The water quality is good in this area, but, unfortunately, housing developments are slowly creeping into this rural setting. However, wildlife is still more commonplace than river front homes in this section, and it is common to see beaver, ducks, muskrat, and mink in the area.

The streambed offers both sandy shallows and deep pools along the bends, which probably will produce bream, perch, bass, and crappie for the persistent angler. There are also a few rocky ledges along the way. These drops of 0.5 to 1.5 feet provide modest challenges.

Hanover County is rich in history, and, like other nearby rivers, the Little River reveals dam, mill, and foundry

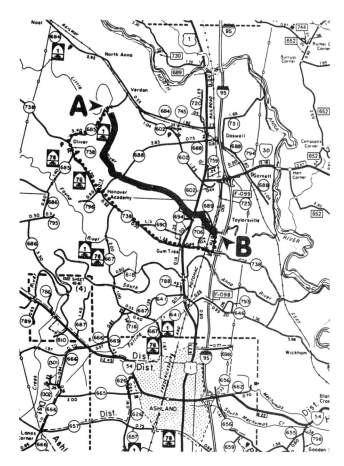

remains. The attractive stone construction and architecture is striking.

You can vary the length of your trip as there are several access points. About 3 miles from Route 685 is Route 688. Those primarily interested in running the falls can take out here. Another couple of miles farther is the Route 1 take-out, followed shortly by the Route 689 take-out. Both are on river right.

There is not much to recommend the Little River below Route 689. The gradient drops back to 3 feet per mile, there are occasional trees across the stream, and you have a long trip to the next two access points, one 14 miles downstream after the Little joins first the North Anna and then the Pamunkey. The other is 8 miles downstream after the Little joins the North Anna and requires a 1-mile paddle up the South Anna. If you brave this lower section, one of the "highlights" is the Doswell waste discharge station near where the Little and North Anna Rivers join.

Concerning water levels, there is a canoeing gauge on the Route 685 bridge. You need a good 0 on this gauge. A rough indicator of a minimum level is the Culpeper gauge, which should be about 2 feet.

Section: Rt. 685 to Rt. 689

Counties: Hanover

USGS Quads: Hewlett, Hanover Academy, Ashland

Suitable for: Day cruising

Skill Level: Advanced/experts at Little River Falls; novices below

Months Runnable: Winter, spring, and early summer

Interest Highlights: Remains of old mills and foundries; fishing

Scenery: Pretty in spots to pretty

Difficulty: Class I–II with 1 Class IV–V rapid

Average Width: 20 to 45 feet

Velocity: Generally moderate

Gradient: Up to 12 feet per mile; the first mile is 40 feet per mile

Runnable Water Levels:
Minimum: 0 feet on the put-in gauge (Rt. 685); perhaps 1.8 feet on Culpeper gauge
Maximum: 3 feet on the put-in gauge; perhaps 5 feet on Culpeper gauge

Hazards: Class IV–V Little River Falls just below put-in; perhaps an occasional tree in river

Scouting: Little River Falls (Class IV–V) on river left

Portages: Perhaps Little River Falls on river right

Rescue Index: Accessible to remote

Source of Additional Information: National Weather Service, Culpeper gauge (703) 260-0305

Access Points	River Miles	Shuttle Miles
A–B	6	8

Access Point Ratings
A–Rt. 685, if running Little River Falls, good; if not, fair to poor
B–Rt. 689, fair

Alan Taylor running the last drop of Little River Falls. Do not take this route—it resulted in a pin! Photo by Stephen Ensign.

Mattaponi River

The Mattaponi is a unique river in many respects, beginning with its name which comes from the names of four tributaries: the Mat, the Ta, the Po, and the Ni. Logicians and crossword puzzle nuts in particular will enjoy putting these tributaries together. Going from south to north, you first have the Mat and the Ta, which join to form the Matta River. Just north of these two rivers you have the Po and Ni, which meet to form the Poni River. Then the Matta and Poni combine to form the Mattaponi. Would that the rest of the world were so orderly!

It is possible to paddle these tributaries, but the full blown Mattaponi is better. The tributaries are not as pretty, and numerous trees cross them which results in many portages. Also, the 10-mile stretch from the confluence of the Matta and Poni Rivers to Route 207 has too many trees. There is much bird life and animal activity here (particularly beaver and muskrat), but the price of numerous portages is a bit steep.

Consequently, it is best to put in at Milford (Route 207) or below and work your way toward Aylett (US 360). There are fewer trees blocking this stretch and wildlife still abounds. During a typical day-trip you may have to slide or lift over from five to ten logs. The only other inconvenience is mosquitoes in season. You will have four direct take-outs in the 55 miles between Milford and Aylett: US 301 at 8.5 miles, Route 654 at 13 miles, Route

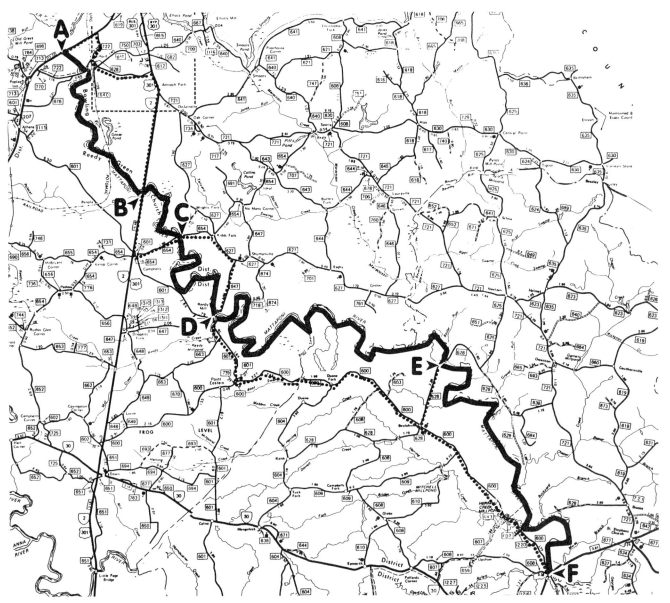

647 at 20.5 miles, and Route 628 at 39 miles. As a result, you have several day-trip or easy overnight camping options on a river that is perfectly suited for families and beginners. Perhaps the prettiest and most remote part of the Mattaponi is the first part of the last 16-mile section from Route 628 to Aylett. The second prettiest part is the stretch below Route 647.

Along with the Pamunkey River, the Mattaponi is the heart of the most pristine freshwater complex on the Atlantic Coast. Indeed, the Mattaponi and Pamunkey River systems have been identified as a national wetland priority by The Nature Conservancy under its National Wetland Conservation Program. Indicative of the crucial importance of these systems, the W. Alton Jones Foundation in 1986 announced the award of a $150,000 challenge grant to The Nature Conservancy for protecting the Mattaponi and Pamunkey Rivers.

With no cities at the fall line, unspoiled freshwater tidal systems, and a full development of plant and animal species, these rivers are irreplaceable living museums. For more than 300 years, the Mattaponi and Pamunkey have guarded nesting bald eagles, ospreys, herons, geese, ducks, and other marsh birds as well as the young of commercial and recreational fish and shellfish. The Virginia Wildlife Magazine has reported that there may be more bird species on the Mattaponi than anywhere else in Virginia. These rivers have also protected a group of plant species so rare that today they are found in only a handful of places worldwide. One species, the water hyssop, apparently occurs only on these two Virginia rivers. One of the most significant aspects of the water hyssop is its indicator value: it can grow only along rivers that are still relatively unspoiled and pristine. Another species, the sensitive joint vetch, is almost as rare.

After putting in at Milford for a relaxing day-trip or overnight journey, you will be struck by the clear green water and sandy bottom. For dropping only 2.5 feet a mile, the Mattaponi has a surprisingly good current. However, do not look for rapids for there are none on this Class A stream. The banks are mainly red clay; they range in height from a few feet to 10 feet or more, in some places forming impressive bluffs. Trees from both sides of the river often meet overhead, creating an intimate natural tunnel through which to paddle. There is also a small, interesting cave below Route 654 and occasional small cliffs with fossils.

After Aylett, the Mattaponi enters a swamp and passes a reservation for the Mattaponi Indians. Here the Mattaponi is tidewater as it journeys to join the Pamunkey and form the York River at West Point.

The surrounding area has an interesting history. First, it was and is now the home of the Mattaponi and Pamunkey Indians; both tribes have reservations in this area. Second, the swamps formed by these two rivers were an impenetrable barrier to road construction during colonial times and the Civil War. Having been spared from development, these two river systems now provide a unique opportunity for naturalists and lovers of the outdoors.

Section: Milford (Rt. 207) to Aylett (US 360)

Counties: Caroline and King William

USGS Quads: Woodford, Bowling Green, Ruther Glen, Penola, Sparta, Beulahville, Aylett

Suitable for: Day cruising or overnight camping

Skill Level: Beginners and novices

Months Runnable: Entire year

Interest Highlights: Wildlife, birds, fishing, quiet remoteness

Scenery: Pretty to beautiful in spots

Difficulty: Class A; no whitewater

Average Width: 50 to 100 feet

Velocity: Slow

Gradient: 2 feet per mile

Runnable Water Levels:
   Minimum: If you can paddle comfortably just above the Rt. 628 bridge, there is sufficient water.
   Maximum: Maybe high flood stage

Hazards: Trees in river

Scouting: None

Portages: None, except for occasional trees in river

Rescue Index: Accessible to somewhat remote

Source of Additional Information: None

Access Points	River Miles	Shuttle Miles
A–B	8.5	9
B–C	4.5	4
C–D	7.5	4
D–E	19.0	12
E–F	16.0	9

Access Point Ratings:
A–at Milford (Rt. 207), good
B–at US 301, very good
C–at Rt. 654, good
D–at Rt. 647, very good
E–at Rt. 628, good
F–at Aylett (US 360), excellent

North Anna River

The unique feature of the 10-mile section of the North Anna from Butler's Ford Bridge (Route 601) to Fox Memorial Bridge (US 1) is its isolation. Other than a couple of houses and one power line, the river belongs to you. The remains of an old mill are passed halfway through the trip. If it weren't for two rapids, this would be a delightful trip for novice paddlers. However, in the last third of the trip there is a long Class II rapid (with an optional Class II–III section) followed over a mile later by a long Class III–IV rapid. Consequently, this is an intermediate trip at moderate levels—particularly since there are no alternate take-outs during the journey.

The remoteness of the North Anna is a definite asset. For example, there are numerous signs of beaver throughout the trip. The paddler often sees either freshly gnawed branches or muddy trails on the bank where beavers slide into the river. Additional critters include deer, ducks, and the ubiquitous great blue heron. The river generally has sandy banks of 5 to 10 feet, which support a forest of primarily beech, river birch, and mountain laurel. The rocks in the river and the rock formations along the banks are usually granite or its larger-grained igneous cousin, pegmatite. Quartz dikes are often visible.

The Butler's Ford Bridge (Route 601) man-made put-in on river left is most convenient. However, this gently sloping launching point has a small price. It belongs to Pete Arnett who requests that you pay a dollar for each boat launched—a nominal fee for such a good service. There is also a canoeing gauge on the upstream piling of the bridge at the put-in. A reading of this gauge can be obtained by calling Lindsay Koenig at (804) 449-6701. Lindsay is a fellow paddler who lives by the river. The river is fed by the dam at Lake Anna, which was created by the Virginia Electric and Power Company (Vepco), which uses a nearby controversial nuclear power plant to generate electricity.

There are two items of historical interest at the put-in. On river left of the Butler's Ford Bridge are the remains of Jericho Mill. Take time to inspect these ruins. This was also where Union troops in 1864 crossed to successfully attack Confederate forces at Beaver Dam Station.

Shortly below the riffles at the put-in is a 1.5-foot ledge. After more than a mile of paddling, there is a nice beach on the right followed by a stone wall and two small ledges. Then comes a hill covered with mountain laurel and two more tiny ledges. Some impressive rocks are seen on the right 2 miles into the trip. Soon after these rocks are several nifty large and small islands in the river; go left of the first large island for the most interesting passage. After a half mile, the islands end with a series of riffles. Nearly a mile

later is another impressive rock formation on the right followed by a power line. Less than another mile later the river turns right with some striking rocks on the left.

Soon thereafter are two small ledges which mark the halfway point of this trip. Pull your boat over to the left bank just below these ledges and just above the remains of a wall on the left and an island in the center of the river. Between 25 and 100 yards from the river are the remains of an old mill complex where several walls and two chimneys still stand. This is Quarles' Mill. The hill on which this mill sits is an interesting place to explore, but be careful—the sandstone chimneys and some of the walls are no longer very stable.

After this delightful respite, run the chute just below the mill. You then pass an island and a couple of small ledges, the second of which has some moderate surfing possibilities. Below this are two more pretty rock formations on the left nearly a half mile apart. The first one has a good sized cedar tree growing directly out of the rock.

About a quarter mile beyond the second rock formation is the longest series of rapids of the trip (primarily Class II). It begins with an easy 200-yard-long rock garden that has a Class II drop at the end. Shortly below is a 1-foot ledge followed by a small staircase. You then go left of an island, negotiate another 1-foot ledge at its end, and reach a second island. The rapids end with a gentle passage to the right of this island (Class I–II) or a more vigorous technical channel to the left (Class II–III), which requires some boat control to pick a way through.

This sequence of islands ends soon after you work your way over a shallow, wide spot on the river. A half mile later the river turns right. As it does, look for an old grey house with a red metal roof high on the hill forming the left bank. (It might be hard to see when there is foliage on the trees.) Just below are some rocks in the river and a horizon line. You have paddled roughly 8 miles.

This is your signal to get over to the right bank for scouting. You have reached Fallsline Rapids (Class III–IV), which drops 10 feet over Paleozoic granite/gneiss for 100 yards. This set of rapids is best run on the right (and upright). The first drop that gets your attention is a 3-foot ledge. It is perhaps best run 15 to 20 yards off the right bank—just right of the steepest part of the ledge. Scout it to determine the best passage. Set a throw rope below this ledge if you have some shaky intermediate paddlers.

After 50 yards of less difficult stuff, there is another more serious 3-foot drop near the right bank where the water funnels directly into a large rock and then pillows off into a narrow channel to the right. Scout this lower drop carefully and set throw ropes/rescue boats using the huge pool below. The big problem here is the possible pinning of a boat in this narrow passage. Good boat control is a must to safely run this bottom drop. Those wishing to portage Fallsline Rapids should do so on river left after a careful ferry across the river. At higher levels these rapids become tougher and require more care. From the left bank at Fallsline Rapids, there is a steep trail that goes to a road. Unfortunately, this trail has allowed thoughtless people to walk in and dump much trash at the base of the rapids.

During early spring, paddlers are treated to a special fish phenomenon here. Below Fallsline Rapids you may see hundreds of fish, each about a foot long. These are alewives, an edible herringlike fish that swims upstream to spawn. They are stopped by Fallsline Rapids and mass here. Also, immediately east of the large island below Fallsline Rapids is Ox Ford, where General Robert E. Lee anchored his southern defenses during the Civil War Battle of the North Anna in May 1864.

From here to the take-out there are primarily higher banks and woods where you can see beaver slides and other evidence of these furry creatures. Less than one-half mile from the take-out are some old bridge pilings marking the old Chesterfield Bridge. The takeout is on the southeast side of the Fox Memorial Bridge (US 1) twin spans, on a site owned by Hanover County. The County's Department

of Parks and Recreation was instrumental in preserving use of this area for paddlers. Please help reward their efforts by contributing to the maintenance of this area. Paddlers should probably park shuttle vehicles in the turnoff area north of the Route 1 crossing which was formerly a VDOT Wayside.

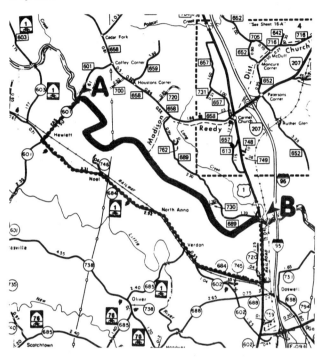

Section: Butler's Ford Bridge (Rt. 601) to US 1

Counties: Hanover

USGS Quads: Hewlett, Ruther Glen, Ashland

Suitable for: Day cruising

Skill Level: Intermediates

Months Runnable: Winter, spring, and early summer

Interest Highlights: Surprisingly remote, remains of old mills

Scenery: Pretty to beautiful in spots

Difficulty: Class I–II with 1 Class III–IV rapid

Average Width: 75 to 100 feet

Velocity: Generally moderate

Gradient: 8 feet per mile

Runnable Water Levels:
  Minimum: Maybe 3 inches on the put-in (Rt. 601) gauge
  Maximum: 2.5 feet (for intermediates) on the put-in gauge

Hazards: Occasional trees in river; Fallsline Rapids at high water

Scouting: Fallsline Rapids (Class III–IV) on river right

Portages: None, except perhaps Fallsline Rapids at high levels

Rescue Index: Accessible to remote

Source of Additional Information: Call Coastal Canoeist Lindsay Koenig, who lives by the river at (804) 449-6701; North Anna Dam, you want medium flow (several hundred cfs) at (804) 771-3000

Access Points	River Miles	Shuttle Miles
A–B	9.5	11

Access Point Ratings:
  A–at Rt. 601, excellent
  B–at US 1, good

Pamunkey River

If you want serenity, try the Pamunkey River. Although it has no whitewater, there is sufficient current to provide a great float trip on which one can fish, camp, relax, observe nature, and listen to the quiet of the wilderness. These features cause many veteran paddlers to return to the Pamunkey time and again.

Indeed, the Pamunkey and its nearby gentle river brother, the Mattaponi, provide good canoeing for even the most inexperienced paddler. Both rivers also have unique ecosystems. Specifically, the Mattaponi and Pamunkey River systems have been identified as a national wetland priority by The Nature Conservancy under its National Wetland Conservation Program. See the description of the Mattaponi in this chapter for more information on the special nature of these river systems.

The Pamunkey is reasonably wide and somewhat deep with flat water and slow, relaxing currents dominating. It winds along in a most restful way and gives a feeling of splendid isolation. The scenery along the riverbanks varies as the landscape fluctuates between open farmland and wooded areas dominated by river birch, sweet gum, and oak.

You have a variety of put-ins and take-outs on this mellow scenic river, which is created when the North Anna and South Anna rivers join. First, you can put in on Route 738 on the South Anna River. This is just 1 mile before the Pamunkey is created at the North/South Anna confluence. From here you have about 7 more miles to the first take-out at the US 301 bridge, thus making an 8-mile, easy day-trip.

Alternatively, you can put in on the North Anna at Route 30 and paddle 6 miles to the confluence and another 7 miles to US 301 for a 13-mile trip. This would provide a fuller day-trip or a really laid back overnight camping trip.

However, if you are a purist and want to paddle only the Pamunkey, put in on US 301 for either a 15-mile trip to Route 615 or a 33-mile trip to US 360 where the river enters a scenic swamp not too far from the Pamunkey Indian reservation.

The section most popular among local paddlers is the 13-mile trip from the North Anna (Route 30) put-in to US 301. Along here, as on other sections, you will find clear water and a sandy bottom. The only real difference is that the river is narrower here (40 feet), before the North and South Anna join. Also, overnighters will love to camp on the numerous sandy beaches along the river.

However, a significant portion of this land is posted, so please obey the "no trespassing" signs. The sand deposits here are large and thick, having shifted over the years as flood waters have moved and redeposited them.

While camping, relaxing, and floating down this serene river, keep a lookout for wildlife. Deer, beaver, muskrat, and raccoons are often seen. There is also significant bird life, particularly turkeys, ducks, great blue herons, little green herons, and occasional hawks. Bring your tackle if you are an angler. Bass, perch, sunfish, bream, and carp abound in these clear waters. Just throw the small ones back so others can enjoy fishing, too. For the sharp-eyed explorer, there is a special treat about 2 miles upstream of the US 301 bridge. On river right when the river makes one of its bends to the left, erosion has exposed an old clay bank that contains thousands of ancient fossilized sea shells. One can even find fossil shark's teeth here—some up to an inch long! There are also two lesser fossilized cliffs close to US 301.

The Pamunkey has a strong flavor of more recent history. For example, a historical marker on the lawn of a landowner bordering the Pamunkey states the following: This is the site of ". . . Hannoverton, a once thriving village which in 1761 by a small vote missed being the state capital of Virginia. Here on May 27, 1864, the Federal Army under Lt. General Grant crossed the Pamunkey in its movement from the Wilderness to the James..."

The Pamunkey takes its name from the Pamunkey Indian tribe which was one of the several tribes in the Powhatan Confederacy during the 1700s. Other tribes in the Confederacy having river names in this area are the Mattaponi and the Chickahominy. The Pamunkey and Mattaponi are clearly the better two of these three flatwater rivers to paddle. The scenery is better, and there are substantially fewer fallen trees to contend with.

Indeed, the main minor logistical difficulty on this peaceful trip is an occasional downed tree in the river. However, these are no real problem (except at high water) because of the slow current. You also have to be careful of the slippery muddy banks. Finally, mosquitoes can be a problem seasonally—especially off the river in the woods where it is shaded, cooler, and damper: here they can be merciless.

Section: Route 30 (North Anna) to US 360

Counties: Hanover, Caroline, King William

USGS Quads: Ashland, Hanover, Studley, Manquin

Suitable for: Day cruising or overnight camping

Skill Level: Beginners and novices

Months Runnable: Entire year; can be run even in summer

Interest Highlights: Wildlife, fishing, quiet remoteness

Scenery: Pretty to beautiful in spots

Difficulty: Class A; no whitewater

Average Width: 25 to 90 feet

Velocity: Slow

Gradient: 2 feet per mile

Runnable Water Levels:
 Minimum: Maybe 1.2 feet on the Culpeper gauge, but this is not too relevant
 Maximum: Flood stage

Hazards: Occasional trees in river, particularly at high water

Scouting: None

Portages: None, except for occasional trees in river

Rescue Index: Accessible to somewhat remote

Source of Additional Information: None

Access Points	River Miles	Shuttle Miles
A–B	13	7
A¹–B	8	7
B–C	15	8
B–D	33	17

Access Point Ratings:
A–at Rt. 30 (North Anna), fair
A¹–at Rt. 738 (South Anna), fair
B–at US 301, very good
C–at Rt. 615, fair
D–at US 360, good—but limited parking

Bill Micks running the first major ledge of Fallsline Rapid on the North Anna.

Larry Gross avoiding the potential pinning rock at the end of Fallsline Rapid on the North Anna.

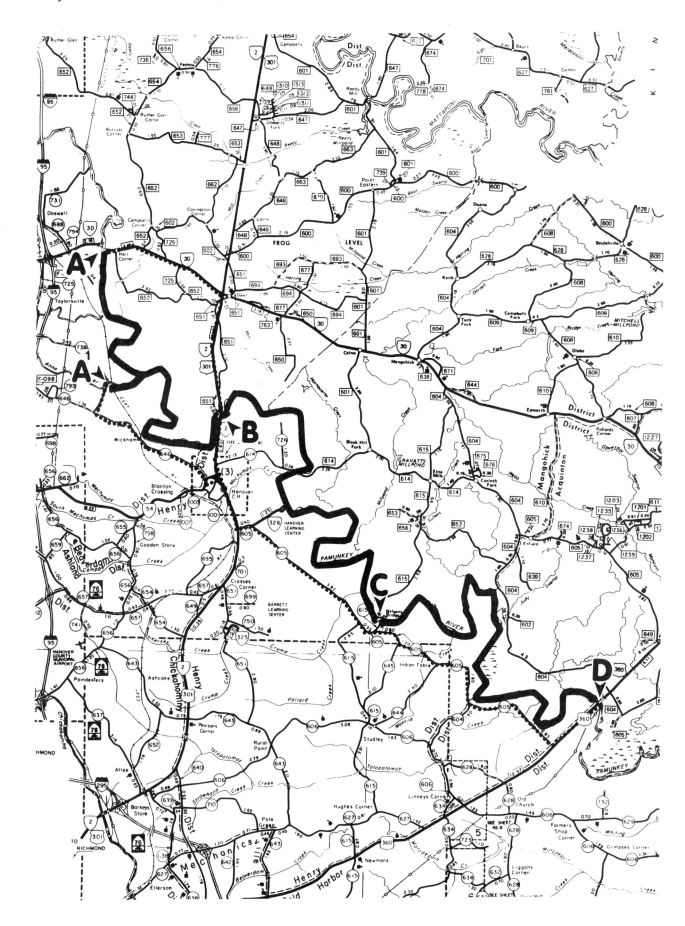

South Anna River

The most accessible and best whitewater section of the South Anna is between US 33 and Route 54, where there is ample parking and easy access to the river. There is more whitewater upstream, but the bridge at Route 673 has posted "no trespassing" signs. Also, the next bridge downstream from Route 673 is on a single-lane dirt road with little parking, and you only get one ledge for all this trouble.

When you put in at US 33 (Ground Squirrel Bridge), there is parking and easy access on river right (the east side). Carry or slide your boat down a short slope to the river. At this point the river is quiet. There is current but no whitewater, the scenery is pleasant if not awe inspiring, and one can pretty much kick back and relax for a spell. Soon you will come to a few islands with some fast water if you go right of them.

You reach the first bona fide whitewater about 1.5 miles (a half-hour paddle) into the trip as you round a left bend. Here the river drops over several easy small Class I–II ledges. Run left of center. After a short calm stretch, the next part of this rapid offers you two choices. First, you can take the main route down the middle of the river and end up with a split decision to go either side of a midstream boulder. Alternatively, if there is enough water, you can take the route on the far left between the left bank and an island. This path is more technical and requires some quick turns. Both routes are Class II+ with no hazards as of this writing.

There are no other rapids of note until nearly 3 miles into the trip (an hour of paddling) when you approach a one-lane wooden bridge (Gilmans Bridge) at Route 657. Here the river widens, and there are a couple of houses on the right bank and a picnic area on the left. Unfortunately, this picnic area is on private property, and boaters must refrain from using it.

These landmarks indicate the longest stretch of rapids, a Class II+ section. The best two routes are on river right and at midstream. This rapid ends with an easy S-turn into another slow section which continues until you arrive at the Route 657 bridge a short distance downstream.

Here is the fall line of the South Anna—with the best Class II+ rapids of the trip dropping over Paleozoic granite/gneiss. There are several choices, but perhaps the best route starts center, moves right, and then left back to center. After a short pause, head down the right bank and then over to the left bank to finish in a pool where the best lunch stop on the trip is found on an island. Eat here instead of at the private picnic ground mentioned above. It's prettier and will keep landowners from being rightfully angry at paddlers.

There are a few more easily seen, enjoyable ledges below here on either side of midstream islands. After this the river again calms down with alternating sections of slow current and fast riffles until you reach the blue metal bridge which is Route 54 and the take-out. There is a low-head dam just above the bridge, but at moderate water levels highly experienced paddlers will not find it a serious problem. Those with "damophobia" can scout and/or take out at an obvious spot on river right just above the dam. Or you can run the dam (with speed please), and take out just below. When parking at the take-out, use the gravel parking area on Route 54 just up the hill from the bridge on the westbound lane. Do this because there are still rumors of cars being towed when left at the Water Treatment Plant parking area beside the river.

This is a pleasant trip well suited to novice boaters. Scenery is good, although the development of riverside property in recent years is spoiling the remote nature of this river in some spots. Also, there is some logging going on in places—a definite eyesore. It's too bad there aren't any continuous heavy duty rapids to take your mind off these distractions from an otherwise scenic Piedmont river. However, if you are quiet, you will still encounter beaver, deer, turkey, waterfowl, and maybe even an occasional sunbather in their respective haunts.

There is a canoeing gauge at the US 33 put-in. You can easily read it from the water's edge as you launch your canoe. Speaking of canoes, advanced boaters may well want to bring a Grumman without flotation to make this trip more interesting.

Section: US 33 to Rt. 54

Counties: Hanover

USGS Quads: Hanover Academy

Suitable for: Day cruising

Skill Level: Novices

Months Runnable: Winter, spring, and early summer

Interest Highlights: Scenic Piedmont river, wildlife, technical fall line rapids

Scenery: Pretty in spots to pretty

Difficulty: Class I–II+

Average Width: 40 to 60 feet

Velocity: Generally moderate

Gradient: 8 feet per mile

Runnable Water Levels:

Minimum: 0 feet on the put-in gauge (US 33); maybe 1.2 feet on Culpeper gauge
Maximum: 3 feet on the put-in gauge

Hazards: Occasional trees in river; low-head dam just above Rt. 54 take-out

Scouting: None, except perhaps low-head dam on right

Portages: None, except perhaps low-head dam on right

Rescue Index: Generally accessible

Source of Additional Information: National Weather Service, Culpeper gauge (703) 260-0305

Access Points	River Miles	Shuttle Miles
A–B	7	9

Access Point Ratings:
A–at US 33, very good
B–at Rt. 54, good

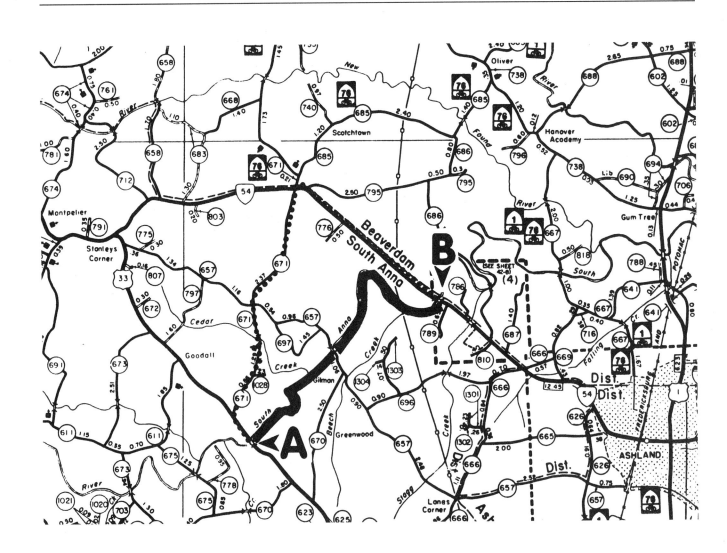

Rappahannock

Conway River

The Conway (also known as the Middle River) is a very busy tiny creek. If you choose to run it you will be very busy, too. The gradient is over 100 feet per mile for the first 2 miles and 60 feet per mile for the last 4 miles of this 6-mile section. Not only will you have to be constantly alert as you plunge down the continual (mostly Class II and Class III) drops of this creek, but you will have to lug your boat around numerous obstacles, many of which are in the middle of these rapids: a dozen trees, two fences, and a bridge with too low clearance. Consequently, this is a stream for advanced paddlers or alert, aggressive intermediates with good boat control. With all these obstacles, make sure you have a helmet on your head and flotation in your boat for safety. At lower levels, there are sufficient small eddies for boaters to stop. At higher levels, the creek becomes more of a flush, and the boater has to be extremely vigilant to avoid certain disaster with these numerous strainers. In the 1960s, heroic efforts by paddlers and Boy Scouts cleared this river of trees. However, with the passage of 20 years and the flood of November 1985, the fallen trees have returned with a vengeance.

For put-ins, you have several choices. You can put in at Kinderhook for a 4-mile trip. There is a gauge here on the left abutment of the Route 613 bridge crossing the Conway. Alternatively, you can put in 2 miles upstream at Fletcher where the gradient is 40 feet per mile steeper. If you put in at Fletcher, get permission first because most of the land is posted. Even though the land is not posted at Kinderhook, it would be wise to get permission there, too. Also, remember that this river is like a naughty child playing hide and seek in the upper 2 miles. When close to the road, it shows you the easier drops and fewest strainers. However, when it goes out of sight, the drops are larger and the strainers more numerous. Finally, competent boaters really feeling their oats could follow the road next to the river and put in upstream of Fletcher where the gradient reaches 150 feet per mile. (See the end of this Conway narrative if you are so inclined.)

At the Fletcher put-in the Conway is only 15 to 20 feet wide. In the first quarter mile most of the rapids are straightforward Class II–III drops with one exception. Here the river turns sharp right over an abrupt 4-foot drop against a large boulder on the left. The left bank here has caved in (probably from the November 1985 flood) and moved this large boulder over to create a narrow drop. Scout it from the right first, not only to make sure you can get over the nasty rocks in this steep drop but also to be sure there isn't a tree blocking it. A portage on the right is an honorable option.

A few hundred yards below this drop, you will come to the first bridge. Within the next mile or so you will come to two other bridges, the first with a man-made stone wall just below it creating a 2-foot ledge, and the second with insufficient clearance underneath and a mandatory portage on the left. Be careful with this last bridge, particularly at high water. By now you should be thoroughly warmed up, having carried around several trees and experienced numerous vigorous rock gardens and cobble drops.

After 2 miles you reach the Kinderhook bridge and can go over to the nearby store for a snack or Gatorade to replace your lost body fluids after so much work. So far, the river has been somewhat intimate and gorgelike as it played tag with the road. Below Kinderhook, the river opens into a wider valley as the gradient lessens. The bank often consists of granite boulders. However, despite less gradient, there are also more trees, including at least one real mess of debris blocking the entire river and (as of this writing) two barbed wire fences. The real shame of all these trees is that they are often in the middle of nice Class II rapids.

About halfway through this lower 4-mile section you will come to a juicy Class III rapid with several hydraulics to punch. Very shortly below this, look for a large flat rock on the left bank and the river turning right. Get your boat over to either bank and scout the Class III–IV rapids dropping a good 5 feet below. There is one tricky hole on the top left to avoid (right or left). Then you set up for the largest drop. At moderate levels at least, there is a tongue in the center that takes you into the heart of the rapids and then a left turn to finish. By all means avoid a huge, nasty hole on the bottom right. Set throw ropes on the left and portage on the left. Less than 50 yards below this rapid is a good 2-foot ledge. Then you will resume your battles with the trees, including probably one long carry around a fallen mess. The take-out on river right is a welcome relief after all this work. Because of the portages, allow more than a couple of hours for this 6-mile trip. For example, a recent trip for this section took nearly 5 hours.

If you are in good shape and have the right attitude, this river is a delight. The Pedlar granite, gneiss, and other igneous rocks forming the bed and banks of this river plus the evergreens (mostly hemlocks and pines) and hardwoods give you a feeling of remoteness. Wildlife abounds. On one winter trip a flock of six wild turkeys was flushed; several great blue herons spooked at close range; and kingfishers, ospreys, hawks, and many other bird species seen. Deer and beaver were also present.

If you want to paddle this river, note that the Conway goes up and down quickly. The minimum level is at least 3.5 feet on the Culpeper gauge. An example of the Conway's volatility follows. One morning the Culpeper gauge was 3.6 feet; that evening it was 5.8 feet. The following morning it had dropped to 4.1 feet and by nightfall was 3.4 feet. The watershed is so small that you generally have only 24 hours after a hard rain to be sure you catch the Conway. However, if you love nature, are in good shape, and want to test your mettle against the Conway, do so in the company of a small group of like-minded boaters. For those who are into trees and small rivers, remember that the Upper Rapidan is only 2 miles or so away from the Conway. Running both of these in one long day would be macho-man's delight.

Like the nearby Upper Rapidan, it is possible to put in on the Conway upstream of the usual Fletcher put-in, depending on nerve, experience, and water level. About 1.5 miles above Fletcher, Route 667 has a low-water bridge crossing the Conway. When this short uppermost section has enough water in it, the water is usually too high and the current too swift to drive across this bridge. On the other hand, you can scout this 1.5 mile top section from the road the entire distance upstream from Fletcher. While on the shuttle, be sure to check out the tight rock gardens nearly a mile below the Route 667 low-water bridge. This top section becomes a real flush at very high water levels. However, it is not quite as difficult as the 2-mile section of the Upper Rapidan above Graves Mill a few miles away.

Steve Ettinger runs an almost typical rapid on the Conwa—there are no trees in it.

Section: Fletcher (Rt. 667) to Rt. 230 bridge

Counties: Madison, Greene

USGS Quads: Fletcher, Stanardsville

Suitable for: Day cruising

Skill Level: Advanced paddlers and very alert intermediates

Months Runnable: Winter and spring following a heavy rain

Interest Highlights: Very busy tiny river

Scenery: Pretty to beautiful in spots

Difficulty: Class II–III (because of fallen trees and obstacles) with 1 Class III–IV rapid

Average Width: 15 to 25 feet

Velocity: Fast

Gradient: Top 2 miles at 100 feet per mile; last 4 miles at 60 feet per mile

Runnable Water Levels:
Minimum: 0 feet on the Kinderhook gauge (Route 613) and a solid 3.5 feet on the Culpeper gauge
Maximum: 3 feet on the Kinderhook gauge and 7 feet on the Culpeper gauge

Hazards: Perhaps a dozen trees in river; 2 barbed wire fences; 1 low-water bridge

Scouting: Boat scout the entire river for fallen trees and fences; abrupt 4-foot drop less than 0.25 mile below Fletcher put-in; big Class III–IV rapid about 2 miles below Kinderhook

Portages: Numerous carries to avoid fallen trees, 2 fences, and low-water bridge

Rescue Index: Accessible first 2 miles; accessible to remote last 4 miles

Source of Additional Information: National Weather Service, Culpeper gauge (703) 260-0305

Access Points	River Miles	Shuttle Miles
A–C	6	6.4
B–C	4	4.4

Access Point Ratings:
A–at Fletcher (Rt. 667), very good
B–at Kinderhook (Rt. 667 & 613), very good
C–at Rt. 230, very good

NOTE: The summer flood of 1995 struck the Conway as this book was being reprinted. There may be significant changes to this run.

Ed Evangelidi entering and exiting the big rapid on the Conway.

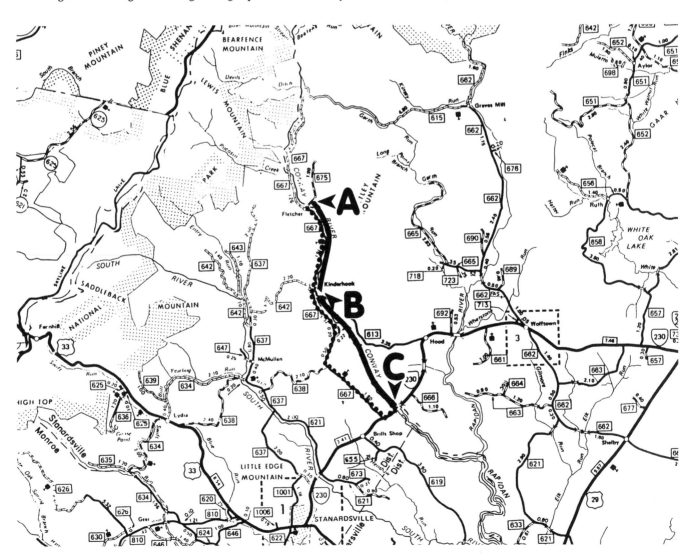

Covington River

This exciting trip is for competent intermediate boaters who do not get claustrophobic on small tight streams. It is best begun at the Route 622 bridge where there is a new Randy Carter gauge. One can paddle this 4.5-mile section of the Covington at 0 on this gauge, but 4 to 5 inches give a very comfortable trip.

On this superb voyage, the Covington is clear and passes through a small gorge before joining the Rush and, later, Thornton Rivers. This section, from Route 622 to Route 626, is generally characterized by pretty woods with trees and ancient Cambrian granite rocks forming the riverbanks.

The put-in is in an area of farmland but the riverbank is lined with trees. The trip begins with a 100-yard Class II rock garden. A couple of minutes later there is a house on the right. This signals a strong Class II double ledge in low water which is a Class III in high water. Below this there are steady Class II rock gardens. As you paddle, please note the lichen covered big rocks and mountain laurel on the banks.

About a mile from the put-in there are a pair of 2-foot ledges roughly a minute apart. The Route 621 bridge is reached a quarter mile further. Right after this bridge, there is a 50-yard Class II rock garden. This is followed by a right turn next to a big rock on the left bank.

About 50 yards later there is another right turn and another big rock forming the left bank. This signals a very tight Class III rapid which gets tougher above 6 inches on the gauge. At moderate levels it is entered on the left next to the face of this rock with the current flowing right. Immediately thereafter one needs to make a hard 90 degree left turn through a narrow chute to avoid a Volkswagen-sized rock in the center of the river. At middling levels this turn can become exceedingly difficult. At higher levels you can run the entire rapid to the right of this nasty rock. Scout this rapid the first time it is run.

Just below, there is a short, low Class III rapid that is best entered in the center. Scout this, too: at levels of perhaps 5 inches you need to angle your boat 45 degrees to the left after entry and pillow off a small curler parallel to the boat near the bottom of the rapid. Otherwise, one may be blown too far right by the current and hit a nasty rock just above water on the bottom right of the rapid. This could pin a boat in such a small chute.

Shortly after this excitement, the paddler comes to an island. The left channel is blocked by a big, dry ledge in low water, so one should run the nice, little ledge to the right. A couple of minutes later there is a nice, diagonal Class II ledge (in moderate water) followed by a Class II chute to the right. This is followed by some large, pretty rocks on the banks. The river continues with Class I riffles for a half mile before the Rush River joins on the left.

After this confluence, there are six nice, little ledges in the mile before the take-out. These ledges (particularly the very last) create pleasant low-penalty surfing holes. You, too, can explore the world of a small hole sitting parallel, perpendicular, or upside down. Shortly below the sixth ledge the Thornton River joins from the right, and you are at the Route 626 take-out bridge.

If you are observant, there is wildlife. A recent trip found boaters playing tag with a great blue heron and flushing a wild turkey. Although there were no fences across the river then, one should be alert to this possibility. Also, watch for downed trees: several years earlier I found a tree 6 feet in diameter across the river. Fortunately, it is now gone.

The section of the Covington above the put-in is not recommended because branches, trees, and perhaps fences block the river. Below the confluence with the Thornton there is little whitewater of note.

Section: Rt. 622 bridge to Rock Mills (Route 626)

Counties: Rappahannock

USGS Quads: Washington

Suitable for: Day cruising

Skill Level: Intermediates

Months Runnable: Winter and spring after a rainy period

Interest Highlights: Scenic little gorge

Scenery: Pretty to beautiful in spots

Difficulty: Class II–III

Average Width: 15 to 25 feet

Velocity: Moderate to fast

Gradient: 38 feet per mile

Runnable Water Levels:
  Minimum: 0 feet on Rt. 622 gauge; 5.8 feet on Remington gauge
  Maximum: 3 feet on Rt. 622 gauge; 8 feet on Remington gauge

Hazards: An occasional tree and maybe fences across river

Scouting: 2 tight Class III rapids just below the Route 621 bridge (a mile into the trip)

Portages: None

Rescue Index: Accessible to remote

Source of Additional Information: National Weather Service, Remington gauge (703) 260-0305

Access Points	River Miles	Shuttle Miles
A–B	4.5	3

Access Point Ratings:
A–at Rt. 622, good
B–at Rt. 626, very good

Ed Grove backs through Volkswagen Rock Rapid on the Covington. Photo by Sam Chambliss.

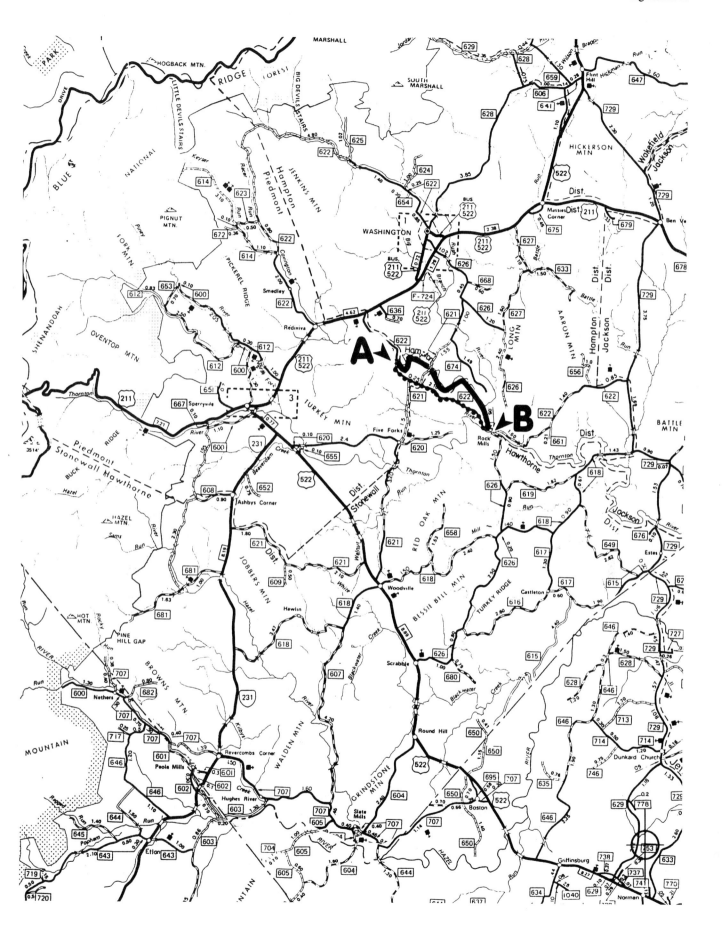

Hughes and Hazel Rivers

This is one of the nicest trips to Boston we know of—Boston, Virginia, that is. The metropolis of Boston is essentially one building which contains a modern general store and a very folksy post office. The store is less than a mile from the take-out near where US 522 and Route 707 join. It is a good place to take a break during the shuttle or after paddling the river.

The Hughes (which joins the Hazel nearly halfway through the trip) is a pleasant Class II stream for novices which is very similar to its nearby whitewater brother, the Thornton (though the gradient of the Hughes is somewhat less and the scenery not quite as spectacular). Like the Thornton, the Hughes has only one whitewater section. There are too many fences or fallen trees above the put-in, and the Hazel is not really whitewater below the US 522 take-out.

However, the Hughes holds its water longer than the Thornton and is a good alternative when the Thornton is running just below 0 on its Fletchers Mill gauge. In addition, do consider the Hughes if the nearby Covington River is also too low.

The Route 603 put-in for this trip is just downstream of a low-water bridge. If you like feathered friends, this put-in is made for you, because it is next to a chicken farm where hundreds of these white critters are strutting about. Also, if you haven't had your Wheaties for this 9-mile trip, you can take out at bridges crossing the Hughes roughly 1.5, 3, and 4 miles into the trip. The last of these three bridges is a low-water bridge and should be approached with care. Portage right or left. The shuttle is also easy. After the put-in on Route 603, Route 707 parallels this section until the take-out on Route 522. For a reasonably comfortable run on this section, there should be at least 1 foot on the US 522 gauge at the take-out.

This enjoyable trip flows mostly through farmland and wooded areas. It is distinguished by 17 (count 'em) Class I–II ledges and various mild rock gardens nicely spaced throughout the trip. Here and there these ledges create nice holes in which the adventurous can play. If you get a late start, look for a very pretty lunch stop nearly 45 minutes into the trip at moderate levels. Here you will find a very large, flat rock on river right where the Hughes makes a sharp left turn.

Nearly halfway through the trip and shortly after the low-water bridge portage mentioned above, the Hazel River joins the Hughes on the left. Roughly a mile below this confluence is the best whitewater section of the river. Here one finds four ledges reasonably close together. The first of these is the largest and best of the trip. This solid Class II ledge should be run to the left at moderate levels and has surfing opportunities below. The last of these four ledges also has a nice surfing wave.

After another mile or so, on river left, you come to a scenic hill on top of which a very striking building sits. This is the Freedom Studies Center which trains foreign officials to counter subversion and maintain democratic institutions in their own countries. From here to the take-out (about 2 miles downstream) the river is generally calm.

Mort Smith runs the largest ledge on the Hughes.

The only negative aspects of this relaxing trip are occasional downed trees blocking the river and debris. On one trip I saw several old tires and a rusting camper top resting upside down in the river.

However, there is more wildlife than the chickens at the put-in. Kingfishers, turkey vultures, and hawks are usually seen, while turkey and deer have been sighted during late fall trips. In addition, anglers catch at least suckers in the clear Hughes/Hazel waters.

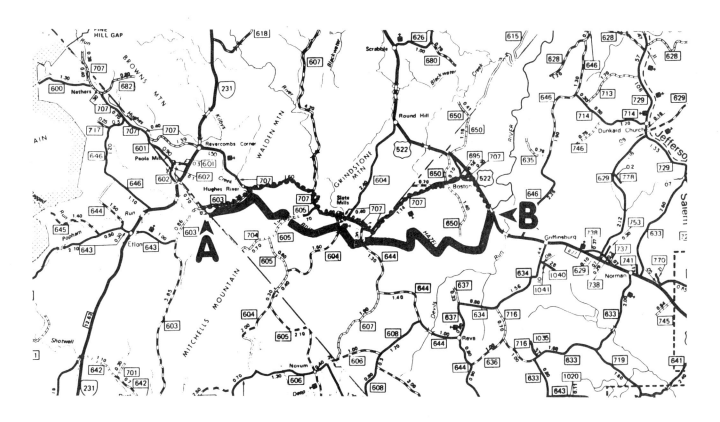

Section: Rt. 603 to Boston (US 522)

Counties: Rappahannock, Culpeper

USGS Quads: Woodville, Castleton

Suitable for: Day cruising

Skill Level: Novices

Months Runnable: Winter and spring, but can be run in early summer after an extended rain

Interest Highlights: 17 ledges, wooded area, scenic farmland

Scenery: Pretty in spots to pretty

Difficulty: Class I–II

Average Width: 25 to 35 feet

Velocity: Moderate

Gradient: 15 feet per mile

Runnable Water Levels:
Minimum: 1 foot on old US 522 gauge; 0 feet on new Hughes gauge on US 522; 4.6 feet on Remington gauge
Maximum: 3 feet on US 522 gauge; 7.5 feet on Remington gauge

Hazards: An occasional tree in river

Scouting: None

Portages: 1 low-water bridge 4 miles into trip

Rescue Index: Generally accessible

Source of Additional Information: National Weather Service, Remington gauge (703) 260-0305

Access Points	River Miles	Shuttle Miles
A–B	9.5	7

Access Point Ratings:
A–at Rt. 603, good
B–at US 522, very good

Rapidan River

Graves Mill to Route 230 Bridge

If you like fences and downed trees, you'll love this 6 mile section of the Rapidan. There are a good seven cattle fences and at least the same number of downed trees to work your boat around, under, or over. However, the carries are worth it! Here the Rapidan is a tiny, picturesque river flowing through scenic farmland backed by beautiful rolling hills and forests. The water is clear, and the riverbed is continuous cobble bars and small boulder ledges. Trees (primarily sycamores) and ancient Pedlar granite boulders line the riverbank, which is often low enough to provide good views of the pretty countryside.

Although the rapids are only Class I–II at lower levels, this section is not for beginners. The swift flowing water with a gradient of over 40 feet per mile often passes under downed trees and fences that suddenly appear around tight bends. Good boat control and fast reflexes are needed so paddlers do not get swept into these obstacles. At higher levels the rapids are more difficult and your reflexes must be faster. Because of the frequent portages, this river is more suitable for open canoes than decked boats. However, if problems develop, Route 662 is on the right for the first two-thirds of the trip.

The Graves Mill put-in is unique. Immediately after Route 615 turns off to the left, you come to the Graves Mill post office. This lonely, tiny white building was the smallest post office in Virginia, but was washed away in the summer flood of 1995.

After putting in on this 20-foot-wide stream, you will be on swift flowing water that often drops over easy cobble bars. The first 1-foot cobble ledge is about a half mile from the put-in and a 1.5-foot ledge comes a half mile later. You probably will have carried around a couple of trees by now, and the first fence is about 1.5 miles into the trip. The cobble bars, tight turns, and occasional ledges come in comfortable succession until you have gone 2 miles. Then the river suddenly braids, and you have to squirm through narrow passages caused by a thicket of brush. Look this section over before committing yourself to it.

After this, the pattern of cobble bars and occasional small ledges resumes. The only pain and strain comes from the continued carries required by fences and downed trees. About 3 miles into the trip, the fences ease up, but the gradient begins to lessen. Nevertheless, the small cobble drops and downed trees are still numerous enough to provide interest and exercise. Having paddled 4 miles, you come to the Route 662 bridge. This is a convenient take-out if you are pooped from the carries or have begun this trip in late afternoon. (I thought I could go from Graves Mill to the Route 230 bridge in 2 hours. However, the numerous portages and fading daylight on one trip forced me to take out at the Route 662 bridge after 2.5 hours of paddling.)

After you go under the Route 662 bridge, the gradient drops to 23 feet per mile and the rapids ease up. However, there is one main hazard to worry about in the remaining 1.5 miles. Midway between this bridge and the Route 230 bridge take-out is a 3-foot dam with a bad hydraulic below. The strenuous portage is on the right. Some paddlers have run this dam close to the right, but inspect this drop carefully before attempting it.

There are two problems at the take-out. First, there is a fence just below the Route 230 bridge. Second, this spot is posted with "no parking" signs, so you will need permission from one of the nearby landowners to park a shuttle vehicle.

In addition to the benignly gazing bovines you encounter along the way, other wildlife will greet you along the river—particularly birds. Kingfishers and great blue herons are perhaps the most striking species seen.

Incidentally, you must act quickly to catch this river since it drains a rather small watershed. The Culpeper gauge should be at least 3.5 feet. If the gauge is close to this minimum and no rain is forecast, do not wait a day because the river will be too low. (For example, on one trip several years ago, the Culpeper gauge dropped from 4.1 to 2.9 feet in 12 hours!) One nearby river alternative needing similar amounts of water is the Conway which joins the Rapidan downstream of this section.

If the Upper Rapidan is really cooking, and you want to extend your trip, you can start up to 2 miles above Graves Mill, depending on the water level, your nerve, and group experience. The river parallels the road with nonstop rapids the entire way so you will know exactly what is in store for you. Here the gradient is 100 feet per mile for the first mile and 70 feet for the second mile. One mile upstream of Graves Mill is the Rapidan Ranch bridge. This property is posted, so choose another put-in further upstream. A quarter mile above Rapidan Ranch the road changes to a Class III cobble as you enter Shenandoah National Park. If you plan to fish in the park, be aware that all fish must be thrown back and that anglers must use artificial lures with barbless hooks.

Just before the highest put-in you go through a beautiful grove of hemlocks. When the road crawls away from the river, you have reached the put-in at the confluence of the Staunton and Rapidan Rivers. Just below the put-in, at moderate levels, on this upper section are two Class III–IV drops twisting between large boulders. Scout these drops carefully should you choose to run them. Set throw ropes below on the right. There are other goodies downstream so make sure you look this stretch over carefully on the shuttle. The heaviest rapids are in the two third-mile stretch of Shenandoah National Park where the river is in a small gorge. Below the park and gorge, the countryside opens up to farmland, the gradient eases, and the rapids become more mellow.

On very rare occasions at very high levels this river can become a narrow, expert, decked boater flush with roller coaster velocity, spiced with big waves and holes, particularly just below the top put-in. The presence of downed trees coupled with high water velocity add to the danger.

Incidentally, I was on the bank of the river one day at very high water and heard an ominous clunking sound. The volume and speed of the river were so intense that the cobble bottom was moving. Also, the river was so high within its cobble bank that the road was lower than the river! It is an eerie feeling to be driving along a road looking up at a river. Expert decked boaters who are into tight high-water flushes should also check out the Upper Conway a few miles away when the world is in flood.

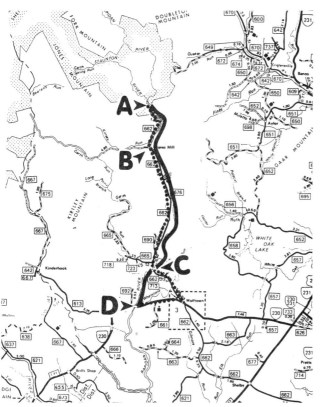

Section: Staunton River (Rt. 662) or Graves Mill (Rt. 662/615) to Route 230 bridge near Wolftown

Counties: Madison

USGS Quads: Madison, Rochelle

Suitable for: Day cruising

Skill Level: Alert intermediates at moderate levels below Graves Mill; advanced/expert paddlers above Graves Mill depending on levels

Months Runnable: Only in winter and spring after heavy rain

Interest Highlights: Gorge above Graves Mill; picturesque woods and farms

Scenery: Pretty in spots to beautiful

Difficulty: Class I–II+ at moderate levels below Graves Mill, but good boat control is mandatory; Class III–IV above Graves Mill depending on water level and put-in

Average Width: 20 feet

Velocity: Moderate to fast

Gradient: 85 feet per mile for 2 miles above Graves Mill; 44 feet per mile for next 4.5 miles; 23 feet per mile for last 1.5 miles

Runnable Water Levels:
Minimum: 3.5 feet on Culpeper gauge
Maximum: Nearing flood stage

Hazards: Numerous trees and fences across river; a 3-foot dam near the end of the trip

Scouting: 1 braided section of the river; 3-foot dam; above Graves Mill scout entire river from road for heavy rapids and trees in high water

Portages: Numerous carries around trees and fences

Rescue Index: Accessible

Source of Additional Information: National Weather Service, Culpeper gauge (703) 260-0305

Access Points	River Miles	Shuttle Miles
A–B	2	2
B–C	4.5	4
B–D	6	7

Access Point Ratings:
A–at Staunton River (Rt. 662), good
B–at Graves Mill (Rt. 662/615), very good
C–at Rt. 662, good (hard to park)
D–at Rt. 230, good

Note: The summer flood of 1995 struck the upper Rapidan as this book was being reprinted. There may be significant changes to this section.

US 522 to Germanna Ford (Route 3)

The 15-mile trip from US 522 to Germanna Ford on the Rapidan will surprise you. It is a perfect blend for a family canoe trip during most of the year. There is pretty scenery, lots of nature, and plenty of opportunities for kids to get out and play. The few rapids are mostly gentle gravel bar riffles of Class I or less. You have long stretches of shallow, crystal clear water flowing over a sandy bottom, and you can get out and explore numerous small sandy islands along the way. There are also nice rocky areas with good fishing holes. The best fishing is for bass, bluegill, and redbreast sunfish. This is a quiet trip along a river which has very little development among large tracts of farmland. The banks are moderately high and often covered with hardwood trees. These features give the feeling that the Rapidan here is a small, even intimate river. When finished, you feel you have touched the trees and banks.

When putting in at US 522, you have two choices downstream of the bridge. If it is not raining, put in on river right from a dirt road in a cornfield. However, if it is wet or muddy the dirt road is a mess, and you should put in on river left by walking 100 yards to a little stream that soon enters the Rapidan.

A better alternative is to put in on river right at Raccoon Ford (Route 611). The Route 611 put-in is about 1.5 miles downstream from the US 522 put-in and gives you a 13.5-mile trip. The remains of an old dam mark Raccoon Ford. However, be careful here because an island divides the river, and sometimes there are fallen trees on the river right side just below this put-in. Also, parking is very limited, and the area is very isolated at both US 522 and Route 611. Consequently, it is recommended that you do not leave shuttle vehicles at either place.

When water levels are low in July and August, this is a full day-trip. Nevertheless, you can usually paddle this stretch when the Rappahannock from Remington to Fredericksburg is too low. In May and June, however, the Rapidan usually moves right along, taking up to 5 hours of paddling time depending on how long you have to play and relax. Unfortunately for campers, the land is private; so there is no camping unless you happen to know one of the owners and have his/her permission.

The gauge for this run is Culpeper. Open boaters with hiking boots can run/walk this stretch down to 0.8 feet on the Culpeper gauge. However, for a comfortable trip you need 1.5 feet of water. The Rapidan gets pushy at 3 feet and starts to leave its banks. This is the recommended cut-off for novice boaters.

Section: US 522 or Raccoon Ford (Rt. 611) to Germanna Ford (Rt. 3)

Counties: Culpeper, Orange

USGS Quads: Unionville, Culpeper East, Germanna Bridge, Mine Run

Suitable for: Day cruising

Skill Level: Novices and families

Months Runnable: Most of the year except after a long summer drought

Interest Highlights: Tree lined banks and farmland; intimate river

Scenery: Pretty in spots to pretty

Difficulty: Class A to I

Average Width: 50 to 60 feet

Velocity: Slow

Gradient: 3 feet per mile

Runnable Water Levels:
  Minimum: 0.8 feet on Culpeper gauge
  Maximum: 4 feet on Culpeper gauge

Hazards: An occasional downed tree

Scouting: None

Portages: None

Rescue Index: Accessible to somewhat remote

Source of Additional Information: National Weather Service, Culpeper gauge (703) 260-0305; Rappahannock Outdoor Educational Center (703) 371-5085

Access Points	River Miles	Shuttle Miles
E–G	15	13
F–G	13.5	15

Access Point Ratings:
  E–at US 522, fair to good
  F–at Raccoon Ford (Rt. 611), very good
  G–at Germanna Ford (Rt. 3), excellent

Germanna Ford (Route 3) to Elys Ford (Route 610)

These 8 miles are certainly not a whitewater trip, but like the section just upstream, it is perfect for families, youth groups, or any novice paddler wanting to get a first taste of moving water.

It is virtually impossible to get lost. The trip is from one bridge at Germanna Ford (Route 3) to another bridge at Elys Ford (Route 610). It is also short enough to relax through the entire day. There are many diversions: the scenery is good and there are numerous sandbars that invite you to stop, lay in the sun, swim, and have a leisurely lunch.

The fishing is good also. As with the Raccoon Ford to Germanna section upstream, you can try your luck for bass, bluegill, and redbreast sunfish. Wildlife on both these sections is plentiful, too. You may spot deer, beaver, muskrat, raccoons, and skillpot turtles sunning themselves. However, there also may be some water snakes and perhaps a rare copperhead sighted if you stop near a brush pile. The more impressive birds are great blue herons, ducks, hawks, and kingfishers. In the early morning, small groups may even see wild turkeys.

The woods along here contain river birch, tulip poplar, sycamore, and oak trees with some occasional mountain laurel and rhododendron. In the spring, there is a riot of wildflowers, including trout lily, bluebells, Dutchman's britches, and early saxifrage.

After a relaxing trip, the good take-out at Elys Ford (river right, downstream) is reached. While floating this section of the Rapidan, take note of its interesting history. Germanna was a settlement in the 1700s named for the German Queen Anne. Later, during the Civil War in 1864, Union forces pursuing troops of Confederate General Robert E. Lee used Germanna Ford and Elys Ford to cross the Rapidan just before the bloody battle of the Wilderness.

Section: Germanna Ford (Rt. 3) to Elys Ford (Rt. 610)

Counties: Culpeper, Orange, Spotsylvania

USGS Quads: Germanna Bridge, Mine Run, Chancellorsville, Richardsville

Suitable for: Day cruising

Skill Level: Novices and families

Months Runnable: Most of the year except after a long summer drought

Interest Highlights: Tree lined banks and farmland; intimate river

Scenery: Pretty in spots to pretty

Difficulty: Class A to I

Average Width: 60 to 80 feet

Velocity: Slow

Gradient: 3 feet per mile

Runnable Water Levels:
  Minimum: 0.8 feet on Culpeper gauge
  Maximum: 4 feet on Culpeper gauge

Hazards: An occasional downed tree

Scouting: None

Portages: None

Rescue Index: Accessible to somewhat remote

Source of Additional Information: National Weather Service, Culpeper gauge (703) 260-0305; Rappahannock Outdoor Educational Center (703) 371-5085

Access Points	River Miles	Shuttle Miles
G–H	8	12

Access Point Ratings:
  G–at Germanna Ford (Rt. 3), excellent
  H–at Elys Ford (Rt. 610), good

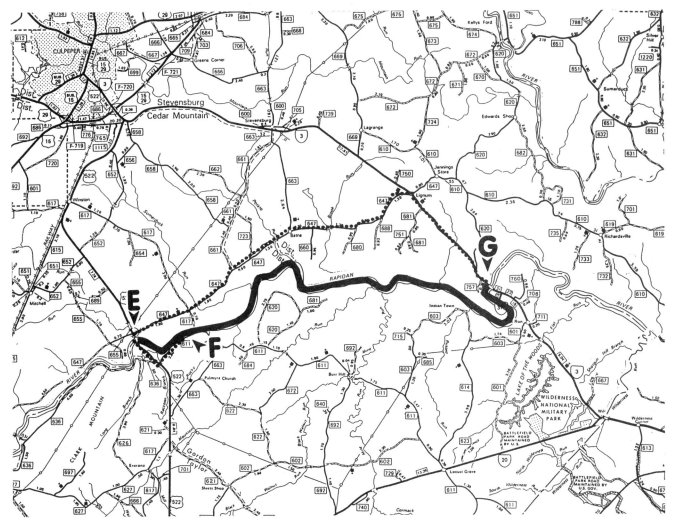

Elys Ford (Route 610) to Motts Landing

This beautiful stretch of a good sized river is for novices who are comfortable with moving water and ready to try some whitewater. In particular, shepherded beginners who have paddled the 13-mile stretch just upstream from Germanna Ford (Route 3) to Elys Ford will find this a good step up at moderate levels. However, when the river is high, novices and campers with bulky gear should stay off this section. Because of its length, the 15-mile stretch from Elys Ford to Motts Landing is either a long day-trip or an overnight trip at medium and lower water levels.

The journey starts with several miles of relatively flat water. Then there are several rapids (primarily Class II with one Class II–III) mainly concentrated just above and below the confluence of the Rappahannock and Rapidan at miles 6 and 7. The river then calms down again for the last 8 miles with occasional rapids (Class I and II) spaced to spark interest. Before describing this scenic journey in detail, some background is necessary. This trip in a wilderness setting is possible because the City of

Fredericksburg owns 5,000 acres on the banks of the Rapidan and Rappahannock Rivers and requires that this land remain undeveloped. As a result, you have campsites galore (with a few posted exceptions) and substantial wildlife along the river.

Deer, raccoons, opossum, otters, rabbits, flying squirrels, and even foxes can be seen. Beaver have burrowed into the riverbanks, and paddlers often see freshly gnawed branches and trees as signs of their activity. Many species of birds, including ospreys, red-tailed hawks, turkey vultures, great blue herons, green herons, bitterns, kingfishers, mallards, pintails, goldfinches, and even pileated woodpeckers soar above. Fishing is excellent. Record size smallmouth bass have been caught in the Rappahannock-Rapidan Rivers as well as bluegill sunfish, crappies, perch, carp, and even pickerel. The woods on the bank are a changing and rich mixed evergreen and hardwood forest. The evergreens are primarily hemlock, cedar, rhododendron, mountain laurel, and Virginia pine. Deciduous trees most often found along the bank are sycamores, river birch, box elders, beech, oak, and

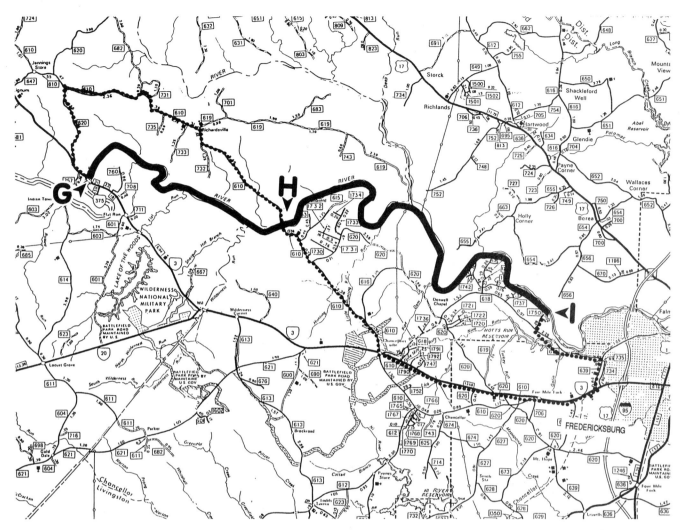

hornbeam. In sum, this is a great river for observing nature while fishing, floating, and camping.

At the put-in there is a gauge on the downstream side of the bridge abutment in the center of the river. It should read between 0 and 1.5 feet. Here the river flows through a wooded valley and has silty banks 6 to 10 feet high. For the first 1.5 miles the river is calm until you come to a riffle with a beach on the left which forms a good fishing spot. A half mile later is a small ledgy drop that is best run left, and after another half mile is another ledgy drop best run right. Shortly below this and about 3 miles into the trip is Todds Ford ledge. This 2-foot ledge (Class II) is best run from center toward the left. Soon thereafter is another smaller ledge, also best run center.

A quarter mile below on the left, as the river turns sharply right, a striking granite rock formation 100 feet high and covered with rhododendron comes into view. A mile below this another pretty rock formation on the right is graced with hemlocks. Shortly thereafter are some small ledges that can be tedious to negotiate at low water levels. Then, after passing a gravel bar and an island, the paddler

comes to a 200-yard Class I–II rock garden—run it center. You have now entered a half mile of nicely spaced whitewater. Just below is a good sized rock on river left which has a good fishing hole just above it and a good chute to run left of center. Then comes another minor rapid (run center) followed by a 100-yard Class II rock garden (Granite Shoals), which is best run to the left of a large rock in the center. Now you will see some large transmission lines and the Rappahannock entering from the left.

The wedge of land between the Rappahannock and the Rapidan is an excellent place to camp after 6 miles of paddling from Elys Ford. In the past year Boy Scouts working on conservation projects have made a good natural campsite better by providing rock fire rings and metal grates for cooking. The campsite is named in honor of Dr. George Brumble, an enthusiastic paddler who introduced canoeing and his love of the outdoors to many young people. If you camp here, please follow the simple rules proposed by Friends of the Rappahannock, a group of concerned citizens devoted to the protection, preservation, conservation, and responsible use of the Rappahannock/Rapidan for recreational purposes. Carry out all litter, be sure all fires are thoroughly extinguished before you leave, and do not destroy living trees and foliage.

Just below is Confluence Rapids (Class II–III) and, on river right, a rocky wall over 100 yards long—the remains of the historic Rappahannock Canal. Immediately downstream of this wall (also on the right) is another superb campsite cleared by industrious Boy Scouts. This site is named for Dr. Lloyd Little, another individual interested in young people and the outdoors. For the description of Confluence Rapids (which novices should scout) and the 9 miles below to Motts Landing, please see the Kellys Ford to Motts Landing section of the Rappahannock River in this chapter.

This section holds its water for most of the year. Indeed, you can paddle the Rapidan more often than you can the Rappahannock above the confluence of these two rivers. The minimum level for this section is 1.1 feet on the Culpeper gauge, which equates to 0 on the Elys Ford put-in gauge. Also, you should check the Remington gauge, which should be at least 3.3 feet. This section gets difficult for beginners when the Elys Ford put-in gauge is over 1.5 feet, the Culpeper gauge over 2.5 feet, and the Remington gauge over 5 feet. Please check both the Culpeper and Remington gauges, because one gauge may be substantially higher, which can markedly change the river below the confluence. If paddlers have the time and inclination, there is a gauge on US 1 in Fredericksburg that measures the Rappahannock and Rapidan after they join. It should be between 0 and 1.5 feet for novice paddlers. During the day, a reading of these gauges can be obtained from the Rappahannock Outdoor Educational Center at (703) 371-5085.

Section: Elys Ford (Rt. 610) to Motts Run Landing

Counties: Culpeper, Stafford, Spotsylvania

USGS Quads: Richardsville, Chancellorsville, Salem Church

Suitable for: Long day cruising or overnight camping; great 2- to 3-day fishing trip

Skill Level: Shepherded novices at moderate levels

Months Runnable: Winter and spring; after a rain in July/August

Interest Highlights: Great campsites, wildlife, fishing

Scenery: Pretty to beautiful in spots

Difficulty: Class I–II at moderate levels with 1 Class II–III

Average Width: 75 to 125 feet

Velocity: Moderate

Gradient: 8 feet per mile

Runnable Water Levels:
  Minimum: 1.1 foot on Culpeper gauge, 3.3 feet on Remington gauge, 0 feet on Route 1 gauge in Fredericksburg
  Maximum: 2.5 feet on Culpeper gauge; 5 feet on Remington gauge; 2.5 feet on Rt. 1 gauge in Fredericksburg

Hazards: None except Confluence Rapids at high water

Scouting: Confluence Rapids for novices (Class II–III); from river left at point where 2 rivers meet at moderate levels and on right bank of Rapidan at higher levels

Portages: None

Rescue Index: Generally remote

Source of Additional Information: National Weather Service, Remington and Culpeper gauges (703) 260-0305; Rappahannock Outdoor Educational Center (703) 371-5085; Rappahannock River Campground (540) 399-1839, no pets allowed

Access Points	River Miles	Shuttle Miles
H–I	15	12 or 14

Access Point Ratings:
  H–at Elys Ford (Rt. 610), very good
  I–at Motts Landing, very good

Rappahannock River

The Rappahannock River shares the distinction with the James and the Potomac of being inextricably intertwined with the history of the state and the nation. After Captain John Smith sailed up this river to near Fredericksburg in the early 1600s, some of the earliest settlements on the continent were founded on the banks of the Rappahannock estuary. George Washington warned Congress during his presidency that if measures were not taken to improve the navigation of the Rappahannock below the falls at Fredericksburg then the day might come when that city would be overshadowed as a seaport by the upstart village of New York. It is the Rappahannock over which Washington in his youth, according to legend, threw a silver dollar.

Throughout most of the Civil War the Rappahannock and Rapidan formed the de facto border between the Union and the Confederacy. Along the banks of the Rappahannock four major battles were fought during the war. The battles of Fredericksburg, Chancellorsville, the Wilderness, and Spotsylvania Courthouse resulted in the deaths of over 100,000 Americans between December 1862 and May 1864. John Wilkes Booth, having murdered President Lincoln, ran south through Maryland, crossed the Potomac near what is now the Route 301 bridge, and entered Virginia. Passing through King George County, he crossed the Rappahannock to Port Royal, on the banks of that river, and was shot in a burning barn near the village.

Also of historical note is the Rappahannock Canal. This 50 mile-long canal was built from Fredericksburg to Waterloo beginning in 1829. Its purpose was to move raw agricultural goods from the interior to the coast and to return finished products from the coast to the markets inland. The canal system when completed had 47 locks, 20 dams, and 15 miles of canal. Unfortunately, as with the C and O Canal on the Potomac, insufficient funding and the coming of the railroad led to its failure. However, remains of the Rappahannock Canal can be seen periodically from Waterloo to Fredericksburg.

The Rappahannock is born in the coves and gaps of the eastern slope of the Blue Ridge in Fauquier, Rappahannock, and Madison Counties. The waters of the Thornton and Hughes/Hazel Rivers join the upper Rappahannock above Remington while the Conway River joins the Rapidan near Stanardsville, before it finally merges with the Rappahannock near the battlefield of Chancellorsville.

Route 647 to US 211

This 13.5-mile section of the upper Rappahannock offers an appealing combination of convenience, wilderness values, and natural beauty. It affords the further advantage of being runnable when other small streams in the Rappahannock and Shenandoah watersheds are not. Although this is a novice level trip with a mild 7-foot-per-mile gradient, it has a surprising number of riffles and small swift chutes to hold the paddler's interest, particularly at low water levels.

The first half mile below the Route 647 put-in at Orlean is the least enjoyable part of this trip due to the pollution of the stream and the trampling of the banks by cattle. However, the terrain soon becomes too rugged for cattle, which are replaced by deer, beaver, muskrat, and a variety of waterfowl and raptors. Also, numerous hemlocks now grace the streambanks. The only hazards on this part of the trip are one or two fences in the first half mile and a few fallen trees in the first 3 miles, one of which has accumulated enough flotsam over the years to require portaging. After 6 miles you reach Route 645. The 7.5-mile section starting at Route 645 is punctuated by large boulders and small ledges. It is particularly well suited to the novice looking for a place to work on eddy turns and braces.

The best rapid on the trip is about 2 miles below the Route 645 bridge. Just beyond a long pool and a small power line right of-way, the river turns briefly to the right, drops over a small ledge, and then runs diagonally back to the left toward a bus sized boulder that extends from the left bank. The river slows substantially just as it reaches this huge boulder, turns abruptly right, and divides around a small boulder just before making an abrupt turn to the left. Run left of this small boulder at low levels and on either side at medium levels. The large boulder can be seen well in advance. Normally a Class I–II drop, this rapid is a solid Class II at higher water levels. Obstructions (such as fallen trees) have not been a problem here, but should they occur, they would be difficult to spot in advance and could ruin someone's day. Novices can scout this rapid from the right and should definitely do so at high water. There is an easy eddy behind the big boulder which is also a great lunch stop.

About 2 miles above the take-out is a Class I–II drop created by a millrace. In very low water, the only way to run this is on the extreme left. Some care needs to be taken here at almost every level. On the right bank just below this rapid are the remains of a mill house that are worth a stop. The mill, known as Foxes Mill, was the upstream end of the Rappahannock Canal which ran all the way to Fredericksburg. Unfortunately, the mill was burned during the Civil War, but evidence of the Rappahannock Canal can still be seen near Waterloo.

The best shuttle from the take-out for the 13.5-mile trip is to follow US 211 east for about a half mile to Route 688. Turn left on Route 688 and go for about 7 miles until you reach Route 647. Turn left on Route 647 to the put-in. To run the 7.5-mile lower section only, take US 211 west for several miles to Route 645. Turn right on Route 645 to reach the put-in. To run the 6 mile upper section only, take Route 645 north from the upper section take-out for 3 miles until you reach Route 647. Turn left and go about 1 mile on Route 647 to the put-in.

Section: Orlean/Crest Hill (Rt. 647) to Waterloo (US 211)

Counties: Rappahannock, Culpeper, Fauquier

USGS Quads: Flint Hill, Orlean, Massies Corner, Jeffersonton

Suitable for: Day cruising

Skill Level: Novices, families

Months Runnable: Winter, spring, and occasionally early summer

Interest Highlights: Rocky bluffs, hemlocks, remains of Foxes Mill, wildlife

Scenery: Pretty to beautiful in spots

Difficulty: Class I–II

Average Width: 25 to 60 feet

Velocity: Moderate

Gradient: 7 feet per mile

Runnable Water Levels:
   Minimum: 3.6 feet on the Remington gauge; 0 feet on Rt 647 gauge

Maximum: 6 feet on the Remington gauge; 3 feet on Rt 647 gauge

Hazards: Occasional trees in river; 1 or 2 fences in first half mile

Scouting: Class II rapid 2 miles below Route 645 at high water; scout on right

Portages: 1 downed tree or so in first 3 miles

Rescue Index: Accessible to somewhat remote

Source of Additional Information: National Weather Service, Remington gauge (703) 260-0305

Access Points	River Miles	Shuttle Miles
A–C	13.5	11
A–B	6	7.4
B–C	7.5	9

Access Point Ratings
A–at Crest Hill (Rt. 647), good
B–at Tapps Ford (Rt. 645), fair
C–at US 211, fair—short, tough carry

Taking aim at the gap between Target Rock on the left and Face Brace Rock on the right in the Falmouth section of the Rappahannock.

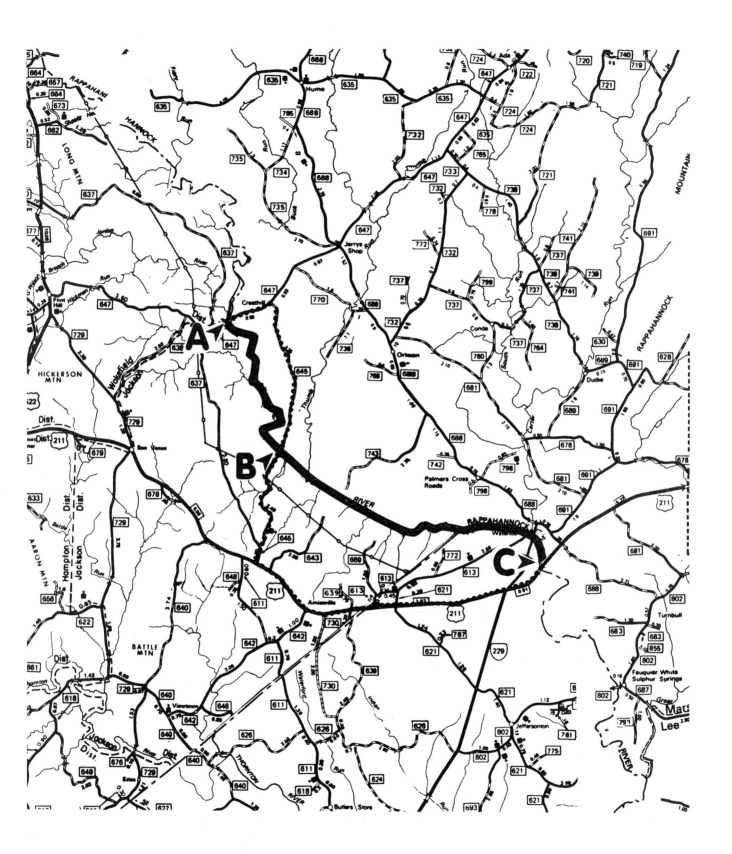

Remington to Kellys Ford

The 4.5-mile run from the old two-lane US 15/29 bridge near Remington to Kellys Ford is an enjoyable trip for shepherded novices and intermediate boaters at moderate levels. The 1.5 miles of Class II–III rapids at the end are worth the 3 miles of flatwater at the beginning. Parking is not allowed next to the old US 15/29 bridge, so paddlers should unload and move their cars very quickly. This is particularly true on the south side of the bridge where local police will quickly issue costly tickets. For those wanting to leave cars near the put-in, there is a parking lot by Ande's Store on the road to Remington not too far from the put-in. Please ask permission of the store's owner first.

Alternatively, before reaching this parking lot, one can go to the first white house by an aluminum gate on the right side of the road from the bridge. This house belongs to Mrs. Virginia Meadows. If you ask permission, she will allow you to park your car during the day or overnight in her backyard. For this service, paddlers may wish to pay her a small amount to show their appreciation. She may even let you put in through her locked gate from which a gravel road goes to the river.

Putting in at the newer four-lane US 15/29 bridge upstream is more difficult and is not recommended. Regarding the take-out, do not leave your car at Kellys Ford overnight; local rowdies may vandalize it in this remote place.

The downstream side of the river left abutment of the put-in bridge has a Randy Carter canoeing gauge. The USGS Remington gauge is just upstream on river left in a tall narrow gauging station building.

Shortly after the put-in, one comes to the first mild rapid just before a railroad bridge. Local folks call this Grandma's Rapids. To the right is a broad Class I riffle drop. To the left (when logs and debris aren't blocking it) is a more interesting little chute.

The best thing about the 3 miles of mostly flatwater during the beginning and middle of this run are the trees on the 10 foot-high banks of the river. With their streamside roots eroded by high water, they tip toward the river. This almost forms a canopy but never succeeds because the river is too wide. White ashes, box elders, silver maples, sycamores, hornbeams, hackberries, and river birches grace the river with their presence. One hardly knows that this almost unbroken line of wooden sentinels on the banks is shielding the paddler from the farms and pastures just beyond.

After 1.5 miles, one comes to some gentle riffles, and on the left are twin red brick barns with sheet metal roofs. There is an alternate put-in here. Ask permission to do so at Ande's Store.

One then begins to play peek-a-boo with the farmhouses and silos behind the trees on the banks. Three-quarters of a mile later, there is a nice flat rock on the right below a farmhouse. Here and there one will smell cattle, reminding you that all is not pristine on this trip.

Another three-quarters of a mile downstream one comes to a gas pipeline crossing. This is marked by a break in the tree lined banks and short black and yellow striped poles on either side of the river. You have now come 3 miles, and the riffles below the pipeline indicate that better rapids will come shortly. Below a foot or so on the put-in gauge many of the rock garden rapids to follow will test the novice and intermediate paddler's ability to read water, because most of the channels have numerous subsurface rocks to dodge.

A quarter mile below the pipeline, one comes to a short, easy rock garden followed by a pool. Then there is another gentle rock garden about 300 yards long. Look for a surfing spot on river right in this area. After another pool, short rock garden, and pool, one sees a line of rocks across the river as it bends left. This indicates Sandy Beach Rapids is ahead.

The rapid should be scouted the first time by novice and intermediate boaters. If the water is below roughly a foot on the Randy Carter put-in gauge, one can scout from the big, flat rocks just above the rapids. Better yet, a small group can have lunch there. If the water is higher or the group bigger, the lunch stop is a sandy beach on the bottom right of the rapids. The sandy beach on the bottom left is posted against trespassing.

Basically, this Class II–III rapids can be run on the right or left at reasonable levels. The right has the cleanest chute, but one should still be careful of rocks on entry and on the bottom right of the runout. If the rapids are run left, either pick your way left all the way down or cut back hard right after entry. This way you will avoid some rocks in the center of this channel, which widens substantially at the bottom.

A few minutes after Sandy Beach Rapids, the river turns right and becomes a good Class II rock garden. This rapid is known to local paddlers as The Maze. Go left or right, but the right has the best small chutes in the bottom through two big rocks.

After the maze, you have several mellow Class I–II rapids. The second of these has surfing possibilities if it is run to the right. The fourth drop is a rock garden. Run it center, but be careful to miss submerged rocks near the bottom.

With the take-out bridge in sight, you are ready for the other main Class II–III rapid of note. This drop is called Piggly-Wiggly by old timers. A good Class II way of running is to enter left of center going toward the right and cutting back left to finish. Alternatively, if you are adventurous and competent, run the extreme left channel after scouting. This channel of pushy water drops 3 to 4

Section: Remington (old US 15/29 bridge) to Kellys Ford (Rt. 620)

Counties: Culpeper, Fauquier

USGS Quads: Remington, Germanna Bridge

Suitable for: Day cruising

Skill Level: Shepherded novices (low levels) and intermediates

Months Runnable: Winter, spring, and after a heavy summer rain

Interest Highlights: Tree lined banks and farms at the beginning; whitewater at the end

Scenery: Pretty in spots to pretty

Difficulty: Class I–II with 2 Class II–III drops

Average Width: 70 to 100 feet

Velocity: Moderate to fast

Gradient: 12 feet per mile

Runnable Water Levels:
  Minimum: 3.3 feet on Remington gauge; 0 on put-in and take-out gauges
  Maximum: 5 feet on Remington gauge; 4 feet on put-in and take-out gauges

Hazards: An occasional downed tree and hydraulics at higher levels

Scouting: Novices should scout the 2 Class II–III rapids

Portages: None

Rescue Index: Accessible

Source of Additional Information: National Weather Service, Remington gauge (703) 260-0305; Rappahannock Outdoor Educational Center (703) 371-5085

Access Points	River Miles	Shuttle Miles
D–E	4.5	5

Access Point Ratings
  D–at Remington (old US 15/29 bridge), good
  E–at Kellys Ford (Rt. 620), very good

feet and is a moderate Class III beause of the rock lurking in the center of the runout waiting to munch errant boats. Indeed, a former local outfitter (Ronnie Meadows) told me that he has pulled several pinned boats off this rock each year.

Only two short, easy drops remain from here to the take-out. The first of these has a surfing spot on the left. Paddlers then go under the bridge and take out on river right.

The 1.5-mile whitewater section of this trip changes markedly with rising water levels. From 0 to 2 feet on the put-in gauge it is a Class II–III run suitable for shepherded novices and intermediates. Between 2 and 3.5 feet it becomes a continuous Class III run for experienced boaters. Approaching 4 feet it changes to a continuous Class IV run—the recommended limit for advanced open boaters.

Besides the trees at the beginning, rapids at the end, and fishing spots galore, there is also bird life along the river. Not only are several species of birds constantly flitting about (such as swallows and goldfinches), but one may be fortunate enough to see an osprey or great blue heron. Indeed, during one trip I ran the last half mile of rapids while trying to sneak up on a great blue heron. However, this magnificent bird always flew another couple of hundred yards downriver just before coming into good camera range.

Kellys Ford is very interesting historically. During the Civil War, troops of both sides forded the Rappahannock near here, and many skirmishes took place close to this strategic river crossing. One North-South battle was along an old wall that extended from river right above Sandy Beach Rapids to Route 674. Also, from the start of the rapids to the take-out, the trace of the old Rappahannock Canal from Fredericksburg to Waterloo comes close to the river at various places on river left.

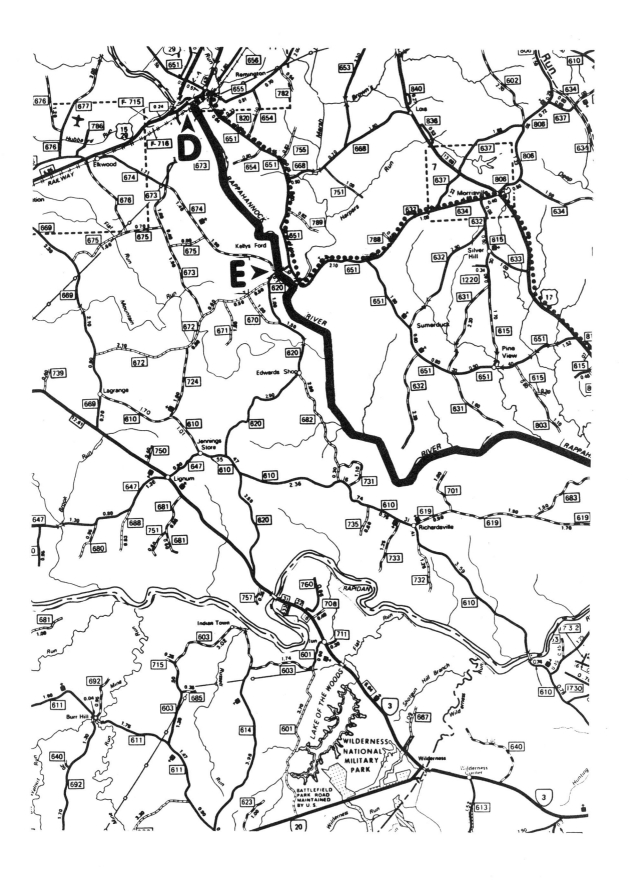

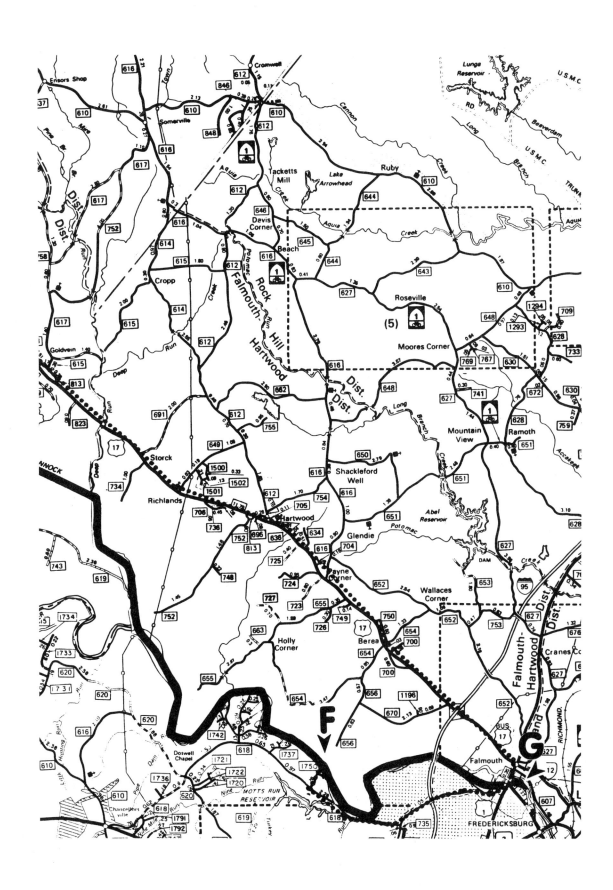

Kellys Ford to Motts Run Landing

This section starts and ends as an angler's float trip at reasonable water levels. Here anglers can try their luck for smallmouth bass, bluegill, perch, catfish, or carp. However, there are several nicely spaced Class II rapids well into the trip that beginning and novice paddlers should look at and be shepherded through.

In addition, paddlers should check two gauges before starting—the Remington gauge for the Rappahannock and the Culpeper gauge for the Rapidan—since this river joins the Rappahannock 16 miles into this 24-mile trip. Checking both gauges is important. On a summer trip several years ago a scout troop found the Rappahannock at a nice moderate paddling level. However, they were rudely startled when the Rapidan joined the Rappahannock at a much higher flow because of heavy thundershowers in the Rapidan watershed. Fortunately, the group had good leadership and was able to get down the rest of the river safely.

Paddlers and anglers owe a vote of thanks to the City of Fredericksburg which owns about 5,000 acres of virtually undeveloped nearby land—much of which borders the Rappahannock. As a result, most of the 24-mile stretch from Kellys Ford to Motts Run Landing is akin to wilderness with large sycamores, box elders, river birches, and other large trees guarding the banks of the river for most of the trip. Only occasionally is this tree wall broken by farms or pastures that reach the riverbank. Indeed, this section is so special that the heart of the stretch from Deep Creek to the Fredericksburg has recently been added to the State Scenic River System of Virginia.

The trip starts on river right just below the picturesque green, one-lane Kellys Ford bridge on Route 620. Because this bridge is quite old, plans are apparently are being made to replace it. After a couple of miles, there is one noteworthy patch of rocks and evergreens on the right. The first riffles and miniledge are about 3 miles into the trip. Shortly after this, there is some pastureland on river right. On hot days herds of black Aberdeen Angus cattle seek shelter under the trees by the riverbank and quietly observe passing paddlers.

One then passes an island on either side and at about 4 miles goes underneath a power line that buzzes loudly—a reminder that civilization is not too far away. There were only two other eyesore signs of "progress" seen recently. One was occasional tires in the river. The other was a bizarre place in the first few miles on river right where, inexplicably, the

Scott Gravatt running a typical drop on the Kellys Ford section of the Rappahannock. Photo by Glenn Gravatt.

front end of four cars buried deep in the riverbank stared blankly out through their hollow headlight rims.

A couple of miles further downstream one comes to a nicely manicured farm on the left—a temporary break from the tree lined banks. A mile below this (at roughly mile 7) is the first Class II rapid, which should be run on the left. The rock on the left of this rapid is called Snake Castle Rock. Another mile later is a second Class II drop followed shortly by a third, smaller drop.. Both of these should be run left too.

Then about 10 miles into the trip is a nice long Class II slalom run on the right. At the bottom of this slalom a long island splits the river on the right. On the right bank is the Rappahannock River Campground, a must camping spot for large groups. Indeed, it is about the only place where there is a phone, water, outdoor bathrooms, and even a coke machine. Make sure you get right at the end of the rapid before this island or you will miss the entrance to the campground.

If you wish to stay there during busy paddling season weekends (particularly Memorial Day), make your reservations early to ensure getting one of the wooded camping sites at this reasonably large campground. One can rent canoes and shuttle service here as well as from the Rappahannock Outdoor Educational Center in Fredericksburg and Clore Brothers Outfitters just downstream of Motts Landing. For the adventurous, there are numerous primitive campsites along the river. However, one should camp on public land as private owners have posted signs prohibiting trespassing at several places along the banks. Any of the three aforementioned outfitters can give paddlers guidance concerning prospective campsites.

After several minutes of paddling below the campground, the island ends. A few minutes later there are two small ledges, a quarter mile or so apart. Now the rapids are becoming more frequent. About a half mile below these ledges is an easy rock garden, followed by four short Class II drops which are each about 5 minutes apart and quite technical in moderate water. Novices should look these over to find a path. The first two perhaps should be run right, the third on the left, and the last toward the center. Shortly after this last drop is a nice long Class II rock garden slalom. This should be run on the right as the river splits around a large island and rejoins after the slalom ends. Just under a mile later is a small rocky ledge run left. Less than another mile below this ledge, the paddler will notice numerous good sized rocks liberally sprinkled across the river. This is where the Rapidan River joins the Rappahannock on the right. The confluence of these rivers is 16 miles into the trip and about 5.5 miles below the Rappahannock River Campground.

Section: Kellys Ford (Rt. 620) to Motts Run Landing

Counties: Culpeper, Stafford, Spotsylvania

USGS Quads: Germanna Bridge, Richardsville, Storck, Chancellorsville, Salem Church

Suitable for: Overnight camping

Skill Level: Shepherded novices

Months Runnable: Winter, spring, and after a good summer rain

Interest Highlights: Great float trip with good camping and fishing; moderate rapids

Scenery: Pretty to beautiful in spots

Difficulty: Class I–II with 1 Class II–III

Average Width: 75 to 125 feet

Velocity: Moderate

Gradient: 6 feet per mile

Runnable Water Levels:
   Minimum: 3.3 feet on Remington gauge, 1.1 feet on Culpeper gauge, and 2.4 feet on Fredericksburg gauge; 0 feet on US 1 paddlers gauge in Fredericksburg

Maximum: 5 feet on Remington gauge, 2.5 feet on Culpeper gauge, and pushing 5 feet on Fredericksburg gauge; 2.5 feet on US 1 gauge in Fredericksburg

Hazards: None, except novices should be careful of Confluence Rapids at high water

Scouting: Novices should scout Confluence Rapids (Class II–III)

Portages: None

Rescue Index: Generally remote

Source of Additional Information: National Weather Service: Remington, Culpeper and Fredericksburg gauges (703) 260-0305; Rappahannock Outdoor Educational Center (703) 371-5085; Rappahannock River Campground - no pets allowed (540) 399-1839 or 1-800-784-PADL (reservations only)

Access Points	River Miles	Shuttle Miles
E–F	24	21

Access Point Rating
   E–at Kellys Ford (Rt. 620), very good
   F–at Motts Run Landing, very good

This juncture marks the best rapid of the trip. Called Confluence Rapids (for obvious reasons), this is a long solid Class II at moderate levels. It is best to work your way toward the center as the two rivers join and finish to the right of a rock island in the center of the river at the bottom of the rapid. At low levels, river right has the most water. Alternatively, there is a nice ledge if one chooses to run this rapid on the left. It is a Class III in high water and can be avoided by staying against the left bank. This rapid can be very technical and picky at lower water and very pushy at higher water. Accordingly, novices should scout it first and follow more experienced boaters to avoid getting hung up (lower levels) or in trouble (higher levels). You can camp here at the confluence of the rivers. Please see the Elys Ford section of the Rapidan for this information.

Just below Confluence Rapids is a long rock wall on the right. This is followed by Clapping Rocks—a delightful Class II chute between two large rocks that resemble huge hands. Then, about a mile after Confluence Rapids, are the remains of a rock wall on the left and an old, open gold mine on the right. Several minutes after this one finds the Class II remains of an old dam best run center through some nice bouncy waves. Nearby on river left are the remains of an old lock. A mile later the river splits into three channels around two small islands. Be alert for downed trees blocking one of these channels.

A mile further is another nice, mild, sloping Class II drop run center or left followed shortly by another similar drop run right of center. Interspersed with these drops are occasional riffles and rocks. After the last drop, one essentially has a flatwater paddle to Motts Run Landing, about 2 miles downstream on river right. When the water is high, plan your docking strategy carefully if there are novices and beginners in your group. However, if you miss

Motts Run Landing, the Clore Brothers take out is just downstream and also on the right. Incidentally, do not leave cars overnight at the Kellys Ford put-in or Motts Run Landing take-out—they may be vandalized.

It is fortunate that this section of the Rappahannock is reasonably long and wide. Despite hordes of paddlers and anglers at the put-in/take-out on holidays, river users can spread out sufficiently so they are not overly bothered by others and can still find nice camping spots. Also, the long, flat stretches are good for swimming as the river is not too deep or pushy at moderate levels. This is a particularly enjoyable trip for carefully shepherded and cavorting scouting and youth groups.

Motts Run Landing to Old Mill Park

The two 4.5-mile sections, between Remington and Kellys Ford on the one hand and Motts Run Landing and Old Mill Park on the other, have several striking similarities. These trips start with tree lined banks, have flatwater for most of the trip, and then finish with a whitewater crescendo. However, there are also differences in these two sections. The river is much wider below Motts Run Landing, and there is a 20-foot dam almost a mile below Interstate 95 that must be portaged on river left.

Even though this section is generally a day-trip, do not leave cars overnight at the Motts Run Landing put-in; rowdies might vandalize your vehicles. Cars are safer at the Old Mill Park take-out.

After floating down the quiet, wide river for nearly a mile below the put-in, one comes to the first rapid. Called Pettimans Camp, this Class I–II double drop can be run left or right and has a minor surfing wave near the bottom left. A couple of minutes later there is an interesting 50-foot

Bill Micks surfing a hole at Sandy Beach Rapid. Photo by Stephen Ensign.

Bob Goodall and his son Matthew run a small ledge just below Motts Landing on the Rappahannock. Note the small tugboat keeping their canoe properly aligned. Photo by Stephen Ensign.

yards. However, when the right bank forms a 30-foot vegetation covered bluff, the river gets serious.

You have reached the First Ledge of the Falmouth whitewater section. First Ledge can be run several ways. The conservative way is down the tight left side over a stairstep of rocks. This is a strong Class II at moderate water levels. A little further to the right is an easy Class III chute with a wave to punch below. Further to the right is the toughest Class III tweeze between several nasty rocks. This is not recommended but can be done by very experienced boaters. Finally, procrastinators can take the last Class III channel nearly all the way to the right. There are good surfing spots at various levels and places at the bottom of First Ledge. First timers should scout this rapid from river left.

After a longish wave field followed by a pool, one has a choice. To the right is the infamous Class III rapid known as Target Rock. The river goes over a 40 yard rock garden before crashing into two large flat rocks 5 feet apart. The rock on the left is Target Rock, and it has pinned many a boat. The rock on the right is called Face Brace Rock. Maneuvering is required to keep your boat from ramming either of these rocks as you attempt to enter the 5-foot gap between them. Once through the gap you have about 10 yards before your boat crashes into another rock below. To avoid this last rock, you have to make a tight right turn down a chute just before reaching it. After this, you must quickly make a tight left turn to finish. Target Rock starts getting really pushy at 1.5 feet on the US 1 gauge and should not be run above 2 feet. In any case, scout this potentially pinning rapid the first time it is run. Please satisfy yourself that you have the requisite boat control to run it and that logs or debris do not block your passage. Indeed, when the river is running at a good level, debris can pile up here from week to week. Also, local nonpaddlers will sometimes lay logs across this area at lower levels to get out to the river. Accordingly, one should always scout this rapid and follow someone through the first time it is run.

rock face on river right that peeks out among the trees. Shortly thereafter one comes to Maze Rapids—so named for the jumble of rocks suddenly appearing on the river. Start this Class I–II rapid near the center, follow a line of rocks to the right, and then cut back left near the bottom. A mile later, another Class I–II rapid, aptly named Interstate Z, appears as you sight the I-95 bridge. The "Z" here consists of entering right of center, making a tight right turn, and then finishing with a quick left turn. Those who don't want to zig and zag can run this rapid on the left near an island.

Once you go under the I-95 bridge, notice the dam house visible downstream on river right. Now you must work left and stay left for your portage around a 20-foot dam, which creates nearly a mile of flatwater below the interstate.

The over 100 yard, or 10-minute, portage on the left is not too bad except for a muddy creek near the beginning. This creek may not have a bridge across it, and on one occasion was fouled by sewage. Step carefully, please!

Once below the dam and after all the flatwater and minor stuff upstream, get ready for Falmouth—a mile-long whitewater section of individual rapids broken mostly by short pools. Here the gradient picks up to 30 feet per mile as opposed to the 13 feet per mile above the dam.

If you go to the right just below the dam, you first encounter a gentle drop. Not too far below this is a nice surfing wave which develops at about 2 feet on the US 1 gauge. Things are peaceful for the next several hundred

If one opts not to run Target Rock, the alternative on the left is Second Ledge. This is a Class II drop at lower levels over a broken wier into a respectable rock garden.

Below Second Ledge is Corner Rapids. The biggest drop of this Class II–III rapid is a 2-foot ledge just to the left of a big rock affectionately called Turtle Rock by locals. Be careful running this drop, however, because Boat Catcher Rock is just 2 canoe lengths below Turtle Rock in the main channel. Several yards further to the left the drop is not as abrupt. However, it is unrunnable below 6 inches on the US 1 gauge and develops a good hole at 1.5 feet on this gauge. Still several yards further to the left is a third alternative requiring quick left and then right maneuvering to hit the right two chutes in low water. There is a nice surfing spot below the main drop several yards to river left of Boat Catcher Rock.

About 50 yards below Corner Rapids is another ledgelike drop. Then comes a ledge called The Hole. This is similar to the drop just above with one exception. On extreme river right is an excellent but demanding hole (also called Berkey's Hole) for surfers between 6 inches and 1.5 feet on the US 1 gauge. The hole is the length of one canoe and is nicely located between two good-sized rocks. The hydraulic formed below the 2-foot ledge here is a good teacher for decked and open boaters. Please wear helmets while surfing this hole. Moderate folks can surf head-on. The brave of heart and hard of head can try sideways.

The beautiful part about this hole (especially for aggressive open boaters with a good low-brace) is the convenient rock on the right shore next to the hole. Someone on the rock can hold a bow/stern painter and pull the sideways surfer out of the hole if he cannot get out. The hole is the grabbiest at about 1 foot. At this level, open boat sideways sitters have to be especially good to get out by themselves.

Shortly below The Hole is Esther's Washing Machine, a short Class II–III jumble of miniledges, rocks, and playing possibilities at lower levels. Run it center for the most interesting action. Below this are a couple of Class I ledges. Then you go under the US 1 bridge. While doing so, note the gauge on the downstream side of the third abutment from the right. Hopefully, you looked at this gauge before putting in. The Old Mill Park take-out is immediately below the bridge on river right.

Roger Knicely with a nice low brace in boat sized Berkey's hole midway down Falmouth Rapid on the Rappahannock. Note the convenient rocks at either end of the hole for hauling out panicking hole sitters when they have had enough. This hole is particularly sticky at about 13 inches on the Route 1 gauge.

In addition to this classic way of running the Falmouth section, there is one more alternative at the beginning of this section if the US 1 gauge is above 9 inches. Just after the portage around the dam, one can go to the extreme left instead of right. This is definitely a change of pace as you follow a creek-sized river channel which goes around two islands. The route is appropriately called Backside by local paddlers. The first island you pass is small; the second is large and is called Laucks Island.

After a picky rock garden at lower levels, one comes to a good pool. Below the pool is a moderate Class III drop that has a strong hydraulic at the bottom. It is called Bob's Glasses by locals because a paddler named Bob offered his glasses to the river gods while getting munched by this hydraulic. At higher levels, the hydraulic gets bigger and grabbier. If you are really competent and nervy, try your luck surfing this hole. However, please wear a helmet because an upstream flip could really ring your cranial chimes.

Then comes another short rock garden. After this is a drop ending with a milder hydraulic than the one encountered above. This strong Class II is called Shoulder Snapper by local paddlers. One then rejoins the main current of the river for Corner Rapids discussed above.

Paddlers not having time to do the whole 4.5-mile section from Motts Run Landing can instead opt for just

the Falmouth portion. A convenient put-in is by Normandy Street on Fall Hill Avenue roughly a mile from the Old Mill Park take-out or at the Rappahannock Outdoor Educational Center off Fall Hill Avenue just upstream. One can either bomb down this short run in less than 20 minutes or spend a couple of hours playing along the way.

In general, 1 foot is about the best playing level for Falmouth Rapids. At 1.5 feet it begins getting too pushy for open boat playing and is a solid Class III run. Also, 1.5 feet marks where the US 1 gauge changes from green to yellow for "caution." For adventurous and good open boaters, 2 feet is a strong Class III run. Approaching 2.5 feet, the lower rapids (Corner, The Hole, and Esther's Washing Machine) start to merge and become one long, low Class IV rapid. At 3 feet all of Falmouth is a continuous Class IV run. When the gauge reaches 4 feet, this section is a strong Class IV run, which is the recommended limit for most expert open boaters who know the river well. The 4-foot level is also where the US 1 gauge changes from yellow to red for "danger." Above this level expert kayakers and crazed open boaters are definitely on their own.

Now that I have described Falmouth Rapids in detail, please remember that there are other positive aspects to this 4.5-mile trip. As with the two sections above Motts Run Landing, the river banks are covered with sycamores, river birches, box elders, and hornbeams. For anglers, perch and catfish swim below the dam. Just below the Motts Run Landing put-in, big turtles sun themselves on rocks in the river during hot days. On one trip, I also saw five great blue herons. Three of these were together on the Backside channel near the bottom of Laucks Island. Finally, on one spring morning we watched a circling osprey suddenly dive and catch a fish just below Laucks Island.

One final item must be mentioned. Every year, during both Saturday and Sunday of the first weekend in June, the Great Rappahannock Whitewater Canoe Race is held over the 4.5-mile course from Motts Run Landing to Old Mill Park. Those not racing downriver on Saturday can still race on Sunday. This thrilling race features just about all classes of solo and tandem open boats as well as decked boats. Families are emphasized, with such open boat classes as father-son, father-daughter, mother-son, and mother-daughter. There are also classes for younger and older paddlers. Call the Rappahannock Outdoor Educational Center for further information about the race at (703) 371-5085.

This is truly a gala event with first, second, and third place trophies for all classes of winners. Also, drawings for a canoe, life jacket, and paddle are held for race participants only. Finally, there is live entertainment (such as country music bands and cloggers), and even the mayor of Fredericksburg is present on Sunday to award the trophies. All the race proceeds go to a worthy cause—the Fredericksburg Rescue Squad.

Section: Motts Run Landing to Old Mill Park

Counties: Stafford, Spotsylvania

USGS Quads: Salem Church, Fredericksburg

Suitable for: Day cruising

Skill Level: Shepherded novices (low levels); intermediates

Months Runnable: Winter, spring, and after a good summer rain

Interest Highlights: Wide scenic river above I-95; convenient Falmouth section of rapids below

Scenery: Pretty to beautiful in spots

Difficulty: Class I–III at moderate levels

Average Width: 100 to 300 feet

Velocity: Moderate to fast

Gradient: 13 feet per mile; Falmouth section is 30 feet for 1 mile

Runnable Water Levels:
  Minimum: 3.3 feet on Remington gauge, 1.1 feet on Culpeper gauge, and 2.4 feet on Fredericksburg gauge; 0 feet on US 1 gauge in Fredericksburg

Maximum: 5 feet on Remington gauge, 2.5 feet on Culpeper gauge and pushing 5 feet on Fredericksburg gauge; 1.5 feet on US 1 gauge in Fredericksburg for intermediate paddlers; add a foot to each of these gauges for advanced paddlers

Hazards: 20-foot dam 1 mile below I-95; Target Rock (debris) in Falmouth section; occasional tree in river

Scouting: In Falmouth section First Ledge (Class II–III) from river left and Target Rock (Class III) from river right

Portages: 20-foot dam 1 mile below I-95

Rescue Index: Accessible

Source of Additional Information: National Weather Service: Remington, Culpeper and Fredericksburg gauges (703) 260-0305; Rappahannock Outdoor Educational Center (703) 371-5085

Access Points	River Miles	Shuttle Miles
F–G	4.5	5

Access Point Rating
  F–at Motts Run Landing, very good
  G–at Old Mill Park, good

Robinson River

The upper section of the Robinson River is a nice novice to intermediate trip. It primarily passes through farm and pasture with interludes of woods and occasional rocky banks (particularly toward the end). Although the river in many places appears to be channelized, the gradient is sufficient in the first half of this section to produce relatively frequent Class I–II ledges and cobble bars. There is also a Class II–III series of three ledges just over 2.5 miles into this 8-mile trip.

It is possible to put in at the confluence of the Rose and Robinson Rivers (where Routes 600 and 670 also join) or farther upstream. However, we strongly recommend against this. First, there are several barbed wire/wood cattle fences across this part of the river. More importantly, the owner of the surrounding pastureland adamantly requests that paddlers put in at the Route 649 bridge, which is roughly a half mile downstream from the confluence of the Rose and Robinson Rivers. Apparently, disrespectful boaters and anglers previously damaged his fences, thereby allowing his cattle to wander unattended.

Soon after the river right put-in at the Route 649 bridge one is greeted by a little ledge. This is followed by a mild surfing spot and a footbridge. Then one slips through Criglersville and comes to another small ledge. A footbridge and low-water bridge (Route 641) are immediately thereafter. Next are a couple of Class II slaloms and mild surfing spots.

Just over a mile into the trip, one goes under another footbridge and over two small ledges. Immediately below is a third, larger ledge (which may be skirted on the right) and a rock garden. The second low-water bridge occurs at 1.5 miles. After more cobble rapids, a ledge or so, a third footbridge, and some bouncy waves, one reaches the Route 231 bridge—nearly 2.5 miles from the start.

A few minutes below this bridge is the best rapid of the trip—a Class II–III series of three ledges. The first ledge drops about 2 feet and can be run over a cobble on the right or a tongue on the left. The second ledge—about 30 to 40 yards downstream—is slightly bigger. It can be run center but also has a respectable surfing hole on the right for those feeling venturesome. About 50 yards further one comes to the last and largest ledge. It is a good 3 feet and should be run on the left. More timid souls should scout this last ledge from river left as the water at moderate levels is funneled diagonally left into a good-sized curler at the bottom.

Shortly below this is a Class II slalom sandwiched between two small ledges. Then comes a concrete embankment on the left. Those who like whitewater only should take out on river left just before the concrete embankment. The road here is Route 609; you are only a quarter mile downstream from the Route 231 bridge. The last of the big ledges can be seen upstream from this potential take-out, for those interested in a peek at the three

Frank Moritz negotiates a mellow ledge on the pretty Robinson River. Photo by Ron Knipling.

ledges before running the river.

After the concrete embankment, there is another Class II drop and some pretty rocks on the right. The riverbanks first get higher and then lower so one can see more of the valley being transited. In this section, with lower gradient, channelization is evident. During the spring, many swallows build their nests in the channelized riverbank.

Downed trees are the only hazard on this part of the river. The only other rapids of note are a couple of small ledges/moderate surfing spots just above the Route 638 bridge, roughly 7 miles into the trip. During the eighth and last mile of paddling one will encounter another footbridge, some pretty rock banks, and fewer signs of channelization. Then comes the river right take-out on Route 636, which is just upstream of four-lane US 29. However, remember that Route 636 is not directly accessible from Route 29.

There is abundant bird life on the Robinson. I was alternately escorted by an osprey and several kingfishers on a spring trip, while many other feathered friends (such as spotted sandpipers and swallows) flitted by. This river is also stocked with trout for fishing season—so late March or the first Saturday in April are definitely not good times to paddle this river. The Robinson is a nice but gentle alternative when the tougher sections of the nearby Conway and the Upper Rapidan become too low to run.

Section: Rt. 649 bridge to Rt. 636 (just upstream of US 29)

Counties: Madison

USGS Quads: Madison, Brightwood

Suitable for: Day cruising

Skill Level: Shepherded novices

Months Runnable: Winter and spring after a rainy period

Interest Highlights: Small valley; farm and pastureland with woodsy interludes

Scenery: Pretty in spots to pretty

Difficulty: Class II with 1 Class II–III set of 3 ledges

Average Width: 20 to 40 feet

Velocity: Moderate to fast

Gradient: 24 feet per mile

Runnable Water Levels:
    Minimum: 2.2 feet on Culpeper gauge
    Maximum: 5.5 feet on Culpeper gauge

Hazards: Maybe a barbed wire fence and an occasional downed tree across the river

Scouting: Novices should scout at least 1 of the 3 ledges 2.5 miles into the trip

Portages: None

Rescue Index: Accessible

Source of Additional Information: National Weather Service, Culpeper gauge (703) 260-0305

Access Points	River Miles	Shuttle Miles
A–B	8	9

Access Point Rating
    A–at Rt. 649 bridge, very good
    B–along Rt. 636 upstream of US 29, very good

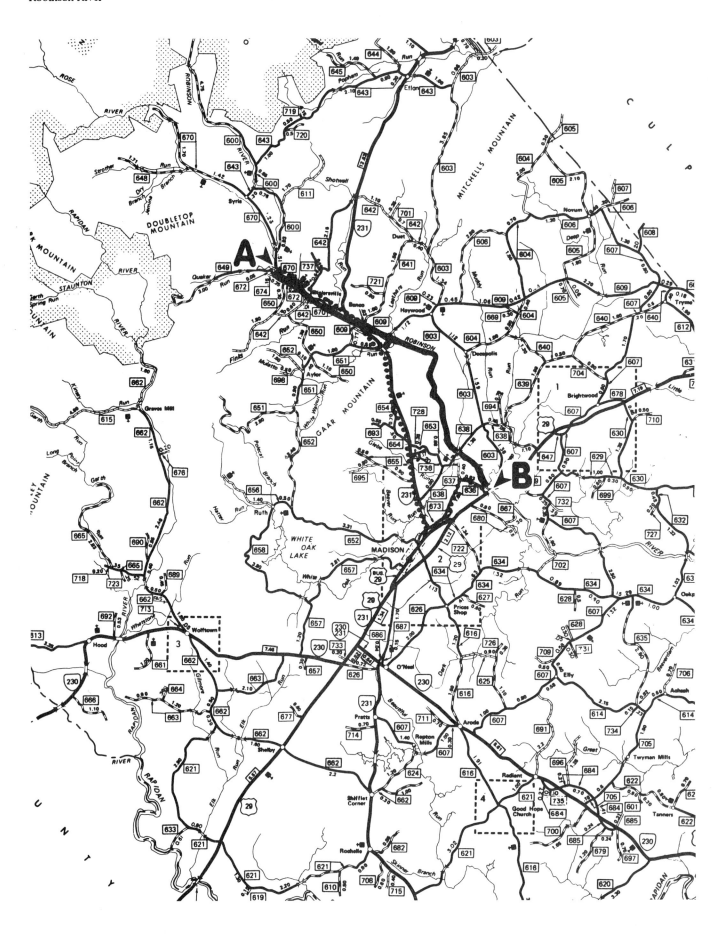

Thornton River

The Thornton River forms at the confluence of its North and South Forks in the tiny historic village of Sperryville. Both tributaries of the Thornton cascade eastward off the Blue Ridge in Shenandoah National Park. The butternut clad legions of the Confederacy traveled over Thornton Gap and along the South Fork of the Thornton. Southern troops camped beside the Thornton at Sperryville on several occasions and must have certainly drunk the clear waters of the stream. The tiny creek that now provides recreation was once, like so many of the streams of Virginia, a source of sustenance, a geographic barrier, a highway, and an important landmark for the men who fought and bled across the state in the 1860s.

After gathering its forks the Thornton slides between Turkey Mountain on the north and Poortown Mountain on the south, and then runs hard up against Red Oak Mountain on its eastward course. After passing Fletchers Mill the stream continues in a southeasterly direction before joining the Hazel River shortly before the Hazel flows into the Rappahannock just above Remington.

One of the most enjoyable aspects of the Thornton is that the drive to and from the river, from any direction, is through some of the most attractive and prosperous countryside in Virginia. The Skyline Drive is just a few miles west of the put in and should not be missed by anyone new to the area. The apple orchards and horse farms of the surrounding region are scenic and pleasant. Sperryville is an apple-processing center, and good local

jams and cider may be gotten there in the fall. A native wine industry is also beginning to grow in the region, for which all enthusiasts of the grape may be grateful. Perhaps what Jefferson referred to as "a champagne country" may soon become so, as literally as it is now figuratively.

The best hassle-free and consistent whitewater section of the Thornton is between Fletchers Mill and Rock Mills. This is a generally scenic trip where the river plays tag with rolling pastureland and increasingly large rocks or cliffs covered with hemlocks.

Above this section there are problems, and below it the Thornton becomes too tame for real whitewater action. Between 1 and 2 miles upstream of Fletchers Mill (along US 211) there is nearly always too little water and simply too many fences, low bridges, and backyards to contend with, even though the gradient is double that of the section below Fletchers Mill. One mile above Fletchers Mill, where US 522 meets US 211 (next to a big store called The Sperryville Emporium), the fences and bridges are gone, but there often is not enough water. Indeed, the gauge at Fletchers Mill clearly refers to downstream, and when it says 0 the only way to paddle the 1 mile just upstream is with incessant scraping and continual trying to squeeze a 3-foot-wide canoe through shallow, rocky 2-foot chutes. Also, Beaverdam Creek at the put-in usually adds a significant volume of water to the trip.

This very pleasant, basically Class II run has lots of moderate action beginning with the rapid below the put-in.

Running Boulder Ledge Rapid on the Thornton–years ago this drop was called Prepare to Meet Thy God Rapid (after a sign which hung above its entry). Photo by Ron Knipling.

Section: Fletchers Mill to Rock Mills

Counties: Rappahannock

USGS Quads: Washington

Suitable for: Cruising

Skill Level: Intermediate

Months Runnable: January to mid-April

Interest Highlights: Scenery, whitewater

Scenery: Pretty to beautiful in spots

Difficulty: Class II with 1 Class III

Average Width: 20 to 30 feet

Velocity: Fast

Gradient: 24 feet per mile

Runnable Water Levels:
   Minimum: 0 on Fletchers Mill gauge, 2.2 feet on Culpeper
      gauge, 4.8 feet on Remington gauge
   Maximum: 3 feet on Fletchers Mill gauge, 5 feet on
      Culpeper gauge, 8 feet on Remington gauge

Hazards: Strainers, cattle fences

Scouting: Class III Boulder Ledge Rapids

Portages: None

Rescue Index: Accessible

Source of Additional Information: National Weather
   Service, Culpeper and Remington gauges (703) 260-0305

Access Points	River Miles	Shuttle Miles
A–B	3	3
B–C	4	4.5

Access Point Ratings:
   A–Fletchers Mill (Rt. 620), good
   B–Rt. 621, fair
   C–Rock Mills (Rt. 626), very good

Paddlers will be pleased to note that all but one (in the first mile) of the fences referred to in previous literature have (at least as of this writing) been removed. Also, be alert for at least one downed tree across the river.

The rapids for the first few miles are basically ledges (one a 2-footer) interspersed with short rock gardens and one hard turn. However, about 1.25 miles into the trip (after almost 30 minutes of paddling in low water) one comes to the lone Class III of the section (which is a marginal Class III in low water). Boulder Ledge Rapids, a descriptive if slightly redundant name, can be recognized by a long pool and a short rocky cliff forming the right bank as the river makes a hard right turn. Also, about 50 to 100 yards back from the left bank of the river is a much higher rocky bluff. The novice/intermediate paddler should get out and scout this rapid on river left. One should not only observe the main 4- to 5-foot bumpy drop (usually run right to left) but also look downstream to see if any other obstacles are lurking. In the 1960s, Boulder Ledge was known as "Prepare to Meet Thy God Rapid" because of a small religious sign on the right bank which is now gone.

There is a nice little double ledge several minutes later followed by the first of several pretty lunch stops where the riverbank on one side or the other becomes huge rocks with hemlocks growing out of them.

The first bridge (Route 621) is reached after 2.5 miles or as one approaches the halfway point of the trip. Just above this bridge there is a picturesque cliff on the left with a small surfing wave below at moderate levels. For the remaining 4 miles below the bridge the small ledges and pretty cliffs and boulders adorned with hemlocks and evergreens become more frequent. Perhaps the best spot is halfway between the Route 621 bridge and the take out. Here, below a beautiful cliff, the river funnels to the left for an entertaining 50-yard run with a hole at the bottom left at lower levels. Two nice ledges with a surfing hole follow about 10 minutes later. The Class II action with cobble bars, ledges, and very good scenery continues to the take-out bridge (Route 626) on this very relaxing trip.

If there is not enough water on the Thornton, check the nearby Hughes River as an alternate; the Hughes usually holds its water longer than the Thornton.

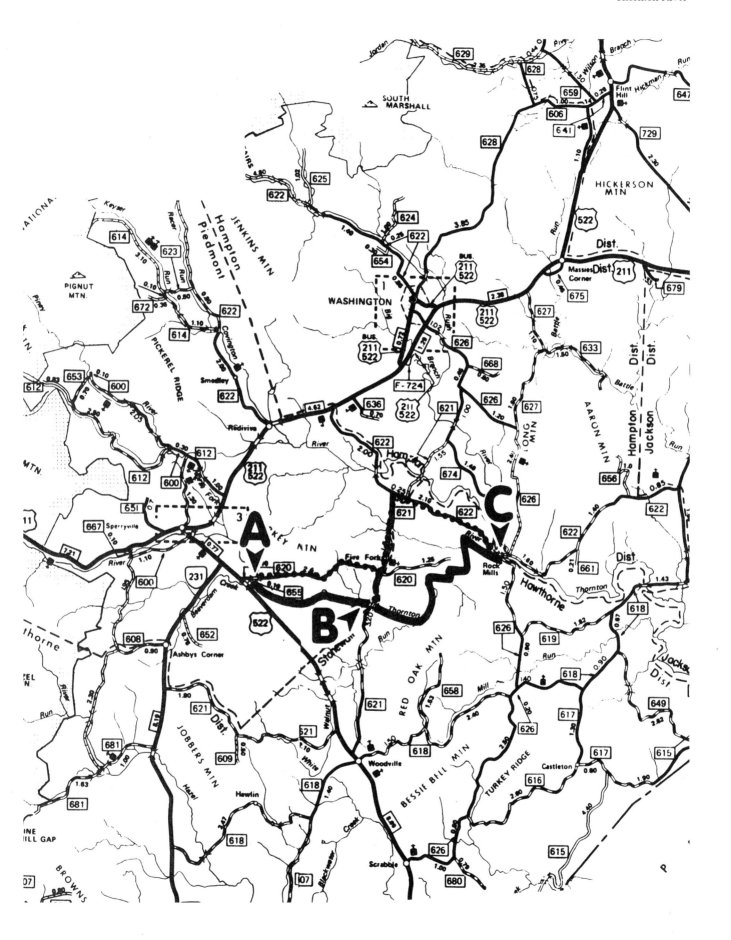

A typical scene on the Thornton River.

Potomac

Aquia Creek

Aquia Creek is one of those little known gems that delight the heart of the whitewater paddler. It is a beautiful small stream and is similar to the Thornton River near Sperryville on the eastern edge of Shenandoah National Park. Located only 30 miles south of Washington, Aquia Creek promises little based on the land surrounding it. The environs of the creek are mostly agricultural land to the south and the Quantico Marine Base to the north. However, once on the river the paddler is in for a day of surprise and delight. Aquia Creek is one of the most scenic and enjoyable small streams east of the Alleghenies.

You have two options of either a 9-mile or a 3-mile trip. For the longer trip, put in at Route 610. Here Aquia Creek is a tiny sand-and-mud-banked creek. The flow moves along swiftly over a sandy bottom, but the only drops are where the stream flows over fallen logs. Fallen logs of the nonsubmerged variety are a significant problem for the first couple of miles, but at most water levels one should be able to lift over them or pass underneath with little trouble.

A couple of miles into the trip a concrete bridge is approached with three large culverts running through it. Barring any accumulation of debris in the pipes, and sufficient clearance depending on water level, any of these passages may be run safely.

Be very sure of clearance before entering because, although the current through the bridge is not particularly swift, a broach in the pipe could be very serious indeed. This bridge is property of the Marines, and if you break it they'll be very mad at you. It was built to handle heavy military traffic and looks it.

After passing under the bridge, Aquia Creek begins to gradually steepen. This process continues all of the way to the lake near the take-out. Also, in the vicinity of the bridge several tributaries enter, and the stream doubles in width becoming a much more respectable size. Soon the paddler begins to notice that the banks are showing some rock mixed in with the sand and clay, and eventually the rock begins to predominate.

The slopes on the left bank rise high above the stream, and rhododendron begins to populate the stream's edge serving notice that the geomorphological environment has changed significantly. Aquia Creek has entered the fall line area where all of the eastward-flowing streams drop off the bedrock of the continent onto the sedimentary soils of the Coastal Plain. Some of the small streams in this area pack all of their drop into a small area, like the Little River, creating rapids with 4- and 5 foot drops. Aquia Creek, however, distributes its gradient more evenly, creating a stream more suitable to the intermediate paddler.

As the creek passes downstream the slopes rise higher and higher on both sides, spectacular rock formations appear, and hemlocks tower over the stream, jutting dramatically from the rock. About a mile above Route 641 the rapids become steeper but not nasty, and the relaxed paddler will find his or her adrenal glands beginning to stir into activity. The drops consist mostly of ledges up to 3 feet in height, some with rather complicated routes, many dropping over very tight turns into picturesque little pools at the bases of high rock cliffs. None are tougher than a stiff Class II. On the inside of bends white sandy beaches invite the paddler to linger and soak up the sun.

The Route 641 bridge is reached after 6 miles. While this bridge would make a convenient take-out, doing so here would deprive the paddler of the best part of the trip. Indeed, those wanting to run the heart of Aquia Creek should put in here for a 3-mile trip to the dam on Smith Lake. Between this bridge and Smith Lake, Aquia Creek has nearly all pluses and no minuses. The downed trees of the far upper section are virtually gone, the gradient continues to steepen, and the ancient igneous cliffs, hemlocks, and rhododendrons are at their most spectacular. The wildlife in this area is equally pleasing. On one trip we saw deer, kingfishers, ospreys, hawks, great blue herons, and various waterfowl. Late afternoon paddlers may even see a beaver, though no beaver dams are evident. The scenery is reminiscent of some of the upper Cheat tributaries in West Virginia, such as Red Creek, minus the high mountains in the far distance.

For 1.5 miles below Route 641 the Class I–II action builds to a crescendo until Aquia drops into Smith Lake. The best rapid is about 1 mile below Route 641. Here you have a mellow Class III on a left turn with a 3-foot drop at the bottom. However, be vigilant for fallen trees; this rapid had a tree in it during 1992. Once at Smith Lake the paddler must pay for his enjoyment upstream with a 1.5-mile paddle across the lake.

The route across the lake is not immediately obvious since the dam is earth fill and has the same look as the rest of the shoreline. Just keep paddling straight ahead and look for the take-out at the right end of the lake. There is a concrete spillway on the left edge of the dam. Give the entrance to the spillway a wide berth as there are not warning signs or buoys.

The dam itself is about 100 feet high and rather impressive. The lake is relatively small for such a large dam, indicating that the gradient of the creek under the reservoir must be quite large. Doubtless some fine rapids were sacrificed to create the water supply for Stafford

County. The upstream end of the reservoir is silting in very heavily, so whitewater paddlers may look forward to the distant day when the lake will be filled by sediment and the creek will reassert its authority over its own destiny.

Below the dam Aquia Creek is rather unattractive, and the remaining 1.5 miles to US 1 are not recommended. Although it still drops at a good rate, the creek passes by some dismal scenery and the odor of sewage as one passes a trailer court on the left is depressing.

The land on the left bank for most of the trip is part of the Marine Base and is posted against trespassing. It would seem best, then, to arrange lunch or suntanning spots on the right bank to avoid any possible federal entanglements. Also, the Marines will occasionally entertain the paddler with low level jet and helicopter flights over the creek. What you thought was the blood pounding in your ears may turn out to be the sound of huge helicopter blades.

You need a heavy rain in the spring to paddle Aquia Creek. The upper section requires more water than the lower section. For the lower section, if you can paddle the riffles below the Route 641 bridge, you can make the entire trip to Smith Lake (Aquia Reservoir). For the upper section, if it looks runnable at the Route 610 put-in, Aquia is runnable the entire 9 miles to Smith Lake.

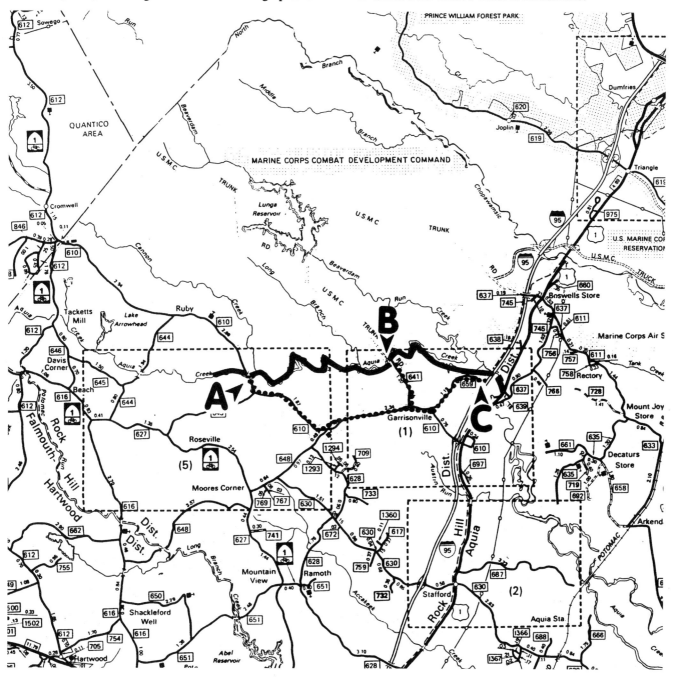

Bill Gordon surfs a wave at one of Aquia Creek's fine fall line rapids.

Section: Rt. 610 to Rt. 659

Counties: Stafford

USGS Quads: Stafford

Suitable for: Cruising

Skill Level: Intermediates

Months Runnable: Winter and spring after a heavy rain

Interest Highlights: Scenery, wildlife, whitewater

Scenery: Beautiful

Difficulty: Class I–II with one Class III

Average Width: 15 to 50 feet

Velocity: Fast

Gradient: 15 feet per mile

Runnable Water Levels:
  Minimum: Upper section: riffle runnable below Rt. 610 bridge; lower section: riffles runnable below Rt. 641 bridge
  Maximum: Perhaps moving toward flood stage

Hazards: Several felled trees between Rt. 610 and Rt. 641; maybe a couple of downed trees between Rt. 641 and Smith Lake

Scouting: None

Portages: None except around downed trees where necessary

Rescue Index: Accessible

Source of Additional Information: None really. This is a hard stream to catch up. If in the area check out the creek. If it looks runnable at the put-in on Rt. 610, it's runnable all the way.

Access Points	River Miles	Shuttle Miles
A–B	6	5.5
B–C	3	3.0

Access Point Ratings:
A–Rt. 610, good
B–Rt. 641, very good
C–Rt. 659, very good

Broad Run

For experienced paddlers on their way to or from other rivers, the 1-mile stretch of Broad Run from Route 628 to Route 55 offers a quick (if not cheap) thrill. In general, Broad Run is a placid creek that calmly meanders its way from aptly named Watery Mountains to Lake Manassas. However, the 1-mile stretch in Thoroughfare Gap is quite feisty and challenges aggressive, shepherded intermediates or advanced paddlers with rapids that steadily build up to strong Class III action. No wonder—Broad Run drops 75 feet in this 1 mile!

You need to exercise care and discretion at the put-in and take-out. The Route 628 put-in bridge is heavily posted. Consequently, park nearby where Route 55 and Route 628 meet. The easiest put-in is on river right downstream of the Route 628 bridge. The Route 55 take-out bridge has no parking signs near it so you need to park shuttle vehicles well away from these signs and the bridge. Having taken care of the logistical necessities, you can begin this quick trip. The first quarter mile gives you a good warm-up with good moving water and several turns on a tight little stream. For the next quarter mile, the action picks up to steady Class I–II rock gardens—with a couple being solid Class II.

Then things get more interesting when you reach the wooded part of this short gorge. The current marker for this change is a tall, dead tree by the river. For the next quarter mile the gradient is over 100 feet per mile. First, there is a Class II–III twisting drop, which in 1988 was blocked by a tree and required a portage on the left. Just below is a tight Class III over a covered rock garden. First timers should scout this second drop from the left to determine the route and to ascertain if trees are blocking any portion of it.

Less than 100 yards below this Class III rapid you will see a horizon line. Catch an eddy on the left and get on the left bank to scout or portage. Here you have a 4-foot ledge. The right side has some nasty rocks and pinning possibilities. Consequently, the more abrupt sliding slot on the left is the best route at moderate water levels.

Basically, this is a straight shot over a half-foot ledge and then the main drop into a squirrelly hole. Be sure you pay attention to the flow of the current and run this strong Class III drop and hole as straight as possible. At low water you may have to carry this drop, because the flow of water from right to left over this jagged ledge creates pinning possibilities.

You should set a throw line just below this ledge on the left, because after a pool there is a 3-foot ledge only 30 to 40 yards downstream. Paddlers who want to do the first ledge more than once have a relatively easy carry on the left.

The second ledge should also be considered a strong Class III because recently there was a tree blocking the runout on the left side and a pinning rock 10 to 20 yards downstream in the middle of the stream to catch the boats of those who screw up. The best route over this ledge appears to be on the right where the ledge is more shallow. On the extreme right is a Class II–III sneak slot. Carry and scout on the right. Also, set throw ropes on the right below this ledge.

After a bouncy Class II below the second ledge, and after passing historic stone Beverly Mill on the left, you go under Interstate 66. However, the fun is not yet over. Just below the bridge you have a 50-yard Class II rock garden. About 100 yards below this rock garden you will see a big rock in the river. This is your entry into a tight Class III drop over a 50-yard rock pile. First timers and intermediates should perhaps look at this tight slalom before committing themselves—particularly since a tree may be blocking it. Soon after this finale and a minor rock

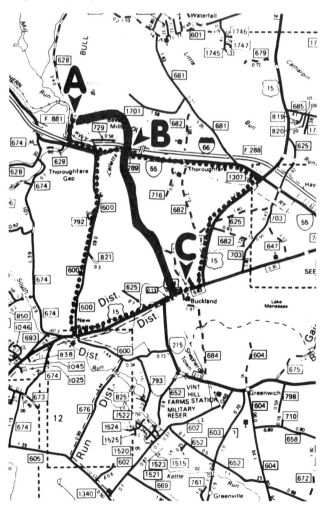

garden you go under the Route 55 bridge. The best take-out is on river left just downstream of this bridge.

The main hazard of this mile run is the potential for downed trees—particularly in the more difficult rapids. Recently, there was only one fallen tree; but this could change. You can scout almost all of this section while driving west on Interstate 66 or after taking Route 55 to 628 and walking down the railroad tracks on river left (be alert for trains). The only other drawback to this fine, short run is that you need a fair amount of water for this part of Broad Run to be up. The Culpeper gauge should be 3 feet or so and the Remington gauge in the 6- to 7 foot range.

Paddlers can continue this trip for 5.5 miles from Route 55 down to Buckland. However, the action simmers down substantially. The section below Route 55 starts off with its best rapids—two Class II drops in quick succession, which immediately follow the first turn within sight of the put-in. The next best rapid is a Class II ledge within sight of the take-out at the US 29/211 bridge. This rapid (the remains of Buckland Mill dam constructed in the 1800s) is best run on the right at higher levels and on the left at lower levels. The option on the left does require a very sharp turn. Novices might want to scout.

In between these entry and exit rapids are a variety of interesting riffles and scenery that is frequently, although not consistently, good. There are some memorable shale outcroppings and green swards which serve as a welcome counterpoint to the mud banks seen elsewhere on the trip. Wildlife along the stream is fairly abundant and includes ducks, geese, deer, herons, and beaver.

There is one "permanent" strainer at about the midpoint of the trip. It consists of a large tree and accumulated debris. It can be seen in advance, but the most convenient portage is over the top, although the footing is a bit tenuous. Given the size of the stream and the softness of its banks, other fallen trees and undercut banks with dangling barbed wire fences can also be expected. The take-out is on river left just upstream from the US 29/211 bridge. A road parallels the stream about 50 yards away.

This is the best of Broad Run. Above Route 628 there are few rapids and the river meanders under numerous fences as it goes through farmland. Below Buckland, Broad Run dumps into Lake Manassas.

Thoroughfare Gap is of geographical and historical interest. This gap, which cuts through 1,300-foot Bull Run Mountain on the north and 900-foot Pond Mountain on the south, funnels Interstate 66, Route 55, and the Southern Railway together on the easiest route between these mountains. During the Civil War, Confederate Generals J.E. Johnston and "Stonewall" Jackson came through Thoroughfare Gap on July 19, 1861, to fight in the first battle of Manassas (also called Bull Run). Then, just over a

Section: Rt. 628 to Rt. 55 and to Buckland (US 29/211)

Counties: Fauquier, Prince William

USGS Quads: Thoroughfare Gap

Suitable for: Day cruising

Skill Level: Shepherded, aggressive intermediates/advanced boaters for 1 mile above Route 55; novices below Route 55

Months Runnable: Winter and early spring after a good rain

Interest Highlights: Scenic, tight gorge and an old mill in upper mile; beaver in lower 5.5 miles

Scenery: Fair to pretty to beautiful in spots

Difficulty: Class II–III with 2 strong Class III ledges in upper mile; Class I–II in lower 5.5 miles

Average Width: 15 to 35 feet

Velocity: Fast in first mile; moderate below Rt. 55

Gradient: 75 feet per mile in the first mile from Rt. 628 to Rt. 55; 13 feet per mile from Rt. 55 to US 29/211

Runnable Water Levels:
  Minimum: 0 feet on new Rt. 66 gauge; for upper mile, perhaps 3 feet on Culpeper and 6 to 7 feet on Remington gauges; for lower 5.5 miles, perhaps 5 feet on Remington gauge
  Maximum: For upper mile, 2 feet on new Rt. 66 gauge and perhaps 6 feet on Culpeper and 8 to 9 feet on Remington gauges; for lower 5.5 miles, perhaps 3 to 4 feet on new Rt. 66 gauge and perhaps 7 feet on Remington gauge

Hazards: Occasional trees in river; 2 strong Class III ledges close together in upper mile; high water

Scouting: 2 strong Class III ledges and Class III above them in upper mile; Class III between I-66 and Rt. 55

Portages: Around occasional strainers; maybe 1 of the ledges in upper mile

Rescue Index: Generally accessible

Source of Additional Information: National Weather Service, Culpeper and Remington gauges (703) 260-0305

Access Points	River Miles	Shuttle Miles
A–B	1.0	1
B–C	5.5	7

Access Point Ratings:
A–Rt. 628, very good
B–Rt. 55, good
C–Buckland (Rt. 683 off US 29/211), good

Historic Beverly Mill on Broad Run–which can be seen from Interstate Route 66 while driving through Thoroughfare Gap.

year later, on August 26, 1862, General Jackson repeated his trip through the gap. He was followed two days later by General Longstreet. Both generals participated in the second battle of Manassas on August 29, where the South again defeated the North.

Do also check out historic Beverly Mill below the two ledges. This six-story mill has a rusty waterwheel on its upstream side. It was built before the Civil War and apparently operated until World War II.

Ed Grove tackles the first big ledge on Broad Run just above Beverly Mill. Photo by Steve Ettinger.

Bull Run and Cub Run

During the Civil War, Bull Run played a significant role in U.S. history. Here, the first real battle of the Civil War was fought at First Manassas in July 1861, and "Stonewall" Jackson, the great Southern general, earned his nickname. The battle of Second Manassas occurred a year later in August 1862. Both battles were defeats for Union troops.

The South viewed the nearby Orange and Alexandria Railroad as the path to the nation's capital. Meanwhile, the North saw this area as the gateway to the vital Shenandoah Valley by way of Manassas Gap, Thoroughfare Gap, and the old stone bridge that carried soldiers over Bull Run along the Warrenton Turnpike. So much history happened and so many soldiers died here that perhaps only the Rappahannock is more important to Virginia's Civil War history than Bull Run.

Incidentally, today's roads to Bull Run have an ironic historic parallel. Union forces had difficulty retreating after First Manassas because the roads were choked by Washingtonians who mistakenly thought they were going to see the North whip the South. The same clogged road conditions can be found today with the grand opening of yet another shopping center.

There is another irony to Bull Run: it is a key water source for roughly one million people at the same time that it serves as an unprotected dump for the urban area. In fact, at low water level one is more likely to find refrigerator and automobile strainers than the wooden kind. Nevertheless, remember the history! And yes, there is some good scenery on this historic stream.

The usual put-in for this 11- or 12-mile trip to Kincheloe Road is either at Bull Run Regional Park (on Bull Run Drive) or at Compton Road (Route 658) on Cub Run, a major tributary. In winter you have a tough choice: the closed park is gated and a quarter-mile carry results; or you can put in on Cub Run and later carry several strainers. However, with more daylight, there is an easier third alternative. This other Bull Run put-in is just off US 29/211 at the old stone bridge 2.5 miles upstream of Bull Run Regional Park and gives you a 14-mile trip. Because fees may be required at the old stone bridge put-in (it's on federal land!) or at Bull Run Park in season, bring some pocket change if you plan to use either of these alternatives.

The nearly 3-mile stretch of Cub Run from Compton Road to the Cub Run-Bull Run confluence begins with low wooded banks on river right and an interstate "whoosh-way" on river left. After you cross underneath Interstate 66, be alert for a low-water bridge. Eventually, Cub Run becomes steep banked on both sides with a narrow route. The shooting range here should remind you of the intense battles fought over a century ago. The only other difficulty is an occasional strainer.

If you choose the Bull Run Park put-in on Bull Run, you have urban "yuck" on river right and parkland on river left where there are wildflowers (especially bluebells!) in later spring. For most of the trip, the left bank is preferable as it is parkland from the put-in to the take-out. Don't be surprised if your neck is sore from facing left so much on the first part of this trip. Also note that the banks of Bull Run are clay and the bottom generally sand and mud. It's about 2 miles from the Bull Run put-in to the confluence with Cub Run.

At this confluence the stream widens considerably. After 1.5 miles more of paddling, you will have passed under the first two bridges—Ordway Road (Route 616) and Route 28 soon thereafter. Below Route 28 the scenery on river right improves, so check your neck to make sure it can still turn right.

You have now gone a third of the way. Note that Route 28 can be an alternative put-in for a shorter 8-mile trip. From here, it is a good 3-mile paddle to the Southern Railway (formerly the Orange and Alexandria Railway) Bridge and where Class I–II Popes Head Creek enters. This section features riffles and pools (some short and others long). But now come some treats. Below the Southern Railway Bridge the rapids become more abundant and almost Class II; the scenery improves substantially from the confluence of Popes Head Creek on river left to the take-out. Below Popes Head Creek the forest is impressive pines and hemlocks. Some of the hemlocks (mostly on river right) are reputed to be over 300 years old. Also, the curious old concrete works on river left make up the oldest electric generating plant in Fairfax County which served the bustling town of Clifton when it was built in 1929. About 100 feet downstream from the generating plant is a staff gauge on river left which can be accessed (with difficulty) upstream from Yates Ford Road (Route 615). The gauge should read at least 3 feet. From here only a handful of riffles remain until flatwater. But as the creek widens, numerous side swamps provide noisy bullfrogs and tail-slapping beaver in late spring. This area is a popular place for migratory waterfowl also. Other wildlife seen on this section of Bull Run are deer, quail, wood ducks, ospreys, eagles, turkeys, great blue herons, and bluebirds.

The Kincheloe Road take-out is often frozen over in the winter, so check it out before launching. Another warm weather take-out occurs nearly a mile downstream at Bull

Run Marina (Route 612), which is open on weekends April through Labor Day. Incidentally, paddling the 2 miles or so upstream from Bull Run Marina or Kincheloe Road to the hemlock overlook and back makes a good circuit trip.

There is a nearby upstream bonus for experienced paddlers. The 1-mile section of Cub Run from US 29/211 to the normal Compton Road (Route 658) put-in has an interesting quarter-mile long gorge with rocky Class III rapids and a gradient approaching 80 feet a mile.

However, run this gorge with care because a swim could be quite bruising. If you want to run the short, feisty Cub Run Gorge, the gauge at the US 29/211 put-in must read 0; you need a hard rain to get this technically demanding section up. You can scout this gorge because Fairfax County has made a trail through it and plans to build a bridge over Cub Run at the top of the gorge. The best level for first timers in the gorge is between 1 and 1.5 feet. In early spring the profusion of bluebells is incredible.

Section: Bull Run Regional Park or Cub Run (Rt. 658) to Kincheloe Road

Counties: Fairfax and Prince William

USGS Quads: Manassas, Gainsville, Independent Hill

Suitable for: Day cruising

Skill Level: Novice paddlers (with wetsuits in winter); only strong intermediate/advanced paddlers should attempt the short Cub Run Gorge just above this section

Months Runnable: Generally fall, winter, and spring

Interest Highlights: Civil War Battles (First and Second Manassas), old power plant, 300-year-old hemlocks

Scenery: Poor in spots to pretty in spots

Difficulty: Class I; short Cub Run Gorge just above this section is Class III

Average Width: 30 to 60 feet

Velocity: Slow to moderate; fast in Cub Run Gorge

Gradient: 5 feet per mile; short Cub Run Gorge above is up to 80 feet per mile

Runnable Water Levels:
Minimum: For Bull Run or normal Cub Run (Rt. 658) put-ins you need 2.8 feet on Goose Creek/Leesburg gauge, or 3 feet on staff gauge off Yates Ford Road (Rt. 615), or pipe below Cub Run gauge on Rt. 658 should be just in water; for short Cub Run Gorge just below US 29/211, Cub Run gauge on US 29/211 should be 0 and a heavy rain is needed.
Maximum: Flood stage, e.g., riffles above Compton Road (Rt. 658) are gone; for Cub Run Gorge, 3 feet on US 29/211 gauge for Cub Run

Hazards: Occasional strainers and low-water bridge below I-66 on lower Cub Run; occasional strainers and foot-high concrete pedestals crossing the stream at two places in Cub Run Gorge below US 29/211

Scouting: Kincheloe Road take-out in winter–may be frozen; maybe Cub Run Gorge

Portages: Low-water bridge on Cub Run

Rescue Index: Somewhat remote

Source of Additional Information: National Weather Service, Goose Creek/Leesburg gauge (703) 260-0305; Bull Run Regional Park, Spring Bluebell Hike and Summer Bull Run Country Jamboree (703) 631-0550

Access Points	River Miles	Shuttle Miles
A–D	14	12.5
B–D	11	11.5
B–E	12	12.5
A^1–B^1	1	4.0
B^1–D	12	8.5
B^1–E	13	9.5
C–D	8	8.0

Access Point Ratings:
A–Old Stone Bridge (US 29/211), very good
B–Bull Run Park, excellent (but only rated good in winter because park is closed and a quarter-mile portage is necessary)
A^1–Cub Run on US 29/211 (for gorge), very good
B^1–Cub Run on Compton Road (Rt. 658), very good
C–Rt. 28, good
D–Kincheloe Road, good unless frozen; limited parking
E–Bull Run Marina (Rt. 612), excellent when open (weekends, April through Labor Day)

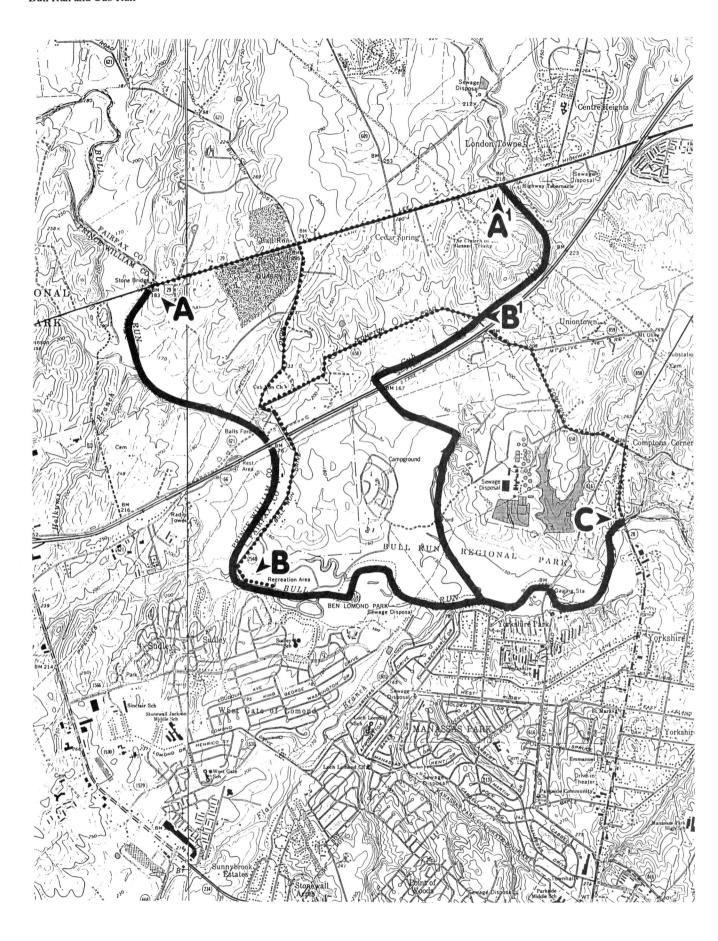

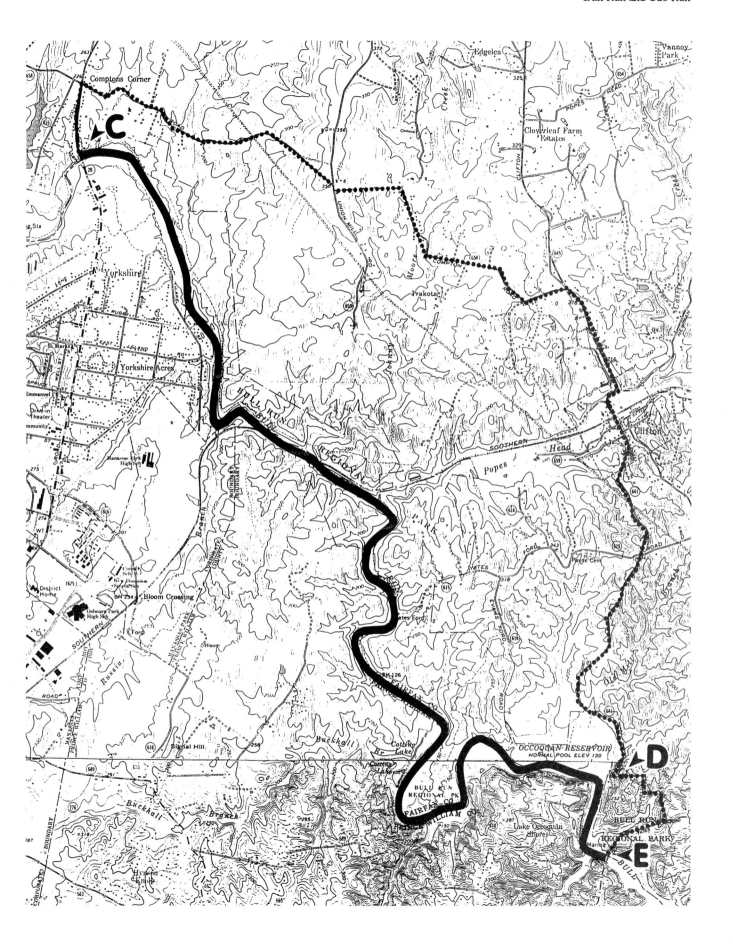

Catoctin Creek

Catoctin Creek is a real sleeper. Located close to Washington, D.C., and Baltimore, Maryland, it provides an enjoyable novice trip with beautiful and varied scenery. At Waterford you start with an intimate stream that flows through rolling farmland and then goes into a woods filled with many bird species. Later in this relaxing journey the well-groomed Firestone Estate is sandwiched between some incredible rock formations. The rapids are easy Class I–II chutes, rock gardens, and small ledges, which are best at the end of the trip.

The main problem is access. To avoid a hassle with owners of the 2,000-acre Firestone Estate, you can neither put in or take out at the most convenient point (Route 673) on this 15-mile trip. Consequently, you either have a long 15-mile day trip (from Waterford to the Potomac River) or a short 4-mile trip (from Taylorstown to the Potomac).

The only other problem is trees. Novices in particular should have enough boat control to avoid occasional strainers, especially in fast water. Don't commit yourself to a rapid unless you can see the bottom.

You have a choice of put-ins in Waterford, a very quaint (but expensive) old town. (Incidentally, Waterford has a memorable craft fair every fall, and proceeds are used to restore the historic buildings there.) You can put in at the Catoctin Creek South Fork just out of town on Route 698. This is the easiest put-in, but a long paddle on a tributary that can be shallow at low water. Alternatively, you can cross the South Fork, turn right immediately on Route 681, and drive a mile to put in on the North Fork. This trip is shorter but the put-in is more difficult—over barbed wire fences. Before putting in at either place, check the ledge beneath the Route 673 bridge between Taylorstown and Waterford. If this ledge is runnable, you will have sufficient water for the whole trip. Again, you can't put in on either side of the river at the Route 673 bridge because of strenuous objections by owners of the Firestone Estate.

After putting in on a 15-foot-wide tributary, the 5-foot high sandy banks shielded by trees will give you a feeling of intimacy. The farmland changes to woods once the North and South Forks join. As you begin this trip, and for its entire length, be prepared for a continuing symphony from the abundant bird life along the river. I assume this is because of the intermingling of woods, farmland, and creek. On a recent trip, I was escorted by a series of kingfishers for almost the entire 15-mile trip, saw three ospreys, and flushed numerous other large birds such as ducks, hawks, turkey vultures, and great blue herons. One special treat was watching a pair of Canadian geese successfully run a rapid just 50 feet ahead of my boat.

Smaller birds, particularly downy woodpeckers, cardinals, and robins, were abundant, too. There were also numerous swallow nest holes along the banks.

The trees along the river spark interest, too. In addition to other river trees such as box elders, beeches, and river birches, the sycamores are particularly striking. There are often big holes forming interesting patterns at the bases of large sycamores that are clinging to the bank. Beaver signs are abundant, too.

In the first 6-mile segment, from the North Fork put-in to the Route 673 bridge, you will primarily pass through woods with a couple of pretty rock formations along the way. The most interesting rapids are a couple of small ledges nearly 2 miles into the trip followed by two good Class I–II drops after you begin the third mile. Then, as you reach the Route 673 bridge, you enter the well-manicured realm of the Firestone Estate. Crisp, black wooden fences border immaculate fields and buildings. The primary purpose of the estate is to raise registered cattle and fine race horses. Indeed, Genuine Risk, the 1980 Kentucky Derby winner, came from these stables.

In the next 5-mile segment to Taylorstown Bridge (Route 663), there are often fences, houses, and other signs of ownership by Firestone and other estates. However, this does not detract from the scenery which still features pretty rock formations here and there—particularly 3 miles into this section on a long turn to the left where huge hemlock-covered rocks appear on the right. The rapids are still mild and pleasant—most notably a couple of tight turns midway into this section and a nice 50-yard rock garden about one-half mile from the Taylorstown Bridge.

As you approach Taylorstown you will see an interesting stone wall on the left followed by a restored historic mill on the right at the Taylorstown Bridge. If you wish, you can take out here or walk up the hill on the right to the Taylorstown General Store for some refreshment. If you put in or take out here, please do so on the left side of the river upstream of the bridge; the remaining land is posted.

However, you shouldn't take out here because the best of the Catoctin scenery and rapids are on the remaining 4 miles to the Potomac! Only a half mile from Taylorstown is a beautiful rock formation on the right and three nice drops close together. Someone must have thought this place especially beautiful, because midway up this rock formation on one trip was a white chair from which one could survey the view.

In the next mile come two more striking rock formations. Less than a mile below this are yet two more formations, with shallow caves this time—a good place for shelter in bad weather. About a half mile after these comes the good Class II rapids to finish the trip. You first have a rock garden followed by a ledge-chute-ledge combination. Then comes a 50-yard-long rock garden, which is the finale of the trip. Note the last gorgeous "holey" rock formation as you run these last rapids. A quarter mile below is the first take-out, the Route 672 bridge. However, this is not recommended because of the steep 20-foot high

banks here. Instead, paddle another couple of hundred yards to the Potomac and then a quarter mile downstream to the Game Commission landing just upstream on river right of the US 15 bridge crossing the Potomac. The take-out is trashy and can be muddy, but be thankful for a gentle walk to your car. However, if it has rained heavily, be sure your car doesn't get stuck on this muddy road and parking area.

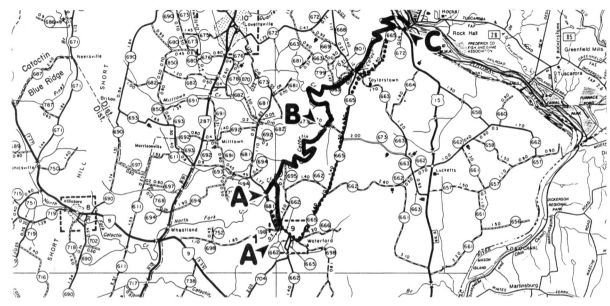

Section: Waterford (Rt. 681 or Rt. 698) to Potomac River (US 15)

Counties: Loudoun

USGS Quads: Purcellville, Waterford, Point of Rocks

Suitable for: Day cruising

Skill Level: Novices

Months Runnable: Winter and spring generally

Interest Highlights: Rock formations; Firestone Estate; bird life

Scenery: Beautiful in spots to beautiful

Difficulty: Class I–II

Average Width: 15 to 40 feet

Velocity: Moderate

Gradient: 8 feet per mile

Runnable Water Levels:
  Minimum: 2.5 feet on Goose Creek/Leesburg gauge; ledge under Rt. 673 runnable

Maximum: 5 feet on Goose Creek/Leesburg gauge; flood stage

Hazards: Occasional tree in the river

Scouting: None

Portages: None

Rescue Index: Generally accessible

Source of Additional Information: National Weather Service, Goose Creek/Leesburg gauge (703) 260-0305

Access Points	River Miles	Shuttle Miles
A–B	10.5	7.0
A[1]–B	12.0	6.0
A–C	15.0	9.5
A[1]–C	16.5	8.5
B–C	4.5	2.5

Access Point Ratings:
  A–at Rt. 681 (North Fork), good
  A[1]–at Rt. 698 (South Fork), good
  B–at Taylorsville Bridge (Rt. 663), good
  C–at Potomac River (US 15), very good

Goose Creek

Goose Creek was the first whitewater stream I ever paddled. Nevertheless, I still find it an interesting and enjoyable experience. Although the trip from Fairfax Dam to Route 7 is less than 3 miles, this best part of Goose Creek has several Class II and one Class III rapids of interest to the shepherded novice paddler and the relaxed intermediate. The sections above and below this short section have few Class II drops and much flatwater. However, one can continue 9 miles below Route 7 (primarily on the Potomac) to reach a take-out at Algonkian Regional Park.

This is also a great stream for those who like to fish. In fact, most of the cars parked at the put-in belong to anglers. Hard core anglers can put in above the 17-foot Fairfax Dam and fish in its lake for largemouth bass, crappie, bluegill sunfish, catfish, and carp. Just make sure you don't get too close to the spillway of the dam.

Indeed, fishing paddlers without whitewater experience can avoid the whitewater on Goose Creek if they wish. For the first half of the day they can fish on the lake above the dam. Then, for the second half of the day, they can drive to the river left take-out on Route 7 and put in 100 yards upstream. Here, Tuscarora Creek enters next to the public golf course, and you are at the bottom of a pool over a half mile long. You can work your way up this pool fishing for smallmouth bass, bluegill, catfish, and carp. For the inexperienced, there is one note of caution. Just be sure the river isn't too high or the current could take you from the bottom of the pool into a Class II rapid underneath the Route 7 bridge. Incidentally, Tuscarora Creek has one claim to fame. It is said that President Grover Cleveland often fished in it near Leesburg.

After carrying down below the dam and putting in on river right, pause to enjoy the 17-foot man-made waterfall here. You have plenty of time to warm up, because, after a couple of riffles, the first ledge (1 foot) is a third of a mile into the trip. Just below this is a long Class I–II rock garden, and then you will pass what appears to be a canal lock on the right. Soon you should see a quarry on the right and drop over a short Class II rock garden best run center or right. This is the trickiest of the Class II drops on this section. The low-water passage on the right requires some tight maneuvering, and there are some cross currents to deal with. The muddy clay banks along here are about 5 feet high, and the river is bordered by a forest of sycamores, tulip poplars, birches, oaks, and other hardwoods.

About a mile into the trip you will go under a striking high bridge 278 feet long that was used by the Washington

and Old Dominion Railroad when it operated off and on from 1858 to 1968. During the railroad's 110-year existence, it hauled Civil War troops, tourists going to the Shenandoahs in the early 1900s, and most recently, commuters who called it the "Virginia Creeper" because of its slow service. Now the roadbed has become a well used bike trail that goes from Mount Vernon all the way to the small town of Purcellville at the foot of the Blue Ridge Mountains. Notice the colorful red sandstone (from local quarries) that support this bridge. A couple of hundred yards below the high bridge and just after a power line, is another nice Class I–II drop. You will then have a good pool over a quarter mile long on which to drift, fish, and generally goof off. However, once you come to a large house on the right and the broken remains of a dam on the right and left banks of the river, pull over to river right and scout. You have arrived at Golf Course Rapids. While scouting, notice a sign high on a tree in the yard of the house: it indicates how high Goose Creek was in 1972 when Hurricane Agnes struck. If you have time, paddle to the left side of the river and explore the remains of Cooks Mill, a canal lock and mill race at the top of the rapids.

Golf Course Rapids is 100 yards long and starts in a mellow way. However, it really gets your attention before it ends. Over halfway down, the right side of the river is a diagonal line of three pourovers and holes. Accordingly, the most conservative way to run this rapid is clearly left of center. However, once below the diagonal line of holes, you should cut back right to miss the shallow left end of the rapid and catch some nice standing waves on the right. For those so inclined, the bottom of this rapid is a good place to practice peelouts and ferrying. If you take the conservative route on the left, this is a Class II–III rapid. However, if you want to tweeze between or challenge the line of holes on the right, this is a Class III effort. Below the Golf Course Rapids is a long pool over a half mile long which continues to the take-out. The muddy clay banks increase in height to about 10 feet. The golf course is on the left and woods are on the right. Break out the fishing rod and enjoy the float.

At the end, you have two take-out alternatives. You can take out on river left at the aforementioned spot 100 yards above the Route 7 bridge where Tuscarora Creek enters. Then you can drag your boat over a field to the parking lot. However, if you have reasonable boat control, you can run the first part of the Class II rapids going under the bridge and catch an eddy on the left quite close to the parking lot. You will have to pull your boat up the sloping 10-foot bank, but this shouldn't be too difficult. While running the shuttle, pick the take-out which suits you. The right side of the river is a more difficult take-out than these two alternatives, and the road here has "no parking" signs. When parking at the Route 7 take-out, be sure to get permission from the managers of the Golf Course. Permission will be easier to get if you mention you belong to a canoe club.

Those intrepid, patient souls wanting to continue can do so. Below the Route 7 bridge, it is a mere 9 miles to the Algonkian Park take-out—2.5 miles on Goose Creek and 6.5 miles on the Potomac. There are only two Class II rapids before nearing the Potomac—a long rock garden and a 2-foot ledge. However, all is not dreary. Rumor has it that there used to be a great blue heron rookery somewhere along this stretch of Goose Creek before it enters the Potomac. Also, roughly a mile below Route 7 are the remains of Claphams Mill (described below). Once you reach the Potomac, you have over 6 miles of paddling before you reach the Algonkian Park take-out on river right. This section is described in the Point of Rocks to Violettes Lock segment of the Potomac elsewhere in this chapter.

Goose Creek was quite important to the canal history of the Potomac. Between 1849 and 1854, the Goose Creek and Little River Navigation Company constructed 12 miles of canal on Goose Creek from its confluence with the Little River to the C and O Canal (where Goose Creek enters the Potomac at Edwards Ferry). Unfortunately, the railroads forced the Goose Creek Canal out of business in 1857. However, remains of this canal are worth seeing. Perhaps the most striking remnants of this canal are found at Cooks Mill (above Golf Course Rapids) and Claphams Mill (downstream of Route 7 on river right). At Claphams Mill (on Xerox property) is a 1-mile canal and impressive two stage lock.

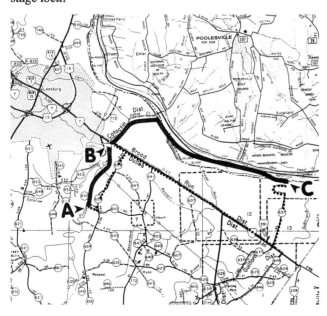

Section: Fairfax Dam (Rt. 642) to Rt. 7 or Algonkian Park (Rt. 637)

Counties: Loudoun

USGS Quads: Leesburg, Sterling

Suitable for: Day cruising

Skill Level: Alert/shepherded novices at moderate levels

Months Runnable: Winter, spring, and perhaps early summer

Interest Highlights: Fishing, scenic dam put-in, mill/canal ruins

Scenery: Fair to pretty in spots

Difficulty: Class I–II at moderate levels with 1 Class II–III

Average Width: 60 to 80 feet

Velocity: Moderate

Gradient: 9 feet per mile to Rt. 7; 1 foot per mile below Rt. 7

Runnable Water Levels:
Minimum: A good 2 feet on Goose Creek/Leesburg gauge; at least 3.6 feet on Remington gauge
Maximum: 4 feet on Goose Creek/Leesburg gauge; 6 feet on Remington gauge

Hazards: None except high water and perhaps a tree or so in river

Scouting: Golf Course Rapids (Class II–III) from right

Portages: None

Rescue Index: Accessible

Source of Additional Information: National Weather Service, Goose Creek/Leesburg and Remington gauges (703) 260-0305

Access Points	River Miles	Shuttle Miles
A–B	2.5	4
B–C	9.0	11
A–C	11.5	14

Access Point Ratings:
A—at Fairfax Dam (Rt. 642), good
B—at Rt. 7, good
C—at Algonkian Regional Park (Route 637), very good

Laurel Fork of the Potomac

"Fantastic! A gem for advanced and expert paddlers waiting to be discovered!" This is what Ollie Fordham of Charlottesville thought about this creek back in the early 1970s when he first saw it on a USGS topographic map. Later he became ecstatic when he found that the reality of paddling this creek was just as great as his fantasy. This was in 1979 when Ollie led a group of Coastal Canoeists on one of the first trips down the Laurel Fork. Since then, he and the Coastals have been back to continue this fantasy come true.

Imagine a small, intimate creek with crystal clear water running through a total wilderness in the Monongahela National Forest. Add to that the excitement of a Class III–IV whitewater stream that has a total drop of 760 feet in its 9.5 mile course, and you have the Laurel Fork. However, be warned! Don't get on this creek unless you can read turbulent, fast water from your boat and are in good physical shape. Otherwise, you may be in for a long day with several nasty swims.

The Laurel Fork watershed has been considered for wilderness designation on several occasions, but local opposition has prevented this. Except for the put-in and take-out, the only access to the stream is by foot trail. It runs through a small isolated valley between two 4,000-foot high mountains—the Allegheny Mountain range on the west and Middle Mountain on the east.

Outstanding features of this run are a rhododendron and hemlock forest (which overhangs the creek in its upper stretches); high gradient (80 feet per mile—which means a lot of action); a hard rock bottom; clear, clean water; and many good rapids. Incidentally, rhododendron is known locally as "laurel;" hence the name of this creek. Regarding wildlife, you may get to run a beaver dam or two, deer are abundant, and the Laurel Fork is considered excellent for trout fishing.

The trip starts at the Route 642 bridge deep in the George Washington National Forest at a stone house that appears to have been a water mill many years ago. It ends 9.5 miles later on Route 644 when the Laurel Fork joins Straight Fork—just above a low-water bridge with a nasty rock jumble below it. Both the put-in and take-out are on private land so get permission first.

You also need to deal with fallen trees. Before the flood of November 1985 only one deadfall blocked the creek, and it was located within a mile of the take-out. However, in 1987 the first and last miles of this run had extensive log jams created by the 1985 flood, making at least five portages necessary.

At low water the Laurel Fork is a good Class III run, and you may have time to enjoy its beautiful scenery. At high water, this is a solid Class IV trip, and you may ask, "What scenery?" With an average gradient of 80 feet per mile, the current is fast and the rapids continuous for 9.5 miles! So, be in shape, be alert, and keep your group as small and tight as continuous whitewater will allow. If you are not adept at scouting from your boat, jamming bank "eddies," and don't command all other abilities of the confirmed advanced/expert "creek freak" paddler, then you don't belong on the Laurel Fork in high water. When the water is high, this creek is particularly dangerous for decked boaters because of the high possibility of being pinned by fallen trees.

Rapids on the Laurel Fork come in many forms and shapes. However, they are all hard to scout because of the thick rhododendron lining the banks and the swift current that makes stopping difficult. The toughest are two Class IV–V drops (Class IV in low water and maybe Class V in high water). These are U-Turn (midway through the run) and Triple Drop (about 3 miles farther downstream near where Vance Run enters the Laurel Fork).

U-Turn is a steep 5-foot drop which is compounded by the river bending 180 degrees to the right next to a rock wall forming the left bank. You cannot really scout U-Turn. The rapid comes up quickly, and the current is so swift that you are committed to it before you can take any other action. Go with the flow but drive hard to the right because the current is trying to push you into the wall on the left. Indeed, water, canoes, and canoeists tend to pile up on this wall, which makes for some mighty furious paddling.

Triple Drop has three big 3-foot ledges. These ledges are about 15 to 30 feet apart with big holes below each of them. Generally, these ledges are run right or right of center. It is also impossible to scout Triple Drop because of the thick rhododendron on both sides of the creek.

You will certainly remember these two rapids. Concerning the lesser rapids, the Laurel Fork is so small that there is usually only one obvious route to take. However, your abilities to read turbulent water and react quickly must be razor sharp, especially at high water.

Once you reach the Route 644 take-out, I hope you will agree with Ollie Fordham that this is a fantasy come true.

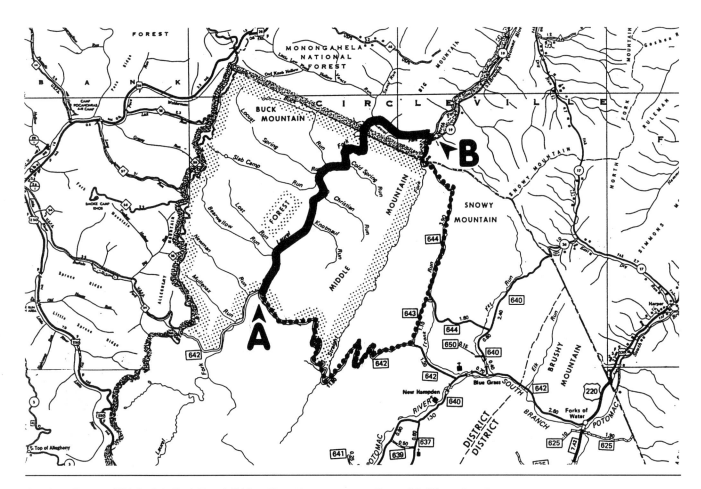

Section: Rt. 642 (VA)/Buffalo Fork Road (WV) to Rt. 644 (VA)/Rt. 19 (WV)

Counties: Highland (VA), Pendleton (WV)

USGS Quads: Thornwood, Snowy Mountain

Suitable for: Day cruising

Skill Level: Advanced (moderate levels) and expert (high levels)

Months Runnable: Winter and spring after a moderate rain or during snow melt

Interest Highlights: Beautiful rhododendron/hemlock gorge through total wilderness

Scenery: Beautiful

Difficulty: Continuous Class III–IV with 2 Class IV–V rapids

Average Width: 20 to 40 feet

Velocity: Fast!

Gradient: 80 feet per mile!

Runnable Water Levels:
Minimum: No gauge–visually check water at put-in and take-out
Maximum: Well below flood stage; this is a killer at flood stage

Hazards: Trees in river (mainly in first and last mile)

Scouting: Not really possible; U-Turn and Triple Drop–try to boat scout as you enter; if you can't read turbulent water in fast current from your boat, you don't belong here

Portages: Around downed trees, particularly in first and last mile

Rescue Index: Remote wilderness

Source of Additional Information: None

Access Points	River Miles	Shuttle Miles
A–B	9.5	28.8
		(Class II WV roads)
		13.7
		(Class IV VA roads)

Access Point Ratings:
A–Rt. 642 bridge, very good; get permission
B–Confluence with Straight Fork (along Rt. 644/Rt. 19) very good; get permission

Potomac River

The Potomac River forms the northern border of Virginia, separating the Old Dominion from Maryland and the District of Columbia. Throughout the history of the United States the Potomac has functioned as an important highway for communication and commerce as well as a barrier to the many military forces, foreign and domestic, that have campaigned throughout this area. In more recent years the Potomac has found new duties as a premier recreational area for the millions that live in the region. Whitewater paddling is the most recent of these activities, but the old river has proven to be a superlative location for the enjoyment of this relatively new sport. The Potomac provides whitewater of all degrees of difficulty throughout its length, from the small headwater streams of West Virginia and western Maryland, through the Blue Ridge at Harpers Ferry, and across the Piedmont between the mountains and the coast.

Upper Potomac: Shinham Road to Point of Rocks (US 15)

The 14- to 16-mile section of the Potomac from just above Harpers Ferry to Point of Rocks offers interesting variety for the paddler. The first 5 to 7 miles of the trip (depending on where you put in) feature Class II whitewater (with one Class II–III) at moderate levels. The remaining 9 miles are all relaxing flatwater—perfect for easy drifting and fishing. One advantage of this stretch is that it has several put-ins and take-outs for those who want shorter trips.

You have a choice of two put-ins. First, you can put in just 2 miles above Dam Number 3 on the Potomac River at Shinham Landing launching ramp on the Maryland side of the river. To reach this put-in, take Sandy Hook Road upstream on the Potomac after turning off US 340 in Maryland. After Sandy Hook Road goes up and away from the river, look for a left on Shinham Road and take it down to the river. There you will find a large parking area and boat ramp. From here you have just over 2 miles of flatwater before reaching Dam Number 3.

For an alternative put-in you can continue west on US 340 and first cross the Potomac into West Virginia. Soon you will cross the Shenandoah River on a second bridge. Go another 1.5 miles until you reach a four-way intersection at Bakerton Road. Turn right and go another 1.5 miles to a railroad underpass. Turn right immediately and go 200 yards down a dirt road to the put-in on the West Virginia side of the Potomac. You are now just below John Brown's Cave. If you wish, you can climb up the railroad grading and check out the cave. Here, in 1859, John Brown

met with his followers to plan his ill-fated raid on Harpers Ferry. This put-in also has two disadvantages: the parking area is small, and your shuttle vehicles are exposed to theft and vandalism in this isolated area.

Once you reach Dam Number 3, get out on the left to scout the dam. Be sure to notice the spikes at the top of the dam while you scout. At moderate water levels, there are a number of runnable Class II+ breaks in the dam. However, be sure no debris blocks the bottom of the break you choose. The best channel is usually on the left. If you can't see a place to run the dam safely, you will have to portage on the left when the Hancock gauge is over 5 feet. Between 3 and 5 feet on this gauge, you can lift over the dam on the left.

Having run or lifted over this 4-foot dam, you now enter the Needles—an enjoyable 1.5-mile series of Class II rapids at moderate levels. For the first third of a mile you will be negotiating a long, intricate Class II rock garden and ledge series. This is followed in the next mile by several wave trains with pools at the end of each one. While in the Needles, be on the lookout for numerous interesting surfing spots. However, don't try the Needles if the Hancock gauge is under 3 feet or the Point of Rocks gauge under 0.9 feet. The water is simply too low, and you will be doing more hiking and scraping than paddling. At this low level, most of the water goes down a feeder canal on the right (West Virginia) side of the river to an old power plant. On the other hand, novices should not run the Needles at high water. Continuous big waves and hydraulics would mean a long and dangerous swim on this big river in cold weather.

After running the Needles, you soon come to the confluence of the Potomac and Shenandoah Rivers. On your right is the picturesque and historic town of Harpers Ferry. (See the Bull Falls and the Staircase section of the Shenandoah for more on this interesting town.) On your left side is Sandy Hook and the Elk Bluff overlook, which gives a splendid view of the confluence. To reach the Elk Bluff overlook on the Maryland side, take the mile-long trail which begins from Sandy Hook Road a half-mile above the confluence on the Potomac. For a view on the Virginia/West Virginia side of the Potomac, cross the river on US 340. Near the boundary between these two states is a sign for the Appalachian Trail on the south side of US 340. This trail will take you to Split Rock Trail overlook.

The next mile begins with an easy Class I set of waves with a good surfing spot on the left. However, be careful at low water here because there may be debris from a metal bridge deposited by a flood years ago. A couple of minutes below these waves you'll encounter a pleasant 50-yard run

World champion Jon Lugbill running the Spout during the First Great Falls Race on the Potomac in 1988. (Level was 3.0 on the Little River Falls gauge). Photo by Matt Esparza.

of Class I–II waves known as Mad Dog Rapids. Shortly below these waves the river flows between two large rocks on the left with some impressive waves below. This is Whitehorse Rapids. At the top left are a couple of surfing possibilities at reasonable levels, and below are about 50 yards of vigorous Class II–III waves, which become Class III at higher levels. There are also two routes to the right of Whitehorse that should be looked at before being run.

After you pick up the pieces in the calm water below Whitehorse, you will approach the US 340 bridge. There is a take-out 100 yards above the bridge on river left at Sandy Hook and a more difficult take-out across the river on the right at Patoma Wayside. These two take-outs are described in more detail under the Bull Falls and the Staircase narrative in this book.

The 11-mile section from Sandy Hook, West Virginia, to Point of Rocks, Maryland, is a distinct change from the whitewater sections above (Bull Falls and the Staircase on the Shenandoah and the Needles on the Potomac). With the exception of three Class II drops near the beginning of this stretch, the river now relaxes after punching through the Harpers Ferry area and novices can enjoy the scenery, fishing, and camping during a pleasant float trip.

After paddling under the US 340 bridge just below Sandy Hook, keep to the extreme right as a large island will separate a small piece of the Potomac for your enjoyment. This channel usually sports a variety of waterfowl (great blue herons, Canadian geese, and mallards) and less head wind! At the bottom of this island channel work to the left of the river. About 1.5 miles downstream from the US 340 bridge you come to the next possible take-out on river left at Weverton, Maryland, which is at Lock 31 on the C & O Canal. Unfortunately, Weverton is a poor access point because it requires a long portage, may be hard to find, and has limited parking. As you pause here, note that the C & O Canal from Sandy Hook to Weverton is part of the 2,000-mile Appalachian Trail which runs from Springer Mountain in Northern Georgia to Mount Katahdin in north central Maine.

Just below Weverton are the prime rapids for the lower part of the trip—three Class II drops, each over 100 yards apart. The first of these (Weverton Rapids) should be run right at moderate levels. The second (File Factory—an old mill dam) should be run center. The last rapid (Knoxville Falls) should be run center or left (most conservative). At higher levels other options are available. As you run these three rapids, notice that they cut through mountains on both sides of the river. On the left in Maryland is South Mountain; the Appalachian Trail follows the ridge at its top. On the right in Virginia is Short Hill; it is capped by Buzzard Rock, which towers nearly 1,000 feet above you. Finally, in the midst of these drops, keep a sharp eye on the Maryland shore for the ruins of the Weverton Manufacturing Company which operated in the early 1800s.

Less than a mile below this bouncy interlude, you come to Knoxville. This take-out is now closed. Folks running the Needles (Potomac) and the Staircase (Shenandoah) upstream used to take-out here. If you have camping gear and want to avoid the Class II rapids upstream, put in downstream at Brunswick. Several islands and channels add interest to the next two miles.

Knoxville is followed 2.5 miles later by a great take-out at Brunswick—also on the left by Lock 30 (Sigafoos Lock) of the C & O Canal and near the Maryland Route 17 bridge (which is Route 287 in Virginia). About 100 yards above the Route 17 bridge at

Nolan Whitesell running the Spout on the Virginia side of Great Falls in July 1986. This was the first time Great Falls was run in an open canoe (level was 2.96 feet on the Little River Falls gauge). Photo by Steven Michael Lowe.

Brunswick, look for a small channel on river left. This pleasant little side channel (except for automobile tires) leads right up to the Brunswick take-out and your car. If you miss the upstream entry of this channel, you can get to the downstream entry just below the US 17 bridge.

Called Berlin until 1890, Brunswick was a thriving canal town and an important Potomac crossing during the Civil War. The Union Army crossed here after the battles of Antietam and Gettysburg. For boaters on the Potomac and hikers and bikers on the C & O Canal, Brunswick has numerous stores for supplies.

In the 6 miles below Brunswick and the Route 17 bridge you will pass more bluffs, wooded banks, and fishing holes. One mile past Brunswick is Brunswick Riverside Park with camping and excellent river access on river left for those so inclined. About 2 miles further the Maryland version of Catoctin Creek enters from the left. Here you will see the Catoctin Creek Aqueduct on the C & O Canal. Also known as Crooked Aqueduct (because boats had to make a sharp turn immediately upstream), this 130-foot span unfortunately collapsed in the early 1970s. Catoctin Creek is also a great Class I novice spring trip, as detailed by Edward Gertler in his book, *Maryland and Delaware Canoe Trails*. Nearly 1.5 miles below Catoctin Creek Aqueduct is the Bald Eagle Island hiker-biker on the C & O Canal. There should be potable water and restrooms here, but check with canal headquarters in Sharpsburg to be sure.

Toward the end of this stretch, the islands in the river get much larger and you will pass through a gap in Catoctin Mountain just before you reach the Point of Rocks take-out. About 1.5 miles above this take-out the river is split by two long islands. If you go left, you will reach Lock 28 on the C & O Canal a mile above the take-out. This interesting lock is made of local red sandstone. Laborers who built it in the 1830s earned less than a dollar a day. If you take the right channel, the Virginia version of Catoctin Creek enters from the right less than a half mile before the take-out. This pretty creek for shepherded novices has some good Class I–II rapids and is discussed earlier in this chapter. As you pass through the Catoctin Mountain gap, note that the Maryland side towers nearly 1,000 feet above you. The take-out at Point of Rocks is on river right at the launching ramp off US 15. There is also a gauging station on river left just downstream of the bridge. If it has rained heavily, be sure your car does not get stuck on the muddy take-out road.

Upper Potomac: Point of Rocks to Violettes Lock

The 26-mile stretch of the Potomac from Point of Rocks to Violettes Lock is a delight for campers, float anglers, birders, and history buffs. No natural rapids exist on this section, and it is made for lazy drifting. On river left there are five hiker-biker campsites with potable water and toilets on the Maryland C & O Canal for those who want to camp. However, check with the National Park Service at the C & O Canal National Historical Park in Sharpsburg, Maryland, first to see if the facilities on these hiker-bikers are working. Also, carry a good map because these hiker-bikers can be hard to locate from the river. More rugged folks can camp on the numerous islands (some quite large) along the way. Incidentally, these islands all belong to Maryland since the Maryland state line is on the Virginia bank of the Potomac. Anglers catch primarily smallmouth bass, catfish, and sunfish with an occasional largemouth bass rearing its head. Birders have opportunities to see such diverse large birds as turkeys, ospreys, herons, and pileated woodpeckers. Historians can poke around the several aqueducts and locks on the C & O Canal and note the several ferry crossings used during the Civil War.

The Potomac passes through a scenic valley before it drops over the falls line from the Piedmont to the Coastal Plain. There are some wooded bluffs and hills in the distance on this section, but tree lined banks are the rule. Silver maples, box elders, sycamores, and river birches predominate.

Sluggards putting in quite late in the day can breathe a sigh of relief. Calico Rocks, the first hiker-biker, is only a half mile downstream. Near here is Kanawha Springs which used to be a watering place for mules on the C & O Canal. A half mile downstream from the hiker-biker are the real Calico Rocks composed of colorful limestone breccia.

About 2.5 miles farther is Nolands Ferry. Discovered by settlers around 1750, this shallow spot was used during the Revolutionary War by British and American troops. Later, in 1862, Confederate troops crossed here to join General Lee at Frederick during the Antietam Campaign. You will also find a picnic area and boat ramp here, but overnight camping is not allowed.

Two miles below this respite is Indian Flats, the second hiker-biker for late launching paddlers. Only a quarter mile further is a real treat—the Monocacy River Aqueduct. This is perhaps the most striking aqueduct on the C & O Canal. Built of white granite from nearby Sugarloaf Mountain, this structure is 560 feet long and has seven arches. It was completed in 1833 by Irish stone masons. Here also (via Mouth of Monocacy Road from Route 28), you have boat ramps, parking, and picnicking but not overnight camping. The Monocacy is also a leisurely float trip, as described in Edward Gertler's book, *Maryland and Delaware Canoe Trails*.

About three-quarters of a mile below the Monocacy is Lock 27 (Spinks Ferry)—another red sandstone marvel on the C & O Canal. Over a mile below this you reach the Pepco Dickerson Powerplant on river left. At low levels (less than 3 feet on the Little Falls Gauge), a large volume of water discharged by the power plant generates a lively chain of man-made waves. Enjoy it because it is the only rapid on this 26-mile section.

Incidentally, the managers of the Dickerson Powerplant and two creative members of the Canoe Cruisers Association of Washington, D.C., have made history. On December 19, 1991, PEPCO executives and the U.S. Whitewater Team dedicated a new artificial whitewater slalom course which was created using the 900 foot concrete drainage culvert for water discharged from the plant. Conceived by local paddlers Scott Wilkinson and John Anderson, this artificial course dropping 16 feet was constructed just in time to train for the 1992 Summer Olympics at Seu d'Urgill, Spain. Using large concrete "gumdrops" and "flounders" (which were poured on land and then lowered into the course by huge cranes—see the photo at the end of this chapter) construction workers

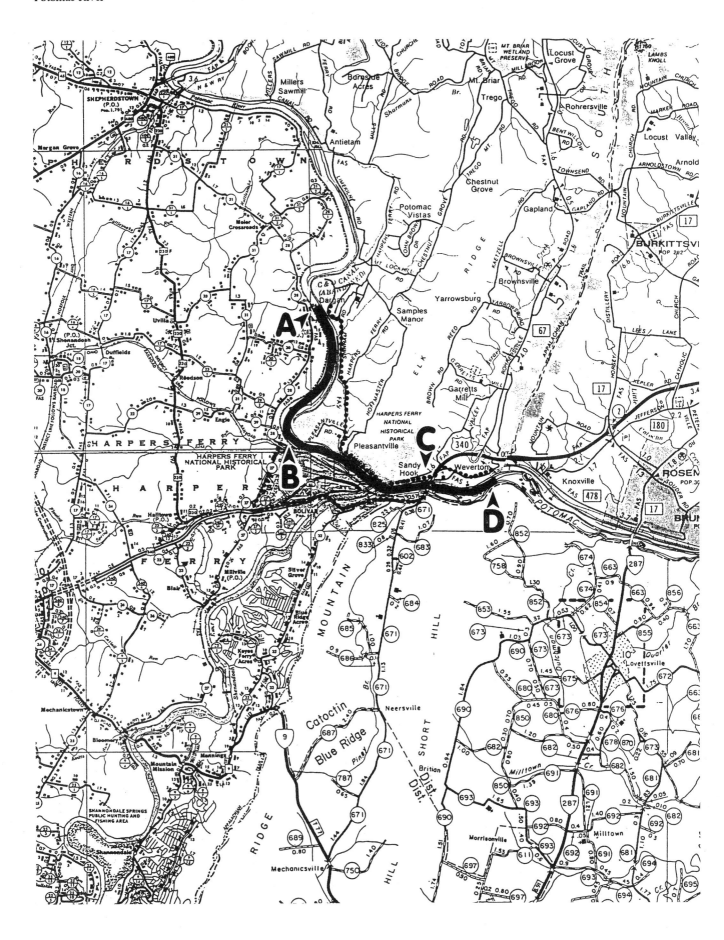

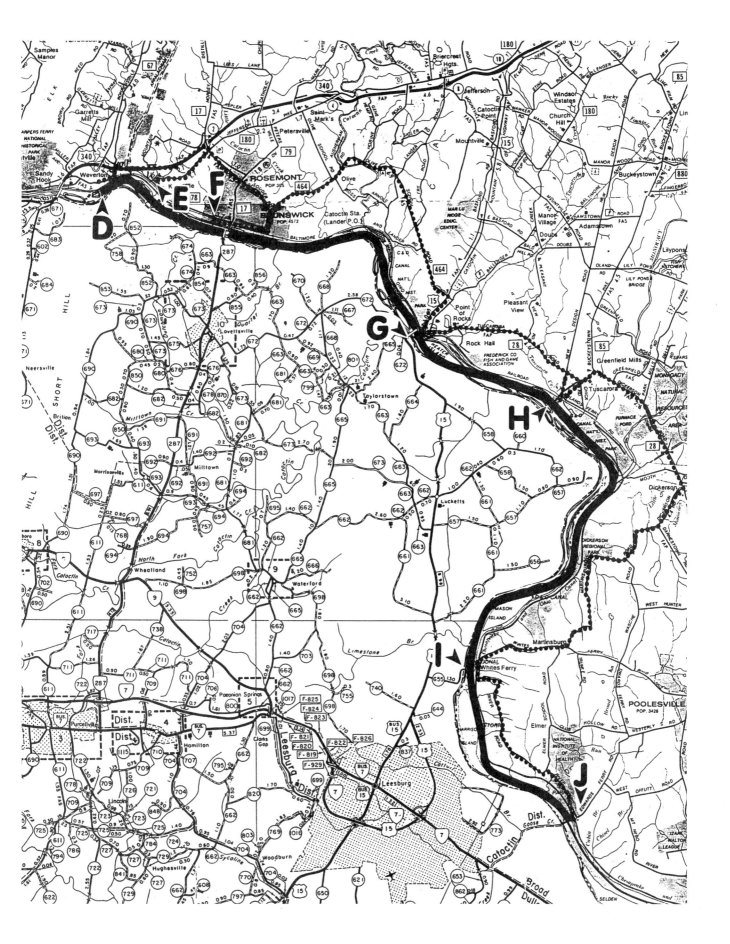

Section: Near Sandy Hook (Shinham Road) to Point of Rocks (US 15)

Counties: Frederick and Washington (MD), Loudoun (VA)

USGS Quads: Harpers Ferry, Point of Rocks

Suitable for: Day cruising and camping

Skill Level: Shepherded novices/intermediates–5- to 7-mile upper section at moderate levels; novices–9-mile lower section

Months Runnable: Needles part of upper section winter, spring, and maybe early summer; entire year below Potomac/Shenandoah confluence

Interest Highlights: Harpers Ferry; great fishing/camping; C&O Canal

Scenery: Pretty to beautiful in spots

Difficulty: Class II for first 5 to 7 miles with 1 Class II–III; Class A for last 9 miles

Average Width: 300 to 2,000 feet

Velocity: Moderate in upper section; slow in lower section

Gradient: Generally 2 feet per mile; however, Needles, Whitehorse Rapids, and 1 mile between Weverton and Knoxville are 10 feet per mile

Runnable Water Levels:
 Minimum: 1.5 feet on Shepherdstown, 3 feet on Hancock, and 0.9 feet on Point of Rocks gauges for Needles; 2.5 feet on Little Falls gauge and 0.5 feet on Point of Rocks gauge for remainder of trip
 Maximum: 5 feet on Hancock and Little Falls gauges

Hazards: Dam Number 3; metal bridge debris on right below Potomac/Shenandoah confluence at low water; high water

Scouting: Dam Number 3

Portages: Maybe Dam Number 3

Rescue Index: Reasonably accessible

Source of Additional Information: National Weather Service: Shepherdstown, Hancock, Point of Rocks, and Little Falls gauges (703) 260-0305; National Park Service (Harpers Ferry) (304) 535-6371; C & O Canal National Historical Park (Sharpsburg) (301) 739-4200; River and Trail Outfitters (301) 695-5177

Access Points	River Miles	Shuttle Miles
A–C	5.0	5.0
B–C	3.0	5.0
C–D	1.5	1.5
C–E	2.5	2.5
C–F	5.0	5.5
C–G	11.0	15 -19

Access Point Ratings:
 A–Dargan Bend Boat Landing at Shinham Road above Sandy Hook, excellent
 B–at Bakerton Road (WV), good but vandal problems
 C–at Sandy Hook, fair
 D–at Weverton (Rt. 180), poor
 E–at Knoxville (Rt. 478), poor and closed
 F–at Brunswick, excellent

created a dynamic Class III+ course worthy of training for world competition. This course also has a unique bonus. Since the water discharged from the powerplant is 20 to 30 degrees warmer than the river temperature, U.S. team members can work out in the dead of winter when the Potomac is shrouded in ice.

Just below the Pepco Powerplant is Whites Ford. It was used during the Civil War by confederate troops at least three times—by Robert E. Lee in the Antietam Campaign of September 1862, by "Jeb" Stuart after a raid a month later, and by Jubal Early after a raid in July 1864.

Only a half mile below Whites Ford is Cherrington where folks fish nearly the entire year because of the warm water there. A half mile further brings you to a marble quarry on the left. Active before 1820, this quarry provided limestone breccia to make the striking columns of Statuary Hall for the U.S. Capitol in Washington, D.C.

After 2 more miles of paddling, you reach Whites Ferry. Here there is a charming little automobile ferry, named the Jubal Early, which operates during the day to connect Maryland Route 107 with Virginia Route 655 and US 15. If you just want a 12-mile day-trip from Point of Rocks, Whites Ferry is a good take-out, although there is a fee to do so there.

The 14 miles from Whites Ferry to Violettes Lock contain many of the same charming features found upstream. However, there is also a launch fee if you put in here. Just below Whites Ferry the river is split by 2 mile-long Harrisons Island. Near the upstream beginning of the island, the Civil War Battle of Balls Bluff took place in October 1861 on the Virginia (right) side of the river. Balls Bluff National Cemetery, commemorating this battle, is the smallest national cemetery in the United States. It can be found just east of US 15 about a mile south of Whites Ferry.

If you go left of Harrisons Island, you will reach the Turtle Run hiker-biker a mile below Whites Ferry. Two miles farther downstream (just over a mile below the end of Harrisons Island) is Broad Run Trunk, the only wooden flume on the C & O Canal. It carries the canal over Broad Run. Two miles more and you reach Edwards Ferry, 5 miles below Whites Ferry. Some minor Confederate and

Union troop crossing occurred here during the Civil War. If you are tuckered, take out here at Edwards Ferry Road by Lock 25. Just below Edwards Ferry is Goose Creek River Lock, which allowed boats from Goose Creek in Virginia to cross the river and enter the C & O Canal through three sets of gates. The best section of Goose Creek is described earlier in this chapter. Immediately below Goose Creek River Lock is Chisel Branch, the fourth hiker-biker.

Three miles or so below Chisel Branch, just after an island begins on the right, is Sycamore Landing on river left. This access point is reached from River Road. A mile below this is Horsepen Branch, the fifth hiker-biker. After 3 more miles and passing a couple of good-sized islands, you reach Seneca Creek Aqueduct on the Maryland side. This 114-foot-long structure has three arches. Lock 24 (Rileys Lock) is less than a mile below the aqueduct. Access to the Seneca Creek Aqueduct is from Rileys Lock Road. On the Virginia side of the river opposite Seneca Creek Aqueduct are the Seneca Red Sandstone Quarries which provided building materials for the Smithsonian "Castle" in Washington, D.C., and numerous C & O Canal locks. Just downstream of the quarries there is a swamp. Here cut sandstone was loaded into canal boats. The swamp is now an excellent bird watching site.

The Violettes Lock take-out on river left is a half mile below Rileys Lock and just above the ruins of Dam Number 2. Keeping watch over Violettes Lock is Guard Lock Number 2 which admitted water into the canal, allowed canal boats access to the slack water above Dam Number 2, and gave some protection to the canal at high water.

For those wanting a Virginia take-out, you can take out at Algonkian Park, a mile above Seneca Aqueduct. However, the shuttle is much longer since all the other access points are in Maryland.

Violettes Lock to Great Falls

Just below Violettes Lock, the Virginia Canal/Seneca Rapids stretch of whitewater on the Potomac is always raved about as a "find" by novice paddlers exploring new opportunities and is appreciated more quietly by intermediate paddlers using this familiar stretch to try out a new boat or new techniques. Indeed, this 1-mile Class I–II section of the river gives a great opportunity to practice river reading, ferrying, and general boat handling skill. The intermediate boater should paddle here in spring at medium levels (3.5 to 4.5 feet on the Little Falls gauge), while the novice paddler can practice here all summer at low water levels (2.7 to 3.5 feet on this gauge).

To take this most popular short trip, drive out River Road (Route 190) well past Potomac, Maryland. Less than half a mile before you reach the stop sign at Route 112, turn left onto Violettes Lock Road. After reaching the Violettes Lock parking lot, cross the first bridge only. Then turn right onto the C & O Canal towpath. A well worn path on the left will lead to a small cove. Just downstream is a nice 3-foot drop through guard Lock Number 2. Be careful of the rock in this drop if you run it.

From the cove you should ferry across the river above the ruins of Dam Number 2. Paddle far enough upstream so that the wind or current will not sweep you over the rubble dam below. Once you reach the Virginia side, you will enter a little side channel perpendicular to the river, which starts well above the dam.

This 1-mile-long pleasant channel is called the Virginia Canal or Seneca Bypass and was part of George Washington's Patowmack Canal system. The Seneca Bypass operated from 1790 to 1830. Today, it will take you over many easy Class I–II riffles and rocky rapids. About three or four rapids down, on river right, is a hole that's somewhat user-friendly. A few rapids farther is a gentle ledge of nearly 2 feet that causes problems for unwary novices because it is a surprise. Just right of this ledge is a tricky "Z" turn that more experienced paddlers can try. Further down, the last rapid can cause difficulty because the rocks are inconveniently placed just under a canoe length apart.

At this last rapid, look on the left for an arrow on a tree directing you upstream. This channel takes you to the upper end of Elm Island, which is nearly half a mile long. Less ambitious folks can follow the arrow slightly upstream to the head of Elm Island, paddle to the main channel of the river, and then ferry across the slack water to the well worn clay beach on the Maryland side, which is known as Blockhouse Point. Those who are hungry can stop at aptly named Lunch Stop Island in the middle of the river. More ambitious paddlers will go farther upstream of Elm Island, angle their boats facing upstream with a 10 to 30 degree tilt toward Maryland (depending on wind and current) and ferry straight across the bottom of Seneca Rapids. Upon reaching the Maryland bank, both groups of paddlers will find an easy carry to the C & O Canal and a pleasant 1-mile paddle back to the Violettes Lock parking lot. The total trip is 3 miles, with nearly a mile spent going back and forth across the wide Potomac.

Incidentally, the island on your left just before Elm Island is Patowmack Island—the only island on the Potomac belonging to Virginia. This man-made island was carved from the Virginia shore when the Seneca Bypass was constructed nearly 200 years ago. All natural islands along the Potomac here belong to Maryland.

Section: Point of Rocks (US 15) to Violettes Lock (Violettes Lock Road)

Counties: Frederick and Montgomery (MD), Loudoun (VA)

USGS Quads: Point of Rocks, Buckeystown, Poolesville, Waterford, Leesburg, Sterling, Seneca

Suitable for: Day cruising and camping

Skill Level: Novices

Months Runnable: Entire year

Interest Highlights: Great fishing and camping; C & O Canal in Maryland; artifical whitewater slalom course for U.S. team at Dickerson Powerplant

Scenery: Pretty to beautiful in spots

Difficulty: Class A with 1 artificial Class I–II rapid

Average Width: 1,000 to 2,000 feet

Velocity: Slow to moderate

Gradient: 1 foot per mile

Runnable Water Levels:
  Minimum: 2.6 feet on the Little Falls gauge; 0.5 feet on Point of Rocks gauge
  Maximum: 5 feet on Little Falls gauge

Hazards: None except high water

Scouting: None

Portages: None

Rescue Index: Reasonably accessible

Source of Additional Information: National Weather Service, Little Falls and Point of Rocks gauges (703) 260-0305; National Park Service (Great Falls) (301) 299-3613; C & O Canal National Historical Park (Sharpsburg) (301) 739-4200

Access Points	River Miles	Shuttle Miles
G–H	4	5
G–I	12	10
G–J	18	16
G–K	26	27–30

Access Point Ratings:
  G–at Point of Rocks (US 15), very good
  H–at Nolands Ferry, very good
  I–at Whites Ferry (Rt. 107), very good
  J–at Edwards Ferry, very good
  K–at Violettes Lock, very good

After reaching Violettes Lock, a second circuit can then be initiated by paddling down the main body of the Potomac. Paddlers can drop over the rubble remains of Dam Number 2 and continue through Seneca Rapids with many route variations. One route in the middle of the river will lead you to a good Class II–III drop with big waves that can swamp boats at medium levels. However, when the Little Falls gauge is below 3 feet, the ruins of Dam Number 2 get scrapey. After reaching Blockhouse Point again, use the C & O Canal to return.

A third variation of this delightful trip is to paddle back up Seneca Rapids on the Potomac rather than use the C & O Canal. You can do this at low to moderate levels. However, if you cannot dip your entire paddle into the main channels on the upward trip, the water is too low. Working the mile up the Seneca Rapids to Dam Number 2 should take from 20 minutes in a kayak to 40 minutes in a solo open boat. In picking channels to work upstream, be sure to avoid dead-end channels or "box canyons."

Remember that you are surrounded by history at this pretty place. The 1-mile Virginia channel is but one segment of George Washington's Patowmack Canal. More impressive are the remains of another mile-long segment 8 miles downriver. This Great Falls Skirting Canal used five locks to bypass the 77-foot drop of Great Falls. The Patowmack Canal was part of Washington's grand scheme to develop the interior of the country, and functioned from 1802 to 1830. Unfortunately, Washington only built these two parts of his canal around the Seneca and Great Falls Rapids, thereby leaving canal boats on the river at the mercy of the Potomac's ever-changing flow. Consequently, his canal only operated 30 to 45 days a year. At other times the Potomac was too high or too low.

The successor to Washington's limited planning efforts was the elaborate C & O Canal on the Maryland side of the Potomac which began operation in 1830 and continued until 1924. The separate channel of the C & O Canal was not generally at the mercy of the Potomac water levels and opened up more of the country to navigation since it ultimately stretched 184 miles from Washington, D.C., to Cumberland, Maryland. Dam Number 2 and Guardlock Number 2 at the Violettes Lock put-in provided the main intake for the C & O Canal from here to the Washington, D.C. boundary, 17 miles downstream. Finally, you should note the C & O Canal here also transported from a nearby quarry the striking red sandstone that was used to build the picturesque Smithsonian Institution "Castle" on the Mall in Washington, D.C.

For those paddlers interested in longer trips, this trip can be lengthened with upstream and downstream alternatives. About one-half mile upstream of Violettes Lock on the Maryland side is the Mouth of Seneca—where the Seneca

Aqueduct crosses Seneca Creek as it joins the Potomac. If you take Seneca Road (Route 112) to Route 28 and turn left, you will soon cross Seneca Creek. There is a staff gauge just below Route 28. If it reads at least 2.2 feet, then you can add a pleasant Class I paddle on this creek to your trip. A good put-in is here or on Greater Seneca Creek at Blackrock Mill. This is on Blackrock Road (Route 107) east of Route 28 and 7 miles from Mouth of Seneca. Other put-ins farther upstream on Seneca Creek can have very bad strainers, usually in winter and spring.

Nearly 1.5 miles downstream of Blockhouse Point is Pennyfield Lock (Lock 22)—the first and most interesting take-out. Make sure you get over to the left side of the river just below Blockhouse Point, or 3.5-mile-long Watkins Island will prevent you from getting to Pennyfield Lock. To find this take-out look for a small stream on the Maryland side. Make the easy paddle up it and under the C & O Canal. For the shuttle take Pennyfield Lock Road from River Road to reach the parking lot at Pennyfield Lock.

Three miles farther downstream is Swains Lock, which is near the end of Watkins Island. Just before you get to Swains Lock, a pipeline crosses the river at the lower end of Watkins Island causing a riffle. Fishing is great on this stretch—especially near Claggett Island, which is halfway down the Virginia side of Watkins Island. Swains Lock is accessible from River Road, and you can rent canoes and rowboats there.

The next take-out is at Great Falls, Maryland—another 2 miles and accessible from Falls Road. (You can also take out a mile below Swains Lock on the Virginia side at Riverbend Park, but the shuttle is ridiculously long.) Note that the Swains Lock and Great Falls take-outs are not obvious and should first be scouted from shore when running the shuttle. Also, please be aware that the Great Falls take-out is nervously close to the nasty 6-foot Great Falls Dam that signals the beginning of Great Falls. Be sure to get to the left of Conn Island, which begins a half mile above Great Falls. Novices should not use this take-out at high water (above 5 feet on the Little Falls gauge).

The grandest trip of all for this section is 22 miles. You would start at Blackrock Mill on Seneca Creek, paddle down to Great Falls, and then paddle 7.5 miles back up the C & O Canal to Violettes Lock.

Paul Marshall runs the first drop (Tumblehome) on the Maryland side of Great Falls (level was 2.9 feet on the Little Falls gauge).

Even though you are near a major city, this is a special place for flora and fauna. For example, in late September knowledgeable paddlers can explore many side channels near Violettes Lock and the C & O Canal for delicious paw-paws. If you paddle slowly, you can spot those oblong greenish-yellow fruits among the oblong green leaves of the paw-paw trees. A slight shake of the tree (not the fruit) with the paddle will drop the ripe fruit from the tree. If you have to beat the tree violently, you will only get very green, unripe fruit. Also, during migratory season, you will see lots of waterfowl taking a break here or in the many nearby sanctuaries. There are numerous hawks, ospreys, and other raptors in the area. Indeed, there recently was a nesting pair of bald eagles just above Great Falls. Finally, you can occasionally spot a deer or two crossing the river on such a trip.

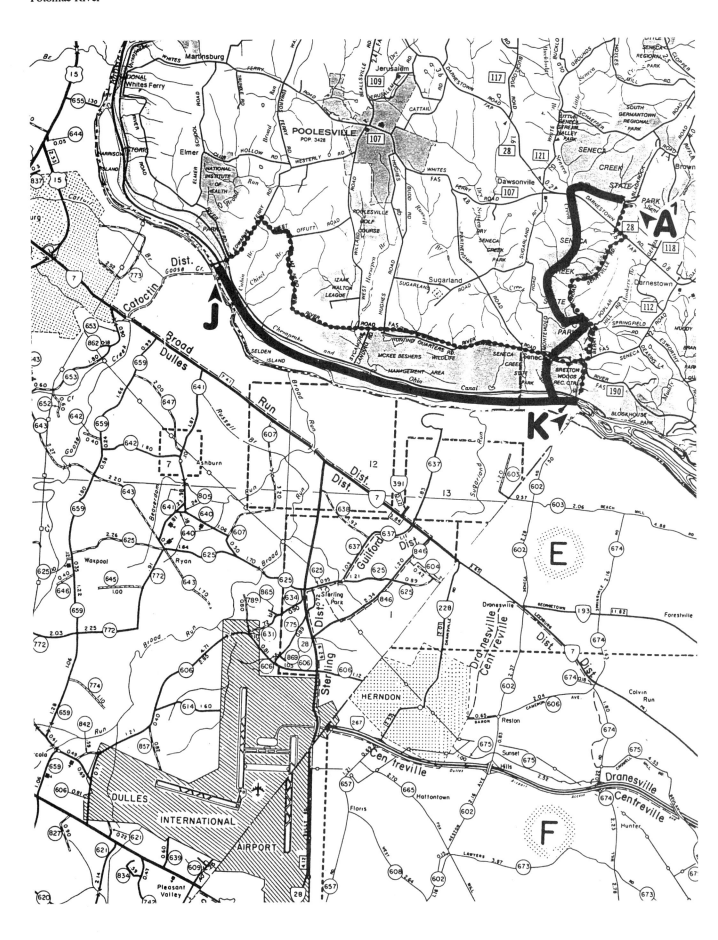

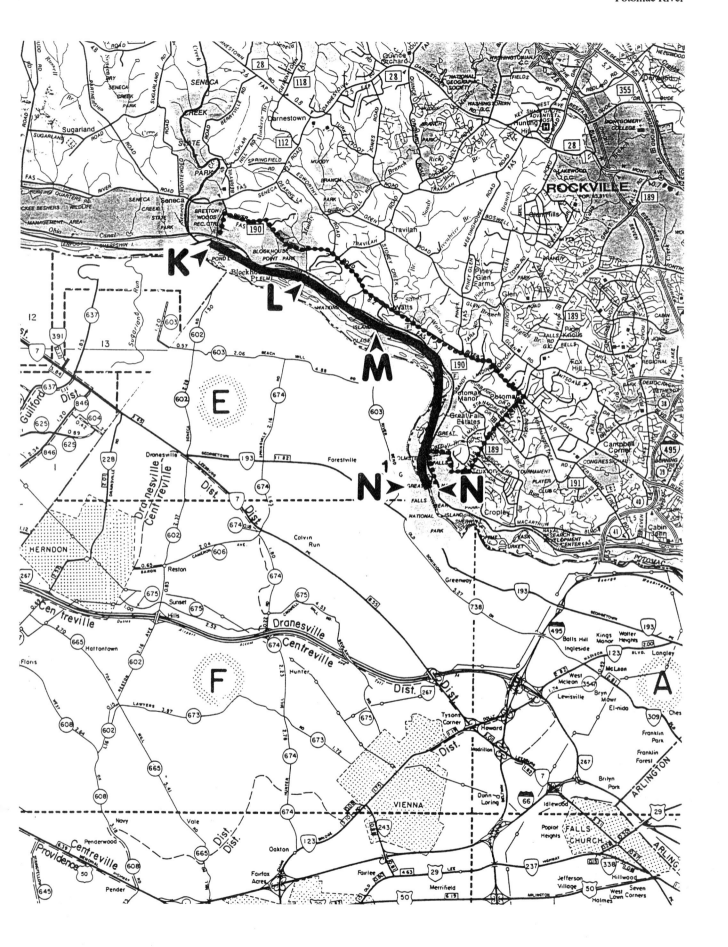

Cold weather surfing brings a smile to Wendy Stone at Observation Deck Rapid just below Great Falls on the Virginia side of the Potomac. Photo by Bob Combs.

Great Falls, Mather Gorge, and Little Falls

The most heavily used section of the Potomac is the stretch between Great Falls and the tidal estuary at Washington, D.C. Access to the river in this area can be had in many spots. The C & O Canal follows the river on the Maryland shore between Washington and Great Falls, Maryland, and provides public access and parking at many locations. The Virginia side of the river is almost entirely in private ownership and public access is rare. Between Great Falls and Washington the most important access points are Great Falls, Maryland, and Old Anglers Inn, both on MacArthur Boulevard, and Carderock Park and old Lockhouse Number 6, both on the Maryland Clara Barton Parkway. All of these points are accessible via the Capital Beltway (I-495) at the Maryland Clara Barton Parkway exit. Note: The George Washington Memorial Parkway on the Virginia side provides no access to the river. The original plan called for the

parkways to be joined by a bridge at Great Falls, but this plan was fortunately scrapped due in large part to the efforts of the late Chief Supreme Court Justice William O. Douglas, who was also instrumental in preserving the 184-mile C & O Canal from Washington, D.C., to Cumberland, Maryland.

Great Falls

Along the northern border of Virginia lies the largest rapid in the state and one of the largest runnable rapids anywhere. This drop was named by the earliest colonists and has retained through the centuries the designation given to it by them: the Great Falls of the Potomac.

The Falls are created where the Potomac, like all other rivers that flow eastward into the Atlantic, drops over the edge of the continental bedrock onto the sedimentary soil of the Coastal Plain. The fall line proper is actually located farther downstream, at Roosevelt Island in the estuary between Rosslyn, Virginia and the District of Columbia. However, the entire section of the river between this spot

Two's company but three's a crowd on the First Wave at Rocky Island a half mile below Great Falls on the Potomac. Photo by Bob Combs.

and the Great Falls, a distance of some 9 miles, is a result of the headward, i.e., upstream, erosion of the riverbed by the stream. The present location of the falls represents the latest manifestation of this unending process.

All of the rapids downstream—Observation Deck Rapids, S-Turn Rapids, Rocky Island Rapids, Wet Bottom Chute, Difficult Run Rapids, Yellow Falls, Stubblefield Falls, and Little Falls—are the locations of particularly resistant rock strata where the falls may have once paused in their ever-slow but inexorable upstream migration. The present-day Great Falls of the Potomac display the steepest and most spectacular fall line rapids of any eastern river.

Before beginning a description of the Great Falls section it must be pointed out most emphatically that this area is extremely hazardous. The danger of the rapids is close to the highest of any rapids currently run. The most advanced paddlers in the country examined these drops for years before the first attempt was made in 1976, and although the passage of time has increased the number of paddlers completing the run, it has not decreased the objective

hazards presented by these falls, as proven by many documented deaths which have occurred here of individuals inadvertently washed over the Falls. No one should attempt such a run without the highest degree of skill and confidence, particularly a very fast and sure roll and previous experience in vertical waterfall running. Most importantly, the newcomer should only paddle the Falls with someone who has previously completed a successful run; the choice of the wrong route would almost surely be fatal. Finally, the park rangers who administer the land on both shores require that paddlers register with the Maryland Department of Natural Resources and police. Also, runs should be made only before 9 a.m. and after 6 p.m. (preferably on weekdays) to avoid a public spectacle and the encouragement of unqualified individuals to run the Falls. A run that turns into a circus or results in a death or costly rescue operation by the National Park Service would almost surely cause the NPS to close this incredible resource to those who are best able to appreciate it.

Section: Violettes Lock (Violettes Lock Road) to Great Falls Park (MD)

Counties: Montgomery (MD)

USGS Quads: Germantown, Seneca, and Rockville (MD)

Suitable for: Day cruising

Skill Level: Novices at low water; intermediates at higher water

Months Runnable: Entire year

Interest Highlights: Violettes Lock; remains of Virginia Canal; C & O Canal in Maryland

Scenery: Pretty to beautiful in spots

Difficulty: Class I–II with 1 Class II–III rapid in first mile; Class A–1 for rest of trip

Average Width: 1,000 to 3,000 feet on Potomac; 20 to 30 feet on Seneca Creek or Virginia Canal

Velocity: Moderate

Gradient: 10 feet per mile for first mile; 2 feet per mile thereafter

Runnable Water Levels:

Minimum: 2.6 feet on the Little Falls gauge for Potomac (Virginia Canal); 2.2 feet for Seneca Creek on Rt. 28 gauge

Maximum: 5 feet on Little Falls gauge; 5 feet for Seneca Creek on Rt. 28 gauge

Hazards: Maybe an occasional tree in river; high water

Scouting: None

Portages: Trees on Seneca Creek

Rescue Index: Accessible

Source of Additional Information: National Weather Service, Little Falls gauge (703) 260-0305; National Park Service, Great Falls Park in Maryland (301) 299-3613 or in Virginia (703) 285-2966

Access Points	River Miles	Shuttle Miles
A[1]–K	7.5	6.0
K–L	2.5	4.0
K–M	5.5	7.0
K–N	7.5	12.5
A[1]–N	15.0	19.0

Access Point Ratings:
A[1]–Blackrock Mill (Seneca Creek), good
K–at Violettes Lock, very good
L–at Pennyfield Lock, good
M–at Swains Lock, very good
N–at Great Falls (MD), very good

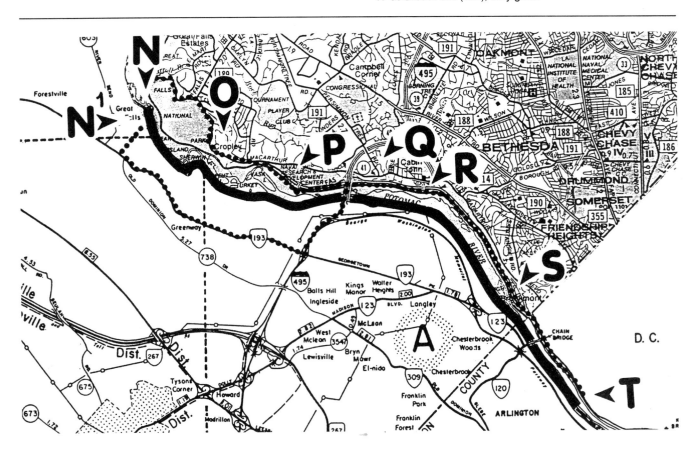

The Potomac flows along lazily all of the way from Harpers Ferry, some 35 miles upstream, across the Piedmont with generally only the lightest riffles disturbing its placid green surface. Seneca Breaks, 5 miles upstream from the falls, marks briefly the new sentiment of the river, but the Potomac resumes its pastoral quality below Seneca. Only 4 miles from the Capital Beltway and without further prelude the river drops over the Great Falls Dam, a 6-foot stone structure built in the 1850s to provide drinking water for the District of Columbia. The structure still serves in its original capacity, the water thus stored being pumped by gravity through the aqueduct running under the equally aged MacArthur Boulevard into the city. The Potomac pools briefly below the dam and then begins its rush to the estuary in earnest.

Below the 6-foot Great Falls Dam, the next third of a mile drops 60 feet and is known as Great Falls. It begins with gentle rapids. Immediately the channel, 2,500 feet wide at the dam, is split by the long and narrow Falls Island, which separates the main part of the Falls from the Fish Ladder channel, adjacent to the Maryland shore. Just downstream, the Fish Ladder channel is split again by Olmsted Island, which separates the Fish Ladder from an equally steep but unnamed channel between Olmsted and Falls Islands. In years past Olmsted and Falls Islands were linked with the Maryland shore by footbridges allowing visitors to the Maryland Great Falls Park, known officially as a unit of the C & O Canal National Historic Park, the opportunity to walk across Fish Ladder channel and the main section of the Falls.

In June of 1972, the flood caused by Hurricane Agnes destroyed these extremely sturdy steel and reinforced concrete bridges, located 25 to 40 feet above the normal water level, and made the islands and their spectacular views of the Falls the exclusive preserve of the wildlife and whitewater boaters at all but the lowest water levels.

However, the bridges have been reconstructed and were reopened on schedule in 1992. Both the Fish Ladder and the unnamed channel waters were altered by the Corps of Engineers around the turn of the century in an attempt to allow fish to migrate upstream of the falls. The resulting channels have concrete ramps which have weathered to expose the aggregate rock and look like magnified views of emery cloth, with knife-edged boulders in mid-channel, and impossible tight turns.

These hazards, combined with the extremely high gradient, make both these channels horrifyingly dangerous and they should not be considered.

The main channel, separated from the Fish Ladder channel immediately below the dam, falls over unnamed drops of increasing severity for a couple of hundred yards. These drops, reaching Class IV in difficulty, would be significant enough to be named and paddled often anywhere else, but here they are mere prelude and warning of the main event which awaits just below.

C-1 paddler enters the right (Virginia) side of Little Falls of the Potomac at a low level (2.75 feet on the Little Falls gauge). Note boat-hungry Cleaver Rock next to the paddler downstream.

The Falls proper begins on a front approximately 600 feet wide. The Maryland Falls, running alongside Falls Island, reach their full development first, running swiftly to the brink of a convex-curved 20-foot vertical drop. This is called Tumblehome by local paddlers. Go with someone who has run this drop before to determine the narrow center route. Below Tumblehome the river immediately regathers its strength and within a few boat lengths drops over a straight-lipped 10-foot drop that is not quite vertical. This drop is known as Charlie's Hole by locals and is probably the most deadly drop when Great Falls is low enough to run. Here the river creates a heavy chute which drops into a very terminal hole. The main way out of this hole, even for the most expert paddlers, is by a rope. Those crazy enough to run this drop must go with someone who has done it before and must have a safety rope on the rock next to the hole on river right.

The river again "pools" while moving at a rapid pace and turns sharply right and drops over a concave-edged 10-foot falls known as Horseshoe Falls, which has a very wicked hydraulic at the bottom and many broken boulders. This hydraulic has kept boats and boaters for uncomfortably long periods of time. Indeed, while there have been no boater fatalities here at the time of this writing, the hole has kept a couple of pilot-less boats on a permanent basis, tearing them to pieces in lieu of releasing them to their bedraggled owners.

Levels are critical in running the Maryland side of Great Falls. The range of 2.65 to 2.9 feet on the Little Falls gauge is best for Tumblehome; anywhere within this narrow range is still bad for Charlie's; and the "best" levels for Horseshoe Falls are even narrower—between 2.7 and 2.85 feet.

To the right of Maryland Falls the channel known since George Washington's time as the Streamers extends its flat section a few dozen feet farther downstream of the Maryland Falls and then proceeds to drop through a chaos of boulders, narrow twisting chutes, and vertical falls that defies description. At the top of this channel is a very interesting phenomenon: a small chute drops a distance of several feet and apparently runs onto a sharply sloped rock at the base, causing the flow to bubble straight upward in a natural water fountain fully as high as the height from which the water originally fell. This entire section of the river is ridiculously dangerous-looking and has only recently been run by a few deranged experts. The name of this section apparently comes from the last drop in the sequence. A relatively small amount of water, at summer-type levels, falls over a rocky lip that is fairly regularly notched at the top, creating dozens of tiny waterfalls at intervals of 1 foot or so, falling a vertical distance of about 10 feet.

Even farther to the right, against the Virginia shore, is the section known as the Spout, named possibly by George Washington or at least current at the time of the writing of his diaries. The Spout is separated from the Streamers by a 100-yard long rock island called The Flake. This channel extends even farther downstream than the Streamers before becoming unruly, but it makes up for any tardiness with extra effort at being horrendous, awesome, and even downright bodacious. After the initial pool, the channel flows over a drop of 7 or 8 feet from a lip that has the shape of about 120 degrees of a circle; the paddler drops from the outside to the inside of the circle. This concentration of the resulting hydraulic makes it extremely strong and it tends to back-pop-up or back-ender the paddler, thoroughly frustrating the carefully constructed plans the boater has made for surviving the following drops. This drop is called U Hole Falls or Norman's Leap by local paddlers. Most paddlers of this falls eschew the entire left side of the drop and enter on the far right, even though this necessitates a very sharp right turn at the bottom. You need to be careful on the approach to U Hole Falls because it is very scrapey.

The channel runs straight downhill to the next drop which splits at the top. The right two-thirds consist of another concave lip and a very nasty looking hydraulic at the bottom. The far left side is a rightward-slanting slide and is actually easier than it looks. Immediately the channels converge and crash together violently against a rock wall straight ahead. The paddler must make a 90-degree turn to the left, proceed over a 5 foot drop, make an immediate 90-degree turn to the right, and then drop a couple of feet. The whole sequence of this rapids from the slanting drop through the two sharp turns, usually lumped together as the second of three major drops in the Spout, occupies the linear space of only about three boat lengths and drops some 10 to 12 feet. Called Z-Turn by local boaters, this drop is exponentially more vicious than another rapid called S-Turn just below Great Falls. A flip here, even with the quickest and surest of rolls, could be disastrous, particularly in view of what lies downstream. If you run Z-Turn, be sure to grab Catch Your Breath eddy on river right just below this drop.

After twisting through Z-Turn, the river forms a moving pool 60 feet in length before delivering the coup de grace. The third and final drop consists of a single vertical falls of 22 feet. Local paddlers call it The Spout. The right two-thirds of the falls drops onto a slanting ledge halfway down and then strikes a flat boulder or ledge at the bottom. The exact configuration of the slanting ledge and flat ledge at the bottom are unknown but the surrounding rock is heavily fissured and potholed, suggesting the presence of many nooks and crannies in which the bow of a boat might become wedged, trapping the paddler under an enormous weight of water pouring over his boat and body. Rescue from such a situation would appear to be quite impossible due to the steepness of the shoreline and the tremendous power of a large amount of water flowing over a lip only about 12 feet wide. Only the farthest left portion of the falls drops into clear water. Reaching this clear slot requires a turn at the top of nearly 90 degrees, virtually in mid-air. In addition, the paddler must simultaneously raise the bow of the boat to avoid a tiny, almost invisible rock at the bottom which is hidden by the curtain of water at all but the lowest levels. This small rock has taken a heavy toll in sterns from those who failed to notice it and achieve some degree of arch to their fall from the lip. Fortunately, within the very narrow range of water levels in which runs of the falls are possible, the hydraulic at the base of the last drop is not a safety problem. The long fall, however, results in a deep penetration of the pool at the base and the water pressure at these depths has popped the seams of some fiberglass boats.

As with the Maryland side, levels for running the Virginia side of Great Falls are very narrow. The optimal range for U Hole Falls is 2.8 to 2.95 feet on the Little Falls gauge; there is no good level for running Z-Turn, technically the most difficult of the three Virginia drops; the range for The Spout is between 2.75 and 3.0 feet.

After this orgy of descent the river pools very briefly and runs down to the heavy but more normal rapids of Observation Deck or "O-Deck" as it is known locally. The origin of the name "The Spout" will be obvious to anyone who views this huge rapids. Survivors of such a run will certainly know that they have done something. We must again emphasize that, for anyone but those who just can't sleep nights without having run Great Falls once in their lives, the best advice is to forget it. Or, to repeat a phrase heard repeatedly on many rivers, "Let's not, and say we did."

For years the myriad of paddlers who played in the rapids below the Falls gazed up from Observation Deck Rapids and wondered about the possibility of a successful run through some section of the very complex drops of the Falls. Many hours were spent discussing the merits of each of the almost infinite number of possible routes through the maelstrom. Most paddlers considered any attempt to verify these hotly contested assertions to be tantamount to suicide, a notion reinforced by the steady incidence of fatalities incurred by ill-advised swimmers and rock scramblers. Each year several of these unfortunates were swept accidentally into the Falls and, without exception, met death in the foamy green chaos of the 200-yard-long stretch of whitewater. For many years it seemed that the Great Falls of the Potomac would

forever remain outside the ken of whitewater paddlers, unexplored and unknown. In 1976 this changed.

Two internationally known paddlers, who prefer to still remain anonymous to the general public, studied the Falls along with many others and wondered whether a run was possible, and, if so, which route would be most feasible. These two, one a C-1 paddler and the other a kayaker, chose a route down the Spout section and, based upon experience gained in running smaller waterfalls during the development of waterfall running during the early 1970s, decided to attempt it. An additional factor in this decision was their plan to run a steep river in the Himalayas in the near future and their feeling that the Great Falls bore a resemblance to the 300-foot-per-mile gradients they would encounter in the canyons of Asia. Thus, the first run of one of the most feared drops in the region was, in point of fact, a mere training run for more severe rapids in Nepal! After the initial run it was two years before another attempt was made in 1978. In late August of that year two more paddlers, both kayakers this time, successfully ran the Spout. The following year the Maryland Falls was successfully run for the first time. Since that time the number of paddlers completing the run and the variations of route and water level have multiplied. No one has been killed purposely running the falls so far, but there have been an increasing number of close calls and many destroyed boats. As mentioned above, the first fatal run could be the last legal run of all, so let's be careful out there.

Mather Gorge through Little Falls

If you can hack the portages, this stretch of the Potomac is a classic for rapids, scenery, and history. There are numerous access alternatives to this section, and you can vary your trip length from 2 to 12 miles. At low summer levels (2.5 to 3.2 feet on the Little Falls gauge) this is generally an intermediate Class II–III trip. At middle spring levels (3.2 to 4.5 feet), the Mather Gorge and especially Little Falls segments are advanced Class III–IV trips. See the data sheet for specifics.

The first possible put-in is on the Virginia side of Great Falls Park. Make sure you have $4.00 because the Virginia side of Great Falls currently charges this admission (per car) to enjoy this lovely park. The portage to the Virginia side below Great Falls is a 300-yard hike, and the last 75 yards are tough—over big rocks down to the river.

Nevertheless, it's all downhill with rewards at the end, and you have a magnificent view below Great Falls. At medium levels, (3.5 feet on the Little Falls gauge) the put-in is energetic Class III water which becomes much more mellow at low summer levels. However, at about 4 feet on the Little Falls gauge, the put-in becomes somewhat difficult, as you have to contend with fast water, standing waves, and very squirrelly current.

Here below Great Falls, the Potomac drops over Observation Deck or "O-Deck" Rapids, named for two tourist overlooks on the Virginia side of the river. At levels between 3.6 and 3.9 feet on the Little Falls gauge, the upper end of these rapids provides large, ender-sized waves for the delight of the aggressive paddler. The sure presence of hundreds of amused, awed, and puzzled spectators on sunny weekends provides the hot-dog paddler with an unparalleled forum for the display of his skills. One such kayaker, a few years ago, apparently in search of female companionship, painted in large letters on the stern deck of his boat his name and phone number, preceded by the message, "For a date call ..." The effectiveness of this technique is unknown.

In spring, be sure to attend the exciting S-Turn Slalom Race which starts here and continues a half mile downstream. Nationally ranked paddlers are the heart of this competition. You can get a great view of the race from the cliffs on the Virginia side of the river here.

About 100 yards below O-Deck Rapids is Class II–III Fish Ladder Rapids—so named because of the fish ladder built just downstream of this drop on the Maryland side of the river. Run these rapids left for the most conservative route. At low levels there is a substantial hole in the center of the river followed by a rock. Fish Ladder is a great place to pause because there are several surfing spots less strenuous than those of O-Deck upstream. At higher levels, Fish Ladder Rapids washes out, but the water just below from the Maryland fish ladder churns in strongly from the left, so prepare to brace accordingly.

Once you reach the Maryland fish ladder, you are near the put-in for paddlers starting on the Maryland side below Great Falls, which also costs $4.00 per car to enter. Paddlers taking the nearly half mile hike down the towpath to put in on the Maryland side below Great Falls can put in below and to the left of the Maryland fish ladder at a beach called Catfish Cove—so named because this is a summer fishing spot. To reach Catfish Cove, hike 800 yards down the C & O Canal towpath from Great Falls Tavern past three locks to Lock 17.

Then, by C & O Canal milepost 14, drop off the towpath on a trail to the right that winds 100 yards to the sandy beach of Catfish Cove on a pool separated from the main Virginia channel of the river by Rocky Island.

If the river level is under 3.8 feet on the Little Falls gauge, folks putting in on the Maryland side have to paddle up the pool or drag over rocks to enter the main channel of the river on the Virginia side. At levels above 4 feet, you have two other options to the main Virginia

channel. First, you can paddle straight ahead and take a slot between Rocky Island and its island neighbor on the left. This strong Class III slot has two rocky drops, the first of which is nearly 4 feet. Enter it left of a rock at the top. Alternatively, you can go to the extreme left by the Maryland bank over a bumpy Class II–III slalom, which washes out at higher levels. In the 5- to 6-foot range, a powerful hydraulic develops near the end of these rapids on the left side of the river.

Meanwhile, if you enter the Virginia channel from the Catfish Cove put-in, remember this can be quite dynamic and requires a vigorous ferry to the right at levels above 3.8 feet. Here you rejoin the path described for paddlers putting in on the Virginia side of Great Falls. The main river bends right here and you enter S-Turn Rapids. At levels of 3.5 feet and above the water wants to push you into the rocks on Rocky Island, which forms the left bank of the river channel here.

S-Turn Rapids is a strange little place. The rapids are created not so much from a high gradient as from the concentration of the entire Potomac River into a channel only 60 feet wide. At levels between 3.2 and nearly 4 feet on the Little Falls gauge a nasty hole forms behind a boulder on river right at the beginning of the S-Turn. At lower levels this boulder becomes exposed. It is known as Judy's Rock after the late Judy Waddell, a local paddler and Great Falls Park Ranger. At all but the lowest levels, the S-Turn sequence is full of moving waves, whirlpools, and cross currents. About 200 yards below S-Turn Rapids is Rocky Island Rapids, a great surfing spot between 3.8 and 4.6 feet when S-Turn approaches Class III–IV and the waves at Rocky Island reach 5 feet. The first wave is very regular; I have seen the bow paddler of a C-2 team juggle several tennis balls while surfing this wave. The second wave is much more irregular and at 4 feet on the gauge pulsates and breaks, providing an exciting aftermath for those who slip off the first wave. Just below is a nice series of standing waves at above 3.5 feet. However, the whole rapid is only moving water at low summer levels, below 3 feet.

At the base of Rocky Island, the middle and Maryland channels rejoin the river and you come to a moderate Class II rocky ledge called Wet Bottom Chute. There are several possible routes, all easy. At low and medium levels, an interesting surfing wave forms on river right. About 200 yards below Wet Bottom Chute the cut of George Washington's mile-long Great Falls Skirting Canal enters the river on the right. As you pass, remember that this cut was blasted by black powder at a time when the use of this explosive was highly dangerous. While paddling in Mather Gorge, its vertical rock walls 50 to 200 feet high, you might see several rock climbers clambering up the steep cliffs of metamorphic metagraywacke on the Virginia side.

Coach Bill Endicott puts members of the U.S. Whitewater Team through their paces at the Feeder Canal slalom gates near C&O Canal Lock 6 on the Potomac. Photo by Bill Snead.

Billy Goat Trail, a very aptly named popular but strenuous rock hiking trail, is on the Maryland side.

Below Wet Bottom Chute you have roughly a mile paddle down the Mather Gorge as the vertical rock walls recede. Then you come to Class II Difficult Run Rapids where the river splits three ways—Virginia, Center, and Maryland Chutes. The Virginia Chute is a pleasant drop with some surfing possibilities. The Center Chute is a modest rock garden—a summer challenge for paddlers who want to eddy-hop their way upstream. The Maryland Chute is the most straightforward and abrupt of the three—a ledgy drop of 2 to 3 feet with good surfing and quasi-ender possibilities at moderate levels. A flock of turkey vultures makes this place their summer home, and they watch errant beginning boaters in the Maryland Chute with anticipation.

Incidentally, just below the Virginia Chute, Difficult Run enters from the right. For those who want to see some very spicy rapids, the short, aptly named Difficult Run Gorge is a short hike. Upstream access to this 1-mile gorge of ascending difficulty (from Class II to Class V) is from

Georgetown Pike (Route 193) and can be easily bank scouted from a path left of Difficult Run.

Below Difficult Run the river flattens and runs placidly between wooded shores. One-half mile below the rapids the Old Angler's Inn put-in appears on the left shore. A parking area on MacArthur Boulevard across from the Old Angler's Inn restaurant provides access to the river. Paddlers park here for trips both upstream and downstream on the river and on the C & O Canal. Hikers, bikers, bird watchers, and other outdoor types park here also, so in anything approaching good weather arrive early to secure a parking spot. Be sure not to block the emergency gates in the lot because the rescue squad and park rangers use these access points regularly on busy weekends. Also, forget getting a drink or a bite to eat at Old Angler's Inn in paddling clothes. The place is strictly for the yuppy trade, and gnarly looking river rats will be shown the door immediately.

At low summer levels paddlers put in at Old Angler's Inn and paddle upstream to Difficult Run for a workout without a shuttle. Aggressive decked and open boaters can also paddle upstream to O Deck (at low levels), though a carry may be needed around Fish Ladder Rapids. Alternatively, even less experienced boaters can paddle up the C & O Canal a good 1.5 miles from Old Angler's Inn to Lock 16. This flatwater paddle is a delightful experience because immediately upstream from Old Angler's Inn is "Widewater"—a scenic half-mile-long section of the C & O Canal that is up to 500 feet wide and 40 feet deep. One difficulty is portaging around Lock 15. However, those into running waterfalls with plastic boats can run the 8-foot drop created by Lock 15. Soon you will reach Lock 16. Then, just after you carry around Lock 16 and pass a stop-lock (to divert flood waters from the canal), you reach a bumpy portage a good 200 yards over the blue-blazed Billy Goat Trail down to a put-in on the Potomac near the base of Rocky Island. Walk this rocky path first so you will know the route. This put-in is the starting point of another spring race—the 7-mile Annual Potomac Downriver Race to Sycamore Island. Sponsored by the Canoe Cruisers Association of Washington, D.C., this race has several open and decked boat classes.

Below Angler's Inn, the river splits around Offut Island. Go left for a pleasant Class II drop when the Little Falls gauge is between 3.5 and 4.5 feet. There are good surfing opportunities here—particularly at 4 feet. Below 3 feet this channel dries up into a rocky maze, and above 4.5 feet the rapids wash out. If you paddle right of Offut Island, there are only riffles. After passing Offut Island and two side-by-side islands at its base (Perry and Hermit Islands), get to the right of the river, particularly at low summer

---

Section: Great Falls Park (Maryland or Virginia) to Little Falls

Counties: Fairfax (VA), Montgomery (MD)

USGS Quads: Vienna, Falls Church, Rockville, Washington West, D.C.

Suitable for: Day cruising

Skill Level: Intermediates (low summer levels), advanced (middle spring levels), experts (high levels)

Months Runnable: Entire year

Interest Highlights: 2 Great Falls Parks (Virginia and Maryland), George Washington's Virginia Canal, Maryland C & O Canal, Mather Gorge, rock climbing, hiking, birding

Scenery: Mostly pretty to beautiful; spectacular in spots

Difficulty: Low summer levels (2.5 to 3.2 feet): Mather Gorge and Middle Section Class II—III, Little Falls Section Class III with 1 Class III—IV; middle spring levels (3.2 to 4.5 feet): Mather Gorge Class III—IV, Middle Section Class II—III, Little Falls Section Class IV; high levels (4.5 to 6 feet): Mather Gorge Class IV; Middle Section Class II—III; Little Falls Section Class IV—V

Average Width: Up to 1,500 feet, except at Mather Gorge and Little Falls where river constricts down to 60 feet, particularly at low summer levels

Velocity: Moderate to fast in Mather Gorge and Little Falls; slow to moderate in Middle Section

Gradient: O-Deck to Stubblefield Falls—4 miles at 8 feet per mile; Stubblefield Falls to Brookmont Dam—4.5 miles at 3 feet per mile; Brookmont Dam through Little Falls—1.3 miles at 26 feet per mile

Runnable Water Levels:
 Minimum: 2.5 on Little Falls gauge
 Maximum: For most paddlers, 6 feet in Mather Gorge; 7 feet in Middle Section; 5 feet at Little Falls (see narrative on high water)

Hazards: Lethal hydraulic below Brookmont Dam; high water—heavy rapids/holes in Mather Gorge and Little Falls

Scouting: S-Turn and Rocky Island at middle to upper levels; Yellow Falls and Stubblefield Falls for intermediates at low to middle levels; ruins of Dam Number 1 and Little Falls at all levels

Portages: Brookmont Dam at all levels! Perhaps Little Falls and some other rapids at high levels

Rescue Index: Accessible

Source of Additional Information: National Weather Service, Little Falls gauge (703) 260-0305; National Park Service, Great Falls Park in Maryland (301) 299-3613 or in Virginia (703) 285-2966; Fletcher's Boathouse (202) 244-0461

Access Points	River Miles	Shuttle Miles
N[1]–O	2.5	10.5
N–O	2.0	2.5
N[1]–P	4.5	8.5
N–P	4.0	4.5
O–P	2.0	2.0
O–Q	3.5	3.5
O–R	4.0	4.0
O–S	6.5	7.0
S–T	3.0	2.5

Access Point Ratings:
 N[1]–at Great Falls (Virginia side), fair
 N–at Great Falls (Maryland side), fair
 O–at Old Angler's Inn, good
 P–at Carderock, fair
 Q–at Lock 10, good
 R–at Lock 8, good
 S–at Lock 6, very good
 T–at Fletcher's Boathouse, excellent

levels. In the distance you should see a house high up the hill on the right. Here, go right of Turkey Island, which creates a large river right channel. Soon you will see a horizon line and a row of white quartz rocks extending from the right bank. Get behind this row of white rocks and scout because you have come to Yellow Falls—a Class II to III drop, depending on water levels. This rapid is a 1-foot ledge followed a couple of boat lengths later by a 2-foot ledge. The only problem is a boat-hungry rock in the runout below the 2-foot ledge. It is easy for experienced boaters to avoid this rock. However, novices should be sure they have sufficient boat control before running this drop; the rock below has pinned an impressive number of boats. At middle levels (3.7 feet) the ledges are covered and you have two sets of standing waves to negotiate. About 50 yards below Yellow Falls at lower water is a 2-foot ledge (Class II), which provides a good, tight right-to-left move if you run it in the center. Paddlers going left of Turkey Island will instead experience Calico Rapids, a stiff Class II boulder slalom somewhat longer than Yellow Falls. At low levels (say 2.8 on the gauge) there is a nice shallow 15-foot slide near the top right of this rapid. Calico Rapids leads you between two large islands—Turkey Island on the right and Vaso Island on the left.

After the river rejoins below these islands, get on the right side of the river. Less than a half mile downstream, Scott Run enters the Potomac on the right. This little creek is a delightful, scenic place in which to cool off during the summer and to admire the rest of the year. Here Scott Run tumbles 25 feet over a rocky cascade into a quiet pool. The water temperature of this small stream is at least 10 degrees cooler than the tepid bathtub temperature of the Potomac in the hot summer, and you can either take a bracing shower in the cascade or swim in the nice pool below. Be careful when walking here because the rocks are slippery with algae. Also, don't be tempted to drink this "clear" water: upstream from here, Scott Run passes through an urban area.

When leaving Scott Run, work over to the left center of the river. After less than a half mile, you will reach Stubblefield Falls—a good Class III drop over a submerged boulder field, which is bumpier and tougher at lower levels. Center is generally the best route, and at modest levels you can scout it from a rocky island on the right if you wish. There is a challenging surfing hole on the bottom right of Stubblefield Falls at lower levels. At middle levels (3.7 feet), these rapids change to a vigorous wave train, which washes out above 5 feet.

If you are taking out below Stubblefield Falls, immediately get over to the left side of the river and line your boats upstream in the small channel on the extreme left, or begin portaging on the path next to the river upstream to the nearest Carderock parking lot. This is a good quarter mile walk if you take the path. If you line your boat upstream, continue past where a small stream enters. About 50 yards upstream is a small clearing with a 7-foot sloping bank. Once you get your boat over this bank it is about 200 yards to the lower Carderock parking lot.

Those who left Old Angler's Inn without a shuttle can (from the pool and beach on river left below Stubblefield Falls) follow a path up to the C & O Canal. This is a stiff 200-yard portage. Check the path first before you start stumbling into the brush with your boat. Alternatively, you can park at Carderock, paddle up the canal 2 miles to Old Angler's Inn, and downstream on the Potomac for a 4-mile circuit. This gets the flatwater done early and gives you a sure parking place.

From Stubblefield Falls to Brookmont Dam is 4.5 miles of flatwater with pretty islands and hardwood forested banks. Here you will see not only water loving sycamores and silver maples, but also great oaks, ashes, hickories, and tulip poplars. The bird life on this stretch is impressive. On one trip we saw over a dozen great blue herons and a half dozen ospreys as well as lesser birds such as ducks and swallows, which darted about the river in profusion.

Nearly a mile below Stubblefield Falls, you go under the Cabin John Bridge on the Washington Beltway (Route 495). The Seven Locks section of the C & O Canal begins here. Seven Locks (Locks 8—14) raise the canal 56 feet in 1.25 miles. Just below this bridge on the left is Plummers Island, a great birding spot. Below Plummers Island and a good half mile below the beltway bridge is the Lock 10 take-out on the left. The 100-yard take-out portage at Lock 10 is easier than the one at Carderock. However, regardless of which alternative you take, please check the Carderock or Lock 10 take-out during the shuttle so you will know exactly where to bring your boat ashore. Shortly below is another, tougher take-out at Lock 8. Near Lock 8 the left bank of the Potomac forms a narrow, intimate channel—a nice change. However, the main section of the river passes some pretty rocks and islands with Class I riffles and channels that will also keep your interest.

About 1.5 miles below Lock 8 is Ruppert Island. Just past Ruppert Island is Sycamore Island where there are boat storage facilities that are property of the Montgomery Sycamore Island Club. In the distance on the left you should see the Little Falls Pumping Station for Brookmont Dam. The pumping station is an example of stark 1930s architecture. This windowless monolith would make a great prop for a Hollywood horror film. The pumping station and several warning signs in the river are your signal to get to the left bank and lift over into the C & O Canal. You can also take out here—over a bridge and then a stiff climb up to a parking lot. This is not recommended.

Rather, you should paddle 1.25 miles downstream on the C & O Canal to avoid Brookmont Dam and reach an easy take-out at Lock 6.

At Brookmont Dam the river is split by a long, skinny island, aptly named Snake Island. On the right of Snake Island the dam is 6 feet high; on the left it is a deceptively perilous 2-foot drop. Although the Corps of Engineers has placed large grout-filled bags in the backwash to break up the lethal hydraulic on the left below Brookmont Dam, it can be dangerous and caution is still advised. The best advice is to avoid the dam by taking the C & O Canal. This will insure that you are not ticketed by the local police who have now made running the Brookmont Dam illegal. The problem is that those likely to get into trouble probably don't know it is illegal, and those who know it is illegal probably have the experience to safely navigate it—preferably immediately to river left of Snake Island.

You have three choices below Brookmont Dam and its concrete pumping station. As mentioned earlier, you can paddle on the C & O Canal to Lock 6 and take out there. This is 9 miles below the Virginia Great Falls put-in. Second, you can get back in the river, run the feeder canal forming the far left of the river here, and take out at Lock 6 about 200 yards downstream on this feeder canal. The top of the feeder canal is where the Canoe Cruisers Association has set up a series of slalom gates for the U.S. Whitewater Team and lesser mortals to practice their technique in Class II water. This might be a good place for you to hone your skills, too. Just below this course is a 75-yard path on the left that leads to Lock 6. If you live nearby, the gates here at the feeder canal make an ideal place for an evening workout. You may even be lucky enough to see the U.S. Whitewater Team practicing.

The left bank at the feeder canal and dam ruins is also important historically. It was here that President John Quincy Adams dedicated construction of the C & O Canal on July 4, 1828, comparing it to the pyramids of Egypt and the Colossus of Rhodes. Ironically, on this same date, Charles Carroll (a signer of the Declaration of Independence) also broke ground for the Baltimore and Ohio Railroad. Nearly 100 years later, this railroad and a flood finally put the C & O Canal out of business.

The third alternative is to run the ruins of Dam Number 1 just below Brookmont Dam and continue 1.3 miles down through Little Falls. This clearly is not a trip for novice paddlers, even at low levels. When the river is low, the best place to run these ruins is to paddle upstream from the feeder canal or lift over from the C & O Canal so you are between the 2-foot drop of Brookmont Dam and the dam ruins below. At moderate levels, there is a good pool between these two drops. If you are running the dam ruins, be sure not to get sucked into the Brookmont Dam

hydraulic, which reaches a surprising distance downstream. In the summer (at 3 feet and below on the Little Falls gauge), the water mainly flows through the dam ruins next to long, narrow Snake Island in the center of the river. About 25 yards left of this island is a slanting concrete slab. Paddle up to it and turn tight left on it to slide 3 vertical feet into a pool above the remainder of the dam ruins. Below this pool is a rocky slalom that drops 4 feet into the Potomac. Thread your way through this Class III slalom carefully. At higher levels there are other possibilities for running this dam ruins, which is a sloping 3 foot ledge followed by a long rock garden. Scout carefully before picking a route because at reasonable levels the rocks are still thinly covered and iron bars poke dangerously through the rubble in places. Incidentally, the Little Falls gauge is on river left just upstream of the concrete Brookmont Dam pumping station.

If you don't want to run the dam ruins, there is an alternative. Below the slalom gates on the feeder canal and just opposite the 75-yard path leading to Lock 6, there is a channel on the right. Water funnels over a rocky Class II–III slalom course to the main river here. The last drop in the slalom has a nasty rock in the center to avoid.

Once below the dam ruins, work your way right. After about 150 yards, you will enter a long Class II–III rock garden of similar length. Below this is a nice peaceful stretch. Then you come to the first and best of four sets of standing waves that alternate with calm moving pools. After the second set of standing waves, a small channel comes in from the left and drops over a boulder pile. This generally strong Class III channel (called Beaver Hole Drop) is runnable at moderate levels. Scout this drop before carrying your boat to the top.

Shortly below the fourth set of standing waves you come to a fifth drop—a ledge on the left and chute of standing waves on the right. Soon below this drop, you will hear an impressive roar. Get over on the left bank to scout Little Falls just below. An island splitting the river here gives you two options; your choice will be influenced by water levels and tides. The more conservative route (a good Class III at low levels and Class III–IV at middle levels) is the left channel on the Maryland side. This is more of a straight shot in which you dodge a couple of rocks/holes before going over a rocky 3- to 4-foot drop at the end. However, at 3 feet and above, the current is deceptive; you need to vigorously work left to keep from being washed right of the jagged island in the center of the river. Throw ropes for the Maryland side should be set below the final rocky drop on the left.

The more adventurous route is on the Virginia side. This is Class III–IV at low levels (2.75 on the Little Falls gauge) and gets markedly tougher as the river rises. The object here is to work far right of the island in the center of the river. This can be difficult at lower levels because rocks/holes guard the right side of the river near the top of the rapids. Consequently, you have to cut back hard right after paddling these rocks/holes. As the river gets above 3 feet, it becomes rather difficult to make this move. At this point, those choosing the Virginia side can eddy out on the left parallel with these rocks/holes and ferry to make this turn. Do not get close to the right side of the island because of the nasty rocks (one is called The Cleaver!) and a big hole there, which becomes larger and wider as the river rises. Paddlers sucked into the clutches of this hole at even moderate levels have reported seeing Chinese farmers before being released from its vast depths. After missing the big hole next to the island, you need to vigorously work left to avoid being slammed into the right bank.

You can also scout from the Virginia side if you choose to run the right channel. At low water there is a lift over on the far right, which becomes a sneak at higher levels. At levels of 4 feet, the Virginia run is much more straightforward, but the hole on the right side of the island is really dangerous. Rescue boats for the Virginia side (at moderate levels) should be below the big hole by the island.

Below Little Falls all is flatwater except at high levels (above 6 feet), when the jagged island in the center is covered and big waves and holes continue down to Chain Bridge and beyond. A dangerous hole develops behind the center abutment of Chain Bridge above 7 feet.

There are three reasonable shuttle choices when putting in at Lock 6 and running Little Falls. You can have a nearly 3-mile circuit trip if you carry a quarter mile up a concrete culvert on river left just below Little Falls and then paddle a mile back up the C & O Canal to Lock 6, portaging Lock 5 on the way. Alternatively, you can go up the culvert and paddle a quarter mile downstream on the canal to a parking lot just upstream of Chain Bridge. Finally, you can paddle 1.5 miles below Little Falls and Chain Bridge to take out on river left at Fletcher's Boathouse. This is the easiest portage. The only problem is that the shuttle road turn into Fletcher's Boathouse is an illegal tight right turn when driving downstream on Canal Road. To enter Fletcher's Boathouse, you must be travelling upstream on Canal Road to make a left turn.

There is a fourth alternative which is not recommended. You can take out on river right at Chain Bridge, but this requires a nasty uphill carry just below the bridge. Also, parking on the spur road off the Glebe

Road approach to Chain Bridge is limited and generally claimed by fishermen.

Remember that a small change on the Little Falls gauge (which is at a wide point of the river) can make a big change in constricted Little Falls and Mather Gorge upstream. Also, be aware that the river can rise quickly; nonboaters have been trapped on rocks by rising waters in both places. Specifically, going from 2.7 to 3.7 feet on the gauge can change Little Falls from a strong intermediate to a strong advanced run. A level of 3.2 feet is a reasonable intermediate/advanced open boat run. Above 4.0 feet, this clearly is advanced/expert boater territory. Those paddling Little Falls for the first time should do so in the company of competent paddlers who have done this section before. It is interesting to note that the highest water velocity ever recorded in nature was seen at Little Falls during the massive flood of 1936.

Similar changes in Mather Gorge are not as dramatic. Most rapids are at their best at 3.5 to 4.5 feet. Shepherded intermediates can handle the lower part of this range and advanced open boaters the upper part. Mather Gorge becomes advanced decked boater territory at the 5- to 6-foot level. Paddlers should also remember that this is a big river. A long swim at high levels in this swift water, especially when it is cold, could be deadly. Incidentally, the 3-mile stretch of the C & O Canal from Fletcher's Boathouse to Lock 6 is built over an older canal—the Little Falls Skirting Canal of George Washington's Patowmack Canal system. Completed in 1795, this skirting canal served for three decades until it was covered by the C & O Canal.

Those interested in flatwater at low levels can put in at Fletcher's Boathouse and either enjoy the Virginia bluffs from a huge pool in the river or paddle on the C & O Canal. In the summer, the Canoe Cruisers Association conducts paddling classes at Fletcher's (for a small fee), which has an armada of good gray Grumman canoes for rent.

Lovers of flatwater also have two opportunities downstream. They can put in at Theodore Roosevelt Island (just above Theodore Roosevelt Bridge) and paddle down to see the Washington skyline from the river. This is particularly impressive on Fourth of July evenings when there is a spectacular fireworks display on the Mall. In addition, there is a 1.7-mile Annual Ramblin' Raft Race farther downstream in August. All forms of creative craft take part in this homemade raft race. Speed is not essential, and participants must often brave water balloon salvos from rogue rafters.

Potomac River Below Great Falls: High Water Information

This narrative is for highly experienced boaters only. In the 5- to 10-foot range of the Little Falls gauge, the Potomac below Great Falls takes on the characteristics of true big water paddling—with the full spectrum of boils, moving whirlpools, and pulsating wave action. No wonder: at 5 feet the Potomac has the normal flow of the Colorado in the Grand Canyon!

At levels over 5 feet, carefully scout the exit from the put-in on the Virginia side of Great Falls. The current slams into the Virginia shore at several points and a ferry across to the "relatively" tranquil Maryland side is a severe test of power paddling. At these levels, the Virginia channel S-Turn just below Great Falls becomes squirrelly indeed, with whirlpools capable of standing a boat on end. The Maryland and Middle Channels here offer more conservative routes down from what remains of Sandy Beach. Catfish Cove is no longer a cove but part of the Maryland Channel and is a much easier put-in than the Virginia side below Great Falls.

Good surfing is available at the bottom of the Maryland Channel in the 7- to 8-foot range. Meanwhile, in the Virginia Channel, the surfing wave at Rocky Island washes out above 4.7 feet. Below the convergence of the Maryland, Middle, and Virginia Channels, Wet Bottom Chute is completely washed out over 5 feet. The rest of Mather Gorge is very fast and squirrelly but essentially flat.

At levels over 9 feet, things begin to get quite interesting between the bottom of Mather Gorge and Difficult Run. Mather Gorge is over half filled with water at about 8 feet and begins to act as a big stopper, backing up water until Great Falls starts becoming submerged. At levels in the 13- to 15-foot range, Great Falls contains no distinguishable drops. Mather Gorge is full and there are just 30-foot explosion waves! At 8 feet and above, much of the elevation normally lost at Great Falls occurs roughly 1.5 miles downstream. This is where the river widens from 50 yards to several hundred yards and is just below Cow Hoof Rock (on river right) a quarter mile above Difficult Run. In this stretch there are waves of 8 to 10 feet at levels over 9 feet, along with the entire spectrum of big water turbulence. A conservative route would follow the right half of the river to avoid the mega-holes created where the river is flowing over the island usually separating the Maryland Chute of Difficult Run from the Middle Chute. Be advised, however, that you will have to work hard in very squirrelly stuff to get to the right side of the river.

At higher levels the preferred surfing waves and play spots differ. In the 6-foot range, good waves are found at the bottom of the Middle Chute in Difficult Run and at Buzzard Rock on river right just upstream of the Old Angler's Inn put-in. Playable whirlpools form at the bottom of the Maryland Chute at 6 to 8 feet.

The stretch of river between Old Angler's Inn, the Route 495 Beltway bridge, and on to Brookmont Dam is fast and flat at higher levels since all the normal rapids are washed out. Exercise caution, however, since the strong current flows through the trees at many points, providing the opportunity for a cellulose slalom to those inclined to risk penalties greater than the 5 seconds per gate touch in slalom racing.

Brookmont Dam should be avoided. In spite of the multimillion dollar backfill completed by the Corps of Engineers, which greatly reduced the hydraulic below the dam, it is still dangerous at higher levels. Running Brookmont Dam is also now illegal at any level. Over the objection of the Canoe Cruisers Association and the U.S. Whitewater Team, boating is prohibited immediately upstream of Brookmont Dam, the Great Falls Aqueduct Dam, and several other dams further upstream on the Potomac. The CCA and the U.S. Team noted that the uninformed rafters and fishermen likely to get into trouble at such dams were unlikely to know about the regulation and that knowledgeable boaters were fully capable of evaluating for themselves the degree of risk at these locations.

The rubble dam below Brookmont can be run at many points at higher levels. Then you have a fast run through minor wave action down to Little Falls proper.

Little Falls at higher levels may actually be easier than in the 4- to 5-foot range, when you have both powerful water and rocks to avoid. At just over 5 feet, the island in this rapid goes under water, and Little Falls becomes a wave train of 8- to 10-footers extending to Chain Bridge. It is very similar to the major rapids on the Grand Canyon—big, but straightforward. As with most such water, it's usually easier to run the middle than to sneak. At levels over 7.5 to 8 feet the bridge pilings on Chain Bridge have an enormous pillow on the upstream side and a terminal hydraulic on the downstream side.

A word of warning to those enjoying the Potomac at higher levels. The National Park Service and other public officials often have little knowledge of recreational boating. Consequently, they generally take a dim view of boaters enjoying rivers at higher levels—which are clearly hazardous to inexperienced paddlers. Consequently, these authorities have occasionally tried to declare the Potomac closed at levels as low as 7 feet. On one infamous occasion Park Police sought to eject boaters when the river was rising rapidly from 3 to 4 feet. While the legal authority for closing the Potomac is tenuous, it behooves the boating community to be polite to these public officials and, most importantly, not to strengthen their argument by doing something silly—like drowning or requiring a rescue. The Potomac at higher levels must be the preserve of highly experienced paddlers with a completely reliable self rescue capability in heavy water conditions. Finally, paddlers running this section of the Potomac at high water should go with someone familiar with the river at these levels.

Great Falls Park

Paddlers putting in below Great Falls on the Virginia or Maryland side of the river are in for a real treat. Both of these put-ins contain unique historical places well worth a visit before or after running the river.

On the Virginia side of Great Falls is a tasteful visitors center with history and nature exhibits. Not only do you get a magnificent view of Great Falls, but you also can walk along a one mile segment of George Washington's Patowmack Canal built to bypass the 77-foot drop of Great Falls. This stretch of the canal (known as the Great Falls Skirting Canal) operated from 1802 to 1830. It represents a key part of George Washington's lifelong commitment to a Potomac canal system that would commercially bind states west of the Appalachians to the original 13 colonies. Take time to look at the remains of this canal, which has been described as the greatest eighteenth century engineering development in the United States. The canal begins with the remains of a wing dam a third of a mile upstream from the visitors center. You can reach this starting point from

the middle of the second parking lot above the center. The wing dam supplied water for the canal. Following the trace of the canal to just below the visitors center, you come on the site of Briggs Grist Mill and 500 feet farther the remains of Potts-Wilson Ironworks. About a quarter mile downstream are the remains of Matildaville—a small canal town named for the first wife of Light Horse Harry Lee, who was the father of Robert E. Lee. In this area are the ruins of Meyers Tavern (also known as Dickey's Inn), which reputedly served all U.S. Presidents from George Washington to Theodore Roosevelt. Unfortunately, it burned down in 1942.

Below Matildaville, the last quarter mile of the canal has the remains of five locks. You can still see Seneca red sandstone in Locks 1 and 2. However, all that remains of Locks 3, 4, and 5 is an impressive cut through the metamorphic metagraywacke of Mather Gorge. These last three locks drop over 50 feet before the cut ends on the Potomac River.

The Maryland side of Great Falls is also most interesting, Here you have the 184-mile-long C & O Canal and towpath, which in 1830 succeeded Washington's Patowmack Canal for nearly 100 years until floods and the B & O Railroad did it in. Be sure to visit historic Great Falls Tavern, which is now a museum. In the summer, there are trips on restored canal boats towed by mules. The towpath of the C & O Canal is a great place for hiking, jogging, biking, and birding. Just below Great Falls Tavern is the Six Locks section of the C & O Canal, where Locks 15–20 change the canal elevation 41 feet. Those taking the nearly half-mile portage (ugh!) to Catfish Cove on the Maryland side can also check out the heavy turbulent rapids forming the narrow Maryland fish ladder of Great Falls.

World Champion Jon Lugbill tries out the new Dickerson whitewater slalom course above Whites Ford on the Point of Rocks to Violettes Lock section of the Potomac.

Rock Creek

Running right through the heart of Washington, D.C., the 7-mile section of Rock Creek from Military Road to the Potomac at K Street is of interest primarily to local paddlers looking for a quick run after work or for a few hours on a weekend. After placidly passing through Montgomery County in Maryland, Rock Creek suddenly becomes quite feisty as it flows through a shallow gorge in the nation's capital before emptying into the Potomac. Most of the action (including five Class III drops in the first half mile) is concentrated in the 2-mile wooded segment between Military Road and Pierce Mill. The remaining 5 miles from Pierce Mill to Thompson's Boathouse on the Potomac is a Class I-II trip with one low-water bridge to carry a half mile below Pierce Mill.

It normally takes nearly an inch of rain to bring Rock Creek up—and it may stay up for only a few hours. There is a gauge on the river left of Rapids Footbridge—which is a half mile below Military Road. The very scrapey minimum on the gauge is 0 feet, and the maximum is 2 feet. Even though the gauge goes several feet higher, it is highly recommended you don't put in if it is over 2 feet. Low levels are very technical. At high levels there are big holes and waves requiring more advanced big-water skills.

In the half mile between Military Road and the appropriately named Rapids Footbridge and its gauge, there are five Class III rock garden rapids. Depending on the level, there may be one or several routes through each. It's advisable and easy to scout this section along Rock Creek Drive because strainers can easily collect in the narrow chutes.

The action begins about 100 yards below Military Road, after you pass beneath a bridge and make a sweeping right turn in front of Rock Creek Park Headquarters. After running a few quick warm up drops you come to a Class III irregular ledge of 3 feet and then more fast water. Shortly below is the longest Class III rapid—over 100 yards with four or five distinct drops. Then comes a short Class III culminating in a 4-foot irregular ledge. Within sight of the Rapids Footbridge are the last two Class IIIs—a short exciting one and then another 60 yards long. At moderate levels, the cleanest and safest route through all the rapids is following the main current down the center or somewhat left of center. There are some exciting, tortuous routes on the far right, but these sometimes trap strainers.

Below Rapids Footbridge is about a half mile of continuous Class II rapids. Then, just before the next bridge and after a grabby surfing ledge, you reach a 4-foot

Section: Washington, D.C. (Military Road) to Thompson's Boathouse on the Potomac (off Rock Creek Parkway)

Counties: Washington, D.C.

USGS Quads: Washington West

Suitable for: Day cruising

Skill Level: Intermediates/advanced (first 2 miles); novices (last 5 miles)

Months Runnable: After an inch of local rain

Interest Highlights: Rock Creek Park and Washington D.C., buildings and bridges; Class III whitewater in first half mile

Scenery: Pretty to beautiful in spots

Difficulty: Class III first 2 miles (at moderate levels); Class I-II last 5 miles

Average Width: 30 to 40 feet

Velocity: Moderate to fast

Gradient: First 0.5 mile is nearly 100 feet per mile; next 1.5 miles are 20 feet per mile; last 5 miles are 10 feet per mile

Runnable Water Levels:
  Minimum: 0 feet on Rapids Footbridge gauge a half mile below Military Road; maybe 3 feet on Dawsonville gauge
  Maximum: 2 feet on Rapids Footbridge gauge

Hazards: 7-foot Pierce Mill Dam 2 miles into trip; low-water bridge a half mile further; trees in river; high water

Scouting: Perhaps several of 6 Class III rapids between Military Road and Pierce Mill

Portages: 7-foot Pierce Mill Dam and low-water bridge below

Rescue Index: Accessible

Source of Additional Information: National Weather Service, Dawsonville gauge (703) 260-0305

Access Points	River Miles	Shuttle Miles
A–B	2	2
B–C	5	5

Access Point Ratings:
  A–at Military Road, very good
  B–at Pierce Mill (Tilden St./Park Rd.), very good
  C–at Thompson's Boathouse on the Potomac (off Rock Creek Parkway at end of Virginia Avenue), very good

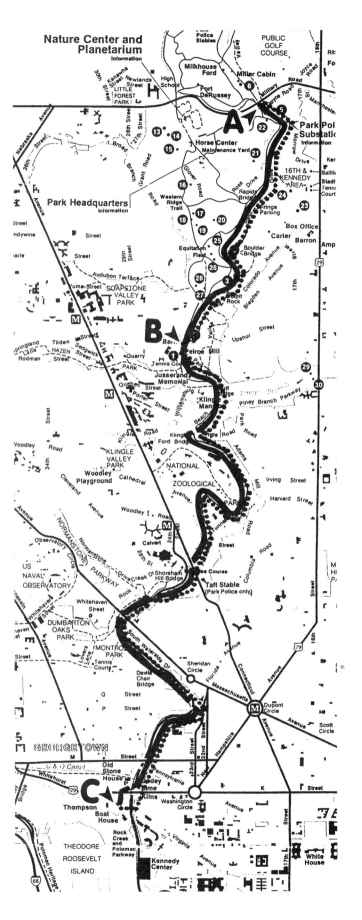

Class III drop over a man-made dam which also should be scouted. Below this dam, the Class II rapids resume for another half mile. Yet a half mile farther is Pierce Mill Dam, a 7-foot drop into a potentially lethal hydraulic. This 7-foot dam is easily seen and carried on either side. Take out here if you only want the zestiest 2-mile part of Rock Creek.

Advanced paddlers have run this dam. However, the hydraulic at the bottom is nasty and gets increasingly dangerous at high water. Those tempted by the dam should run it only at low water (4 to 6 inches over the dam) with full safety precautions (including throw ropes set below the dam). Above 6 inches, the hydraulic quickly becomes dangerous even though it may not look that way. Paddlers should also be aware that if an accident occurs in running the dam, the Park Police could close Rock Creek to boaters.

For paddlers doing the remaining 5 miles to the Potomac, the main concern is a low-water bridge a half mile below Pierce Mill Dam. Carry it on the right. There are also scrapey fords and pipe crossings. Other than these hazards, the 5 miles from Pierce Mill to Thompson's Boathouse on the Potomac is Class I–II water. The highlights are some easy Class II drops as you go through and below the National Zoo.

There are numerous parking areas alongside Rock Creek Drive. However, the two parking areas just above Military Road and just above Pierce Mill are the usual put-in and take-out, respectively, for those interested in only the best rapids. Thompson's Boathouse (off K Street) is the best take-out for paddlers who continue another 5 miles down to the Potomac.

Above Pierce Mill both banks are generally wooded, and the scenery is surprisingly rustic except for the road alongside. Below Pierce Mill the city gradually intrudes more, but this actually increases the interest of the trip, especially with several dramatic bridges in Rock Creek Park followed by the lovely sight of Watergate and the Kennedy Center.

The only real negative is water quality. During heavy rains, sewer overflow pollutes Rock Creek and its tributaries. I've not known anyone to get sick from this yucky water, but it certainly discourages playing.

On the bright side, the National Park Service no longer requires permits to run Rock Creek. However, please stay off this creek during rush hour. Otherwise, delays by rubbernecking motorists may lead to new paddling restrictions.

For hard core paddlers looking for really ephemeral thrills, Rock Creek has several interesting short tributaries that are extremely hard to catch up. All of these tributaries should be scouted on foot beforehand and reached before the downpour finishes, as they may stay runnable for only a very short time thereafter. Broad Branch, (1.8 miles), Joyce Road Branch (0.5 miles), and Piney Branch (0.5 miles) all have gradients of about 70 feet per mile, no serious strainers (except for a dangerous collapsed bridge on Joyce Road Branch), and some exciting Class III drops. Pinehurst Branch and Fenwick Branch would also be enticing except that they have too many strainers. However, the real challenge is Soapstone Branch (0.7 miles). It has a gradient of 130 feet per mile, one genuine Class IV rapid, a pair of Class III–IV drops, and two trees across it (at the time of this writing) in dangerous places. After the trees are removed, Soapstone Branch will make a short but exciting run for good paddlers.

Court Ogilvie at Pierce Mill Dam on Rock Creek in the heart of Washington, D.C. Photo by Kevin Baughan.

Tearcoat Creek

Tearcoat Creek ("tear" as in "rip"), located in West Virginia along US 50 about 12 miles from the Virginia border, is a creek to savor for small stream connoisseurs. It offers a truly enchanting combination of lovely scenery and lively rapids.

Tearcoat Creek is a tributary of the North River which runs into the Cacapon. It runs about 3.5 miles from the village of Pleasant Dale, West Virginia, where it crosses under US 50, to its confluence with the North. With a gradient of 44 feet per mile, it has virtually continuous Class II action and five or six Class II–III ledges. Just below the Pleasant Dale put-in, Tearcoat enters a cozy, isolated, twisty gorge. There are fern- and moss-covered limestone rock formations and pristine woodlands throughout the run. The only complaint about Tearcoat is that it is hard to catch up. Even during the wettest months

of the year, you have to catch this stream within one or two days of a hard rain.

The best put-in is at US 50 (downstream, river left). It is also possible to start the trip one-half mile above US 50 where county Route 50/17 fords the creek. Adventurous small-stream paddlers armed with detailed local maps might venture even further upstream. There are no memorable rapids in the half-mile stretch above US 50, but there are two difficult cattle fences just above the bridge that make the extra half mile rather arduous and unrewarding. Putting in at US 50 is a better choice.

Like any small, fast stream, water levels are critical to the difficulty level and excitement of the trip. No gauge exists, but a close inspection at the put-in should suffice. Because of the high gradient and many tight turns on this run, the difficulty level increases significantly with

Leslie Knipling enjoying a typical drop on Tearcoat Creek. Photo by Ron Knipling.

Section: US 50 to ford on Rt. 50/19 located 0.25 miles above confluence with North River

Counties: Hampshire (WV)

USGS Quads: Hanging Rock

Suitable for: Day cruising

Skill Level: Intermediate

Months Runnable: January to mid-May following very heavy rain

Interest Highlights: Tiny, twisting, scenic gorge

Scenery: Beautiful throughout

Difficulty: Class II–III

Average Width: 15 to 25 feet

Velocity: Fast

Gradient: 44 feet per mile

Runnable Water Levels:

Minimum: 120 cfs (estimate); 5 feet on Great Cacapon gauge

Maximum: 400 cfs (estimate); maybe 7.5 feet on Great Cacapon gauge

Hazards: At this writing, no significant hazards, however, many blind turns and possibility of log strainers

Scouting: None required if skilled lead paddler at moderate levels; otherwise, scout blind turns

Portages: None except for possible downed trees

Rescue Index: Accessible to remote

Source of Additional Information: National Weather Service, Great Cacapon gauge (703) 260-0305

Access Points	River Miles	Shuttle Miles
A–B	3.5	2.5

Access Point Ratings:
A–US 50, fair to good (watch for traffic on US 50)
B–Rt. 50/19, good (if dirt road at take-out is muddy, be careful not to get car stuck at bottom of hill at creekside)

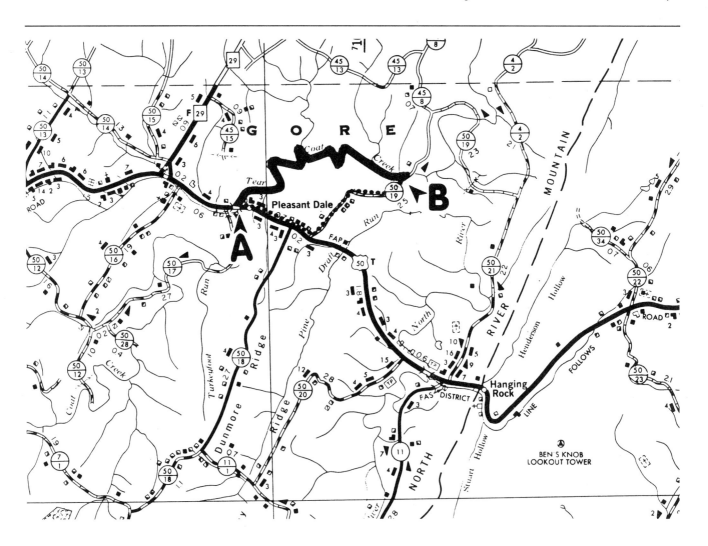

increases in water volume. The difference between zero and the maximum safe water level is probably no more than 15 inches. If in doubt, scout downstream from the put-in. There are enough rapids in the first few hundred yards to let you know what you're in for.

To run the shuttle, drive east on US 50 from the put-in about 0.75 miles to country Route 50/19. Turn left onto 50/19. After about 1.5 miles on this dirt/gravel road, you come to a fork in the road. Bear to the left and park near where this road fords the creek. Near the creek this road is steep and may be muddy. Don't get stuck! This take-out spot is about 0.25 miles above the confluence of Tearcoat and North River. You can paddle to the confluence, but that involves a take-out across private property at some cottages. You can also paddle on the North River for another 7 miles to the Capon Bridge/Slanesville Road near North River Mills. The first 4 of these 7 miles are forgettable, but the last 3 are scenic and have a few decent Class II rapids.

The current is fast throughout this run. The first significant rapid, an easy Class II–III ledge, is about 200 yards below the put-in. From there on the rapids, mostly Class II ledges, are very frequent. The overall stream difficulty is roughly comparable to the Passage Creek Gorge in the Shenandoah Watershed. Tearcoat has a steeper gradient and more ledges, although there are probably two or three rapids on Passage that are a bit harder than anything on Tearcoat. The creek bottom is rock, and there are enough boulders for plenty of practice maneuvering. Although Tearcoat has many rapids, none exceeds Class II–III, and none presents major hazards. One particular rapid deserves mention. About halfway through the run, there is a short, flat stretch followed by a turbulent Class II bend that starts right but then makes a blind turn to the left. Around the bend is a picturesque overhanging rock face on river right. Below the rock face are two mattress sized boulders that block most of the stream. The recommended route is the tight but uncomplicated chutes down the middle between the two boulders. There is also a runnable chute on river right, but it's a super hero squeeze right against the rock face. River left is an easy, shallow sneak route. As you approach these rocks from around the bend, be ready to bail out left if the center chute is blocked. For photographers, this spot is probably the best of many photo opportunities on the run.

Altogether, there are six to eight sharp, blind turns with the potential hazard of sudden strainers. At this writing, there is only one such strainer, a downed tree just below a rock garden on a left turn near the end of the run. Aside from potential strainers, many of the sharp turns have vertical or overhanging rock walls on the outside of the bend, offering the possibility of a bump on the head to the paddler who is lazy in making turns. A helmet might be a worthwhile safeguard, particularly for paddlers without small stream experience.

Tearcoat Creek is memorable for its intimate scenery and for the easy delight of its rapids. At moderate water levels it doesn't press the skills of the intermediate level paddler, but it sure provides a chance to exercise them. If you get to run this creek, run it twice! The second time down, you won't be worrying about what's around that next blind turn and will have a chance to revel in the diminutive splendor of this little-known creek.

Trout Run

Trout Run is a delightful, tiny slalom tributary to the Lost River. The only problem with this trip through the pretty little gorge described here is that it is not possible more often. You have to wait until the Lost River has at least 2.5 feet of water on the Route 55 gauge above Wardensville before you have several inches of paddling water on the Trout Run gauge–also on Route 55.

The 7-mile trip from Trout Run Road to Route 55 near Wardensville starts with nice Class II–III drops on which to warm up. Then, once you're in the gorge, the difficulty is mainly Class III with a couple of Class III–IV rapids at moderate levels. This simmers down to Class II action after leaving the gorge and until the take-out is reached.

Lining the banks at the start are sycamores and igneous rocks. In the gorge there are more evergreens, particularly hemlock, cedar, white pine, and Virginia pine. Before the take out, the rocks change to sedimentary shale.

To reach the put-in, take Trout Run Road until just over 5 miles from Wardensville. Here a small road turns right and the put-in bridge is less than a quarter mile from the turn. If the water is high enough, venturesome boaters can put in a mile or so further upstream.

After you've put in, you'll find some easy Class II–III bouncy waves and slalom action for the first 1.5 miles. The main hazard here is downed trees. On one trip four were encountered; fortunately, they were two pairs close together. Also, you should be alert for possible barbed wire fences. Shortly after this, when you realize you are now in a gorge, there are three nice long Class II–III slaloms followed by a good Class III slalom.

The river is dropping steeply now at over 100 feet per mile and care is necessary. After another Class II–III slalom, stop and scout because you will encounter a difficult Class III–IV slalom with nasty rocks in the bottom. The paddler must work over to the right of the river and run the final drop tight right to miss these very nasty rocks.

Just below this drop it's Class III city beginning with two ledges that should also be run tight right. However, after running the second ledge, immediately work left to finish this rapid. Then come two drops—the first a tight channel and the second a 2.5-foot ledge.

Not too far below this you will go through a tight tweeze between two large rocks on the left. The right rock is like a flat table top. Eddy out just below this table top rock and begin boat or bank scouting. After leaving the eddy, work to the far left side of the river. Scout the drop just below, which is on the extreme left and requires an immediate 90-degree right turn as you enter it. Just below is a nice pool.

Stop and scout the large Class III–IV drop just below this pool. Basically you dodge several boulders in entering this drop and run the 5-foot sloping ledge at the end of it in the center, if there is enough water. Just below is the last of the major rapids—a tough Class III slalom requiring good boat control. After this slalom, you reach an island. Go left.

Jerry Salzman running the biggest drop on Trout Run.

Section: Bridge off Trout Run Road (Rt. 23/10) 5 miles from Wardensville, to Rt. 55 near Wardensville

Counties: Hardy (WV)

USGS Quads: Baker, Wardensville

Suitable for: Day cruising

Skill Level: Shepherded intermediates; advanced paddlers

Months Runnable: Winter and early spring after a very heavy rain

Interest Highlights: Gorgeous small gorge; tight slalom rapids

Scenery: Pretty in spots to beautiful

Difficulty: Class II–III for first 2 miles; Class III with 2 Class III–IV's in gorge at moderate levels; Class I–II at end

Average Width: 20 to 30 feet

Velocity: Fast

Gradient: 75 feet per mile in upper 4 miles (with 1 mile over 100 feet per mile); 27 feet per mile in lower 3 miles

Runnable Water Levels:
Minimum: 0 feet on Trout Run Rt. 55 gauge west of Wardensville; maybe 5 feet on Cootes Store gauge
Maximum: Maybe 2.5 feet on Trout Run Rt. 55 gauge west of Wardensville

Hazards: Trees in river; tight rock slaloms; maybe barbed wire fences

Scouting: At least two Class III–IV rapids in gorge

Portages: Perhaps one or more of the Class III—IV rapids, depending on water level

Rescue Index: Accessible to remote

Source of Additional Information: National Weather Service, Cootes Store gauge (703) 260-0305

Access Points	River Miles	Shuttle Miles
A–B	4	3.5
B–C	3	2.0

Access Point Ratings:
A–at Trout Run Road Bridge (Route 23/10) 5 miles west of Wardensville, very good
B–at low-water bridge, good
C–at Rt. 55, good

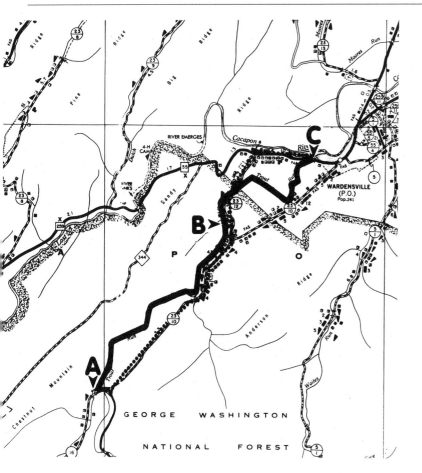

Shortly below is a 2-foot low-water bridge. This is followed by two Class II rapids next to 25-foot splintered shale cliffs on the left. About a half mile below this is a 1-foot low-water bridge and another half mile of bouncy Class II action next to more shale cliffs. When you come to two low-water bridges, you have reached the first take-out on river right. The first bridge is 2 feet high; the second is 3 feet. You can run one or both of these bridges if you wish; just look them over first to be sure there is sufficient water and that the channel is clear. Water just barely running over the first bridge is also a 0 level for the section upstream.

From here to the Route 55 take-out and its confluence with the Lost River, Trout Run is a pleasant Class I–II stream with the only obstacles being a fence or two. Be sure to check the Trout Run gauge on the downstream side of the Route 55 bridge middle abutment before launching.

The picturesque Route 720 covered bridge on the North Fork of the Shenandoah.

Historic Fort Stevens on Cedar Creek.

Shenandoah

Cedar Creek

Star Tannery (Route 55) to Fort Stevens (Route 628)

Cedar Creek is perhaps the best trip for shepherded novices in the state of Virginia. Although the upper 10-mile section is more scenic and slightly more difficult than the lower 10-mile section, both are classic trips.

The generally Class I–II 9.5-mile upper section is characterized by cedar-studded Devonian shale cliffs on the right and farmland on the left for the first third of the trip. The middle of this journey features cedar- and hemlock-covered hills alternating on both sides of the river. Finally, the best rapids (one strong Class II and one Class II–III) and most spectacular cliffs, rock formations, and caves are in the last third of the trip. While enjoying the clear water of Cedar Creek, you will encounter surprisingly long and deep green pools in which you can see fish darting about.

Al Thompson pauses at the waterfalls created by an old millrace dropping into Cedar Creek just above pentagon shaped Fort Stevens and Route 628.

Before putting in, be sure you check the canoeing gauge on the downstream right abutment of the Route 628 take-out bridge and get permission to park because it is privately owned. If you don't get permission, take out at the Route 623 low-water bridge upstream. Because the rapids are generally Class I–II cobble bars and turns requiring some boat control, only the more significant drops will be mentioned. One drawback is that most of the land is posted, so use discretion when stopping for lunch and other purposes. Other than perhaps a grumpy landowner, the only other hazards are an occasional downed tree and a low-water bridge 8 miles into the trip.

Be discreet when putting in from Route 604 just after Route 55 crosses Cedar Creek. Except for this nice put-in on river left 50 yards downstream from the bridge, the land on both sides is posted. There is parking on Route 604 and by the Route 55 bridge for shuttle cars.

Less than a quarter mile after starting you come to a pretty pool on the right side of the creek and a left turn. The right bank is a striking shale rock face 20 to 50 feet high covered with cedar trees. Although it disappears briefly, the shale rock face on the right soon reappears with ferns and moss now gracing it. About a mile into the trip, a Class I–II rock garden is encountered, followed a quarter mile later by a Class II 2-foot ledge. The best passages are on the left or right side of this ledge in moderate water. Look the ledge over before running it because a tree blocked the left side recently.

Shortly below, the striking bedded shale rock face resumes on the right, the river turns left, and 2 miles into the trip you come to a classic farm–complete with red barn–on the left. Soon below is an island; the left channel was blocked on one recent trip. Then, less than a half mile below this island, the river turns left against the face of a hill. Here the left bank is guarded by a line of sycamore trees stretching over 100 yards along the creek. These ghostly white trees are quite striking from a distance in the winter. After making this turn, you reach yet another 50-foot-high shale rock face on the right while the left bank opens up so that you soon see a beautiful mountain in the distance.

About 3 miles into the trip is a rugged, 200-foot-high, steep hill on the left covered with cedars clawing for a foothold on its precarious slopes. In the next half mile you pass another farm while floating through some long, deep, clear pools. Then, three-quarters of a mile farther, the creek turns left against a beautiful 200-foot hill on the right covered this time with hemlocks. While paddling next to this gorgeous hill, you will have to dodge a few rocks in a long stretch that is almost a rock garden. This can be very technical at low water.

A good half mile below this you will come to an eye-catching rock bed which looks like building blocks sloping into the river on the left. Shortly below this is another hemlock-covered rock face on the right and a 50-yard Class I–II rock garden. A quarter mile farther is a surfing spot on the left immediately followed by a pretty red shale rock lunch stop on the right. Then comes a large, brown, stone house (posted), another farm, and a debris island. Right was the least obstructed channel recently. Then, about a half mile later is the biggest eyesore of the trip: a 4-foot-high fence 100 yards long of (ugh!) old tires.

A quarter mile below this eyesore, the river slowly turns right. Look for a 20-foot-high rock on the left bank and a horizon line. Novices should pull over on the right bank to look at this strong Class II, man-made ledge of a good 2 feet. It is best run center and perhaps has surfing possibilities for aggressive, skilled paddlers below. A good couple of hundred yards below this is the toughest rapid of the trip–a Class II–III rock garden with some nasty rocks to avoid. Pull over to the right bank to scout this one also. The best route is to enter right of center between two offset rocks at the top. Immediately below these rocks you will have to tweeze between or go right of two rocks at the bottom of the drop.

About 300 yards below this rapid you come to the Route 623 low-water bridge. Portage this please! Carry on either side: the left is steeper but shorter. This Route 623

Section: Route 55/604 to Route 628

Counties: Shenandoah, Frederick

USGS Quads: Mountain Falls, Middletown

Suitable for: Day cruising

Skill Level: Shepherded novices

Months Runnable: Winter and spring after an inch of rain

Interest Highlights: Rocky bluffs, limestone formations, caves, waterfall, and historic fort (on private property) at take-out

Scenery: Beautiful in spots to spectacular

Difficulty: Class I–II with one strong Class II and one Class II–III

Average Width: 20 to 40 feet

Velocity: Moderate

Gradient: 13 feet per mile

Runnable Water Levels:

Minimum: 0.1 feet on Route 11 gauge; 3.3 feet on Cootes Store gauge; 3 inches below bottom blue line on Route 628 gauge (see Additional Information below)
Maximum: Perhaps 6 feet on Cootes Store gauge

Hazards: Low-water bridge nearly 8 miles into the trip; an occasional tree in the creek

Scouting: Novices should scout Class II ledge 1 mile into trip and strong Class II and Class II–III about 7.5 miles into trip

Portages: Low-water bridge nearly 8 miles into the trip—carry on left or right (left is steeper but shorter)

Rescue Index: Generally accessible

Source of Additional Information: National Weather Service, Cootes Store gauge (703) 260-0305. There is a painted gauge on the river right downstream abutment on Route 628. The bottom blue line is 3 inches above paddling 0, and the top red line is 9 inches above paddling 0.

Access Points	River Miles	Shuttle Miles
A–B	9.5	8

Access Point Ratings:
A–at Rt. 55/604, very good
B–at Rt. 628, good

Al Thompson paddles through a small cave near Panther Cave on Cedar Creek about a mile above Route 11.

bridge can also be the take-out if you don't get permission to take out at Route 628.

Once below this bridge you can relax and prepare for a spectacular finale in the last 2 miles of the trip. Shortly you will come to some 30-foot-high shale cliffs on the right which contain numerous interesting holes and indentations. Immediately below the shale changes to limestone, and you pass some bigger holes, caves even, in a limestone rock 30 feet high. After this the left bank takes its turn for scenery. Big cedars are first seen and then spectacular cliffs 200 feet high. Soon the river turns left, and you see an undercut minicave and a triangular hole in another limestone rock face on the right. A quarter mile later you pass an old gauging station on the left.

Immediately thereafter you will see some big chunks of the left bank that have fallen into the river to create some strange islands of Conococheague limestone. Stop and look at these and the left bank. Here from the comfort of your boat you can enjoy stalactites, stalagmites, and other rock formations usually seen only in limestone caves. Please don't damage them so future paddlers can enjoy them also.

A final scenic treat occurs just below on the left: a 25-foot waterfall from an old mill. Get your camera out because you can get shots of fellow paddlers slipping behind this waterfall without getting wet. On warm days experienced paddlers can even attempt to paddle through a gap in the falls.

The take-out is next on river left, just upstream of the Route 628 bridge. However, the land here is private and posted so get permission first to take out here and/or leave a shuttle vehicle. While taking out please notice the five-sided building on the left (also on private land). This is Fort Stevens, built in 1752 and a three-story miniature ancestor of the Pentagon in Washington, D.C. The top story was used to defend against Indian attacks. The remaining two stories are underground: one was for women and children and the other for supplies.

You will particularly enjoy this trip on a clear winter day and experience true solitude. If there has been a recent snow storm, the ice formations on the rock faces will be spectacular. Also, birds abound on Cedar Creek: hawks, ospreys, kingfishers, turkey vultures, herons, and particularly ducks–including mallards, black ducks, and gadwells. Indeed, a kingfisher led me on a merry chase for 2 miles, and I must have flushed 50 ducks on one memorable winter trip. Besides stocked trout, which have drifted down from upstream, there are bass, sunfish, and catfish in this river. The wooded banks support cedars, hemlocks, pines, and deciduous trees such as oaks, hickories, sycamores, and tulip poplars. The rock cobbles are composed primarily of varied shale, sandstone, quartz, and chert. In sum, this is a positively delightful trip for all who love nature.

Fort Stevens (Route 628) to US 11

This 10.5-mile section of Cedar Creek is also one of the prettiest trips in Virginia for the shepherded novice paddler. A historic fort, waterfall, caves, clear water, limestone formations, rocky bluffs covered with cedar trees, and even rocky arches to walk or paddle through–this stretch of Cedar Creek has it all. The only drawback is that this delightful stream is not up more often.

The put-in at Route 628 is most scenic. As you look upstream from the bridge, there is a 25-foot waterfall on the right less than 100 yards away, which was created to run a now defunct mill. Venturesome paddlers can paddle behind it carefully without getting wet. As you look at the waterfall, notice the rock formations near it. The Conococheague limestone here has been dissolved by water to form stalagmites, stalactites, and other features that you usually see only in underground caves.

The land on both sides of the put-in is privately owned, so get permission from the landowners before putting in or parking your vehicles. If you don't get permission to put in here, go upstream and put in at the Route 623 low-water bridge. Past abuses by careless paddlers have caused at least one of these landowners to put "no trespassing" signs on this land. Historic Fort Stevens is also here at the put-in; it is a five-sided building next to the road on the same side as the waterfall. However, it is on private land, so permission must be obtained to view it. Before putting in, check the canoeing gauge on the downstream right abutment of the Route 628 bridge. The lower blue mark is 4 inches above 0; the upper red mark indicates 10 inches of paddling water.

After putting in and paddling up to marvel at the waterfall and limestone formations, you will go over a small rocky ledge just below the bridge. In the first mile you will pass some well tended farms and pretty rock bluffs. A half-mile later you will come to some spectacular 100-foot rocky cliffs on the right. Shortly after this you will understand where the name of this creek came from, as you pass a hill full of cedars on the left. Just below is a tight right turn with some interesting cavelike formations on the left followed by some more cliffs and cedars.

Then comes a half mile of flatwater before you reach a 1-foot rocky ledge and a 50-foot syncline in the rocks on the right. About a quarter mile below this was a sign recently warning about stray bullets. Apparently a local resident has set up a shooting range here.

Nearly 2 miles farther is the Route 622 bridge, midway through the trip. A pair of 1-foot rocky ledges occurs just above and just below the bridge. These are followed 100 yards later by a 1.5-foot ledge which should be run center and a pretty rock cliff on the right. As you pass by some of the farms notice the rope swings; apparently this stream keeps enough water in the summer for some nice swimming holes.

A half mile below is a striking, slanting rock block formation that slides into the river on the left. Three-quarters of a mile later is a tight right turn by 100-foot-high cliffs and then a shallow cave on the left. You go beneath a power line a half mile later and some

Section: Rt. 628 to US 11

Counties: Shenandoah, Warren, Frederick

USGS Quads: Middletown, Strasburg

Suitable for: Day cruising

Skill Level: Shepherded novices

Months Runnable: Winter and spring after an inch of rain

Interest Highlights: Limestone formations, caves, rocky bluffs; waterfall and historic fort (on private property) at put-in

Scenery: Beautiful in spots to beautiful

Difficulty: Class I–II with 1 Class III below US 11

Average Width: 40 to 50 feet

Velocity: Moderate

Gradient: 11 feet per mile

Runnable Water Levels:
Minimum: 0 feet on Rt. 11 gauge; 3.2 feet on Cootes Store gauge; 4 inches below lower blue mark on Rt. 628 gauge

Maximum: Perhaps 6 feet on Cootes Store gauge

Hazards: Low-water bridge over 8 miles into the trip; an occasional tree in the creek

Scouting: None

Portages: Low-water bridge over 8 miles into trip—carry right

Rescue Index: Accessible to remote

Source of Additional Information: National Weather Service, Cootes Store gauge (703) 260-0305. There is a painted gauge on the river right downstream abutment on Route 628. The bottom blue line is 4 inches above paddling 0 and the top red line is about 10 inches above paddling 0.

Access Points	River Miles	Shuttle Miles
B–C	10.5	11.5
B–D	13	11
B–E	14	12

Access Point Ratings:
B–at Rt. 628, good
C–at US 11 wayside, good
D–at Rt. 635, good
E–at Rt. 611, good

nice standing waves shortly thereafter. A quarter mile below these waves you come to a low-water bridge; portage on the right. You then pass under a railroad bridge and by a minor surfing spot.

Just a few hundred yards below is the best rapid of the trip. You go left of an island and the river turns right. As it does so it goes over a Class II double ledge on the right and a single 2-foot ledge on the left. About 50 yards below this is another Class II drop where the river narrows and two rocks divide the creek into three channels. Decide early which channel you want.

Less than a half mile below here you come to Panther Cave on your left. This huge hole in Ordovician limestone goes back 25 feet. Stop and explore it. The photo opportunity gets better because a few yards downstream from the cave is first a rocky mini-tunnel which you can walk through and then a rocky arch just below through which you can usually paddle.

After this scenic stop, there are only a couple of minor rapids until you reach the take-out a mile later on river left between the two bridges of US 11. There is a campground on river left just above these two bridges, and a Randy Carter gauge on one of the bridges which

should be at least 0. Do be aware that you need a recent wet period to run this beautiful stream; the Cootes Store gauge should be at least 3.2 feet and holding.

If you want bigger action and don't mind some flatwater, continue on below US 11. Two miles below US 11 and only a tenth of a mile above the Route 635 low-water bridge is a Class III sandstone/shale ledge of 3 feet. The most conservative route (Class II–III) over this washboard ledge is on the left. The more exciting route is over the right. The center is nastiest and most abrupt. Scout from river left.

You can take out at Route 635 (limited parking on the right) or continue 1 mile to Route 611, where Cedar Creek joins the North Fork of the Shenandoah.

Incidentally, Cedar Creek has some interesting Civil War history. The Battle of Cedar Creek was fought in 1864 near the section below Fort Stevens. In it, Union General Sheridan just barely turned back a surprise attack by Confederate General Jubal Early. The Union victory (despite heavier losses) essentially ended the Civil War in the Shenandoah valley. The map for this lower section is in the narrative on the upper section.

Al Thompson checks out Panther Cave on scenic Cedar Creek.

Gooney Run

Gooney Run is one of the premier whitewater runs near the Washington, D.C. area to challenge the advanced or expert paddler. If you live near the nation's capital, why travel several hours to a West Virginia river when a short drive and simple shuttle can have you on the river and off again for an easy day trip five miles south of Front Royal. This enjoyable trip is clearly tougher than Trout Run but somewhat easier than Johns Creek—both of which are also described in this book.

However, please remember that Gooney is for the hard core and patient paddler. When you have a 2-inch rain and other rivers are bank full or above, that is the time to target this stream. To determine if Gooney is runnable, call one of the three local paddlers listed under Source of Additional Information in the Gooney data sheet.

The classic 6-mile section of Gooney Run from Browntown to US 340 begins with 4 miles of Class II–III rapids. Then the bottom drops out as the stream enters an intimate, tight Class III–IV gorge for the last 2 miles.

The upper 2-mile stretch from Browntown to Boyds Mill (where Route 622 crosses Route 649) should be run by macho intermediate paddlers who can quickly eddy out above the several strainers and at least one barbed wire fence here. Nevertheless, this part of Gooney Run is otherwise pleasant and seems easier than the 55 feet per mile gradient indicates.

If you put in at Boyds Mill, you have a 2 mile warm-up before entering the 2 mile gorge. Nevertheless, don't enter the gorge unless you can handle numerous long and complex Class III and IV rapids or enjoy long, rocky portages. Also, there are many technical turns which can be difficult for a full sized tandem canoe. The gorge cuts through ancient Precambrian Pedlar granite gneiss and is full of hemlocks, pines and varied hardwoods. The water quality is superb as it flows over and around boulders of every size and shape.

The frequency and complexity of the rapids in the gorge require constant scouting. The drops are blind and strainers may clog them. However, at moderate levels there are usually pools between the drops in which to recover boats and bodies. Although you can't see the hills above this tight, lush gorge, Dickey Ridge towers 1,500 feet on the right and Buck Mountain rises nearly 1,000 feet on the left. Finally, if you must carry a rapid, make sure that you scout the carry all the way: the rapids are long and some cannot be portaged from one side.

However, before jumping on this steep creek (which drops 200 feet in the 2 mile gorge!), please stop at the Route 340 Bridge where Gooney joins the South Fork of the Shenandoah and check the gauge. This paddlers gauge is on a rock face on river left downstream of the bridge. Be careful of traffic when checking the gauge. You need about 3 inches on the gauge for a comfortable paddling level of zero. Between 3 and 9 inches on the gauge, this is a Class III–IV trip as described below. Moving from one to two feet on the gauge, the Gooney Gorge goes from Class IV to Class V because of the relentless gradient and rapids.

After checking the gauge, drop off as many shuttle cars as possible at Karo Landing. The road down to the landing is well marked and just north of the Route 340 Bridge. To reach the put-in, go north on 340, take a right on Route 605 (Poor House Road), then another right at Route 649 (Browntown Road) and drive 2.5 miles to Boyds Mill where Route 622 crosses Route 649. After you arrive, check the gauge on the upstream river right piling of the Route 622 Bridge which indicates a true paddling zero.

Ed Grove bumping down the last drop of Surprise Rapids on Gooney Run. Photo by Bob Walsh.

You can put in a mile downstream at Glen Echo, but parking is more limited and landowners have objected on occasion to paddlers launching here. If you insist on putting in at Glen Echo, get permission if possible and leave only one shuttle car.

Once on the creek at Boyds Mill, the first mile to Glen Echo is a pleasant paddle with one 2 foot dam and two low water bridges as the main rapids. After this, you start downhill through Class II+ rapids that continue for about 3/4 of a mile. Then, as the river bends sharply to the left and enters the gorge, be on the look out for trees in the river. (One protruded into the right side of the river here recently.) Soon below this bend the rapids change from Class II to Class III.

As you begin to work through these rapids, the remoteness and smallness of the gorge make you feel like this is your own personal world of rock and water, Soon you reach a pool formed by a rock pile. Run this 1.5 foot drop center to set up for the Class II rapid below. After a quarter mile of Class II–III action climaxed by the Class III+ double drop of Entrance Rapid and a pool, you reach First Falls. Below a foot on the put-in gauge, First Falls is a boulder sieve that should not be run. Portage on the right. However, above a foot or so, a Class IV route opens. Scout it from the right and run it right.

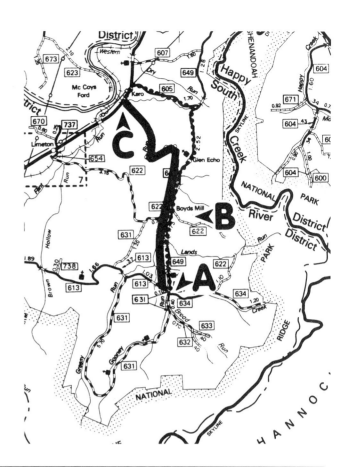

Section: Browntown (Rts. 649/613) to US 340

Counties: Warren

USGS Quads: Chester Gap

Suitable for: Day cruising

Skill Level: Intermediate paddlers with good boat control for the first 3 miles; advanced and expert paddlers for the last 3 miles in the gorge

Months Runnable: After a local rain of at least 2 inches

Interest Highlights: Intimate but very challenging gorge

Scenery: Pretty in spots to beautiful

Difficulty: Class II–III from Browntown to Glen Echo; strong, complex Class III–IV in gorge below with boulder sieve First Falls to carry

Average Width: 20 to 40 feet

Velocity: Fast

Gradient: From Browntown to the gorge 4 miles at 55 feet per mile; the 2 mile gorge averages 100 feet per mile with one mile pushing 120 feet per mile!

Runnable Water Levels:
  Minimum: 3 inches above 0 on gauge just below Route 340 and 0 at gauge on Route 622 bridge, 4 miles above take-out (upstream river right piling)
  Maximum: 2 feet on Route 340 and Route 622 gauges

Hazards: Boulder sieve First Falls (below 1 foot on gauge) near beginning of gorge; several trees in river; high water

Scouting: All major drops, particularly to avoid trees

Portages: Perhaps one or more of the Class IV rapids and boulder sieve First Falls at low water

Rescue Index: Browntown to Glen Echo is accessible; the gorge is remote

Source of Additional Information: Steve Marchi (540) 635-2003; Trace Noel at River Rental Outfillters (540) 635-5050; Don Roberts of the Front Royal Canoe Company (540) 635-5440. Potomac Appalachian Trail Club Map Number 9

Access Points	River Miles	Shuttle Miles
A–B	2	2
B–C	4	4.5

Access Point Ratings:
  A–at Browntown (Rts. 649/613), excellent
  B–at Boyds Mill (Rt. 649/622), good

About 100 yards further downstream is Class VI Second Falls (also known as Folsom Falls). Get out on river right above a room sized rock to scout it. The best line is not easy to reach. Start left of center, then go right behind the flat rock midstream and work to right of center. After this, you follow a tongue of water just to the right of some small rocks midstream, go over a four foot boulder studded ledge, and punch the hole at the bottom.

Below Second Falls, Gooney is a steady mellow slalom course for 75 yards. This is followed by a 50 yard Class III+ drop with two parts—a boulder garden requiring tricky maneuvering at the top followed by a second boulder garden with an eroded ledge at the bottom.

Now you are in one of the few pools in the gorge. Stop on the left above the next drop to scout Ain't No Place to Swim—a long Class III-IV rocky rapid. Start right or left and then move center. After avoiding some rocks you go over a three foot drop into a good sized hole. Eddy out behind the car sized boulder in the center to the left of the hole. Then, take the left channel from the bottom of the eddy and work center as you run the final pair of rocky ledges to finish the rapid. There is a vigorous play hole at the bottom left.

After 3 solid Class III drops is another good Class III-IV rapid—On the Rock. Scout it on the left. If you don't make the tight slot on the left halfway through this rapid, you'll probably get washed up on the van sized rock in midstream and have to finish the rapids backwards through a tighter slot between two rocks in the center of the river. This is not fun because directly below is a two foot drop quickly followed by a three foot drop. After a small pool, the next rapid has a good surfing wave at the bottom.

After about 10 more good rapids is a long Class III-IV boulder garden. Run it from right to left. Below is a pool above a small picnic/campground area followed by Up Against the Wall—a Class III 4-foot sloping ledge. At moderate levels the best place to run this ledge is center angled left.

Surprise (Class IV) is next. It is the last big rapid and forms two long channels around an island. The left channel is best; it starts out as the river bends right through a boulder garden, drops over a couple of 2 foot ledges, and ends with a tight, bumpy 5 foot drop. Just after the pool below is a center/hard left/right S-turn over a corkscrew ledge.

Within sight of Gooney Creek Campground and at the bottom of the last good rapid (Class III) is Catfish Hole—a big hydraulic on the left half of Gooney Run that doesn't easily let go of errant paddlers.

Please note that the Gooney Gorge is well posted against trespassing along Route 649. However, paddlers camping at the campground where US 340 and Gooney meet can easily access the Gooney or hike up its gorge to scout. Also, the river banks in the Gorge are periodically posted, so be discreet.

Gooney Run was originally called Sugar Tree Creek. However, in the 1700s Lord Fairfax lost his favorite hound Gooney here when the dog accidentally drowned in the creek. In Gooney's honor, Lord Fairfax renamed the creek Gooney's Run—a wonderful memorial to man's best friend.

Finally, paddlers should keep their groups small (a maximum of 6 boats) because of the tight, continuous nature of this stream and the ever present potential for new strainers.

Jeff Jarriel running Second Falls on Gooney Run. Photo by Bob Walsh.

North River

The North River Gorge is one of the best trips in Virginia for advanced paddlers. This pristine river begins in a spectacular small gorge in the George Washington National Forest and after 6 miles emerges into pleasant farmland and woods for another 4 miles. The only trouble with the gorge is that the river is so busy you may not have time (particularly at high water) to view the scenery.

The best put-in is at the pretty Forest Service campground on Forest Service Route 4, just after you cross the North River. Do not go a mile upstream to put in at the base of the Staunton Dam. At moderate levels there are few rapids from the dam to the campground, and your passage will be substantially hindered by occasional brush. However, at high levels, adventurous paddlers can put in at various places between the dam and the campground. They should scout the blind turns first, however.

The gauge is on the downstream left abutment of the Route 4 bridge where the North is only 15 feet wide. Despite the 1985 flood, the gauge remains quite accurate, and its range of 0 to 2 feet indicates the difference between minimum and flood levels. If you are running the river at 2 feet, have a very strong party of advanced paddlers. In particular, be alert for alder thickets at several places in this stream which create very dangerous strainers at high water.

Frank Fico in the heavy duty rock garden 30 yards upstream of the five-foot ledge on the North River. Photo by Ron Knipling.

Section: Forest Service campground (F.S. Rt. 4) to Rt. 731

Counties: Augusta

USGS Quads: Stokesville, Parnassus

Suitable for: Day cruising

Skill Level: Advanced

Months Runnable: Generally winter and spring after a good rain

Interest Highlights: Beautiful gorge, Natural Chimneys nearby

Scenery: Beautiful in spots to spectacular

Difficulty: Class II–III with several Class III–IV rapids in 6-mile gorge section; Class I–II in 4-mile section below gorge

Average Width: 15 to 40 feet

Velocity: Fast in gorge; moderate below

Gradient: 48 feet per mile for 6 miles; 40 feet per mile next 4 miles

Runnable Water Levels:
  Minimum: 0 feet on the put-in gauge (F.S. Rt. 4); 3.8 feet on Cootes Store gauge
  Maximum: 2 feet on the put-in gauge (F.S. Rt. 4); 5.8 feet on Cootes Store gauge

Hazards: Several alder thickets in river; occasional trees in river; continuous rapids and hydraulics in high water

Scouting: Class III–IV ledge-rockpile-ledge 3.5 miles into trip and Class III rapids just below (both on river right); Class III–IV rock garden 5 miles into trip (island in center); Class III–IV 5-foot sloping ledge just below (left at moderate levels)

Portages: None, except maybe 1 or more of the Class III–IV rapids

Rescue Index: Remote in gorge; accessible below gorge

Source of Additional Information: National Weather Service, Cootes Store gauge (703) 260-0305

Access Points	River Miles	Shuttle Miles
A–B	6	7
B–C	4	4

Access Point Ratings:
A–at Forest Service campground below Staunton Dam (F.S. Rt. 4), excellent
B–at Stokesville (Rt. 730), good
C–at Rt. 731, good

Ed Grove slides down the sloping five foot ledge on the North; a good left brace helps here.

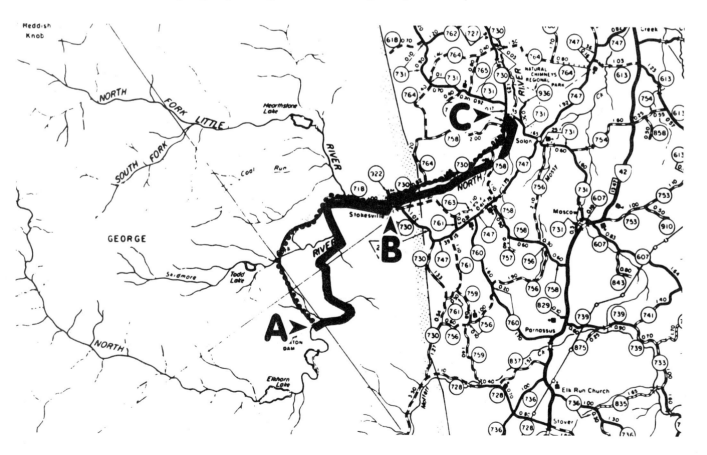

In addition to these alder thickets, be alert for occasional downed trees.

After putting in underneath the hemlocks of this very scenic campground (which is filled on a first-come, first-served basis), you will start dropping over several 1- to 2-foot ledges. Pause and admire the hemlock, rhododendron, and mountain laurel growing here and there as you begin to descend this tight gorge which slices between Trimble Mountain on the left and Lookout Mountain on the right. Between 1 and 1.5 miles below the put-in you will reach a feisty 2-foot ledge and a couple of zesty Class II–III drops followed by a 3-foot ledge.

For the next mile it is ledge city. You first hit a double ledge and then 2 diagonal ledges with squirrelly water. Just below this is a drop through alders that grow in the river; so be careful here, particularly at high water. Toward the end of this mile you make a sharp left turn and then reach a five-ledge sequence. The last two ledges are the largest (2 feet each) with good hydraulics to punch.

Just below this five-ledge sequence you reach a great lunch stop (at least at moderate levels). Here the pink Devonian shale/sandstone forming the banks and riverbed for the entire gorge creates a nice long shelf on the right side of the river. This is just above a nifty, long, flumelike chute with a punchable stopper at the bottom. You really build up velocity in running this drop, so put on your flying goggles and enjoy it.

The next mile eases up somewhat with easier ledges. You then come to an island and a 2-foot drop. Shortly below this and about 3.5 miles into the trip, the river turns right beginning with an innocent-looking rock garden. Get on the right bank and scout the heavy Class III–IV rapid below this easy rock garden entry which features a diagonal 2-foot ledge near the top, a rock pile below this, and a 3-foot ledge at the bottom *perpendicular* to the direction of the river. On a low level run recently, the base of a tree in the river on the left was catching the bow of paddlers running the first diagonal ledge and momentarily trapping them between the tree and the hydraulic formed by the ledge. Also scout the next stiff Class III rapid below this ledge-rockpile-ledge sequence to see that you have a clear path through it, too.

About a half mile below these two rapids is another place with alders in the river; be careful here. In the next three-quarters of a mile you pass an island and several rock gardens. Then you reach a short section with boulders in the river.

About a quarter mile below this or 5 miles into the trip, the left bank becomes a 40-foot-high dirt face. Just downstream the left bank changes into a rock face. Stop on the island in the center of the river by this rock face and scout. On your left is a Class III–IV nasty, intense rock garden that drops 4 feet or so in a short distance. At low levels this rock garden is very technical, requiring precise moves and a center entry to avoid a pin. At higher levels you can enter more to the right but need to avoid being blown into the rock wall at the bottom left of this rapid. For those wishing to avoid this turbulent channel, there is a sneak on the right side of the island which was created by the 1985 flood.

Be ready to rescue boats and bodies quickly because there is a Class III–IV 5-foot ledge 30 yards below. This second drop can be scouted from the left (or right at high water) and is best run tight left with the bow angled right to miss rocks on the left bank. Have a left brace ready at the bottom as you ride the curler down this exciting sloping ledge. There is a great opportunity to take photographs in the center of the river below the second drop. Here you can capture a paddler running the sloping ledge with the nasty rock garden upstream in the background.

In the last mile you will go under a couple of foot bridges while running a ledge and a mellow Class II–III drop. Here the 5-foot banks change to dirt and stone as you leave the gorge. After a zesty chute and a pretty rock formation, you reach the Route 730 bridge at Stokesville which is the first take-out. The left bank is posted, so get permission if you plan to take out there.

Below the bridge the river is channelized with 5-foot cobble banks. The rapids are straightforward Class I–II cobble bars as you pass through woods of Virginia and white pine, sycamore, tulip poplar, and occasional hemlocks. Soon you will smell the essence of cows and know that you are in farm country. On this 4-mile section there are many deep pools as well as occasional trash in the form of tires, a truck, and even a tractor-trailer on the bank. Near the end of this section, below the first bridge, are some striking rocks thrusting high into the sky–this is Castle Hill. After going through a mild alder thicket you reach the final take-out at Route 731. The river below the Route 731 take-out loses gradient and is clearly less interesting. However, if you go river right on Route 731 for a quarter mile southeast of the North River, you are in for a treat. Turn left at the sign there and go a half mile farther to arrive at Natural Chimneys. Here, seven towering limestone columns rise over 100 feet. Nearby are over 100 campsites (even open in winter) and an Olympic-sized swimming pool (open in summer). There is also a special event at Natural Chimneys of interest to history and sporting buffs: on the third Saturday of each August there is jousting on horseback–an event which started way back in 1821. Contestants try their luck spearing three hanging steel rings while galloping full tilt.

Passage Creek

The northern part of the Shenandoah Valley is bisected by the intimidating massif of Massanutten Mountain. From Harrisonburg to Strasburg, Massanutten holds apart the respective valleys of the North and South Forks of the Shenandoah until at Strasburg the North Fork abandons its northeasterly course and turns east to join the South Fork near Front Royal. From the floor of either valley the Massanutten appears as an abrupt, even-topped wall separating the lowlands surrounding it. A look at a map, however, reveals that the Massanutten is itself cleaved throughout its northern half by the defile of Passage Creek. The upper part of Passage Creek provides a restful trip for novices at moderate levels. However, as Passage Creek tumbles from its high repose in the Fort Valley to join the North Fork of the Shenandoah it becomes briefly a cascading torrent that will delight the strong intermediate whitewater paddler.

Upper Passage Creek

Although the Class II–III gorge is the best-known part of Passage Creek, there are over 20 miles of beautiful Class I–II water above the gorge. If you like your streams tiny, tight, cozy, and off the beaten track, then Upper Passage Creek is for you. And, oddly, you can often paddle Upper Passage when Lower Passage (the gorge) is too low. This is mainly because Upper Passage has a lower gradient (12 feet per mile) than the gorge section; also, there are more pools and fewer rock gardens to scrape over in low water.

Passage Creek flows northward through long and narrow Fort Valley between Massanutten Mountain to the east and Green Mountain to the west. Fort Valley is about 4 miles wide and 25 miles long, and Passage Creek runs through its entire length. Since it meanders, Passage Creek is about 35 miles long, of which about 25 to 30 miles can be paddled. The creek flows mostly through pastoral farmland, but there are also numerous hills and Devonian shale cliffs that pop out of the valley along the banks of the creek.

Along its length, it flows through both wooded areas and stretches of open rolling farmland. The land in the valley is privately owned farmland and woodland, but the mountains surrounding the valley are almost all part of George Washington National Forest.

The rapids of Upper Passage Creek are mostly small ledges; often they occur at sharp turns to add to the fun. There are no rapids harder than Class II, but at moderate to high water levels Upper Passage Creek can present some nasty strainers and other obstacles.

There are many access points and thus many possible trips. You can put in as far upstream as Route 769 near Kings Crossing, but the first stretch with reasonably reliable water is that beginning at Route 775 near the village of St. Davids Church.

The 6 miles between St. Davids and Route 758 near Seven Fountains is perhaps the prettiest section of Upper Passage. Zero for this section is about 3.1 feet at Cootes Store or 48 inches vertical clearance under the Route 775 bridge. You can eyeball it from the riffles near this bridge. If the water is 18 inches higher (i.e., 30 inches vertical clearance), it's too high for most boaters. This 6-mile section has great variety–tranquil farmland, dark hollows, picturesque bluffs, and grand views of Massanutten Mountain on your right. One enchanting spot is about a mile below the put-in. The creek leaves an area of open farmland and turns right past two or three shale cliffs and then left through a hollow. On the left in a secluded glen is a quaint, tranquil farmyard. It's hard to understand how such a timelessly-beautiful spot can have such an unfriendly owner. He's usually not around, but if he is, be charming–or quiet–or quick.

About one-half mile below this spot is the potentially dangerous Route 769 bridge near a village called Carmel. At low levels you can go under the bridge with no problem. At moderate to high levels there is not enough clearance, and it could really catch you. After passing a section of open land on the right you enter a wooded area and approach the bridge through a series of small Class I–II turns. You'll see the bridge when you are perhaps 50 yards upstream of it. It's best to work to the left bank for the portage. It is recommended that you scout this bridge from the road before you begin your trip. About a quarter mile below Route 769 there is another low-water bridge that is less hazardous but which will also require a short portage.

About one-half mile farther downstream, a farmer has built two fences across the creek to create a corral for cattle watering. It's easiest to portage them both at once on the left. About a half mile farther there is a steep slope on the left that's dotted with shale outcroppings and beautiful trees and wildflowers. It's just dazzling on an April morning when the redbud and phlox are in bloom.

Route 758 crosses Passage Creek twice. Both are good access points. However, it's worthwhile to paddle on to the second bridge which is near Seven Fountains and about 300 yards off Route 678 (Fort Valley Road). If you paddle on past the second Route 758 bridge, you will have a 100-yard portage. This low-water bridge itself must be

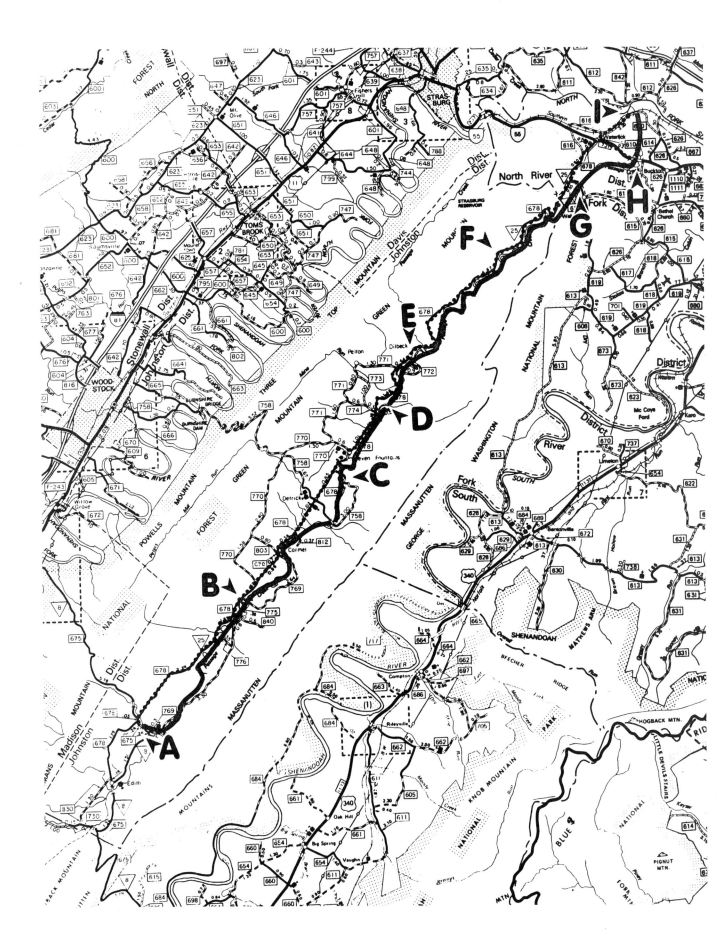

Doug White working to make Z-turn on Passage Creek.

it's a bit bigger here, there are fewer obstacles. There is one wrecked low-water bridge about a mile below Route 774 that requires a carry. Farther downstream, beginning about a half mile from the picnic area, the stream begins to pick up some speed and gradient, giving you a hint that the character of Passage Creek is about to change.

The effects water levels have on stream hazards are dramatically illustrated by a stream like Upper Passage Creek. At low to moderate water levels, there are really no significant hazards except the typical obstacles that one encounters on small streams. On Upper Passage, these are easily negotiable by intermediate or even novice paddlers. It's a perfect stream for kids or novice paddlers. At higher water levels, the character of the stream changes sharply. Overhanging branches that otherwise would be brushed aside suddenly loom large as boat and people catchers. The low-water bridges now have

portaged, and there are two cattle fences just downstream of the bridge. Portage all three obstacles to the left.

The 8-mile Upper Passage trip from Route 774 to the Elizabeth Furnace Picnic Area is also scenic and is the easiest section of Passage Creek to catch up. It's similar in terrain and scenery to the section described above, but the stream has perhaps 50 percent more volume. Because

Section: Kings Crossing (Rt. 769) to Elizabeth Furnace Picnic Area (Rt. 678)

Counties: Shenandoah

USGS Quads: Rileyville, Toms Brook, Strasburg

Suitable for: Day cruising

Skill Level: Novices at moderate levels

Months Runnable: January to mid-May or following a heavy rain

Interest Highlights: Fort Valley and surrounding Massanutten Mountain

Scenery: Pretty to beautiful

Difficulty: Class I–II

Average Width: 10 to 30 feet

Velocity: Moderate

Gradient: First 5 miles, 20 feet per mile; last 16 miles, 10 feet per mile

Runnable Water Levels:
Minimum: 4-foot vertical clearance under Rt. 775 bridge (access point B); 3.1 feet on Cootes Store gauge

Maximum: 2.5 vertical clearance under Rt. 775 bridge (access point B); 5 feet on Cootes Store gauge

Hazards: Several low-water bridges, strainers, high water

Scouting: Before trip scout Rt. 769 bridge for clearance

Portages: Several, mostly short, portages around low-water bridges, footbridges, or obstacles; 100-yard portage at second Rt. 758 bridge (access point C)

Rescue Index: Accessible

Source of Additional Information: National Weather Service, Cootes Store gauge (703) 260-0305; Appalachian Trail Club Map "G"

Access Points	River Miles	Shuttle Miles
A–B	5.0	4.0
B–C	6.0	4.0
C–D	2.0	2.0
D–E	2.5	2.5
E–F	5.5	4.5

Access Point Ratings:
A–at Kings Crossing (Rt. 769), very good
B–at St. Davids Church (Rt. 775), very good
C–near Seven Fountains (Rt. 758), very good
D–Rt. 774, very good
E–Rt. 772, very good
F–Elizabeth Furnace Picnic Area (Rt. 678), very good

the potential to entrap the careless boater. Sharp and tight turns that normally add to the easy delight of the trip suddenly become ominous because of churning currents and possible unseen strainers just beyond. Normally Upper Passage Creek is an easy stream. But Ron Knipling tells this story of his most harried paddling experience ever–on this stream.

"As a novice, I led a group of three tandem open boats, each with one novice and one beginner, and none with extra flotation. Cootes Store was at 5 to 6 feet. Where we put in the water was only about a foot deep and no hazards were apparent. We had scouted the creek at a couple of bridges downstream but didn't perceive the danger. Within a half mile of the put-in, all three boats had capsized trying to avoid a low-water bridge just past a blind turn. One boat broached against the footbridge, and it took the (unprofessional) efforts of all six of us to get it out. At this point the whole group was cold and shaken up. We had three more spills and several more bad bouts with strainers before we were forced to abort the trip just before nightfall. We had paddled about 3 miles in 4 hours. It was bad judgment born of inexperience. The combination of high water, a small, twisty stream, and novice boaters produced a formula for disaster. Fortunately we made it with only the ill consequences of wet clothes, cold bodies, lost glasses, and an embarrassed leader (me). Paddling the stream at normal canoeable levels you wouldn't think it could possibly be that dangerous."

High water can be a hazard on any type of river, but it is particularly hazardous on small streams like Passage

Louis Matacia running Out-of-Sight Rapid on Passage Creek in the early 1970s when aluminum canoes and horse collar life vests were state-of-the-art whitewater gear.

Creek, primarily because of possible entrapment by strainers.

If you like to add some hiking to a day's canoeing, there are numerous trails through the surrounding mountains of George Washington National Forest. One of the prettiest and easiest is the hike to Kennedy Peak on Massanutten Mountain. Drive out of Fort Valley on Route 675 heading toward Luray. When you reach the top of the mountain range, park and take the fire trail north toward Kennedy Peak. The first part of the hike is unspectacular, but as you near Kennedy Peak the hike gets steeper, the vegetation more interesting, and the view more spectacular. At the top of Kennedy Peak is an observation platform that gives you a striking view down the length of Fort Valley and, to the east, the Shenandoah River South Fork, its surrounding valley, and the Blue Ridge looming beyond. It's about a 1.5- to 2-hour round-trip hike.

Lower Passage Creek

Only slightly over an hour from Washington, D.C., the lower part of Passage Creek rewards the paddler with clear water, easy access, towering cliffs and rock formations, rhododendron thickets, and tight, intricate rapids. There is a price, however, and the price is an ever-changing maze of fallen trees at the end of the lower part of the run. Fortunately the worst part of this labyrinth is in relatively calm water so at moderate levels it is more of an inconvenience than a death trap. Route 678 follows the creek throughout the length of the trip. Although it occasionally wanders some distance from the stream, a rescue or a walk-out will not be a disaster.

Upon reaching the Elizabeth Furnace Recreation Area, the mountain closes in on both sides, and Passage Creek begins to head downhill. Putting in at the picnic area the paddler is treated to a swift current and occasional Class I–II gravel bars and rock gardens for a mile or so.

Just after Passage Creek approaches the road, the good stuff begins. The first Class II–III ledge is a tight right turn with a turbulent approach. This is followed by a long rock garden and a 2-foot ledge. You then negotiate a short rock garden as the creek nears the road again nearly 2 miles into the trip.

Now the good stuff gets better for a half mile or so. You first have a low Class III rapid where you stay right for two drops, cut sharply left, and finish in an eddy on the left below a large rock shelf that slopes from the road down into the water. During nice weekends this sloping rock is a favorite hangout for anglers and sunbathers. It's worth noting this spot because just below is Z Turn–the toughest technical rapid on the creek. Here you have a tight Class III right-left-right move, which you can boat scout at moderate

Section: Elizabeth Furnace Picnic Area (Rt. 678) to Rt. 55 or Rt. 610

Counties: Shenandoah and Warren

USGS Quads: Strasburg

Suitable for: Day cruising

Skill Level: Strong intermediates at moderate levels; advanced at higher levels

Months Runnable: January to mid-May or following a heavy rain

Interest Highlights: Pretty gorge

Scenery: Beautiful

Difficulty: Class II–III at moderate levels; Class III–IV at high levels

Average Width: 20 to 45 feet

Velocity: Moderate to fast

Gradient: 40 feet per mile average; 60 feet per mile in steepest section

Runnable Water Levels:
Minimum: 0 feet on Rt. 55 gauge; 3.3 feet on Cootes Store gauge

Maximum: 3 feet on Rt. 55 gauge; 6 feet on Cootes Store gauge

Hazards: Difficult rapids, logjams, strainers, anglers, dam

Scouting: Scouting from road possible for most difficult rapids; Out-of-Sight Rapids

Portages: Dam at fish hatchery; probably some logjams to carry around below dam

Rescue Index: Accessible

Source of Additional Information: National Weather Service, Cootes Store gauge, (703) 260-0305

Access Points	River Miles	Shuttle Miles
F–G	3.5	4
G–H	2.5	2
F–H	6	6
F–I	7	7

Access Point Ratings:
F–Elizabeth Furnace Picnic Area (Rt. 678), very good
G–at Fish Hatchery Bridge (Rt. 613), good
H–at Rt. 55, good
I–at Rt. 610, very good

levels. The key to running Z Turn successfully is making the hard left as you enter the steep middle part of the rapid. This hard left move is a great spot for right handed paddlers to practice their cross bow draws.

Below Z Turn, Passage Creek again pools and moves away from the road. A high rock wall appears on the right bank. You have now arrived at Class III Out-of-Sight Rapids. Scout from the left and set throw ropes on the left for nervous first-timers. At low levels the main current goes over a drop on the left and then over a drop/hole on the right. However, there are several routes through this rapid. There is a good surfing spot just below the main two drops of this rapid at moderate levels. Incidentally, Out-of-Sight Rapids got its name in a very interesting way. A hard core motorcyclist was standing on the bank and looking at Passage Creek one day. Suddenly, he saw a canoe run this rapid and immediately exclaimed, "Out of Sight!" So, although this rapid is away from the road, it actually got its name from a phrase popular at the time.

After Out-of-Sight Rapids the creek pools and drops over a tight Class III chute which is probably the biggest abrupt drop in the trip. You can look it over from the left, too. Just below is a lesser but busy Class II–III rocky drop. This is followed shortly by two Class II–III rock gardens. The river then returns to the road by a masonry wall. Here you have a Class II–III drop with a hole on the left. The pool below is called Blue Hole.

Paddlers just looking for the best rapids and a quick trip can take out here. However, at high water all boaters should take out at this spot because of what lies below. First, a quarter mile later comes the fish hatchery dam–a 6-foot-high wier. The right side of the dam looks like the proper portage route but this is not the case! Years of paddlers walking over this area have severely eroded the soil there and portaging on the right side of the dam is prohibited. Carry on the left side with care. In high water beware of the flow going over the dam.

Below the hatchery dam the stream begins to flow with a decreased gradient and the load of rock rubble and timber carried by the creek through the steep section above is deposited. You encounter two very long Class II rock gardens just after the dam. Next comes the Fish Hatchery Road Bridge which can be an emergency take-out if the current doesn't blow you by at high water. Below this bridge you have another long rock garden and pretty Silurian shale cliffs appear on the right. However, after you reach these shale cliffs, Passage Creek divides around numerous small islands, and between these islands there may be tangles of fallen trees, debris, and branches. These obstacles are the other reason for taking out above the fish hatchery dam at high water. Even though the gradient has decreased, high water can make the wooded tangles very dangerous. However, at moderate levels, the section below the dam has some good Class II drops for alert paddlers. Nevertheless, use extreme care when choosing which route to run between the islands and always be prepared to get to shore quickly. The route through this maze changes with every high-water season, so the paddler is on his own in negotiating the puzzle. Below the jackstraw pile the creek flows swiftly between wooded banks until the Route 55 bridge at Waterlick heaves into view. This road is a heavily used truck route, so take out just above the bridge on river right even though you have to muscle your boat up a steep slope to the dirt road there.

Since Route 55 is a rather tough take-out, you can make things easier on yourself by paddling a mile and a quarter farther to an easier take-out by Route 610 just beyond the tracks of the Southern Railroad. This is a couple of hundred yards before Passage Creek joins the North Fork of the Shenandoah River. On this short stretch, Passage Creek continues with Class I–II rapids. However, there are two hazards other than the occasional trees and debris in the stream. First, there are two barbed wire fences for which to be alert. Recently, the last fence was just above the take-out. The second hazard is the Route 610 low-water bridge at the take-out. Look it over while on the shuttle (particularly at high water), and make sure you eddy out above this bridge. Also, parking is tight at both Route 55 and Route 610 take-outs, so be prepared to leave only one or two shuttle cars there.

Passage Creek is a heavily fished trout stream, stocked, as one would expect, from the hatchery at the exit from the steep section. Along with most of the small streams in the state, we highly recommend that Passage Creek not be paddled when the river is heavily used by trout fishermen (perhaps some times in early spring).

A high-speed collision with a wading angler would be a disaster in both the physical and public relations areas, especially since there may be many canoeist-hating anglers standing by in the event of a mishap.

For those with a propensity for hiking near Lower Passage Creek, a trip to Signal Knob via the Signal Knob Trail will certainly be worthwhile. The trail begins at a small parking area off the road on the west side of the canyon near the Elizabeth Furnace Campground and leads to a prominent peak used as an observation post by both sides during the Civil War.

The Massanutten Trail heads south from the fish hatchery and follows the crest of Massanutten Mountain all the way to Route 33 east of Harrisonburg. This entire area lies within the George Washington National Forest which is a public hunting area, so wear bright clothing when hiking during hunting season.

Other streams in the area include Cedar Creek, flowing into the North Fork from the north nearby; South Fork of the Shenandoah to the south; and the Lost River just over the West Virginia line to the west. Two great short trips that can be fit into one day are the Passage Creek Gorge and the Lost River Gorge—which is described by the author in *Applachian Whitewater: Volume II - The Central Mountains.*

Ron Knipling running a juicy drop on Passage Creek.

Shenandoah River

The Shenandoah River is legendary throughout the world. In song, story, and among canoeists it is part of the vocabulary of the English-speaking world. The valley through which it flows is synonymous with agricultural richness, particularly in apples, and the very name conjures images of pastoral serenity and farm living. For the paddler the Shenandoah offers mostly mild whitewater and provides a beautiful river experience, running through a combination of scenic farmland and steep mountain forest. The Shenandoah was beloved by the Indians who lived and traveled here before the coming of the Europeans. The valley seems to have been largely conserved as a hunting ground in the years immediately preceding the arrival of the colonists, although prehistoric villages continue to be found along the South Fork. The aboriginal villages were very small and tended to revolve around cave dwellings in the limestone cliffs of the valley. The inhabitants of these villages greatly predated the Susquehannocks and Catawbas of popular legend and were apparently not related culturally or racially to these later Indians.

The identity of the first European to see the Shenandoah Valley is a matter of controversy. There is evidence that French Jesuits visited the area before 1632. John Lederer, the early geographer, certainly was there in 1669. Later, German, Dutch, and Scottish immigrants from Pennsylvania began settling in the valley of the Shenandoah. The names of their descendants are still evident on the mailboxes along Route 11 and other roads in the valley. During the Civil War, the Shenandoah Valley was of critical importance to both sides. The farms of the valley provided a large portion of the foodstuffs necessary to keep the armies of the Confederacy operating, and the strategic location of the valley meant that an army unchecked there could easily threaten Washington, D.C. As a result the valley was the site of constant fighting throughout the war. The most famous of the campaigns fought there was Stonewall Jackson's campaign in the spring of 1862. During this period, Jackson tied up Federal armies of several times his own strength, weakening the Northern attempt to take Richmond and keeping the Federal leadership in constant anxiety for the safety of the Northern capital. Later in the war, when Southern fortunes began to sink, Federal General Philip Sheridan was charged with the duty of reducing the valley to such an extent that, "a crow flying over the valley would have to carry his own rations." Following a scorched earth policy, Sheridan destroyed every barn, burned every crop, and killed animals throughout the length and breadth of the valley, causing great hardship among the inhabitants.

When, as predicted by Stonewall Jackson, the valley was destroyed, so went the Confederacy.

Morgan Ford (Route 624) to Berrys Ferry (US 50)

This relaxing, easy 12-mile trip on the Shenandoah is a great day-trip for beginning paddlers. The scenery is good–well-tended farms and summer homes in a large scenic valley. The landmarks along this section have truly eye-catching names and entice the paddler to make this run just to check them out. Specifically, you will pass by such exotic places as Treasure Island, Lovers Leap, Robinson Crusoe Island, and (would you believe?) The Blue Ball. There are also a couple of nice Class I–II ledges and a few other minor rapids to occasionally spice up the trip. However, this stretch is mostly flatwater with good current.

The put-in is on river right below the low-water bridge at Morgan Ford on Route 624. Just below is an easy Class I rapid. There are two similar rapids at the end of the first and second mile. Three miles into the trip, as you pass the summer homes of Shenandoah Farms on the right shore, start looking for a horizon line. This signals a Class II 2-foot ledge–the best drop of the trip. Beginners should look this ledge over before running it. A quarter mile downstream is a 1-foot ledge as the river bends right. A mile and a half below this ledge and halfway through the trip comes Treasure Island. This is followed by mile-long Hardin Island. The larger river channel is to the left of these islands.

Shortly after Hardin Island, the river turns sharply right. Just after this turn are some high rocky bluffs on river left called Lovers Leap. When the trees are bare, you can see several small caves in these bluffs.

A mile below Lovers Leap you will see a hill on river right with an amazing name–The Blue Ball. Just below the Blue Ball is a large rock in the river called White Horse Rock. Stop and check this rock out. Less than half a mile below this rock is Swift Shoals, a long, easy Class I descent.

After Swift Shoals, you pass Gibson Ridge on the right and then Robinson Crusoe Island on the right. The take-out is another half mile downstream on river left where Route 622 goes under Berrys Ferry Bridge (US 50).

A good level for this trip is 2 feet on the Front Royal gauge. At 3 feet, all rapids are washed out. The bare minimum is 1 foot on the gauge. One final good point about this trip is that the Shenandoah is runnable most of the year. Only after an extended dry spell (or in the dog days of summer) is it too low to paddle.

Section: Morgan Ford (Rt. 624) to Berrys Ferry (US 50/Rt. 622)

Counties: Warren and Clarke

USGS Quads: Linden, Boyce

Suitable for: Day cruising and camping

Skill Level: Beginners except at high water

Months Runnable: Most of year except late summer

Interest Highlights: Pretty valley, Blue Ridge Mountains, caves

Scenery: Pretty to beautiful in spots

Difficulty: Class I–II

Average Width: 100 to 130 feet

Velocity: Moderate

Gradient: 5 feet per mile

Runnable Water Levels:
 Minimum: 1 foot on the Front Royal gauge
 Maximum: 4 feet on the Front Royal gauge

Hazards: Occasional trees in river

Scouting: None, except beginners should look at 2-foot ledge 3 miles into trip

Portages: None

Rescue Index: Generally accessible though somewhat remote in spots

Source of Additional Information: National Weather Service, Front Royal gauge (703) 260-0305

Access Points	River Miles	Shuttle Miles
A–B	12.5	11

Access Point Ratings:
 A–at Morgan Ford Bridge (Rt. 624), very good
 B–at Berrys Ferry (Rt. 50/622), very good

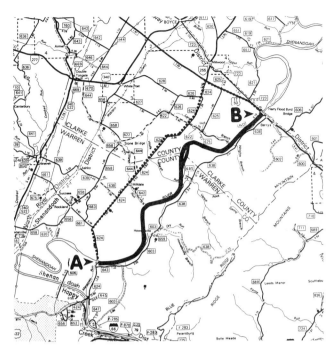

Berrys Ferry (US 50) to Castleman Ferry (Route 7)

This 15-mile section is an excellent trip for beginning paddlers who would like to camp overnight on the river. Here the Shenandoah passes through a large valley with the Blue Ridge Mountains visible in the distance. In particular, scout troops and other youth groups will find this a good first experience with moving water. The only warning is for beginners to stay off this river in high water (above 4 feet on the Front Royal gauge) and away from downed trees (strainers) where the current is fast. With a gradient of only 3 feet per mile this section is basically flatwater, particularly at the start and end of the trip. Only an occasional ledge or riffle breaks the calm. On the other hand, this section is runnable for most of the year–except after a long dry period or in the dead of summer.

The put-in is from Route 622 where it goes under the Berrys Ferry (US 50) bridge. A half mile downstream is Burwell Island–the largest island on the Shenandoah. Take the channel to the right of this 1.5-mile-long island and be alert for downed trees. At the end of Burwell Island, you can go left back to the main channel of the river or go right around a second island only a quarter of a mile long.

After another mile, the river begins to make a 180-degree turn at Calmes Neck. About a mile later you round this bend, and after some riffles you'll find good access on river left from Route 621 about 5 miles below Berrys Ferry. Below this access the riffles continue and less than a quarter mile downstream is a cave in a rocky bluff 100 feet above the river. The entrance is 10 feet square, and energetic paddlers can climb up to check it out. The view from the front of the cave is impressive. When foliage is on the trees, however, this cave is hidden.

Minor riffles and ledges continue for a half mile below this cave. Another half mile and you reach a V-shaped Indian fish dam. About three-quarters of a mile downstream (as the river begins to make a big horseshoe bend) is an interesting side trip on river right. Here there are two sinkholes not far from the right bank. Nearly a mile below these sink holes and after the horseshoe bend are a

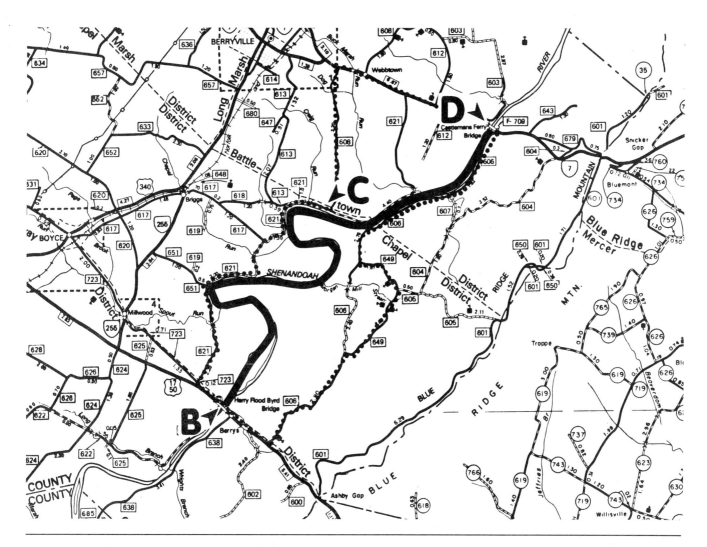

Section: Berrys Ferry (US 50/Rt.622) to Castleman Ferry (Rt. 7/606)

Counties: Clarke

USGS Quads: Boyce, Ashby Gap, Berryville

Suitable for: Day cruising and camping

Skill Level: Beginners except at high water

Months Runnable: Most of the year except late summer

Interest Highlights: Pretty valley, Blue Ridge Mountains, cave, Indian fish dam

Scenery: Pretty to beautiful in spots

Difficulty: Class A-I with 1 Class II

Average Width: 110 to 140 feet

Velocity: Moderate

Gradient: 3 feet per mile

Runnable Water Levels:
  Minimum: 1 foot on the Front Royal gauge
  Maximum: 4 feet on the Front Royal gauge

Hazards: Occasional trees in river

Scouting: None

Portages: None

Rescue Index: Generally accessible though somewhat remote in spots

Source of Additional Information: National Weather Service, Front Royal gauge (703) 260-0305

Access Points	River Miles	Shuttle Miles
B–C	10	9
C–D	15	11

Access Point Ratings:
  B–at Berry Ferry (US 50/Rt. 622), very good
  C–at Lock Landing (Rt. 621), excellent
  D–at Castleman Ferry (Rt. 7/606), very good

couple of mellow small Class II ledges. Then the river bends right, goes for a mile, and then bends right again. A half mile below this bend and 10 miles into the trip is Lock Public Landing (Route 621) on river left. For those not wanting to camp overnight on the river, this makes a good day-trip take-out.

Just below Lock Public Landing are two islands. The first is only a few hundred yards long. The second is about a mile long. Go right of this island for better scenery. Just below the second island is a long series of riffles which mark Old Shepherd Ford. A mile below Old Shepherd Ford are some more riffles and then flatwater for 2.5 miles until the last set of riffles just before the take-out at Castleman Ferry on river right where Routes 606 and 7 cross.

The best water levels for this section are between 1 and 3 feet on the Front Royal gauge–the same as for the section just upstream.

Castleman Ferry (Route 7) to Bloomery (Route 9)

This 14-mile section of the Shenandoah is much like the section just above except that there are more mini-ledges along the way. However, this trip can be shortened more easily because there are three river left access points in West Virginia before you get to Route 9: Riverside (4 miles), Meyerstown (7.5 miles), and Shannondale Road (10 miles). They are on three successive bends in the river.

This trip is primarily in West Virginia. On your right there are the 1,500-foot-high Blue Ridge Mountains with the scenic Appalachian Trail following their ridge lines. Two miles into the trip you pass some large islands; then you enter West Virginia. Just past the first access point at Riverside is the site of Old Boyds Ferry. Over a mile later is a half-mile stretch of tiny ledges which are covered at high water. A mile below this you pass the Meyerstown access point at Avon Bend and the site of Old Meyers Ferry. In the next couple of miles there are a few ledges before you reach Shannondale Road and the old site of Shannondale Ferry as the river makes another large bend

to the right. About a mile below Shannondale Road is the best rapids of the trip - a Class II set of ledges which you run center. The last 2 miles to Bloomery is flatwater.

The best camping spots are the big islands near the beginning of this stretch just before you enter West Virginia. Elsewhere most of the land is privately owned, and it could be difficult to get permission to camp.

The fishing is great on this stretch—particularly between Riverside and Shannondale Springs (a mile below Shannondale Road). The best fishing is for smallmouth bass and catfish. Muskie also lurk in the deep pools near Shannondale Springs and below.

When you reach Route 9, the best take-out is on river right just below the bridge. Paddling the section from Route 9 to Millville is not recommended. The scenery changes for the worse, and there is a 20-foot dam that has a difficult portage on posted land.

Bull Falls and the Staircase

One of the true classic Class II–III trips for accomplished intermediates and shepherded novices who want to sharpen their paddling skills is Bull Falls and the Staircase. If you are willing to pay the admission price of 2 to 3 miles of flatwater, the remaining 3.5 miles of whitewater make the trip worthwhile. But the flatwater also has a positive side: it's a lazy start for rafters, boaters, and experienced tubers

Grant Grove tubing through a narrow slot at Bull Falls on the Shenandoah.

Greg Grove running the classic route through Bull Falls (third slot from the left bank) with the rooster-tail by his paddle.

as well as a perfect opportunity to sharpen novices on whitewater strokes they will soon need.

Almost halfway through the trip, Bull Falls (Class III) starts off the more serious whitewater with a bang. Below Bull Falls there are fairly continuous Class I and Class II rapids through the Staircase until Harpers Ferry (emergency take-out only!) is reached. Below this point

there still is Whitehorse Rapids (Class II–III) before the usual take-out at Sandy Hook. The trip from Millville to Sandy Hook is a very scenic one. The low hills where the Shenandoah and Potomac Rivers merge are very pretty, and there is the charming and historic town of Harpers Ferry to poke around in after the trip. Also, this is a dependable trip because the rivers hold their water for

---

Section: Castleman Ferry (Rt. 7/606) to Bloomery (Rt. 9)

Counties: Clarke (VA), Jefferson (WV)

USGS Quads: Ashby Gap, Berryville, Round Hill, Charles Town

Suitable for: Day cruising and camping

Skill Level: Beginners except at high water

Months Runnable: Most of year except for a prolonged dry period in late summer

Interest Highlights: Pretty valley, Blue Ridge Mountains, numerous little ledges, fishing

Scenery: Pretty to beautiful in spots

Difficulty: Class I–II

Average Width: 200 to 400 feet

Velocity: Slow to moderate

Gradient: 2 feet per mile

Runnable Water Levels:
 Minimum: 1 foot on the Front Royal gauge
 Maximum: 4 feet on the Front Royal gauge

Hazards: Maybe an occasional tree in river

Scouting: None

Portages: None

Rescue Index: Generally accessible

Source of Additional Information: National Weather Service, Front Royal gauge (703) 260-0305

Access Points	River Miles	Shuttle Miles
D–E	14	13

Access Point Ratings:
 D–at Castleman Ferry (Rt. 7/606), very good
 E–at Bloomery (Rt. 9), good

virtually the entire year. The only dangerous time is when the river is too high on occasion in winter and spring and rarely during other times of the year.

For the put-in on Bloomery Road, launch underneath the power lines by the transformer station at the outskirts of Millville, or, to avoid some of the flatwater, put in farther downstream. About the last put-in is River and Trail Outfitters—a good one and a quarter miles below the transformer station. However, you should get permission from the Outfitters and join an organized club trip if possible. Finally, be careful about leaving shuttle cars at isolated spots on Bloomery Road; thieves have broken into unattended cars on numerous occasions. Having a gracious camper or outfitter keep an eye on your shuttle cars would probably be very wise.

Wherever you put in along this stretch, notice that there are many camping spots on river left. Also, silver maples, sycamores, cottonwoods, box elders, and occasional ashes line the riverbanks. The Route 340 shuttle road is lined with royal paulownia trees, which are breathtaking in mid-spring when they are covered with large, light purple flowers. From the put-in to Bull Falls 2 to 3 miles downstream the river is popular for fishing in

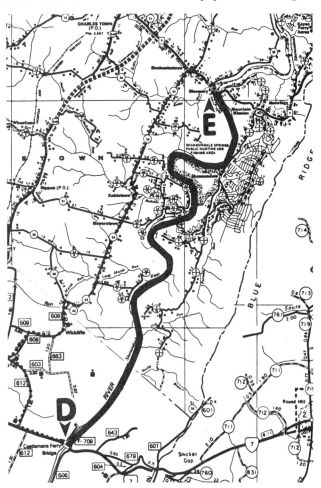

canoes, johnboats, and other watercraft. Smallmouth bass, bluegills, channel catfish, and the omnipresent carp are the primary fish that swim these waters. Also, be alert for bird life: great blue herons, turkey vultures, ducks, geese, and swallows dart above the paddler. On one trip a majestic pileated woodpecker was even sighted.

Just below the power line put-in the paddler has the choice of running a Class I channel between two islands in the center of the river or continuing down the left to Class I riffles at the end of the second island. About a half mile downstream you will pass the Millville gauge on the left which is followed by the put-ins for various outfitters on the left and summer homes on the right.

Over 2 miles from the power line put-in, some small islands appear on the right, and you will be heading straight toward a hill roughly 200 feet high. Approaching this hill several minutes later you'll see rocks across the right and center of the river with a long Class II rock garden on the left. Notice the nice stone wall supporting the railroad track and the interesting rock formations on the left when passing through this rapid. There are also one or two mild surfing spots near the bottom of this slalom.

Then, in the pool below this rapid, look for an exposed broad, flat ledge blocking most of the river. This is your signal to stop on the 50-foot-long section of the rock ledge between the current flowing through a narrow notch on the right and diagonally from right to left over a more powerful drop to the left. Novices should be shepherded as they ferry to catch this ledge in fast moving water.

Congratulations. After 3 miles of warm-up you have arrived at Bull Falls and novices can now start quivering. At low and medium levels the long, low ledge here is a perfect place to beach boats, rafts, and tubes before scouting, eating lunch, or watching the continuous parade of boats and bodies go over the falls. However, in 1991 there was a huge tree on this ledge (now gone) which reduced spaces for boats.

The most classic route here is the 3- to 4-foot Class III drop immediately to the left of the large, low scouting ledge. The paddler should start this run reasonably close to the scouting ledge to prevent being carried too far left by the current. Upon reaching the drop, notice that there is a just exposed rock (low water) or a rooster-tail (higher water) about 5 feet from the scouting ledge. Turn hard right 90 degrees and run this drop on the tongue just to the left of this rock/rooster-tail. The reason for running this drop tight right is simple: the farther left one goes the more chance there is of hitting a submerged rock in the channel.

After running this drop, keep your boat parallel with the current because at lower levels a hydraulic about 25 feet below can flip those who drop into it sideways. Incidentally, this hydraulic is a great teacher for those who

Section: Millville, WV to Sandy Hook, MD

Counties: Washington (MD) and Jefferson (WV)

USGS Quads: Charles Town, Harpers Ferry

Suitable for: Day-trip cruising

Skill Level: Shepherded novices and intermediates (moderate levels); advanced paddlers (high levels)

Months Runnable: Most of the year except for extended dry periods

Interest Highlights: Scenic confluence of Shenandoah and Potomac Rivers; historic town of Harpers Ferry

Scenery: Pretty to beautiful in spots

Difficulty: Class II–III at moderate levels; Class III–IV at high levels

Average Width: 250 to 1,000 feet

Velocity: Moderate to fast

Gradient: 10 feet per mile; 3.5 miles at 15–20 feet per mile

Runnable Water Levels:
  Minimum: 1.8 feet on Millville gauge
  Maximum: 5.5 feet on Millville gauge

Hazards: Occasional trees in river

Scouting: Bull Falls (Class III)

Portages: None

Rescue Index: Accessible

Source of Additional Information: National Weather Service, Millville gauge (703) 260-0305; River and Trail Outfitters (301) 695-5177

Access Points	River Miles	Shuttle Miles
F–G	6.5	8

Access Point Ratings:
  F–at Bloomery Road, excellent
  G–at Sandy Hook Road, fair - however the railroad closed this takeout in 1995; call River and Trail Outfitters for current status

want to explore the world of sideways hole sitting. It is gentle enough not to be a keeper but tough enough to bounce boaters around a bit; sometimes considerable effort is required to exit. If you plan on sitting in it sideways, have flotation in your boat and wear a helmet–the ledge is shallow. Also, have a rescue boater nearby to pick up the pieces in the pool below. As the Millville gauge reaches 3 feet, this hole starts to wash out and is not as grabby.

Getting back to Bull Falls, the classic drop described above is actually the third runnable slot from the left bank. To run the other two, either scout them from below after running Bull Falls the classic way or look them over from the railroad tracks on the left after beaching your boat upstream. The drop closest to the railroad tracks is basically two drops (Class II–III), which can be run center. The second drop from the left (low Class III) can also be run, but scout it first to avoid a nasty rock near the bottom.

The fourth slot (on the right of the scouting rock) is a Class II–III rapid with a 1-foot ledge on the top into a narrow slot below that drops 2 to 3 feet. Novice paddlers and tubers too nervous about the classic drop just to the left of the scouting rock can run this one if they have good boat control. Incidentally, this slot also has a small surfing spot near the end at moderate levels. Also, this chute was blocked in early 1992 by a large tree (now gone).

The adventurous can explore other drops farther to the right on this riverwide ledge. The first of these is a straight drop which used to have a tree lodged in the normal runout. The next drop is a narrow slot with a nasty rock to dodge

immediately below entry. There are perhaps four other possibilities farther to the right that are unrunnable at low water and may be possibilities at high water, particularly a rocky slalom on the extreme right.

The great thing about Bull Falls is that the easy carry over the scouting rock allows paddlers many opportunities to run this rapid. They can either take alternate routes or try again if they don't run it right the first time. However, at really high levels, this riverwide ledge is covered, and parts of Bull Falls take on Class IV characteristics.

After a hopefully invigorating stop at Bull Falls, one reaches a 50-yard pool before hitting 50 yards of Class I–II standing waves called Bulls Tail Rapids. These are followed by another 50-yard pool and a Class II ledgy drop (Lunch Stop Ledge) best taken on the far right at lower levels. A nice long pool follows, and then the river splits in several places over the remains of an old diversion dam built about 1800. Going from right to left, the first three splits are straightforward Class I–II drops over covered cobbles with some riffles below. The last alternative on the extreme left, a small Class I–II slalom, gives one the feeling of running a creek.

From the long pool below the splits you can clearly see the first US 340 bridge. You are now about to begin the well-known Staircase—so named because it is a stairstep-like series of ledges which continue for a good mile. At lower levels this mile is generally Class II, but at high levels it starts taking on Class IV characteristics because of its length, strength, complexity, and the big holes that develop.

The US 340 bridge marks 4.5 miles from the transformer station put-in and is about halfway down the Staircase. At low levels the upper half of the Staircase tests one's water-reading ability because it is very picky. Perhaps the best route at lower levels is to start on the left and then work toward the center. Just above the center abutment of the bridge is a 1.5-foot ledge which can be run to the right or left of the abutment. The ledge also offers surfing opportunities.

After getting a breather by the center bridge abutment, paddlers can continue their Staircase descent. Just below the abutment to the right is another nice 1.5-foot ledge followed by 100–200 yards of little ledges. Then there is a spicy Class II–III double drop in river center over two 2-foot ledges called Hesitation Ledge by local paddlers. Another 100 yards of small ledges follow, and you then find yourself in a series of nicer Class II ledges and surfing spots until you reach a 10 foot-high wall with a 10-foot circular hole in it on river left. These are the ruins of an old cotton mill. Just below this wall is the Harpers Ferry beach.

However, because of congestion, the National Park Service will no longer let paddlers take out here and discourages boaters from stopping here except in emergencies. So, continue downstream and within a half mile you will reach the confluence of the Potomac and the Shenandoah. Greeting you at this confluence are the abutment remains of an old bridge on the Shenandoah, a working railroad bridge over the Potomac, a striking hill

1,200 feet above the river, and a railroad tunnel. Once past the confluence, look back upstream at the pretty village of Harpers Ferry nestled in the trees.

The last mile begins with an easy Class I set of waves with a good surfing spot on the left. A couple of minutes later you'll encounter a pleasant 50-yard run of Class I–II waves (Mad Dog Rapid). Shortly below these waves the river flows between two large rocks on the left with some impressive waves below. This is Whitehorse Rapids. At the top are a couple of surfing possibilities at reasonable levels and below are about 50 yards of vigorous Class II–III waves which become Class III at higher levels. There are also two routes to the right of Whitehorse that should be looked at before being run.

Just below Whitehorse, pick up any errant boats and boaters and begin looking for a wall on the left. The second Route 340 bridge looms just below. After several minutes you will notice a sandy beach and a 3- to 4-foot sandy hill instead of a wall. This is the first possible take-out at Sandy Hook, but if you go a couple of minutes farther downstream and remain about 100 yards or so upstream of the bridge, you will find another beach. This is the preferred take-out because the walk takes you over more gradual terrain. This 125-yard portage first goes over the C & O Canal towpath (which is also the Appalachian Trail here), then continues down across some broken cross ties over a muddy stream (the old canal), and finally over the railroad tracks to Sandy Hook Road. Be very careful when crossing the tracks here; freight trains pass frequently at a good clip.

Grayson Grove at the scenic confluence of the Shenandoah and Potomac at Harpers Ferry.

Unfortunately, it is hard to find a place to park cars at Sandy Hook. You basically have a few sloping places next to the railroad track or in people's driveways on the other side of Sandy Hook Road, but parking in driveways is not recommended unless you get permission. So leave as few cars as possible and watch your valuables; there have been some thefts here, too. Perhaps the best way of dealing with the shuttle for this trip is by conning a couple of shuttle bunnies (or bucks) to do the chore. However, in 1995 the railroad closed the Sandy Hook take-out. Call River and Trail Outfitters to see if it has been reopened.

One can also take out on river right just above the Route 340 bridge at Patoma Wayside, but the portage is longer, you cannot leave shuttle vehicles there, and you have to carry up a nasty little hill at the very end. On the other hand, a nice little cascade from a nearby stream provides welcome wet relief on hot days.

Harpers Ferry is rich in history. The first settler, a trader named Peter Stephens, arrived in 1733 and set up a primitive ferry service at the junction of the Potomac and Shenandoah Rivers. Robert Harper, a millwright and the man for whom the town is named, settled here in 1747 and built a mill. The original ferry and mill are long gone. In the 1790s George Washington was instrumental in establishing a national armory here. By 1801 the armory was producing weapons, and arms produced at Harpers Ferry were used by Lewis and Clark on their famous westward expedition of 1804–1806. The arrival of the C & O Canal and the B & O Railroad in the 1830s generated prosperity, and by the 1850s Harpers Ferry had 3,000 residents.

In 1859, however, John Brown's raid on the eve of the Civil War thrust the town into national prominence and set the stage for its eventual decline. When the Civil War began in 1861, the armory and arsenal buildings were burned to prevent them from falling into Confederate hands. Because of the town's geographic location and railway system, both the Union and Confederate forces occupied the town intermittently throughout the war. Discouraged by war damage and fewer jobs, many people soon left. The finishing blow to the town was dealt by a series of devastating floods in the late 1800s.

Harpers Ferry has since been restored by the National Park Service and today is a delightful place to visit. Besides restored streets, shops, houses, and public buildings, there are other points of interest. On the Shenandoah side above the town is Jefferson Rock. Here, in 1783, Thomas Jefferson was so taken with the view he thought it was "worth a voyage across the Atlantic." Not far from this rock is the grave of Robert Harper and a very interesting cemetery. On the left side of the Potomac River across from Harpers Ferry is the Appalachian Trail and the C & O Canal towpath for day hikers and backpackers.

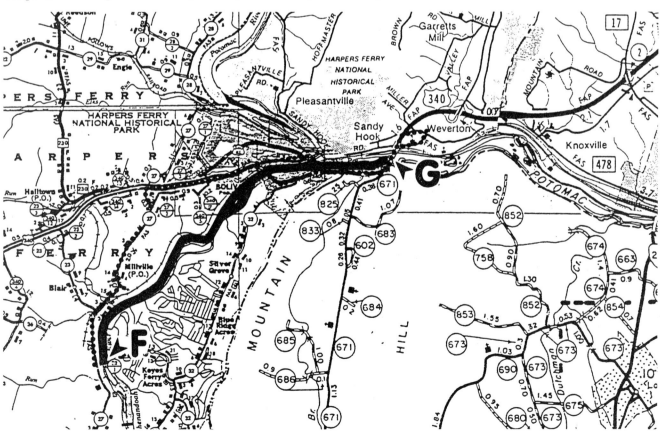

North Fork of the Shenandoah

Riverside Church (Route 921) to Cootes Store (Route 259)

Although the flood of November 1985 significantly damaged the riverbed and banks of the North Fork of the Shenandoah, this is still a scenic and worthwhile trip providing an interesting variety of water. The 9 miles from Riverside Church to Cootes Store primarily drops over cobble bars with numerous chutes and turns. Novice paddlers should be shepherded because of the danger of occasional downed trees in these chutes. Without the trees, these cobbles, chutes, and turns are Class I–II in moderate water. The second half of the trip (beginning at the Route 612 bridge) provides better scenery and more interesting rapids. On the other hand, if there is a fair amount of water, and if you want a longer trip, you can put in at Bergton (Route 820) several miles upstream of Riverside Church. The rapids on this upper section are similar to those just below Riverside Church.

The preferred put-in is Riverside Church. However, when unloading your boat, you may wonder where the church is. It's gone! The flood of November 1985 swept it away, and only part of its white foundation remains. This area is now a parking lot for anglers who want to try to catch the rainbow, brown, and brook trout stocked in this river.

Incidentally, be careful when there are many fishermen using the North Fork–perhaps in early spring. Also, when putting in at Riverside Church, you may need to tread lightly; a flock of geese inhabited this area recently and their dark deposits made the area a minefield for folks who don't watch their step.

While putting in, you will find yourself in a broad valley with mountains in the distance. For the first half of the trip you will paddle through farmland with occasional clots of houses near the several bridges you pass. At the beginning you'll be tempted to call this river the Cobble River: the riverbed, banks and rapids are primarily cobbles. You may still see signs of how the November 1985 flood scoured the riverbed and banks and left behind many downed trees.

The rapids are Class I–II chutes and cobble drops which sometimes occur on tight turns. Look before running each drop to be sure a tree is not in it. During this trip, you probably will have to carry around two or three tree strainers in the river. Interspersed with these frequent drops are nice pools, some surprisingly deep. Haul out your fishing line if you are so inclined.

After 2 miles you will go under the first (Route 819) bridge. Less than three-quarters of a mile below this bridge is a low-water bridge in fast water. Pull out well upstream for the portage on either side. Only at very low levels can experienced boaters carefully sneak underneath the bridge.

After another mile you will come to the third bridge (Route 818), and the river will split into two channels around a huge cobble bar. Here the Little Dry River enters on river right. About a quarter mile below this is a very interesting rock formation on the left with several striking holes in it. About three-quarters of a mile later is the Route 612 bridge and an intriguing black shale rock formation on the left and the Ruritan Club on the right. Again, this is an alternate put-in if you want a short trip and the best scenery.

The cobble bars continue, and about three-quarters of a mile below the Route 612 bridge is a nifty series of small (Class II) ledges and a hemlock-covered rock wall on the right. Another three-quarters of a mile farther is an even more impressive hemlock-covered shale rock face 40 feet high. However, about one-quarter of a mile below this rock face you should become alert. Here a huge cobble bar has channeled the river to the right. At the bottom of this long channel are two diagonal holes (at least at moderate levels). Be sure to avoid them or punch them squarely. Aggressive boaters may try to surf the lower hole if they are so inclined. Just below is a pretty, undulating series of shale rock beds on the right.

Less than a mile later you will come upon another impressive sight. You will be paddling straight toward Little North Mountain–which is over 2,000 feet high and scarred only by a switchback road. At the base of this mountain you will turn left and experience a half-mile-long, mellow rock slalom where you will dodge occasional rocks at moderate water levels. There aren't enough rocks in this slalom for it to be a true rock garden. Not too long after this long, pleasant passage you will see Chimney Rock on the left–a narrow rock formation over 100 feet high.

The river turns right as you run a short rock garden (called Chimney Rock Garden, naturally). Here the river and the road next to it knife through Brocks Gap in Little North Mountain. If you are hungry or thirsty, there is a restaurant on the left bank and a park on the right. However, watch your step in the park because there are geese there, too. While relaxing, notice another interesting cliff on river left just upstream of the restaurant here at Brocks Gap. About half a mile and two chutes below the restaurant is a beautiful cedar and fern covered cliff on the

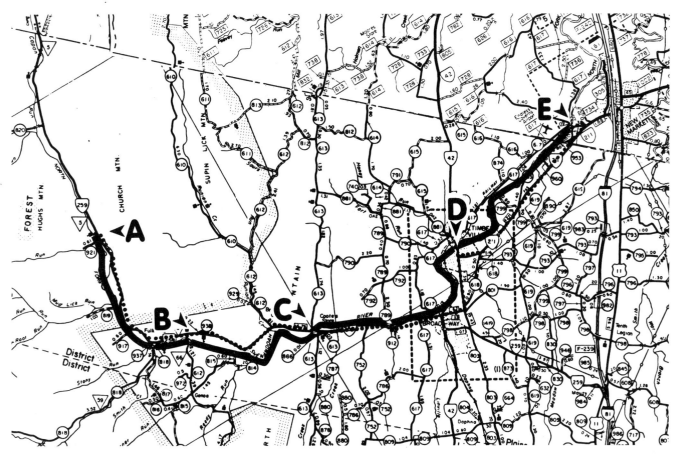

right. In winter the water seeping from this cliff turns to ice which makes it even more spectacular.

A couple hundred yards beyond this cliff rocks block the right side of the river. Here you have a left-to-right

Class II chute. Check it before committing yourself. A tree jammed in the drop made this a more difficult run recently. Another 200 yards below this drop is a river-wide man-made ledge of 2 feet. Here the famous Cootes Store

Section: Riverside Church (Rt. 921) to Cootes Store (Rt. 259)

Counties: Rockingham

USGS Quads: Fulks Run, Timberville

Suitable for: Day cruising

Skill Level: Shepherded novices and intermediates

Months Runnable: Winter and spring generally

Interest Highlights: Brocks Gap, Chimney Rock

Scenery: Pretty in spots to beautiful

Difficulty: Class I–II

Average Width: 30 to 40 feet

Velocity: Moderate

Gradient: 29 feet per mile

Runnable Water Levels:
  Minimum: 3.3 feet on Cootes Store gauge

Maximum: Perhaps 6 feet on Cootes Store gauge

Hazards: Low-water bridge less than 3 miles into the trip; an occasional tree in the river

Scouting: None

Portages: Low-water bridge less than 3 miles into the trip—carry on either side

Rescue Index: Accessible

Source of Additional Information: National Weather Service, Cootes Store gauge (703) 260-0305

Access Points	River Miles	Shuttle Miles
A–C	9.5	8
B–C	4.5	3.5

Access Point Ratings:
A–at Riverside Church (Rt. 921), very good
B–at Rt. 612, very good
C–at Cootes Store (Rt. 259), good

gauge is on the right bank. Take out on the right or left at the Route 259 bridge, if you get permission. Otherwise, continue less than one-half mile downstream and take out at the Riverside Garage by Route 259.

Cootes Store (Route 259) to Route 617

If you are bonkers over birds, you should thoroughly enjoy this trip in the spring. I am not a hard core bird watcher, but during a 3-hour paddle on this trip of 12 miles, I saw or heard many different species. There were kingfishers, herons, hawks, bobwhite quail, mallards, teal, white domestic ducks, Canadian geese, domestic geese, woodpeckers, red-winged blackbirds, robins, and cardinals. I also chased a very friendly osprey down the river for about half the trip!

However, even if you are not a friend of John James Audubon, this section has much of interest for the intermediate paddler and the shepherded novice. Basically, it is a surprisingly nice Class I–II trip with a couple of Class III's thrown in for spice. The only real danger is a 6-foot dam, but more about that later.

The trip starts on a rather dismal note at the Cootes Store or downstream at the Riverside Garage on Route 259. If you have permission, put in on river left at Cootes Store below the riverwide Class II ledge and the gauge on river right. Immediately below is a car graveyard on the left and then several not too charming houses on the high riverbank. Fortunately, the scenery soon changes to rock walls and farms.

About three-fourths of a mile into the trip, a highway bridge over a stream entering on the right marks a low-water bridge on the river. This drop can be run in the center after a quick peek. Just below this are three nice moderate surfing waves/holes on the right. Shortly thereafter is an island with runnable channels to the right or left and a pretty rock wall on the right. A second island is immediately below; go right here for nice bouncy waves and a good surfing spot at the bottom. One rock formation here contains a large, almost cavelike hole, and another is an anticline.

A real cave is then soon seen on the right; this is about 2 miles into the trip. The sedimentary bedrock here consists of slanted blocklike slabs that slope into the river. Shortly thereafter one comes to two good, river-wide ledges that each drop a foot. These offer good surfing possibilities for the mildly adventurous.

One then reaches the second low-water bridge; this is a 1.5 foot ledge best run in the center after a quick look. Following this bridge, go left around another island to be rewarded by nice waves and scenic flat rocks. A farm, cobble bar, and bouncy 1- to 2-foot waves follow shortly. After over an hour, or 4.5 miles into the trip, you'll pass abandoned railroad tracks and a 75- to 100-foot-high cliff on the right. There is a well-kept dairy farm on the left. The big pool here warns that you are coming to a 6-foot dam. Near the dam is a tall, narrow building on the right.

Upon reaching the dam, there is a choice. The easiest route is a short portage on the left, as bovine spectators look on. Alternatively, the dam can be run on the extreme

The five foot dam with a runnable slot on river right above Timberville on the North Fork of the Shenandoah.

Charming old patchwork Arbogast Mill above Route 617 on the North Fork of the Shenandoah. This historic mill was built in 1835 and is the oldest mill in the Shenandoah Valley still in operation.

right. Here it changes from a nearly river-wide drop of 6 feet to a 20-foot-wide lesser drop of 3 feet (Class III) with no nasty hydraulic at moderate levels. Do not run the main dam because of the terminal looking hydraulic below.

If you choose to run the 3-foot dam slot on the far right, scout it to be sure fallen trees do not block your path. The channel for 100 yards below the right side of the dam is like a small millrace which then rejoins the main river. Paddle this channel carefully as trees or branches may block your path.

Below the dam is a big, flat, monster lunch rock on the left. Here also are a couple surfing waves and perhaps some cows from the nearby pasture for lunchtime entertainment. After this there are a couple of more surfing waves before you reach the railroad bridge a good 5 miles into the trip. Then comes a 50-foot cliff on the right before arriving at the Route 42 bridge in Timberville. There is a parking lot by the Gulf station on river left for those folks who want to end the trip at 6 miles here. The next convenient take-out is another 6 miles downstream.

The river becomes relatively calm for about a mile or so below the Route 42 bridge, except for some riffles and bouncy waves. Then, when you see three tall silos plus their midget brother, you will come to a 1.5-foot ledge and a nice surfing wave/hole. This is followed by some moderate waves.

Later, just over halfway through this lower section, there is a rock wall on the right with a dark orange-colored building on the top. This and the roar downstream herald

the best rapids of the trip–a Class III ledge of 3 feet with a couple of good 2- to 3-foot waves below. The best route is left of center, while the sneak is on the extreme left. Advanced and nervy intermediate paddlers may not want to scout the ledge. Timid intermediates and novices should scout it from river left.

Shortly below this ledge is a huge old building (Arbogast Mill) on the right, its walls formed by a metal patchwork of the ages. Below this there is only a mile of some mild Class I–II stuff before the take-out at the Route 617 bridge.

In parting, I should mention that there is more than bird life to be seen on the river. Stocked trout swim in the clear waters near the put-in, while perch and suckers are below the farms and dam. Also, turtles and woodchucks are found along the bank in the early spring sun, and youngsters will enjoy the numerous cows, sheep, and other farm critters along the way.

Route 617 to Strasburg (Route 648)

Below the Route 617 bridge the river flows at a more moderate pace for 68 miles to Strasburg. There are numerous access points on this stretch which are made to order for novices and families at moderate water levels. However, access at several points is bumpy or on private land, so take this into account when planning your trip. The water is generally clear throughout this long section and the bottom is most often sand.

Route 617 to Route 730

This first segment is the 6 miles from Route 617 to Route 730. After you put in, Route 617 parallels the river on the left for about a mile. Along here you have occasional Class I–II cobble bar rapids, and the North Fork continues its pleasant journey through farmland. The banks are reasonably high and lined with sycamores and box elders. Oaks, ashes, and other hardwoods grow farther back from the bank. Along this stretch you will also find some Ordovician limestone rock formations. The most striking one is on the right, 2 miles downstream from Route 617. Here you run a nice 50-yard Class I–II boulder garden with a ledge or two as you pass limestone bluffs 200-feet high.

This is the site of New Market Battlefield, where on May 15, 1864, General Breckinridge of the South (a former U.S. Vice President) ordered 247 cadets from Virginia Military Institute at Lexington to face Union troops under General Sigel. The cadets were supposed to be kept in reserve, but in the heat of battle they were placed in the front lines, and their heroism helped defeat General Sigel's veteran troops. Each year this battle is reenacted the second Sunday in May at the battlefield, which is on Route 305 one mile north of Interstate 81 at Exit 264.

About 2.5 miles after this battlefield you reach the Route 767 bridge just past an island. Roughly 1 mile below this you go underneath Interstate 81; you arrive at the Route 730 bridge 0.75 miles later. The main significance of this bridge is that Shenandoah Caverns is 1.5 miles away on river left. These caverns are one of the prettiest in the Blue Ridge.

Among spectacular formations in them are Diamond Cascade and Grove of the Druids. The caverns are open the entire year.

The Route 730 bridge is a convenient take-out. There is a small parking lot upstream of the bridge on river right, but be discreet: you must cross private land from this lot to the river. If possible, go by boat or shuttle car another 1.25 miles downstream to the striking Route 720 bridge. This covered wooden bridge is an incredible piece of construction. Take time to check out the graceful arch and interior woodwork of this classic bridge. Unfortunately, this take-out is also on private property and parking is very limited.

Route 730 to Route 675

For the 15 miles from Route 730 to Route 675 near Edinburg, the river passes through a pretty section of the Shenandoah Valley. The low banks afford pleasant views of the farmland and the mountains to the right in this historic valley. The rapids consist of occasional Class I gravel bars at the end of long pools. The main problems on this stretch are a couple of low-water bridges.

There are numerous access points along here. Less than a mile below the Route 720 covered bridge is busy US 11. After another mile Smith Creek enters on the right. Less than 2 miles later you reach Mount Jackson. Be prepared for a low-water bridge here. Soon thereafter Route 698 parallels the river on the right offering numerous access points for the next couple of miles. A mile later is another bridge

Section: Cootes Store (Rt. 259) to Rt. 617

Counties: Rockingham, Shenandoah

USGS Quads: Timberville, Broadway, New Market

Suitable for: Day cruising

Skill Level: Shepherded novices and intermediates

Months Runnable: Winter and spring, generally

Interest Highlights: Bird life, rock formations, caves

Scenery: Pretty in spots to beautiful

Difficulty: Class I–II with 2 Class IIIs

Average Width: 40 to 50 feet

Velocity: Moderate

Gradient: 10 feet per mile

Runnable Water Levels:
Minimum: 3 feet on Cootes Store gauge

Maximum: Perhaps 6 feet on Cootes Store gauge

Hazards: 6-foot dam 4 miles into the trip; maybe an occasional tree in the river

Scouting: 2 Class IIIs

Portages: None, if the Class III slot to the right of the 6-foot dam is runnable

Rescue Index: Accessible

Source of Additional Information: National Weather Service, Cootes Store gauge (703) 260-0305

Access Points	River Miles	Shuttle Miles
C–D	6	6
C–E	12	11

Access Point Ratings:
C–at Cootes Store (Rt. 259), good
D–at Timberville (Rt. 42), good
E–at Rt. 617, good

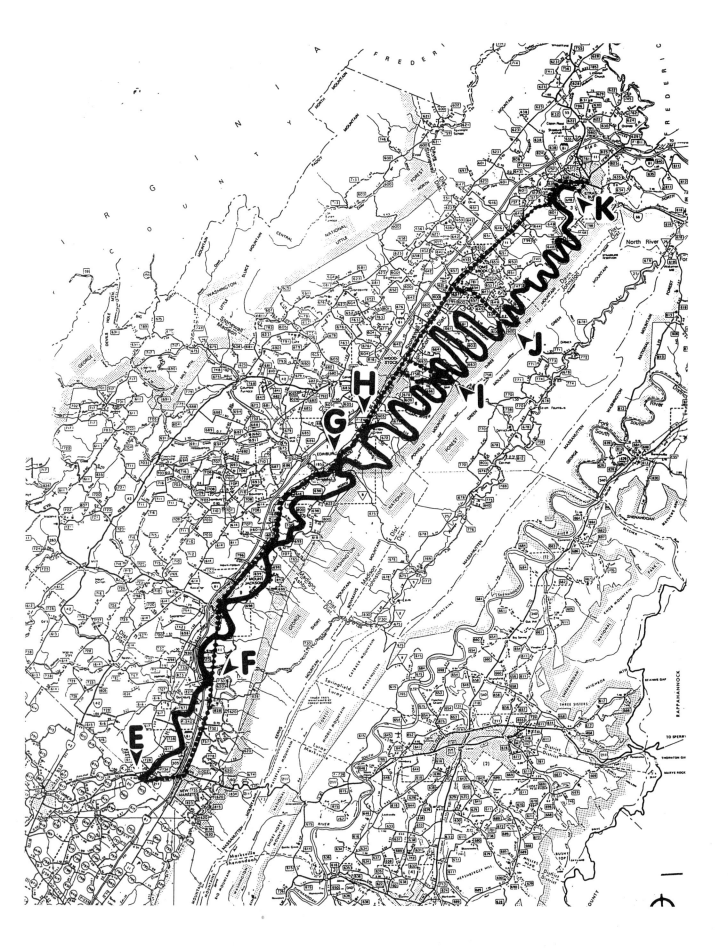

bridge below which Route 698 again nestles next to the river for a half mile. For the next 4 miles, you don't have roads quite so near the river and you can enjoy 2,800-foot Short Mountain in the distance on your right. Also, you will pass two 150-foot bluffs, the first on the right, the second a mile farther on the left.

Approaching Edinburg you go under the Route 698 bridge. Just over 1 mile below this is a low-water bridge. Almost 1.5 miles farther is your take-out at the Route 675 bridge in Edinburg. This river left take-out upstream of the bridge is fair at best: it involves a 100-yard portage up a 50-foot hill to the narrow parking area. Just above the take-out, Stony Creek (described later in this chapter) enters on the left.

Route 675 to Burnshire Bridge (Route 758)

Below Route 675 you enter the famous Seven Bends section of the North Fork which stretches from Edinburg past Woodstock to Maurertown. For the first four of these graceful bends you have 2,500-foot Powell Mountain on the right, which you are incessantly going toward or away from. For those who love short shuttles and miles of paddling, you can paddle the 30 miles of the Seven Bends from Route 675 to Route 654 yet have only a 13 mile shuttle on Route 11! On this stretch the river makes 14 (count 'em) 180-degree turns.

This slowly twisting section is very pleasant for drifting, fishing, and camping. However, there is very little whitewater (Class I riffles) during these 30 miles. On the other hand, in the first half of the Seven Bends section you have (ugh!) three dams 10- to 15-feet high that create long pools and three portages on this 17 mile trip.

The first dam is less than a mile below Route 675. Then, on a left bend nearly 3 miles below Route 675, you have some scenic 500-foot-high bluffs on the right. Two miles later you reach Chapman Landing (Route 672). This is an excellent take-out on river left, and there is a nice rock face on the right.

Section: Rt. 617 to Strasburg (Rt. 648)

Counties: Shenandoah

USGS Quads: New Market, Hamburg, Conicville, Edinburg, Rileyville, Woodstock, Toms Brook, Strasburg

Suitable for: Day cruising

Skill Level: Novices and families at moderate water levels

Months Runnable: Winter, spring, and maybe early summer

Interest Highlights: Beautiful Shenandoah Valley; Seven Bends

Scenery: Pretty in spots to beautiful

Difficulty: Class I–II with 1 Class II–III (broken out dam) just above Rt. 663

Average Width: 40 to 70 feet

Velocity: Slow to moderate

Gradient: First 21 miles, 8 feet per mile; last 47 miles, 5 feet per mile

Runnable Water Levels:
  Minimum: 2.3 feet on Strasburg and 2.6 feet on Cootes Store gauges to Maurertown; 1.5 feet on Front Royal gauge from Maurertown to Strasburg
  Maximum: Perhaps 5 feet on Strasburg and Cootes Store gauges to Maurertown; 3.5 feet on Front Royal gauges from Maurertown to Strasburg

Hazards: Three 10- to 15-foot dams between Edinburg (Rt. 675) and Burnshire Bridge (Rt. 758); low-water bridges; occasional tree in river; high water; broken out dam above Rt. 663

Scouting: 1 Class II–III (broken out dam right of an island) and Class I–II (sneak left of this island) just above Rt. 663

Portages: Three 10- to 15-foot dams between Rt. 675 and Rt. 758—one a mile below Rt. 675, one 3.5 miles below Chapman Landing (Rt. 672), and one just above Rt. 658; low-water bridges

Rescue Index: Generally accessible

Source of Additional Information: National Weather Service, Cootes Store and Front Royal gauges (703) 260-0305; Potomac Appalachian Trail Club Map "G"

Access Points	River Miles	Shuttle Miles
E–F	6.0	6.0
F–G	15.0	10.0
G–H	5.0	2.5
H–I	12.0	6.0
I–J	13.5	8.5
J–K	16.5	11.0

Access Point Ratings:
E–at Rt. 617, good
F–at Shenandoah Caverns (Rt. 730), good
G–at Edinburg (Rt. 675), fair
H–at Chapman Landing (Rt. 672), excellent
I–near Woodstock (Burnshire Bridge, Rt. 758), fair
J–at Maurertown (Rt. 654), good but private
K–at Strasburg (near Rt. 648), fair to good

The stretch below Chapman Landing is character building. The second dam (Chapman Dam) is 3.5 miles beyond Route 672–after you pass a long island and then a huge bend to the left. Portage with care. About 1.5 miles later, after a right bend, you reach Route 609. Then you go 6 miles and, after passing a bridge and three left bends, you reach the third dam which is nearly 20 feet high. There is a difficult short portage next to a shale hill on the right and an easier but much longer portage on the left. Both portages are on private property, so get permission first. Just below the third dam is the Route 675 Burnshire Bridge where you can take out 17 miles below Route 675 if you are becoming disoriented from all these turns. No wonder: while doing the Seven Bends you head every direction of the compass except south. However, at Burnshire Bridge the road spur on the right above the bridge is closed, and no parking is allowed there. Consequently, please use another road spur on river left by a picturesque hydropower plant (which looks like an old mill/barn) next to the dam. This is on private land, so get permission to park. If you put in here, the best place is downstream of Burnshire Bridge on river left.

Burnshire Bridge (Route 758) to Maurertown (Route 654)

Those who want to finish the Seven Bends below Route 758 can continue another 13.5 miles around the last three bends to Maurertown. After Route 758, you have two access points–at Route 663 (5 miles) and Route 661 (10 miles)–before reaching Route 654 near Maurertown. Along the right bank Powell Mountain is replaced by 1,900-foot Three Top Mountain. The main rapids of concern along here occur 200 yards above the Route 663 low-water bridge. Here there are the remains of a 2- to 3-foot dam (Class II–III) to the right of an island. Rather than running this dam, less experienced paddlers should go left of the island where there is a short Class I–II, mellow rock garden. The ruins of Stonewall Mill are on river right just below this dam. There are one or two more low-water

bridges to contend with below Route 663. Indeed, the take-out near Maurertown is also a low-water bridge. The land is private, and the only room for parking is away from the bridge on river left, so get permission.

Route 654 to Strasburg (Route 648)

Below Route 654, the North Fork continues on a lazy 16.5-mile meander to Strasburg. The access points are not as frequent, and you still encounter an occasional low-water bridge. Interestingly enough, this stretch also has seven bends which are not as pronounced as the Seven Bends section just upstream.

On this section, scenic Three Top Mountain continues on your right for most of the trip. After the first couple of bends, Toms Brook enters from the left after passing through the town of Toms Brook to the west. Here Big Blue Ridge Hiking Trail goes east to the summit of Three Top Mountain. The only reasonable access points are Route 744 (11 miles) and the first Route 648 bridge (13 miles). The second Route 648 bridge is somewhat convenient and is 3 miles farther near the town of Strasburg. The bridge has no parking, but you have two river left options. You can take out downstream at the parking lot of Strasburg High School or upstream off a road spur: turn left at High Street and left again at the Route 1202 sign.

Incidentally, a mile west of the Route 648 take-out is the site of the 1864 Battle of Fishers Hill. In this Civil War battle, Union forces under General Crook and future president Colonel Rutherford Hayes soundly defeated the Confederates.

You can go the remaining 13 miles from Strasburg to Front Royal where the North Fork joins the South Fork. However, there is not much to recommend this trip. The scenery deteriorates and there are two dams to portage. However, in this last section, two tributaries (Cedar Creek and Passage Creek) join the North Fork. These two streams (described elsewhere in this chapter) provide a delightful whitewater experience.

South Fork of the Shenandoah River

The South Fork of the Shenandoah has probably been paddled by more beginning and veteran paddlers than any other Virginia stream. Boy Scouts have wetted their paddles in the South Fork for generations, and outing groups of all varieties continue to do so in droves. For any Virginia paddler a trip down the South Fork of the Shenandoah continues to be an essential part of the Old Dominion experience.

The present-day paddler on the South Fork of the Shenandoah will see things much as they might have been before the Civil War with the addition of the occasional concrete bridge, power line, and tractor. The business of the land, farming, takes place in much the same area it did during earlier years. Some of the fields have been plowed within the same fence-rows for generations. Battle sites can be visited that are nearly identical to their wartime appearance, not due to protection, but because the land is still being used for the same purpose.

The river contains numerous fish dams built by prehistoric Indians. These structures, only visible at low water, are V-shaped arrangements of rocks pointing downstream. The people of the hunter-gatherer culture would place nets at the downstream end of the V and gather the fish funneled in from upstream. Some paddlers grumble about running man-made rapids, but who can be offended by a ripple produced by a thousand-year-old pile of cobbles. It is interesting to think that the stones placed so laboriously by hand long ago now bear the multi-hued streaks scraped off the aluminum and plastic pleasure craft of today.

The river is a sterling example of a geomorphologically mature stream, and it meanders back and forth between the Blue Ridge and Massanutten Mountains. As a result, the view and the orientation of the light are constantly changing, and the paddler is presented with a feast of visual entertainment alternating between steep forested slopes, limestone cliffs, cow-tenanted fields, and shady bowers between sandy islands.

Camping is possible in many places along the river, although the "No Trespassing" signs proliferate more and more each year. If there is any doubt as to whether camping is permitted in a particular spot, it would be wise to locate the nearest farmhouse and inquire.

The river is heavily used in this area and littering is a severe problem for some of the landowners; therefore, protect the relationship between paddlers and riparian landowners by utilizing courtesy, discretion, and a large trashbag.

Newport (US 340) to Luray (US 211)

This 9-mile stretch of the South Fork has the best gradient (8 feet per mile) and the most rapids. It is also perhaps the most scenic stretch with striking Ordovician limestone rock formations and well-groomed farms along the way. This section is an excellent day-trip for shepherded novices and holds sufficient water for most of the year. The toughest rapids are at the beginning (a Class II drop formed by the rubble left from an old dam) followed somewhat downstream by two nice long series of ledges (Class I–II). For the rest of the trip, the remaining Class I–II drops and ledges are less frequent but nicely spaced.

Paddlers have a choice of two excellent put-ins: across from Kite's Store at a campground or at Newport Public Boat Landing less than a half mile downstream. There is a small fee for putting in at the campground where you can spend the night from April through early November.

Just below the campground and the river left put-in is the aforementioned 3- to 4-foot Class II drop formed by the remains of Foltz Mill dam. Beginners should scout this straightforward washboard drop on the left. Do not run the narrow far left channel which is clogged by big nasty gears and other obstructions from the old mill.

Less than a half mile downstream of this rapid and just below the river left Newport Public Boat Landing put-in is Foltz Cave. Look for it in the pretty rock cliffs high above on river left. The adventurous can best enter the cave from the top of these cliffs.

A half mile below this is a good set of small ledges several hundred feet long. Then, after another half mile, comes the longest and best stretch of ledges and minor drops which lasts for nearly a mile.

You will pass under the US 340 bridge about 3 miles into the trip. A mile below this on river right are the remains of Fort Long–an ingenious fort built by a German settler in the 1700s. Rocky cliffs form the left bank of the river, and there is a pretty waterfall in one of the nearby narrow ravines. Several interesting minor drops come before and after Fort Long. After another half mile the river turns right. There are a couple of nice drops in the mile below this bend. Then things are relatively peaceful for the next 2 miles until you come to a nice ledge on the left upstream side of an island; continue left around this island.

Things are mellow for the final mile until you get to the excellent take-out at Whitehouse Public Boat Landing on river left off Route 646 just upstream of the large dual US

Section: Newport (US 340) to Luray (US 211)

Counties: Page

USGS Quads: Stanley, Hamburg, Luray

Suitable for: Day cruising and camping

Skill Level: Novices

Months Runnable: Winter, spring, and often early summer

Interest Highlights: Well-groomed farms, rock formations, Foltz Cave

Scenery: Pretty to beautiful in spots

Difficulty: Class I–II with 1 Class II at beginning

Average Width: 75 feet

Velocity: Moderate

Gradient: 8 feet per mile

Runnable Water Levels:
Minimum: 1.3 feet on US 211 take-out bridge; 1.4 feet on the Front Royal gauge

Maximum: 3 feet on US 211 take-out bridge; 3.5 feet on the Front Royal gauge (all rapids washed out)

Hazards: Occasional trees in river; clogged far left channel of Foltz Mill Rapids

Scouting: Foltz Mill Rapids (Class II) just below Kite's Store put-in for novices

Portages: None

Rescue Index: Accessible

Source of Additional Information: National Weather Service, Front Royal gauge (703) 260-0305; Kite's Store and campground (540) 652-8174; Shenandoah River Outfitters (540) 743-4159.

Access Points	River Miles	Shuttle Miles
A–B	9	7

Access Point Ratings:
A–at Kite's Store and Newport Public Boat Landing (both on US 340), excellent
B–at US 211 bridge (off Rt. 646), excellent

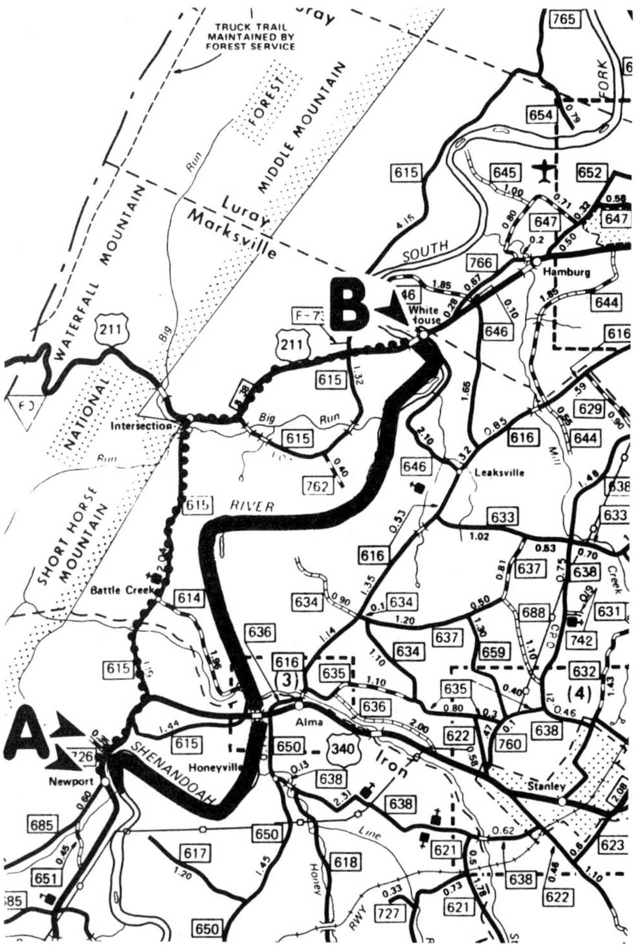

211 bridge. This take-out was named for the whitewashed house nearby which was built about 1760.

The adventurous can extend this trip a mile further downstream and take out at a dirt road on river right. However, the only rapid in this mile is a Class I–II drop formed by the remains of a dam and mill.

Below this take-out are 4 miles of flatwater and a 20-foot dam. This stretch is not recommended. However, for hard core flatwater paddlers, there are two take-outs before the dam and its nasty left side portage. The first is on river left at Massanutten Public Boat Landing after 2 miles of this flatwater, and the second is on river left at Route 654 just above the dam. However, the Route 654 take-out is on posted property, so get permission first.

There is a canoeing gauge on the river left bridge abutment by the US 211 Whitehouse Landing take-out. The rapids tend to wash out when this gauge gets well above 3 feet or when the Front Royal gauge rises above 3.5 feet. For a run free of much scraping, the Front Royal gauge should be at least 1.5 feet.

Bixler Bridge to Karo Landing

This mellow 36-mile section of the South Fork is excellent for novice overnight trips or can be broken into four roughly equal day-trips. Good scenery and easy Class I–II rapids are found throughout this section. The most significant whitewater is Compton Rapids (Class II) 17 miles into the trip. Other attractions on this section are the

Compton Rapids and the cliffs of Golden Rock on the South Fork of the Shenandoah.

numerous caves, V-shaped cobblestone Indian fish dams, Indian archaeological sites, and remains of frontier settlements and mills. There are many primitive campsites and no portages caused by dams or other obstructions.

Bixler Bridge (Rt. 675) to Goods Mill (Rt. 684)

The put-in is on river left below the Route 675 bridge and the remains of a one-lane low-water bridge at Bixler Bridge Public Landing. You will see two old canoeing gauges on the second and fourth Route 675 bridge abutments from the left. After a mile of quiet water you come to Will Mauck Cave on river right. The entrance to this cave is high above the river. When rain and other precipitation cause the water level in the cave to rise enough, a striking jet of water shoots from the cave into the river. The river bends right after the cave, and there are several small drops soon thereafter. A half mile below this Hawksbill Creek comes in from the right just as the river bends sharply left at Sandy Hook.

Hawksbill Creek Cave is a quarter mile downstream in the cliffs on river right. Another three-quarters of a mile and one comes to Fort Stover, also on the right. Fort Stover was built in the late 1700s by a settler named Samuel Stover. Today it consists of a restored fort and home.

For the next couple of miles the small ledges and rapids are more frequent. About 4.5 miles into the trip and continuing for a short distance, the left bank of the river is

Forest Service land open to public camping. The best camping area is opposite a series of several ledges where a group of small islands lies along the left bank. A short distance downstream on river right are commercial cabins for those who like less primitive facilities. Here also is a V-shaped riffle which was probably an Indian fish dam many years ago.

After 2 more miles of mostly flatwater you come to a half-mile series of riffles. Precisely at the end of these riffles and a few hundred yards below a river left island, is Bealers Ferry (Route 661) on river right. This is a good take-out for those on a lazy day-trip of 8 miles, but it's easy to miss if you're not alert. If you plan to take out here, look this place over while running the shuttle so you can identify it from the river. If your sense of direction is really bad, tie something brightly colored to the trees or brush on the riverbank so you don't miss this take-out.

A mile below Bealers Ferry is a cave high above the right bank. Those wanting to see the cave should first get permission from its owners. Just below here the action picks up for 2 miles. This series of ledges (from very tiny to 2 feet) culminates in Goods Falls–a mile-long section of small ledges that ends just after Goods Mill (Route 684) is passed on river right. At low water this stretch is very picky, requiring much maneuvering and good water reading ability. For day-trippers, the 11.5-mile paddle to Goods Mill is worth it. This river right take-out is better than Bealers Ferry because it is open and easier to see, has more parking space, and the trip there gives the paddler more rapids. However, the Goods Mill take-out is on private property, and a small fee is required.

Goods Mill (Rt. 684) to Burners Ford (Rt. 664)

Rileyville, a half mile below Goods Mill on river right, is in a stretch with many caves. One of these is Keyser Cave (on river left), over a quarter mile downstream from where the river bends left at Rileyville. This cave contains a burial site for a nearby prehistoric village which was unearthed by archaeologists in the early 1940s.

After another mile and a couple of minor rapids, the river bends right, and you pass around an island. A mile below this is an emergency access on river right where a spur of Route 663 runs next to the river for a quarter mile. This access is significant for two reasons. First, from here to the Bentonville take-out the left bank is now all part of George Washington National Forest. Although there are private homes within the park, camping is allowed for most of this stretch. If in doubt about a possible campsite, please ask permission at the nearest house and leave the site cleaner than when you arrived.

Second, three-quarters of a mile below Route 663 is the biggest rapid of the trip–Compton Rapids (Class II). As the river turns left there is a railroad bridge high in

the sky and a gorgeous Ordovician limestone rock cliff (Golden Rock) just below on river right. The cedars clawing for a foothold on this 200-foot-high rock face make it even more impressive. Novice paddlers should take out on river right above the rapids to scout. The easiest route is on the right through some good standing waves with perhaps a couple of moderate holes to punch. Beginning paddlers who have another night to spend on the river should make sure their gear is in waterproof bags and tied down securely because there is a good chance of taking on water while running this rapids. There is a nice recovery pool and lunch stop below Compton Rapids at the base of the large rock cliff. However, a canoe livery owns this spot so get permission to stop here.

The adventurous can drag their boats upstream and run the rapids again during a lunch stop. The cobble bar at the top right of these rapids sports a feast of multicolored sedimentary rocks–sandstone, limestone, shale, and conglomerate.

In the next 2 miles you pass Indian Grave Ridge on the left. This ridge appears to be named for two stone mounds on its tip which are said to be Indian burial sites. There are several mellow rapids on this stretch, primarily V-shaped Indian fish dams. The last of these cobble dams is just before the river turns hard right. After this turn there is a mile-long mini-staircase before another take-out at Burners Ford (Route 664) on river right. This is a good 9 miles

Section: Bixler Bridge (Rt. 675) to Karo Landing (US 340)

Counties: Page and Warren

USGS Quads: Hamburg, Luray, Rileyville, Bentonville

Suitable for: Day cruising and camping

Skill Level: Novices

Months Runnable: Winter, spring, and often early summer

Interest Highlights: Caves, Indian fish dams, rock formations, frontier and archaeological sites

Scenery: Pretty to beautiful in spots

Difficulty: Class I–II with 1 Class II (Compton Rapids)

Average Width: 70 to 150 feet

Velocity: Moderate

Gradient: 5 feet per mile

Runnable Water Levels:
Minimum: 1.2 feet on the Front Royal gauge

Maximum: 3.5 feet on the Front Royal gauge (all rapids washed out)

Hazards: Occasional trees in river

Scouting: Compton Rapids (Class II)

Portages: None

Rescue Index: Accessible

Source of Additional Information: National Weather Service, Front Royal gauge (703) 260-0305; Shenandoah River Outfitters (703) 743-4159.

Access Points	River Miles	Shuttle Miles
C–D	11.5	10
D–E	9	6
E–F	7	6
F–G	9	6

Access Point Ratings:
C–at Bixler Bridge (Rt. 675), excellent
D–at Goods Mill (Rt. 684), very good but private
E–at Burners Ford (Rt. 664), good but limited parking
F–at Bentonville (Rt. 613), excellent
G–at Karo Landing (by Gooney Run off US 340), very good

from Goods Mill. Like the Bealers Ferry take-out, Burners Ford may be hard to recognize from the river, so check it out first and perhaps even mark it. Also, parking is limited on the narrow Burners Ford road with room for only one shuttle vehicle or so.

Burners Ford (Rt. 664) to Bentonville (Rt. 613)

After a minor rapid below Burners Ford, the river becomes calm and deepens. This spot is a haven for anglers; bass, sunfish, and carp are caught frequently. This area is known as Overall Eddy by locals.

After the river turns left at Overall Eddy, it becomes more shallow and swift. Here one will find a few nice ledges. The best ledge (2 feet) is a mile below Overall Eddy and 2 miles below Burners Ford. Novices should look the ledge over before running it. A quarter mile below this ledge is another V-shaped fish dam. Two miles downstream (4 miles below Burners Ford) is a U.S. Forest Service campground on the left bank of the river near Hazard Mill.

Hazard Mill is just below this campground. To see Hazard Mill, go left of a large island–taking a small channel that once was its mill race. Near the end of this channel are the remains of Hazard Mill which operated until 1870 when a flood destroyed it. Nearby is an early Indian village which was excavated extensively in the mid-1960s.

After the island ends, the river slowly makes a gradual 180 degree turn to the right in the next 1.5 miles. About a half mile below this bend is the last set of minor rapids. Another half mile and you are at the Bentonville Landing take-out which is a low-water bridge. The view looking back upstream here is pleasant, so pause and enjoy it. For those not ready to go home, there is camping at the Indian Hollow Campgrounds on river right just upstream from the Bentonville Landing take-out, 7 miles below Burners Ford.

Bentonville (Rt. 613) to Karo Landing (Rt. 340)

If you wish, you can go another 9 miles beyond Bentonville to another take-out at Karo Landing. However, this is not as pleasant a trip for several reasons. The river is flatter, the rapids are not as exciting, and there are often heavy winds blowing upstream for the last 2 to 3 miles above Karo Landing. Although there are many small ledges on the Bentonville to Karo Landing section, they are washed out above 1.5 feet on the Front Royal gauge. This section is best only at about 1.3 feet on the gauge. At 1 foot one will need hiking boots instead of a canoe for the entire run from Bixler Bridge to Karo Landing.

Karo Landing is on river right just after Gooney Run enters the river. You can recognize it from the river by the low, black railroad bridge crossing Gooney Run. Incidentally, Gooney Run has a challenging gorge for advanced paddlers and is described elsewhere in this chapter. Gooney Creek Campground is on the other side of US 340 from Karo Landing.

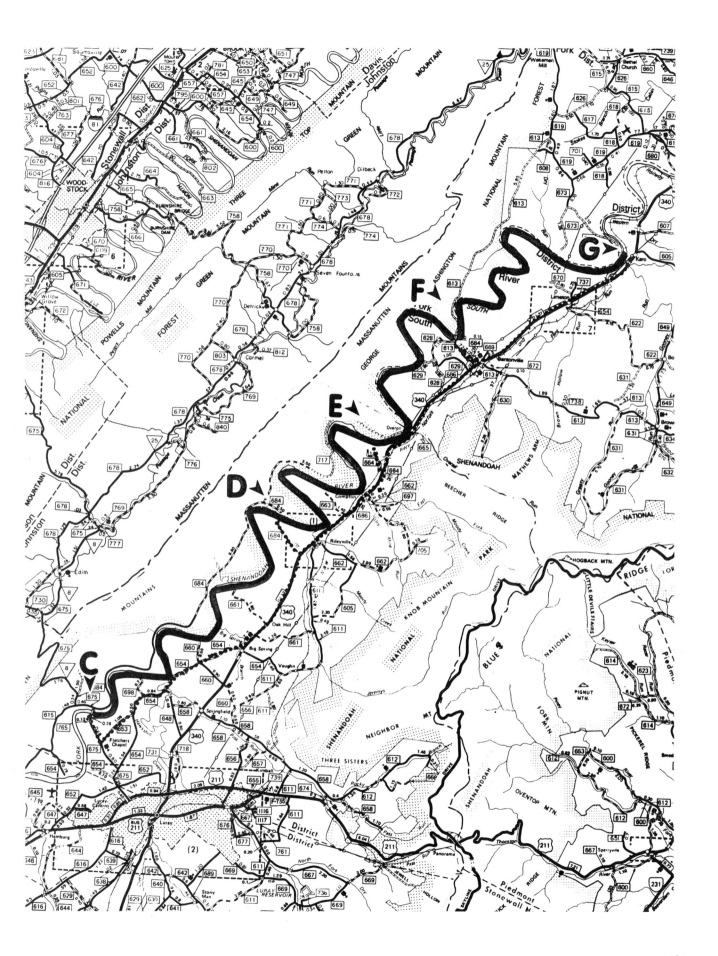

South River

Crimora (Route 612) to Port Republic (Route 659)

The South River from Crimora to Port Republic is a real sleeper. This 15-mile Class I–II trip (with one Class II–III) is perfect for shepherded novices. The relaxing voyage takes you through woods and farmland where there are occasional open spots giving a pretty view of the Blue Ridge Mountains on river right as the South flows north. The riverbed is mostly sand and gravel; the banks are often 6 to 7 feet high. Three historic caves near the town of Grottoes and a rich history of frontier boats (called "gundalows") add spice to this river trip.

Previous accounts of pollution do not appear to be true; there are fish in the South River and the water is generally clear. Also, this section is far enough downstream from Waynesboro that dilution minimizes the effects of pollution.

Although the gradient is only 8 to 9 feet per mile with several long pools, the river moves well and keeps the paddler's interest throughout the trip. This journey can be shortened by using one of three intervening bridges for put-ins or take-outs. However, two of these bridges–at Routes 778 and 256–are high bridges with steep carries. For partway put-ins or take-outs use the Route 844 bridge to Grand Caverns or Route 825 on river right just below Harriston. Just remember that when Grand Caverns are closed (in winter), the Route 844 bridge is closed, too. The only negative aspects of the trip are a couple of downed trees that may necessitate a carry or two and an additional portage if you pick the wrong channel when the river occasionally divides around several islands.

When putting in at the Route 612 bridge at Crimora, be aware of two things. First, there is not much room for parking, so leave a minimum number of vehicles here. Second, the put-in on river left upstream of the bridge is small: large boating parties will have to phase their launching. The best take-out in Port Republic is just downstream on river left of the Route 659 bridge. However, this is private property, and you must get permission from one of the two or three property owners to take out or park your cars here. If you don't get permission, an alternative is to float down 2.5 miles farther on the South Fork of the Shenandoah to Lynnwood (Route 708). On the way you will pass Great Island–the largest island on the South Fork. Go right for the best channel. Just above Lynnwood is an 8-foot dam; portage on left.

After putting in you will encounter farmland and bovine spectators on the right. Watch for frisky calves in the spring. The forest soon shields the farmland, and this continues for most of the trip. About 1.5 miles below the put-in on the left is a millrace and a nice chute. These are the remains of an old mill. Roughly 3 miles into the trip the river divides around an island. The smaller right channel is an enticingly intimate path that beckons to you. Don't take it! At moderate levels it will sucker you into dragging your boat over an intermittent stream bed for at least a quarter mile after the first 100-yard spur of water.

Soon after taking the left channel around this big island you will see the river divide again around a much smaller island. The left is a ledgy drop and the right is a straightforward cobble bar. After this island, note the interesting shale rock face on the left. Shortly below the

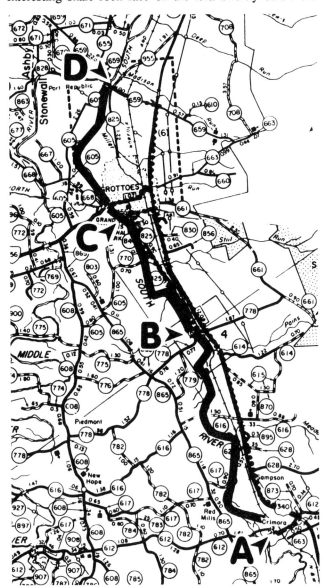

river opens up, and you can see the Blue Ridge Mountains on your right.

About one-third mile below this some pleasant rapids begin. First are a couple of 1-foot ledges a quarter mile apart with a surfing spot in between. Another one-third mile farther is a better set of Class I–II rapids–a rock garden followed closely by two 1-foot ledges. A mile later, 200 yards above the Route 778 bridge, is a nice Class II ledge and rock garden combination.

If you haven't previously checked the rough canoeing gauge on the upstream face of this bridge's second river left abutment, please do so as you pass. Below the Route 778 bridge at Harriston (which is nearly 7 miles into the trip), the woods and long pools continue. Nearly 2 miles downstream (after passing an alternative put-in/take-out on river right on Route 825) is a nice, wooded, steep hill on

Ed Evangelidi running the longest rapid on the South.

the left. This is Patterson Ridge. A half mile below this you come to some interesting rocks in the river–one with an intriguing hole through it. Just below is a nice short rock slalom, and the countryside opens up again.

After passing some islands and a choice of two Class II chutes (right is zestier), you reach the Route 844 bridge to Grand Caverns. At this point you've done 10 miles of paddling. At the top of the last island before the Route 844 bridge are some bleachers and an overlook on the left. Here you can beach your boat on the left bank of the river and walk 100 yards downstream on a trail to a lime kiln.

Left of the Route 844 bridge is Cave Hill. This mound of Conococheague limestone is just before the aptly named town of Grottoes and contains three major caves. The largest and most well-known cave is Grand Caverns,

supposedly the oldest commercial caverns still open in the United States. The cave was first called Weyers Cave because a chap named Bernard Weyer found it in 1804 while chasing a groundhog that had stolen one of his traps. Later it was called Grottoes of the Shenandoah and, finally, Grand Caverns. As well as being a tourist attraction in the 1800s, these caves were used by both Union and Confederate troops (Stonewall Jackson's) for shelter at different times during the Civil War. Grand Caverns (and the alternate take-out at Route 844 here) are open from March through October. Also on Cave Hill is Madison's Saltpeter Cave, named for James Madison and allegedly mined for saltpeter during the War of 1812. Finally, there is Fountain, or Weasts Cave, which was also active in the early 1800s.

Only a half mile below this bridge, as you near the town of Grottoes, are the best rapids of the trip–a 75-yard Class II–III rock slalom. The river bends left before reaching these rapids and turns right midway through them. Novices should scout this slalom from the right and may want to carry it. At moderate levels the rapids are technical and require good boat control. Nervous novices may want to walk 300 yards upstream from the Route 256 bridge on the shuttle to check out this drop.

Just after the Route 256 bridge (after 11 miles of paddling) is another nice series of Class I–II rapids. First come two 1 foot ledges with surfing possibilities; shortly thereafter are two more ledgelike drops. Finally, a couple of hundred yards below this, is a 2-foot ledge cobble best taken on the right if the passage is clear.

Over a mile farther the river splits three ways as you work through a series of islands. Enter center or right and stay right for the best channels. Recently, about one-half mile after this island series ended, there was a rusty but working waterwheel on the left. A couple of hundred yards below is a 100-yard, gentle rock slalom followed a half mile later by the Route 659 take-out. History buffs should look for an old cemetery on the left bank as they approach Port Republic.

Incidentally, this tiny burg has quite a history. Founded in 1802, Port Republic was created as a river port. Originally it was the farthest upstream point for cargo boats travelling to Harpers Ferry on the Shenandoah. Later, the clearing of channels extended this river highway farther upstream to Grottoes.

Boats used here and for commerce downstream were called "gundalows"–a frontier corruption of the famous "gondolas" used in old world Venice. These boats were up to 90 feet long and 9 feet wide. Constructed near Port Republic, they were loaded with such staples as iron, lumber, flour, corn, potatoes, apples, and brandy. Boaters piloting these craft used unique horns 8 feet long; the hair-raising sound of these horns could be heard for several miles. Upon arrival at Harpers Ferry, 160 miles downstream, boat and cargo were sold and the boater had to trudge all the way back to Port Republic–after being paid the princely sum of $15 for the 5-day trip downstream and the long walk back upstream.

In addition to caves and history of the South, there is wildlife. On hot sunny days many turtles sun themselves on the numerous rocks and trees in the river. Snapping and painted turtles are most common. On a recent trip I saw two huge specimens and spooked several beaver who had left much evidence of their presence (slides and gnawed branches).

This is a good river for fishing, too. Perch predominate, but there are smallmouth bass and sunfish also. Bird life also abounds. Spotted sandpipers continuously flit ahead of the paddler and large hawks, herons, and ducks (wild and domestic) are common. On one trip we startled a huge flock of two dozen turkey vultures.

Trees along the banks include the usual river denizens–sycamore, silver maple, and box elder. But other trees are present also: ash, basswood, catalpa, cottonwood, oak, and cedar, to name a few.

This is not a heavily traveled river. If you want a nice uncrowded alternative to the South Fork of the Shenandoah, try the South. It does not require much more water: the Lynnwood gauge should be at least 3.3 feet. Be sure to also check the crude canoeing gauge (upstream side) on the Route 778 bridge at Harriston before putting into the river.

Section: Crimora (Rt. 612) to Port Republic (Rt. 659)

Counties: Augusta and Rockingham

USGS Quads: Crimora and Grottoes

Suitable for: Day cruising

Skill Level: Shepherded novices

Months Runnable: Winter, spring, and maybe early summer

Interest Highlights: Well-groomed farms, wooded banks, wildlife, Grand Caverns

Scenery: Pretty in spots to beautiful in spots

Difficulty: Class I–II with 1 Class II–III just above Rt. 256 bridge

Average Width: 50 to 70 feet

Velocity: Slow to moderate

Gradient: 8 feet per mile

Runnable Water Levels:
  Minimum: 2.7 feet on Waynesboro gauge; 3.3 feet on the Lynnwood gauge; 0 feet on Rt. 778 gauge
  Maximum: 6 feet on the Waynesboro and Lynnwood gauges; 3 feet on the Rt. 778 gauge

Hazards: Occasional trees in river; 8-foot dam below Port Republic and just above Lynnwood

Scouting: Class II–III rapids 300 yards above Rt. 256

Portages: None

Rescue Index: Generally accessible

Source of Additional Information: National Weather Service, Waynesboro and Lynnwood gauges (703) 260-0305

Access Points	River Miles	Shuttle Miles
A–B	7.5	7.5
A–C	10.0	9.0
A–D	15.0	12.0
B–D	7.5	7.5

Access Point Ratings:
  A–Crimora at Rt. 612 bridge, good
  B–Rt. 825 (river right) just below Harriston, very good
  C–Grand Caverns (Rt. 844) bridge, very good (closed in winter when caverns not open)
  D–Port Republic at Rt. 659 bridge (river left; with permission), good

---

Stony Creek

Like nearby Cedar Creek and the North Fork of the Shenandoah, Stony Creek is a fun trip. It is a very scenic 14 mile journey through farmland and woods with striking rock formations and hillsides to add spice. The rapids are cobble drops, rock gardens, chutes, and several small ledges–basically Class II (with an occasional Class II–III) at moderate levels.

However, this is not a novice trip because of several hazards. There are at least seven low-water bridges and three dams. The water flowing under several of the low-water bridges is fast, even at low water. In high water, the low-water bridges are even more dangerous, and the hydraulics below the dams become more perilous. Also at high water, the occasional alder patches and downed trees in the river become dangerous. Consequently, good boat control is essential for this trip.

The Stony is very aptly named. With numerous cobble bars along the way, there are quite a variety of rocks for amateur geologists to study. The shapes and colors of the rocks are particularly interesting. The primary rocks are shale and sandstone in a variety of colors. You'll also see an interesting man-made slag rock that looks like obsidian (volcanic glass) and small white crystals in veins cutting through various ancient gray limestone rocks. Sharp-eyed folks can also find fossils in some of the shales.

Put in on river left by the Route 691 one-lane metal bridge just before Riles Run joins Stony Creek. (Going north on Route 691, cross Riles Run just before you reach the put-in.) Here you are in George Washington National Forest. If the Stony doesn't look too scrapey at the put-in, you will have sufficient water for the entire trip. The woods, composed of cedars, pines, hemlocks, sycamores, tulip poplars, birches, and maples, usually shield the paddler from the surrounding farmland. A spring trip is made more glorious because of blooming redbud, dogwood, wild cherry, and occasional apple trees.

As with nearby Cedar Creek and the Shenandoah North Fork, the bird life is prodigious. Ospreys, kingfishers, great blue herons, hawks, ducks, goldfinches, downy woodpeckers, and spotted sandpipers are only a few of the species seen. I particularly enjoyed the numerous sandpipers flitting close to the water ahead of me and then

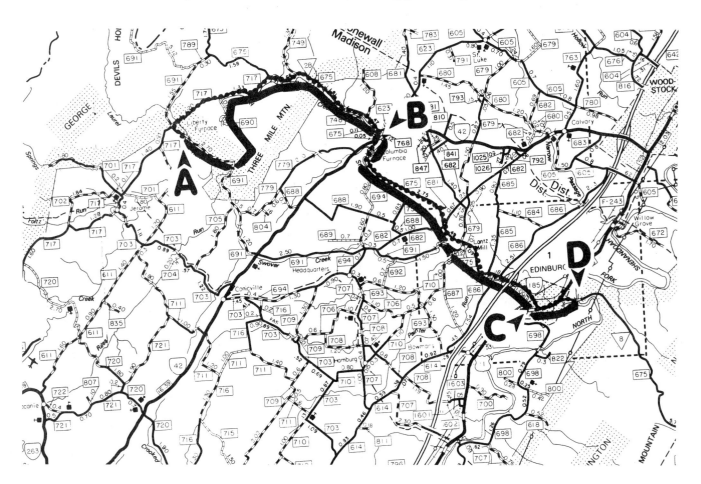

Section: Rt. 691 to Edinburg (US 11)

Counties: Shenandoah

USGS Quads: Conicville, Wolf Gap, Edinburg

Suitable for: Day cruising

Skill Level: Intermediates, maybe carefully shepherded novices at low levels

Months Runnable: Winter and spring generally

Interest Highlights: Pretty rock formations, bird life

Scenery: Pretty in spots to beautiful

Difficulty: Class II with at least 1 Class II–III

Average Width: 30 to 40 feet

Velocity: Moderate

Gradient: 22 feet per mile

Runnable Water Levels:
　Minimum: 3.3 feet on Cootes Store gauge
　Maximum: Perhaps 6 feet on Cootes Store gauge

Hazards: At least 7 low-water bridges, 2 dams of 2 feet and 1 dam of 5 feet (between Rts. 691 and 710), an occasional tree in the river

Scouting: 2 dams of 2 feet; approaches to low-water bridges warrant care

Portages: 7 low-water bridges and a 5-foot dam, perhaps 1 or both 2-foot dams

Rescue Index: Generally accessible

Source of Additional Information: National Weather Service, Cootes Store gauge (703) 260-0305;

Access Points	River Miles	Shuttle Miles
A–B	7	7
A–C	13	12
A–D	14	13

Access Point Ratings:
　A–near Liberty Furnace (Rt. 691), good
　B–Rt. 675 (near Rt. 42 bridge), very good
　C–Edinburg (US 11), good
　D–confluence with North Fork (Rt. 675), very good

stopping on nearby rocks to bob their backsides up and down. Toward the end of the trip you'll see numerous domestic geese and ducks (note the "giant" mallards).

The trip begins with a drop over small ledges and Devonian sedimentary rock cobbles while you paddle toward Three Mile Mountain which towers 800 feet above

you. Then you make a tight left turn and have a nice rock slalom.

At the end of the first mile you come upon cobble banks and more open countryside. Shortly thereafter you reach the first "dam." Recently, this was a wooden damlike structure (2 feet high on the right and 1.5 feet on the left) that blocked the river. The "dam" is easily runnable on the left at low levels. However, paddlers should check the strength of the hydraulic below the dam at middle and upper water levels. Below the dam there are a couple of nice chutes, pretty rock walls (first right and then left), two tight turns, and a 1.5-foot ledge.

After 2 miles you come to the first (unnamed) road bridge. Just below it is a nifty rock on the right with a tree clinging to it. In the spring pink phlox also graces this rock. Soon a dirt road runs next to the river and then a paved road. The latter is Route 717, which later changes to Route 675. Just after the road leaves the river, look for various-sized layers of Devonian gray shale slanting into the river.

Then, about 4 miles into the trip, when the left vista opens up and after you've passed some houses, you come to a real 2-foot dam which is abrupt on the right and sloping on the left. Scout it if you wish to run it.

In the next quarter mile or so you drop over a small ledge and run a couple of nice chutes (one with mild surfing possibilities) while passing some pretty rocks on the right. Just below this is the best rapid of the trip. At lower levels it begins with a rock slalom entry, has a nice chute in the middle, and finishes with a 100-yard-long Class II–III technical rock garden.

The next mile features several rock gardens and chutes. Here you are cutting between Three Mile Mountain on your right and Little Sluice Mountain on your left. The tallest peak of Little Sluice (called Little Schloss) is over 2,600 feet high–1,600 feet above you. Then, 6 miles into the trip, you come to a nice cobble bar on the left and a striking, low rock formation on the right. This makes a great lunch stop where you can poke around the rocks and enjoy the scenery.

Below this you will pass some houses on the left and then a footbridge. About a quarter mile below the bridge, after running a nice technical Class II rapid and passing a big rock of banded shale on the right, you come to another 2-foot dam. The most conservative route through this dam is a broken out slot on the right. In any case, scout the dam from the right to determine the best route or whether to carry.

Just below the dam are a rock garden, a couple of 1.5-foot ledges, and some chutes (one with surfing possibilities). Shortly thereafter is the first (Route 675) low-water bridge with the Route 42 high bridge less than

Ron Knipling running a small tongue in the five foot dam on Stony Creek below Columbia Furnace. This dam should only be run at modest water levels by experienced paddlers with all safety precautions. Photo by Gary Knipling.

100 yards farther. You have come 7 miles or halfway. Folks can put in or take out here if interested in a shorter trip. The remaining six low-water bridges are in the second half of this section.

After going under the Route 42 bridge you come to a large pool which is a great fishing hole for stocked trout (rainbow and brown) and smallmouth bass. The left bank consists of two huge rocks, one with an interesting triangular cave at its base.

Although you'll see some trash, this is a great place to stretch your legs or toss out your line. Incidentally, trout are stocked in most of this 14-mile section of Stony Creek during the spring, So be careful in early spring when the creek may be heavily used by anglers. Also, on the right bank here are the remains of Columbia Furnace, an historic iron works.

There are a couple of nice Class II rapids before reaching the second Route 675 low-water bridge less than a half mile later. If the cobble rapids just below this bridge are not too scrapey, there is sufficient water for the entire trip. You then run a nice Class II and go under a footbridge sporting "no trespassing" signs. Over a half mile below this you come to a third low-water bridge. The easiest portage at low levels is on the left.

Only 300 yards below are the remains of a fourth low-water bridge. Even at low levels a steel girder crosses the entire creek a foot above water. Portage on the right. Be careful as you approach this because the banks are lined with brush and at high water this brush wall could create a dangerous situation with no escape.

About a quarter mile below this bridge go right around an island to see some nifty rocks. Over a half mile below this is a ledge with a gentle surf spot, and a fifth low-water bridge (Route 682) follows. Carry on the left at moderate water.

Less than a half mile later is the sixth low-water bridge (Route 691). It is probably best to carry this one on the right. This bridge is an important landmark–particularly if you take Route 691 (via Route 675 and Route 809) for most of the shuttle. Only 100 yards downstream is a 5-foot dam. Look it over, if you wish, before running the river. On the river you'll recognize it by some concrete steps (on the left bank) and a very impressive horizon line. Carry on the left at moderate levels.

Another 200 yards downstream of the dam is a pipe blocking the right side of the river and creating a twisty chute on the left. The pipe can create quite a hydraulic at high levels. Just below this chute is the seventh (Route 710), and last (gasp!) low-water bridge.

You then enter the tiny village of Lantz Mills. Check out some of the huge, sprawling, abandoned houses on the riverbank here as you pass by. Almost a half mile and a couple of nice Class II rock gardens later, you come to three pretty limestone rock slabs on the left bank. Just below are some striking rocks on the right with a neat 1-person cave at their base.

Over half a mile later you go under Interstate 81 and over a 1-foot ledge. Within the last mile you pass under a railroad bridge and finally reach the US 11 take-out on river right.

You can continue for the next mile until the Stony joins the North Fork of the Shenandoah. After the first half mile there is a low-water bridge that was recently jammed with debris. A few hundred yards below this is a diagonal ledge and another low-water bridge. Between this bridge and the confluence is one more diagonal ledge. There's good smallmouth and largemouth bass fishing where the Stony and the North Fork join. However, the best take-out is on river right by Route 675.

There are currently no gauges on the Stony. However, if the Cootes Store reading is a good 3.3 feet, there is probably sufficient water for a minimal level trip.

Trout fishing is great on Stony Creek.

James

Appomattox River

Route 616 bridge to Route 626 bridge below Hixburg

This 11 mile trip is a relaxing journey for novice paddlers and includes nothing tougher than Class I rapids. You put in either river right or left at the Route 616 bridge in Appomattox County.

The first section of the trip is 6.5 miles of Class I rapids—numerous gravel bars and riffles. However, because of this stream's small size and its gradient (13 feet per mile), there is much maneuvering required.

The scenery of forest and farmland is quite good. The stream takes you through Appomattox-Buckingham State Forest for much of the trip, but you also pass beautiful pastureland. In particular, you will see large hemlocks on various bluffs along the way. Be on the lookout for turkey, beaver,

and deer. The only hazards are an occasional tree in the river and perhaps a few fences. You can take out at the Route 618 bridge (at Hixburg) on the left.

If you wish, you can continue below Hixburg for another 4.5 miles to the Route 626 bridge. The gradient is less here (8 feet per mile) and the scenery is not as nice.

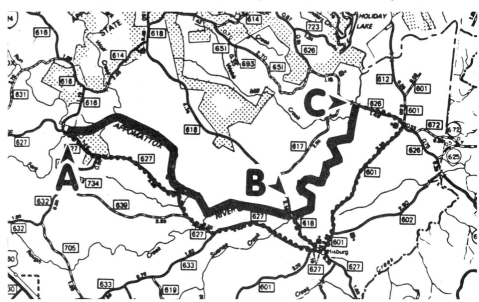

Section: Rt. 616 bridge to Rt. 626 bridge (5 miles below Hixburg)

Counties: Appomattox

USGS Quads: Pamplin

Suitable for: Day cruising

Skill Level: Novices

Months Runnable: Winter, spring, and early summer (following a wet spell)

Interest Highlights: Appomattox-Buckingham State Forest, pretty pastureland, Appomattox Courthouse National Historic Park (on Route 24 near the put-in)

Scenery: Pretty to beautiful in spots

Difficulty: Class I

Average Width: 20 to 30 feet

Velocity: Slow to moderate

Gradient: 13 feet per mile in upper section; 8 feet per mile in lower section

Runnable Water Levels:
  Minimum: None. If the river looks runnable at the put-in, it should be runnable for entire trip
  Maximum: Flood stage

Hazards: Occasional trees in river and a few fences

Scouting: None

Portages: None

Rescue Index: Accessible to remote

Source of Additional Information: Appomattox River Company (804) 392-6645

Access Points	River Miles	Shuttle Miles
A–B	6.5	8
B–C	4.5	6

Access Point Ratings:
  A–at Rt. 616, good
  B–at Hixburg (Rt. 618), good
  C–at Rt. 626, very good

However, this lower section is still worth the trip for the beginning paddler. The river has Class I rapids for the first part of this stretch and flatwater near the end. The scenery continues as farms and woodlands. However, be sure to take out on river right at the Route 626 bridge because the Appomattox is log strewn for many miles below here.

There is a very important historic spot on Route 24, about a ten-minute drive from the put-in. This is Appomattox Courthouse National Historic Park, where General Robert E.

Lee surrendered to General Ulysses S. Grant to end the Civil War in April 1865.

Giles Mill (Route 609) to Genito (Route 604)

The 8.5-mile stretch of the Appomattox from Giles Mill to Genito is a great novice trip for paddlers looking for a relaxing time. This is a good first river trip for paddlers wanting to try moving water and is runnable virtually the entire year. Indeed, you can even consider this river during a long dry spell. You may not be able to get your entire paddle in the water, but the river bed is so even that you probably will not have to get out of your boat. The gradient is only a foot per mile, so there are no rapids except for a Class I just below the take-out.

One put-in is on river left (north) just upstream of the Route 609 bridge. Better yet is a nearby jeep trail also on the north side of the river, which can get you closer to the river and which offers better parking.

This is a good trip for just drifting and letting your fishing pole dangle for largemouth and smallmouth bass, bream, crappie, or catfish. The banks are often

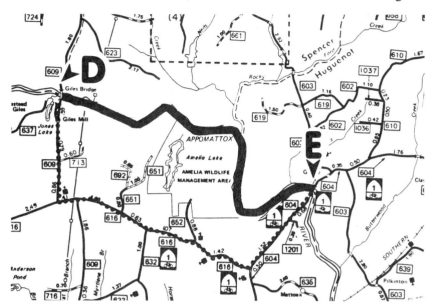

Section: Giles Mill (Rt. 609) to Genito (Rt. 604)

Counties: Powhatan, Amelia

USGS Quads: Chula, Clayville

Suitable for: Day cruising

Skill Level: Beginners and novices

Months Runnable: Virtually the entire year

Interest Highlights: Surprisingly remote and wooded, fishing, Amelia Wildlife Management Area

Scenery: Pretty to beautiful in spots

Difficulty: Class A with 1 Class I just below the take-out

Average Width: 30 to 40 feet

Velocity: Slow to moderate

Gradient: 1 foot per mile

Runnable Water Levels:
  Minimum: No gauge; if runnable at put-in, this section is runnable for the entire trip
  Maximum: Flood stage

Hazards: Maybe an occasional tree in river

Scouting: None

Portages: None

Rescue Index: Accessible to remote

Source of Additional Information: Appomattox River Company (804) 392-6645

Access Points	River Miles	Shuttle Miles
D–E	8.5	10

Access Point Ratings:
  D–at Giles Mill (Rt. 609), good
  E–at Genito (Rt. 604), very good

wooded (on occasion with mountain laurel), and the water quality is good.

Perhaps the best thing about this trip is that, after 3 miles, you have the Amelia Wildlife Management Area on the right bank for most of the remainder of your journey. This is a great place for hunting, fishing, and other outdoor activities. Bird hunters have a variety of environments for dove, quail, and ducks. Also hunted are rabbit, squirrel, deer, and turkey. There is a fishing lake in the Wildlife Management Area as well as a pond. Amelia Pond is stocked with bass and bluegill, while the 100-acre lake has crappie and channel catfish as well.

Between 5 and 7 miles into the trip you come to a couple of scenic bluffs between 50 and 100 feet high. Other than that you mostly see woods, particularly in the Wildlife Management Area.

The only rapid is just below the take-out. This is a Class I drop over bowling ball-sized boulders, which are the remains of an old mill dam. You can run the rapid and get back to the take-out with minimum hassle. If you don't run the rapid, take out on river right below the Route 604 bridge.

Chesdin Road or Matoaca Bridge to Route 36

For history buffs, this 6.5-mile intermediate whitewater trip is a classic. Here the Appomattox really shows you what the United States was like in simpler times—when canals played a crucial role in our country's transportation network and when water power was the engine that drove many mills in the bustling communities along this waterway. Starting with steady Class I-II rapids at the beginning, the river builds to two Class III rapids in the last half mile of this journey.

Petersburg (with its many historic buildings) and the Appomattox River have much to offer Civil War and American history fans. General Robert E. Lee and his Confederate army retreated from Petersburg along this stretch of the river in April 1865 as he made his way to Appomattox Courthouse where he would surrender to Union forces under General Ulysses S. Grant. Earlier, during the Revolutionary War, the British general Benedict Arnold brought Redcoats here before the final Yorktown Campaign. His opponent, commanding the Colonial Irregulars, was the Marquis de Lafayette. Still earlier, this was the domain of Powhatan, an Indian chief who in about 1600 established a powerful confederacy before the first English colonists settled this area.

Section: Chesdin Road (Rt. 669) or Matoaca Bridge (Rt. 600) to Campbells Bridge (Rt. 36)

Counties: Chesterfield

USGS Quads: Sutherland, Petersburg

Suitable for: Day cruising or camping

Skill Level: Intermediates

Months Runnable: Winter, spring, and early summer

Interest Highlights: Old mill remains, canals, dams, and islands

Scenery: Pretty to beautiful in spots

Difficulty: Class I-III

Average Width: 75 to 100 feet

Velocity: Generally moderate

Gradient: 13 feet per mile on river

Runnable Water Levels:
   Minimum: 2.4 feet on NWS Matoaca gauge; 0 feet on Matoaca Bridge gauge

Maximum: 6.4 feet on NWS Matoaca gauge; 4.5 feet on Matoaca Bridge gauge

Hazards: Occasional trees in river, spikes near Spiked Dam, 6-foot dam with hydraulic 200 to 300 yards below Rt. 36 (take-out) bridge. At high water, a whirlpool develops under Rt. 36 (take-out) bridge. Possible vandalism if parked on Petersburg (south) side of river at take-out.

Portages: Vepco Dam about 1.5 miles after either put-in

Rescue Index: Accessible

Source of Additional Information: National Weather Service, Matoaca Gauge (804) 226-4423

Access Points	River Miles	Shuttle Miles
F–H	6.5	8
G–H	3.5 or 6.5*	4 or 0*

Access Point Ratings:
   F–at Chesdin Lake Dam (Rt. 669), excellent
   G–at Matoaca Bridge (Rt. 600), good
   H–at Rt. 36, good

*Includes 3-mile circuit up Appomattox Navigation Canal and down Appomattox

192

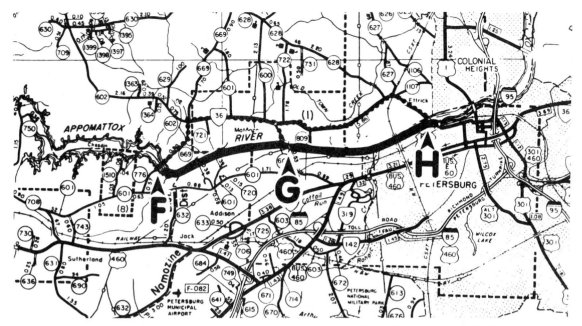

Even though this section of the Appomattox is on the outskirts of Petersburg, nature lovers will thoroughly enjoy it too. The abundant wildlife and unique beauty of this river as it winds around numerous islands is truly memorable.

Interestingly enough, the paddler has a choice of two put-ins. If you want to go in style, put in on river left (the north side) below the 35-foot-high Brasfield Dam on Lake Chesdin. Here, Chesterfield County has spared no expense to construct the Cadillac of canoe put-ins. You then have a 1.5-mile flatwater paddle to a 6 foot second dam, which was constructed in 1807 for the Appomattox Navigation Canal. It is now called Abutment Dam or Vepco (Virginia Power and Electric Company) Dam. On the right, no more than a quarter of a mile from the put-in, are the remains of Caudles Lock, one of 27 boat locks that formed a 100-mile canal-river navigation system in the 1800s from Farmville downstream to Petersburg. A few hundred yards below this (also on the right) are the ruins of Clarks Mill, which apparently was active until 1921. After reaching the Vepco Dam, you then portage on the left bank or line your canoe down a fish ladder near the left side of the river.

The alternative put-in is in the Navigation Canal on river right (south side) of Matoaca Bridge (Pickett Avenue/Route 600). From here you paddle 1.5 miles up the canal to just below the aforementioned Vepco Dam, portage over the towpath, and enter the river from the right bank. The Canal has more scenic flatwater then the Brasfield Dam to Vepco Dam stretch, and you have a shorter shuttle. Indeed, the old 30- to 40-foot-wide Navigation Canal is a visual treat. The left (south) bank consists of hardwood forest behind large chunks of moss-covered Petersburg granite. The right (north) bank

is a 5-foot fence of planks—wooden battens made to hold the earthen wall forming this bank and towpath when the canal was dredged out. All of this contributes to a quiet, intimate paddle down the canal.

The Navigation Canal is still known as the Upper Appomattox Canal; it was built between 1795 and 1816 to bypass the fall line of the Appomattox River. In 1970, the City of Petersburg was given the 6-mile Navigation Canal by Vepco. One provision of this gift was that Petersburg construct a park next to this canal for recreational purposes. This park and the pond next to it are the first sights you will see as you begin your paddle upstream on the Navigation Canal. Incidentally, in the early 1900s this park was the site of Ferndale Amusement Park, which featured a merry go-round, bowling alley, shooting gallery, ice cream parlor, dance hall, and silent movie theater. The current park (now open) is called Appomattox Riverside Park.

Before starting, check the Matoaca Bridge gauge on the downstream side of the color-coded center abutment. Green (0 to 1 foot) is for very carefully shepherded novices: yellow (1 to 3 feet) is for intermediates with good boat control; red (3 to 4.5 feet) is for advanced paddlers; and black (above 4.5 feet) is the time to take an alternative trip. (See the data sheet for the National Weather Service Matoaca gauge, which you can get by telephone.) There is a nice river right stair path to view the gauge after leaving a nearby parking lot for shuttle cars. One other advantage of the Matoaca bridge put-in is that you get a nice 3-mile shepherded novice circuit trip that requires no shuttle: you paddle 1.5 miles upstream on the flatwater canal and then 1.5 miles downstream on a Class I–II section of the Appomattox to your starting point.

After crossing the road from the parking lot to the canal put-in, take some time to paddle around the pond by the park. In summertime many turtles sun themselves on fallen trees.

Continuing upstream on the placid canal, pause to enjoy the lichen- and moss-covered Petersburg granite blocks forming the 10-foot-high left bank. The weathered granite is pink from large amounts of feldspar in it. Look for birds and other wildlife in the hardwood forest of oak (white, black, red, and chestnut), beech, and birch continuing beyond the bank. After paddling three-quarters of a mile, you will go under a run-down I-beam bridge and soon thereafter come to a mound of silt that has washed into the canal—an easy lift over. In the next three-quarters of a mile you pass under another bridge, go by a 6-foot-high concrete overflow wall on the right bank, and reach the Vepco Dam.

Steve Thomas takes aim to avoid Target Rock in the distance on the Appomattox.

After portaging over to the river, pause to marvel at the big rusty gears that used to control a sluice gate on the dam here. Nearby is a hand winch used to pull logs off the gate. Once on the river and staying near the right, you will drop over three 1 foot ledges in the first 100 yards. Just after this is a 2–3 foot drop (Class II). Then comes a long, mellow rock slalom. At the end of this slalom is Picnic Rapid (Class II+)—so named by all the float anglers who used to picnic and fish here. Enter this rapid left of center and work right toward the end to avoid some sneaky rocks in the runout. There's a good recovery pool at the bottom, and nervous novices can look Picnic Rapid over from the right

bank before running it. You then pass Woodpecker Island on the left after a river channel enters from the left. Woodpecker Island is a great spot to relax and camp for those so inclined. The river then breaks into three channels; the middle or right routes are generally best.

After the channels converge, paddle through a rock garden toward a large rock on the left bank. As you approach this rock you will see the Matoaca Cotton Mill Canal wing dam. The right half of the river bypasses the dam. It has two Class II channels running through it. Less experienced paddlers can take this route. If you continue on the left within the wing dam, you will go down the canal under a powerline and enter Jughandle (Class II–III) as the current bends right and breaks out of the canal. You can scout Jughandle from the island on its right to make sure there are no trees in this bumpy 3- to 4-foot drop. Also, while you're on the island, notice the remains of the headgate of the Matoaca Mill Canal on the left and visualize the Matoaca Mill Dam, which was built across to the island in 1830. Jughandle gets its name because the left side channel and island forming this rapid look like a jughandle on a map.

You enter a long Class II rock garden just below Jughandle, so try to pick up the pieces of errant paddlers quickly. Halfway down this rock garden is a 2-foot ledge. Just below this ledge, get over to river left for a very pleasant lunch stop if your stomach is growling.

After the rock garden ends, you reach Matoaca Bridge. There are two historic items of interest on river left here. First, if you walk a short distance north on Route 600 and turn left on Ferndale Road, you will see three buildings that were Matoaca Mills—a busy cotton mill complex that operated for 100 years and employed 200 workers. Second, slightly downstream of Matoaca Bridge are the abutments from an old wooden toll bridge, which charged a nickel for pedestrians and 15 cents for horses and wagons at the turn of the century.

A quarter of a mile below the bridge you enter a maze of delightfully beautiful islands with some very large pine trees growing on them. Weave your way through the smaller maze of rocks in the right channel passing by these islands. Relax and enjoy this scenic mile while you look for great blue herons and other critters. There is good fishing here, too. The river reforms after these islands, and you may be able to see a silo on your left. This is a part of the Randolph Farm, which, in the late 1700s, was the childhood home of "John Randolph of Roanoke," a U.S. congressman and senator.

You then see a Vepco transformer station high on the right and go underneath some powerlines. Here Rohoic Creek (formerly called Indian Town Creek) enters on the right. This was the last Appomattox Indian village site. Indian Town Aqueduct (which was 42 feet high) used to support the Appomattox Navigation Canal as it crossed Rohoic Creek. Four toll locks upstream from the aqueduct lowered boats 33 feet from the upper canal.

After going under the powerlines (you're now 2 miles below Matoaca Bridge), look for a sign on an island warning of dam spikes. Go left of the island and run a Class II drop center as you do so. Don't worry about the spikes, you won't reach them for a half mile. Soon after this island you can take a far left channel (which has a 2- to 3-foot drop in it) around a second island, or go right of the second island. If you go right, stay near the right bank. Soon you will see a horizon line formed by the remains of Spiked Dam (a crib dam that diverted water to a mill race on the right side of the river) and see a small channel (an old mill canal) to the extreme right. You have a second choice. You can take the intimate Class I–II old canal channel or look for a place to carefully bump down Spiked Dam. Although this is technically a Class II–III drop, look out for spikes and nasty rocks if you decide to run it. Many boats have been damaged here. After the initial 3-foot drop, there are a couple of rocky passages to negotiate before reaching the pool below.

Soon you cross under a railroad bridge. Notice the newer bridge built on top of the much lower, older bridge. After a good quarter of a mile you will pass a rock garden with stone canal walls on the right. Not far below you will see the twin stone arches of a mill and a dam warning sign on the left. After exploring these twin arches, stay tight right. Just below is a 5-foot dam (Battersea Canal), which, like Spiked Dam, diverts water to millraces on both sides of the river. You will see a pipeline on the right bank and a canal alongside it. After about 50 yards, the current breaks left through the canal

wall into Pipline Rapids—a mellow Class III of two good drops best run right of center to avoid the rocks in the left side runout. There is an eddy on the right at the top of the rapids. Here you can scout Pipeline, after pulling your boat up on the large granite boulders on the right side of the canal break that leads into Pipeline Rapids.

After getting your act together below Pipeline, you will soon come to a 1- to 2-foot ledge. About 50 yards below this on the left is Target Rock, a tougher Class III and very aptly named because paddlers without good boat control tend to crash into the center of this large rock at the bottom of the rapid. If the current isn't too pushy, you can scout from an island in the center of the river to the right of the rapid. Otherwise, you need to pull over to the left bank and get over to the rocks forming the left side of the rapid to scout. Paddlers generally run Target Rock Rapids on the left and catch a big eddy on the left below the main drop before being blown into Target Rock. This eddy is a great place to practice ferrying, if you can avoid intimacy with Target Rock. On river left below Target Rock notice the striking 12-foot cascade as another canal break enters the river. Take the right side of the river to sneak Target Rock Rapids. However, beware of a large hole that develops on the right at higher water.

Shortly below Target Rock you cross underneath Campbells Bridge (Route 36) and take out less than 100 yards below on river right. At high water, when a large, moving whirlpool forms beneath it, you may want to take out on river right well above the bridge. You don't want to swim the whirlpool at high water because a 6 foot dam with a keeper hydraulic is lurking only 200 to 300 yards below the Route 36 take-out bridge.

Spend some time poking around the take-out. There are mill ruins on both banks of the river. On river right are the remains of Battersea Cotton Mill, which was several stories high, had a bell tower, and operated for over 75 years until 1918. On the hill overlooking the left side of the river is the campus of Virginia State University. This used to be known as Fleet's Hill—a famous duelling site in colonial times.

However, do not leave vehicles unattended on the Petersburg (south side) of the river at the final take-out. There have been numerous instances of vandalism here.

Back Creek

Back Creek is a pure delight and certainly one of the most outstanding Class II–III intermediate whitewater runs in Virginia. Unfortunately, there are two obstacles that slightly tarnish Back Creek's perfection.

The main obstacle is the need for a permit to run this pristine creek. Specifically, you must obtain written permission to paddle Back Creek from the Boiling Springs Rod and Gun Club (which owns land on both sides of the gorge), and have this permission with you on the river. To obtain this permission, you should write to Mr. William J. Loth III, 304 Yorkshire Avenue, Waynesboro, VA 22980.

Paddlers writing to Mr. Loth should adhere to several guidelines. First, their group should be small (under 10 boats). Boaters wanting to do this trip with a canoe club should contact the Coastal Canoeists, a state-wide club centered in the Richmond area, or the Blue Ridge Voyagers, who hail from Washington, D.C. suburbs.

Second, interested parties should apply several months in advance, as daily launches are limited. Also, you may not use the river after April 15 or in the summer.

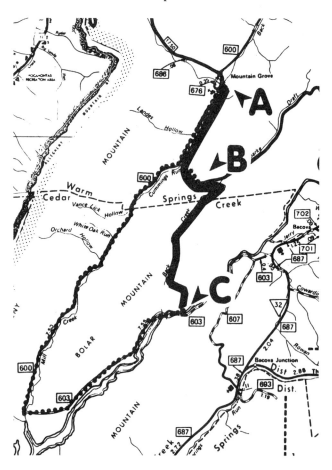

However, the latter part of March is great because it is also the time of the Highland County Maple Syrup festival described below. Third, while on the river, paddlers should be very respectful of fishermen and not antagonize them in any way. Finally, since the Boiling Springs Club stocks the river with its own trout, paddlers are not allowed to fish in the river.

Take this warning about securing prior permission seriously. The local laws allowing such exclusion are well established, and some Boiling Springs Club members and residents don't like canoeists. You will indeed be stopped if you do not have the requisite paperwork.

The only other flaw in Back Creek's perfection is its long shuttle for a short canoe trip. The 13-mile shuttle is about three times as long as the 4.5-mile trip through the gorge.

If you obtain permission, the late March Highland County Maple Syrup Festival is a good time to run this stream along with the Richardson Gorge of the Jackson River. Both trips have a common take-out, but you also need permission from the Boiling Springs Rod and Gun Club to run this beautiful section of the Jackson. The buckwheat pancakes, country sausage, and locally manufactured maple syrup served at various locations during the maple syrup festival are reason enough to make this trip, but one might consider wearing two life jackets after such a breakfast to support the added ballast. The most popular spot to stoke up before running the Back Creek and Jackson Gorges is the Ruritan Club on the west side of Route 220 about 16 miles south of Monterey on the way to Warm Springs. Get there early in the morning before it gets too crowded.

Having secured permission from the rod and gun club and endured the shuttle, the paddler is in for a real treat. Back Creek starts off with a bang and keeps its momentum all the way to the backwaters of Lake Moomaw—named for Ben Moomaw, a former Secretary of the Covington Chamber of Commerce.

Most paddlers put in at the gauging station on Route 39. For a nice comfortable run the gauge should be 3 feet. Other boaters put in a mile upstream at the bridge where Route 600 leaves Route 39. Still other folks put in another 1.5 miles upstream at Mountain Grove where Route 39 turns west. Here Little Back Creek joins Back Creek and adds significant volume to the river. At high water, the paddler can put in even further upstream.

For the first 2.5 miles below Mountain Grove, Back Creek is a mellow trip over occasional mild rapids. After reaching the gauging station on Route 39, however, things

Running the vertical drop of the second big ledge on Back Creek; the more gradual alternate route is in the foreground on river left.

get more interesting. This is why the gauging station (for a 4.5-mile trip) is the preferred put-in.

The first significant drop is the 2-foot ledge just below the gauging station. In the first half mile there are three small ledges and several rock gardens on which to warm up. Then the paddler reaches another 2-foot ledge, which can be tricky; it is usually run left of center. Below this are several more rock gardens, a 1-foot ledge, and another rock garden. Meanwhile, the road leaves the river at Blowing Springs Campground.

After this last rock garden, and a mile below the gauging station, you reach the first 3-foot ledge. Here the river narrows and creates a drop having the best concentrated water volume in the trip. Be careful and scout from the right because the hydraulic at the bottom of this ledge is squirrelly. You are now in a Devonian limestone and sandstone gorge with 1,000-foot-high, steep hills, which are often graced with hemlocks and rhododendrons. You will also see signs of beaver here.

The next half mile has a couple of 2-foot ledges bracketing a long rock garden. Then there is a 2-foot ledgy drop followed by a long pool. At the end of this pool, and three-quarters of a mile below the first big ledge, you will see a horizon line. Get over to the left and scout the second 3-foot ledge. On the left it is a 2-step drop, which you can run with care. If there is enough water, you can also run it in one abrupt drop using a slot in the center. Be sure to avoid the big rock just below and between these two routes.

After the next three-quarters of a mile, which features a long pool and rock garden, you will see another horizon line. Scout this last 3-foot drop on the left. You can run it center (which is a bit bumpy) or on the extreme left, making sure you miss a sharp rock in the ledge.

The next 1.5 miles start with a pretty limestone rock formation, continue with hemlocks and rhododendrons clinging to the banks, and end with several rock gardens and one 2 foot ledge. Then comes an interesting short section with big boulders in the river. Shortly below this the Jackson River joins on the left, and you enter Lake Moomaw. From here it is about 500 yards to the river left take-out upstream of the McClintic Bridge (Route 603).

Section: Mountain Grove (Rt. 600) to McClintic Bridge (Rt. 603)

Counties: Bath

USGS Quads: Sunrise, Warm Springs, Mountain Grove

Suitable for: Day cruising

Skill Level: Novices (first 2.5 miles), intermediates (last 4.5 miles)

Months Runnable: Winter and spring, generally

Interest Highlights: Stunning Back Creek Gorge (last 4.5 miles)

Scenery: Beautiful in spots to spectacular

Difficulty: Class I-II first part, Class II-III second part (with 3 ledges of 3 feet)

Average Width: 40 to 60 feet

Velocity: Moderate for first part, often fast for second part

Gradient: 22 feet per mile for first 2.5 miles, 27 feet per mile in 4.5-mile Back Creek Gorge

Runnable Water Levels:
  Minimum: 2.5 feet on gauge by Rt. 39, Buena Vista gauge 3.5 feet
  Maximum: 5.5 feet on gauge by Rt. 39, Buena Vista gauge 6 feet

Hazards: Maybe a tree in the river

Scouting: 3 Class III ledges (first on right, last 2 on left)

Portages: None

Rescue Index: Accessible above Gorge, remote in Gorge

Source of Additional Information: National Weather Service, Buena Vista gauge (703) 260-0305. Obtain permission from Mr. William J. Loth, III, 304 Yorkshire Avenue, Waynesboro, VA 22980.

Access Points	River Miles	Shuttle Miles
A–B	2.5	2.5
B–C	4.5	13.0

Access Point Ratings:
  A–at Rt. 600 (Mountain Grove), very good
  B–at Rt. 39 (gauging station), very good
  C–at Rt. 603 (McClintic Bridge), good

Buffalo Creek

Buffalo Creek is a nifty 13-mile Class I–III intermediate trip just a few miles southwest of Lexington, Virginia. It can be broken into two parts—a mellow 8-mile upper section and a much busier, 5-mile lower section. Unfortunately, it is hard to catch with sufficient water and is generally only runnable in winter and spring after rains of 2 or more inches. The Maury River usually should be over 5 feet at the James River Basin Canoe Livery gauge on Route 60 near Buena Vista before Buffalo Creek is worth a look. Call the Livery at (703) 261-7334 to be sure there is sufficient water.

The put-in for the full 13-mile trip is near the Route 251 bridge at Effinger (where Colliers Creek and Buffalo Creek join), about 15 miles west of Lexington on State Route 251 on the way to Collierstown. Put in here along Route 251, using any spot that is convenient and out of the way. Be discreet because Buffalo Creek is technically on private property and, unless you're on the state right-of-way, so are the access points. There have been no recent reports of problems with landowners, but, as with any stream, take care not to anger them.

About a mile below the put-in and before passing under the steel bridge on Route 251 at Murat, you'll reach Murat Ledge, a Class II–III double drop of first 2 and then 3 feet that can be easily scouted and run on the extreme left. You can also check out these two ledges on the shuttle if you are so inclined.

About a half mile below the Murat bridge is a dairy farm and the most dangerous challenge of Buffalo Creek—possible electric fencing. Obviously, being in the water is a real problem if the fences are turned on. However, remember you are on private property, so don't damage the fence.

Another mile below the dairy farm you'll come to a low-water bridge. There will be a second low-water bridge (Route 674) in the next mile and a third a mile later. After 2.5 more miles comes a fourth low-water bridge (Route 610). All four bridges can be seen easily and portaged. However, if you have a large group, be sure all boats get out of the river quickly since the eddies above the bridges are small.

Section: Effinger (Rt. 251) to Rt. 700

Counties: Rockbridge

USGS Quads: Collierstown, Natural Bridge, Glasgow

Suitable for: Day cruising

Skill Level: Intermediates at moderate levels

Months Runnable: Winter and spring following a heavy rain

Interest Highlights: Pretty cliffs and good ledge series below Interstate 81

Scenery: Pretty to beautiful in spots

Difficulty: Class I–III at moderate levels

Average Width: 50 to 60 feet

Velocity: Moderate to fast

Gradient: 25 feet per mile

Runnable Water Levels:
  Minimum: No gauge; if runnable at take-out, last 5 miles is runnable; Buena Vista gauge should be 5 feet
  Maximum: Maybe 2–3 feet of water; inspect rapids at take-out and below I-81; maybe 8 feet on Buena Vista gauge

Hazards: Electric fence at dairy farm one-half mile below Murat, occasional tree in river, several low-water bridges

Scouting: Class II–III rapids at Murat (from left), Class III just below I-81 (right), Class III one-half mile below Rt. 700 low-water bridge (right), Class II–III below Rt. 608 (right)

Portages: 5 low-water bridges, maybe an electric fence, maybe an occasional tree

Rescue Index: Accessible to remote

Source of Additional Information: National Weather Service, Buena Vista gauge (703) 260-0305; James River Basin Canoe Livery (703) 261-7334

Access Points	River Miles	Shuttle Miles
A–B	8	10
B–C	5	6 or 8

Access Point Ratings:
A—at Effinger (junction of Colliers Creek and Buffalo Creek), excellent
B—at Rt. 678, excellent
C—at Rt. 700, excellent

One of the great ledge sequences on Buffalo Creek. Photo by Howard Kirkland.

After the fourth low-water bridge, things pick up a little with a few play holes and some Class I rapids. About 2.5 miles below the fourth low-water bridge and 8 miles into the trip, you'll see Route 678 on the right bank. This road comes off US 11 and is a good put-in for those wanting a shorter trip and more rapids.

The last 5 miles below Route 678 pass more quickly and contain several Class III rapids at moderate levels. As you continue down from Route 678, the creek passes under US 11 after a mile or so. Along here there are only a few Class II rapids, even at high water. However, be patient—better things are soon to happen.

Just a mile after US 11 the twin bridges of Interstate 81 come into view high above Buffalo Creek. The biggest gradient of the creek is over the next half mile, which contains several series of ledges. The first ledge series is before you reach the Interstate 81 bridges and can be run on the extreme right or left. Even though you can't see this entire Class II–III rapid from the eddies at the top, don't worry—there should be no big surprises.

The biggest drop on the entire trip is just after the second I-81 bridge. This strong Class III must be run on the right; most of the water heads this way—over a 4-foot drop followed immediately by a 2-foot drop into a squirrelly hole. The water then kicks hard back to the left across a few shorter ledges. Be ready to brace through all this. At higher water you can run this rapid farther left to miss the hole and avoid the turbulence, which really increases in higher water.

The next several hundred yards run over a number of small ledges. The scenery here is outstanding, with a high cliff over the right bank. Part of this cliff hangs 2 to 4 feet above the water with a small stream that drops through it—beautiful! Buffalo Creek then turns sharply left against the face of a sheer cliff 100 feet high. The roar around the bend is only a nice play spot and should present no problem for the intermediate paddler. Both right and left bank cliffs are still in view of Interstate 81.

The next half mile has a number of nice play spots at some ledges that are half the width of the river. Then you reach the easily spotted Route 700 low-water bridge. There are two small eddies on the left and right and the portage is easy. As with the low-water bridges upstream, paddlers in large groups need to get out of these small eddies quickly.

There is a good strong Class II rapid immediately as you put in below the bridge.

After another half mile you reach a Class III set of rapids—three drops spaced 20 to 30 feet apart. The first drop is 3 to 4 feet and should be taken to the right. Trees have a tendency to block the extreme left of the second drop. Consequently, you need to make an "S" turn in the last two drops: cut left after you run the first ledge, back right to run the second, and center to run the third. The second and third ledges are 2 to 3 feet each, and there are a few play spots here.

Another mile and Route 608 crosses Buffalo Creek just below the last drop. This Class II–III rapid is very similar to the ledgy drop just before the twin Interstate 81 bridges. Run this drop on the right. There is an island immediately below it, straddled by the Route 608 bridge. If you've gotten too far right you'll have to run the right channel. Unless a tree is stuck there you should have no trouble. Use the large bank eddy and hop out for a quick look to be sure no obstruction lurks below.

When you set your shuttle, you can look at this last rapid from the bridge. If there's enough water, there will be enough for at least the 5-mile trip from Route 678. Nothing on the creek is much tougher than this rapid, so you can use it to decide whether you should paddle Buffalo Creek.

It's only a half mile to the last low-water bridge and the river left take-out on Route 700. To return to the put-ins drive upstream to Route 608 and go left across the bridge. Continue about a mile to the top of the hill and go right on Route 680. It's paved, so enjoy it as you go about 1.5 miles to Route 679 at Falling Springs Church. Here you can either go right for a 2-mile, unpaved ride to US 11 or continue straight on a paved road for 3 or 4 miles to US 11.

When you reach US 11, turn right (north) in either case. As you start down the long hill to Buffalo Creek, Route 678 turns sharply left and goes a half mile to the short put-in before it dead-ends. For the long trip, continue on US 11 for several miles more to Route 764. Turn left and continue on route 764 until you reach Route 251. Turn left and go west to Murat, being sure to take the right turn Route 251 makes 100 yards after the bridge crosses Buffalo Creek. Effinger and the upper put-in are just 1.5 miles away.

Have a good run, and don't forget, you're on private property.

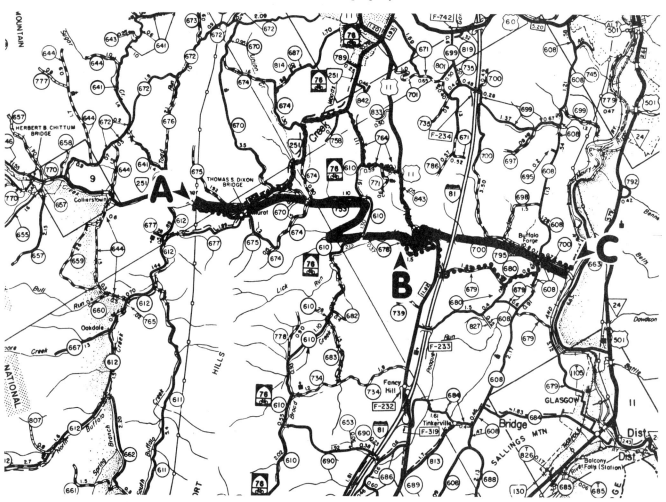

Bullpasture

It's great to shoot the Bullpasture! The scenic feature for most of the 14-mile section from McDowell to Williamsville is a series of high bluffs, mainly along the left side of the river. However, the scenery is most beautiful and the rapids most challenging (Class III–IV) in the last 3 miles, where you go through the Bullpasture gorge of Devonian limestone and Silurian sandstone.

The Bullpasture is clear and flows over a bed of solid rock. It passes through a very scenic valley. On your right are colorfully named Buck Hill, Bear Mountain, and Little Doe Hill. On your left is Bullpasture Mountain, until you enter Bullpasture Gorge, which cuts through this mountain. The Bullpasture is a 25-foot wide trout stream at the McDowell put-in, but reaches a more mature 40-foot width at the take-out.

Be careful of paddling the Bullpasture during the first few days of spring when many fishermen converge on the river to catch brown, rainbow, and brook trout. Also, there have been problems with landowners above the gorge, so you should use the US 250 and Route 612 put-ins described below and be very alert and respectful of using the riverbanks before you reach the gorge.

Shepherded novice and intermediate paddlers can do the 10 mile stretch from McDowell (Route 250) to where Route 678 rejoins the river a mile above the Bullpasture Gorge. The first 6 miles of this stretch are generally Class I–II drops—occasional cobble bars and small ledges. The river wanders close to hemlock studded hills on the left and farmland on the right for the first 2 miles. When it crosses the valley and gets close to the road, there is a nice series of Class II mini-ledges and rock gardens. After this, the river goes away from the road for the next 4 miles.

Having paddled 6 miles, you reach Route 612—a nice alternate put-in. For the next 4 miles the river continues to wind through farmland with the left bank occasionally bumping against pretty shale rock formations covered with hemlocks. Be alert for water birds along here: great blue herons, kingfishers, and ducks. The occasional rapids are similar to those in the first 6 miles.

Route 678 joins the river after this 4-mile section. Novice paddlers should take out here, but intermediates can continue on for another mile. Now the river picks up gradient and the scenery changes. You leave farmland, and hemlock-studded rock formations become more frequent. A half mile or so after Route 678 comes back to the river, you come to a 2-foot ledge (run right) followed by a good Class II–III rock slalom. Just over a quarter of

a mile below this are two ledges close together: 1 is 2 feet and the other is 3 feet.

Soon you arrive at a campground on the right which marks the entrance to the Bullpasture Gorge. This clearly is the zestiest part of the Bullpasture. Here you are committed to nearly continuous Class III ledges and rock gardens for 3.5 miles. The Gorge and its rocky slalom drops will give you a good workout. Accordingly, shaky intermediates

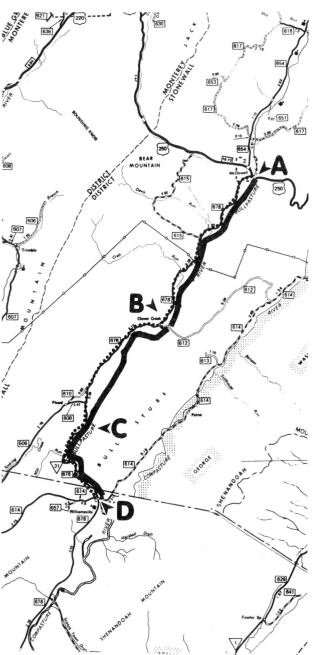

Dave Jeffrey dropping into the juicy hydraulic formed by the second ledge of Double Ledge in the Bullpasture Gorge. Photo by Mayo Gravatt.

should take out here. However, strong shepherded intermediates can continue at low water levels, and advanced paddlers can put in here for this delightful section.

Less than half a mile below the campground (after passing under a footbridge), you are in the gorge and see a beautiful 100-foot-high rock face on the right covered with hemlocks and ferns (in spring). You can stop for lunch on the left bank in a patch of hemlocks to marvel at this formation.

The rapids (mostly Class III) start in earnest just below this stop. First, there is a ledge combination followed a half mile later by three ledges. Then, it is slalom city. You begin with a good Class III S-turn which is followed by a 100-yard rock garden. Below this are two longer rock gardens.

At the end of this last rock garden and about a half mile above the take-out you should notice a sloping rock formation with a 40-yard overhang creating a long shallow cave on the left bank. Immediately below this formation is a big slab of rock blocking the left side of the river as well

as a big rock in the right side of the river. Proceed cautiously and pull over to river right to scout: you have reached an impressive horizon line! Another indicator that you are approaching this drop is a cable crossing the river about 250 yards upstream.

Here you have a double ledge with two healthy Class III–IV sloping Tuscarora sandstone ledges close together. The first ledge is a 3 foot drop into a modest hydraulic. Then, after a 20-foot pool where you can reorient yourself, there is a 4-foot drop into a more feisty hydraulic. The best route for these two ledges (and their hydraulics) is in the center. There is a nice recovery pool below the second ledge where you can set throw ropes and rescue boats. Aggressive boaters can poke their noses into the lower hydraulic for dynamic surfing at moderate levels. There is also a nice surfing hole 50 feet below these two ledges; it is formed by a rock ledge just below the surface of the river and exists at ten inches and above on the Route 614 take-out gauge.

Pick up the pieces of errant boats and bodies quickly because 100 yards below is a 5-foot drop over another

John Williams running the five foot vertical ledge which is the next rapid after Double Ledge. Photo by Tom Gray.

sandstone ledge. The best passage at moderate water levels is the third vertical drop from the left bank (Class III–IV). Just right of this route is a more gradual but squirrelly passage on the right side of the river with a big hole and a stern-smacking rock at the bottom, which is hard to avoid at very low levels. Scout both routes carefully. Most paddlers run the vertical drop option: it is a straight shot with more airborne time and a lower penalty. There is a good pool below both options for rescue.

After these two big rapids, the river simmers down to a few Class II–III ledges and rock gardens for the remaining quarter mile of the trip. There is a particularly nice rock garden just above the take-out.

Before paddling, please check the gauge at the take-out on the upstream side of the right abutment of the Route 614 bridge. Be very careful of this run (particularly the 3 miles in the Bullpasture Gorge) as the gauge approaches 2 feet. At this level the Gorge gets really big and pushy and is for advanced to expert paddlers only.

You can easily scout the two big rapids near the end before running the Bullpasture Gorge. Simply go a third of a mile upstream on Route 678, up the hill from the Route 614 bridge take-out in Williamsville. Once your odometer registers 0.3 mile you will see the remains of a road going diagonally toward the river. Park and walk 150 yards down this track to see the 5-foot ledge of the lower big drop. Continue 100 yards upstream to view the double ledge of the upper big drop.

To reach Wallace Track Campground on the Cowpasture River take Route 678 for 2.2 miles in the other direction from Williamsville (south) and turn left on Forest Service Road 282. This is just about three-quarters of a mile south of the state fish hatchery. During the March maple syrup festival, float fisherman camp here as do fellow paddlers running Back Creek and the Jackson River—gentler streams than the Bullpasture Gorge. (However, Back Creek and Jackson River require permission from the Boiling Springs Rod and Gun Club of Bacova; see the descriptions of these two streams for further information.) Incidentally, if you want to gorge yourself on gorges you can run the Bullpasture, Back Creek, and Jackson gorges all on the same day; the latter two are only 25 miles or so from the Bullpasture. It is also possible that one could do the Goshen Pass of the Maury in the same day for a fourth gorge. The nearby Cowpasture River is not covered in this book and is not recommended as a trip because of landowner problems. The Bullpasture joins the Cowpasture shortly below the Williamsville take-out.

Section: McDowell (US 250) to Williamsville (Rt. 614)

Counties: Highland and Bath

USGS Quads: McDowell, Monterey, Williamsville

Suitable for: Day cruising

Skill Level: Shepherded novices/intermediates (first 10 miles); shepherded intermediates (low levels)/advanced (last 4 miles)

Months Runnable: Winter and spring generally

Interest Highlights: High bluffs and mountains, Bullpasture Gorge

Scenery: Beautiful in spots to beautiful

Difficulty: Class I–II first 10 miles; Class III last 4 miles, with 2 Class III–IV drops

Average Width: 25 to 40 feet

Velocity: Generally fast, particularly at the end

Gradient: 28 feet per mile for first 10 miles; 40 feet per mile for last 4 miles (including 3-mile Bullpasture Gorge)

Runnable Water Levels:
  Minimum: 0 feet on Rt. 614 gauge; 2 feet on Maury gauge at James River Basin Canoe Livery; 3.5 feet on Buena Vista gauge

Maximum: 2 feet on Rt. 614 gauge; maybe 6 feet on Maury gauge at James River Basin Canoe Livery; maybe 7.5 feet on Buena Vista gauge

Hazards: Perhaps trees in the river; holes in high water

Scouting: Class III–IV double ledge (7 feet total drop); Class III–IV ledge (5 feet) 100 yards below double ledge

Portages: None

Rescue Index: Generally accessible except for Bullpasture Gorge

Source of Additional Information: James River Basin Canoe Livery (703) 261-7334 for Maury gauge there; National Weather Service, Buena Vista gauge (703) 260-0305

Access Points	River Miles	Shuttle Miles
A–B	6.0	4.5
B–C	4.5	4.0
C–D	4.0	4.0

Access Point Ratings:
A—at US 250 (McDowell), very good
B—at Rt. 612, very good
C—at Rt. 678 (1 mile above Gorge), very good
D—at Rt. 614 (Williamsville), very good

Calfpasture

The 6-mile trip on the Calfpasture from Route 688 to Route 692 near Deerfield is a great trip at moderate levels for shepherded novices wanting to improve their skills and intermediates who want some continual action not exceeding Class II. Novices must be shepherded because of occasional downed trees and brush near the banks in or at the bottom of Class I–II rapids, which can cause problems for those who don't have good boat control.

The scenery in this section is most pleasant. Low shale cliffs studded with evergreens (hemlock and pine) alternate with views of a gorgeous pastoral valley of rustic farms and pretty mountains in the distance. Indeed, Roger Corbett, in the 1977 edition of his Virginia whitewater guidebook, said, "About 3 miles below the route 688 bridge, there is a spot that may be the most beautiful scene on any river in Virginia." Not all paddlers may agree with Roger, but his statement indicates what a special trip this is. The water is crystal clear and the pools between rapids are incredibly deep for such a small stream—a paradise for trout! The rapids are generally Class I–II drops over multicolored sandstone and shale cobble bars, some with tight turns at the bottom. Occasionally, there are interesting modest shale ledges parallel, diagonal, and even perpendicular to the current for added spice.

The only problem with this trip is access. Ideally, you should keep your group small. The put-in is posted, but you can probably leave one shuttle car there. If you see anyone, ask permission to launch. The best put-in is river left, downstream of the Route 688 bridge. You should also take out river left, downstream of the Route 692 bridge. You can probably park two shuttle cars here, but again, ask permission if possible. There is currently no gauge. Canoeing zero is probably when the water is even with the left abutment footing at the Route 688 put-in.

The put-in is quite interesting; you have some Class II ledges mainly going perpendicular to the water flow. This creates some interesting currents. Generally, you should run this first ledgy drop on the left and the second drop just below in the center. After that you'll see a pretty rock face with hemlocks clinging to it and a house nestled under it.

You are now in the first pool, and you can admire its depth and the water's clarity.

Soon you begin entering long Class I–II cobble bars alternating with deep pools. The Route 808 ford is reached just over a mile into the trip. Then, you have the road and a high shale bluff on the right. About a quarter of a mile after a long cobble bar you'll come to a 2-foot ledge and just below that, some nifty little ledges with minor surfing possibilities. Two more small ledges soon follow.

Then you get back into gravel bars again. You are in a broad valley now, and despite the rather high banks, you can pause and admire this beautiful sight of rolling terrain, well-manicured farms, and scenic mountains in the distance on the right. After a couple of gravel bars is a diagonal 1.5-foot ledge.

Over a half mile below this ledge is a cobble bar that blows into some brush on the right. Be careful here. A couple of hundred yards below this is a short set of ten tiny shale ledges—a fun miniature staircase with interesting shale bedding on the left. A gravel bar about three-quarters of a mile farther warrants care: stay away from the small, clogged far left channel. Less than a mile below this is another shale rock face with hemlocks and pines. The river mellows out for the last mile before the take-out. Recently, there was a patch of brush to avoid on the left just above the take-out.

Concerning other attractions of the Calfpasture, it is first a great trout stream with its deep pools. Bird life is also good with primarily ducks and kingfishers escorting you down the river. For hikers, there are great trails, such as Ramsey's Draft.

You could conceivably put in at the US 250 bridge several miles upstream of this section. This is not recommended because the Calfpasture is much tinier there and usually doesn't have enough water. Also, access is even tighter than below. Alternatively, you can continue below Route 692 to the Route 687 bridge 15 miles downstream, which is also posted. But this is not a great trip: it is quite long, not as scenic, and has fewer rapids.

Section: Rt. 688 to Rt. 692

Counties: Augusta

USGS Quads: Deerfield, Elliott Knob

Suitable for: Day cruising

Skill Level: Shepherded novices and intermediates

Months Runnable: Winter and spring following a good rain

Interest Highlights: Beautiful wide valley, mountains in the distance, shale rock formations with hemlocks, deep pools, interesting ledges

Scenery: Pretty to beautiful

Difficulty: Class I-II

Average Width: 40 to 60 feet

Velocity: Moderate

Gradient: 22 feet per mile

Runnable Water Levels:
  Minimum: Level with left abutment footing at put-in, perhaps 3.5 feet on Buena Vista gauge
  Maximum: Maybe 2 to 3 feet above left abutment footing at put-in, perhaps 6 feet on Buena Vista gauge

Hazards: Occasional trees in river

Scouting: Only for trees in or just below rapids

Portages: Occasional trees

Rescue Index: Generally accessible

Source of Additional Information: National Weather Service, Buena Vista gauge (703) 260-0305

Access Points	River Miles	Shuttle Miles
A–B	6	7

Access Point Ratings:
  A–at Rt. 688, good
  B–at Rt. 692, very good

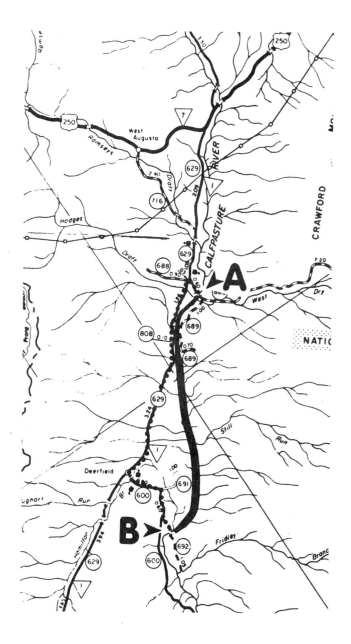

Catawba Creek

If you don't mind carrying a few dams and like limestone gorges, Catawba Creek is for you. This basically Class II stream has a couple of Class II–III spots and even a Class III rapid at certain levels.

To begin this 32-mile section of Catawba Creek, you could put in at Route 311 near the tiny berg of Catawba. However, this is on private property, so it might be better to put in roughly 3 miles below here at the Route 779 bridge. Putting in here will also avoid numerous fences and cattle gates just upstream.

At the Route 779 put-in you have a pastoral creek with low banks affording a good view of a beautiful valley. Don't worry if it is scrapey at the put-in; you will have plenty of water as you work toward the take-out. Soon after launching you will enter a pretty limestone gorge where you encounter Class II rapids, which are generally full to broken ledges and boulders with drops of up to 3 feet. Still in the gorge, you come to a second Route 779 bridge 1.5 miles below the first bridge.

After leaving the gorge, the scenery remains beautiful as you go another 1.5 miles to the third bridge (Route 663). The fourth significant bridge (Route 779 again) is 4.5 miles downstream. This is the first reasonable take-out after a 7.5 mile trip. There is a USGS gauge upstream on river right of this bridge. In this stretch you have frequent easy rapids and a great view of the open valley and surrounding mountains. Along here there is also a 1-foot weir with a strong roller to punch near a footbridge.

Just below the Route 779 bridge with the gauging station you pass a cement plant. Around the bend below the cement plant is a 6-foot dam. Carry it, please, on river right. Soon you will go under a fifth bridge (Route 600), and the sixth bridge (Route 666) is reached 2.5 miles later. In this area the scenery is rural with a touch of low density residential housing.

About 4.5 miles below the sixth bridge you come to a ford at Route 670. Less than a mile below this ford you have your work cut out for you. First, there is a 6-foot dam which is shortly followed by a 9-foot dam. Carry both dams on the right. As you pass over the dams and under the bridges notice that the banks are becoming higher. The only consolation for these two dams between the sixth and seventh bridges is that there is one section of Class II–III ledgy rapids. Two miles from the Route 670 ford (and roughly a mile below the two dams) you go under the seventh (Route 606) bridge. You reach the eighth (US 220) bridge 3 miles later.

In the vicinity of the US 220 bridge, just north of Fincastle, high muddy banks dominate and the water is

Section: Catawba (Rt. 779) to James River (Rt. 726)

Counties: Roanoke, Botetourt

USGS Quads: Catawba, Daleville, Oriskany, Salisbury

Suitable for: Day cruising

Skill Level: Intermediates

Months Runnable: Winter and early spring generally; a heavy rain is also needed for the upper section

Interest Highlights: 2 limestone gorges

Scenery: Pretty in spots to beautiful in spots

Difficulty: Class II–III with 1 Class III in second gorge near end

Average Width: 20 to 40 feet

Velocity: Generally slow to moderate; fast in 2 gorges

Gradient: 37 feet per mile in first 7.5 miles (with 60 feet per mile in first gorge); 22 feet per mile in next 12.5 miles and 10 feet per mile in last 12 miles (with 20 feet per mile in second gorge)

Runnable Water Levels:
  Minimum: scrapey at put-in near Catawba; lower sections by inspection
  Maximum: Perhaps 2 feet above minimum

Hazards: 3 dams: 1 (6 feet) below cement plant and fourth bridge (Rt. 779); 2 (6 and 9 feet) 1 mile above Rt. 600 bridge; occasional tree in creek; low-water bridge at end (Rt. 726)

Scouting: Strong Class III ledgy drop over halfway through second gorge near end

Portages: 3 dams: 1 (6 feet) below cement plant and fourth bridge (Rt. 779); 2 (6 and 9 feet) a mile above seventh bridge (Rt. 600)

Rescue Index: Generally remote in upper section, becoming more accessible in lower sections

Source of Additional Information: None

Access Points	River Miles	Shuttle Miles
A–B	7.5	6.0
B–C	12.5	14.5
C–D	12.0	11.0

Access Point Ratings:
  A–near Catawba (Rt. 779), good
  B–Rt. 779 near gauging station, good
  C–Fincastle (US 220), very good
  D–Rt. 726 (2 choices), good

mostly smooth. This is 20 miles below the first recommended put-in and 12.5 miles below the Route 770 bridge and gauging station. You can take out here if you're pooped or put in for a 12-mile trip if you are fresh. About 5 miles below Route 220 you pass under the Route 635 bridge. The rapids soon intensify as you enter another limestone gorge. There are some lush stands of arborvitae here—evergreen trees of the cypress family that resemble cedar. The gorge contains about 2 miles of good Class II–III rapids, primarily ledges. At least halfway through the

gorge you will encounter a strong Class III (Class III–IV at high water), intense, ledgy drop. Perhaps you should scout this one (possibly from the left) before committing yourself.

Soon after the rapid you leave the gorge and subsequently arrive at a low-water bridge nearly 12 miles below US 220. This take-out has Route 726 and the ruins of old Salisbury Furnace on the left. Alternatively, you can paddle less than a half mile to where the Catawba enters the James and take out at Route 726 on the left.

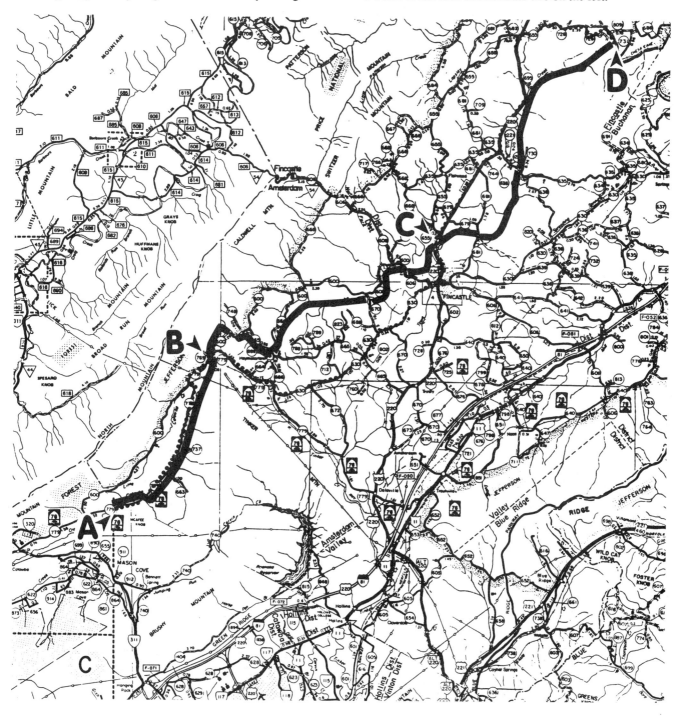

Dunlap Creek

Dunlap Creek is a small stream with some generally nice surprises for alert intermediate and advanced paddlers with good boat control and a penchant for short hikes. This ledgy and cobble bar Class II trip is interspersed with at least one Class IV and several unrunnable drops—some man-made and some natural. Most importantly, there is a spectacular double waterfall near the beginning of this 29-mile stretch of river. There are numerous take-outs, so many different trips are possible along Dunlap Creek.

The first put-in is less than half a mile into West Virginia where this stream is called Cove Creek. You follow VA Route 603 into West Virginia for about a third of a mile. You turn left and reach the put-in bridge (Route 3/14) a tenth of a mile later. Here the creek is fast with small sloping ledges and sharp turns. The fast velocity means you must have good boat control to make the turns and to stop before portaging several fallen trees in the first stretch of this trip.

After a nice warm-up of nearly 2 miles in the remote and pretty valley of Cove Creek, you come to the first bridge in Virginia (Route 603). The walls soon close in, and less than a mile below this bridge you arrive at a ten-foot waterfall. Stay alert because this drop approaches suddenly, and you need good boat control to get to the left bank for your portage.

Having grunted and groaned down the portage, you are in store for a treat: Cove Creek has entered a limestone chasm. Just below your portage Sweet Springs Creek joins on the right as a second waterfall—a 28-foot drop called Beaverdam Falls. The twin waterfalls from Cove Creek and Sweet Springs Creek are a spectacular scenic delight, so bring your camera. Also, the limestone walls here are travertine and sport interesting stalactites and stalagmites, adding to your visual feast. If your eyes are sharp, you will see a giant living arborvitae tree in this vicinity. This evergreen looks somewhat like a cedar but has its own unique and appealing characteristics.

The stream is called Dunlap Creek after this confluence. Stay alert below the waterfall junction because you soon arrive at a third waterfall. You should also portage this 5-foot drop on the left. Below here Dunlap Creek bumps over a few nice moderate ledges and then dashes over

Bob Whaley admiring one of the gorgeous falls on Dunlap Creek. Photo by Ed Gertler.

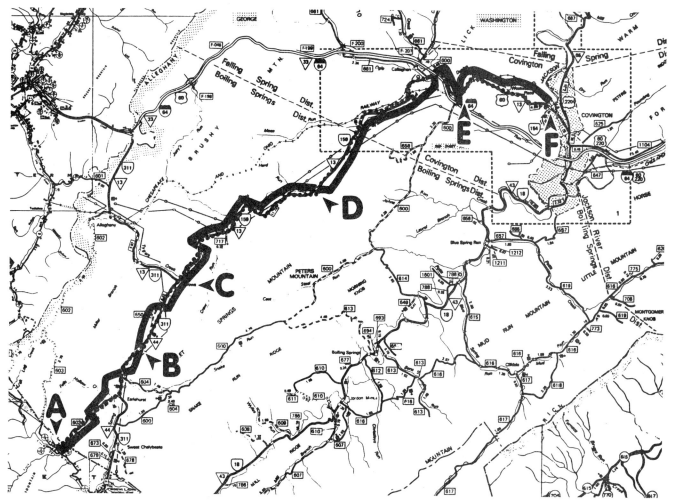

many easy gravel bar rapids. Also, the carries over trees virtually end. If you wish to take out, you can do so just over a mile below the last waterfall at the second bridge (Route 311).

After this, Dunlap Creek continues as a typical ridge and valley stream; unfortunately, it passes houses here and there with unsightly trash heaps near them. Because the creek is already at a high elevation (nearly 2,000 feet), the surrounding mountains do not tower over it. The third bridge (Route 311) is just over a mile below the second bridge, and the fourth bridge (also Route 311) is 2 miles below this.

After 1 more mile (having paddled over 8 miles) you come to a take-out next to Route 311 at the small community of Crows, where Routes 311 and 159 join. Dunlap Creek continues over its rocky bottom, passing woods and rocky bluffs in many places. Soon the creek narrows and develops some quick chutes. Below this it flattens out and the pools are broken by gravel bar rapids.

Nearly 2 miles beyond Crows you reach the fifth bridge (Route 159). Now the creek passes over some small ledges along with gravel bar rapids that break the monotony of the

long pools. Soon you pass the tiny community of Hematite, and Jerrys Run enters on the left after 2 more miles. The second Route 159 bridge appears 2 miles later. It is again time to be alert: the remains of a 6 foot dam come about 200 yards below this bridge. The aged dam is broken out on the right; this is the easiest passage. Not far below this dam is a low pipeline bridge which you should be able to duck under at moderate levels.

As you approach and pass the Interstate 64 and US 60 bridges, a good 6 miles farther, the action picks up with several Class II ledges. Then, about 1.5 miles below this pair of bridges is a 5-foot dam. A portage on either side is generally recommended. However, at low water there is a smooth chute on the left side of the river, which can be run by experienced paddlers.

After another half mile, you next come to this second pair of bridges and two moderate rapids. The first bridge is Humpback Bridge—so named because it is a historic covered wooden bridge of unique design. Many years ago it was part of the James River and Kanawha Turnpike which linked the James River in the east with the Kanawha and Ohio Rivers in the west. On river right is Humpback

Bridge Wayside—a great place for a lunch stop and a history lesson. Just below is the second US 60 bridge which has a locked gauging station just above the bridge on the right but a gauge just downstream on the right. The gauge should read at least 2 feet.

About a mile after this second pair of bridges you must be even more alert. Just below a quarry you will encounter a 20-foot dam. Carefully work your way over to the right above this impressive horizon line and land on the shallow, right side brink of the dam. You now must carry your boat over a steep rock ledge and then gently drop it over a small cliff onto a rock shelf for launching.

Immediately below this dam is a ledgy rapid, which is Class IV at higher water levels. Continue your portage if you are not comfortable with this drop. After another mile you will come to the Route 700 bridge. A quarter of a mile below this bridge is a big sloping shale ledge with a chute carved in the center. This 8-foot drop is a straight shot and has been run at modest water levels. However, be very careful of the giant hole at the bottom. There is an easy portage on the left. Incidentally, this chute is man-made. It apparently cut off a river meander so that the railroad grade paralleling the river could be built over the old stream channel.

About 2.5 miles later you come to the Jackson River and soon reach the third US 60 bridge. The left side take-out at this bridge is steep but convenient.

Section: Just over the West Virginia line (near Rt. 603) to Covington (US 60)

Counties: Monroe (WV) and Alleghany (VA)

USGS Quads: Glace, Alleghany, Jerrys Run, Callaghan, Covington

Suitable for: Day cruising

Skill Level: Careful, strong intermediates and advanced paddlers with good boat control and a penchant for short hikes

Months Runnable: Winter and spring generally; a heavy rain is also needed for the upper section

Interest Highlights: Remote valley and incredible double falls in upper section

Scenery: Pretty to beautiful and even spectacular in spots

Difficulty: Class II with at least 1 Class IV rapid and several sharp drops

Average Width: 20 to 40 feet

Velocity: Fast in upper section; moderate in lower sections

Gradient: 38 feet per mile in upper 8 miles to Crows; 18 feet per mile in lower 21 miles below Crows

Runnable Water Levels:
  Minimum: Riffles runnable at put-in for 8-mile upper section; riffles runnable at Humpback bridge below US 60 for 21-mile lower section; also, there is a USGS gauge on the right downstream of US 60 bridge—it should read 2 feet for lower section
  Maximum: Perhaps 2 feet above minimum

Hazards: 2 waterfalls less than 3 miles down upper section; broken 5-foot dam 200 yards below second Rt. 159 bridge below Crows; 5-foot dam one-half mile above and 20-foot dam a mile below Humpback and US 60 bridges; ledgy Class IV just below the 20-foot dam; 8-foot sloping ledge a quarter of a mile below Route 700; occasional trees in river in upper section and parts of lower section

Scouting: 5-foot dam one-half mile above Humpback and US 60 bridges; ledgy Class IV below 20-foot dam; 8-foot sloping ledge below Rt. 700

Portages: 2 waterfalls in upper section; maybe 5-foot dam one half mile above Humpback and US 60 bridges; 20-foot dam a mile below US 60 and Humpback bridges; maybe ledgy Class IV just below 20-foot dam; maybe 8-foot sloping ledge a quarter of a mile below Route 700; occasional trees in river

Rescue Index: Generally accessible

Source of Additional Information: None

Access Points	River Miles	Shuttle Miles
A–B	4.0	4.5
A–C	8.0	8.0
C–D	8.0	6.0
D–E	8.5	7.0
D–F	13.0	10.5

Access Point Ratings:
  A–just over WV line (Rt. 3/14) near Rt. 603, good
  B–by second Rt. 311 bridge, good
  C–at Crows (Rt. 311), good
  D–by second Rt. 159 bridge, good but steep
  E–at Humpback and US 60 bridges, excellent
  F–Covington (US 60), good but steep

Historic Humpback Bridge over Dunlap Creek—a key part of the James River and Kanawha Turnpike which linked the James River in the East with the Kanawha and Ohio Rivers in the West. Photo by Ed Gertler.

Don Bowman getting covered up in the first big drop of Irish Creek.

North Fork of the Hardware River

Like its nearby South Fork brother, the North Fork of the Hardware starts out placidly and then suddenly, the bottom falls out. In the case of the North Fork, this is about 2 miles downstream from the put-in near the big quarry at Red Hill. Unfortunately, it takes a lot of rain to get this small stream pumping. Once it is, however, advanced paddlers' adrenaline will also begin pumping as they contemplate the huge Class IV–V rapids encountered partway into the trip.

Things start peacefully enough with a swift flowing current and a low-water bridge in the first mile below the put-in. After this the river moves into a broad valley, but the paddler can see little because of the high banks. Then, there is a long Class II rock garden as the valley changes into a gorge.

Once in this gorge the paddler hears a roar below and is entreated to stop on river left to scout the large rapids making this noise. Saner souls wishing to carry this long rapid can do so on the left with some difficulty. When the leaves are off the trees, this main rapid of the North Fork can also be clearly scouted from Route 708 during the shuttle. After trees have leafed out, paddlers will have to scout from the riverbank.

The big rapids of the North Fork drop over ancient horneblende gabbro—a most erosion resistant rock. The main difference between the two Class IV–V drops of over 20 vertical feet on the two forks is that the South Fork rapids are only 50 yards long, whereas the North Fork kin are perhaps three times that length.

These tough rapids begin with a U-shaped 3- to 4-foot dam; the bottom of the shallow U-shape faces upstream. With a foot of water going over the dam, there is a short but very nasty, violent hole formed just below. Immediately after this is a rat's nest of ugly rocks dropping another 3 feet. Thus, paddlers wanting to run the dam should pick their path carefully to avoid pinning their boats. Members of the Kamikaze Kanoeing Klub can inspect a 7-foot break in the dam on the extreme right if they want to contemplate running this upper drop all at once.

About 50 yards below the dam are two more 3-foot ledgelike drops 10 to 15 yards apart. Then, there are another 50 yards before the *piece de resistance*. The river suddenly drops about 8 feet over a 30-yard nasty rock and ledge jumble on the left and a 20-yard even nastier rock and ledge jumble on the right. With enough water, the left looks less difficult; but please carefully scout this drop (while meditating and paying up your life insurance) before attempting it.

There are a couple of minor drops just below this ledge, and the river calms down as the paddler goes underneath a private bridge about 200 yards downstream. Shortly below this bridge is a good Class III double drop, which is perhaps easier on the left. You then reach the Route 708 bridge.

About a mile below the Route 708 bridge and over a quarter of a mile below a 2-foot ledge, prepare to meet a natural steep ledge that drops 5 feet over about 15 feet of river. This is runnable through a notch in the left-center of the steep rock outcrop. Exercise caution and scout this ledge, because trees or other debris often block it. Just below the ledge is a 20-foot pool and then a gentler 5-foot drop over 70 feet. After this last rapid, the action is basically Class I–II rock gardens and a 2-foot ledge just before the Route 631 bridge.

Shortly below this bridge the rapids end. Like its South Fork brother, the North Fork begins meandering; one now encounters high banks and an increasing number of downed trees. Paddlers who love whitewater and hate scrambling over trees should take out at Route 631. Those who are masochists at heart can take out 4 miles farther downstream, at either the next Route 708 bridge (just before the North and South Fork join) or the Route 20 bridge, another painful mile below that.

For advanced paddlers interested in whitewater only, the upper sections of the North and South Forks of the Hardware make a good 1-day combination because they are so close and the shuttles are so short. However, unless you love endless meanders and intimate contact with trees, make sure you take out at the right bridges.

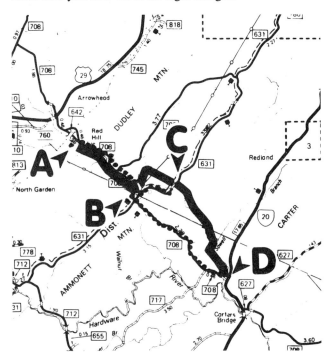

Section: Red Hill Quarry (Rt. 708) to second Rt. 708 bridge

Counties: Albemarle

USGS Quads: Alberene

Suitable for: Day cruising

Skill Level: Advanced paddlers

Months Runnable: Spring after a heavy rain

Interest Highlights: Huge, long Class IV–V rapids below a 3-to 4-foot dam

Scenery: Pretty in spots to pretty

Difficulty: Class II–III with 1 Class IV–V below a 3-to 4-foot dam

Average Width: 20 to 30 feet

Velocity: Moderate to fast

Gradient: 4 miles at 32 feet per mile (which has one-quarter-mile at 100 feet per mile); 4 miles at 15 feet per mile

Runnable Water Levels:
  Minimum: Scrapey at big Class IV–V rapids
  Maximum: Perhaps 1 foot of water at big Class IV–V rapids

Hazards: Trees in river; 3-to 4-foot dam; Big Class IV–V rapids just below this dam; 5-foot ledge (which may have debris blocking it) 1 mile below first Rt. 708 bridge

Scouting: Big Class IV–V rapids about 2 miles into the trip below a 3- to 4-foot dam; 5-foot natural ledge a mile below first Rt. 708 bridge

Portages: 3-foot dam; perhaps big Class IV–V rapids just below this dam; 5-foot natural ledge (if blocked by debris) a mile below first Rt. 708 bridge

Rescue Index: Accessible to remote

Source of Additional Information: None

Access Points	River Miles	Shuttle Miles
A–B	2.5	2.0
A–C	4.0	3.5
A–D	8.0	5.0

Access Point Ratings:
  A–at Red Hill (Rt. 708), good
  B–at first Rt. 708 bridge, good
  C–at Rt. 631, good
  D–at second Rt. 708 bridge, good

The big Class IV–V rapid on the North Fork of the Hardware River.

South Fork of the Hardware

The only serious whitewater found in the South Fork of the Hardware River is the 2-mile section between the South Garden bridge (Route 631) and the first bridge downstream (Route 712). However, this section starts out with a monstrous bang because it has what is probably Virginia's most humongous put-in rapids. Accordingly, it is advanced paddler territory. About 50 yards from the put-in, and after crossing a Class I–II ledge for a quick warm-up, there is a spectacular drop of at least 20 feet over about 50 yards. This is a good Class IV in low water and certainly tougher at higher water. Fortunately, it is very easy to scout from either side, and the rocks on river left can act as bleachers from which the masses watch the strong at heart. One could liken these rapids to the big drops on the Chauga River in South Carolina, except that the Chauga drops are more benign and often have moss, which eases the long rock slides.

Basically, this 20-foot drop is a cascade over ancient granite broken into three sections. There is only one way to run these rapids at low levels. The first section is a narrow rocky chute that drops a good 5 feet; it is entered at a 45-degree angle to the right, about 3 feet from the right bank. Having entered this chute, the paddler must immediately begin drawing left. This is necessary to prevent the bow from hitting the right bank in the micropool below the drop, and to move the boat sufficiently left to run the 5-foot rocky face of the second drop straight.

Then, at low levels, there is a 15-foot pool in which one works the boat hard left about 30 feet across the river for the final large drop of the rapids. Any paddler unfortunate enough to continue further down the right side will be funneled into a nasty rocky chute at the bottom of the rapids, which is too narrow for bodies and boats. The final big drop on the left is best described as a rocky washboard dropping 10- to 12-feet. At shallow levels it has a small hydraulic in the middle and a final larger hydraulic at the bottom. At these levels boats (particularly those of the aluminum genus) can hang up halfway down this last drop. Rescue ropes should be set on river right by the second 5-foot drop and on river left below the last 10- to 12-foot drop.

At higher levels these big rapids get much nastier. The 15-foot pool before the last 10- to 12-foot drop all but disappears, and the nasty rocky chute at the bottom right of the main drop becomes even more terminal. Accordingly, expert paddlers are advised to run the entire rapids on the left as a straight shot when the water is higher.

After this last big drop, there is a 30-foot pool. Then comes a final narrow 3- to 4-foot Class III twisty drop over rocks. It is best entered by a notch on the right and has a final runout requiring a right and then hard left turns. Shortly following these rapids are at least three good, Class II, twisty 3-foot drops through a wooded mini-gorge. After these, the river calms down for 10 to 15 minutes of paddling. Then, there is another Class II drop entered tight left with a hard right turn to finish. This is followed by a nice Class II slalom 5 minutes later.

After several more minutes, start looking for a small white building across the road on the left. This marks the pool before a strong Class III+ rapid, which is further

Ed Grove entering the last part of the BIG rapids on the South Fork of the Hardware. Photo by Neil Groundwater.

indicated by a large white house on the left next to the rapid itself. This rapid should be scouted either from the road while running the shuttle or from the left riverbank before running the rapid.

At moderate levels, the paddler enters right or center, then angles left and cuts back hard right over a 2- to 3-foot drop. Then, because there's a rock just below this drop, the paddler must quickly cut hard left to miss it. Just below are

Section: South Garden bridge (Rt. 631) to Rt. 712 or Rt. 717 bridges

Counties: Albemarle

USGS Quads: Covesville, Alberene

Suitable for: Day cruising

Skill Level: Advanced paddlers

Months Runnable: Spring after a heavy rain

Interest Highlights: Huge 20-foot slide rapids at put-in

Scenery: Pretty in spots to pretty

Difficulty: Class II–III with a Class IV–V at put-in and Class III–IV a mile into the trip

Average Width: 20 to 30 feet

Velocity: Moderate to fast

Gradient: 2 miles at 37 feet per mile (with first quarter-mile at 100 feet per mile)

Runnable Water Levels:
 Minimum: Scrapey at big slide rapids at put-in
 Maximum: Perhaps 1 ft of water at big slide rapids at put-in

Hazards: Many trees across river in last 6 miles; Class IV–V put-in rapids

Scouting: Huge 20-foot slide rapids at put-in (Class IV at low levels and Class IV–V at higher levels); rapids a mile into the trip (Class III+ at low levels and Class IV at higher levels)

Portages: Perhaps put-in rapids

Rescue Index: Generally accessible

Source of Additional Information: None

Access Points	River Miles	Shuttle Miles
A–B	2	2
A–C	8	5.5

Access Point Ratings:
 A–at Rt. 631, good
 B–at Rt. 712, good
 C–at Rt. 717, good

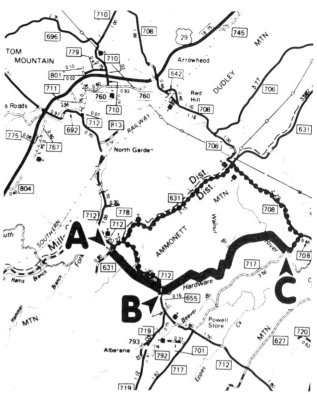

Although the river flows through farmland and woodland below the bridge, it suddenly changes character dramatically. Specifically, it starts a seemingly endless series of tight meanders within 10-foot-high silt banks. The only break in this pattern is an increasing number of trees to carry over or around. Other than a mini-ledge and sporadic riffles, the only rapids are a Class II rock slalom over halfway between the Route 712 bridge and the second take-out at the Route 717 bridge. Besides trees, one needs to watch for occasional cables hanging across the river (probably the remains of cattle fences). There are some signs of beaver along the way, but the silty river does not appear very hospitable for fish.

The trip below the big rapids to the Route 712 bridge is about half an hour at moderate levels. However, it is 2 to 2.5 hours at least (depending on downed trees) from the Route 712 bridge to the Route 717 bridge. The only other hazard (eyesore) on one trip was a vintage 1940s rusted car embedded in the bank. Hopefully, it will soon be gone from this interesting trip, which starts with a bang but ends with whimpers as frustrated paddlers carry over increasingly numerous trees across the river.

There do not appear to be any gauges for this river. If there is enough water for the big entrance rapids to be runnable, there is sufficient water for the trip. Advanced whitewater paddlers can run the South Fork and the upper North Fork of the Hardware on the same day because they are so close together and the shuttles so short.

at least a couple of juicy hydraulics to end these rapids. While heaving a sigh of relief after punching these hydraulics, look out for shallow rocks in the center and right of the river. These rapids certainly get meaner at higher levels and become a Class IV at least.

After these rapids, there are only a couple of Class IIs before the Route 712 bridge where there are the broken remains of a cattle gate. Take out here if your prime interest is whitewater.

Irish Creek

This is a little creek with BIG ideas. Unfortunately, it is very hard to catch up. When most other rivers are moving toward flood stage and the Buena Vista gauge for the Maury is approaching 6 feet, this is the time to target Irish Creek. The giddy gradient (80 feet per mile) of the stream keeps the paddler constantly working. With several big drops (mostly at the top), it's a good river for the advanced boater. Other than a couple of big drops, the main dangers to avoid on this 5- to 7-mile trip are several fallen trees and strainers. Helmets and flotation are *de rigueur*, especially if one runs the large drops.

You have a choice of two put-ins. More experienced boaters can put in at a cemetery parking lot 7 miles above the take-out. If you want to avoid the two large drops in the first 1.5 miles, you can put in just below the three large ledges as the river turns left. One nice safety feature of Irish Creek is that the road follows it the entire 7 miles of this trip. Consequently, you can see the largest rapids by careful inspection during the shuttle.

Just after putting in at the cemetery parking lot on Route 603, there is a nasty boulder garden that requires care. Then after numerous other Class II–III boulder-studded drops, you come to a tough Class IV rapid a half mile into the trip. Scout this sloping 5-foot ledge, which would entail a nasty swim if a paddler flipped at the top. When you look

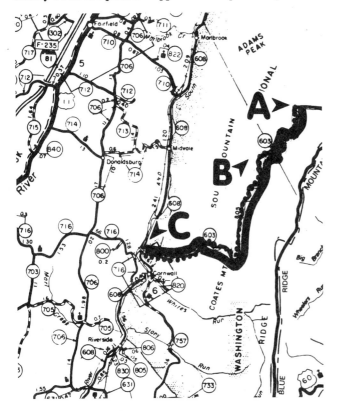

down on it from the road it doesn't look too difficult, but it is quite impressive when seen from the river bank. After a technical entry, the general route is skidding down the right side of the ledge rock face into a usually benign, but slightly squirrelly, hole at the bottom. Set rescue ropes just below, because there is a nice recovery pool here. This big ledge is very shallow; make sure you have enough water to run it.

About a quarter of a mile below this ledge you reach the first bridge. Then, after another three-quarters of a mile of several lesser but still significant Class II–III rapids, you come to a second bridge. A few hundred yards below this bridge is the pool above three big ledges that drop at least 12 feet in 50 yards. Scouting is a must at these Class IV–V rapids, which have a most eye-catching feature. You can't help but notice that the right bank of the river here is a unique levee. Many years ago, a group of very patient people loaded "jillions" of fist-sized boulders into large, long, wire mesh cages 4 feet high and 4 feet wide. Then these cages were stacked on top of one another and wired together to form a levee for keeping Irish Creek in its bed. You will see these levees at other spots on Irish Creek, but the three ledge levee is the most impressive.

Generally, paddlers run the three ledges from center to right. They drop over the first ledge in the center and then work right to drop over the best parts of the last two ledges. The first ledge is 4 feet, the second 3 feet, and the last 5 feet. The last ledge (because it is largest and sloping) has the worst hole, which can be quite grabby. Make sure you have a good head of steam and run these ledges squarely. Fortunately, there is a good recovery pool in which to set ropes and rescue boats and pick up bodies and boats. Be careful on the steep, rocky rip-rap of the right bank just below the last ledge; these big rocks are loose and the current is fast.

The rapids simmer down but are still Class II–III challenges as you head toward the third bridge. The biggest worries here are strainers and trees in the river. Below the third bridge is a nice sloping ledge on the right with generally low penalty surfing opportunities. Then, on the way to the fourth and last bridge, you will meet with some good roller coaster opportunities (particularly at high water) and, just above the bridge, a series of hydraulics formed by ledges. Immediately below the last bridge is the toughest rapid of the lower section. It is a steep Class III–IV drop which is generally best taken to the right of a rock in the center of the river. Scout it from the left. Just below this rapid is a feisty Class III drop with a sneaky hole spanning most of the

C-1 paddler running the last drop of Triple Drop Rapid on Irish Creek. Note the mesh basket levees filled with stones.

After this, the river is a mile or so of easy Class II cobbles until you reach the take-out at the bridge where Routes 603 and 608 join and Irish Creek enters the South River. Take out upstream of the bridge and on river left by a parking lot, which hopefully still is not posted. Below the bridge is private property, and the owners do not want paddlers taking out there. Incidentally, the Irish Creek gauge is on the upstream abutment of this bridge; hopefully you checked it out before putting in upstream.

Generally, Irish Creek is quite pretty even though it follows a road. It skitters down the ancient backbone of the Blue Ridge Mountains starting with Precambrian gneiss and ending with Cambrian sandstone. The banks are lined with hemlocks, pines, and hardwoods. Trout are stocked in this stream, and there are many camping places along it, as long as you stay away from posted areas.

One good day or weekend combination is to do Irish Creek on the west side of the Blue Ridge Mountains and then go over to the east side and do the Tye River. This is a larger stream than Irish Creek, but it requires almost as much rain to be runnable in its upper, Class III–IV section. For example, one day when the Buena Vista gauge read 6.5 feet, Irish Creek had over a foot of water, and the Tye River had a good 2 feet.

With enough water, paddlers can put in a mile above the cemetery at a church just below the junction of Irish and Nettle Creeks for a vigorous Class III slalom.

bottom left and center which is lurking to grab inattentive paddlers. Go well right to miss the hole.

Section: Cemetery (Rt. 603) to Rt. 608

Counties: Rockbridge

USGS Quads: Cornwall, Montebello

Suitable for: Day cruising

Skill Level: Advanced

Months Runnable: Winter and spring after a heavy rain

Interest Highlights: Beautiful steep creek, 3 big ledges

Scenery: Pretty in spots to beautiful

Difficulty: Steady Class II–III with 1 Class III–IV, 1 Class IV, and 1 Class IV–V rapids

Average Width: 20 to 30 feet

Velocity: Fast

Gradient: 80 feet per mile

Runnable Water Levels:
   Minimum: 0 feet on the take-out gauge (Rt. 608) bridge; 4.5 to 5 feet on Maury gauge at James River Basin Canoe Livery; 5.5 to 6 feet on Buena Vista gauge

Maximum: Maybe 2 feet on the take-out gauge (Route 608) bridge; mayble 7 feet on Maury gauge at James River Basin Canoe Livery

Hazards: Occasional trees in river; 2 Class IV–V rapids; high water

Scouting: 2 Class IV–V rapids (river right); 1 Class III–IV (river left)

Portages: Perhaps 1 or both of the 2 Class IV–V rapids

Rescue Index: Accessible

Source of Additional Information: James River Basin Canoe Livery (703) 261-7334 for Maury gauge there; National Weather Service for Buena Vista gauge (703) 260-0305

Access Points	River Miles	Shuttle Miles
A–C	7	7
B–C	5.5	5.5

Access Point Ratings:
   A–at Rt. 603 cemetery, very good
   B–at Rt. 603 below 3 ledges, very good
   C–at Rt. 608 bridge, very good

Jackson River

Hidden Valley Section

If someone were searching for the perfect fastwater float trip with excellent trout and bass fishing, fairly continuous Class I–II rapids, and hemlock-shaded camping spots galore in a remote uninhabited wilderness gorge, then an ideal choice would be the Hidden Valley section of the upper Jackson River.

Unlike the classic bigwater canyons with steep rocky walls and, usually, a railroad track and swarms of rafts, this is a place of great silence where you can drift along with a nice current and listen to the call of every kind of bird and hear even the slightest turbulence ahead. The scenery has, as Randy Carter says, "an intimate beauty of rocks, high mountainsides, and unmolested, unvisited forests and glens." On one side of the stream or the other there are, almost always, grassy meadows or shady groves of hemlocks, pines, or hardwoods. Just about all the wildlife you'll ever see in the East is here. Hidden Valley is, in fact, reminiscent of the scenic North River gorge, only about a class less difficult.

The rapids are mostly Class I–II rock gardens and low ledges, many on sharp turns up against rocky bluffs, and there are occasional limbs or trees across the fast current. There are only a few long pools (150 to 200 yards), and at the end of each one is a sharp turn out of sight followed by a feisty Class II+ rapid—with one exception. This is the first pool, which is about 2 miles below the put-in at US 220 and 1 mile below the preferred alternative put-in at Route 623. This pool is easily remembered because of the large grassy area on the right and the entrance to the 4-mile-long gorge ahead. At the end of this pool is a blind turn to the left and then a horizon line about 60 feet ahead. Get out on the right before the turn and scout, or better carry, the complex Class III+ double ledge dropping 5 feet with no really good passage. This is an obvious boat buster except in high water.

About a mile above the take-out, or about 7 miles into the trip, the river fans out into many small channels through gravel bars and islands—a confusion probably caused by the 1985 flood. Each of the channels was blocked by trees and appeared unrunnable recently. This is a good place to practice lining your canoe, as the portage on either bank is rather roundabout.

This is not a stream to run when it is too low, not only because the waves are smaller and it's scrapey, but also because at low levels there will not be enough water depth to hug the insides of sharp bends. If in doubt, stop and look at any blind turn to be sure the passage isn't blocked.

Though the run is only about 8 miles long, it could well be done as a overnighter by those who might be tempted to check out the classic trout pools that lie at the foot of almost every rapid and the beautiful, level, pine-needled, primitive campsites. If you had to hide out from the law for

Section: US 220 to Forest Development Road (FDR) 241

Counties: Bath

USGS Quads: Burnsville, Sunrise, Warm Springs

Suitable for: Day cruising and camping

Skill Level: Shepherded novices and intermediates

Months Runnable: Winter and spring after a moderate rain

Interest Highlights: Beautiful gorge, great fishing, wildlife

Scenery: Beautiful to spectacular in spots

Difficulty: Class I–II at moderate levels with 1 nasty Class III

Average Width: 30 to 50 feet

Velocity: Moderate

Gradient: 24 feet per mile (4 miles in gorge at 40 feet per mile)

Runnable Water Levels:
  Minimum: 1 foot below left downstream abutment of Rt. 623 bridge; 4.5 feet on Buena Vista or Petersburg gauges
  Maximum: River above left downstream abutment of Rt. 623 bridge

Hazards: Major 5-foot ledge 2 miles below US 220; several trees in the river, mainly on sharp turns; low-water bridge at take-out

Scouting: 5-foot double ledge 2 miles below US 220

Portages: Maybe 5-foot ledge 2 miles below US 220 on right

Rescue Index: Generally remote

Source of Additional Information: National Weather Service, Buena Vista or Petersburg gauges (703) 260-0305; Buddy Murray at Sportsman's Inn on US 220 (703) 839-2689

Access Points	River Miles	Shuttle Miles
A–C	8	12
B–C	7	12

Access Point Ratings:
A–at US 220, good
B–at Rt. 623 wooden bridge, very good
C–at FDR 241, very good

awhile, this is one of the few places left where it appears you could actually live off the land (and river). The trout fishing is superb and smallmouth bass fishing is good, too.

There is excellent primitive camping on the right side of the river in a big meadow area (along Route 623) just before entering the gorge, and also along the river after entering the gorge. You can also camp at the grassy area at the Forest Development Road (FDR) 241 low-water bridge take-out, but this can be rowdy. Better than this is Hidden

Valley Campground, a fine U. S. Forest Service facility on FDR 241 (river left) one-half mile from the take-out.

Incidentally, there is a trail system that provides excellent hiking in the area. The Hidden Valley Trail starts at Hidden Valley Campground, and the Rock Shelter Trail starts on river right at the take-out bridge. Both trails join 2.5 miles upstream of the take-out and continue along the river into the gorge. There are also some interesting side trails. For example, Bogan Run Trail leaves Rock Shelter

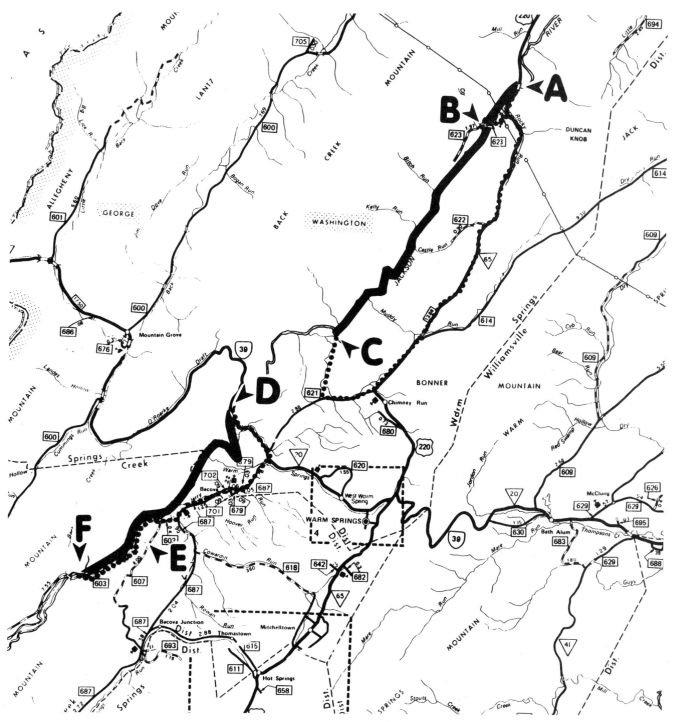

Tom McCloud and friends survey the cliffs on the lower Jackson below Gathright Dam.

Trail near the take-out and climbs scenic Back Creek Mountain, which is 3,000 feet high.

Wildlife and bird life are abundant. Be on the look out for beaver, mink, deer, big snakes, and perhaps even a mountain lion. There are also huge snapping turtles in this river. One was so large it made Dan Elasky quite nervous ("Jaws syndrome") as he paddled his low-volume C-1 on this trip. The larger birds include wild turkeys, grouse, hawks, and perhaps even bald eagles.

Currently, there is no painted gauge for the Jackson. Good paddling levels will be found when the left downstream abutment of the wooden bridge on Route 623 (the alternate put-in) is 2 to 8 inches out of the water. However, be careful if the abutment is covered. A zero paddling level is about 12 inches below the top of this abutment. As a rough correlation, a reading of 4.5 feet on either the Buena Vista or Petersburg gauges will probably suffice for a good run. For current river information, call Buddy Murray, the owner of the Sportsman's Inn on US 220 a couple of miles from the take-out. He is quite fond of the Jackson and will be able to tell you water level and fishing conditions. He will also help you with a shuttle or supplies. His phone number is (540) 839-2689.

Hidden Valley is most interesting historically. Archeological excavations on the northern side of the Jackson River show that Indians were present as early as 6500 B.C. This fertile valley was first settled by Europeans in the 1740s who were plundered in 1754 by the French and Indians. Jacob Warwick settled in Hidden Valley in 1788. Later, in 1848, the Warwick Plantation

home was built by slaves using bricks of mud from the banks of the Jackson. The plantation prospered until the Civil War began in 1861. Warwick House is listed with the National Register of Historic Homes and is on river right at the take-out.

Paddlers can continue another 3 miles below the take-out to Route 39, but this is not recommended. The river is much flatter and less scenic here. Also, and very important in this locale, the land on every corner of the Route 39 bridge is posted or fenced.

Route 39 to McClintic Bridge (Route 603)

Like nearby Back Creek, this 5.5-mile section of the Jackson River is a delight. The most energetic part of the Jackson is found in the last half of this trip: here you go through Richardson Gorge, which begins next to Route 603 about 2.5 miles upstream of the McClintic Bridge take-out. The gorge is not only pretty, but has continuous Class II–III rapids for 2 miles.

Those wanting a more placid start can put in on Route 39. Here the Jackson meanders in its open valley for 3 miles below Route 39, dropping over easy gravel bars until it enters Richardson Gorge. As it enters the gorge, the Jackson passes the Boiling Springs Rod and Gun Club next to Route 603 and drops over a low-water bridge. This area is property of the Rod and Gun Club, which only allows paddlers carrying written permission to enter the stream on its property.

The paddler who gets as far as the club without securing said permission may well become a guest of the county at the local "Steel-Bar Lodge" for a period, and a return trip to Bath County will be necessary to pay the local magistrate for these very Spartan accommodations. As with nearby Back Creek, local laws allow ownership of the river proper in fee simple, and they don't cotton to outsiders who trespass without permission. One way to obtain a pass is to hook up with a group from the Blue Ridge Voyagers or Coastal Canoeists—canoe clubs that often schedule a trip every year in mid-March. Please see the Back Creek narrative in this chapter for guidelines to get permission for paddling Richardson Gorge.

Also, try to avoid the height of fishing season when numerous anglers try their luck for trout (rainbow, brown and brook), chain pickerel, and bass. This trout stream is highly prized by anglers, so please be on the alert for nimrods and give them every courtesy.

Having passed the gauntlet of the rod and gun club, the paddler will find that the crystal clear waters of Richardson Gorge are full repayment for such trouble. The Jackson drops over intricate low ledges and rock garden rapids at

Section: Rt. 39 to McClintic Bridge (Rt. 603)

Counties: Bath

USGS Quads: Warm Springs, Mountain Grove

Suitable for: Day cruising

Skill Level: Novices (first half); intermediates (second half)

Months Runnable: Winter and spring generally

Interest Highlights: Richardson Gorge (second half)

Scenery: Beautiful in spots to beautiful

Difficulty: Class I–II first half; Class II–III second half

Average Width: 35 to 45 feet

Velocity: Moderate for first half; fast for second half

Gradient: 25 feet per mile (2 miles in Richardson Gorge are 40 feet per mile)

Runnable Water Levels:
Minimum: 0 feet on Rt. 39 gauge; Buena Vista gauge 3.5 feet
Maximum: 3 feet on Rt. 39 gauge; Buena Vista gauge 6 feet

Hazards: Several trees in the river

Scouting: None

Portages: None

Rescue Index: Generally accessible

Source of Additional Information: National Weather Service, Buena Vista gauge (703) 260-0305. Obtain permission from Mr. William J. Loth, III, 304 Yorkshire Avenue, Waynesboro, VA 22980.

Access Points	River Miles	Shuttle Miles
D–E	3.0	5.0
E–F	2.5	2.5

Access Point Ratings:
D–at Rt. 39, very good
E–at Rt. 603 (Rod and Gun Club), good
F–at Rt. 603 (McClintic Bridge), good

40 feet per mile for the next 2.5 miles, passing through a gorge of unsurpassed beauty. Steep forested slopes crowd the stream on both sides, and spectacular rock formations tower over the river. Small tributaries tumble into the stream over steep cascades, adding a tinkling soprano to the river's baritone rumble. None of the rapids present particular problems, but be prepared for nearly constant maneuvering in Class II–III whitewater.

Look out for fallen trees in the gorge. A broach on one of these would be deleterious to your boat's structural integrity, and possibly to that of your tender pink or brown flesh. On various trips, there have been several downed trees, often in fast water. Fortunately, the gorge section can be scouted from Route 603, which follows the river closely on the left bank. The rough dirt road carries little traffic and is unobtrusive, barring a ballistic beer can from recreating young drivers.

Having reached the put-in for the 2.5 mile trip through the gorge, you get a third of a mile to warm up, and then things get active after you drop over a 2-foot ledge. Below this ledge the river is pretty busy for 2 miles as it goes over mainly rock gardens with a couple of juicy 2- to 3-foot drops. All too soon Back Creek enters from the right and the current gives up the ghost in the backwater of Lake

Moomaw. McClintic Bridge (Route 603) looms in the middle distance and from here it is a 500-yard lake paddle to the take-out on river left at the parking lot upstream of the bridge.

The Jackson River is a great combination with Back Creek for a one day paddling adventure. You can paddle both Richardson Gorge and Back Creek Gorge and have a common take-out. The main difference between these two streams is that Back Creek has more ledges (including three that are 3-foot drops) and more pools in its gorge section. Also, Back Creek is more remote: there is no road in Back Creek Gorge and the mountains, hemlocks, and rhododendron are perhaps more spectacular.

Approaching the Richardson Gorge via auto, one passes through the village of Bacova. This extremely picturesque little town was founded in the 1920s by a wealthy industrialist who settled families there and established cottage industries for the support of the people. These industries still operate, manufacturing a variety of articles (from mailboxes to furniture) and "exporting" them to nearby Hot Springs where they are retailed. The large wooden structure by the road just northeast of the village is an abandoned abattoir (that's slaughterhouse to you, buster).

Section: Gathright Dam, (Rt. 605) to near Covington (Rt. 687)

Counties: Alleghany

USGS Quads: Falling Spring, Covington, Rucker Gap, Callaghan

Suitable for: Day cruising

Skill Level: Shepherded novices

Months Runnable: Winter and spring generally (constant dam release)

Interest Highlights: Beautiful cliffs, deep pools, pretty open valley

Scenery: Beautiful in spots to beautiful

Difficulty: Class I–II

Average Width: 40 to 60 feet

Velocity: Moderate

Gradient: 5 feet per mile

Runnable Water Levels:
  Minimum: Dam release 200 cfs, 8.8 feet at put-in gauge

Maximum: Dam release 750 cfs, maybe 12 feet on gauge

Hazards: None except maybe a rare tree in the river

Scouting: None

Portages: None

Rescue Index: Accessible

Source of Additional Information: Gathright Dam (during the day) for cfs (703) 962-1138 or recorded message at (703) 965-4117

Access Points	River Miles	Shuttle Miles
G–H	3.5	5
G–I	7.5	10
G–J	10	8
G–K	13	11

Access Point Ratings:
  G–below Gathright Dam (Rt. 605), very good
  H–at Rt. 638, very good
  I–at Rt. 721, good
  J–at Rt. 687/641, fair
  K–at Rt. 687, good

Gathright Dam to near Covington (Route 687)

The 13-mile stretch of the Jackson from below Gathright Dam to Covington is a very pleasant scenic trip for shepherded novices. The gentle rapids (no stronger than Class II) are nicely spaced, allowing time to view the scenery of periodic high bluffs and an open valley. The water quality is quite good, and numerous deep pools hide trout that have washed down from Gathright Dam. Other fish also swim these waters, particularly sunfish and good sized smallmouth bass.

The only drawback to this relaxing trip is a history of landowner problems. Early deeds in this area allowed ownership of the land under the river, and owners have had to pay taxes for this land. So, it is understandable that they feel very possessive about it. However, a court case several years ago established the right of boaters to float these waters because the Jackson below Gathright Dam was determined to be a navigable river. To underscore this right, the U. S. National Forest Service asked a group of Coastal Canoeists in the spring of 1988 to run this stretch. This small armada of boaters had no problem and only elicited an occasional scowl from a disgruntled landowner or two on the bank.

On the other hand, the swimming and fishing rights are still up in the air. The Virginia Fisheries folks want to

stock these ideal waters with brown and rainbow trout, but in 1995 an Alleghany judge banned public fishing on the Jackson where land ownership predates the Revolutionary War. Accordingly, float the Jackson with discretion and do not step out of your boat in posted areas.

The scenic put-in just below Gathright Dam on river right gives you a good introduction to the trip. On the left bank are high cliffs containing interesting caves. A stiff Class II+ rock garden is clearly visible at the put-in. This is the toughest rapids on the trip, and if you can run it comfortably you should have no further problems. Basically, This rock garden can be run left or right, picking your way down.

About 100 yards below this rapid is a gauge on river left. It should read 9 feet (roughly 250 cfs) for a pleasant trip. The minimum is maybe 8.8 feet (200 cfs) for a very scrapey run. Because this is a dam release river, call the Gathright Dam keeper at (703) 962-1138 to be sure the release is above 200 cfs. Recorded cfs is at (703) 965-4117.

Below the gauge, go right of an island with Class I–II drops at the beginning and end. Notice the rhododendron, hemlock, and pines on the left along here. Next comes a mellow Class I–II rock garden. A quarter of a mile below this is a Class II ledge of 2 feet; the best slot is right of center. Nervous novices can scout from the right bank.

In the next mile you will have some pleasant Class I–II rock gardens and well-rounded hills on the right. About 3

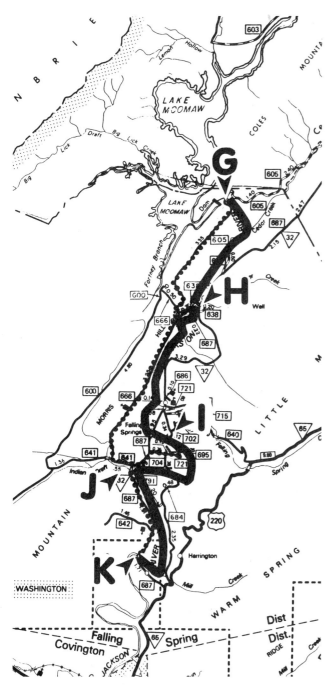

right off a spur road from Route 638. There is good parking in a field here and easy access for your boats. Across from the take-out is a private home: be considerate because the landowner as had troubles with noisy late night revellers who have abused this access point.

Soon you will come to an island. Go right and notice yet another shale and limestone formation with hemlocks and rhododendron. Enjoy the deep pools here. You then have a mellow Class II rock garden as you head toward a pretty hill. About a half mile later geology buffs should note a shale formation on the right with some large boulders trapped in it. Below here some houses intrude for a mile as you continue the pattern of pretty bluffs and Class I–II rock gardens.

After 7 miles, you come to the Route 687 bridge. However, don't take out here. If you must end this pleasant trip, continue past a couple of modest ledges (the second with surfing possibilities) and take out at the next bridge (Route 721) a half mile downstream. Limited parking is on river right, but take-out on river left because it is not nearly as steep.

About a half mile below the second take-out on the left is the biggest bluff of the trip—over 500 feet high. Then comes a gravel bar chute and another two ledges with limited surfing possibilities. About 1.5 miles farther, which include a couple of good rock gardens and several houses, you reach a third possible take-out on river right. This is not a great take-out: you have to drag your boats across a long field, and there is very limited parking on Route 641 a quarter of a mile downstream—just above the Route 687 bridge over Indian Draft before it enters the Jackson.

Rather than struggle with this take-out, you really should continue for the last 3 miles. About a half mile farther is a footbridge with an interesting rock formation containing caves on the left. A mile later it is "eyes left." Here, you have an open view with a beautiful mountain in the distance. Unfortunately, the right bank is trashy. Rock formations and occasional rapids continue for the remaining 1.5 miles to the final take-out on river left at the Route 687 bridge. The field below the bridge is public land, so you can park shuttle vehicles here. However, you can avoid the steep slope below the bridge by getting permission from the kindly nearby store owners to take out on river left above the bridge.

miles into the trip you will go under the first bridge (Route 638). Rock formations with hemlocks are on the right near here. After another Class I–II drop, there is a beautiful shale and limestone formation on the left with cedar trees. Just below is the first take-out or alternate put-in on river

James River

As Roger Corbett says, the James River is the "heart of Virginia." It flows through the center of the state and four of its five geographic regions. The James is rich in scenery, history, and variety. You can paddle this large river for virtually the entire year, and there is a stretch for every skill level. Intermediate paddlers can enjoy the modest whitewater of the Balcony Falls section on the upper James near Buena Vista; novice paddlers, anglers, and families can take relaxing float trips on the middle James; and expert paddlers can run the fall line of the lower James in Richmond at high water levels with boaters who know the river well.

Iron Gate (Route 727 or US 220) to Saltpetre Cave (Route 688)

The 25-mile section of the James from Iron Gate to Saltpetre Cave can begin on the Jackson River at the Route 727 bridge in Iron Gate with a steep put-in. Or, you can put in roughly a mile downstream on the south side (river right) of the James River below the US 220 bridge. Putting in at the Route 727 bridge will give the paddler a quarter of a mile on the Jackson River. Then

the Cowpasture River enters on the left and mixes its clean, clear mountain water with the dark, stained water of the Jackson to form the James River.

Unfortunately, the stained water of the Jackson overcomes the clear Cowpasture before the first Class II ledge, located just above the US 220 bridge. The easiest route over this ledge is by the right bank. The river then winds its way to Glen Wilton 4 miles downstream through low farmland on river left and occasional steep bluffs on the right. The Class I–II rapids are spaced enough to keep the paddler's interest as the river winds past Glen Wilton. The rapids on this stretch are mostly low gravel bars and diagonal ledges.

The 7-mile section from Glen Wilton to Gala is a meandering float through low farmland and offers some of the James River's best smallmouth bass fishing areas. More citation smallmouth bass (5 pounds and over) are caught in the Upper James than in any other river in Virginia. The best fishing is usually accomplished in and below riffles using artificial lures and live bait. Live bait works best in the slower, deeper holes of the James.

At Glen Winton, there is access on river left at the Route 633 bridge. When you reach Gala, another access

---

Section: Iron Gate (Rt. 727) to Saltpetre Cave (Rt. 688)

Counties: Botetourt

USGS Quads: Clifton Forge, Eagle Rock, Salisbury, Buchanan

Suitable for: Day cruising, camping

Skill Level: Novices

Months Runnable: Winter, spring, and early summer

Interest Highlights: Great smallmouth and muskie fishing; remains of the James River and Kanawha Canal; occasional bluffs

Scenery: Pretty to beautiful in spots

Difficulty: Class I–II with flatwater

Average Width: 60 to 110 feet

Velocity: Slow to moderate

Gradient: 4 to 5 feet per mile

Runnable Water Levels:
　Minimum: Over 2 feet on river left gauge one-half mile below where Maury joins the James
　Maximum: Maybe 6 feet on this gauge

Hazards: High water; occasional trees in river (particularly on outside bends)

Scouting: None

Portages: None

Rescue Index: Accessible to remote

Source of Additional Information: Call James River Basin Canoe Livery (703) 261-7334 for gauge; another outfitter is James River Runners Canoe Livery (804) 286-2338

Access Points	River Miles	Shuttle Miles
A[1]–B	16	11
A–B	15	10
B–C	9	5 or 7

Access Point Ratings:
　A[1]–Iron Gate (Rt. 727), fair
　A–Near Iron Gate (US 220), good
　B–Craig Creek near Eagle Rock (US 220), excellent
　C*–Saltpetre Cave (Rt. 688), good-limited parking

*Note: For this access point you have to cross the railroad tracks and the railroad company currently frowns on this.

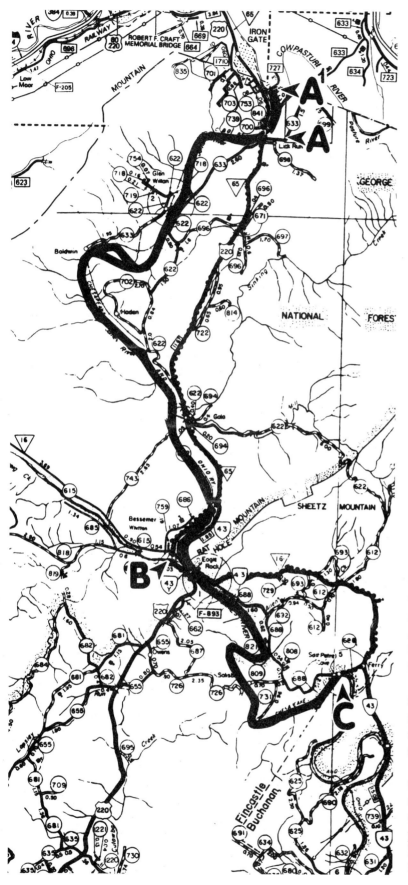

point is behind the Columbia Gas Company Transmission Pump Mill on US 220. You can put in or take out under the C & O Railroad bridge on Mill Creek. In the 4 miles from Gala to Eagle Rock, the paddler passes farmland on both banks. The rapids in this section are mostly small cobble bars. After passing under the US 220 bridge, the river turns right as it heads toward Eagle Rock.

Just above Eagle Rock on river right is Craig Creek, a major tributary of the James. The Virginia Highway Department maintains an excellent access point here near the US 220 bridge over Craig Creek. Paddlers and anglers may be tempted to paddle up Craig Creek, which is a beautiful, clear stream. However, do not do so because of landowner problems. Instead, head downstream, and you will be rewarded by some nice Class II ledges just below this access point.

The James slows its pace as it reaches the small town of Eagle Rock, with its towering multicolored shale cliffs. The water quality gets better with each passing mile, but, if you look closely, paper particles from the Westvaco Mill in Covington are ever present. Also, the river's bottom is stained and silted from previous years when water pollution controls were lax.

Nevertheless, fishing for smallmouth bass, sunfish, rockbass, and catfish is still excellent. The best bass fishing is still in and below the riffles and rock gardens that start as the river bends away from Eagle Rock.

There are no difficult rapids in this section. At higher water, most rapids wash out and only a little wave action remains. However, during low water in summer and fall, beginner canoeists may have trouble with the many rock gardens and shoals along here. Often these occur in the bends of the James as the faster water sweeps along the outside bank. Paddlers should also be alert for strainers on the outsides of these bends.

As the James flows south from Eagle Rock, the river banks alternate between low farmland and steep hillsides. The C & O Railroad tracks are on river left until below Saltpetre Cave, where they cross to river right.

The James River below Eagle Rock is part of the Virginia Scenic Rivers system. Beginning approximately 3 miles below Eagle Rock and continuing for 16 miles is the newest section protected by state law from development. However, a Maryland developer recently still hoped to place a 21-foot earthen dam along here.

The scenic, tranquil upper James near Eagle Rock. Photo by Ed Gertler.

Numerous islands occur in this section. Although small, they could be used for camping when there is no threat of sudden high water. Here the river meanders past steep cliffs, which alternate with high-banked fields. The Class I–II rapids range from small, eroded ledges to cobble bars. Many of these small ledges are the remains of an aborted effort to extend the James River and Kanawha Canal system to Covington.

Virginia State biologists have found that after initial stocking years ago, the muskie population is now naturally reproducing in this area of the James River. Indeed, this stretch is known among serious anglers as "Muskie Alley," and Virginia State Fisheries Department officials report that the James is the premier Virginia river for citation muskie catches. Also, the smallmouth fishing remains excellent, and a new "slot limit" on smallmouth bass will enhance the fishery even more in the coming years. ("Slot limit" fish are fish 11 to 14 inches long, which must be released because they are the best reproducing fish.)

One alternate access point for the lower section is 6 miles below Eagle Rock on Route 726 where Catawba Creek enters the James on river right. Be sure to hug the

right bank as you near this access point or several large islands in the river will cause you to miss it.

You reach the last take-out for this section at Saltpetre Cave on Route 688, a very short distance from Route 43. Parking is very limited at this access point which is located where the road first meets the railroad track and turns left.

Saltpetre Cave (Route 688) to Natural Bridge Station (Route 759)

Like the 25-mile stretch just upstream beginning at Iron Gate, this 32-mile section from Saltpetre Cave to Natural Bridge Station is made for fishing, camping, and drifting. It's a relaxing 3-day float if you do the whole distance. However, you have access at several places on this stretch so you can vary the length of your trip. There are access points at Route 43 (5 miles), Springwood (8 miles), Buchanan (13 miles), Alpine (24 miles), and Gilmore (29 miles) before you get to Natural Bridge Station. Also, occasional Class I–II rapids spaced throughout this section keep up your interest. The best of these drops are the remains of low dams built for the James River and

Kanawha Canal, the first navigable canal system in the United States. This historic canal was started at Richmond in 1789 and had stretched 197 miles from Richmond to Buchanan by 1851. However, the Civil War did serious damage to the canal, and heavy competition by the railroads finished it off soon thereafter.

I offer one word of caution for campers. You can only camp in certain areas along this wild and scenic stretch of river because most of the banks are privately owned. However, at several private places you can camp for a small fee. Also, the Jefferson National Forest forms the right bank of the river at various spots, and camping is allowed there. Look for yellow National Forest Service boundary markers. The rules for camping in the Jefferson National Forest are simple: (1) no camping on trails or on the river bank; (2) no fires between midnight and 4 p.m. from March 1 to May 15; (3) extinguish all fires, and spread the ashes; and (4) pick up all your trash, and bring it out in your canoe. For more specific information on current camping locations and rules, call the James River Basin Canoe Livery at (703) 261-7334.

The put-in on river left at Saltpetre Cave is over the railroad tracks and down to the river. There are two nice Class I rapids in the first mile. About 1.5 miles later you reach Camp Oxbow Farms on river left and can camp there for a small fee. Another 1.5 miles farther, after the river completes a large horseshoe bend to the left, you reach two long islands. The best channel is on the left.

A mile below these islands, after another horseshoe bend to the right, is the first take-out on river left at Route 43. You have two Class I drops in the next mile and then reach an old dam site of the James River and Kanawha Canal. When the river is up, there is a 3-foot drop and a Class II rapid here. The best route is left of center. For those with heavy camping gear, the right channel is shallower and less abrupt.

Soon after the dam site you cross under a C & O Railroad bridge. This is noteworthy because just below on river right is a good place to catch catfish. After this fishing break, you have 2 miles of slow water before you reach Springwood. Just above Springwood take the right channel for the best water and a Class I drop.

Once you reach Springwood, it's time to talk about the great fishing on the James. First of all, muskies have been stocked from Springwood to Alpine. Bring appropriate tackle if you are after these fearless fighting fish. Also, this section of the James is famous for citation catches of other game fish. (For those who are not anglers, a citation fish is big!) For example, 4 to 7 pound smallmouth bass have been caught in this section as well as 10 pound channel catfish and 20 pound flathead catfish. Good sized bluegill sunfish and redeye perch are also present.

John and Janet Williams enter Balcony Falls near Snowden on the upper James.

The 2 miles below Springwood is slow water. Soon after going under Interstate 81, the river turns left. Here, at the site of an old railroad bridge on the left, a stretch of fast water breaks the monotony. Two miles below Interstate 81 you reach the pleasant town of Buchanan. This was the terminus of the James River and Kanawha Canal. (Efforts to build another 50-mile stretch to Covington were never completed.) Goods traveled overland from Buchanan through the Alleghanies to Kentucky on the 208-mile-long James River and Kanawha Turnpike. US Route 60 currently follows this route. Incidentally, local folks do not pronounce the name of this town like the 15th president of the United States; they pronounce the name Buck-han-on. At Buchanan the Norfolk and Western Railroad reaches the right bank so you now have railroad tracks on both sides of the river. Take out in Buchanan if you are only interested in a long summer day float. Otherwise, take a break, replenish your supplies, and continue.

A mile below Buchanan is a Class I rapid. Over 2 miles below this, just after the river turns right, is another old James River and Kanawha Canal dam site with a good Class II drop of 3 feet. The best route is left of center. A mile downstream of this dam site the right bank enters the Jefferson National Forest. For the next mile you can camp on the right bank. Yet another mile farther and soon after you leave the Jefferson National Forest, the river turns left and then begins to turn right. Here you reach an island. The channel on the left has the most water and is a good Class I–II rapid; the right channel is a Class I drop.

Section: Saltpetre Cave (Rt. 688) to Natural Bridge Station (Rt. 759)

Counties: Botetourt, Rockbridge

USGS Quads: Buchanan, Salisbury, Arnold Valley

Suitable for: Day cruising, camping

Skill Level: Novices

Months Runnable: Virtually the entire year

Interest Highlights: Jefferson National Forest; remains of James River and Kanawha Canal; Natural Bridge; fishing and camping

Scenery: Pretty to beautiful in spots

Difficulty: Mostly flatwater with occasional Class I–II rapids

Average Width: 90 to 110 feet

Velocity: Slow to moderate

Gradient: 4 to 5 feet per mile

Runnable Water Levels:
  Minimum: 2 feet on river left gauge one-half mile below where Maury joins the James
  Maximum: Maybe 6 feet on this gauge

Hazards: High water

Scouting: None

Portages: None

Rescue Index: Generally accessible

Source of Additional Information: Call James River Basin Canoe Livery (703) 261-7334 for gauge; another outfitter is James River Runners Canoe Livery (804) 286-2338

Access Points	River Miles	Shuttle Miles
C–D	5	3
C–E	8	6
C–F	13	9
F–G	11	14
G–H	5	5
G–I	8	8

Access Point Rating:
C*–Saltpetre Cave (Rt. 688) good, limited parking
D*–Rt. 43, excellent
E–Springwood (Rt. 630), good but private
F–Buchanan (US 11), excellent
G*–Alpine (Rt. 608/622), very good
H*–Gilmore Mills (Rt. 608), good
I*–Natural Bridge Station (Rt. 759), good

*Note: for these Access Points you have to cross the railroad tracks and the railroad company currently frowns on this.

A good mile farther, as the river bends right, you will come to Indian Rock on the left. Near here is an old stone lock and dam abutment of the James River and Kanawha Canal. If you want to poke around this area a bit and soak up some history, you can camp at Breeden's Campground on river right just upstream of Indian Rock, for a small fee.

Just beyond Indian Rock is another island. Take the left channel for the most water and a Class I–II drop. The right channel does not usually have enough water.

Three miles below this you reach a take-out near Alpine at Route 608/622. Soon thereafter you come to a cobblestone reef. Take the left channel and go from left to center over a Class I–II drop. As with the previous island, the right channel is generally too low.

Soon below Alpine the right bank enters the Jefferson National Forest again, and there is good camping for a mile or so. Also, a mile below Alpine is another James River and Kanawha Canal dam site. You have several Class I–II channels to pick from. A good mile below here, Jefferson National Forest and camping possibilities return on the right bank. Five miles below Alpine is another river left take-out at Gilmore Mills on Route 608. Another mile later is a nice 1.5-foot drop, best run in the middle or on the extreme right. Two miles below this

rapid you come to the Route 759 Natural Bridge Station take-out on the left. You go under a railroad bridge just before the take-out.

Before or after this trip be sure to visit nearby Natural Bridge—a limestone arch 215 feet high, 90 feet long, and 50 to 150 feet wide. US 11 is built over this natural wonder, and Cedar Creek flows under it. You cannot see the bridge from US 11; use Route 130 to gain access.

Natural Bridge is the remains of a huge prehistoric cavern system, and has quite a rich history. It was worshipped by the Monocan Indians as "The Bridge of God." Later, George Washington surveyed it and carved his initials in it. Thomas Jefferson bought the bridge from King George III in 1774 for 20 shillings and built a cabin for visitors. During the Revolutionary War, the bridge was a shot tower. Later, while the War of 1812 and the Civil War were raging, a nearby mine supplied ingredients for gunpowder. Natural Bridge is open daily from 7 a.m. to dusk for a fee.

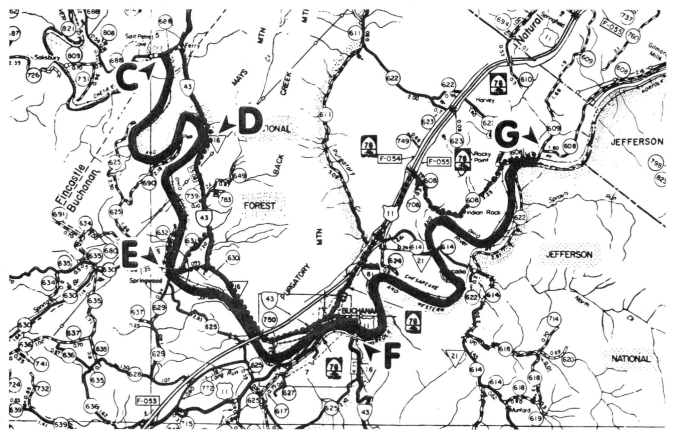

Natural Bridge Station (Rt. 759) or Locher Landing (Rt. 684) to Snowden

If so inclined, paddlers can put in at Natural Bridge Station from a road spur of Route 759. However, other than some occasional riffles and moderate waves, there is only one rapid of note (a Class II 2 foot ledge—run center) near the end of the 3.5 mile stretch between Natural Bridge Station and Locker Landing where the Maury River enters the James. Instead, most paddlers choose to run the 5.5 mile stretch from Locker Landing (near Glasgow) to Snowden, which has the best whitewater of the upper James River. It is suitable for intermediate boaters, and has several Class II and Class III rapids. After a Class III rapid at the put-in where the Maury joins the James, this trip is calm for a while, builds up to the heaviest rapids at Balcony Falls, and then tapers down through less difficult rapids to nearly 2 miles of flatwater at the end.

The scenery is spectacular as the wide James cuts through beautiful mountains in Jefferson National Forest, which are nearly 3,000 feet high. Sycamores, silver maples, and river birches line the banks. The rocks are igneous and contain lots of quartz. The trip is marred only by a powerline cutting through the mountainous forest on river left. Also on river left is the active Chesapeake and Ohio railroad, on the

other side of which are traces of the James River and Kanawha Canal which ran from Glasgow to Richmond.

The Locker Landing put-in for this trip is at the end of Route 684, which is half a mile from US 501 and the first left turn after crossing the Maury River and then some railroad tracks while on Route 130 heading for Glasgow (South).

After sliding down a nice sloping bank, going under a railroad bridge, and paddling less than 100 yards on the Maury River, the paddler is confronted with a Class III rock garden just as the Maury joins the James. This is just the ticket for competent paddlers to get their kinks out quickly. First timers should get out and scout this rapid from the rocks in the center at moderate levels and the left bank at higher levels. The far left passage is easier and more straightforward with two successive 2-foot drops. The right side is for the more adventuresome paddler with good boat control. After entry on the right, you must go smartly to the right of first one and then another of two rocks roughly 10 yards apart in the main channel.

Once on the James, the paddler will immediately experience a very gentle surfing wave and see an impressive white rock face on the right downstream. As you reach a quarter of a mile from the put-in there are two items of note. First, it's hard to believe, but there used to be an 18-foot dam on this placid section. Second, there is a gauge on river left below an old, large, white house; it should be 2 feet for a canoeing level of zero. A few hundred yards past this gauge are some stone wall remains of the old James River and Kanawha Canal.

Less than 10 minutes after passing the large white rock face you'll come to some large white rocks in the river (predominantly on the right), which come in some interesting shapes. They are worth a stop and announce a Class I–II drop of about 2 feet. The most direct passage through this drop is in the center.

Several minutes later one comes to a staircase of Class I–II ledges which require maneuvering (at least in lower water) to avoid getting hung up. These are followed shortly by an easy Class II ledgelike drop with various surfing possibilities here and there.

At this point the paddler will notice a large stone wall on the left bank of the river. Just downstream of this wall is a scenic mountain ridge coming down to the river. On the right bank is a large rocky ledge extending into the river. Go over to this big rocky ledge and scout. You have arrived at Balcony Falls after paddling roughly a mile and a half. There is more than one way of running this bumpy Class III rapid which quickly drops about 4 feet. The most conservative route at moderate levels is a tongue just to the left of a nearly submerged rock on the right side of the rapids. Several good sized standing waves follow. Folks

who enjoy surfing can try their luck in these 2- to 3-foot waves, which form the lower part of Balcony Falls.

Just a few minutes below Balcony Falls is a Class II rock garden, which can be run center, left, or right. This drop is a 2- to 3-foot ledge on the extreme right, which slowly converts to an easy gradual boulder garden on the far left. Look for a couple of good surfing spots just below. The best spot is formed by a small ledge just above a big boulder in the center of the river. If one runs just to the left of this boulder, there is another surfing wave followed by a Class II–III drop where maneuvering is required.

Just below are two very large rocks on river right which make a good lunch and swim stop. While stopped here, history buffs should ferry their boats across the river and park them on the rocky left bank formed by the railroad bed. After hiking up this bank and crossing the railroad track, paddlers will first find a depression up to 10 feet deep. This is the path of the aforementioned James River and Kanawha Canal. Walk along the railroad track about 100 yards upstream. Here you will see the remains of a wall that formed one of the canal's locks. In the underbrush directly behind this lock are two stone monuments. One was erected in the late 1800s and the other in 1975. They honor Frank Padget, a slave who in 1854 used a dory to save the lives of a canal boat captain and others marooned

Section: Natural Bridge Station (Rt. 759) or Locher Landing (Route 684) to Snowden (Route 501/130)

Counties: Rockbridge, Amherst

USGS Quads: Glasgow, Snowden

Suitable for: Day cruising

Skill Level: Intermediates

Months Runnable: Virtually the entire year except for very dry summers

Interest Highlights: Beautiful large gap in Blue Ridge Mountains; traces of James River and Kanawha Canal; monument to Frank Padget

Scenery: Pretty to beautiful in spots

Difficulty: Class II–III at moderate levels

Average Width: 100 to 200 feet

Velocity: Moderate

Gradient: 2 feet per mile from Natural Bridge Station to Glasgow; 11 feet per mile from Glasgow to Snowden

Runnable Water Levels:
Minimum: 2 feet on river gauge one-quarter mile below Locher Landing; 4 feet on James River gauge recorded by James River Basin Canoe Livery; a good 1 foot on Cartersville gauge
Maximum: Maybe 5 to 6 feet on the river gauge below Locher Landing; maybe 6 to 7 feet on gauge recorded by James River Basin Canoe Livery

Hazards: High water

Scouting: Balcony Falls (Class III) on river right rocks

Portages: None

Rescue Index: Generally accessible

Source of Additional Information: James River Basin Canoe Livery (703) 261-7334, National Weather Service, Cartersville gauge (703) 260-0305

Access Points	River Miles	Shuttle Miles
I–K	9.0	10
J–K	5.5	7

Access Point Ratings:
I–Natural Bridge Station (Rt. 759), good
J–Locher Landing (Rt. 684), very good
K–Snowden (US 501/Rt. 130 below railroad bridge), very good.

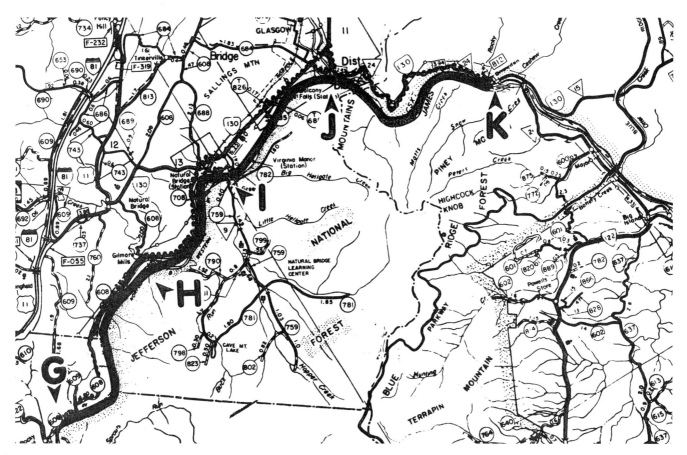

on a rock after their boat washed over Balcony Falls in high water. It is ironic that this canal boat was unharmed after its trip through Balcony Falls and subsequent rapids. Just after rescuing this first group of marooned individuals, Frank Padget lost his life trying to save another slave who was marooned on a different rock.

After this history lesson, the paddler comes to an easy Class II rock garden a few minutes downstream. This is followed over half a mile later by a bunch of rocks scattered across the river. The easiest passage through this Class I rapid is to the right. A few minutes later, the rocks end and an island begins on the left. In the center of the river, you will find a good moderate surfing wave just above a flat rock in a mild Class II rapid. You can go right or left of the rock after your careful surfing efforts. If you go left, watch out for a rock in the center of the channel.

Shortly thereafter, the first island ends. A second island on the right ends a few minutes later. All that is left now is nearly 2 miles of paddling on a dam-formed lake. The take-out at Snowden is on river left up a little stream immediately after going under a railroad bridge. Afternoon winds blowing upstream can make this paddle to the take-out a character building experience. Note that the Appalachian Trail is on the mountain ridges to your right

and left; it crosses the James not too far downstream of the take-out.

There is a fair amount of bird life and other action on the river. Ducks, kingfishers, bitterns, spotted sandpipers, and other water birds were sighted on recent trips. Snowy egrets have even been seen in the area on occasion. Also, anglers use john boats in the upper and lower parts of this section to fish for smallmouth bass, bream, and catfish. Finally, experienced tubers with life vests run this section at lower levels.

Bent Creek (US 60/Route 26) to Scottsville (Route 20/6)

This is a delightful, long stretch of the James for novice paddlers and families. Camping, fishing and lazy drifting are the main activities for this trip. From the put-in at the Bent Creek Bridge, the James River meanders for 40 miles to the take-out at Scottsville. Alternatively, if you need to rent equipment and/or want experienced help in planning your trip, you can use the James River Runners, Inc. This most able outfitter is on river left 2.5 miles upstream of Scottsville at Hatton Ferry (Route 625). For paddlers not wanting to do the full 40 miles over several days, there are several access points for long day trips. The best are Wingina (15 miles) and Howardsville (27.5 miles).

Two monuments to Frank Padget (on the James just below Balcony Falls on river left)—a slave who saved several lives here in the 1854 flood before losing his.

Boaters just interested in paddling the river will have an easy 3-day outing, with plenty of time to enjoy lounging in the mellow Jacuzzi-like rapids of the James. Anglers who expect to float much of the way should allow 5 days to pursue the James's abundant stock of channel catfish, smallmouth bass, and bluegill sunfish.

This is a year-round trip—except in high water, when paddlers should stay away. Even in August, when the James runs fairly shallow (depth ranging from 2 to 8 feet), it is navigable through the entire course. Most of the occasional whitewater is Class I with a couple of Class IIs to add interest. While these rapids may not be exciting to the experienced paddler, this stretch of the river compensates with beautiful scenery and a relatively mosquito-free environment. Most of the land on both banks is privately owned, but campers will find little difficulty in pitching tents on islands that dot the James at regular intervals.

The put-in is at Bent Creek from Route 26 near where US 60 crosses the James. If you've forgotten anything, you can get a fairly wide range of camping accessories at the Bent Creek Convenience Store, approximately 60 yards from the put-in ramp. For the novice paddler, the 15-mile stretch to Wingina eases you into your trip with very few, mild whitewater situations to navigate. This easy first stretch will prepare beginners for more challenging situations below Wingina.

In the first couple of miles you pass several long islands, and David Creek enters from the right. You then have a long calm stretch. After passing more islands and some occasional Class I rapids, you pass some pretty rock

bluffs on the right. The Tye River enters on the left two-thirds of the way to Wingina. Soon below this you pass a huge island (Cunningham's Island—owned by The Nature Conservancy) and then the Wingina Bridge (Route 56) where day trippers can take out. Approximately a half mile from the Route 56 take-out at Wingina Bridge was a convenience store. Unfortunately, it is now closed and the owners, Mr. and Mrs. Wood, can no longer charm you with their hospitality.

The next stretch is 12.5 miles, from Wingina Bridge to Howardsville Landing on Route 602. About 1.5 miles below the Wingina Bridge is a beautiful campsite on Swift Island. Just below Swift Island, 500 feet from the river, are the ruins of an old mill. Two miles below Wingina is access to the river at James River Wildlife Management Area. Soon below here you will pass Yogaville Shrine on river right which you can see in spring and fall when the foliage is gone.

After passing the temple you enter a 5-mile stretch of very slow moving water. The best advice for dealing with this part of the river is "grin and bear it." At the end of this slow stretch you will be rewarded by an entertaining series of Class I rapids and small islands between Buford Island and Dog Island. Although privately owned, Dog Island is a delightful spot at which to lunch or swim; there are big sunning rocks and more challenging Class II rapids nearby. Just below Dog Island on river left is an attractive camping spot on the last of three tiny islands; you can see Howardsville Bridge in the distance. Because of the steep slopes, you will want to unload your gear on the upstream point of the third island. Just below the Howardsville

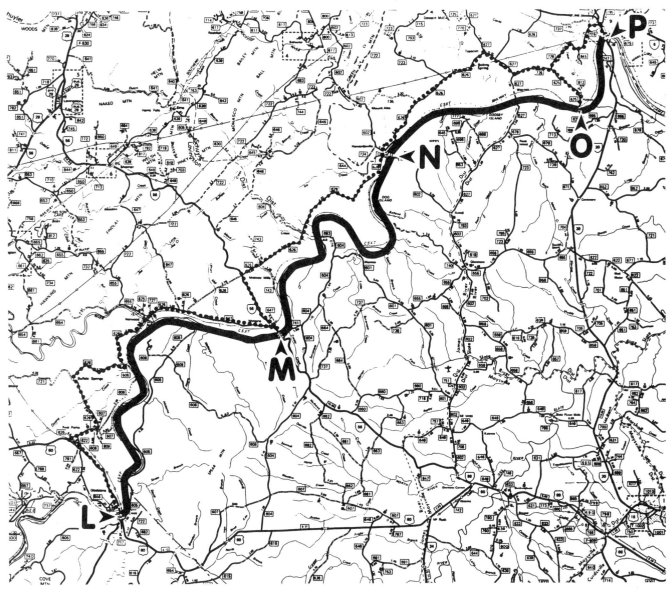

Bridge is a take-out by Route 602 and a convenience store about a quarter of a mile up the road. Pay a fee at this store for very limited camping at this privately owned place.

The section from Howardsville to Scottsville is 12 miles (9 miles if you take out at James River Runners). After 3 miles or so of calm water you will come to a white house on river left and a long skinny island on river right. The easiest and lowest passage is a Class I route between the right bank and the skinny island. For those looking for more action, there is a Class II drop on the left side of the river. This is the most exciting rapid on this 40-mile section of the James. Campers with gear will probably need to bail after running this drop. After a calm stretch, there are two alternatives on the left side of the river. The first is a Class I mellow course between the left bank and an island. The second is a Class II drop to the right of the island.

After another calm section you will go underneath a telephone cable spanning the river, which means you are 6 miles below Howardsville. There is access on river left at Warren Ferry (which is not operating); however, this public right-of-way to the river has very limited parking. Roughly a mile farther downstream you have a couple of interesting Class I channels to run on the center right side of the river. On the far left the river is quite shallow between the left bank and a log narrow island (Rock Island). However, just below the two Class I channels and to the right of Rock Island is a spectacular lunch spot (Little Rock Island) situated on a 100-foot-high bluff in the very middle of the river. Access is on the left side of Little Rock Island, but be careful as the path to the top is clogged with poison ivy. The upstream view from the top gives a full panorama of the James River: a great photo opportunity. Do not jump off the cliff; it is dangerous!

Section: Bent Creek (US 60/Rt. 26) to Scottsville (Rt. 20/6)

Counties: Appomattox, Nelson, Buckingham, Albemarle

USGS Quads: Gladstone, Shipman, Howardsville, Glenmore, Esmont, Scottsville

Suitable for: Day cruising, camping

Skill Level: Novices

Months Runnable: Virtually the entire year

Interest Highlights: Pretty islands for camping; some rocky bluffs

Scenery: Pretty to beautiful in spots

Difficulty: Mostly flatwater with some Class I–II rapids

Average Width: 200 to 300 feet

Velocity: Slow to moderate

Gradient: 3 to 4 feet per mile

Runnable Water Levels:
　Minimum: Maybe 3 feet at Bent Creek gauge; 3 feet at James River Runners gauge
　Maximum: Maybe 6 feet at Bent Creek gauge; 6 feet at James River Runners gauge

Hazards: High water

Scouting: None

Portages: None

Rescue Index: Accessible to remote

Source of Additional Information: James River Runners, Inc., Canoe Livery (804) 286-2338; National Weather Service, Bent Creek Gauge (703) 260-0305 or (804) 226-4423

Access Points	River Miles	Shuttle Miles
L–M	15	15
M–N	12.5	11
N–O	9	12.5
N–P	12	15

Access Point Rating:
　L–Bent Creek (US 60/Rt. 26), excellent
　M–Wingina (Rt. 56), excellent
　N–Howardsville (Rt. 626/602), excellent
　O–James River Runners (Rt. 625), excellent
　P–Scottsville (Rt. 20/6), excellent.

Also, be considerate because this island is private property. Camping is not permitted.

From Little Rock Island to the take-out is about 2 miles of calm water that end with a nice Class I–II rapid just opposite James River Runners, Inc. The best channel for this rapid is left of center. Take out on river left downstream of Hattons Ferry here. Below this rapid it is less than 3 miles of calm water to the Route 20/6 take-out on river left (north) at Scottsville, which also has a general store for supplies.

Scottsville (Route 20/6) to Bremo Bluff/New Canton (US 15)

This popular 13-mile novice section of the "Piedmont" James, offers a good number of ledges, riffles, and shoals at moderate water levels. The beauty and remote character of the middle 5 miles of this Class I–II trip make it ideal for float fishing, wildlife observation, camping, or just a leisurely paddle away from the hustle and bustle of everyday life.

The quiet town of Scottsville is about 65 miles west of Richmond on Route 6, a Virginia byway. You might like to spend a few moments in the town's museum, pick up some last minute provisions, or talk with one of the local townsfolk about early river days or the floods of recent years.

For the put-in, go just downstream of Route 20 on Route 6. Between the railroad station and the river left (north) shore of the river, the Virginia Fish and Game Commission maintains an excellent access point with ample parking for shuttle vehicles.

For the first 2 miles or so, as you traverse the second half of long Horseshoe Bend, the river is wide, flat, and offers a chance to get one's "sea-legs" while working on paddling technique. You then reach what looks like a river-wide ledge, but which is actually a submerged pipeline. Soon thereafter some small islands and riffles appear. After 4 miles, you arrive at a large island on river left that offers some open space for lunch or camping; approach it midway down the left shoreline.

Numerous islands separated by Class I small ledges and riffles soon follow as you approach the next access point near the mouth of the Hardware River. If you take out here, 6.5 miles from the put-in, be sure you are on the river left (north) side. Islands can obscure your view of this access point if you are on river right. However, the river left access point here is easier to locate than the Hardware's mouth, which is several hundred feet farther downstream.

About a mile below the Hardware, the James divides into numerous channels as you approach Seven Islands—a pleasant half-mile Class I paddle through pretty isles. Immediately below this is 2-mile-long Big Island. The river left (north) channel around Big Island is reached by staying hard left as you enter Seven Islands. Conversely, working right through Seven Islands and subsequent islets will place you in the large channel that passes Big Island on river right (south). The left side is easier, but both north

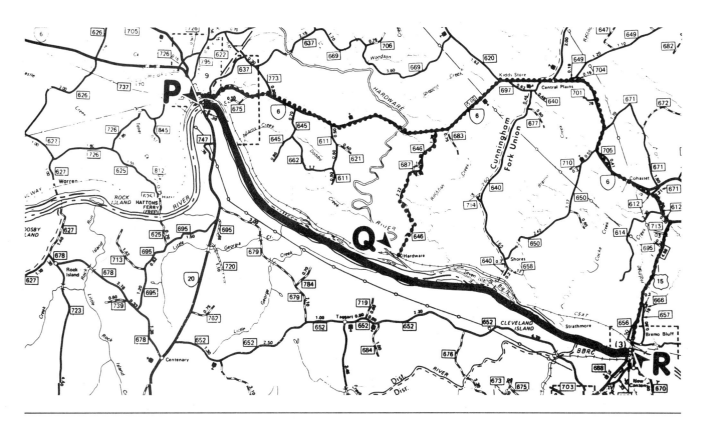

Section: Scottsville (Rt. 20/6) to Bremo Bluff (US 15)

Counties: Fluvanna, Buckingham

USGS Quads: Scottsville, Diana Mills, Arvonia

Suitable for: Day cruising, camping

Skill Level: Novices (moderate levels), intermediates (high levels)

Months Runnable: Entire year except for very dry summers

Interest Highlights: Middle 5 miles of trip remote, including wooded, island passages; good fishing, wildlife

Scenery: Pretty to beautiful in spots

Difficulty: Class I with 1 Class II–III rapid in high water

Average Width: 100 to 200 feet, with many narrow channels between islands in the middle part of trip

Velocity: Slow to moderate

Gradient: 5 feet per mile

Runnable Water Levels:

Minimum: Enough water in first mile means sufficient water for trip
Maximum: Flood stage

Hazards: High water

Scouting: None

Portages: None

Rescue Index: Accessible to somewhat remote; railroad follows river on left (north) shore

Source of Additional Information: James River Runners (804) 286-2338

Access Points	River Miles	Shuttle Miles
P–Q	6.5	10
Q–R	6.5	15
P–R	13.0	21

Access Point Ratings:
P–Scottsville (Rt. 20/6), excellent
Q–Hardware River (Rt. 646), excellent
R–Bremo Bluff/New Canton (Rt. 687 off US 15), very good

and south channels around Big Island sport several Class II rock gardens and ledges for 2 miles. If you take the left channel, swift current may require an upstream ferry to reach the main channel below Big Island. However, if you take the right channel and go right of an island that parallels the last half-mile of Big Island, you will have a mean Class II–III

S-turn with a pinning rock to avoid. More experienced paddlers can go next to the far right (south) bank of the river near the end of Big Island. Here you will find a stiff Class III, 3- to 4-foot drop onto a shallow rock. You must work to find this abrupt drop because the main channels of the river don't go there. (See map of Seven Islands, below.)

Some of the higher islands on this stretch offer delightful campsites for small groups. There is little posted land in this area, and you can find a place to camp on any of the islands. However, keep campsites clean, fires drowned, and noise levels low to ensure the continued patience and generosity of the individuals who own these islands. Be sure to constantly watch the river levels while camping here; higher water at night can be a very unpleasant surprise. The river banks would be safer places to camp if the river is rising, but, unfortunately, most of them are posted.

At the end of Big Island, the north and south channels of the river rejoin. The last several hundred yards of both north and south channels before the confluence offer the best whitewater of the trip, and at higher levels the standing waves (easier on the left) approach Class III. You should also watch for downed trees, which occasionally hang up in this area.

The final 3 miles to Bremo Bluff is flatwater. Midway through this last section you can see Bremo Mansion on a hill on river left about half a mile away. Soon after passing this mansion, you will see the Slate River enter on the right. Unfortunately, the noise and dust of a Solite Mining Corporation mine are noticeable here.

A final island and the sighting of the high John H. Cocke Memorial Bridge on US 15 announce the trip's end at Bremo Bluff. Be alert for the last Class II rapid—a river-wide ledge with boulders that extend under the bridge. This ledge is known as Phelps Falls and has a surfing wave in the main center chute at low levels. There used to be no formal access at Bremo, and paddlers generally were allowed to park on either shore several hundred yards below the bridge. Try to have someone watch your car because there have been break-ins here. The village of Bremo is on river left, and this was the traditional take-out. However, there is a new take-out on river right. From US 15, take three left turns on Routes 688, 670, and 687 to just downstream of the US 15 bridge in New Canton.

The wildlife is great along this stretch: deer, muskrat, mink, beaver, opossum, and an occasional otter are seen. There are many raccoons at night so store your food carefully. Bird life is also impressive: great blue herons, wild turkeys, ospreys, ducks, geese, kingfishers, and numerous songbirds are seen. For fishing, smallmouth bass is king—along with bluegill, crappie, catfish, and a few largemouth bass. A rare muskie or walleyed pike can even be creeled. Some locals enjoy fishing for gar and carp.

There is no formal gauge for this section of the river. However, you can call James River Runners at (804) 286-2338 to be sure water levels are neither too low nor too high. Also, if you have enough water in the first mile, you will have sufficient water for the entire trip. Nevertheless, water levels in the late summer can be quite low. Canoeists will find that flat-bottomed ABS canoes are best then. Aluminum canoes and V-bottom boats can be a pain at low levels.

The Chesapeake and Ohio Railroad on the north (left) bank and lesser roads here and there provide reasonable access. There is one note of caution: the railroad owners are getting testy about access at unauthorized places. Be alert when you're on railroad property: a few people have gotten trespassing tickets.

Hunter Marrow (bow) and Nolan Whitesell (stern) run Hollywood Rapid on the lower James in Richmond.

James River — Seven Islands

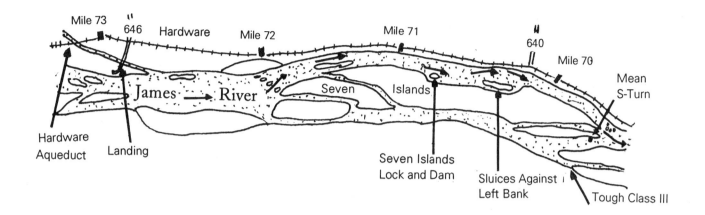

Map courtesy of W.E. Trout, III and the Virginia Canals and Navigations Society.

The James at the Fall Line in Richmond

The James at Richmond qualifies as one of the great whitewater streams of Virginia by virtue of its popularity with paddlers from all over the area, especially those from the southern half of the state. This river defines the concept of proximity to a populated area, as the run described lies entirely within the city limits of Richmond. The river is only occasionally too low to run—primarily after extended periods of drought in late summer. At levels of 3.4 to 3.8 feet on the Richmond-Westham gauge, the river is hardly runnable and definitely not fun. Therefore, we recommend a bare minimum of 3.9 feet for the lower section below Reedy Creek and 4.2 feet for the upper section from Pony Pasture to Reedy Creek. On the other hand, the paddler should beware of too much water during the winter and spring. The James can rise extremely rapidly to a dangerous level. The ledges and broken dams that create the whitewater sport on this section of the James can become deadly when large amounts of water pour over them creating dangerous hydraulics of great width. When the Richmond-Westham gauge reaches levels of 9 feet and above, expert paddlers must obtain a permit from the City Fire Department Chief at 501 N. 9th Street, Richmond, VA 23219. Failure to obtain this permit can result in fines, and, if rescue is required, these fines can be substantial. This permit costs $10.00 and is good for 2 years.

Having set these parameters, further discussion of the Richmond-Westham gauge is necessary. You can get the level for this gauge by calling (804) 226-4423 or (703) 260-0305. In the opinion of most local boaters, the best level for all types of boating is 4.5 feet to 6.5 feet, with shepherded strong intermediates paddling at the lower end of this range and advanced paddlers boating at the upper end. Above 7.5 feet, this section should not be attempted in open boats except by the most experienced and highly advanced paddlers, nor should it be attempted by similar decked boaters who do not have a bombproof roll. Although some hair boaters have run this section over 20 feet, several trips above the 12-foot flood stage have ended in life-threatening incidents. The river here is almost one-half mile wide and rescue is extremely difficult at high levels. Because of these difficulties, those who want to run the river at high levels should only go with someone who is familiar with the river and its dangers at these levels. See the section below on high water information.

As with the rest of our eastward-flowing rivers, the James meanders for many miles through farmland with no appreciable gradient before it reaches the edge of the bedrock underlying North America. Here the river tumbles off the continent onto the Coastal Plain, creating whitewater for our enjoyment. The city of Richmond was located here in colonial times to take advantage of the free power available from the falling water. Many low dams were built across the river to collect water for use in

An open boat surfer contemplates the incongruous skyline of Richmond at Second Break Rapid.

years of insane destruction, and Richmond would lie in ruins at the end of this struggle. Factories on the fall line in Richmond churned out weapons, gunpowder, and supplies for the Southern armies, and Yankee prisoners were incarcerated at Libby Prison on the left bank of the James and on Belle Isle in midstream. In the end the greater strength of the North prevailed, and the nation, begun in Virginia and symbolically rent asunder there, was restored. Students of ecology will notice while traveling through the countryside between Richmond and the Potomac that the land of Virginia is still recovering from the depredations suffered during the Civil War. Think of these things while paddling through the modern metropolis of Richmond on the James River.

running various mills and industrial operations. In 1969 Hurricane Camille wreaked havoc on these dams and restored the river to a largely natural course. However, the remains of these dams still present hazards to paddlers.

This part of the James River comprises the heart of the state of Virginia. Along its banks were created the earliest English settlements in the western hemisphere. The tidewater planters modeled a society on English laws and traditions, establishing the pattern for the continent-wide society that grew from these initial plantations. Nathanial Bacon, an early settler of the area, led his neighbors in a revolt against a disinterested and aloof aristocracy in 1676, burning the capital of Jamestown to the ground and striking the first blow in the struggle against colonialism that would culminate 100 years later in the establishment of the United States. Patriot and English armies marched and countermarched through the James basin in the War for Independence establishing Virginia as the birthplace of the American nation and presaging it as the cockpit in the Civil War, which nearly destroyed that same nation.

When the Southern states seceded from the Union in late 1860 and early 1861, Richmond was chosen as the capital, both to bring the border states into the war on the Southern side and to emphasize the preeminence of Virginia among her Southern neighbors. As a result of this decision, the state became the center of the most destructive event in the history of the country. The banks of the James became the goal of the Northern armies for 4

The put-in is on Riverside Drive on the south bank of the James at a parking area called Pony Pasture (which did have ponies at one time). This parking lot is downstream from Hugenot Bridge and over a mile upstream of Powhite Bridge. Unless otherwise noted, the rapids below are described at the 5-foot level.

Just above the put-in is Pony Pasture Rapid. For those carrying upstream to run this rapid, the route is center and then right or left through small holes into a rock garden. This is a Class II at 5 to 7 feet on the gauge. However, there are fantastic surfing waves here at the 8- to 10-foot level.

Below here the river flows quietly for a mile or so to Powhite Ledge. This is a Class II river-wide ledge and boulder field about 250 yards above Powhite Bridge. Run it in the center through 2-foot waves. At 6 to 7 feet on the gauge there are several good open boat surfing waves here.

After passing under Powhite Bridge (which used to have painted "X" marks showing the best channel) and then an arched concrete railroad bridge, you come to appropriately named Choo-Choo Rapid. This rapid includes the remains of Grants Dam, which was built before 1800. It is a Class II at all water levels and has excellent surfing waves at most levels.

There is a low-head dam (Coopers Island Dam) 200 yards below Choo-Choo Rapid. It is best run at its easternmost (right) extremity. Boulevard Avenue Bridge is visible just downstream. However, you will pass over another concrete-lined pipe (which resembles a low-head dam) before reaching the bridge. Beware the water flowing *under* this hazardous pipeline.

Below Boulevard Bridge is a Class II–III wave field called Mitchells Gut. Soon below here on river right, you pass Reedy Creek—a put-in for those who want a short trip to run just the heaviest of the rapids on this section (where the river drops 80 feet in 3 miles) and a take-out for nervous novices at low water and for intermediates at high water. To keep things easy it may be best to not park on the Reedy Creek access road or carry your boats over the railroad track. Instead, after walking the 50 yards from the small parking lot to the railroad tracks, carry your boat under these tracks through a culvert. Then follow the creek below the culvert to the put-in. However, be wary of leaving shuttle vehicles at the Reedy Creek parking lot, because there have been break-ins there.

Several hundred yards below Reedy Creek in the right center of the river you come to a dam on your left with two breaks in it. This is Hollywood Dam which is just upstream of Belle Isle. The first break you reach is called Variation

by local paddlers. At most levels this 3- to 4-foot drop is a Class II. Beware of a hole on the left (usually stuffed with kayaks) and another hole in center right two or three waves into the rapid. The best approach is to start center. Then either angle 45 degrees left to go left of the surfing hole, or angle 45 degrees right to go between the surfing hole and the hole on center right.

Most paddlers do not run Variation but continue downstream along the dam a couple of hundred feet farther. Soon you reach the other break (called First Break) which approaches Class III at higher levels. The sneak is on the far left. Alternatively, you can sneak just to the right of the main flow or attack this 3- to 4-foot drop head-on for a big roller coaster ride. If taking this head-on route, beware of a fairly large hole about three waves into the rapid. First Break has good surfing at most levels. However, at low water do not take the far right or the head-on slot—rebar and concrete lurk there.

You now are nearing the more serious rapids. Below Variation and First Break you have two alternatives. The first option is Cemetery Rapids which is run by few paddlers. You reach this impressive set of drops by

Stephen Ensign gets an ender at Pipeline Rapid on the lower James in Richmond. Photo by Corbin Ensign.

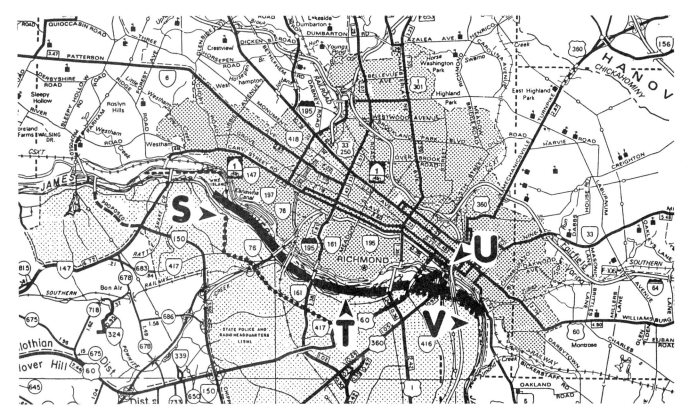

ferrying river left a couple of hundred yards from Variation. Cemetery is Class III–IV at levels under 6 feet and at least Class IV at higher levels. However, it cannot be scouted from the river. It is marked by large, irregular, broken waves and three or four holes that can easily swamp or dump a boat. Start on the left, angle right to miss the first hole, and then cut back to the left to avoid additional holes. The best advice is to run Cemetery the first time with a paddler who knows it. Cemetery is too dry at levels below 4.2 feet.

The second, more popular alternative is to stay river right below First Break and hug Belle Isle. Soon you hit Hollywood Entrance—a long Class II–III rapid at lower levels which ends just before the more difficult Hollywood Rapid. The heaviest part of Hollywood Entrance is on the left with easier routes close to the right bank. There are several nice surfing spots in the holes and waves here. The final drop in the center above Hollywood has three linked holes collectively called Stripper Hole. It becomes well formed somewhere over 5 feet and has been known to keep rafts at levels over 6 feet. At higher levels, especially with a boat full of water from Entrance, it is difficult to ferry to the right bank to dump before running the 7 foot drop of Hollywood.

Hollywood Rapid is the river's most impressive rapid. At very low levels this is a technical Class III–IV. It becomes a Class IV as levels move toward 6 feet and approaches Class V at levels over 6 feet due to high waves

and a very difficult rescue. Scout from the right bank. The general route at medium levels is to start close to the right bank with the boat's hull just touching the foam on the edge of a tongue of smooth water. In high water, ride this tongue until it breaks down and cut left. At lower water, hard draws to left are necessary to miss rocks in the middle of the runout. However, at lower levels you can also go right of the boulders at the bottom. Go either way, but make your mind up early. There are lots of entertaining waves and holes here, but be sure to miss the big hole on the left at the top.

Speaking of entertainment, Belle Isle is often a busy place. In summer, all types of bodies (nubile and otherwise) come here to catch the sun and action. Belle Isle is a great lunch stop where paddlers can observe activities, both on the river and on the island. Incidentally, while on Belle Isle, check out the numerous round holes in the Petersburg Granite created by revolving rocks during high water.

Just below Hollywood Rapid is Hollywood Shoals, a Class II rock garden with several good surfing holes extending 100 yards below the rapid. After passing under the Robert E. Lee Bridge, you reach the Vepco Levee Dam. This is an easy drop if you know where to go. The correct place is near the center of the river. Look for markings (currently a faint red "X") on the levee and scout from your boat as well as from the Manchester Bridge prior to your trip. An alternative way to run Vepco Levee

Section: Pony Pasture Parking Area (Riverside Drive) to 14th St. bridge

Counties: Henrico, Chesterfield, and City of Richmond

USGS Quads: Richmond

Suitable for: Day cruising

Skill Level: Strong shepherded intermediates and advanced paddlers at lower levels; advanced and expert paddlers at higher levels

Months Runnable: Virtually the entire year except for very dry summers, but beware of high water in winter and spring

Interest Highlights: Historical Belle Isle; whitewater in urban setting

Scenery: Fair to pretty in spots

Difficulty: Above Reedy Creek Class II–III; below Reedy Creek Class II–IV at moderate levels and Class IV–V at high levels

Average Width: 1000 to 2000 feet

Velocity: Moderate to fast

Gradient: 15 feet per mile overall with one-half mile at 30 feet per mile in lower half of trip

Runnable Water Levels:
Minimum: 3.9 feet (2000 cfs) on Richmond-Westham gauge, but over 4.5 feet guarantees an enjoyable trip
Maximum: 9 feet (21,000 cfs) on Richmond-Westham gauge; permit is required on the river above 9 feet for expert paddlers

Hazards: High water and hydraulics, huge river, Vepco Levee hydraulics at high water; rebar in Second Break, dangerous hydraulic in drop to right of Second Break, maybe trees or debris in major drops after high water, Pipeline at high water

Scouting: Hollywood Rapid–Class III to V depending on water levels (from right); Second Break–Class IV (from left at lower levels only); Pipeline Rapid–Class III to V depending on water levels (from left)

Portages: Perhaps 1 or more of big rapids at high water or if obstructed by trees/debris

Rescue Index: Accessible

Source of Additional Information: National Weather Service, Richmond-Westham gauge, either (804) 226-4423 or (703) 260-0305; Richmond Raft Company (804) 226-RAFT; James River Park (804) 780-5311

Access Points	River Miles	Shuttle Miles
S–T	4	5
T–U	2.5	3.5
T–V	3.5	4

Access Point Ratings:
S–Pony Pasture parking area (off Riverside Drive), good
T–Reedy Creek, fair
U–Reynolds Metals parking lot above 14th St. bridge on left (north), good
V–Ancarrow's Marina a mile below 14th St. bridge on right (south), very good; Richmond Raft Company (with permission) on river left (north) across the river from Ancarrow's, very good

is 30 yards or so to the left of the "X" under a sign which says "channel." This leads you (via two ledges called "Fish Ladders") to Pipeline Rapids (discussed later) and avoids Second Break (discussed next).

Soon you will see the Manchester Bridge overhead and approach Second Break Rapids. From Vepco Levee Rapids, paddle river right approximately 100 yards until you are about 100 yards from the right (south) bank. Do not go too far right, however; a second break closer to the south bank has a death trap hydraulic. At lower levels you can pull out to the left of this rapid, on the dam, and scout. At higher levels you don't have this luxury and should scout from Manchester Bridge during the shuttle. Best of all, be sure you run this rapid with someone who knows that Second Break is a 4- to 5-foot drop through a break in the old Vepco (Virginia Electric Power Company) dam.

Second Break is a straightforward drop with a fun wave at the top and tenacious wave/hole at the bottom. However, it is the nastiest rapid on the river because dead ahead at the bottom of these rapids are broken-out chunks of concrete with exposed steel reinforcing bars (rebar).

You can sneak this rapid either left or right, but the right sneak requires a difficult ferry across the rocky runout if you are going river left to Pipeline Rapid downstream. Second Break may be run head-on, but it is very shallow at lower levels. At high levels, a steep wave at the bottom of the drop tends to swamp open boats unless you hit an almost invisible tongue that angles left from the center after the first big wave above the drop. At water levels above 6 feet a hole to the left of center can hold paddlers. Because of the concrete rebar rubble and difficult wave/hole at the bottom, Second Break is a solid Class IV at moderate to medium levels and approaches Class V at higher levels.

Those not wishing to run Second Break, particularly at low water, can run the aforementioned Fish Ladders (a.k.a. Left Side). After running the Vepco Levee, go straight to reach this Class II sneak route. Here the old Vepco dam is anchored to a group of boulders that create a two-step drop over two ledges of 1 to 2 feet.

After Second Break, the river is divided by Mayo's Island. You have two options if you go right of Mayo's. The first is Southside Rapid. This is 100 yards downstream of Second

Break to the right of a rock island and near the right (south) bank. Southside is a delightful rock garden and an excellent place to practice eddy turns and ferrying. If you run left of the rock island (at levels of 5.5 feet and above), you have Double Dip. This rapid is seldom run because: (1) you can only do it above 5.5 feet on the gauge; and (2) most paddlers opt for the gentler Southside or Pipeline Rapid (on the left of Mayo's Island). Double Dip is two drops: the first is over a 3- to 4-foot ledge, and the second is a hard left twister after a shallow rock garden. This is a strong Class III–IV, at least.

Paddlers going left (north) of Mayo's Island will reach Pipeline. At higher water it can be difficult to work your way left from below Second Break to Pipeline.

This rapid is easily scouted from the large pipeline on the left bank which gives this rapid its name. At very low water this is a Class III, at moderate levels it is Class IV, and at 6 to 7 feet it approaches Class V. Commercial rafting companies will usually not run Pipeline at levels over 8 feet. Water at that level begins to push under the piers of the CSX Railroad trestle near the bottom of the rapid—creating a dangerous strainer.

Pipeline consists of four distinct drops of 2 to 3 feet each. The first drop is 3 feet and requires an S-turn to avoid a nasty hole. The second drop has a tricky pillow and hole at lower levels. The best route is to stay well right until the third drop, where you miss the big rock on the right by about 6 feet, and then cut diagonally left through the big wave. This route holds for all levels, but above 6.5 feet there may be a hole just above the big rock to avoid. The third drop contains a great ender spot at reasonable levels, accessible from the eddy on the left at the bottom. From the eddy, just poke your bow into the hole and hang on tight. However, don't come out of your boat because the fourth drop lies just below and would cause an unpleasant swim. The fourth drop of Pipeline usually is not run, and contains a great deal of metal rebar, broken concrete, and sharp rock. On the left below the third drop there is an outlet under the huge pipeline. This puts you into a canal leading to the canoe/kayak take-out on river left at the Reynolds Metals parking lot. Paddlers who run the fourth drop will have a 50- to 75-yard paddle back upstream to reach this take-out.

To the right of Pipeline Rapid and still on the left of Mayo's Island is yet another fiesty rapids called Triple Drop. You enter this blind Class IV rapid (which consists of three ledges) just right of the base of an electric utility pylon in the river. You can scout the second ledge from river right.

Since Mayo's Island extends 1/4 mile below Second Break, be sure you are on the proper side of the river for the proper take-out just below Second Break. You should be left (north) to reach the Reynolds Metals parking lot (just upstream of the 14th Street Bridge), and right (south) for Ancarrow's Marina a mile below Southside Rapid.

However, new riverfront development may limit access or parking along the falls of the James in coming years. Paddlers may be required to find a takeout on or downstream of Mayo's Island. Ancarrow's Marina, part of the James River Park, is a useful alternative on the south side of the river, but reaching it requires crossing about one mile of character-building flatwater. On the opposite shore is Richmond Raft Company, at 4400 East Main Street. Paddlers are generally welcome to park and take out here—but should ask permission to do so.

In sum, because of the many variations of difficult rapids, huge size of the river, and dangers of high water, paddlers running this section of the James for the first time should be in the company of paddlers who know the river well. This will markedly increase your safety and enjoyment.

Richmond Fall Line: High Water Info

At high water (8 to 17 feet), the James in Richmond is very big, very fast, and very wide. There are no rocks available for rescue, so all rescues will be by boat. Consequently, you will be very alone, and a bombproof roll is mandatory. You must also be very watchful for debris coming down the river. Most importantly, do not run the river unless you go with someone who knows it well at high levels.

For those who might brave the James at high levels, the following information may help. Pony Pasture has large holes and waves for great playing. Powhite Ledge has surfing waves on the far left. Choo-Choo Rapid is safest on river left. On river right above the railroad trestle at levels above 11 to 12 feet, there is a 50-foot-wide surfing hole; but beware of the dangerous whirlpool and gnarly ledges just below the railroad trestle. The river has large choppy waves for a mile or so as you pass Mitchells Gut.

First Break perhaps washes out above 10 feet. However, you can get great enders between 7 to 10 feet. When you reach Hollywood Entrance, be sure to stay right near Belle Isle for calmer water.

The general high-water route through Hollywood is the same as the low-water route, but the water is much heavier. Eddy out before the last drop of Entrance, which now merges into Hollywood. Peel out to center or right of center and quarter the 3- to 4-foot waves here with your bow facing right of the current. Be sure to hit the slot between Stripper Hole on your left and another hole on your right that becomes huge at levels above 7 feet. At 12 feet on the gauge, Stripper becomes a 4- to 6-foot breaking wave hole, while the hole to the right of Stripper becomes a major raft eater. You then head right toward the main drop, which is bigger than it looks from shore. Run the main drop right to left, with a big emphasis on the left. However, be sure you miss (on the right) the terrible terminal hole on the left of the main drop before you work left toward the center of the river for the runout.

The best route for Vepco Levee at high-water is under the red "X" mentioned earlier. However, above 12 feet the holes here become increasingly sticky and dangerous. Don't miss this line because other hydraulics at Vepco Levee (particularly on the right) start taking on lethal characteristics, and Pipeline on the left is very dangerous above 8 feet. For Second Break, run the usual route to the left toward Pipeline Rapid, after missing a large hole in the main drop that forms the left side of the bottom wave. There are tougher routes through Second Break, but discuss them with paddlers who know them first.

Pipeline is not often run above 8 feet. First, it is difficult to get to from Second Break. More importantly, there is a major penalty—a strainer from the CSX Railroad trestle piers above and below the third drop on the left bank. There is less maneuvering in the upper two drops, but the water is very heavy and very fast.

Lynn Aycock-Spangler covered up as she drops over Fools Falls on Johns Creek. Photo by Tim Vermillion.

Tim "Catfish" Vermillion running the third drop of Bambi Meets Godzilla Rapid on Johns Creek.

Johns Creek

This section of Johns Creek is a superb run for the physically ready, advanced or expert paddler. It should only be undertaken with careful attention to the gauge for the river, and paddlers doing it for the first time should go with someone who knows this tight, steep technical stream well. Paddlers familiar with earlier guidebooks should note that the gauge on the river right abutment of the Route 615 bridge in New Castle was revised in 1981 to give a more accurate reading. A level of "zero" is equivalent to 3 inches of water on the old gauge and is a more realistic "zero". Also, please note that a change of a few inches on this gauge can dramatically increase the difficulty of this river.

What can be seen of Johns Creek from the road is misleading. At the put-in it looks like a drainage ditch, while the section immediately above the take-out looks like the Class II–III Nantahala River in western North Carolina. In between, hidden from view, is a ruggedly beautiful 2 mile gorge that has an average gradient of 115 feet per mile, with one mile at 150 feet per mile. This gradient combines with a heavily obstructed riverbed to create a classic trip of very challenging water. The rapids in the gorge of Devonian and Silurian sandstone range from Class III to Class V and are mostly continuous, with only a few short pools offering a breather. Because of possible strainers, all of these rapids should be scouted by boat or land.

After the put-in at the Route 311 bridge (or shortly downstream where the road returns to the river), there are two miles of mostly flatwater leading into the two-mile gorge. The arrival of the heavy section is heralded when the paddler reaches an overhanging rock wall on the right. There the river takes a sharp left bend and quickly picks up to a strong Class III at two drops called Shubaloo I and II. After these "smaller" rapids, the proverbial bottom drops out.

The first major rapid in this hot and heavy section is a steep Class III–IV S-turn from right to left over a succession of rocks, drops and holes for about 75 yards. Locals have christened this Sirius, the Dog Star, an abstract but somehow very appropriate name.

The paddler is soon confronted with the picky entrance to Class III Royal Flush. The entry requires a slalom around rocks and pourovers, setting the stage for a fast blast from left to right where the main flow piles into a boulder on the left. Some very fast ferrys and dynamic eddy hopping can take place at the bottom of this drop.

Immediately after this is an island that splits the river, with a shallow channel on the left and a steep, blind chute on the right. (The left channel is very shallow when the gauge is below one foot.) You enter by dropping down on the right and catching a small eddy on the right bank just downstream of a large rock. Downstream is a rock in mid-channel. Run just left of this rock and quickly cut back right below it to miss a big hole at the bottom left. Running right of the rock is not recommended because strainers are often caught here. Indeed, the whole right channel of the river should be scouted for trees after high water. This tough Class IV rapid has informally been called Coke Island as it is surely "the real thing."

Shortly thereafter is another strong, steep Class III–IV sequence terminating with a large padded rock dividing the current into two chutes. The right chute is more easily run by dropping off at an angle and surfing down a wave/hole into the bottom eddy. The left chute is more difficult and should be looked at carefully before attempting it. Locals have dubbed this rapid Little Heinzerling due to its similarity to Heinzerling rapids on the Upper Youghiogheny River in Maryland.

Just below is the granddaddy of the rapids on Johns Creek. One colorful name (among several) applied to this Class IV–V rapids by local paddlers is Bambi Meets Godzilla. One may assume that "Bambi" is the innocent paddler. This is a real heart pumper with a total drop of about 15 feet in 30 yards. Here the flow channels to the right and narrows, with a tongue that drops over a 5-foot slide into a boiling hole. Then comes another drop next to a boulder and a final drop into another hole before reaching the pool below. Run this last drop right or left to avoid a pinning rock in the center.

Blind Man's Bluff is around the next bend. This Class IV rapid is simply a jumble of boulders. The paddler's predicament is to guess which channel is clear and safe. Watch out for log jams blocking the path. Run the center chute left and then cut back right.

Next is a Class IV rapid called The Separator. Here the river funnels to the left and plunges steeply over a jumble of rocks. Half way down is a 4-foot drop. Immediately below is a screaming right-hand turn to avoid a pillowed boulder. The current then continues over another drop into a hole that requires a sharp left turn. The final chute deposits paddlers into a small pool where they can regain their breath and composure. You can make dynamic ferries below the third drop by surfing its hole back up to the river right eddy—but be careful, it's very shallow here.

Just below a short pool, Typewriter hole spans the width of the stream; sneak it against the far left bank or on the right--or be prepared to punch it in the center. This hydraulic can get very sticky at higher levels, and scouting is advised for first timers.

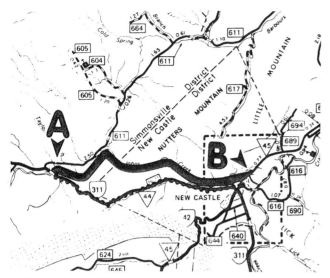

Typewriter is followed by a series of ledges and pourovers known as Found Paddle. Care should be taken here, as the last large drop has a pinning rock in what looks like a clean chute; run tight left to avoid nasty vertical pin.

Fast water carries the paddler from Found Paddle to a smooth horizon line that announces Fool's Falls. This is the last and biggest individual drop; it previously has been described as unrunnable by certain guide books. However, with proper care and appropriate water levels,

a path can be found over this Class IV 6-foot drop into a rock garden. In popping over the drop and overshooting its hydraulic immediately below, proper boat angle is critical to avoid a vertical pin. Run right with your boat pointed to the right. Be really cranking when you go over the drop.

The river changes character immediately after this drop and soon becomes Class II to the first take-out a half mile downstream at the rescue squad station or the second take-out at the Route 615 bridge in New Castle a half mile farther.

The only difficulty with this delightful trip is recent problems with local landowners. From "Bambi" to the take-out the left bank is posted against trespassing while the right bank is posted between Typewriter and a good one quarter mile below Fools Falls. Indeed, local landowners can be very hostile; there have been instances of paddlers being threatened by at least one of these landowners brandishing a shotgun. When planning a run down Johns Creek, check with local boaters to ascertain the latest information about this situation.

I have one final word of warning. At levels above 1.5 feet, John's Creek is one mega-rapid (with very few eddies) from Blind Man's Bluff to Fool's Falls. Consequently, anyone contemplating this run at or above this level should be an expert paddler who makes this trip with fellow experts who know the river well.

Section: Rt. 311 bridge to New Castle (Rt. 615)

Counties: Craig

USGS Quads: Potts Creek, New Castle

Suitable for: Day cruising

Skill Level: Advanced or expert

Months Runnable: Usually in winter and spring or after heavy rains

Interest Highlights: Beautiful gorge

Scenery: Beautiful in gorge

Difficulty: Class I–II for first two miles; Class IV for 2 miles in the gorge (with 1 Class IV–V); Class II–III at the end

Average Width: 25 to 35 feet

Velocity: Fast

Gradient: Average is 60 feet per mile; 2 miles in the gorge are 115 feet per mile with 1 mile at 150 feet per mile!

Runnable Water Levels:
Minimum: 0 feet on Rt. 615 gauge
Maximum: 1.5 feet on Rt. 615 gauge

Hazards: Bambi Meets Godzilla (Class IV–V); numerous Class IV rapids; Fool's Falls; trees in river - 1 was 50 yards above Typewriter in 1995 in a Class II–III drop with only a far left sawed out slot open

Scouting: Boat or land scout all major rapids

Portages: Optional

Rescue Index: Remote (and there are hostile landowners)

Source of Additional Information: Coastal Canoeist Tim Vermillion (703) 389-2613

Access Points	River Miles	Shuttle Miles
A–B	5	4.5

Access Point Ratings:
A–Rt. 311 bridge, good
B–Newcastle (Rt. 615), good (or rescue squad station on Rt. 311 a half mile upstream, also good)

Maury River

The Maury River is referred to on old maps and in old texts as the North River of the James. However, the North River was renamed in honor of Matthew Fontaine Maury, born in Virginia but raised in Tennessee. Maury obtained a commission in the U. S. Navy as a young man and sailed out of Newport News, Virginia. Over the succeeding years he began a study of ocean winds and currents which was to earn him the title of "Father of Oceanography." The Civil War interrupted his scientific career, however, and he devoted his efforts to strengthening the minuscule Confederate Navy and to the destruction of the ships on which he had formerly served. After the defeat of the South, Maury became a professor at the Virginia Military Institute at Lexington on the North River. There he fell in love with the Goshen Pass and requested that when he died his remains be carried through the pass. An honor guard of VMI cadets carried out this wish, and a monument to him stands on the road in the pass today.

While in the area of the Maury, those with a historical bent will not want to miss a side trip to Lexington, Virginia, one of the most historically rich towns in a state that thrives on its past. The Virginia Military Institute, where Stonewall Jackson was a professor before the Civil War; Washington and Lee University, where Robert E. Lee spent his last years after the close of the same war; and a wealth of historic buildings, monuments, and cemeteries will bring the past alive to those who are in tune with such things. The James River and Kanawha Canal reached as far as Lexington until 1895 and provided reliable transportation between the tidewater and the mountains.

The Maury lies virtually at the intersection of I-64 and I-81 and so is easily reached from any area of the state. Other rivers in the neighborhood include Back Creek, Irish Creek, Calfpasture, Bullpasture, and Jackson, all due west of Goshen Pass; the Upper James to the south; and the Tye and Piney over the Blue Ridge to the east.

Mr. "Goshen Pass" (Glenn Rose) cooking his way through Devils Kitchen on the Maury. Photo by Doug Howell.

Goshen Pass to Rockbridge Baths

The Maury River is formed just above Goshen Pass where the Calfpasture and the Little Calfpasture rivers join. Just as the streams merge the now sizable Maury cuts across the spine of Little North Mountain and drops precipitously into the Valley of Virginia. This happy circumstance of a reasonably large amount of water slicing through a steep mountain pass of resistant Tuscarora sandstone and quartzite provides whitewater paddlers with excellent scenery, easy access via interstate roads, splendid rapids, and sparkling water quality in a combination unsurpassed anywhere in the East. Luxuriant rhododendron stands, steep rock cliffs lining the river, and cascading tributary streams create a superb arena for the enjoyment of our sport. The Goshen Pass section of Maury is therefore the quintessential Virginia whitewater stream of advanced paddlers. The only negative aspect of this section is that it is too short.

This trip on the Maury also has one mixed blessing: a paved road closely paralleling the river the length of Goshen Pass. The road, State Route 39, is usually dozens of feet above the stream, however, and so does not detract from the wild character of the scenery to a great degree. The presence of this artery will be appreciated by many who may require assistance, who may be forced to walk away from the river sans boat, or who have friends or family who wish to see what the devil their friend or relative has been doing on weekends for all these years. In addition, the fortunate location of the road provides the Maury with a delightfully short shuttle route, allowing multiple runs of the river in a single day if so desired.

The put-in for this section is shortly below the confluence of the Calfpasture and the Little Calfpasture rivers, where the river runs up against the road and turns left into Goshen Pass. There is a dirt road here that leads the short distance from the paved road to a convenient pool. Parking is limited, so arrange the shuttle to have most of the vehicles at the bottom of the run. Below the put-in the Maury flows swiftly over some entertaining river-wide low ledges for a few hundred yards, a few short rapids and quick ledges, and another 100-yard rapid to the first of the named rapids.

This is Undercut Rock, one-half mile below the put-in. It is a 3-foot ledge, broken on the right and more abrupt on the left. Either side may be run but beware of the boulder on the bottom right which gives this rapid its name.

Shortly below Undercut Rock is Roadside (also known as Doorknob), recognizable by a jumble of low boulders on the left forcing the river to the right against the roadside bank. Take a left course through this drop, easier at high levels when room is created for the passage of conservative

Doug Howell entering Corner Rapid on the Goshen Pass section of the Maury.

boaters. This rapid is a long wave field (50 yards) with a nice surfing wave three-quarters of the way down. Excellent surfing waves are found at the bottom of this drop.

A long and pleasant Class II–III boulder garden appears below Roadside. This is an example of the good nature of the Maury for this rapid seems to be provided as a morale builder for the nervous paddler in preparation for the serious business that lies below. At the bottom of the boulder garden is a pool known as the Blue Hole. Running out of the Blue Hole the river disappears to the left, the road retreats high up on the right bank, and an unusually basso profundo roar may be heard from the stream ahead. These clues and the sight of various numbers of people in brightly colored helmets and nylon clothing scrambling all over the riverbanks should indicate that something unusual lies ahead. Rest assured that this is indeed the case.

Devil's Kitchen is the object of all of these grave portents, and it deserves them. This drop is a 100-yard-long Class IV with almost every conceivable river hazard packed into a short distance. The river drops about 20 feet in this span, with steep drops, limited visibility, strong holes, undercut rocks, tiny eddies, fallen trees, and the possibility of strainers making this by far the most serious rapid on the trip. The complexity of the series makes a detailed description of the route impractical, but the general path is to the left of a quasi-island made up of bus

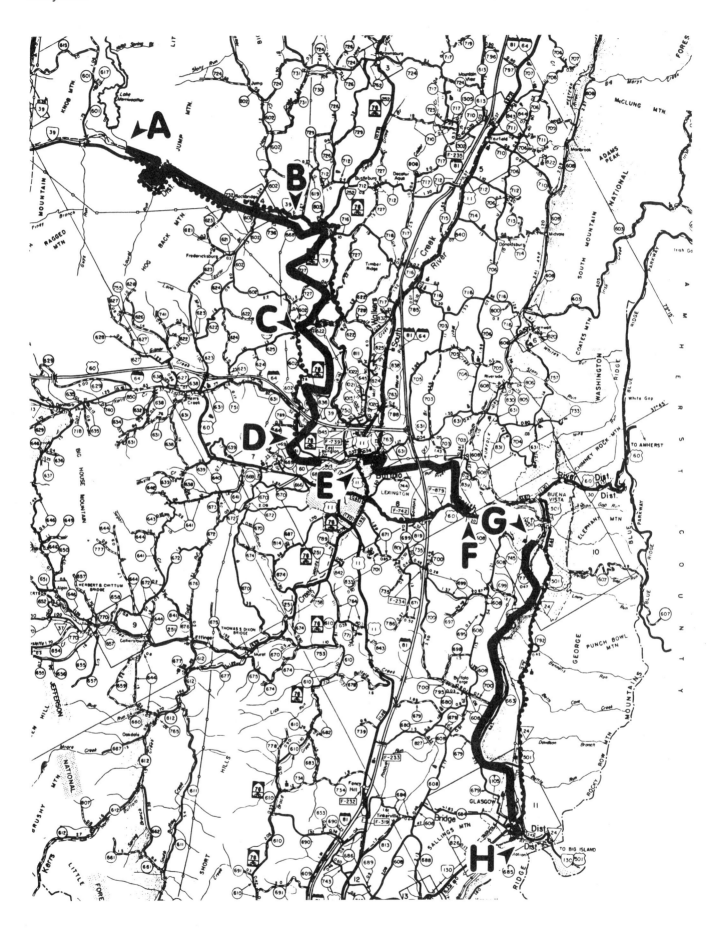

Section: Goshen Pass to Rockbridge Baths

Counties: Rockbridge

USGS Quads: Goshen

Suitable for: Day Cruising

Skill Level: Strong intermediates at moderate levels except for Devil's Kitchen, which is for advanced paddlers only

Months Runnable: Winter and early spring, or other times following a moderately heavy rainfall

Interest Highlights: Scenery, wildlife, history, geology, and whitewater

Scenery: Exceptionally beautiful

Difficulty: Class III with 1 Class IV at moderate levels

Average Width: 40–60 feet

Velocity: Fast

Gradient: 48 feet per mile average; 71 in the Goshen Pass

Runnable Water Levels:
Minimum: 1.3 feet at Rockbridge Baths or at James River Basin Canoe Livery; 2.8 feet on Buena Vista gauge
Maximum: Added congestion makes swims at levels above 3 feet hazardous; runs up to 5 feet are not too difficult for advanced paddlers, and 6 or 7 feet are possible for crazed experts; this is about 5, 7, and 9 feet respectively on Buena Vista gauge

Hazards: Strainers, keeper hydraulics at high levels, difficult rapids, lots of jagged rocks that have been broken off or rolled up and exposed during the November 1985 flood

Scouting: Devil's Kitchen (Class IV); Corner rapids (Class III–IV); Brillo rapids (Class III) just above Rockbridge Baths

Portages: None

Rescue Index: Accessible

Source of Additional Information: National Weather Service, Buena Vista gauge (703) 260-0305; James River Basin Canoe Livery, RFD No. 4, Box 125, Lexington, VA 24450 (540) 261-7334; Randy Lawless, Old Country Store, Rockbridge Baths (540) 348-1300

Access Points	River Miles	Shuttle Miles
A–B	5	5.5

Access Point Ratings:
A–Rt. 39 above Goshen Pass, very good
B–Behind Maury River Mercantile in Rockbridge Baths, very good

The "coffee pot" home of the James River Basin Canoe Livery on the lower Maury.

sized boulders on the right. Basically, you start on the left of the river by a huge boulder and work right over seven to eight drops of 2 to 3 feet each to end up on river right at the end of the run. Avoid the temptation to sneak the heavy stuff by running through the more lightly watered channel to the right of this island because it is festooned with strainers and studded with undercut rocks. Land above the entrance to Devil's Kitchen on the left and take a long hard look at it on foot. The best portage is on the left.

Below Devil's Kitchen the Maury provides another of the delightful Class II–III boulder gardens that make this trip such a pleasure. Run this drop right of the center—the left side is a rock jumble and way over on the right are two pourovers. Below here, paddlers will find themselves at the picnic area where, after Devil's Kitchen, some may wish to make use of the restrooms near the road. Leaving the picnic area, the highway, perhaps sensing more accurately than paddlers what lies ahead, again retreats away from the river and remains cowering high above the canyon floor for over a mile. Just below the picnic area are two 4-foot drops. Run the first on the right at moderate levels and the second left of center.

Soon Laurel Run falls off the right mountainside and enters the Maury, but it isn't noticeable unless you look for it. There are three small drops below Laurel Run that afford nice play spots. Corner Rapid, located just after a sharp bend to the left, is formed from boulders cut from the cliffs on the right. The river is squeezed to the left and through this Class III–IV boulder jumble. Paddlers should run the upper section on the left and then get to the right for the lower section. This rapid has several large holes to punch or avoid, depending on the skill or inclination of the paddler. Scrupulously avoid being pushed too far right at the top as you'll be squeezed into one of two violent channels. Also, the bottom the lower left is ugly, with pinning spots and scraping channels.

After a pool, there are a couple of Class II–III rapids through two diagonal lines of rocks. Then a smoothly sloping rock wall will be seen on the right. This indicates Sloping or Sliding Rock Rapids, a 100-yard-long ledge series. The route is straight through on the far right. The channel is directly next to the sloping rock wall, which runs uninterrupted into the water, and zooming down this bouncy channel with the rock within arms' reach on the right is reminiscent of looking out the window of a speeding subway. The eddies against the wall are very entertaining if they can be caught, and they provide opportunities for dynamic eddy turns, exciting surfing chances, and the possibility of customizing your boat by grinding off the bow on the unyielding stone. There are easier eddies on the left. There are also some nice surfing holes here.

Downstream is a long Class III rapid that has some very nice surfing waves toward the end. About 100 yards later the paddler will reach a calm spot known as the Indian Pool—recognized by a picnic table, a stone stairway, and the road. Below Indian Pool is another Class II–III rock garden almost one-half mile long that becomes rather bony at lower levels. This long rapid has several play spots and a new 4-foot ledge about two-thirds of the way down on river left. It is possible to take out at the bottom of this rapid where the road reapproaches the river, but I recommend continuing on to Rockbridge Baths unless you want to repeat the heavy duty part of Goshen Pass.

Below Indian Pool the canyon opens out into the valley, but the river has tenaciously retained enough gradient to keep the paddler entertained a while longer. Class II–III boulder gardens and ledges continue for a mile with the river occasionally splitting around islands. These islands are deposited material occurring where the steep gradient of the Goshen Pass has receded, reducing the capacity of the stream to carry rock, rubble, and sand. This excess material settles out of the flow and forms the islands and braided channels of this section. These characteristic formations are found wherever a steep stream reaches a level of temporarily decreased gradient. The drops in this area tend to be technical and require careful channel hunting at lower levels. At high levels just blast ahead and devil take the hindmost.

The last two notable drops on the run are easily recognized. They are both within a few hundred yards of the Route 39 highway bridge. The first is called Lava

---

Section: Rockbridge Baths (Rt. 39) to Limekiln Bridge (Rt. 631)

Counties: Rockbridge

USGS Quads: Goshen, Lexington

Suitable for: Day Cruising

Skill Level: Intermediates/shepherded novices first half, novices second half

Months Runnable: Generally winter and spring, early summer after rain

Interest Highlights: Pretty cliffs, scenic woodlands and farms

Scenery: Pretty in spots to beautiful

Difficulty: Class II with several Class II–III rapids in first 8 miles; Class I–II last 5.5 miles

Average Width: 50 to 60 feet

Velocity: Mostly moderate, occasionally fast in upper section

Gradient: 15 feet per mile

Runnable Water Levels:
Minimum: 3 inches on the put-in gauge behind Maury River Mercantile in Rockbridge Baths and similar level on gauge by James River Basin Canoe Livery; about 1.7 feet on Buena Vista gauge
Maximum: Maybe 3 feet on the put-in gauge behind Maury River Mercantile in Rockbridge Baths and similar level on gauge by James River Basin Canoe Livery; about 5 feet on Buena Vista gauge

Hazards: Perhaps an occasional tree in river

Scouting: Perhaps a couple of the Class II–IIIs

Portages: None

Rescue Index: Generally accessible

Source of Additional Information: National Weather Service, Buena Vista Gauge (703) 260-0305; James River Basin Canoe Livery (540) 261-7334; Randy Lawless, Old Country Store (540) 348-1300

Access Points	River Miles	Shuttle Miles
B–C	8.0	8
C–D	5.5	4
B–D	13.5	10

Access Point Ratings:
B–Behind Maury River Mercantile in Rockbridge Baths, or off Rt. 39 bridge, very good
C–At Rt. 622 bridge, very good
D–At Limekiln Bridge (Rt. 631), good

Section: East Lexington (US 1) to Ben Salem Wayside (US 60)

Counties: Rockbridge

USGS Quads: Lexington, Glasgow

Suitable for: Day cruising

Skill Level: Careful novices

Months Runnable: Generally winter and spring, early summer after rain

Interest Highlights: Scenic woodlands, cliffs

Scenery: Pretty in spots to pretty

Difficulty: Class I–II

Average Width: 50 to 60 feet

Velocity: Slow to moderate

Gradient: 5 feet per mile

Runnable Water Levels:

Minimum: 0 feet on the gauge at the James River Basin Canoe Livery; 1.5 feet on the Buena Vista gauge

Maximum: 3 to 4 feet on the James River Basin Canoe Livery gauge; 5 feet on Buena Vista gauge

Hazards: Treacherous lock on left and water sucking underneath Emores Dam 2 miles into the trip; perhaps a rare tree in river

Scouting: None

Portages: None

Rescue Index: Generally accessible

Source of Additional Information: National Weather Service, Buena Vista Gauge (703) 260-0305; James River Basin Canoe Livery (540) 261-7334

Access Points	River Miles	Shuttle Miles
E–F	6	8

Access Point Ratings:
E—East Lexington (US 11), very good
F—At Ben Salem Wayside (US 60), excellent

Falls after the igneous rock intrusion that forms the rapid. Lava is a Class II–III chute, run on the far right. Good surfing waves are found at the bottom at 2.5–3.0 feet on the Rockbridge Baths gauge. Shortly below is Brillo, an abrupt 4-foot ledge. Scouting here is in order since the channel is difficult to see from above. The route of choice at low and medium levels is on the far left, but even a perfect run will likely be accompanied by a grinding sound on the hull of the boat providing an immediate answer to the question of the origin of the rapid's name. Brillo can also be run on the far right.

The Route 39 bridge is now in sight signaling the end of the run. Do not take out at the bridge, however; this is frowned upon by the landowner. Instead, continue downstream 100 yards and take out on river right near Route 602 or another half-mile to the Old Country Store on the left bank in Rockbridge Baths. There is a 150-yard long Class II rapid before the store.

Rockbridge Baths (Route 39) to Limekiln Bridge (Route 631)

After rushing through exciting Goshen Pass, the Maury calms down after crossing under the Route 39 bridge. Indeed, the put-ins just below the Route 39 bridge (on Route 602) or at the Old Country Store in Rockbridge Baths, a half-mile downstream, are downright peaceful. However, the first 8 miles (to Route 622) of this 13.5-mile section are still challenging enough for the intermediate paddler or shepherded novice at moderate

water. There are numerous solid Class II rapids with a few approaching Class III, depending on route taken and water level. The rapids are generally rock gardens with a few ledges. Below Route 622, this trip is a 5.5-mile Class I float with only a couple of Class IIs.

The scenery is quite pleasant in this entire stretch. In some places the banks are low, and you can see woods and farmland. In other places Ordovician dolomite cliffs rise above. Folks interested in fishing will find moderate sized smallmouth bass and sunfish in profusion. Sharp-eyed paddlers may also see deer and beaver.

You have a choice of two put-ins. The first is about 100 yards downstream of the Route 39 bridge on river right off Route 602. After a long Class II rock garden, you reach the second put-in just off Route 39 in Rockbridge Baths. This is on river left just downstream of the Maury River Mercantile. Be sure to check the gauge here installed by Glenn Rose of the James River Basin Canoe Livery. It should be at least 3 inches for this lower section.

Soon below the second put-in, Hays Creek enters on the left, and you reach a Class II rock garden. Immediately following is a second rock garden with a 2-foot ledge lurking in the middle. You then come to an island. The right channel is longer, more gradual, still Class II; the left channel is more abrupt—with a Class II–III double drop of 2 feet that first timers should look over. Both passages approach Class III in high water.

In the next mile you will encounter several Class II rapids. More spectacular are some cliffs with hemlocks on the left, then some minicaves on the right, and last a

500-foot dolomite cliff on the right with a host of cedars clinging to it. Just below is a Class II with a rock at the bottom to avoid. Nearly a half-mile farther and about 2.5 miles into the trip you will come to a tough Class II–III rapid on the left. At low water enter far left but work right at the bottom to miss the nasty pinning rocks hiding there. Toward the end of the next mile the Maury will make a lazy 180-degree right turn. In this mile you will have several Class II rock gardens and some more spectacular cliffs. Then Mouse Run enters from the left and, as the river bends left, you encounter a good long Class II–III with nice wave action. The heaviest water is on the right. After a couple of Class IIs and some more scenic cliffs in the next mile, the river will start a 180-degree turn to the left. At the beginning of this turn, when you see some green cabins on the left, make sure the current doesn't push you into the cliffs on the right at high water.

After a couple of Class II rapids and a cliff on the right at the end of this turn, you will come to two islands. Take the right channels around both. The left channels were plugged by debris from the flood of 1985. About a half-mile further you will come to another island. The left channel is an easy Class II while a 2-foot drop and sharp left turn make the right channel slightly more difficult. Be careful here because there was a nasty strainer on the right recently. After rounding a bend and passing another island you will come to two 2-foot ledges about 100 yards apart. Run them center.

Nearly 2 miles later as the Maury bends left you will come to an island. To the right of the island are a couple of Class I–II rapids. The channel left of the island requires tighter maneuvering over three separate drops and is a Class II–III at moderate levels. Be careful of strainers here. Just below this island is the first take-out on river left below the Route 622 bridge. This makes an 8-mile trip. Intermediates can take out here, and raw novices can put in for a 5.5-mile journey.

A half mile below Route 622 is a Class II drop as the river bends right. For the next 3 miles there are only occasional Class I rapids. Then, as the river makes a long hairpin turn to the left, make sure you avoid a rock in a Class I rapid next to an island. Things are quiet for the next mile until you go under the Interstate 64 bridge. Immediately below is a Class II drop. Soon you will see some red cottages on the right and Limekiln Bridge (Route 631). The take-out is on river left above the bridge. Folks interested in caves should check out Bathers Cave about a quarter mile above the take-out on river left.

East Lexington (US 11) to Ben Salem Wayside (US 60)

To avoid the large 6-foot dam and less interesting paddling below the Limekiln bridge (Route 631), put in just below this dam on river right and upstream of US 11. This 6-mile trip through woodlands to Ben Salem Wayside is for careful novice boaters and has nothing more difficult than Class I–II rapids.

Be careful of the lock on the left at Emores Dam, which you must avoid about 2 miles into the trip. Some of the water here goes left through a treacherous lock with an abrupt drop of 4 feet. Do not attempt to run the lock. Also, a large volume of water is sucked unnoticed under the dam. To stay clear of both of these dangerous places take the Class I channel on the right.

Soon you will come to an island. Take the right channel; the left route is often too low. Then you go underneath Interstate 81 and have a few minor Class I rocks and ledges for the next mile. About a half mile later you come to the remains of the old South River Dam. The water here is fast but shallow. Scattered rocks can make the going tough for beginners. The best channel is down the middle of the river. Please note the old lock from the James River and Kanawha Canal system on the right bank as you negotiate these rapids.

The South River soon joins the Maury on the left. There are two islands here. The easiest route is left of both islands, but this channel is often low. For more excitement go to the right or in between these islands for some Class I–II action. Watch for a big rock after the second island if you take the channels between or right of the islands.

Below these islands you will come to three shelves in the river running roughly parallel to the bank and several hundred yards apart. Cross each of these right of center. The last shelf is a good Class I rapid. The Buena Vista gauging station is just below the second shelf on river right. After another mile of calm water, you will come to the Ben Salem Wayside (US 60) on river right. The Class I–II drop here is the remains of the Ben Salem Navigation Dam; the best channel is on the extreme right. Notice the remains of a lock at this wayside. Just below on the river right is a culvert and the James River Basin Canoe Livery. This eye-catching building is shaped like a coffee pot because it used to be a restaurant. Also at the culvert is the gauge for this section and the next section downstream; it should read at least 0.

Section: Glen Maury Park (Rt. 745) to Locher Landing (Rt. 684)

Counties: Rockbridge

USGS Quads: Glasgow

Suitable for: Day cruising

Skill Level: Careful novices

Months Runnable: Generally winter and spring, early summer after rain

Interest Highlights: Scenic farmland

Scenery: Pretty in spots to pretty

Difficulty: Class I–II

Average Width: 50 to 60 feet

Velocity: Moderate

Gradient: 11 feet per mile

Runnable Water Levels:

Minimum: 0 feet on the James River Basin Canoe Livery gauge; 1.5 feet on the Buena Vista gauge
Maximum: 3 to 4 feet on the James River Basin Canoe Livery gauge; 5 feet on the Buena Vista gauge

Hazards: Goose Neck Dam at high water; Class III rapids just below Locher Landing take-out for novices; perhaps a rare tree in river

Scouting: Class III rapids below Locher Landing

Portages: None

Rescue Index: Accessible

Source of Additional Information: National Weather Service, Buena Vista Gauge (703) 260-0305; James River Basin Canoe Livery (540) 261-7334

Access Points	River Miles	Shuttle Miles
G–H	12	9

Access Point Ratings:
G—Glen Maury Park (Rt. 745), very good
H—Locher Landing (Rt. 684), very good

Glen Maury Park (Route 745) to Locher Landing (Route 684)

To avoid portaging around a 20-foot dam and most of Buena Vista, put in upstream or downstream of Glen Maury Park which is roughly 3 miles downstream from the Ben Salem Wayside. This gives a 12-mile Class I–II novice trip to where the Maury joins the James at Locher Landing. Be very considerate on this trip because the banks are virtually all privately owned.

Just below the Glen Maury Park and the Route 745 bridge (10th Street) are the remains of Keys Mill Dam. Here there is an easy 2- to 3-foot Class I drop. A mile below this is a railroad track with an island just below; the best channel is to the left. Two miles below here the river splits. The remains of an old dam are in the right channel where you can run the Class I break of this ruined dam on the left. Alternatively, you can take the left channel, which has a longer Class I rapid. Two miles later, after a long horseshoe bend, are the remains of Goose Neck Dam. There is a large "12" painted on a big concrete slab there. Paddlers have permission of the property owner here to line their boats over the remains of Goose Neck Dam on the left. There is a 30-foot break on the right side (Class II) that can be run at moderate water, but be careful here at high water—it is very treacherous. Most of the water runs to the left over and through two very ugly pinning rocks and a lot of dam debris. So, at high water run a narrow 2-foot slot to the right of center and just left of the concrete slab with the "12."

A half mile below Goose Neck Dam is a Class II rapid when the water is high. Go right when the water is low. As the river turns left there is another nice Class II drop; stay left of center. Just below this rapid is an island. Opposite this island on the left bank is a freshwater spring located up the 30-foot bank and across a dirt road; this is on National Forest land.

After this refreshment you come to an island and Buffalo Creek, entering from the right. The best channel is to the left of the island. Just below here is another island and a big tree growing out of the right bank just above it. Go right of this island, but be careful of the tree: the current pushes you into it.

About 2.5 miles farther (after a quarry) is another island. Go right here too, but watch for tree limbs on the bank. The left channel is usually too shallow. After passing this island, you will see a gazebo on the left bank, meaning you have 2 miles left. You then cross under one old bridge and then the Route 130 bridge. A half mile downstream you come to the railroad bridge just before the Maury joins the James. Take out above this bridge on river right, here at Locher Landing (Route 684). At high water make sure you take out well upstream of the railroad bridge. There is a rocky Class III rapid just below the railroad bridge, which becomes more difficult with higher water. Experienced boaters may want to run this rapid after looking at it. However, many novice boaters have had their boats pinned here so don't be sucked into this drop.

Mill Creek

Mill Creek is a 1.5- to 4-mile cheap thrill when most rivers are moving toward flood stage and you've got time for a quick trip while you're rushing around in the Goshen Pass area trying to find a stream still low enough to paddle. However, Mill Creek is very busy a good part of this trip, and you need good boat control as you bump your way down this tiny Class II–III stream at moderate levels.

The put-in is at Panther Gap, 4 miles west of Goshen on Route 39. You put in across the road from a grocery store currently called the Walker Mountain Market. The heart of this run is from 1 to 2.5 miles below the grocery store; here you have 1.5 miles of increasingly busy Class II–III water (at low levels), which bumps over an interminable number of small ledges and rock gardens of Silurian sandstone and shale. There are eddies here and there along the banks—if you can find enough room to make an eddy turn on this tiny stream. At medium levels and above, this 1.5-mile rapid becomes Class III and above because of the relentless gradient. The road follows Mill Creek for 1 mile of this stretch, so you can get an idea of what you are in for.

Those who are in a hurry or who want whitewater only can take out less than 2 miles below the put-in, at (or just below) the national forest sign just before Mill Creek leaves Route 39. However, this take-out is only midway

in the 1.5-mile-long rapid. For those continuing, there is a surprise. Very shortly after the road goes away from the river, you come to a 3-foot ledge. You should look this over, particularly at high water, because of the nasty hydraulic below. Just below this ledge on river left are the remains of an old mill. Less than a half mile below the ledge, the 1.5-mile-rapid ends and is followed by a mile of flatwater. This is an opportunity to relax after a long

---

Section: Panther Gap (Rt. 39) to Goshen (Alt. Rt. 39)

Counties: Rockbridge, Bath

USGS Quads: Green Valley, Millboro, Goshen

Suitable for: Day Cruising

Skill Level: Intermediates (low water) advanced (high water)

Months Runnable: Winter and spring after a heavy rain

Interest Highlights: 1.5-mile-long rapid on tiny stream

Scenery: Pretty in spots

Difficulty: Class II–III (low water); Class III and above at high water

Average Width: 15 to 25 feet

Velocity: Fast

Gradient: 31 feet per mile

Runnable Water Levels:
  Minimum: Inspect from road west of Goshen; maybe 5 feet on Buena Vista gauge; maybe 3 feet on Maury River gauge in Goshen Pass or at James River Basin Canoe Livery

Maximum: Perhaps 2 feet of canoeing water; maybe 7 feet on Buena Vista gauge; maybe 5 feet on Maury River in Goshen Pass or the gauge at James River Basin Canoe Livery

Hazards: Occasional trees in river; maybe 1 or 2 fences; 3-foot ledge; 5-foot dam one-half mile before take-out

Scouting: From road before you run 1.5-mile-long rapid; 3-foot ledge just after road leaves Mill Creek

Portages: Maybe 3-foot ledge, and 5-foot dam one-half mile before take-out in Goshen

Rescue Index: Accessible

Source of Additional Information: National Weather Service, Buena Vista gauge (703) 260-0305; James River Basin Canoe Livery (540) 261-7334

Access Points	River Miles	Shuttle Miles
A–B	4	4

Access Point Ratings:
  A–Panther Gap along Rt. 39, very good
  B–In Goshen (Alt. Rt. 39), very good

nonstop rapid: the scenery is pretty with numerous large hemlocks to greet you along the way. The only potential hazard during this flatwater mile is an occasional tree or log dropped over the stream by anglers to create foot bridges. Be careful of these, particularly at high water.

After the mile of flatwater, as you near the outskirts of Goshen, please be alert. Here there is a 5-foot dam. This dam has been run through a small break left of center by advanced boaters at moderate levels, but portaging is the preferred option. Below this dam it is a half mile to the Route 39 (alternate) take-out bridge in Goshen. There are some modest ledges along the way, and just as you reach this bridge at medium levels there is a pleasant Class II wavefield. Take out on river right by the volunteer fire department building.

The first good drop on the Goshen Pass section of the Maury River.

The three foot ledge next to the remains of an old mill on Mill Creek

Moormans River

This 13-mile stretch of the Moormans has two distinct sections: a 4-mile, little slalom, upper section; and a 9-mile, bigger water, lower section where the river is twice as wide. For the 4-mile upper section, the Moormans is a busy, tight, small stream dropping over continual rock gardens and small ledges of precambrian granite and gneiss. Adding spice to this section are occasional barbed wire fences as well as trees in the river (both downed and upright). Macho aggressive intermediates and advanced paddlers who like to hop in and out of their boats while dodging or carrying around numerous obstacles will love this Class II–III run.

Unfortunately, this upper section is almost entirely dependent on releases from the Charlottesville Reservoir for this river which comes out of Sugar and Burnthouse Hollows with 3,100-foot-high Bucks Elbow Mountain to the south. During early spring, the reservoir is usually full and outflow is nearly equal to rainfall and snowmelt inflow. However, at other times, this flow may be held back, leaving the upper Moormans unrunnable while the lower Moormans has ample flow from the Doyles River. There is one final caution about the reservoir: the Rivanna Water and Sewer Authority forbids boats of any kind in it.

Rather than launching just below the Charlottesville reservoir on Route 614, it is perhaps better to use the second Route 614 bridge as you go upstream from Route 810. Put in below a barbed wire fence; there's a nice parking area nearby. This way you will get a flavor of the upper section but have fewer trees and barbed wire fences with which to contend. After 3 miles of Class II small ledges and rock gardens, you will reach Route 810. Be careful of a wood and barbed wire cattle gate just below this bridge.

The 9-mile lower section of the Moormans begins at the Route 810 bridge, where the Doyles River joins the Moormans (from the north) and adds substantially to its

Section: Below Charlottesville Reservoir (Rt. 614) to Free Union (Rt. 601)

Counties: Albemarle

USGS Quads: Browns Cove, Crozet, Free Union, Charlottesville West

Suitable for: Day cruising

Skill Level: Aggressive intermediates or advanced on upper section; intermediates at moderate levels on lower section

Months Runnable: Winter and spring following a rain or snowmelt

Interest Highlights: Beautiful rock cliffs in lower section

Scenery: Pretty to beautiful in spots

Difficulty: Class II–III

Average Width: 15 to 30 feet in upper section; 30 to 40 feet in lower section

Velocity: Fast on upper section; moderate to fast on lower section

Gradient: 60 feet per mile on upper section; 22 feet per mile on lower section

Runnable Water Levels:
  Minimum: Upper section, 9 inches on Rt. 810 gauge; lower section, 0 on Rt. 671 gauge
  Maximum: Upper section, perhaps 2 feet on Rt. 810 gauge; lower section, perhaps 3 feet on Rt. 671 gauge

Hazards: Numerous trees and several barbed wire fences on upper section; occasional trees, cattle gate (by Rt. 810), a low-water bridge (about 7 miles below Rt. 810), and a barbed wire fence or so on lower section; high water on both sections

Scouting: Perhaps eddy scout several ledges a mile below the Rt. 810 bridge at high water

Portages: A low-water bridge (7 miles below Rt. 810); trees and fences, more on upper section than lower section

Rescue Index: Accessible to remote

Source of Additional Information: Charlottesville Dam at (804) 823-4738; Blue Ridge Mountain Sports in Charlottesville at (804) 977-4400

Access Points	River Miles	Shuttle Miles
A–B	1.0	1.0
B–C	3.0	3.5
C–D	3.5	4.0
D–E	5.5	5.0

Access Point Ratings:
A–Below Charlottesville Reservoir (Rt. 614), very good
B–Rt. 614/674 intersection upstream from Rt. 810, very good
C–Rt. 674 on Doyles River off Route 810, very good
D–Rt. 671 bridge, good
E–Free Union (Rt. 601), fair to poor

flow. Since the flow of the Doyles River is not governed by dam release, there will often be water in the Doyles when the upper section of the Moormans is too low. So, rather than put in at the Route 810 bridge, it is usually better to turn right (east) on a gravel road a half mile north of this bridge (Route 674) and put in on the Doyles River. You will also avoid the aforementioned cattle gate at the Route 810 bridge on the Moormans and a shallow 2- to 3-foot ledge, which can bang sterns, just below.

There is a canoeing gauge on the Route 810 bridge (downstream side, river right), which is valid only for the upper section of the Moormans. You should have at least 9 inches on the gauge for a run on the upper section.

About 200 yards below the Route 810 bridge, the Moormans and Doyles Rivers join. The following stretch of river is for accomplished intermediates at moderate water levels.

Here the Moormans passes through hardwood forests though you have occasional glimpses of pasture land. Its runnable season usually coincides with central Virginia's springtime, when the scenery is excellent with swollen maple buds, dogwood blossoms, and new spring foliage.

Shortly after the put-in you have a pleasant, long Class II rock garden, which introduces you to this part of the river. From here on you have continual rock gardens and small ledges. About a mile below the Route 810 bridge, the Moormans constricts somewhat, and the boater must react quickly to navigate through several Class II rock gardens and ledges. There are wide passages, but unless one is familiar with the route, there may be surprises, particularly in high

water when this section approaches Class III. Below this section, the rapids are less demanding.

After 3.5 miles you come to the bridge at Millington (Route 671). On the upstream river left footing of the bridge is the best canoeing gauge for the lower stretch of the Moormans. This Randy Carter gauge registers a true canoeing 0, so be sure you check it on the shuttle. The bridge here can be a take-out for folks who want the best part of the Moormans only or a put-in/take-out for those who only have time for a late afternoon paddle. The ledge at the Millington bridge is all that remains of the dam for a nearby mill (on the left). There are other remains of mills along this stretch. Below the Millington bridge, the river simmers down slightly for the last 5.5 miles of the trip, offering you smaller rock gardens and smaller ledges. Three miles below Millington, you come to a 2 foot ledge made by a road. If the river is high enough, several inches on the Route 671 gauge, you can paddle over this ledge. In past years there was also a barbed wire fence here, but it was gone recently. If the river is lower and you cannot scrape over the ledge with care, portage on either right or left.

The latter half of this trip passes by beautiful rocky cliffs overlooking the river and deep pools for swimming when the weather is warm enough. With the rapids being easier, you can now take time to fully enjoy this pretty place. Although the fishing is not good, there is impressive wildlife. The larger birds often seen are ospreys, red-tailed hawks, great blue herons, geese, turkeys, and ducks. The most commonly seen animals are beaver, muskrat, deer,

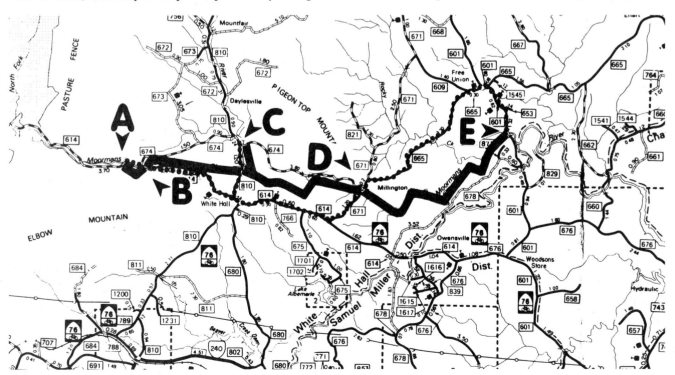

and raccoon (at night). In warm weather, please be careful of snakes.

All too soon you reach the take-out on the right under the Route 601 bridge. Don't continue farther unless you enjoy paddling on the backwater of dams. The next bridge (Route 660) is 6 miles farther, 4 miles of which are the backwater of the Rivanna Reservoir Dam.

The lower Moormans is up perhaps a dozen times a year, while the upper Moormans is up about half that. Although this is normally a winter/spring trip after a rain or snowmelt, you can catch the Moormans (particularly the low section) after a heavy fall storm. The lower section of the Moormans also has numerous good playing spots for experienced boaters, particularly at levels from 2 to 3 feet on the Route 671 gauge. At 3 feet the river is basically bank full, and big holes start to develop here and there. At this level the lower Moormans is the province of advanced paddlers. To see if there will be sufficient water on the upper stretch of the Moormans, call the dam keeper of the Charlottesville Dam at (804) 823-4738 on weekdays between 8 a.m. and 5 p.m. To get the scoop on the lower section as well as the upper, call Blue Ridge Mountain Sports in Charlottesville at (804) 977-4400. Besides providing information, these kind folks also rent canoes and sell paddling gear.

A kayak below a typical rapid on the scenic mellow Moormans. Photo by John Holden.

Ogle Creek

Ogle Creek, pronounced "ugly," is anything but! A short 4-mile section of this creek near Callaghan, Virginia, offers some real fun when the water level is right—generally in winter and spring. The run is mostly Class II rock gardens and ledges of Devonian sandstone and shale except for two series of 2- to 3-foot ledges that are low to high Class III,

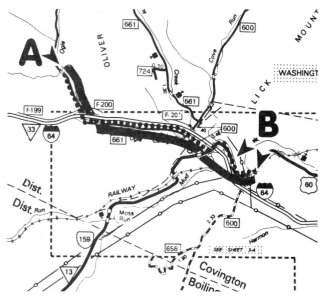

depending on whether the water level is low or high. The ledges are probably formed by resistant chert beds in the Devonian limestone formations found in this area.

Put in on Route 661 about 1 mile from Interstate 64, near where Big Run joins Ogle Creek. Be awake when you launch because the gradient is 45 feet per mile and the continuous Class II action starts immediately. The first set of Class III ledges is behind the town of Callaghan, about 2 miles from the Route 661 put-in. Here you have several river-wide ledges near some houses. They are clearly visible from the river and easily scouted from either bank. Generally, you have to work back and forth between the ledges to pick the cleanest chute.

The second series of Class III ledges occur 1.5 miles farther downstream, just before Ogle Creek enters Dunlap Creek. Ogle Creek narrows here and bumps down about a dozen closely spaced ledges as the water funnels the action down the center of the river. There is an easy scout on the left. However, be alert because this rapid has a way of sneaking up on you. The ledges are near a service station on the left side of the river.

Other than these ledges, the only hazard is perhaps an occasional deadfall in the stream. Ogle Creek can be scouted in many places as it is easily accessible from roads throughout its length. Unfortunately, there are some trashy sections midway on this trip near the town of Callaghan, but they are balanced by some beautiful spots where you pass through an evergreen hemlock forest. All too soon you reach the US 60 bridge take-out on Dunlap Creek about one-quarter mile below the second set of ledges.

Section: Rt. 661 near Callaghan (at or near confluence with Big Run) to US 60 on Dunlap Creek

Counties: Alleghany

USGS Quads: Callaghan

Suitable for: Day cruising

Skill Level: Intermediate

Months Runnable: Winter and spring or after a heavy rain at other times

Interest Highlights: 2 nice sets of ledges; hemlocks

Scenery: Fair to beautiful in spots

Difficulty: Class II with 2 Class III series of ledges

Average Width: 25 to 35 feet

Velocity: Moderate to fast

Gradient: 45 feet per mile

Runnable Water Levels:
  Minimum: No gauge; visually check creek at put-in and take-out
  Maximum: Below flood stage; scout from the road

Hazards: Perhaps an occasional tree in river

Scouting: 2 Class III series of ledges; scout first series from right or left and second series from left

Portages: None except for perhaps an occasional downed tree

Rescue Index: Accessible

Source of Additional Information: None

Access Points	River Miles	Shuttle Miles
A–B	4	4

Access Point Ratings:
  A–Rt. 661 bridge (near Big Run), good
  B–US 60 bridge (over Dunlap Creek), very good

Piney River

The 5-mile upper section of the Piney River offers a challenge for advanced to expert paddlers and the 7-mile lower section is a treat for competent intermediate paddlers as well. Tumbling out of George Washington National Forest, this pristine mountain stream has only one drawback: most of the land along its banks is privately owned. Permission should be obtained to launch or stop wherever the land is posted against trespassing.

If you have a strong desire to bust your body or boat when everything else is in flood stage, the upper section of the Piney is for you. However, be warned! Not only is this river a tough tangle, angry landowners can be even nastier to thoughtless boaters. For example, in the early 1980s the landowner on river right just above the Woodson Bridge (Route 666/827) take-out for the upper section drilled five shots into the hull of a pig-headed boater who infringed on his fishing. The judge upheld the landowner in an ensuing court case. The lesson is clear: macho folks running the upper section should get permission first! Be especially diplomatic with landowners and considerate of private land.

Those contemplating the 4- to 5-mile run (at a gradient of 150 feet per mile) down to the Woodson Bridge have several options, depending on nerve and water level. One nice safety feature is that the road runs near the river for the entire upper section trip so boaters can road scout most of this run before committing themselves. Because of the road and the nonstop intensity of this run, only highlights and landmarks are discussed here.

The uppermost put-in is on Route 827, 5.5 road miles upstream of the Woodson Bridge (junction of Routes 666 and 827), and then several hundred yards down a private dirt road that crosses a low-water bridge. Here the Piney is only 20 feet wide and the low-water bridge is unusable when there is enough water to put in. Those intrepid souls putting in here will find continuous granite and granidiorite boulder piles for the first half mile. Then, as the river runs next to the road again, there is a nasty 5- to 6-foot drop with a narrow center slot into a pool, followed one boat length later by a 3-foot drop into another pool. Scout this by road (and on foot) before committing yourself to this tough drop. A portage on the right is the preferred option.

The boulder piles continue for another half mile. Then comes a second put-in, a mile downstream from the first. This put-in is recognized by a George Washington National Forest sign near a circular turnaround on Route 827 (now a dirt road). There is a trail near this sign that takes you to the river, which still is only 20 feet wide.

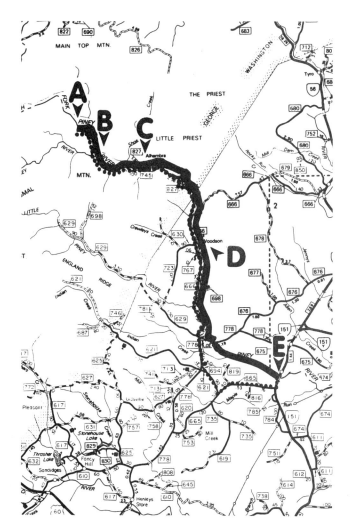

In the next half mile, as you bounce among the boulders, you will pass several houses and an island where most of the water is in the right channel. Just below this is the third put-in—a dirt road in a large grove of hemlocks one-tenth of a mile from Route 827.

Then Route 827 and the Piney go separate ways for nearly a half mile. When you reach the one-lane Route 827 bridge (a fourth put-in, near some houses), be alert. There is a hairy boulder garden just below, followed soon by a low-water bridge and a boulder ledge. After passing a pool and some houses, the river turns left into another severe boulder garden and, like a naughty child, hides from the road for another half mile.

Soon after you and what's left of your boat reach the road, you encounter another island. Take the left channel, please. The right channel has a mangled metal footbridge and low-hanging hemlock branches which make this route quite hazardous at runnable levels. Several hundred yards below this island is another low-water bridge. This is followed by a two-boulder gardens, separated by a pool. Below here the river eases up a bit as it goes under a footbridge and past some houses. After another pool, the Piney drops into a heavy rock garden, under a one-lane bridge, and into a blind, heavier boulder garden just below.

Then comes a pool by a privately owned recreational building and an island which has an easier boulder garden and most of the water in the right channel. After another half mile of boulder piles, the river calmly returns to the road.

When you reach several apparently man-made boulder ledges you have arrived at the Route 666/827 bridge. This is the take-out for macho men and the put-in for more mortal souls. However, get permission before putting in or taking out above this bridge unless you want your boat custom ventilated by a Smith and Wesson! The landowner downstream of the bridge is more reasonable than the gun-toting fellow upstream. The best put-in is on river left just downstream of the bridge. Be ultra considerate so future boaters can put in here, too.

Besides having friendlier landowners and a more "modest" gradient of 55 feet per mile, the lower section of the Piney below the Route 666/827 bridge is runnable much more often. Unfortunately, the Randy Carter canoeing gauge at the bridge in Lowesville is gone, so

inspection of the river is the only way of determining if there is sufficient water. The section beginning at Woodson starts with a bang (albeit a gentler bang than most of the upper Piney). Just below the bridge is an island and a Class III rock garden. The right channel contains more water. Then, just after this rock garden and a scant tenth of a mile below the bridge is an intricate Class III, 4-foot drop through a boulder pile. Intermediates should scout this mean drop on the shuttle or before running it. There is a large, sloping, flat rock slab just below this drop on river right. After this drop there are five bouldery ledges nicely spaced over 100 yards or so. Shortly below this is a Class II–III rock garden.

From here the river simmers down to frequent Class I–II drops as you travel 1 mile to the next Route 666 bridge which is followed a half mile later by a crude one-lane bridge. You will notice that the river is increasingly channelized with porphyritic granite boulders forming the banks. The cobble bars continue and you go under the one-lane Route 698 bridge less than a mile later. One mile below this bridge is a 5-foot dam. Look at it on the shuttle and pull off well upstream for your portage on the right.

Section: George Washington National Forest (Rt. 827) to Piney River (Rt. 151)

Counties: Nelson, Amherst

USGS Quads: Montebello, Massies Mill, Piney River

Suitable for: Day cruising

Skill Level: Advanced/expert (upper section); intermediates (lower section)

Months Runnable: Upper section–winter and spring after a prolonged heavy rain; lower section–winter and spring after a moderate rain

Interest Highlights: Beautiful gorge in upper section

Scenery: Pretty in spots to beautiful

Difficulty: Class III–V in upper section; Class II–III in lower section

Average Width: 20 to 40 feet, upper section; 40 to 60 feet, lower section

Velocity: Fast in upper section; moderate to fast in lower section

Gradient: 150 feet per mile in 4- to 5-mile upper section; 55 feet per mile in 7-mile lower section

Runnable Water Levels:
  Minimum: No gauge, visually check river
  Maximum: Flood stage

Hazards: Numerous boulder piles or drops, 2 low-water bridges, 1 mangled metal footbridge, occasional trees in river, and gun-toting landowners in upper section; a 5-foot dam (a third of a mile above Lowesville) and perhaps an occasional tree in river in lower section

Scouting: Numerous drops in upper section, first 2 drops in lower section just below Rt. 666/827 bridge, and drop just below Lowesville bridge

Portages: Probably several drops and 2 low-water bridges in upper section; 5-foot dam in lower section

Rescue Index: Generally accessible

Source of Additional Information: None

Access Points	River Miles	Shuttle Miles
A–D	5.5	5.5
B–D	4.5	4.5
C–D	2.5	2.5
D–E	7	8

Access Point Ratings:
A—George Washington National Forest at dirt road off Rt. 827, very good but get permission
B—George Washington National Forest sign on Rt. 827 at circular turnaround, very good
C—one-lane Rt. 827 Bridge, very good but get permission
D—at Woodson (Rt. 666/827 bridge, very good but get permission (downstream best)
E—at Shady Land/Piney River (Rt. 151), very good

A third of a mile below the dam you reach Lowesville and the Route 778/666 bridge. Just below this bridge is a feisty, Class III, 50-yard rock shelf which should be run left to avoid a hungry hole on the right. The hole is great for competent boaters to surf but difficult to exit from upright. If you put in or take out here, please do so upstream on river right unless you get permission to do so upstream on river left, which is posted.

For about 2 miles below Lowesville, the rapids are Class I–II gravel bars. When you reach the quarry, the river narrows into a decent Class II–III rapid. The Piney then calms down again for the remainder of the trip except for two Class II rapids just before you reach the settlement of Shady Lane near the town of Piney River and the Route 151 bridge take-out. There is a locked gauging station on river left upstream of the bridge, which is obviously no

help in determining river levels. The best take-out and parking are also upstream on river left. However, this is on private property, so get permission first.

The Piney is truly a scenic river, particularly the upper gorge section. Even if you don't paddle the gorge, it is worth a drive any time of the year. The hemlock groves and rocky riverbed are a real treat. There are occasional pools to swim and cool off in on a hot summer day (when you can contemplate paddlers doing harm to their bodies and boats in the chilly spring). The lower section of the Piney is also pretty; although the hemlocks are gone, hardwoods such as ashes and black locusts shield the privately owned river banks. Abundant bird life will entertain you. Be alert for herons, bobwhite quail, blue grosbeaks, and even wood thrushes trilling deep in the forest.

One of the huge boulder piles on the Upper Piney River at low water.

Potts Creek

Potts Creek has something for everyone. In the upper and middle stretches intermediate and advanced paddlers will find good action. In the lower stretches careful novices who are willing to make a portage or so can find an interesting trip. Generally, you will be paddling with a hill (and occasionally interesting rock formations) on one bank and farmland on the other. Hills and farmland alternate banks with pleasing frequency. The scenery is superb and the water clear on this pleasant stream.

Another great thing about this creek is that you can create your own trip of just about any length. Route 18 crosses the creek 13 times in this 33-mile segment of Potts Creek. It's 24 miles on this efficient shuttle road from the first put-in (Route 311) at Paint Bank to the last take-out in Idlewilde just below a 6-foot dam on the outskirts of Covington. Some of the take-outs are steep or on private

land, so look these over or get permission before using them.

The put-in at the community of Paint Bank gives you a real feel for the outdoor character of this area. The general store a few score yards from the Route 311 put-in is a game inspection station for turkey, deer, and bear hunters in the late fall. Even on a hot summer day, you can see green herons stalking their prey on the bank of Potts Creek in this tiny town of a few buildings. Just a mile and a half south of town on Route 311 is one of five Virginia fish hatcheries, which raises 1.7 million rainbow, brown, and brook trout each year. It is open to visitors from 8:00 a.m. to 3:30 p.m. on weekdays, and you might want to check out some of the lunkers lurking there.

The easy Route 311 put-in is on river right. Stock up at the nearby general store if you have forgotten anything to

The natural ledge (low water) at the beginning of the "Sinks" on Potts Creek below Boiling Springs off Route 694.

eat or drink. Do not put in 100 yards upstream on the Route 18 bridge because the land there is privately owned.

Below the put-in the river flows over a gravel and cobble riverbed. Between the put-in and the first Route 18 bridge the rapids are generally delightful Class II–III rock gardens and ledges with numerous tight passages. Roughly 1.5 miles into your trip the remains of a low-water bridge create a Class II drop. Shortly below,

the river braids with a resulting debris jam. A nice hill forms the right bank for part of this section. Another 1.5 miles later is the beginning of a 1-mile section where you'll find stocked rainbow, brown, and brook trout. Be careful it you run this section in early spring because there may be many fisherman there. The rapids continue to be interesting rock gardens as the creek follows a dirt road and Route 18.

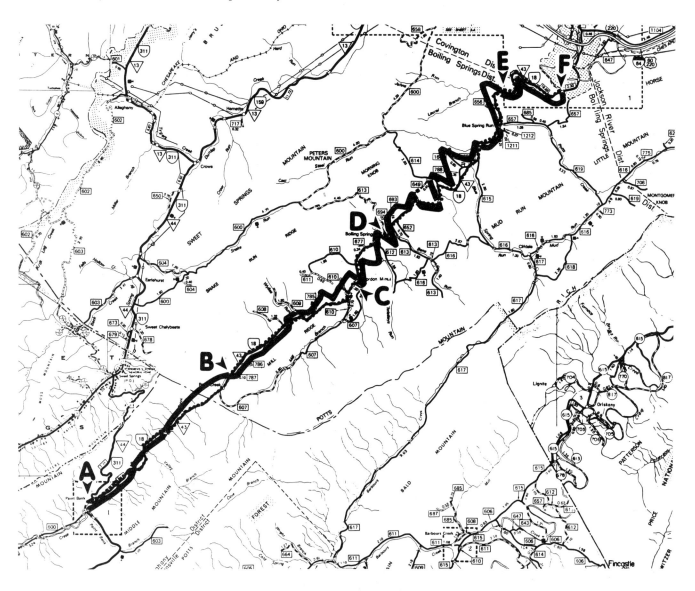

Just after this you will come to Steel Bridge Campground, a superb camping area on river left in a large grove of hemlocks and rhododendrons gracing the river bank. The trout fishing area ends about a quarter mile below this campground. Campground protocol is simple: no fee, no booze, and first come, first served. It's a great place to spend the night if you want to run Potts Creek for two days. However, it is mobbed during the start of fishing season (mid to late March) and can be crowded in hunting season (November–December).

Soon you will come to the first Route 18 bridge. Now the Class II–III rock gardens will lessen somewhat in intensity to Class II as a long hill becomes the left riverbank. A man-made rock wall on the right and a 2-foot ledge signal your approach to the second Route 18 bridge. A bumpy take-out is possible here after a 7-mile trip.

For the next several miles the rock gardens and small ledges are milder (Class I–II) as Potts Creek periodically runs up against Route 18 while hills form the right bank. Be alert for two low–water bridges in the first 1.5 miles below the second Route 18 bridge. Take care here as a couple of hundred yards below this bridge is another low-water bridge (visible from Route 18 on the shuttle). Roughly a mile below the second low-water bridge the river goes under the one-lane, metal Route 785 bridge.

Potts Creek then plays tag with the hills on the left before it gets to the town of Jordan Mines.

In this section, and at many other places along Potts Creek, crumbly black Devonian Shale cliffs form the outside edges of bends. These can be especially scenic in early spring during snowmelt when glimmering cascades of water pour over many of the cliffs.

Shortly below is the fourth Route 18 bridge, which is a good put-in or take-out on placid pools. The river plays tag with hills on the right below this bridge. Bridges five (easy take-out), six (tough take-out, near Route 613), and seven go by in quick succession. Between bridges six and seven you pass the small community of Boiling Springs and the rapids pick up again. Specifically, just above the seventh bridge is a good Class II–III bumpy ledge of 3 to 4 feet. The river left passage is easier and more of a boulder garden. At higher water the river right passage offers some fun surfing and playing spots on the multiple shelves formed between the ledges. The seventh Route 18 bridge is 19 miles below the Route 311 put-in.

Incidentally, the stretch of Potts Creek from bridge five to 1 mile below bridge seven is geologically very interesting. One-quarter mile below bridge five, Boiling Spring gushes into Potts Creek on the left. At higher springtime flows, the water actually boils up from the

Section: Paint Bank (Rt. 311) to Idlewilde/Covington (Rt. 18)

Counties: Craig, Alleghany

USGS Quads: Paint Bank, Potts Creek, Alleghany, Jordan Mines, Callaghan, Strom, Covington

Suitable for: Day cruising

Skill Level: Advanced/intermediates (upper and middle sections); novices (lower sections)

Months Runnable: Winter and spring generally

Interest Highlights: Trout stream near top, occasional pretty bluffs; karst geology and caves near Boiling Springs

Scenery: Pretty in spots to beautiful

Difficulty: Class II–III in upper section; Class II with two Class III–IV ledges in middle section; Class I–II in lower section

Average Width: 40 to 60 feet

Velocity: Fast for first half; moderate to fast in middle; moderate at end

Gradient: 36 feet per mile in first 7 miles; 16 feet per mile for last 26 miles

Runnable Water Levels:
  Minimum: Riffles below Rt. 311 put-in bridge runnable

Maximum: Flood stage

Hazards: 3 low-water bridges below second and third Rt. 18 bridges; two 5-foot ledges just below seventh Route 18 bridge; one 6-foot dam just above last Rt. 18 take-out near Covington; maybe a couple of trees in the river

Scouting: Two 5-foot ledges

Portages: Definitely 6-foot dam and perhaps two 5-foot ledges

Rescue Index: Accessible

Source of Additional Information: None

Access Points	River Miles	Shuttle Miles
A–B	7	6.5
B–C	7.5	5.5
B–D	12	8
D–E	10.5	7
D–F	14	10

Access Point Ratings:
  A–at Paint Bank (Rt. 311), very good
  B–at second Rt. 18 bridge, fair
  C–at fourth Rt. 18 bridge near Rt. 616, very good
  D–at Rt. 694 off seventh Rt. 18 bridge, good
  E–at twelfth Rt. 18 bridge, very good
  F–at thirteenth Rt. 18 bridge, fair

streambed, forming a mound on the surface of the water. This is just one of the many different limestone karst phenomena found in the area.

The seventh bridge is rather high, and from it you can see the aforementioned ledge just upstream. Branching off on river left and following the stream for a short distance is Route 694. This is a good access point but one on private land, so get permission if you put in or take out here.

Just below is a short stretch for advanced paddlers or alert intermediates who should be prepared for some hiking. Roughly two-tenths of a mile downstream from the seventh bridge is a Class III–IV 5-foot ledge composed of Devonian sandstone and quartzite, which is more resistant than the shale rock formation below. This is the site of an old mill dam that washed away. Scout this ledge on the shuttle before committing yourself to this trip; drive down Route 694 for a peek. Again, get permission first because this decaying road is on private property. Be very careful in running this ledge because substantial parts of it are undercut. Perhaps the right has a better choice of routes. Incidentally, the gray Devonian shale rock forming much of the left riverbank is chock-full of fossil shells.

After running this ledge and picking up the pieces below, stay alert. About another 200 yards downstream you will see the tall remains of a bridge abutment on the left. This is the approach to another Class III–IV 5-foot ledge. Make sure you have enough of a bank on the left for scouting or portaging. This dark quartzite ledge is also full of fossils in addition to black chert nodules that form interesting knobs. The right appears to be a safer passage than the left, which has a pinning rock at the bottom, at least in low water. Scout this ledge in any case, and set throw ropes below on the left.

At this point you should be aware of two karst cave phenomena. First, in the big pool above the second ledge, Potts Creek splits. A large part of Potts's water is pirated to the right through a tunnellike entrance to a cave called The Sinks. The water entrance to this cave is usually clogged with debris, but there is a dry entrance to the cave at the top of the hill on river right. The water from the cave rejoins the creek at two spots in the large pool below the second ledge. In at least one of these places you can paddle into the downstream exit of the cave a good boat length or so. The streambed paralleling the cave and going over the second ledge to the left is actually an overflow channel and may be dry in the summer.

Second, Arritt Mill Tunnel and Cave begin at the top of the old railroad bridge abutment on the left side of Potts Creek above this second ledge. The man-made tunnel, which has been abandoned for many years, is 600 feet long, 20 feet high, and 18 feet wide. It is open all the way through the hill. Just after the entrance to the tunnel and along a break in the left wall near the top is a natural cave entrance. It has about 500 feet of passage.

Below the second big ledge is a big pool—a great swimming hole for locals in the summer. Then Potts Creek goes right over a long rock garden which also has a couple of ledges. From here the river mellows out before you get to the eighth bridge more than a mile later. Be sure to check out the pretty shale bluffs on your left before you get to this bridge.

Below the eighth bridge, Potts Creek is an easy novice trip with one carry over a 6-foot dam just before the thirteenth bridge. However, the eighth and ninth bridges are too steep to be good put-ins/take-outs even though the river is placid for the 2 miles between them. After passing the ninth Route 18 bridge and going under the Route 614 bridge, the river again nestles against the hills on the left. At the tenth Route 18 bridge are a high shale formation on river left and a gauging station just downstream (also on the left). There is a good put-in and parking area here. How helpful this gauging station is I don't know. It begins at 9 feet, which is 6 feet above the normal low summer level. Below this bridge, the river snuggles up to some hills on the right for a couple of miles and then reaches the eleventh bridge. The only good take-out here is river right upstream on private land. Be sure to get permission from the owner before taking out over this carefully manicured property.

After another couple of miles, you come to the twelfth bridge which has a easy take-out on river left below the bridge. There is also good parking here. More hardy souls can continue 3.5 miles down to the last bridge and portage the 6-foot dam just above this bridge on river left.

The trees along Potts Creek are a nice combination of river trees (sycamores, river birches, box elders, and willows), hardwoods (oaks, hickories, and ashes), and evergreens (cedars, pines, and hemlocks). There is also abundant bird life (herons, kingfishers, and other waterfowl), and wildlife (muskrat, beaver, and deer). In addition to the trout upstream there are numerous smallmouth bass and bluegill sunfish.

Unfortunately, there is no relevant gauge for Potts Creek. Perhaps the best indicator is the riffles area below the Route 311 bridge. If the riffles are easily runnable, there should be enough water to go all the way to Covington. In addition, because Route 18 crosses Potts Creek so many times, there are ample opportunities to gauge if there is sufficient (or too much) water. At high water, the two big ledges below the seventh bridge near decaying Route 694 should be looked at very carefully.

Rivanna River

The Rivanna is a real sleeper. Not many folks know that this pretty, placid river is one of Virginia's State Scenic Rivers. Despite its high banks you are able to see pleasant woods, farmland, and hills from the river. The 36-mile stretch described here is also surprisingly remote for a Piedmont river, and it has only a few access points which are conveniently spaced for day and overnight tripping. Perhaps the best time to run this Class I–II river is in the spring when the redbuds and dogwoods are popping. Since other trees are just beginning to leaf out, you can also see the nearby hills and their occasional, striking rock faces which are cloaked by the summer canopy.

The shallow, gentle Rivanna has surprisingly good current despite its low gradient. Novices and families will thoroughly enjoy the good scenery, fishing, bird life, and camping opportunities. Views of scenic hills pleasantly alternate with flat farmland and woods. Anglers can try their luck for smallmouth bass, largemouth bass, catfish, pike, and even river gar. Birds are very evident, particularly in spring. You will be escorted down the river alternately by noble Canadian geese, screeching ospreys, soaring turkey vultures, scolding kingfishers, darting or bobbing sandpipers, huge great blue herons, or one of several varieties of ducks. You may even hear a turkey call from the woods. The most common wildlife species are turtles, beaver, and muskrat.

The paddler can choose from numerous wooded campsites below Shadwell. However, the 10- to 15-foot high steep banks, behind which sycamores, river birches, and box elders grow, create some difficulties for the camper. Use good judgement in picking a site and care in climbing the often slippery bank. On the other hand, the land is posted in very few places. To maintain this delightful opportunity for others, be a considerate camper. Carefully extinguish all campfires and pack all litter out. Those not camping overnight can stretch their legs or break for lunch at occasional sand and gravel bars.

There are several cautions for novices paddling the Rivanna. Most importantly, don't get on this river in high water. The high banks covered with trees will not allow you to get to shore and may even cause problems if you try to land. Also, during high water, downed trees collect in debris piles that can be dangerous to novices. Further, novices should be shepherded the 4 miles from the first put-in to Shadwell. The ledges on this stretch can create problems for those who can't read water and don't have boat control. Similarly, there is one Class II–III between Palmyra and Columbia that novices should look at carefully—particularly if they have a boatful of camping

Larry Gross below a mellow rock garden near Shadwell on the Rivanna.

and fishing gear. Finally, the wind blowing upstream can sometimes be a problem, particularly in the afternoon.

The first part of this section is a very nice, quick, 4-mile Class II trip that starts in the back door of Charlottesville and quickly gets you away from civilization as you paddle toward Shadwell. The best put-in is a mile or so downstream of the US 250 bridge. Go south on High Street which is just west of this bridge. Follow High Street for a quarter mile, angle left on Meade Street for a half mile, and then turn left on Market Street for three-quarters of a mile to the river. You will arrive at an 8-foot dam and limited parking. Be sure to get permission first and leave only a couple of vehicles here. On the river left side of the dam is a canoeing gauge that is reasonably accurate.

After putting in below the dam and quickly heading downstream (to get away from the foul smelling effluent from a sewage treatment plant), you will notice on river right an old smokestack nearly 100 feet high. You then hit a Class I series of riffles before going under the Interstate 64 bridge. All is calm as you leave civilization and enjoy the high wooded banks for a mile and a half. Then you come to a Class II ledge. The far left is the most

Rivanna River

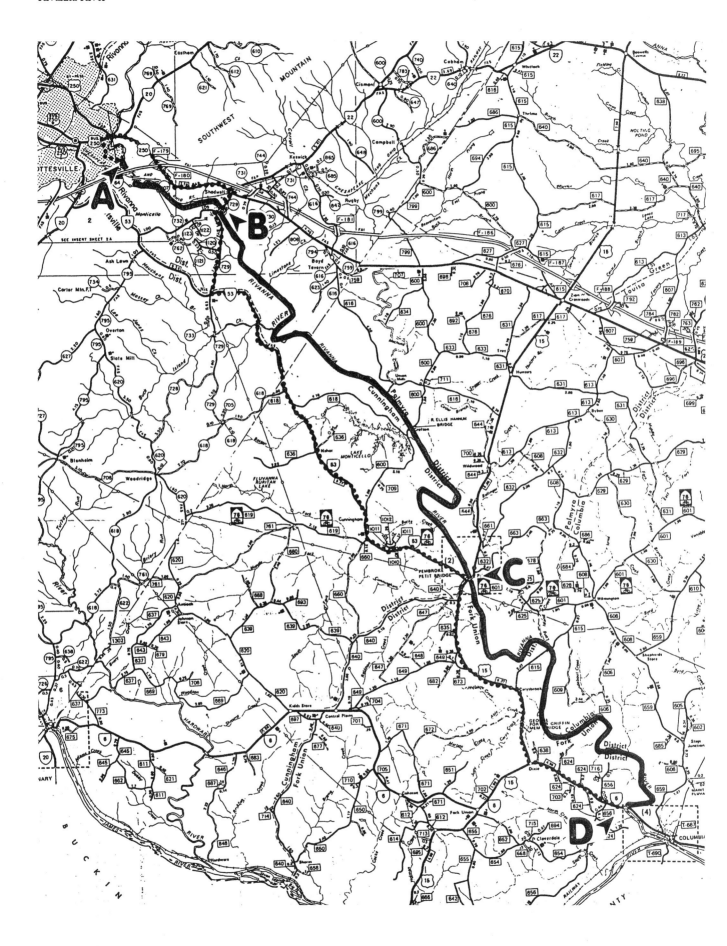

268

Section: Charlottesville (Market St.) to Columbia (Rt. 6)

Counties: Albemarle, Fluvanna

USGS Quads: Charlottesville East, Simeon, Boyd Tavern Palmyra, Columbia

Suitable for: Day cruising and camping

Skill Level: Novices (shepherded in 4 miles above Shadwell)

Months Runnable: Winter, spring, and early summer; last 15 miles below Palmyra is runnable almost the entire year

Interest Highlights: Good fishing, pretty hills and woods, old mill remains

Scenery: Pretty to beautiful in spots

Difficulty: Class I–II, except Class II for first 4 miles to Shadwell and Class II–III drop 11 miles below Palmyra

Average Width: 60 to 100 feet

Velocity: Slow to moderate

Gradient: 7 feet per mile for 4 miles between Charlottesville and Shadwell; 3 to 3.5 feet per mile for remaining 32 miles

Runnable Water Levels:
   Minimum: 0 feet on gauge below dam near Market St. in Charlottesville; Shadwell (Rt. 729 bridge) 1 foot below 0
   Maximum: Flood stage

Hazards: Maybe a rare tree in river; left channel of Class II–III drop 11 miles below Palmyra

Scouting: Novices should scout Class II–III drop 11 miles below Palmyra

Portages: None

Rescue Index: Accessible to somewhat remote

Source of Additional Information: None

Access Points	River Miles	Shuttle Miles
A–B	4	6
B–C	17	15
C–D	14.5	10

Access Point Ratings:
   A–off Market St. below US 250 in Charlottesville, good
   B–at Shadwell below Rt. 729, fair
   C–at Palmyra (US 15), excellent
   D–near Columbia (Rt. 6), good

conservative route. The river resumes its placid pace for almost another half mile, and you come to three ledges as you see a second powerline. Take the first ledge on the left or the right. There are numerous routes for the remaining two ledges on this mellow Class II ledge series.

A quarter mile below this you come to an island. The more conservative route is to the right where there is more water and three Class I chutes to negotiate. The left channel is smaller, and there is a tight Class I–II rock garden at the bottom that may be a problem for beginners. At the bottom of this island, note the remains of an old dam in the river and the rock formations in the hill on the right.

Over a half mile later you will come to another island. Again, go right over a Class I chute but stay away from the undercut right bank. Another half mile later you will see the Route 729 bridge. Here you have another Class II drop; the far right is easiest. Negotiating the open slots in the center will require some boat control.

The only negative aspect of the trip occurs a quarter mile below the Route 729 bridge. The long take-out here is by Randolph Mill Road on the left side of the river. On the shuttle before the trip, note the gauge here, on the upstream side of the second bridge abutment from the right; it is set at least a foot too high. On a recent trip we had a good 6 to 9 inches of water when this gauge read 6 inches below 0. Also, this gauge goes to 12 feet, so if you can't see a gauge here the river is much too high!

Paddlers putting in for the 17-mile Class I trip from Shadwell to Palmyra will pass through farmland for the first 2 to 3 miles. There will still be 10-foot-high clay and sand banks along the way. Then some hills will start coming in from the left, and you will have riffles when the hills switch from left of the river to right. These hills will stay with you for most of the remainder of this section, occasionally showing striking rock faces topped with pines and hemlocks.

After about 4 miles, you will come to the remains of a dam which is broken out on the left and right and offers some Class I riffles. Another 2 miles downstream and you will reach the remains of a wing dam and resultant Class I riffle.

The best visual treat of this section is another 3 miles downstream (9 miles from Shadwell). Here you will find a big canal lock on the right and the remains of a wing dam across the river that forms a Class I–II drop of 2 feet. Stop and poke around or have lunch at this scenic spot.

Shortly below this pleasant place is the Route 600 bridge. Lake Monticello, though not visible from here, is a quarter mile away to the right. The 6.5 miles from the Route 600 bridge to Palmyra are marked by more pretty hills, woods, farmland, and high banks. Unlike the Shadwell put-in, the take-out at Palmyra is an excellent

Virginia Game Commission landing. It's on river right just upstream of the US 15 bridge. There is also a store here for last minute food items.

Paddlers going the 14.5 miles from the Palmyra to Route 6 near Columbia will continue to enjoy this river. Just below the put-in is a 1-foot ledge that offers modest surfing possibilities at moderate levels. For the first 2 miles a pleasant hill with pine trees on its crest borders the left bank. The scenic bluffs then shift to the right of the river, and you go under a railroad bridge 3 miles into the trip. After you pass an island in the next half mile, the countryside opens up on both sides. Another 1.5 miles of paddling brings you to the Route 615 bridge. The best take-outs here are upstream. The one on river left is steeper but closer to the small area where your shuttle vehicle is parked. The take-out river right is gentler but longer. Below this bridge the river stops its gentle meandering and becomes almost as straight as an arrow. The trees lined up along riverbanks here act as silent sentinels shielding the paddler from the surrounding farmland. Unfortunately, one of the few eyesores of the trip becomes apparent here: the shallow river bottom suddenly is sprinkled with beer cans. However, the patient paddler is rewarded 2 miles below the Route 615 bridge. Here the remains of an old dam form a pleasant Class I–II drop and some modest standing waves.

In the next few miles the woods return, and there is a pretty rock face on river right 3 miles below the old dam ruins. Then, a mile below this and 4 miles below the pleasant Class I–II drop, the river bends to the left and you pass some riffles. The roar you hear and the horizon line you see mark the most impressive rapids of the trip—a 50-yard-long, rocky Class II–III dropping 4 feet.

Novices (particularly those with camping gear) should get out on the right and look at this drop. Nervous beginners can also portage right. The best route is down the center of the large right channel, but make sure there is enough water to bump through with a boat load of gear. Stay away from the small left channel of the river because this was recently blocked by a tree. However, once you're below these rapids, paddle back up to this channel as it reenters the river on the left to admire the old mill building there. This is the remains of Rivanna Mills and is definitely a photo and lunch stop. Also, just below these rapids are the remains of an old dam that form two islands.

In the next 3 miles or so to the Route 6 take-out the river continues to show its beauty: pretty hills with occasional rock outcroppings, mountain laurel, a stately row of cedars, and even a few rocks in the river. The take-out near Columbia is a sandy plateau river left and upstream of the Route 6 bridge. Alternatively, you can paddle another mile or so downstream and take out in Columbia just after the Rivanna joins the James River.

The Rivanna was also an important part of the extensive river navigation network in Virginia during the 1800s. Beginning with organization efforts by Thomas Jefferson, a system of sluices, locks, dams, and bypass canals was built for batteaux and other river craft which ultimately extended over 40 miles from Charlottesville to Columbia. The canal system was completed in the 1850s and operated until 1908 when the railroads did it in. You can occasionally see the scattered remains of this system as you paddle the Rivanna. Perhaps the best preserved example is the aforementioned Rivanna Mills building at the Class II–III rapids 11 miles below Palmyra.

Rucker Run

This little ripsnorter is deceptive. From the take-out Rucker Run looks like a harmless creek, but don't be fooled! It has chewed up and spit out several intermediate paddlers. Although basically a Class II–III run, this 4-mile trip is for strong intermediate and advanced paddlers only because of its continuous rapids.

The main reasons for caution are the gradient and the current. The gradient is a giddy 35 feet per mile, creating an extremely swift current as Rucker Run punches through Canada Gap. Indeed, when you pull off the bank, the current is so swift that your boat can be easily overturned. Furthermore, it's hard to get out of your boat and on shore. It takes a large amount of water to get this creek cranked up: you need a torrential rain of several inches. But this wait is well worth it for the patient paddler.

The put-in is on river right where Routes 655 and 653 intersect in Nelson County. Because the road (Route 655) follows the stream for a distance, you can get an idea of the nonstop nature of the run before you start. Once you are launched, Rucker Run gets very busy fast. You begin hitting nonstop Class II drops over ancient metamorphic rocks, and Class II–III rock gardens and ledges begin after you pass under the Route 655 bridge. The scenery is good with several cliffs and thick rhododendron foliage—if you have time to look at it.

In the second half of the trip there are three major rapids. All are Class III and the last (just before the take-out) is a Class IV in high water. Local paddlers have given interesting names to these rapids: W-4, W-3, and W-5. These seemingly odd designations will become immediately clear for paddlers who love alliteration and who are familiar with the old Elmer Fudd and Bugs Bunny cartoons of Warner Brothers.

When you come to a definite horizon line you have reached W-4, the "Wuff Wapid on Wucker Wun." Get out and scout this Class III drop from the right bank. To run W-4, enter center through a Class II approach, then go left after the first 2- to 3-foot drop and stay left for the bottom 2- to 3-foot drop.

W-3 is next after a respectable distance. This "Wapid on Wucker Wun" is a straight ahead Class III. It can be boat scouted in a left eddy below a 15-foot cliff and is located after the river bends right. More conservative paddlers can bank scout from the right.

You come to W-5 a half mile above the take-out. This "Weal Wuff Wapid on Wucker Wun" is the toughest drop on the trip. It is a strong Class III in moderate water and a Class IV in high water. You know you have arrived when you see an impressive horizon line after the river bends right. Scout it from the right bank. To begin W-5 enter center, drop over a 2-foot ledge, and go right. Then cut back left and finish by going right or left. There are several eddies in this rapid, and the 15- to 20-foot cliffs here make W-5 a very pretty spot.

The take-out for this delightful flush down Rucker Run is at the Route 654 bridge just above the Tye River. Take out on river left for a 100-yard carry as you join the Tye. Incidentally, this creek is a great target of opportunity when the Tye is really up. There is no gauge; just check it out if the Tye and its north and south forks are really cooking. If you have enough water at the Rucker Run put-in, you have enough water for the entire run.

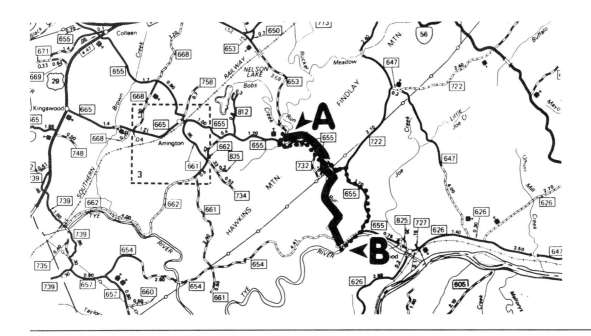

Section: Rt. 655/653 to Tye River (Rt. 654)

Counties: Nelson

USGS Quads: Shipman

Suitable for: Day cruising

Skill Level: Alert, strong intermediates, and advanced paddlers

Months Runnable: Winter and spring after 4- to 6-inch rain

Interest Highlights: Pretty little gorge, cliffs, rhododendron

Scenery: Pretty

Difficulty: Class II–III with 3 Class IIIs at moderate levels

Average Width: 20 to 30 feet

Velocity: Fast

Gradient: 35 feet per mile

Runnable Water Levels:
Minimum: Enough water to run at put-in
Maximum: Maybe flood stage

Hazards: Occasional trees in creek; banks hard to get out in bushes; high water

Scouting: 3 Class III rapids (W-4, W-3, and W-5) from right

Portages: Occasional trees and maybe W-5 (Class IV) at high water

Rescue Index: Accessible for first mile, remote thereafter

Source of Additional Information: None

Access Points	River Miles	Shuttle Miles
A–B	4	4

Access Point Ratings:
A–Jct. of Rts. 655 and 653, very good
B–at Rt. 654 on Tye River, good

Slate River

For good fishing or just a leisurely float through the heart of Buckingham County, the river rat would be hard pressed to locate a more splendid natural stream than the Slate River. Nature has adorned the banks of this northward flowing stream as it winds towards the mighty James River. The two bodies of water blend together approximately 1.5 miles above Bremo Bluff.

The name of the Slate River is associated with the rich bed of slate located near the river to the south. The Monacan Indians, whose hunting grounds were in Buckingham County and surrounding counties, were the first people to take advantage of the flowing water of the Slate. During early settlement by Europeans in central Virginia, the river provided transportation for goods shipped from Buckingham Courthouse to the James River, 30 miles downstream. Various types of locks were used to aid in the batteau navigation. The remains of several of these locks are still visible and at times form riffles and small falls. Grist mills harnessed the waters of the Slate to provide flour and feed to the people of Buckingham.

The Slate supports a great assortment of game fish for the paddler who is float fishing. Largemouth and smallmouth bass, sunfish, catfish, and occasional pike are taken from its waters. Also, on warm sunny days the long-snouted gar fish can be seen lounging close to the surface of deep pools. The traveler also will see numerous nonpoisonous water snakes. These reptiles are more savage in appearance than in aggressiveness and are quite willing to let paddlers pass by unmolested. However, when walking along the banks or exploring the land around the river, beware of the poisonous copperhead. Though not abundant, it is native to this land and is at home in bushy and rocky areas. Likewise, the timber rattler, which is native to the western counties, will occasionally be spotted here. The dreaded water moccasin is not a native of this area, but has been spotted along the lower stretches of the Slate near the James River.

Most sections of the Slate are heavily forested and give the paddler a wonderful wilderness feeling. Great forest canopies shade the traveler from the sun. The banks of the

Ben Johnson and David Martin paddle past the remains of the old stone mill below Preacher's Bridge (Route 676). Photo by Francis Wood.

Slate River vary from flat sandy shorelines to steep ridges covered with mountain laurel. These ridges and rocky bluffs provide a treat to paddlers in the springtime when the mountain laurel is in bloom.

The deciduous forests and flatlands along the Slate offer homes to many native animals. Deer and turkey are abundant and can be seen near the riverbanks, many times within range of gun, bow, or camera. Hunters should be knowledgeable of Virginia game laws concerning hunting from boats before pursuing game in this fashion. Hunting permits can be acquired from the various lumber companies who own and manage large tracts of forestland here, but written permission must be obtained from individual landowners before taking game from property bordering the river. A variety of small game including rabbits, woodcocks, grouse, wood ducks, bobcats, and foxes have been seen during winter canoe hunting and camping trips.

The 10.5 mile section of the Slate from Route 20 to Diana Mills is canoeable mostly during the fall and winter and during periods of substantial summer rains. This section can be leisurely paddled in 6 hours. The canoeist will find the access area on Route 20 in Buckingham rather difficult as a steep roadbank must be negotiated to reach the river. Once on the water the canoeist is engulfed by the mountain laurel. A substantial tributary, Muddy Creek, enters the Slate from the left approximately 1.5 miles downstream. The river is slow moving along this section with an occasional riffle at the remains of old river locks. Approximately 4 miles into the trip the paddler will pass under Route 622 at Melita.

The next 6 miles are heavily forested on both sides and there are very few signs of civilization. The banks become steeper with some 100-foot-high bluffs and occasional rock outcrops which effectively block out the morning and evening sunlight. Although this part of the river is 6 miles by canoe, it is only 3 miles from Route 622 to Diana Mills as the crow flies. This gives an indication of just how sinuous the river is.

The 11-mile section of the Slate River from Diana Mills to its junction with the James River includes a variety of canoeing terrains, from slow-moving flatwater to a few Class II rapids. Access to the Slate at Diana Mills is good and parking is no problem. The remains of the old Diana Mill works are actually visible from the put-in, and the first rapid of this section is caused by the remains of the mill dam. The banks along this section are either forested or cutover. The paddler is, for the most part, removed from the roads and houses in this part of the county. The largest tributary of the Slate, Sharps Creek, is encountered 2.5 miles into the trip.

Section: Rt. 20 to Bremo Bluff (US 15)

Counties: Buckingham

USGS Quads: Diana Mills, Dillwyn, Arvonia

Suitable for: Day cruising or camping

Skill Level: Novices

Months Runnable: Winter, spring, and early summer

Interest Highlights: Fishing, wildlife, remains of old mills, river locks

Scenery: Pretty to beautiful in spots

Difficulty: Class I–II

Average Width: 25 to 50 feet

Velocity: Moderate

Gradient: 4 feet per mile in upper 10.5-mile section; 8 feet per mile in lower 11-mile section

Runnable Water Levels:
  Minimum: No gauge; if runnable at put-ins, there is sufficient water
  Maximum: Flood stage

Hazards: An occasional tree in river

Scouting: Beginners should look at Class II rock garden 1 mile below Preacher's Bridge (Rt. 676)

Portages: Maybe around an occasional tree

Rescue Index: Accessible to remote

Source of Additional Information: Appomattox River Company (804) 392-6645

Access Points	River Miles	Shuttle Miles
A–B	10.5	7.5
B–C	11	11.5

Access Point Ratings:
A–at Rt. 20, fair
B–at Diana Mills (Rt. 671), very good
C–at Bremo Bluff/New Canton (Rt. 687 off US 15), excellent

The right bank of the river from Diana Mills to Route 676 is owned by Continental Investments Corporation and can be hunted with proper permits. Just below the entrance of Sharps Creek the remains of a significant river lock are easily recognizable on the left. Almost 5 miles from Diana Mills the river traveler will encounter a small island which can serve as a rest stop or an overnight camping site. Just below the island a swift-moving chute quickly carries the paddler into a section of slower water. A half mile downstream from this point is a old gauging station and the Route 676 bridge. Here, on a quiet Sunday afternoon, the

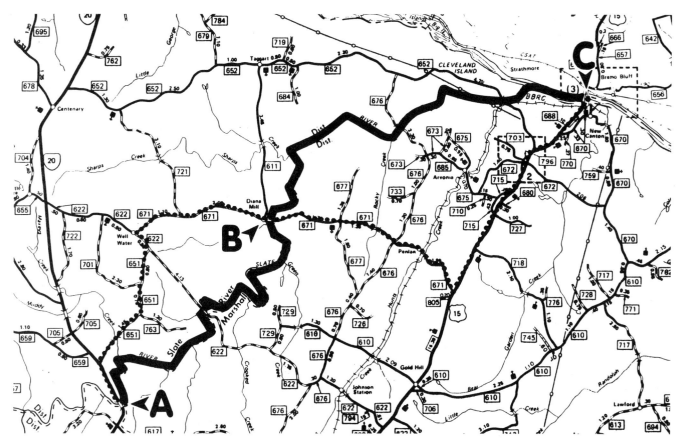

traveler may be greeted by great outbursts of spiritual revelations from a local pilgrim who spreads his holy book on the bridge railing and preaches a fire and brimstone sermon to the waters of the Slate. This bridge is appropriately known as Preacher's Bridge to local canoeists.

About a mile downstream from Preacher's Bridge the paddler will encounter a 100-yard Class II rock garden. It is a good idea to stop and scout; the best course is different at different water levels. This rock garden is the swiftest water on the Slate.

The Slate offers a spectacular view into history approximately 1.5 miles past the rock garden when the remains of a nineteenth-century three-story mill become visible at the water's edge. From a distance, the remains of this once-integral part of the river and community look like a forgotten castle. The mill was built around 1800 by the Williams brothers who were Welsh immigrants. The exterior walls of the structure are constructed of native stone for the first and second stories and locally made brick for the third story. The roof was constructed of slate and was donated to Colonial Williamsburg after the mill became inactive. The remains of the aqueduct system and dam are still very visible. The mill was in operation for about 100 years, providing commerce for the residents of Buckingham County. The property around the mill site is still owned by descendants of the original owners.

Once it passes the mill, the Slate has low banks, deep water, and is relatively slow moving. One-half mile before entering the James, the paddler will pass under Route 652. This is a good take-out, providing one doesn't mind mud. Solite Mining Corporation owns and operates quarrying and processing plants at the confluence of the Slate and James rivers. The paddler will see the company's water pump station just prior to reaching the James.

Entering the James River from a long trip on the Slate is like entering a new world. The wide open space and the large volume of water are an extreme contrast to the Slate. Upon entering the James, the paddler will see the first residence of the trip—the famous Bremo Bluff Plantation. About 1.5 miles below the confluence of the Slate and James rivers is a public access on the south bank at New Canton just below Bremo Bluff. There is adequate parking here. One word of caution: if the James is running high, novice paddlers should take out at Route 652 before they become committed to running this big river.

The Slate River is of the few places in Virginia where several attempts to build a canal system (30 miles from Buckingham to the James River) failed miserably. The last attempt was by the Slate River Company which built 15 dams and locks between 1823 and 1835, when the company failed.

Tye River

The Tye River packs a lot of variety into a comparatively short distance. Beginning at Nash, just a mile or so below the mouth of Crabtree Creek, the Tye starts in a mountain pass, cuts through foothills, and then settles into an open valley. A cross-sectional view of its gradient would be very close to a parabolic curve, a classic geomorphological landform.

There are two good parts of the Tye. The first is the more intense 8 mile section from Nash to Massies Mill. The second is the 24-mile stretch from Massies Mill to Rucker Run which can be broken into two nearly equal parts.

The Upper Tye: Nash to Massies Mill

The Tye River, when it is up, is a roll-your-own trip with bridges galore in the first 8-mile section. There are 11 (count 'em), including the Appalachian Trail foot-bridge, between the first put-in at Nash and the take-out at Massies Mill. A canoeing gauge is on the North Fork at the Route 56 bridge in Nash where the North and South Forks join to form the Tye. The gauge is downstream on a river right abutment. From 0 to 6 inches on the gauge, the first 2 miles or so is a Class III run. However, at 1.5 to 2.5 feet, this upper part is a solid Class IV run. For the best put-in (on the North Fork), take Route 687 for about one-quarter mile from the Route 56 bridge at the confluence to the Evergreen Christian Church. This launching point is recommended because there are numerous "No Trespassing" signs at Nash.

In the first couple of miles below the confluence of the North and South Forks at Nash the Tye is a steep boatbuster with abrupt drops and tight turns through boulder-strewn chutes. The scenery in this section is spectacular, with high rock formations and steep forested slopes on both sides. The road follows the river closely on the left but is not intrusive. The paddler will bless its presence for scouting and in the event of a rescue effort or boat salvage operation. Rapids are almost continuous in this stretch but there are four memorable Pedlar granite ledges that may have to be scouted depending upon water levels. The difficulty of these drops will be Class III in low water and Class IV at higher levels.

After passing under the first bridge at the confluence of Campbell Creek, the Tye relaxes a bit. Rapids continue to appear at regular intervals, but they are not so threatening as those above Campbell Creek. The river valley has widened somewhat and the gradient has lessened as the Tye leaves the mountain pass it has carved

through Pinnacle Ridge at Nash and approaches its alluvial fan east of the mountains.

The rapids in this section consist of gravel bars and occasional sizable ledges where the Tye runs up against

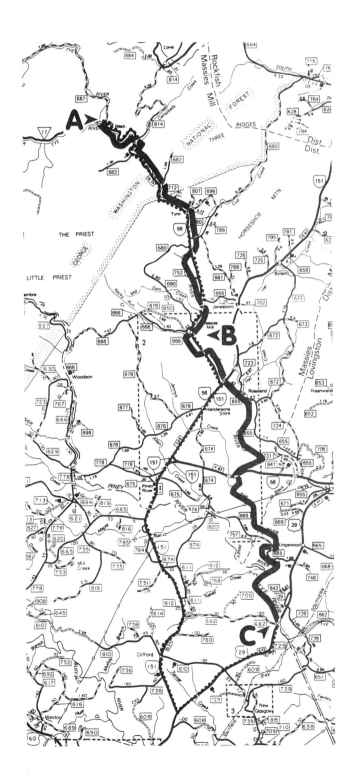

Geff and Lonnie Fisher enter a rock garden on the upper Tye.

Section: Nash (Rt. 56) to Massies Mill (Route 56)

Counties: Nelson

USGS Quads: Massies Mill, Horseshoe Mountain

Suitable for: Day cruising

Skill Level: Advanced in upper section, intermediates in lower section

Months Runnable: Winter and spring following very heavy rain

Interest Highlights: Scenery, geology, whitewater

Scenery: Pretty to beautiful

Difficulty: At moderate water levels, Class III–IV in upper section; Class II–III in lower section

Average Width: 20 to 40 feet

Velocity: Fast

Gradient: 86 feet per mile in first 1.5 miles; 56 feet per mile overall

Runnable Water Levels:
  Minimum: 5 feet on Buena Vista gauge; 0 feet on Rt. 56 gauge near put-in where North and South Forks of Tye join

Maximum: 8 feet on Buena Vista gauge; 2.5 feet on Rt. 56 gauge

Hazards: Strainers; steep rapids; pinning possibilities on boulders; cold, high water; low water bridge near Massies Mill

Scouting: All major rapids scoutable from road

Portages: None

Rescue Index: Accessible

Source of Additional Information: National Weather Service Buena Vista gauge (703) 260-0305; James River Basin Canoe Livery (703) 261-7334; Appomattox River Company (804) 392-6645

Access Points	**River Miles**	**Shuttle Miles**
A–B	8.5	8

Access Point Ratings:
  A–at Nash (Rt. 687 near 56), very good
  B–at Massies Mill (Rt. 56), very good

Dave Swagger catching an ender on the Tye in flood.
Photo by Stephen Ensign.

occasionally dropping over a Class II ledge, a shallow gravel bar, or through a narrow chute around a small island. The channelization in this section is not overwhelming since the river has been kept in its natural course. Hurricane Camille in 1969 caused great damage in the Tye River valley, and the flood caused the stream to relocate its course in this lower section. As Massies Mill is approached the river broadens out over a gravel bed, and at low-water levels the paddler may find him- or herself sliding and/or hiking for short stretches. Be alert for a low-water bridge here.

The water on the Tye is usually brilliantly clear and clean. The river is a popular trout stream, and paddlers should make all possible efforts to avoid conflict with anglers—fellow friends of our rivers. As with many small streams in the state, it is probably best to be very careful in early spring when there may be many fisherman on the Tye. On one trip paddlers were threatened by locals with having their cars towed away because "this is private property and canoeing isn't allowed." This sort of comment is hard to swallow when the banks are lined with dozens or hundreds of anglers who don't seem likely to have secured permission from all the riparian landowners, but remember, the quiet word turneth away wrath. Getting into a shouting match on the banks of a stream is worse than useless. In this particular instance the cars were not towed away, nor have any cars ever been towed according to all paddlers consulted concerning this question.

The Upper Tye drains a very small watershed, which, even though it is virtually completely forested, loses water very rapidly. As a result the Tye can go from too high to too low in a day, and the paddler must be alert and determined to catch this stream with a suitable flow. By the time the Buena Vista or other gauges show sufficient water, to indicate that there may be flow in this area, the Tye has most likely waxed and waned and may be unrunnable. But go take a look anyway; if there is sufficient water it will be worth it, and there are plenty of alternatives in the area if you miss the Tye. Alternatives in the general area include the Piney River and, somewhat farther away, the Maury.

When in the neighborhood of the Upper Tye a short hike is a must for all lovers of falling water. Above the runnable section of the Tye, along Route 56 toward the Blue Ridge Parkway, lies a small Forest Service parking area. From here a trail leads up Pinnacle Ridge along Crabtree Creek to a spectacular cascade high on the mountainside. Crabtree Falls consists of a steeply sloping curtain of water some 100 feet high where Crabtree Creek ends its meandering along the top of the ridge and falls abruptly into the valley of the Upper Tye. The hike to the falls from the parking area is short but very steep,

rock bluffs on either bank. The difficulty of the rapids in this section is a step down from the upper region, in the Class II–III range. The scenery is still good but a few cabins and cleared areas begin to intrude on the view.

As the fourth bridge crossing approaches, the Tye leaves steep terrain behind and begins meandering through a broad valley full of orchards and cattle. Advanced paddlers can take out here, and lesser mortals can put in. The river flows primarily through a channelized trough with bulldozed banks, only

Section: Massies Mill (Rt. 56) to Rucker Run (Rt. 654)

Counties: Nelson

USGS Quads: Massies Mill, Horseshoe Mountain, Arlington, Shipman

Suitable for: Day cruising

Skill Level: Novices to intermediates

Months Runnable: Winter and spring following a rain

Interest Highlights: Scenery, geology

Scenery: Pretty

Difficulty: Class I–II with several Class II–III rapids

Average Width: 40 to 70 feet

Velocity: Moderate

Gradient: 15 feet per mile in 13-mile upper section; 11 feet per mile in 10.5-mile lower section

Runnable Water Levels:
  Minimum: 0 feet on Rt. 151 gauge
  Maximum: 3 feet on Rt. 151 gauge

Hazards: Perhaps some barbed wire fences in upper 13-mile section; 6-foot dam just below US 29, occasional strainers, high water

Scouting: None except occasional Class II–III rapids by novices

Portages: Six-foot dam just below US 29

Rescue Index: Accessible

Source of Additional Information: National Weather Service Buena Vista gauge (703) 260-0305; James River Basin Canoe Livery (703) 261-7334; Appomattox River Company (804) 392-6645

Access Points	River Miles	Shuttle Miles
B–C	13	12
D–E	10.5	8

Access Point Ratings:
  B–at Massies Mill (Rt. 56), very good
  C–at Tye River P. O. (US 29), very good
  D–at Tye River (Rt. 739), very good
  E–at Rucker Run (Rt. 654), good

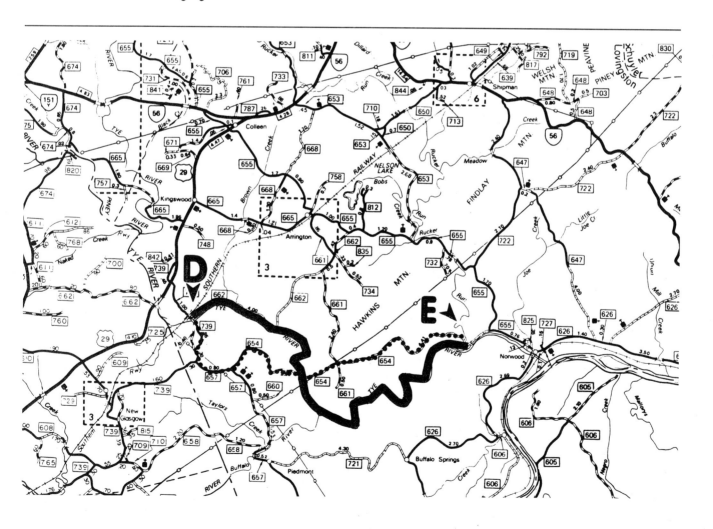

following innumerable switchbacks beside the swift and clear creek. Those who struggle all of the way to Crabtree Falls are amply rewarded by its beauty and by the breathtaking views available from the top of the rock dome over which the creek cascades.

Massies Mill (Route 56) to Rucker Run (Route 654)

This 24-mile section is much easier than the Upper Tye. At moderate levels intermediates find it relaxing, and shepherded novices can polish their skills. The first 13 miles offer a more difficult and more continuous series of Class I–II drops then the last 10.5 miles, but the lower 10.5 miles also have frequent rapids and will challenge novices.

The rapids in the upper section are generally small ledges and cobble bars with an occasional rock garden to add spice. The only hazard is an occasional barbed wire fence. There are several access points, but not nearly as many as on the Upper Tye. The most important points are the first Route 56 bridge (1 mile), the Route 151 bridge (2.5 miles), and the second Route 56 bridge (6.5 miles) before reaching US 29 after 13 miles. Paddlers can relax on this trip as they traverse a wide, pretty valley on a river with clear water. After 11 miles, the Piney River enters on the right. Make sure you stop at the US 29 take-out as there is a 6-foot dam 200 yards downstream.

To run only the last 10.5 miles of this section of the Tye, put in 1 mile downstream of this 6-foot dam at the tiny community of Tye River on Route 739. This stretch of the Tye, from this dam to the confluence with Rucker Run, offers the paddler enjoyable but less frequent Class I–II whitewater. The rapids are primarily gravel bars and a few ledges. The occasional pools of flatwater at the top become more frequent only toward the end of this stretch. The scenery is gorgeous rolling hills, and the remoteness of the area is appealing. However, note that the rocks in the river are stained a light shade of red below the confluence with the Piney—a result of mining practices upstream on the Piney years ago. Paddlers who have run the Cheat Canyon in West Virginia will notice a similarity in color.

After some pleasant rock gardens, you will see a striking angular rock face on river left about three-quarters of a mile from the Route 739 put-in. At an island, take the left channel for more water, and at the end of this quarter-mile-long island is a nice Class II rock garden. The rock gardens continue for the next mile, and 2 miles into the trip you come to a very long rock garden and ledge series which is a miniature version of the famed Shenandoah Staircase (near where the Shenandoah joins the Potomac near Harpers Ferry).

There is a terrific lunch-stop rock on river right about 3 miles into the trip just above a good Class II rock garden. Just under 4 miles into the trip and after another long rock garden is a very pretty rock face covered with moss on the right.

About 4.5 miles into the trip the one-lane Route 654 bridge comes into view. This bridge can be used as a put-in or take-out, but it's a lousy alternative. The banks are very steep and parking is very limited.

Over a quarter mile below this bridge the paddler encounters the toughest rapid of the trip—a Class II–III drop of 3 feet over a short rock pile. At lower water the best slot is in the center with a hard right turn to finish. Scout from the right.

A mile below the Route 654 bridge the Buffalo River enters on the right. Just below this confluence is another Class II–III rapid, if you take the center route. A conservative Class II route is on the left. Below here the river begins to flatten out, and the countryside opens up. There is a great lunch stop at a rock face on river left a mile below the Buffalo River.

About 2 miles below the Buffalo, you come to a rock in the river that looks like Schoolhouse Rock on the Lower Youghiogheny River in Pennsylvania. The rapids are much mellower, however. The conservative Class I–II channel with the most water is on the right, but a series of more challenging bumpy passages are on the left.

Roughly a mile below here start noticing the rocks in the river which are very interesting shapes and colors. The tops of them are green metamorphic rock but the bottoms have been stained red. About a half mile farther is a Class II–III ledge that is best run center. There is a nice surfing wave at the bottom at moderate levels. Another half mile below here a rock formation that looks like a submerged spine stretches across the river.

About a mile below this spinelike feature and 5 miles below the confluence with the Buffalo River, Rucker Run enters on the left. The field on river left just below Rucker Run is the best take-out spot for this stretch as well as for the more difficult 4-mile trip on Rucker Run, which is described elsewhere in this chapter. A bridge crosses Rucker Run about 50 yards upstream (Route 654). For those wanting a long trip, there is a final take-out on the James at Wingina after yet another 5.5 miles—all flatwater.

Despite the stained rocks, the water quality on this last section is good as is fishing for smallmouth bass, rock bass, and redeye sunfish. However, much of the land is posted from the community of Tye River to Rucker Run (particularly the lower few miles), so camping is not advised unless prior permission has been obtained.

Roanoke

Roanoke/Staunton River

The Roanoke River has two names. At its beginning in the western Virginia mountains and at its end in Albemarle Sound on the coast of North Carolina, it is called the Roanoke. This name comes from a tribe of Indians that inhabited an island in Albemarle Sound. However, in the south central part of Virginia, this river is known as the Staunton. It was named for either Lady Rebecca Staunton Gooch, whose husband served as lieutenant governor of Virginia in the mid-1700s or Captain Henry Staunton, who patrolled this river, protecting early settlers from Indian attack.

The pleasant 11-mile, Class I–II stretch of the Roanoke/Staunton River from Long Island to Brookneal is steeped in batteau river history. The word batteau comes from the French word for boat, *bateau*. A batteau is a river boat 7 to 8 feet wide, 50 to 60 feet long, and, weighing 3,000 pounds. It was built to carry cargo without drawing much water. The first batteau was built by Anthony and Benjamin Rucker in 1771 to navigate the shallow waters of the James River. The first recorded batteau trip on the Long Island to Brookneal section of the Roanoke/Staunton was in 1815, when Col. William Clark (brother of explorer George Rogers Clark) floated a cargo of flour on a 340 mile trip from Long Island to Albemarle Sound and then up the Dismal Swamp Canal to Norfolk. With that auspicious event, this section of the Roanoke/Staunton soon became an integral part of the important commercial river artery serving the Virginia-North Carolina boundary. During the mid-1800s, pilots steered batteaux carrying up to 6 tons

of cargo down this section through numerous man-made sluices. These batteaux carried such diverse cargos as livestock, flour, tobacco, and whiskey. Pictures of recreated batteaux are found below and in the short Canals and Batteaux section near the beginning of this book.

Most of the rapids from Long Island to Brookneal are formed by the aforementioned man-made sluices, which often are accompanied by towing walls on the nearby banks. These are hand crafted stone walls at least 5 feet high and 5 feet wide at the base. Boatmen used them and ropes to pull batteaux upstream through swift sections of river when oars or poles could not be used. The walls (as well as accompanying sluices and wing dams) were built in 1826–27 by masons working for Superintendent Samuel Pannill of the Roanoke Navigation Company. As a result of this intensive work, the Long Island to Brookneal section of the Roanoke contains perhaps the most extensive network (2,500 feet of towing walls and nearly 11,000 feet of wing dams) of batteau navigational improvements in the United States.

The paddler's trip begins at a Virginia State Game Commission boat ramp next to Route 761 in the tiny town of Long Island. Put in at a flat pool about a half mile long. This is followed by Hale Islands, which contain Corn Row Falls. The falls are formed by Class I shallow ledges. The best routes are far right and left, although the center channels are passable.

After leaving these islands, you encounter more shallow ledges, which end with Pannills Fish Trap, where the Indians and early settlers trapped fish. About 1.5 miles of

Replica of a batteau navigating the Staunton. Photo by Bo Tucker.

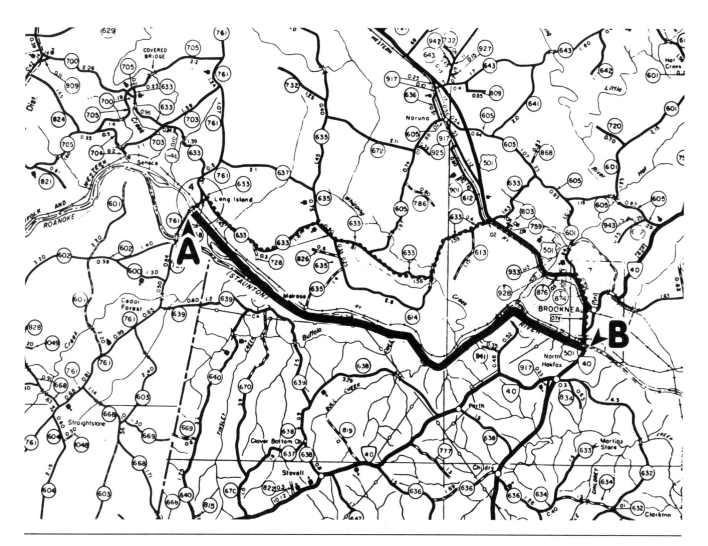

Section: Long Island (Rt. 761) to Brookneal (US 501)

Counties: Campbell, Halifax

USGS Quads: Long Island, Brookneal

Suitable for: Day cruising and camping

Skill Level: Shepherded beginners and novices

Months Runnable: Entire year (dam fed)

Interest Highlights: Historical batteau towing walls and sluices

Scenery: Pretty to beautiful in spots

Difficulty: Class I–II

Average Width: 100 feet

Velocity: Slow to moderate

Gradient: 8 feet per mile

Runnable Water Levels:
  Minimum: None
  Maximum: Flood stage

Hazards: None except an occasional tree in river and high water

Scouting: None

Portages: None

Rescue Index: Generally accessible

Source of Additional Information: Appomattox River Company in Farmville (804) 392-6645

Access Points	River Miles	Shuttle Miles
A–B	11	15

Access Point Ratings:
A–at Rt. 761, excellent
B–US 501, excellent

flatwater follows. This flatwater section begins with the remains of Pannills Bridge piers (circa 1830) and ends with Pannills Falls. The falls consist of a Class I–II rock garden with a chute at the bottom in the center of the river. When running this rapid, notice the opening that was cleared through the rock garden for batteaux and the wing dams forming the chute at the end.

About one-third of a mile below Pannills Falls you near Goose Mountain and encounter large boulders of granite scattered across the river. This flatwater appropriately leads to Flatland Falls. The best route through Flatland Falls is left of center. Enjoy a Class II rock garden and a 2-foot drop at the end. There is also an old batteau towing wall and sluice immediately left of this rapid. At the bottom of the sluice was an old wooden fish trap; you can still see its timbers. This trap gives the rapid its alternate name of Fishtrap Rapids.

The next 1.5 miles, below Flatland Falls/Fishtrap Rapids, contain numerous islands. Stay left of the islands and you will soon encounter Collins Ferry Sluice (Class I–II). This is quickly followed by Eckels Falls Sluice I which is 1,000 feet long. Eckels Falls Sluice I (also Class I–II) begins on river left approximately 75 feet from the bank and runs diagonally right toward several islands. It then empties into a 1/4 mile-long pool. On the right side of the islands in this pool was a wing dam built to channel water into a millrace on the right bank. At the next (unnamed) Class I–II rapid below this millrace you can see partially cut mill stones lying in the river near the islands.

Eckels Falls Sluice II is next. This 2,000-foot-long sluice (Class I–II) was also built diagonally from left to right. The sluice begins with a large boulder on the right side, which contains clearly visible drill holes where it was blasted.

After another three-quarters of a mile you come to Journetts Falls. This Class I–II rapid begins as a rock garden and ends with two small ledges. The rock garden shows evidence of a batteau channel blasted through it. On river left by the two ledges are a 100-foot-long towing wall and a blasted channel sluice. A quarter mile below Journetts Falls is a nice Class II surfing wave on river right. The wave is formed from rock dumped in the river to make a boat ramp. To the left of this surfing wave is a wing dam and sluice, which was blocked to form a fish dam.

About two-thirds of a mile further is Forrests Fish Trap and Sluice. The best route for this Class I riffle is left of center between a large island on the right and a small island on the left. Midway through the next 2 miles of flatwater you will find numerous small riffles. These are the remains of fish dams.

You then come to some shallow ledges that lead over a pipeline. About a quarter mile below the pipeline is Jones Falls Sluice and Towing Wall. This Class I sluice is 1,500 feet long and should be run left of the nearby islands.

Jones Falls is immediately followed by Seven Islands Falls Sluice and Towing Wall, which is also known as Cat Rock Sluice and Towing Wall. This Class II sluice is easily recognized by a nearly river-wide rock ledge. The best channel is the blasted entrance to the sluice on the far right. You will next pass an impressive towing wall, which was placed on the National Register of Historic Places by the State of Virginia in 1978 because it is in such good shape. Nonpaddlers can easily reach this wall by walking up the railroad tracks from Brookneal. Those wanting another Class II alternative to this drop can run left of the rock ledge across a wing dam. This route is 25 feet or so from the left bank.

About 800 feet below this is Salmon Rock on river right and a wing dam opposite it, which together form an interesting passage. Salmon Rock is followed by Class I Brookneal Sluice and Towing Wall. The towing wall here is 250 feet long with a wing dam at its head. Another wing dam is on river left. The US 501 bridge is less than a half mile further and a Virginia State Game Commission boat ramp follows shortly, on the left at Brookneal.

The Staunton is a dam release river and can be paddled the entire year. Indeed, once a year or so, batteaux constructed by members of the Virginia Canal and Navigation Society float down this segment of the Staunton, thus reenacting some colorful history on this special river. Note that the Long Island to Brookneal section has the only whitewater on the Staunton. The river is flat for the 40 miles from Brookneal to Buggs Island Lake, near the North Carolina-Virginia border. It then flows through North Carolina until it reaches Albemarle Sound.

This is an ideal stretch of river for camping, wildlife viewing, and fishing. There are many good camping spots on the islands. Animals seen on occasion are deer, rabbits, squirrels, and foxes. Large birds such as turkeys, great blue herons, ospreys, red-tailed hawks, wood ducks, and mallards are also present. Fishing is good the entire year for catfish, walleye pike, bass, and sunfish. Finally, from mid-April to mid-May, striped bass make their way up-stream from Buggs Island Lake to beyond Brookneal for their annual spring spawning. During this time, striped bass weighing up to 30 pounds can be caught.

Smith River

Of all the Commonwealth's stream sections that have yet to be designated Virginia Wild and Scenic Rivers, the Smith between Route 704 and Philpott Reservoir could perhaps be assigned the highest priority for such recognition. Nowhere in Virginia can a boater so completely escape evidence of human habitation. The Smith flows through Patrick County, one of the least populated (about 2,500 residents) and developed counties in Virginia, passing through a narrow, if fairly shallow, gorge of exceptional tranquility and beauty. No road, utility line, path, or railway is in evidence below the Route 704 bridge. The most obvious sign of human disturbance may be an occasional glimpse of an illicit practice, sometimes highly respected in these parts, and one best ignored by paddlers—the distillation of a Franklin and Patrick County product that is as clear as the waters of the Smith. (A bit of submerged copper tubing, or a small puff of smoke in the woods might be seen.)

Route 704, though it is a good quality paved road and a major route through Patrick County, may not be found on every Virginia Roadmap—nor will the tiny village of Charity (three buildings). There is an excellent put-in on land adjacent to the new 704 bridge. However, a gauge on the bridge footing is overly optimistic, and a reading of 8 inches over 0 should be considered a minimum level for paddling below Route 704. This is a small stream, which is best run immediately after wet periods. The upstream basin is not large, and the Smith runs off quickly.

The section from Route 704 to Philpott Reservoir contains the Smith Gorge which has incredible scenery.

Some parts of the gorge are solid rhododendron which are spectacular in spring. Water quality is excellent, perhaps the best of any stream in the state, although microbial contamination could exist. Rainbow trout spawn and thrive here in one of the few native trout fisheries in this region.

The gorge run is mostly a Class I–II trip, suitable for low-intermediate paddlers at all levels below floodstage, provided weather conditions and White Falls are given proper respect. The total drop from Route 704 to the lake's high-water level is about 100 feet, over about 10.5 miles. In the upper and middle part of the trip are four solid Class II rapids dropping 5 feet each. The first, Little Falls, is a multi-ledge drop which should be run down the center. Next is Black Falls, marked by a black granite outcrop visible from upstream. It requires an S-turn and is best entered river right. Watch for a sharp triangular rock at the bottom. Incidentally, Black Falls is about halfway (5 miles) into the moving water part of the trip and makes an ideal lunch stop. The remaining two rapids are Screaming Left Turn I and II. Oddly, the first of these requires a hard turn to the right!

About 10 miles into the trip and soon after a moderate-sized creek comes in from river left is White Falls, named for the spectacularly white, Paleozoic quartzite of the Alligator Back Formation that it tumbles over. This 7-foot Class III drop consists of a river-wide ledge followed by a sloping shelf, and then by a second ledge whose downstream lip is pierced by several chutes. At the second ledge much of the river flows through a narrow keyhole slot in river center. This is slightly wider

Charles Ware at the bottom drop of White Falls on the Smith.

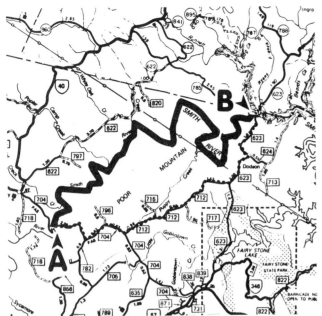

than the average canoe, and an excellent place to trim off gunnels or bodily appendages. There has been a broken shoulder suffered here. It is also possible to run the second ledge on river right, but at low water it is difficult to traverse the sloping shelf above. There's a nice pool at the bottom of the falls to collect errant bodies and boats, and the falls are easily scouted or portaged left or right. The Smith levels out for another mile below White Falls, and then is very flat where Philpott Lake has backed up into the river's channel. It is another 5 miles to the Route 623 bridge over the lake, but the reservoir is fairly narrow in this upper stretch and fairly well protected from wind.

Most of the property along the river upstream of the lake is privately owned. While it might be possible to take out above the lake at several points, it is imperative that boaters respect property rights. Access has been a sensitive issue here, and one should not offend people as nice as those encountered in this area. Incidentally, just a few miles south of the take-out is Fairy Stone State Park where fascinating cross shaped crystals of the mineral staurolite are found.

During the mid-eighties, the Army Corps of Engineers proposed building a high dam at White Falls, creating a reservoir which would have flooded and forced relocation of the Route 704 bridge. This newly created "Charity Lake" (3,100 acres) would have operated in conjunction with downstream Lake Philpott as a pumped storage hydro project. An estimated $410 million project cost, plus determined local opposition, forced the Corps to abandon its efforts—at least for now.

There is another exceptional Class II+ section of the Smith below Philpott Dam and Lake, runnable when power is being generated at the dam. Releases generally occur only on weekdays, although occasional Saturday and rare Sunday releases of COLD water may emanate from the depths of the reservoir. Area paddlers frequently paddle from a Route 905 putin just below Philpott Dam, to Town Creek in Bassett, a distance of about seven miles. The Corps of Engineers will tell you when water is to be released if you call (540) 629-2432. Smith River Valley Canoe Club member Bev Bryant (540) 638-4306) is willing to provide more information about the two sections of the Smith.

Section: Rt. 704 to Philpott Reservoir (Rt. 623)

Counties: Patrick

USGS Quads: Charity, Philpott Reservoir

Suitable for: Day cruising

Skill Level: Shepherded novices or intermediates

Months Runnable: Winter and spring

Interest Highlights: Scenic gorge, rhododendron

Scenery: Beautiful

Difficulty: Class I–II with 1 Class III rapid

Average Width: 30 to 40 feet

Velocity: Generally moderate

Gradient: 10 feet per mile in first 10.5 miles; flatwater for last 5.5 miles

Runnable Water Levels:
Minimum: 8 inches on the put-in gauge at Rt. 704
Maximum: Maybe 3 feet on the put-in gauge

Hazards: Class III White Falls; perhaps an occasional tree in river

Scouting: Class III White Falls

Portages: Maybe White Falls by novices

Rescue Index: Remote

Source of Additional Information: Philpott Dam (540) 629-2432; Smith River Valley Canoe Club (540) 638-4306

Access Points	River Miles	Shuttle Miles
A–B	16	9

Access Point Ratings:
A–at Rt. 704, good
B–at Philpott Reservoir (Rt. 623), good

The New

Big Reed Island Creek

Big Reed Island Creek drains the west slope of the Blue Ridge in Carroll County, carving a peaceful way through a strikingly rugged countryside to join the New River at Allisonia. Although humanity has done its best to farm and settle this area, the creek's two gorge sections have defied most attempts at civilization. Thus, at moderate levels this river offers two short but sweet wilderness interludes. The upper section is generally for intermediate paddlers—offering a 2-mile gorge and interesting whitewater. The lower section is for novices—with easier whitewater but a 13-mile, remote, steep walled gorge.

US 58 to Route 664 or US 221

In its upper section, Big Reed Island Creek runs through a mini-gorge that is a pure delight for the intermediate boater or carefully shepherded novice at lower levels. This gorge is beautiful, isolated, and provides continuous whitewater for about 2 miles. There are two main drawbacks to paddling the 12.5-mile section from US 58 to US 221. First, this stream is runnable only occasionally during the winter and spring. Second, there is no convenient access to the gauge that is painted on the west side of the Route 664 bridge abutment—the first take-out after 8.5 miles of paddling.

The put-in is at the US 58 bridge. Plan your shuttle carefully because there is only limited parking along the road in this area. The stream is very small here—about 20 feet wide. It flows for about 1.5 miles before reaching a pair of Class II ledges. Several routes are possible here.

The next mile consists of Class I rock garden rapids. Near the end of this mile, at the bottom of a long rock garden, the river is constricted by boulders. The Class II rapids formed here mark the beginning of the gorge. From here the river steadily picks up in gradient and paddling intensity; soon the rapids are continuous and technical. Small ledges and boulders in the stream are characteristic of the gorge.

Especially notable is a Class III 4-foot ledge, which is the largest drop on Big Reed Island Creek, occurring roughly 1 mile into the gorge. It is below a cabin on the left side of the stream and may be scouted from the left bank. Here the river suddenly turns left after a troublesome rock garden, and then, being blocked, moves sharply right over a 4-foot drop.

Below this rapid, the river continuously cruises over small ledges and between boulders. After an especially technical rock garden, the volume of the river nearly doubles when a major and runnable tributary, Laurel Fork, enters from the right. The last Class II–III drop in the gorge (Confluence Rapid) is about 100 yards below this confluence. It can be scouted from the left. From here it is a lengthy paddle (roughly 4 miles) to the first take-out at the Route 664 bridge.

Water levels are more important on Big Reed Island Creek than on most streams. From 0 to 6 inches on the Route 664 gauge, the stream is runnable, but scraping and hanging up on several of Big Reed's many rocks is likely. Levels between 6 and 12 inches provide a more enjoyable

One of the smaller drops on Big Reed Island Creek. Photo by Tom Peddy.

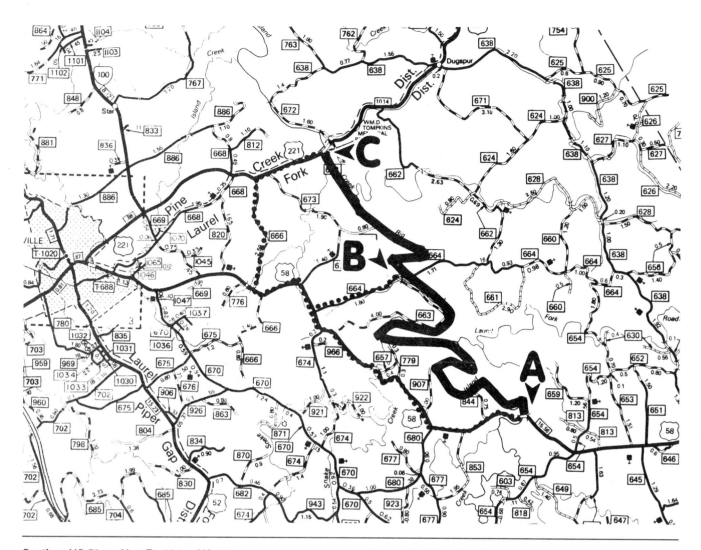

Section: US 58 to either Rt. 664 or US 221

Counties: Carroll

USGS Quads: Laurel Fork, Dugspur

Suitable for: Day cruising

Skill Level: Shepherded novices or intermediates (up to 1.5 feet on gauge); strong intermediates and advanced paddlers (higher levels)

Months Runnable: Winter and spring following a rainy period

Interest Highlights: Beautiful small gorge

Scenery: Pretty to beautiful in spots

Difficulty: Class II–III (up to 2 feet on gauge); Class III–IV at higher levels

Average Width: 15 to 40 feet

Velocity: Moderate to fast

Gradient: 20 feet per mile; 1 mile in gorge at 60 feet per mile

Runnable Water Levels:
  Minimum: 0 feet on Rt. 664 gauge
  Maximum: Flood stage; the Rt. 664 gauge only goes to 2 feet

Hazards: Occasional trees in river

Scouting: A Class III 4-foot ledge halfway through the gorge (on left); Confluence Rapid just below where Laurel Fork joins (also on left)

Portages: None

Rescue Index: Accessible to remote

Source of Additional Information: None

Access Points	River Miles	Shuttle Miles
A–B	8.5	9
B–C	4.0	13

Access Point Ratings:
  A–at US 58, good
  B–at Rt. 664, good
  C–below US 221, very good

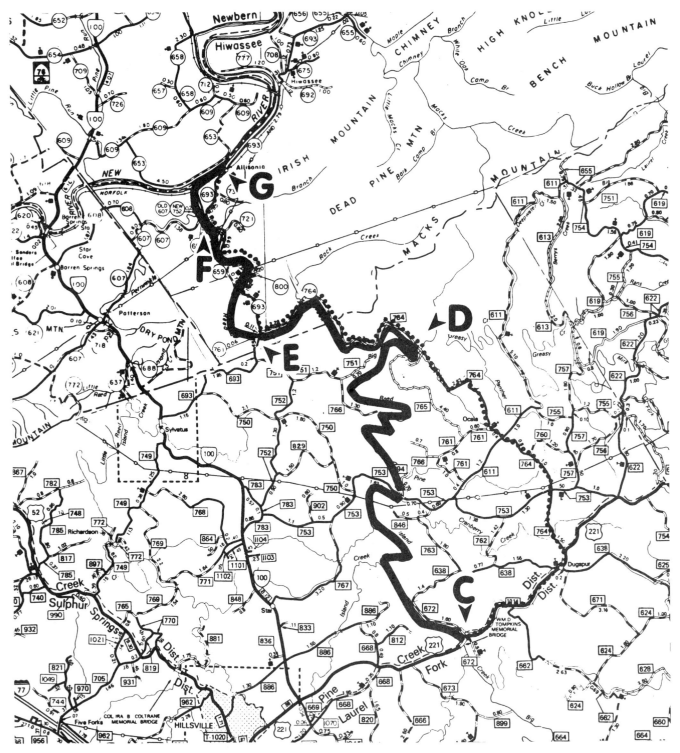

paddle, but from 1 to 2 feet the stream becomes more difficult. Levels between 2 and 3 feet begin to produce Class III–IV water, and mistakes at these levels may result in lengthy swims and broached boats. At 4 feet, the stream is even more pushy and requires very competent boat control to avoid a miserable day.

Because of logging operations in the area, downed trees are common and constitute the greatest hazard of the run. The second greatest hazard is the nearby landowners. Big Reed at one time was a premier, stocked trout stream. However, abuses by anglers led to posting of most riverside land. There have been arrests for trespassing, but only for intrusions on private land. This trip can be

Section: US 221 to Allisonia (Rt. 693)

Counties: Carroll, Pulaski

USGS Quads: Huntsville, Sylvatus, Fosters Falls, Hiwassee

Suitable for: Day cruising

Skill Level: Novices

Months Runnable: Winter and spring

Interest Highlights: Wild remote gorge

Scenery: Pretty to beautiful

Difficulty: Class I–II

Average Width: 50 to 200 feet

Velocity: Moderate

Gradient: 11 feet per mile

Runnable Water Levels:
  Minimum: Enough water to negotiate riffle at US 221 will be enough to get through gorge; add 6 inches for wide shoals below Greasy Creek

Maximum: Flood stage

Hazards: None

Scouting: None

Portages: None

Rescue Index: Generally remote

Source of Additional Information: None

Access Points	River Miles	Shuttle Miles
C–D	13	9
C–E	18	14
C–G	23	18

Access Point Ratings:

C–below US 221, very good
D–at Greasy Creek (Rt. 764), good
E–Rt. 693, good
F–Rt. 607, very good
G–Allisonia Landing, New River (Rt. 693), very good

extended 4 miles by paddling on to the US 221 bridge. Take out below the bridge using a secondary road (Route 672) on river right which follows the creek for 1.5 miles below Route 221. There are three Class II rapids in these 4 miles, but mostly the river flows steadily through some attractive scenery.

US 221 to Allisonia on the New River (Route 693)

After putting in below US 221 (See description of takeout in preceding section.), a secondary road serving a few houses and spawning some streambank trash follows the creek for about a mile and a half. When the road turns northeast up a hollow, the creek enters a wild, remote gorge that extends for the next 13 miles to where Greasy Creek joins Big Reed Island Creek. The walls of the gorge are steep and mostly forested with hemlock and rhododendron dominating the cool northern exposures. A single road bridge and some unfortunate signs of logging activity are the only blemishes on this landscape.

Perhaps the most interesting feature in the gorge occurs about 9 miles below US 221. Look for a small patch of bottomland (rare in this steep gorge). Opposite this, on river left at river level, you will find a tunnel that cuts

through the neck of a big hairpin loop in the river, and which has an attractive waterfall at its downstream portal. This "mysterious" tunnel was drilled in the latter part of the 1800s by local landowners who unsuccessfully tried to construct a waterwheel and grinding operation.

At the tunnel's lower end is the only significant rapid on this gorge of Big Reed Island Creek: a staircase of ledges up to 2 feet high with a rather winding route to navigate them. Otherwise, the stream alternates between shore pools and long gentle riffles descending over little ledges and cobbles.

The gorge opens up into a valley where Greasy Creek enters from the right. It is possible to take out here. The streambed also suddenly widens and begins dropping over a long staircase of tiny ledges, which can be quite tedious at lower levels. Houses now appear again as does some litter, but a spectacular display of huge Cambrian limestone cliffs well justifies continuing on. The first take-out below Greasy Creek is 5 miles downstream at Route 693. The next take-out is at Route 607 less than a mile above where Big Reed joins the New River, and this is also a possible spot to take out. Finally, you can exit on the New at public landings on both sides of the river downstream at Allisonia.

Big Stony Creek

Big Stony Creek is a nonstop, rocket run in the Jefferson National Forest of western Virginia just before it dumps into the New River. This creek defines the limit of navigability; if it were any smaller you could not say you floated it. The heavy duty part of this stream is steep and fast; the gradient is over 100 feet per mile for the first 5 miles! As a result, you have numerous Class III–IV drops with an occasional Class IV–V thrown in for spice.

You need a lot of water for this creek. If all other streams are too high to paddle, then Big Stony may have enough water to float it. A very small size and small watershed make this stream hard to find with enough water. The only time Ron Mullet of Salem has been able to paddle it has been after a winter snow immediately followed by a week of spring rain or during a hurricane season flood. Without these water conditions, this run is a bump and grind suitable for old plastic boats ready for their last voyage.

Also, Big Stony does not have the big sandstone rocks characteristic of many Eastern rivers—those rocks that make the rapids and eddies we all love to play. Instead, this steep creek is similar to a Western-style big flush—like paddling a flume with little chance of a graceful exit. Although the scenery isn't great with a road and houses next to the river, don't worry: you'll be too busy to look at it!

The primary danger in paddling Big Stony at any adequate water level is not its technical difficulty but its continuous nature. Rescue after any mishap is difficult, even though it is only 30 to 40 feet wide. A swim will typically result in a rough ride along the rocky Ordovician limestone creekbed for a quarter mile before the swimmer can escape the fast current. The water is shallow (normally less than 2 feet deep), but the power of the current makes swimming or walking impossible. Any open boaters attempting this creek must exercise extreme caution and quick judgement because the narrow channels mean certain pins if boats drift sideways. Other dangers are occasional strainers and railroad or road bridge abutments.

The only good safety feature of this trip is Route 635, which runs along the creek for almost its entire length. Consequently, you not only have numerous access points, but you also can scout all of Big Stony from the road—which makes a great instant take-out if this creek is suddenly too much for you. However, because of its accessibility, Big Stony is also very popular with local anglers. Be courteous to these people, but watch out for old lines and hooks snagged on overhanging trees.

Because of the continuous nature of this run and the nearby road for mandatory scouting, a detailed description is not attempted here. The first suggested put-in is near an ancient (circa late 1930s) one-pump Texaco station about 3.5 miles after Route 635 crosses the Big Stony for the first time as you drive upstream from Kimballton. (If you cross Route 635 a second time, you have gone too far.) In the first 3 miles, the Big Stony really lives up to its name with numerous braided channels. While there's always enough water to get through without scraping, a mistake in this continual shallow, rocky slalom can result in a broach or a broken paddle.

However, beginning about 3 miles below the put-in, near where Route 635 crosses Big Stony the first time, there are three well-spaced ledges that require extra caution. The first ledge is a quarter to half a mile upstream from the bridge. It resembles a broken dam and should be run on river right. However, in the third drop of this bumpy stair-step ledge, watch out for the sharp rocks at water level pointing upstream in the middle of this right channel. Don't run this ledge on the left. In 1987 David Brown of Knoxville got intimately acquainted with a nasty hydraulic on the left of this ledge when he tried to jump it at high water.

The second ledge is about 200 yards downstream of the Route 635 bridge and directly below a second bridge, on Route 781. At higher water, this ledge forms a perfectly vicious hydraulic; please use Route 635 to portage on river left.

The third ledge is approximately another quarter mile below the second ledge. This is a semiblind drop behind one of the few large boulders in Big Stony. Run this drop far left near the bank. The creek makes a sweeping right turn as it tumbles down this left side.

After these three ledges, the creek becomes less intense. Those interested in only the most difficult part of Big Stony can take out at the gypsum and lime plant less than a half mile below the Route 635 bridge. The next thing the paddler will notice is that the creek changes color after its confluence with Kimballton Branch, which enters on river right. Above this feeder stream Big Stony is clear, pristine water; below it Big Stony is a dirty, concrete-colored creek.

Nevertheless, Big Stony remains steep, and heavy duty rapids continue for 2 more miles below Route 635. However, there are now occasional eddies to catch, and the river is slightly deeper so you can get a full purchase for your paddle in this nonstop slalom. Probably the nastiest rapids on this lower section is a spicy Class IV sequence about 1.5 miles below the Route 635 bridge and between the Routes 739 and 720 bridges.

The next suggested take-out (after a 5-mile trip) is on river left soon after going under the Route 720 bridge and just above a 5-foot dam at a quarry. Below this dam the Stony calms down substantially. Those wanting to continue another 1.4 miles to near the New River will have Class II

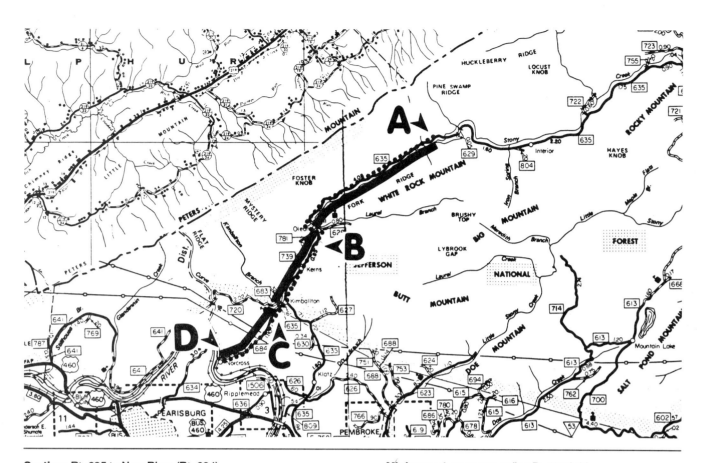

Section: Rt. 635 to New River (Rt. 684)

Counties: Giles

USGS Quads: Interior, Lindside, Pearisburg

Suitable for: Day cruising

Skill Level: Experts only!

Months Runnable: Winter and early spring after a very heavy rain

Interest Highlights: Western-style flush down a continuous rocky slalom

Scenery: Fair to pretty in spots

Difficulty: Continuous Class III–IV with several Class IV–V rapids

Average Width: 30 to 40 feet

Velocity: Fast!

Gradient: Up to 125 feet per mile in upper 3 miles; 80 feet per mile for next 2 miles; 60 feet per mile for last 2 miles above the New River

Runnable Water Levels:

Minimum: 0 on gauge at first Rt. 635 bridge
Maximum: 6 inches or so at first Rt. 635 bridge

Hazards: Occasional trees in river; railroad abutments; bridges; continual, shallow, rocky slalom; big holes; 3 big ledges— the second with a vicious hydraulic at high water; 5-foot dam below Rt. 720

Scouting: 3 big ledges above and below Rt. 635 bridge (from left)

Portages: Any of these ledges, particularly the second at high water; 5-foot dam below Rt. 720

Rescue Index: Accessible

Source of Additional Information: None

Access Points	River Miles	Shuttle Miles
A–B	3.5	3.5
B–C	2.0	2.0
C–D	1.5	1.5

Access Point Ratings:
A–on Rt. 635, very good
B–gypsum plant on Rt. 635, very good
C–just below Rt. 720, good
D–at New River (Rt. 684), very good

rapids until the final take-out next to Route 684 on river left. There is a canoeing gauge on the upstream side of the middle abutment on the Route 635 bridge. Pay careful attention to water levels because a few inches make a whale of a difference on this creek. Zero on the gauge is passable, and 2 to 3 inches is a good level. However, 6 inches is hair water!

Chestnut Creek

Chestnut Creek is born along the Blue Ridge Parkway and passes through Galax on its way to the New River. The only drawback to this pleasant 11.5-mile trip (which starts in Galax) is that this creek must be run during or within a couple of days of heavy rain. Consequently, it is hard to catch up. Be sure you have at least a 0 level on the Route 793 bridge gauge (7 miles into the trip). Also, note that the water level can rise or fall rather quickly due to runoff from the city of Galax. Paddlers wanting a shorter trip can run either the upper 7-mile section or the lower 4.5-mile section.

Put in at Route 726 just before you get to the Route 721 bridge (Cliffview Street) in Galax. The first 7-mile segment of this trip sports two rapids that make it interesting. Otherwise, the creek consists of easy riffles, shallow ledges, and slow moving water. The first of these two significant rapids is 1.5 miles into the trip—three closely related drops that together would rate low Class III. These drops are called Andrews Rapids and generally should be run left of center. First timers can scout from the left if they wish.

After another 1.5 miles, the bottom suddenly drops out of the river. You have reached Six Pack Falls—a Class IV stairstep rapid which is an 8-foot drop. Scout from the left bank to determine which of three options to take. The usual route is in the center. However, you can try the far right, which is more difficult. Finally, a carry on the left bank is an honorable option. Below these two rapids the river runs on slowly to two take-outs. The first is the Route 607

bridge. This cuts off 3 miles of slow water before you get to the second take-out at Route 793.

The first half of the 4.5 miles below Route 793 is busier than the 7-mile section above. Consequently, it is more popular and a great intermediate stretch. The only drawback is that after 2.5 miles of good paddling, you pay the penalty of a 2-mile lake paddle because of the presence of Byllesby Dam on the New River at the take-out.

After 1 mile of slow moving water and riffles on this lower section, you will come to some shallow ledges. These mark the beginning of over 1 mile of fairly continuous Class II and III rapids. After the first half mile of these rapids, you will notice a boulder-choked section. Just below it is Camera Rapid, a solid Class III composed of three ledges; the middle ledge is the largest—a 3-foot drop. Run these in the center, except for the last ledge which requires an immediate right turn to avoid a rock in the center. Scout on either the left or right bank. About a quarter mile downstream you will approach a Class II creek-wide ledge best run left. Then maneuver right because 50 yards downstream is Lunchstop Rapids, a nice Class III where the creek bends right-to-left through a boat-wide channel into a nice punchable hole. Just below this there is the last Class III – a 3-foot drop best run far right. There are a few more ledges and nice little chutes until you get to the flatwater of Byllesby Dam. The 2.5 miles of good water upstream certainly make this character-building, 2-mile paddle worthwhile.

A nice ledge on the lower section of Chestnut Creek. Photo by Tom Peddy.

Section: Near Rt. 721 bridge (Cliffview St. in Galax) to Byllesby Dam boat landing on New River

Counties: Carroll

USGS Quads: Galax, Austinville

Suitable for: Day cruising

Skill Level: Intermediates (moderate levels), advanced (high levels)

Months Runnable: Winter and spring after a heavy rain

Interest Highlights: Several zesty rapids; old railroad bed, which is being converted to hiking trail along river

Scenery: Beautiful in spots to beautiful

Difficulty: Class I–III with 1 Class IV rapid

Average Width: 40 to 50 feet

Velocity: Moderate

Gradient: 13 feet per mile

Runnable Water Levels:
  Minimum: 0 feet on the Rt. 793 gauge (downstream side)
  Maximum: 2 feet on the Rt. 793 gauge

Hazards: Occasional trees in river; Six Pack Falls; hydraulics below ledges at high water

Scouting: Six Pack Falls (Class IV), on river left; Camera Rapid, on river left or right

Portages: None, except perhaps Six Pack Falls

Rescue Index: Accessible

Source of Additional Information: None

Access Points	River Miles	Shuttle Miles
A–B	4	4.5
A–C	7	5.3
C–D	4.5	3.5

Access Point Ratings:
  A–at Rt. 726 near Rt. 721 (Cliffview St.), good
  B–Rt. 607, good
  C–at Rt. 793, good
  D–at Byllesby Dam boat landing, good

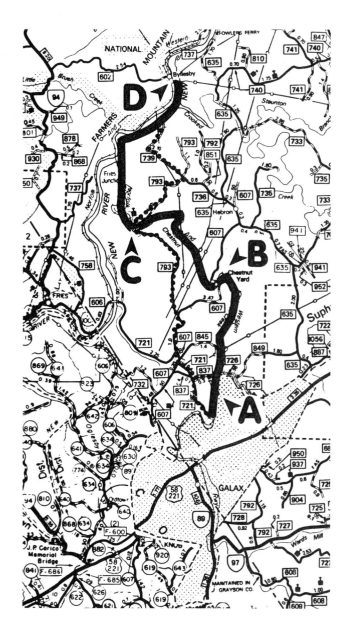

Elk Creek

Elk Creek is a popular Grayson County trout stream that flows quietly through Elk Creek Valley on its way to the New River. However, it's passive nature changes in the last 4.5 miles before the Elk joins the New. Indeed, this section of the Elk is a splendid, small, intermediate whitewater trip that will work up a sweat in a hurry. Unfortunately, it can only be run during rainy periods or shortly thereafter. At low water, this stream is a real boat bruiser, so be sure to check the canoeing gauge located on the upstream side of the Route 274 bridge just before the Elk and New join. It should read at least 0 to avoid pain and strain to your boat.

You could start your trip at the Route 660 bridge, but you would soon encounter three Class VI drops that have not been run as of this writing. Running them is not advised because of the nasty undercut and pinning rocks they contain. In between the big rapids are some nice Class II rapids, but the long carries around the three Class VI drops do not make the easier rapids worthwhile.

The standard put-in is off Route 650 after the three Class VI drops and a rock garden below the Route 660 bridge. From here you will have about 2 miles of Class II and III rapids (with a gradient approaching 80 feet per mile) over small ledges and rock garden chutes of Precambrian granite/gneiss with many right turns required. Keep in mind that this is a small, boulder-choked stream, meaning that the paddler must pick the best slots to avoid being stuck on rocks. The best rapid you get while Route

650 still runs alongside the creek (a half mile below the put-in) is Slicer, a Class III that at low water has a rock jutting upward in the bottom chute. This appropriately named rapid is a 4-foot, sloping drop; it requires the paddler to follow the main channel in a right-to-left, 90-degree turn into a pool. Scout it from the road on the left.

Just below Slicer is a shallow ledge followed by an easy Class III rapid, which is best run left of center while maneuvering toward a big boulder and turning right before you hit this boulder. As the stream leaves Route 650 (nearly a mile from the put-in), it enters a scenic isolated area, which is strewn with boulders and rhododendrons. The high hillside on the right creates a mini-gorge. Be alert because the most continuous ledges and drops are also located here. The most noticeable rapid in this section is Todds Rapid, a Class III distinguished by creek wide boulders. Scout it from the left. The best passage here is to go right over a small drop toward a big boulder and then left around a boulder to go river left through a chute. From here there are several lesser Class II–III rapids until it all ends at a 3-foot, creek-wide ledge (also Class II–III) with three chutes.

After this, you have a 2-mile Class I paddle to the confluence with the New River and then less than another half mile to the public boat landing downstream on the New at the intersection of Routes 94 and 274.

Section: Rt. 650 (below third big rapids) to New River public boat landing at Jct. of Rts. 94 and 274

Counties: Grayson

USGS Quads: Briar Patch Mountain

Suitable for: Day cruising

Skill Level: Intermediates (moderate levels), advanced (high levels)

Months Runnable: Winter and spring after a heavy rain

Interest Highlights: Isolated, scenic mini-gorge with rhododendrons

Scenery: Pretty to beautiful

Difficulty: Class I–III

Average Width: 20 to 30 feet

Velocity: Moderate

Gradient: 21 feet per mile but up to 80 feet per mile for first 2 miles

Runnable Water Levels:
Minimum: 0 feet on the Rt. 274 gauge (upstream side)
Maximum: 2 feet on the Rt. 274 gauge

Hazards: 3 Class VI rapids above Rt. 650 put-in; Elk Creek is a real boat bruiser at low water; occasional trees in river; hydraulics at high water

Scouting: Slicer (Class III) and Todds (Class III), both from left

Portages: None, except 3 Class VI rapids if you put in at Rt. 660

Rescue Index: Accessible to remote

Source of Additional Information: None

Access Points	River Miles	Shuttle Miles
A–B	4.5	5.5

Access Point Ratings:
A–at Rt. 650, good
B–at New River boat landing, Jct. Rts. 94 and 274, excellent

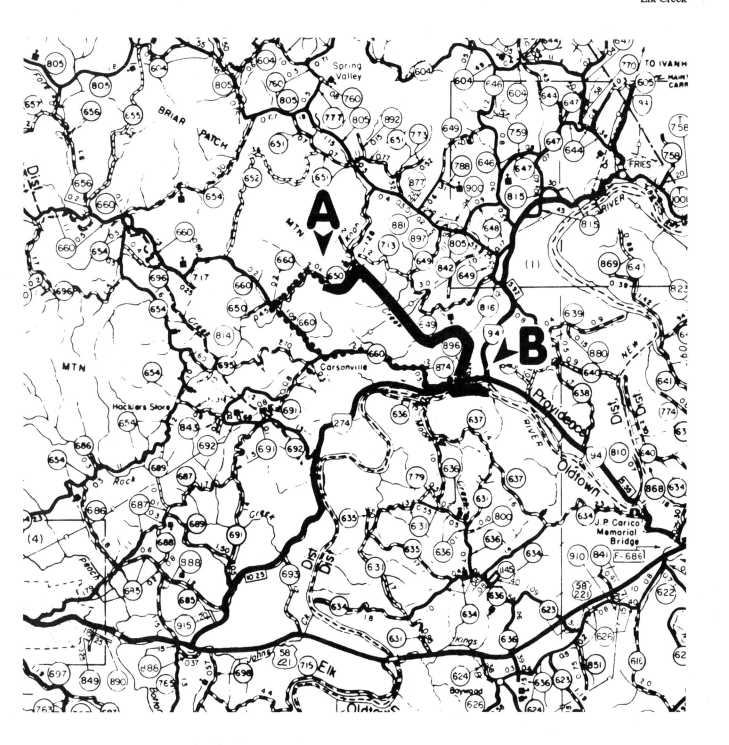

Little River

Route 716 near Route 8 to Route 787

Born at the confluence of its North and South Forks in rural Floyd County, the Little River winds for many miles through pastoral farmland, rolling hills, and over mostly gentle Class I–II rapids before emptying into the New River near the city of Radford. Many an experienced boater from the area first wet his paddle on sections of the Little, and there are places for mild family float trips. The exception to this peaceful tranquility is a short, intense section 2 to 3 miles above Route 787, where the Little drops at a rate of up to 80 feet per mile, creating several rapids in the Class II–IV range.

This intense section is part of the popular whitewater trip that begins at Route 716 under the Route 8 bridge and ends 13.5 miles later at Route 787. In between lies something for many paddlers. Though rated an intermediate trip, advanced shepherded novices, with some judicious portaging, could handle the run at moderate levels.

There is no reliable gauge for the Little, but you can run the river in all except the driest months. If the riffles below the put-in look runnable, it has enough water.

Other than farmland and flatwater with riffles, little else characterizes the first 3 miles of the trip. For the next 3 miles there are Class I cobble bars and tiny ledges punctuated with boulders and rock formations on the banks. After about 6 miles you will pass several small cabins on the right bank. Immediately below these cabins the river widens and cascades over an intricate Class II

Section: Rt. 716 near Rt. 8 to Rt. 787

Counties: Floyd, Montgomery

USGS Quads: Riner, Alum Ridge, Radford South, Indian Valley

Suitable for: Day cruising

Skill Level: Intermediates

Months Runnable: Winter, spring, and early summer

Interest Highlights: Abundant wildlife

Scenery: Pretty to beautiful in spots

Difficulty: Class II–III with 1 Class III–IV and 1 Class IV rapid

Average Width: 30 to 35 feet

Velocity: Generally slow to moderate

Gradient: 8 feet per mile for first 9 miles; 22 feet per mile for last 4 miles with one-quarter mile at 80 feet per mile

Runnable Water Levels:
　Minimum: No gauge; if runnable at put-in, is runnable for entire trip
　Maximum: Maybe bankful at the put-in

Hazards: Maybe an occasional tree in the river; Shoulder Snapper and Bear Falls

Scouting: Maybe Bear Cub Falls (Class II–III), from left; definitely Bear Falls (Class IV), from right; Shoulder Snapper (Class III–IV) in between is difficult to scout before you are committed to it

Portages: Maybe Bear Falls on right

Rescue Index: Accessible to remote

Source of Additional Information: None

Access Points	River Miles	Shuttle Miles
A–B	13.5	15

Access Point Ratings:
　A–at Rt. 716 near Rt. 8, very good
　B–at Rt. 787, good

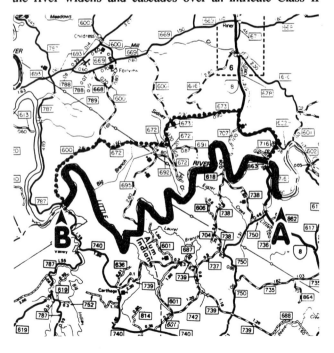

series of shoals and small ledges. At most levels this section will sorely tax your patience and make you question your water reading skills. Many routes exist, but it may help to enter center and work right. As you regain your composure at the bottom, you'll now know why this rapid is known as "Exasperation Shoals." Note that if the water is high enough to easily paddle down these shoals, you're in for quite a ride farther downstream.

The river quickly regains a calm demeanor, but after another 2 miles it begins to narrow as large boulders appear along the banks. Bear Cub Falls is obvious on the approach; the river falls over small ledges and disappears behind a large boulder that obstructs your vision. First timers may scout from the left bank, but beware of snakes, poison ivy, and "No Trespassing" signs. To run this drop just follow the current down the right channel, draw right at the big boulder, and ride the chute to the bottom pool. Consider Bear Cub an easy Class II–III at moderate levels and a Class III at high water. As you run Bear Cub, you will notice a boil left of center that is called Suck Hole by locals.

Things again calm down for about 2 miles until the river dramatically widens and a second set of shoals appears. As its name implies, Class II Deja Vu Shoals is much like its upstream cousin, only longer. It also presents the boater with two choices: either entering center and then heading left or running on far river right. The first choice takes you on a Class II sneak route left of an island. The second choice takes you to the right side and presents you with Shoulder Snapper and another decision. Either stick to the

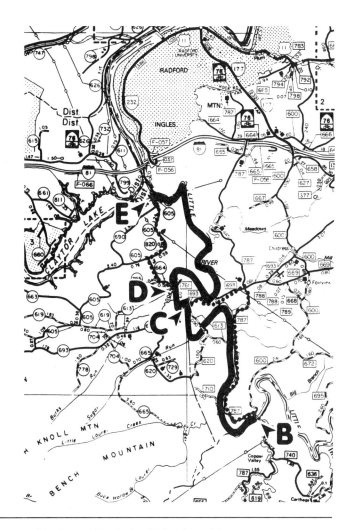

Section: Rt. 787 to Little River Dam (Rt. 605)

Counties: Floyd, Montgomery

USGS Quads: Radford South, Indian Valley

Suitable for: Day cruising

Skill Level: Novices

Months Runnable: Winter, spring, and early summer

Interest Highlights: Abundant wildlife

Scenery: Pretty to beautiful in spots

Difficulty: Class I–II

Average Width: 40 to 60 feet

Velocity: Generally slow to moderate

Gradient: 10 feet per mile

Runnable Water Levels:
Minimum: No gauge; if runnable at put-in, is runnable for entire trip

Maximum: Maybe bankful at the put-in

Hazards: Maybe an occasional tree in the river; Little River Dam near take-out

Scouting: None

Portages: Little River Dam, on left

Rescue Index: Accessible to remote

Source of Additional Information: Radford City Manager (703) 731-3603

Access Points	River Miles	Shuttle Miles
B–C	7	7
B–D	8	8
D–E	8	8

Access Point Ratings:
B–at Rt. 787, good
C–at Snowville (Rt. 693), good
D–at Graysontown (Rt. 664), good
E–below Little River Dam (Rt. 605), fair to good

left channel and drop down a very narrow, twisting chute or stay in the right channel and take a 90-degree left turn drop over a steep 4-foot ledge, landing (hopefully upright) 90 degrees to the rushing current in the bottom channel. This is a very rocky, frothy drop that has earned its name. Be careful whatever choice you take. The narrow left slot is a Class II–III; the right channel with the sharp turn is a solid Class III–IV. Be careful when running these last two drops; it's tough to scout or carry them once you go right of the island and forego the Class II sneak on the left.

Whichever route you take through Deja Vu or Shoulder Snapper, you will end up in the same narrow channel leading into the pool above Class IV Bear Falls. Here a chain of rocks forces the river sharply left, then right in a short heavy Z-turn, which ends between a couple of shark tooth rocks. The drop can be run several ways and is easily scouted from, or carried over, the large rocks on river right. Several boats have broached and pinned here, so use caution and set throw ropes on the right. You can sneak the worst of Bear Falls by starting on the far left, dropping over two small ledges, and then running the last part of the Z-turn between the two shark tooth rocks.

Below Bear Falls and a Class II shoals the river widens and begins its return to civilization and the take-out. It's an easy 2 miles to Route 787. Near the start of this last stretch is a 2-foot ledge with good surfing. Paddle underneath the Route 787 bridge and take out on river left.

Route 787 to Little River Dam (Route 605)

Below the Route 787 bridge are a good 16 miles of river, which are suitable for beginner or novice boaters. The first part is a 7- to 8-mile trip to Graysontown through farmland. The rapids here are mainly Class I riffles and ledges. The only exceptions are a Class II S-turn at the Snowville bridge (the second bridge) and a Class II drop of 3 feet over 20 yards at the Graysontown take-out; the latter is the remains of an old mill dam. Use discretion when taking out at Graysontown because much of this land is private property. Paddlers not wanting to do the entire upper stretch can take out on Route 787, which parallels the Little for several miles after the Route 787 bridge.

The second part of the trip is the 8- to 9-mile section that goes every direction of the compass with two huge meanders and ends at the backwater of the Little River Dam. The most striking feature on this last section is Cracker Neck—a sharp left turn between 400-foot-high bluffs a mile from the dam. The dam impoundment is fairly narrow and heavily silted in. Several caves are accessible by boat on the lake for those so inclined. However, the Little River Dam generates electricity for Radford and permission is needed to use the area for access. Check with the City Manager's Office in Radford at (703) 731-3603. Unfortunately, at low water you will have to drag your boat over yucky mud flats to reach the take-out, a small parking area left of the dam.

Depending on time, desire, and water levels, there are several other good streams in the area, including Big Reed Island Creek and the upper New River. For folks who like lake boating, Claytor Lake is nearby. Virginia's only outdoor drama, "The Long Way Home" (discussed in the New River narrative) is also located near here.

New River

The New River is not new; it is very old! Many geologists believe it is the oldest river in North America. Indeed, some experts think the New is the second oldest river in the world, with only the Nile being older. In prehistoric times the New was known as the Teays River and had one of North America's largest watersheds. It is believed that 180 million years ago in Paleozoic times, the Teays flowed all the way to the Saint Lawrence River on the United States-Canada border. Blockage by glaciers in the much more recent Pleistocene ice ages (less than 1 million years ago) allowed the relatively "new" Ohio River to pirate most of the Teays into its watershed. During it's life, the New has eroded through 4,000 feet of rock, making it the only river that has cut through the entire width of the Appalachian Mountains. Also, the New is one of the few rivers in the world that flow north and is the southernmost river in North American to do so.

Besides being old, the New has great scenery and variety. It begins just south of the Virginia-North Carolina border. For most of its journey through Virginia, the New is a pleasant camping and Class I–II novice canoeing river at moderate levels. However, after it enters West Virginia, its character changes substantially as it goes through the exciting New River Gorge. The gorge is not only one of the best Class III–V big whitewater runs in the East, but near its end is the largest single-span bridge in the United States. Nearly 900 feet high, this bridge is closed to vehicles one day in October for Bridge Day. On this day parachutists and daredevil "bungey" cord artists jump from the bridge—the later folks acting like human yoyos with one end of their cords anchored to the bridge as they launch themselves into space. For information on the New River Gorge, see *Appalachian Whitewater, Volume II, The Central Mountains*, published by Menasha Ridge Press.

The beautiful upper New near Fries in early morning. Photo by Ed Gertler.

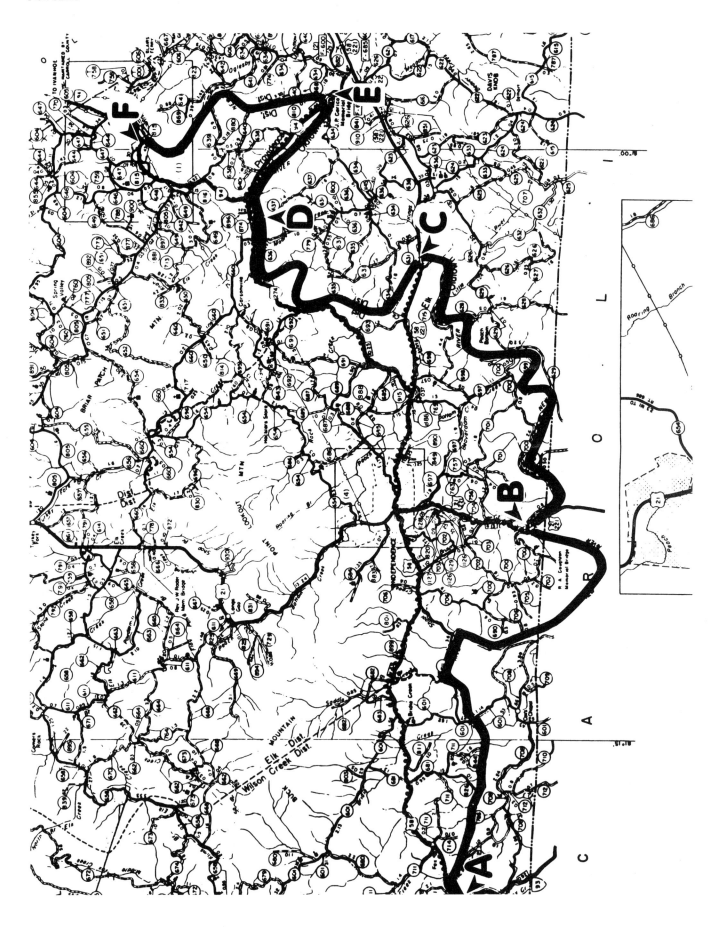

Section: Stuart Dam (US 58) to Fries (Rt. 648)

Counties: Grayson (VA), Alleghany (NC)

USGS Quads: Mouth of Wilson, Briarpatch Mountain, Galax, Sparta West, Sparta East

Suitable for: Day trips and camping

Skill Level: Shepherded novices for upper 14 miles; novices for middle 22 miles and lower 5 miles at moderate water levels

Months Runnable: The entire year

Interest Highlights: Rolling hills and pastureland, oldest river in North America

Scenery: Pretty to beautiful in spots

Difficulty: Class I–II with 1 Class II–III in upper 14 miles; Class I–II in lower 27 miles

Average Width: 200 to 400 feet

Velocity: Slow to moderate

Gradient: 7 feet per mile first 14 miles; 5 feet per mile last 27 miles

Runnable Water Levels:
   Minimum: None, river can be run the entire year
   Maximum: High water

Hazards: Fries Dam (50 feet high) at end of this section; occasional trees in river; high water

Scouting: Novices might scout Class II Molly Osborne Shoals 6 miles into the trip (2 miles below Rt. 601 bridge), from the left; definitely scout Class II–III Penitentiary Shoals just below, from the right

Portages: Novices with camping gear might portage Penitentiary Shoals

Rescue Index: Accessible to remote

Source of Additional Information: New River Canoe and Campground (Independence) (540) 773-3412

Access Points	River Miles	Shuttle Miles
A–B	14	12
B–C	11	10
B–D	18	14
B–E	22	16
E–F	5	6

Access Point Ratings:
A—below Stuart Dam (US 58), very good
B—Doughton Bridge (US 221/21), public boat landing 1 mile downstream on river left, excellent
C—US 58, public boat landing, excellent
D—Rt. 274/94, public boat landing, excellent
E—Carico Bridge (US 221/58), good (private land)
F—Fries (Rt. 94), very good

It's hard to say enough about camping, hiking, and fishing possibilities on the New. There are many camping sites for church, scout, and family groups along the bank and on numerous islands. However, many spots are on private property, so use discretion in choosing your campsite. For those interested in hiking, biking, or horseback riding, New River Trail State Park is a recent development. This trail follows an old railroad bed and is planned to parallel over 50 miles of the New. Currently, it is over half finished—especially the dozen miles from the small town of Fries to the tiny berg of Ivanhoe. Wildlife often seen on the New include deer, beaver, mink, and assorted birds—particularly ducks, geese, herons, and hawks. Fishing is great, too! Between Mouth of Wilson and Byllesby Dam one will find primarily three game fish: smallmouth bass, muskie, and catfish. Below Byllesby Dam to Claytor Lake you can also catch walleye pike.

Both scenery and the sense of history on this river are impressive. For example, near the source of the New at Mouth of Wilson are Mount Rogers National Recreation Area and Grayson Highlands State Park. These parks contain Mount Rogers (the highest mountain in Virginia at 5,729 feet), the Appalachian Trail, camping, picnic areas, trout streams, horse trails, and hiking trails. The scenery continues downstream. For most of its length in Virginia, the New offers pastoral settings and forested hillsides. In many places one finds a splendid isolation broken only by tiny towns that time has forgotten and occasional farmhouses or vacation homes. It is humbling to think that because of its size, the New was an impediment to settlers moving west in the early history of our country.

Finally, the New is a reliable river. You can paddle it the entire year, even during droughts. The Virginia sections are made for summer and early fall paddling when most other rivers have dried up. However, remember that the New is big, one of the largest rivers in Virginia. Novice paddlers should stay off this river during high water and in January or February when ice can also make it dangerous or impassible.

Stuart Dam to Fries

Stuart Dam (US 58) to Route 221/21

The New begins where the North Fork and South Fork join, 3 miles south of Mouth of Wilson, North Carolina. The unique nature of this river was acknowledged in 1976 when 22 miles of the South Fork plus the first 4.5 miles of the New were designated as a National Wild and Scenic

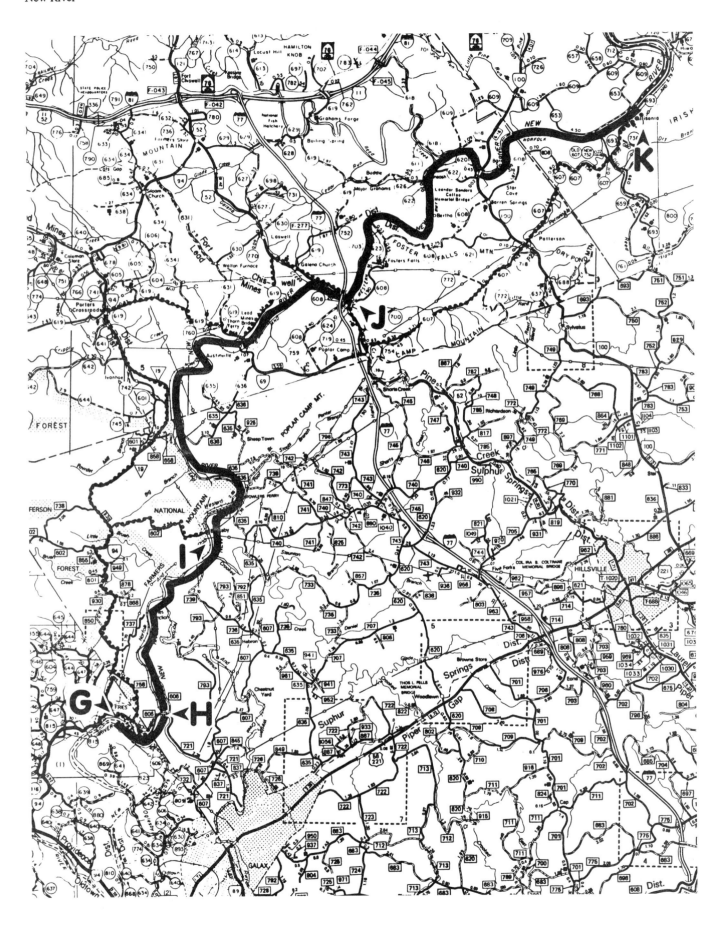

River. Indeed, the gentle South Fork is much more popular than the North Fork for paddling. There are more access points and longer stretches of suitable water (up to Class I), making it ideal for novice canoeists and camping. For more information on the North and South Forks, see *Carolina Whitewater* by Bob Benner, which is published by Menasha Ridge Press.

From Mouth of Wilson to Stuart Dam the New is primarily backwater for the dam and, thus very flat. Paddling this 2.5 miles is not recommended. Instead most boaters use US 58 to put in on river left below Stuart Dam. This introduces the paddler to the first section of the New—a 14-mile trip to the US 221/21 bridge. The river is quite scenic for most of this section as it passes through an open valley of farmland and rolling hills covered with trees. The first 2 miles are flatwater, whereas the second 2 miles feature Class I riffles and a cobble bar near the end.

Just over 4 miles into the trip and after you see Route 711 on the left bank, you will go under the Route 601 bridge. This is an alternate put-in and is also known as Cox's Chapel Bridge. About a mile below the Route 601 bridge is a Class I drop as the river turns right. Now you should begin thinking about the two rapids of note on this section. You reach these rapids after another mile as the river again bends right. The first is a long Class II series of ledges called Molly Osborne Shoals. Run it on the left. If

you are not in a hurry, please note that there are Indian caves on river left just above these rapids.

The second ledgy drop is roughly 200 yards below the first drop and is called Penitentiary Shoals. It is a Class II at low water and a Class III at high water. Here most of the water flows left against a large boulder on the bank. The drop is just beyond this boulder. Scout or portage on the right. Campers with gear especially should be careful. At moderate levels this drop can be run center or river left, but at higher water, run it in the center because a nasty hole develops on far river left. This hole is caused by a ledge that extends from the left bank about 15 feet into the river, and each year at high water, several boats are pinned here by inexperienced paddlers lacking floatation. Incidentally, there was a proposed dam site here for the Appalachian Power Company, but this threat ended when the first 4.5 miles of the New became a Wild and Scenic River.

A half mile or so below these two drops, you will come to an island; go left. As you pass a second island, keep left over a long Class I series of rapids. This will avoid the right side of the second island, which is too shallow. For the last 5 miles of this section there are only two Class I–II rapids of note. The first is quickly reached just as you enter North Carolina; it is called Big Island Falls. Run right of a large island for the best channel. The second rapid is near the end of the section, shortly before you reenter Virginia.

Section: Fries (Rt. 94 below dam) to Allisonia (Rt. 693)

Counties: Grayson, Carroll, Wythe, Pulaski

USGS Quads: Austinville, Galax, Max Meadows, Fosters Falls, Sylvatus, Hiwassee

Suitable for: Day cruising

Skill Level: Shepherded novices at moderate levels

Months Runnable: The entire year

Interest Highlights: New River Trail State Park, oldest river in North America, Old Shot Tower

Scenery: Pretty to beautiful in spots

Difficulty: Class I–II with 1 Class III and 1 Class III–IV

Average Width: 400 to 500 feet

Velocity: Slow to moderate

Gradient: 7 feet per mile for 8 miles from Fries to Byllesby Dam (with Double Shoals 1.5 miles at 20 feet per mile); 5 feet per mile below Buck Dam to Allisonia (with Fosters Falls 0.5 miles at 40 feet per mile)

Runnable Water Levels:
  Minimum: None, can be run the entire year

Maximum: High water

Hazards: Two 50-foot dams (Byllesby Dam and Buck Dam); occasional trees in river; high water

Scouting: Class III Buck Rapids between Byllesby Dam and Buck Dam, from left; Class III Fosters Falls (Class IV in high water) 1.5 miles below I-77, from left

Portages: Two 50-foot dams (Byllesby Dam and Buck Dam), on left; novices may portage Buck Rapids and Fosters Falls at high water, on left

Rescue Index: Accessible to remote

Source of Additional Information: None

Access Points	River Miles	Shuttle Miles
G–I	8	12
H–I	6	10
I–J	12	10
J–K	12	14

Access Point Ratings:
  G–Fries (off Rt. 94 below dam), very good
  H–Fries (Rt. 606), excellent
  I–Rt. 602, good
  J–US 52 off I-77, very good
  K–Allisonia (Rt. 693), very good

This easy series of small ledges is called Farmers Fish Camp Shoals and can be run almost anywhere. Soon below you reach the Doughton Memorial Bridge take-out on US 221/21. The New River Campground is on river right here, and a public boat landing is on river left a mile downstream.

US 221/21 to Route 274 (Carico Bridge)

Those who want a 2- or 3-day camping trip can do the 22 mile section from US 221/21 to Route 274 (Carico Bridge). This stretch of the New is perfect for novice paddlers and their families who want a relaxing experience. The rolling hills and pastureland continue unabated. The occasional rapids on this section are no tougher than Class I–II riffles and rock drops. If you put in or take out at Route 274, get permission if the place you park appears to be privately owned. For others who want a day-trip only, there are several convenient access points. The best are the US 58 public boat landing 11 miles below the US 221/21 bridge and the Route 94/274 public boat landing on river left another 7 miles farther. This second take-out is just downstream of the New River Wildlife and Conservation Club, which promotes wildlife management for hunters.

There are only occasional Class I rapids on this 22-mile section, with two exceptions. The first is a Class I–II drop next to an island 6 miles into this trip; run it center. The second is the Class I–II Joyces Rapid 10 miles farther, which should be run right of center.

There are two noteworthy tributaries. The first is Little River, which is 9 miles from the US 221/21 bridge. This Class I–II stream enters from river left and is described in Bob Benner's Carolina Whitewater. The second is Elk Creek, which enters on river right 4 miles above the Route 274 take-out. The Route 94/274 boat landing is also the take-out for Class I–III Elk Creek described elsewhere in this book.

Route 274 to Fries (Route 94)

If you continue below Route 274, I recommend that you either go 3 miles and take out on the river right public boat landing across (Route 641) from Delps Beach, or go 2 miles farther and take out on river left at Route 94. Otherwise, you will have to portage left around the 50-foot-high Fries Dam by the town of Fries. The main items of interest on this short stretch are islands and a long Class I cobble bar between Delps Beach and the Route 94 take-out.

Fries to Allisonia

Fries (Route 94) to Byllesby Dam (Route 602)

Below Fries Dam (depending on where you put in or take out) is a short, 5- to 8-mile section of the New with a 1.5 mile long rapid called Double Shoals. After that comes Byllesby Dam, another 50-foot-high wonder to portage on the left. You have two put-in choices: off Route 94 on river left in Fries just below Fries Dam or 2 miles downstream on river right at the Route 606 bridge. Similarly, there are two take-out alternatives. The first is on river right off Route 736 about 5 miles below Route 606 but has a complex shuttle. The second and recommended take-out is another mile downstream on river left on Route 602 just above Byllesby Dam.

This short trip contains two highlights. The first is Double Shoals. This is a delightful 1.5-mile section of Class II cobble bars and ledges, which begins 2 miles below the Route 606 bridge. It is similar to the Staircase on the Shenandoah near Harpers Ferry, except that the New is a much bigger river. At higher water, Double Shoals becomes Class III. The second highlight is the scenery: some paddlers believe this is the most scenic section of the New River in Virginia. The terrain becomes more rugged, and the paddler is treated to striking rock formations and beautiful hemlocks. In recognition of this scenic section, the aforementioned New River Trail starts on the left bank below Fries and continues a dozen miles to Ivanhoe. Just below Double Shoals, Chestnut Creek enters on river right. This Class II–III stream is discussed elsewhere in this chapter.

Byllesby Dam (Route 602) to Route 52 off I-77

The 12 miles from Byllesby Dam to Interstate 77 are for paddlers who don't mind some strenuous hiking with their paddling. Campers should probably avoid this stretch unless they love to grunt and groan. In the first 3 miles there are two difficult portages, both on the left. The first is by 50-foot-high Byllesby Dam. The second is nearly 3 miles downstream by 50-foot-high Buck Dam (also known as Byllesby Dam Number Two). After portaging, be sure not to put in too close to the dangerous turbulent waters just below each dam. Also, be warned that water levels below these two dams can rise rapidly. Gates for these dams are sometimes opened automatically and water levels can rise abruptly without warning—e.g., a yard in a few minutes. Campers paddling sections below these two dams must heed this warning; choose your campsites well above the river and don't leave your canoes on the banks overnight.

If you can hack the portages, there are two reasons to run this section. The first is Buck Rapids, which is midway between the two dams. This Class III technical ledge and boulder drop is best run center or left. Scout and portage on the left. The second reason is the scenery—the striking rock formations and hemlocks continue. In recognition of this beauty, the New River Trail continues on the left bank to Ivanhoe. Just below Ivanhoe the trail crosses the river and continues on the right for the last half of the trip.

Below Buck Dam, there are occasional Class I ledges for the next 5 miles. You run the last Class I drop just after Cripple Creek enters from the left and the river turns to the right. Below here are 3 miles of flatwater. Then you reach Shot Tower Rapids. This Class II is a slalom through boulders and cobble bars. About a half mile below this rapid you cross under Interstate 77 and then see the Shot Tower on river right. Just past the tower is the US 52 take-out on river right.

The 75-foot-high Shot Tower was built in 1807 to supply shot for settlers in the nearby frontier. Lead was heated at the top of the tower until molten and poured through a sieve. The resulting pellets then fell 150 feet down a shaft extending 75 feet into the ground below the base of the tower and into a kettle of water. The hardened ammunition was then carried out a tunnel that led to the river. Currently, the Shot Tower is slated to be the headquarters of the New River Trail State Park.

Interstate 77 to Allisonia (Route 693)

The 12-mile section from Interstate 77 to Allisonia (Route 693) is also fairly remote and quite scenic. It is a Class I–II trip with one important exception—Fosters Falls. This Class III, abrupt drop (Class IV at high water) occurs only 1.5 miles into the trip. You know you are nearing this rapid when you see a huge iron cylinder in the river. The river becomes very wide, with many Class II channels, as you enter this rapid. In the entrance, the river drops 8 feet over 100 yards and is a Class III at high water. Stay on the left as you begin to work your way down. Then, less than a half mile from this entry, you will see a horizon line. Get out on the left bank to scout or portage. You have reached the heart of Fosters Falls, where the river drops at least 10 feet over four ledges, each 2 to 4 feet high. The first three ledges are each only 10 yards apart, and the fourth ledge is a good 50 yards downstream. At high water, be sure you approach Fosters Falls on the extreme left (or right) of the river because the holes and drops are largest in the center.

Soon below Fosters Falls you will pass Baker Island. Just after this large island is a nice Class II drop as the river bends right. A couple of miles farther, after the river bends left, you come to the last named rapid—Bertha Shoals. This Class II series of small ledges and cobble bars can be run almost anywhere.

Below Bertha Shoals, there are only occasional Class I riffles and cobbles. You pass under the Route 100 bridge 7 miles into the trip. Those wanting a short day-trip can take out a half mile above Route 100 on Route 618. The only problem with this is that you have to cross private land to take out. Although it is not presently posted, get permission if possible. For those wanting a longer trip,

it's 5 miles from the Route 100 bridge to the Route 693 take-out on river right in Allisonia. About a half mile above the take-out, Big Reed Island Creek enters from the right. This Class II–III stream is described elsewhere in this chapter.

The 20 miles of the New below Allisonia are not recommended for those who like moving water: this is Claytor Lake, formed by Claytor Dam.

Below Claytor Lake Dam to Glen Lyn

In the 45-mile stretch from Claytor Lake Dam (upstream from Radford) to Glen Lyn (near West Virginia) the New River continues as a wide, high volume river. However, at moderate levels, it is a river for novice paddlers, anglers, and campers. There are numerous access points, so you have many options in setting up your trip.

This section of the New does not have a lot of whitewater; it is largely flat with occasional riffles and rapids. There is only one Class III at normal water levels— Narrows Falls below the town of Narrows as you near the West Virginia border. However, at higher levels, the difficulty and danger level of the New increases greatly because of the river's huge size—particularly in cold weather. Also, paddling downstream on this river can at times be an exercise in futility because the wind funnels upstream and overpowers the generally slow current of the river. Fortunately, strong winds are not very common in this area because the hilly terrain tends to limit them.

As a float fishing stream, this part of the New is excellent. It has a large native population of smallmouth bass. Citation size (over 5 pounds) are caught frequently, and it is hard to avoid catching the small fry. Rock bass, catfish, and bluegill are also common. An occasional muskie is even caught. At one time, large walleye pike and ringtail perch were common in the river; but for reasons unknown, the population of these species has been greatly reduced.

The scenery on this part of the river is generally good and at points even spectacular. The river does pass through Radford and lesser populated areas, but one largely has the feeling of being removed from civilization. In and around Radford, which is just below Claytor Dam, the scenery is mostly poor, but it improves for the rest of this 45-mile section. Indeed, 20 miles below Claytor Dam (near Eggleston), the magnificent dolomite cliffs next to the river are spectacular. Also, the water quality is generally good; Claytor Lake has filtered out much of the dirt and trash.

There are some interesting stories associated with this river, which was a barrier to early settlers and the scene of some bridge burning during the Civil War. Just off the right side of the river and below Claytor Dam is an outdoor

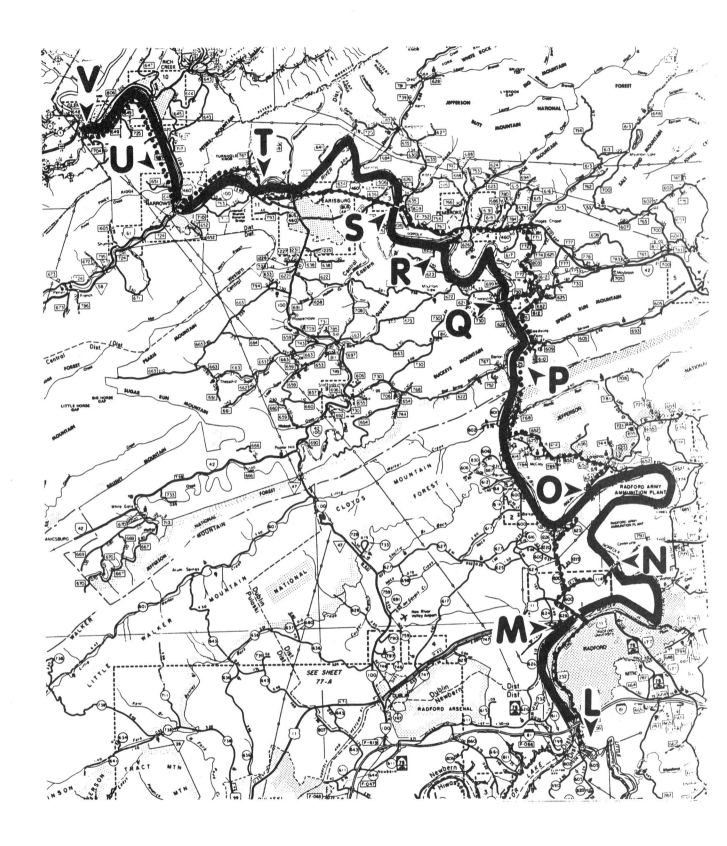

Section: Below Claytor Lake Dam (off Rt. 605) to Glen Lyn (US 460)

Counties: Giles, Montgomery, Pulaski

USGS Quads: Eggleston, Narrows, Pearisburg, Radford North, Radford South, Petersburg

Suitable for: Day cruising and overnight camping

Skill Level: Novices at moderate levels

Months Runnable: The entire year

Interest Highlights: Spectacular dolomite rock cliffs near Eggleston, fishing, camping

Scenery: Fair to beautiful in spots

Difficulty: Class I–II with 1 Class II–III and 1 Class III at moderate levels

Average Width: 200 to 300 feet

Velocity: Slow to moderate

Gradient: 5 feet per mile

Runnable Water Levels:
Minimum: None, river can be run the entire year
Maximum: High water; note that water level fluctuates substantially because of releases from hydropower plant at Claytor

Hazards: High water; unscheduled releases from hydropower plant at Claytor; Class II–III Arsenal Rapids (1 mile below Peppers Ferry Bridge/Rt. 114)—at high levels there is a protruding rock trap on the left side, so run right or center; Class III Narrows Falls, 1 mile below the Rt. 61 bridge at Narrows—a Class IV at high water

Scouting: Narrows Falls (Class III at moderate water and IV at high water), 1 mile below Rt. 61 bridge at Narrows (on left)

Portages: None, except perhaps Narrows Falls

Rescue Index: Accessible to remote

Source of Additional Information: New River Canoe Livery in Pembroke, Virginia (540) 626-7189

Access Points	River Miles	Shuttle Miles
L–M	4	6
M–N	4	3
N–O	6	10
O–P	3	5
P–Q	2	5
Q–R	8	12
R–S	2	4
S–T	8	8
T–U	4	4
U–V	4	4

Access Point Ratings:
L–Public boat landing (off Rt. 605) below Claytor Dam, excellent
M–Private boat landing (off Rt. 626 0.5 mile upstream from US 11), good
N–Peppers Ferry Bridge (Rt. 114), good
O–Whitethorne Public Boat Landing (Rt. 623), excellent
P–McCoy Falls (off Rt. 625), very good
Q–Near Eggleston (Rts. 730/622), very good
R–Pembroke (Rt. 623), good
S–Ripplemead (Rt. 636), good
T–Bluff City (Rt. 680), very good
U–Near Narrows, public boat landing (Rt. 649), excellent
V–Glen Lyn, public boat landing (US 460), excellent

theater where the story of Mary Ingles is told each summer. Mary, a pioneer woman, was captured by Indians near Radford and carried off to Ohio in 1755. She escaped and followed the New River back home. For more details see the play, *The Long Way Home*, about that brave lady at this outdoor theater.

While few and far apart, the rapids on this section of river merit care and caution. If you put in at the state launch facility below Claytor Dam, you will find a long but simple Class II beginning about 300 yards below the Interstate 81 bridge. Run this rapid in the center. About 7 miles downstream and above Peppers Ferry Bridge (Route 114) is another Class II, which at higher levels, sports an interesting whirlpool on the left side. Run this rapid center, too. You reach Peppers Ferry Bridge about 8 miles downstream of Claytor Dam.

Roughly 1 mile below Peppers Ferry Bridge are the infamous Arsenal Rapids. Several lives have been lost at these Class II–III rapids. At higher levels, near the bottom of this

drop, the river pounds furiously into a huge boulder jutting out from the left bank. So, avoid the left side like the plague! The easy route is on the right side as is the portage. However, it's more fun to run down the center of the river, where there are ledges to negotiate.

The 6-mile section of the river from Peppers Ferry Bridge to Whitethorne flows through the Radford Army Ammunition Plant. The banks of the river are fences, and you are not welcome on the land. However, be thankful that the plant failed in its attempt to prohibit river traffic on this navigable stream.

About 2 miles below Whitethorne is a series of small ledges. On the left side is the community of Parrott. These ledges are simple to run if you have enough water. Fishing in this area is excellent, too.

Another mile downriver is the misnamed Big Falls or McCoy Falls. The straightforward run of this Class II is on the right side. At higher levels, an ender hole develops at the bottom of this drop over toward the left side of the river. In warm weather, inner tubing attracts many students from nearby Radford University and Virginia Tech as well as anglers, other river users, and the local gendarmes. Be prepared for a crowd on warm summer weekends. McCoy Falls also gives access to the New via Route 625 on river right. About a mile below Big Falls is a good set of Class I–II ledges, and roughly a mile above Eggleston is a Class II–III ledge on the right of an island.

One of the most spectacular scenes on this river is the multicolored Paleozoic Knoxville dolomite cliffs which begin about 3 miles below Big Falls just after you pass Eggleston and the Route 730 bridge. Do pause to enjoy these 400-foot-high cliffs—particularly 3 miles below Eggleston where they form the right bank on a long horseshoe bend. The river is mostly quiet through here and into Pembroke, which is about 7 miles downstream as these scenic cliffs continue in less spectacular fashion. Then, below the bridge at Pembroke, is a long, fun Class II. In fact, 5 or 6 Class IIs occur in the 10-mile stretch between Pembroke and Bluff City—the best whitewater section of the river from Claytor Dam to West Virginia. These rapids consist of wave fields and are easy and fun to run. The last of these, Clendenin Shoals, is about 9 miles downstream from Pembroke and has a large, glassy wave on the left side that is great to surf. For the adventurous there is also a hungry hydraulic on the right side of a small ledge just above the bridge at Bluff City. It makes for interesting surfing and, usually, swimming.

For the final 8-mile section between Bluff City and Glen Lyn, the river is somewhat polluted and at its slowest, except for one rapid. That is Narrows Falls, located about 1 mile below the Route 61 bridge in Narrows. Be sure to get to shore to scout or carry this rapid when you see a concrete structure on the left bank. This is a genuine Class III drop at moderate levels in a narrow section of the river. This rapid becomes a Class IV at higher levels, so don't attempt it unless you are very good and have rescue capabilities. This short, choppy ledge is usually run by entering from the right and moving diagonally left toward the opening in the center. Expect to find large waves and squirrelly water here. Other routes are possible through this rapid, but they are more difficult.

The last take-out in Virginia is at the river left public boat landing at Glen Lyn 100 yards upstream from the US 460 bridge.

The striking Knox dolomite cliffs on the lower New near Eggleston. Photo by Ed Gertler.

Big Sandy

Russell Fork

Located in the southwest corner of Virginia, the Russell Fork is a river of extremes and superlatives. Its heart, the Breaks Section, is for expert Paddlers only. The Breaks Section flows through Virginia's spectacular Breaks Gorge—a fabulous gorge over 1,000 feet deep that cuts through Pine Ridge Mountain. This incredible chasm with giant vertical walls and pounding whitewater cuts across the Kentucky-Virginia border as the Russell Fork plunges through the mountains near Elkhorn City, Kentucky. First run in 1975, the Breaks Gorge sports nearly 2 miles of the most intense and dangerous Class IV–V+ whitewater in Virginia, gaining the river a national reputation for ferocity.

Nevertheless, the Russell Fork and the Breaks Section are worth a trip by every paddler—if only to peer into the gorge from the high overlooks of Breaks Interstate Park on river right. Breaks Interstate Park is on Route 702, which branches off from Route 80. More adventurous sightseers can also take the Clinchfield Railroad track from Pool Point Tunnel 1.5 miles upstream from Elkhorn City. The railroad crosses to river left just after this tunnel and provides easy hiking into the gorge. However, be very alert for trains and be particularly careful when walking through State Line Tunnel (one-third mile long) and Towers Tunnel (one-quarter mile long). You will be repaid for your hike by fantastic scenery and plenty of action on the river. The beauty of this gorge is truly awesome. Its depth, the gaily colored Pennsylvanian sandstone and the room-sized boulders in the river will captivate you.

Paddlers can put in on the Pound River (a tributary to Russell Fork) at the picnic area off Route 739 at the base of Flannagan Dam. This is a good Class II+ run with flows of 800 cfs or more from the dam. The 2 miles on the Pound

George Mower running Tower Falls of the Russell Fork. Photo by Jim Goddard.

Nolan Whitesell entering Climax Rapid on the Russell Fork.

run through a small wooded gorge with fun waves and playful holes.

There are usually a few downed trees in the river to watch out for but no major obstacles. This is a short, fun run for intermediates and experts alike. For hard core expert paddlers, the journey to or through the Breaks usually begins on river right by the Route 611 bridge, which crosses the river near the small community of Bartlick, Virginia. About 100 yards upstream of this bridge is the confluence of the Russell Fork and Pound Rivers. Just below this confluence and hiding beneath the Route 611 Bartlick bridge and its multiple spans is a sloping 4-foot dam. When running this dam, be sure to run under the second bridge span from the right. This channel has a break through the hydraulic below the dam at all levels. The other slots have very tenacious holes that might result in a nasty swim at most levels. This drop can be seen easily from the Bartlick bridge.

Incidentally, the history of the Bartlick bridge is interesting. The bridge piers were originally used to support gates forming a dam that was used to run logs through the gorge to Elkhorn City. And you thought paddling this river was tough! There is a Corps of Engineers gauge located near the Bartlick bridge below the Russell Fork-Pound confluence. However, you can't read this gauge yourself, but must call the John Flannagan Dam at (540) 835-1438, where you can get recorded cfs readings and the Bartlick gauge in feet.

Below the bridge, the river begins to pick up gradient and the next 3 miles are laced with Class I–III rapids. This section passes through a wide Pennsylvanian sandstone gorge with some beautiful scenery. Each rapid improves over the one

preceding it, plunging through longer and steeper mazes of sandstone boulders and ledges. The scenery maintains a similar pattern and pace with increasingly high and ornate riverside cliffs and rising canyon slopes.

Then the gorge opens up somewhat, and at the end of one large pool, a road can be seen on river right. This pool is called the Garden Hole and serves as the last-chance take-out for the 3- to 5-mile intermediate upper section or as an alternate put-in for the 5- to 7-mile expert run through the Breaks Gorge. The road is controlled by the National Park Service and is open May through October from dawn until 9:00 p.m.

From Garden Hole, the river begins to carve its 1,000-foot deep gorge through the Breaks of Pine Mountain. As the gradient increases markedly and steep sandstone walls rise on both sides, the Russell Fork pounds its way along a giant semicircular loop. Here, hidden by the shadows of the gorge, is a hellish continuum of thundering vertical drops and foam-blasted boulder gardens.

Those entering the Breaks gorge should note that this is very serious technical whitewater. The drops are tight, the water is pushy, and the portages can be difficult. In the heart of this gorge you have Class V–V+ rapids connected by Class IV drops. The rapids of the Breaks are extremely dangerous because so many of its rocks are undercut. This is no place for a swim. It would be very wise to make your first trip with someone who has run the river and knows it well.

As you approach a huge rock cliff on river left, you reach Entrance, a Class IV drop that begins with sloping ledge and ends with a wave/hole. The river then runs over a boulder ledge. Entrance is best run straight down the center or by making a dogleg to the left through the first chute right of center. Before committing yourself, you can scout Entrance from an eddy near the center or an eddy on the right.

The river pools below this drop, and you are looking at the towers rock formation on your left. Much harder to spot is Loop Overlook of Breaks Interstate Park on the right, high above. The next rapid is appropriately named Tower Falls. This Class V drop can be run conservatively near the rocks on the left off a 15-foot sloping ledge or, more heroically, down the center over a 10-foot vertical ledge. Rafts take the left route—about two raft-widths from the

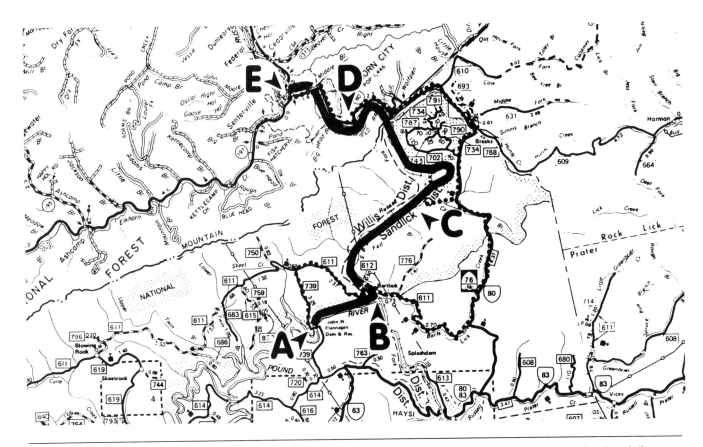

Section: Below Flannagan Dam on the Pound River (Rt. 739) to Elkhorn City, Kentucky (Rt. 197)

Counties: Dickenson (VA), Pike (KY)

USGS Quads: Haysi, Elkhorn City

Suitable for: Day cruising

Skill Level: Experts, except intermediate paddlers can do the 5 miles from Flannagan Dam to just before the beginning of the Breaks Gorge (Garden Hole) at moderate levels (e.g., 800 cfs)

Months Runnable: In fall (October) during Flannagan Dam release and through the spring (occasionally) with natural runoff

Interest Highlights: Incredible Breaks Gorge with its miles of world class whitewater

Scenery: Exceptionally beautiful to spectacular

Difficulty: Class II–III from Flannagan Dam to above the Breaks gorge; Class IV-V+ in the Breaks Gorge

Average Width: 35 to 100 feet

Velocity: Fast!

Gradient: 5 to 180 feet per mile

Runnable Water Levels:
  Minimum: 8.4 feet on Bartlick gauge or 800 cfs (good-first time canoeists); 9.3 feet or 1,350 cfs is optimal for experts

Maximum: 9.5 feet or 1,500 cfs is very pushy, though there have been runs at 10 feet or 2,000 cfs by experts

Hazards: The entire Breaks Gorge can be hazardous to your body and boat. In particular, Fist, Twist and Shout, and Red Cliff/Climax are technical, hard to scout, and difficult to carry. Make your first trip with someone who has run the river and knows it well!

Scouting: See Hazards

Portages: See Hazards; most likely carries are the first drop of Triple Drop, El Horrendo, and Climax

Rescue Index: Remote; accessible only by railroad and steep trails from Breaks Interstate Park

Source of Additional Information: John Flannagan Dam for cfs and Bartlick gauge (540) 835-1438 (recording 24 hrs); (540) 835-9544 or 835-9824 (live 7:30 to 4 pm, Mon-Fri)

Access Points	River Miles	Shuttle Miles
A–B	2	4
B–C	3	9
C–D	5	7
C–E	7	9

Access Point Ratings:
A–Flannagan Dam on Pound River (off Rt. 739) ,good
B–Bartlick bridge (Rt. 611), very good
C–at Garden Hole (National Park Service road), good
D–Ford Rd. off Rt. 80, 2 mi. upstream of Rt. 197, good.
E–Elkhorn City, Kentucky (Rt. 197), very good.

Roger Zbel in the last drop of Triple Drop on the Russell Fork. Photo by Jim Goddard.

left shore. (The right side of this drop looks like a sneak route but don't be tempted: this is a very easy place to wrap a boat.) Tower Falls is scouted from a table rock just above the rapid. This is also the place to scout Fist—the powerful Class V rapid just after Tower Falls.

There is a small pool below Tower Falls. The river then continues at a Class III–IV rate and quickly drops into Fist—a large 6-foot sloping ledge with a hole at the bottom. The right side of the hole piles into a large mound of rocks called (naturally) The Fist. Just below this hole on the left is a house-sized undercut boulder. There is a slot off the right corner of this boulder, which is the only place to run this Class V drop. Below Fist, the river slacks up for about one-quarter mile as you run several Class II–III rapids.

If you feel uneasy now, do not look to the railroad for escape because it has slithered off into the relative security of Towers Tunnel during this trying period. As the gorge begins to narrow, the river becomes boulder choked. The railroad eventually emerges from Towers Tunnel, but the roar you keep hearing is not the train. The river now funnels through Twist and Shout, which you can boat scout. This Class V rock garden is a complex, steep slalom through a maze of large boulders with deceptively powerful crosscurrents and deceptively weak eddies. Do not botch Twist and Shout because it washes into an even more difficult rapid—Triple Drop.

Class V+ Triple Drop consists of three major ledges in which the river drops over 30 feet! These three drops can be run without catching an eddy, if you don't get stuck in the hole at the bottom of the first drop. For those who get

stuck in this hole, the penalty is often a very nasty swim for the next two drops. To avoid this penalty you can easily portage the first drop on the left. Scout Triple Drop from river left, taking out just below the concrete retaining wall. Rafts will have a difficult time catching the small Three Kayak eddy here, so a safety rope should be set.

Triple Drop starts with a river-wide, sloping, 5-foot ledge into a churning, powerful stopper/keeper. Run the top stopper on the far right where it breaks slightly. This is a real power move, so be cranking when you try it. The second drop is a narrow chute, which drops 12 feet as it moves right to left. Eddy left below the second drop. The most conservative route for the third drop is over a 10-foot waterfall on the left. The heavy duty route is the right side of the third drop—a two-stage drop with some very strong currents.

It was Triple Drop where the "Massacre of '87" occurred according to David Brown of Knoxville, Tennessee. On that fateful October day, over 80 paddlers reached the top of Triple Drop in a steady stream. With the top small (Three Kayak) eddy quickly filled, boaters were forced to run the first drop in lemming-like fashion. Barrages of throw ropes were continually launched to stem the steady flow of bodies (along with the debris of boats, paddles, floatation and other gear) that washed through the last two drops. Fortunately, no one was seriously hurt.

The river flows through a large pool below Triple Drop before entering Dave's Rapids (also known as Screamer)—a long, visibly open, steep complex. Enter Dave's Rapids (Class IV+) on river right, move to river left, and run down the left bank. This rapid can be scouted

Brian Homburg dropping into the maw of El Horrendo on the Russell Fork. Photo by Bill Millard.

from the right or boat scouted as you eddy hop. There is a large pool below this rapid, which runs into El Horrendo.

El Horrendo is awesome! Fortunately, there is an easy scout or carry on river right. For the intrepid, El Horrendo is a Class V++, two-stage ledge system, which drops 25 feet and is best entered on the extreme left of the river by dropping over a 5 foot ledge into a small but calm eddy. The second ledge involves a fast and committed ferry across the nearly 100-foot-wide channel to the far right side of the river. This ferry is done above, through, or below a generally benign hydraulic. At higher water it is best for rafts to run the first ledge on river right. The big drop is no problem if you enter far enough right. The entire left side is a powerful drop into a thick boulder pile suitable for serious bodily injury. Run as far right as possible to catch the 6-foot-wide chute. The best spot for rafts is one to two raft widths off the right bank. This trip through heavy but aerated water is a guaranteed adrenalin pump. Paddlers who have run the second drop liken it to a deep (blub) religious experience! Rafts should get right at the bottom of El Horrendo because of an undercut ledge on the left.

Below El Horrendo, the Russell Fork moves through Class IV Fling Falls (also known as Little El Horrendo, Little Heinzerling, or Twister) and begins a twisting descent through Red Cliff Rapids (also known as S-Turn)—so named for the sandstone cliffs on river right. Scout Fling Falls from river left.

Red Cliff Rapids begin as a solid Class V rock garden with 3- to 7-foot ledges. There are several routes through, but if you don't know them, scout Red Cliff from river right.

After a moving pool with an eddy on the right, the last drop of Red Cliff Rapids is appropriately called Climax—a Class V++ steep ledge complex dropping 14 feet. (For rafts, the most conservative approach to Climax is to stay right for the three drops through Red Cliff until the eddy above Climax.) Climax is the largest ledge and has a well-deserved reputation of being tricky and dangerous. You can scout Climax from the rocks on the right after eddying out. The route is down the center slot through a diagonal hole, then over a smaller ledge and hole. The diagonal is the nasty culprit in this drop. You can very easily flip in it, and it is a guaranteed head knocker. Broken fingers, noses, glasses, helmets, and egos are common casualties resulting from a screw-up on this ledge. Do not try the left slot at Climax: it has generated nothing but horror stories by those who inadvertently have paddled or swum that way. After Climax, the river loses most of its steam and mellows to a fun Class II–III run for a couple of miles. There is a ford road takeout on river right near a trailer court just below Route 80. Alternatively, you can go 2 miles farther downstream and take out either at the right end of the Route 197 bridge in Elkhorn City or on the left at the police and fire station. The 2 miles above Route 197 are Class II with one Class III a half mile before Elkhorn City. Both the steep road and boat ramp below Route 80 and the Route 197 take-out recently have been improved by Pike County.

Most paddlers run the Breaks during October weekend water releases that have been scheduled with the Corps of Engineers during the annual fall drawdown of Flannagan Reservoir. The optimum for expert decked boaters is 9.3 feet on the Bartlick gauge, which is 1,350 cfs. The gorge can be run from a very technical 8.4 feet (800 cfs) to a very dangerous 10 feet (2,000 cfs). A good range for highly experienced rafters is 800 to 1,600 cfs, although some decked boaters think the gorge is getting boney at 1,000 cfs (9 feet) and very pushy at 1,500 cfs (9.5 feet). A couple of hundred cfs can make a whale of a difference on the difficult heart of this run so be careful. The upper section from Bartlick to Garden Hole can be run at any level from 8.4 feet (800 cfs) for this upper section.

A typical series of drops on the spectacular Russell Fork. Photo by Ed Gertler.

Tracy Turner entering El Horrendo on the Russell Fork at 800 cfs. Photo by Mayo Gravatt.

Tracy Turner in the jaws of El Horrendo —they treated him kindly. Photo by Mayo Gravatt.

Tennessee

Big Moccasin Creek

Big Moccasin Creek flows west along the north side of Clinch Mountain in Russell and Scott counties and then turns south through Moccasin Gap to quickly reach its confluence with the North Fork of the Holston River. Moccasin Gap is the only break through the entire 125-mile length of Clinch Mountain. Also, Moccasin Gap is where Daniel Boone in 1775 created the Wilderness Road to Bonnesboro, Kentucky, thus opening the way for settlement west of the Appalachians.

Big Moccasin is a very small stream and generally can be paddled only in the winter and spring. Venturesome paddlers can put in at any of a half dozen access points on Route 613 in the 15 miles between the Russell County line and New Hope Church. The only hazard is a 10-foot dam 1 mile upstream of New Hope Church.

However, the best of this creek is the 20 miles between new Hope Church and Slabtown. Mostly, this is a novice run that goes through open pastureland in a fairly wide valley. The one exception is the 3-mile gorge just below Snowflake; this is for intermediate paddlers at moderate levels.

Indeed, the first 10-mile stretch of this creek, from New Hope Church to Snowflake, is quite peaceful. This section is virtually flat as it passes through Big Moccasin Valley's rocky farms and pastures. On your left is 3,000-foot-high Clinch Mountain while on your right is Moccasin Ridge (800 feet lower). The Class I–II rapids on this first section are mostly gentle ledges, although there are a few cobble bars. This is a nifty shuttle: for only 4 miles on Route 613, you get 10 miles of creek. The creek bumps against the road (Route 613), which also crosses Big Moccasin in several places. The only danger is 10-foot McConnell Mill Dam (off Route 687) just over 4 miles below the put-in at New Hope Church. Please carry on the left because the right bank is a cliff.

Things change at Snowflake. The 6-mile section from Snowflake to Antioch Church at Route 669 is for alert intermediate paddlers at reasonable water levels. The best put-in for this section is just upstream of the Snowflake Post Office and General Store on Route 671. At Snowflake the valley narrows and the creek starts to drop more quickly. This is also the most wooded portion of the creek. The gradient more than doubles to 28 feet per mile, and the rapids move up a notch in intensity. Soon below Snowflake, Big Moccasin enters a 3-mile Ordovician limestone gorge and the rapids are now steady Class II ledges. Then, after a vigorous low Class III ledge, comes Charlie's Shoulder. It is the biggest rapid of the trip and occurs about 3 miles below Snowflake where Big Moccasin makes a sharp right turn and high bluffs form the left bank. This drop of three ledges (two 3-footers followed by a 5-footer) is by far the most fun at moderate levels (Class III+), but it becomes the most hazardous rapid on the creek at high water (Class IV) because of a very tenacious hydraulic below the last ledge. It should be scouted at all water levels from river right. The portage is also on the right. Generally, the best route over these ledges is center. However, at high water, be sure you are really lined up and cranking hard to punch the hole below the last ledge. The picture below graphically shows how

Fellow paddlers treating Charlie LeBlanc's dislocated shoulder after his encounter with the hole below the five foot ledge on Big Moccasin Creek. Note that Charlie's boat is still surfing this hole. Photo by Terry Dougherty.

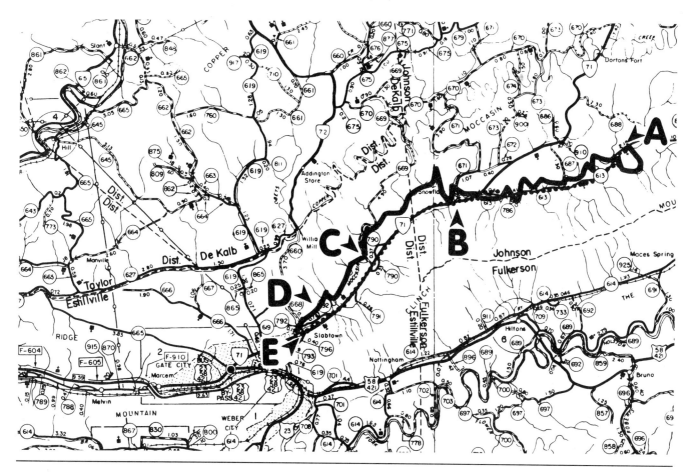

Section: New Hope Church (Rt. 613), or Snowflake (Rt. 671), to Slabtown (Rt. 792 above dam or Rt. 71 below dam)

Counties: Scott

USGS Quads: Mendota, Hilton, Gate City

Suitable for: Day cruising

Skill Level: Novices above Snowflake; intermediates from Snowflake to Antioch Church; novices from Antioch Church to Slabtown

Months Runnable: Winter and spring, generally

Interest Highlights: Pastoral farmland, some woods and cliffs

Scenery: Pretty to beautiful in spots

Difficulty: Class I–II, except gorge just below Snowflake is solid Class II with 1 Class III and 1 Class III–IV rapid

Average Width: 30 to 50 feet

Velocity: Moderate to fast

Gradient: 12 feet per mile above Snowflake; 28 feet per mile between Snowflake and Antioch Church; 22 feet from Antioch Church to Slabtown

Runnable Water Levels:
Minimum: No gauge; if runnable at put-in, is runnable for entire trip

Maximum: Full banks approaching flood stage

Hazards: 10-foot dam 4 miles below New Hope Church; 10-foot dam just above Slabtown; occasional trees in river; Charlie's Shoulder at high water

Scouting: Charlie's Shoulder (Class III–IV) on river right

Portages: 10-foot dam 4 miles below New Hope Church; 10-foot dam at Slabtown; perhaps Charlie's Shoulder at high water, on river right

Rescue Index: Accessible above Snowflake and below gorge; remote in gorge

Source of Additional Information: None

Access Points	River Miles	Shuttle Miles
A–B	10	4
B–C	6	2.5
C–D	4	2.5
C–E	4.5	3

Access Point Ratings:
A—New Hope Church (Rt. 613), good
B—Snowflake (Rt. 671), good
C—Antioch Church (Rt. 669), good
D—at Slabtown (Rt. 792), good
E—at Slabtown (Rt. 71), good

Charlie's got its name. In it, Charlie LeBlanc's right shoulder is dislocated and being treated while his canoe is still trapped in the rapids. It took about 30 minutes to get the boat out. At lower water levels, Charlie's is a notch easier because the keeper hydraulic loses its punch.

After this excitement, the river returns to Class II ledges, which become more mellow as you continue downstream to the next take-out on river right at Antioch Church. If you do the 4 miles below Antioch Church, you will find that the distance between the drops increases as they become even more gentle. I suggest that you take-out on Route 792 about a half mile upstream of the 10-foot dam at Slabtown. The alternative is a portage on the left by this dam and a nearby mill to a take-out on new or old Route 71 just below Slabtown. I do not recommend that you paddle farther downstream to Gate City and then Weber City. Although Moccasin Gap is exciting as it slices 1,000 feet into Clinch Mountain, there are man-made hazards, such as wiers and low-water bridges, and the scenery is not as nice.

This area is also the site of Houstons Fort, the first settlement in Scott County. The original settlement of 1769 was abandoned in 1771 because inhabitants feared an Indian attack. A fort was constructed in 1774 by William Houston to protect settlers. However, in 1776 a large force of Cherokee Indians attacked the fort, killing and scalping at least one person.

Overall, Big Moccasin Creek is a delightful and scenic springtime canoeing stream with Charlie's Shoulder rapid a real challenge to boaters at high water. There are fish here, too. Anglers can try their luck for smallmouth bass, rock bass, and sunfish.

Clinch River

The New River divides Virginia into two vastly unequal parts. East of the New River, most of the Commonwealth drains to the Atlantic primarily via the Shenandoah, Potomac, and James Rivers. The New River cuts off the western tip of the state as it flows north to the Ohio River. This tip of Virginia, west from Wytheville and Bluefield, is on the Cumberland Plateau and contains the headwaters of the Tennessee River.

In this Tennessee watershed, the Clinch River rises on the north side of Clinch Mountain, near Tazewell in southwest Virginia. The three forks of the Holston rise to the south, near Marion, in the big valley between Clinch Mountain and Mount Rogers. The Clinch and Holston flow southeast to Knoxville, Tennessee, where the Holston joins the French Broad to become the Tennessee River. The Clinch starts out small, but by the time it joins the Tennessee River below Knoxville, it is a big, powerful, slow moving river.

In early times, the Clinch was a river of commerce and transportation as well as a source of food. As late as the early 1900s, this river was still a primary means for getting the logs from the vast forests of southwest Virginia to big mills in Chattanooga. In springtime, large rafts of logs were formed near Clinchport and floated down to the sawmills. The arduous trip would take several weeks.

However, because the upper Clinch is an undammed river, it is prone to flooding, and for many of the towns along the river, periodic inundation is a way of life. A good example of this is the former town of Clinchport. In its heyday, Clinchport coped with high water in a variety of ways. One of the more novel devices was elevated wooden sidewalks. These kept folks' feet dry while crossing some parts of the town, even though homes and businesses elsewhere were flooded. Finally, there was one flood too many and the Clinchporters gave up. With the help of the Tennessee Valley Authority they pulled out. Gone are the restaurants, beauty shops, car dealers, department store, drugstore, the bank, and 75 private homes. Some folks moved to a model community established by TVA, but others just disappeared. Other towns have also given up along the Clinch, but none on the scale of Clinchport.

Even though the Clinch does not plunge through a wild and uninhabited gorge, it is still a river of striking scenic beauty. Its banks and shoals provide habitat for many wildlife species. For example, just below Fort Blackmore, the Nature Conservancy has made a preserve out of Pendleton Island because over 40 species of pearly mussels live there. Pendleton Island is discussed in more detail under the Dungannon-Kyles Ford section of the Clinch.

Because the Clinch watershed endures only a small amount of coal mining and very little agriculture, the river is relatively clean and there is a thriving fish population. Indeed, the Clinch supports one of the most diverse riverline fauna in the world—more than 100 species live on this river. The fish in the Clinch, like those elsewhere, can be lured to self-destruction with the correct bait, correctly placed, at the correct time. There is an abundance of game fish (mainly smallmouth bass, channel and yellow catfish, and bluegill sunfish) and rough fish (carp and suckers) along the entire length of the river. By far the most frequently observed activity on the river is fishing. Incidentally, strange as it seems, shooting fish on portions of the Clinch is still legal. It is the only river in Virginia where this practice is allowed.

The Clinch is also very accessible. Courtesy of the TVA and Virginia Game Commission there are convenient boat landings every 6 to 10 miles on the Clinch from Honaker (Route 80) to the Tennessee line.

Much of the Clinch is suitable for canoe camping and most sections can be run the entire year except during severe drought or flood conditions. For the most part, the Clinch is a gentle river. There are only two sections containing rapids that can be a challenge to shepherded novices at moderate levels. One section is above Cleveland between Pucketts Hole and Nash Ford. The other section is between St. Paul and Dungannon.

Pucketts Hole to Nash Ford

For the paddler, the tenderloin of the upper Tennessee drainage in Virginia is the South Fork of the Holston below Damascus and the Clinch above Nash Ford. By the time it reaches Cleveland in Russell County, the Clinch is one of the bigger little streams in the state, with a mean annual flow of 714 cfs. Compare it with the South Fork of the Holston at Damascus (481 cfs), the Bullpasture at Williamsville (142 cfs), the Tye at Roseland (131 cfs), and the Maury at Rockbridge Baths (364 cfs). Because of this larger size, the Clinch holds up well past Memorial Day, when the smaller streams have been reduced to trickles.

There are two put-ins at Pucketts Hole. In dry weather only, put in just above the Route 652 bridge on river left for an extra half mile of river and one nice ledge before the Virginia Game Commission put-in. Downstream the river suffers some typical Appalachian civilization abuses until it turns left, away from the last house on the right, and enters the wilderness.

This is a mountain river with a rock bottom, not sand or silt. It also is "Ledge City." There are hundreds of little ledges, ranging from 1 to 6 inches high and arrayed in every possible angle. At low water, these provide a clinic in precision paddling; at higher water, the smaller ledges wash out while their larger cousins provide chutes, eddies, and waves.

In the upper half of the trip, there is a plethora of good campsites, mostly on river right. Also on river right in places are the remains of an old, hand-laid stone wall. The purpose of this wall is not evident, but its antiquity is. Except near the put-in and at one civilized spot downstream, the scenery ranges from good to splendid. In the latter category, look particularly for the high cliffs, both at the river and on the slopes of the gorge.

Unfortunately, the Clinch also is an Appalachian river, i.e., every collection of driftwood on the banks is punctuated with plastic milk jugs. The clear water makes it harder to fool the fish with a lure but impossible to overlook the beer cans on the bottom. Wherever a road comes near the river, some thoughtless natives have followed the Appalachian custom of connecting the two

with a stream of trash. This stream is lean on junked cars, probably because of its remoteness, but fat with floating trash. Sigh!

About halfway through the trip, the river passes a pasture on the right with a shed and several piles of firewood. It then enters a little gorge with the longest rapids and fastest water of the trip. Whoopee! Then Cedar Creek enters on the left, to warn the paddler of the Big Stuff. Immediately below the junction, there is a Class III series of ledges, dropping 5 feet in about 30 yards. This formation is mostly washed out on river right where it can be run as a long "swooooshhhhhh," followed by a couple of small ledges. On river left, there are bigger ledges, dry at low water and trouble for the unwary at high water.

Still farther downstream, after a beautiful rock wall on the right, a low rumble announces Class III Double Ledge. This is a pair of ledges (1-foot and 2-foot) about two boat-lengths apart. At low water, the obvious way to run this is on the left, where the upper ledge has a pair of slots and the lower has a bit of a tongue. Unfortunately, the

Running Double Ledge between Pucketts Hole and Nash Ford on the Clinch. Photo by John Heerwald.

Section: Pucketts Hole (Rt. 652) to Nash Ford (Rt. 798 at Rt. 645)

Counties: Russell

USGS Quads: Lebanon, Elk Garden

Suitable for: Day cruising and camping

Skill Level: Shepherded novices and relaxed intermediates

Months Runnable: Winter, spring, and early summer

Interest Highlights: Scenic mountain river, dynamite fishing

Scenery: Pretty to beautiful

Difficulty: Class I–II (with 2 Class III rapids)

Average Width: 100 feet

Velocity: Moderate

Gradient: 15 feet per mile

Runnable Water Levels:
 Minimum: 350 cfs at Cleveland gauge
 Maximum: 3,000 cfs at Cleveland gauge

Hazards: Occasional downed trees; pinning rock at lower ledge of Double Ledge in low water

Scouting: Double Ledge (from left)

Portages: Class III Double Ledge for novices

Rescue Index: Remote

Source of Additional Information: Russell County road map; gauge at Cleveland (615) 632-2264 and then press 3 on touch tone phone; Virginia Game Commission (ask for their state map)

Access Points	River Miles	Shuttle Miles
A–B	9	8.5

Access Point Ratings:
 A–Pucketts Hole (Rt. 652), good
 B–Nash Ford (Rts. 798/645), good

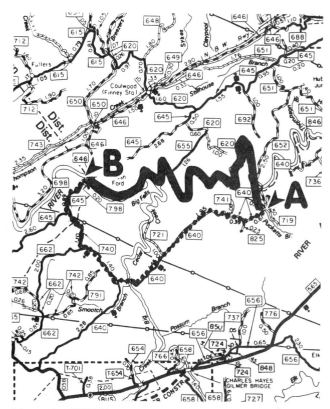

Mountain Wildlife Management Area (open April to Thanksgiving). Drive east from Lebanon on US 19. About 5 miles from the Bonanza Steak House (good food!) east of Lebanon, turn right on Route 80. Now comes the fun part: follow Route 80 up Clinch Mountain; continue to follow Route 80 down Clinch Mountain. Turn left on Route 613 at Hyters Gap. Follow Route 613 a few miles and then turn left again on Route 747. Do not be tempted to stop at the Rainbow Campground. Instead, follow the dirt road and Big Tumbling Creek back up Clinch Mountain. If the concession stand is open, pay there (5 bucks—cheap!); if not, the headquarters is on up the road. Persevere! The campground is almost 30 minutes from Route 613 (longer if you turn off to look at Laurel Bed Lake or if your driver wants to look at the beautiful trout stream alongside the road).

Cleveland to Carterton

From Cleveland to Carterton, the Clinch offers an easy, 7-mile novice day-trip with fair scenery, excellent fishing, and an opportunity to observe the depredations of the Appalachian Power Company.

With its sister streams of the upper Tennessee River basin (the Powell and North, Middle, and South Forks of the Holston), the Clinch is home to indigenous pearly mussels. The molluscan fauna of the Cumberland Plateau is unusually diverse and the Clinch is the richest and most diverse mussel habitat of the area, if not the entire planet. The prime habitat in the Clinch is downstream toward

tongue is shallow and its foam conceals a flat rock that will pin any aluminum boat with its bow in the tongue and its stern on the ledge. Bad news! ABS grease boats, with momentum, should be OK. At higher water, the ledges are just ledges, due the deference their size commands. In any case, there is a nice, grassy bank on the left for scouting and portage. After Double Ledge, it's decrescendo to Nash Ford and the take-out.

If you don't mind a long drive in the mountains (1.25 hours from Lebanon) and would like to stay at the finest state campground around (except for Audra, West Virginia), plan to spend a night at the primitive campground at the Virginia Game Commission's Clinch

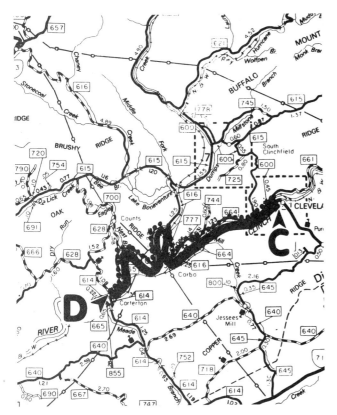

Section: Cleveland to Carterton

Counties: Russell

USGS Quads: Carbo

Suitable for: Day cruising

Skill Level: Must know which end is the bow

Months Runnable: Entire year, except in particularly dry summers

Interest Highlights: Apco's electric generating plant at Carbo; good fishing; endangered freshwater pearly mussels

Scenery: Fair to pretty in spots

Difficulty: Class A– I

Average Width: 80 feet

Velocity: Moderate

Gradient: 4 feet per mile

Runnable Water Levels:
  Minimum: 200 cfs at Cleveland for canoeing (serious anglers can tolerate less)
  Maximum: Until it spoils the fishing; flood stage

Hazards: An occasional tree in river

Scouting: None

Portages: None

Rescue Index: Accessible

Source of Additional Information: Gauge at Cleveland (615) 632-2264 and then press 3 on touch tone phone; Virginia Game Commission (ask for their state map)

Access Points	River Miles	Shuttle Miles
C–D	7	7

Access Point Ratings:
  C–at Cleveland on Rt. 210 near Rt. 664, excellent
  D–at Carterton near Rt. 614, good

Tennessee, particularly near Fort Blackmore and the Nature Conservancy preserve at Pendelton Island—where over 40 species live. (The entire continent of Europe only hosts 12 species.) Nonetheless, there are abundant mussels at Cleveland, including three species that are classified as endangered by federal and state law: the shiny pigtoe, the fine-rayed pigtoe, and the birdwing.

The sex life of these creatures is worth a paragraph here. As the water warms in the spring, the male mussel emits his sperm into the river. A downstream female can collect the sperm from the water with her intake siphon to fertilize the eggs in her gills. The eggs then hatch to larvae that, in turn, are ejected into the river. The few, fortunate larvae that pass through the gills of the right kind of fish (generally a different species for each species of mussel) can attach to the gills and exist as parasites until they mature and metamorphose into mussels. The microscopic (typically 0.15 mm) mussels then drop free and fall to the bottom. Those that land on a cobble bottom in riffle/run areas of the river have a chance to survive to reproduce and complete the cycle. Although the mussels have a foot, they rarely move more than a few yards. Thus, Mr. and Mrs. Mussel probably never meet.

There are several riffle areas downstream of Cleveland that offer good mussel habitat. Live mussels are hard to find without equipment and knowhow: all that shows is the tip of the shell and the siphon that the animal uses to take in river water. The usual clue to mussel habitat is a clean, cobble bottom and the presence of the shells, with the characteristic pearly inside surface. The muskrats and herons see to it that part of the population is converted to shells each year. There are plenty of mussels below Cleveland.

About 3 miles below Cleveland, the river passes beneath a railroad bridge at Carbo and turns north to enter Kiser Bend. On the inside of the bend (river left) is the Clinch River Plant, a 720,000 coal-fired steam electric plant owned by Appalachian Power (Apco). Apco takes up to 14 million gallons per day from the river, depending on the weather, primarily as makeup water for its cooling towers.

Just below the Apco intake structure on river left, Dumps Creek enters on river right. The dismal water quality of this aptly named creek is due to the upstream coal processing operations and to the leaking fly ash impoundments of Apco. In June, 1967, an Apco fly ash impoundment ruptured, depositing some 198 million cubic meters of alkaline fly ash slurry (pH 12) into Dumps Creek and the Clinch. The discharge killed 162,000 fish in the Virginia portion of the river (66 miles) and another 54,000 fish in Tennessee (24 miles). The fish moved right back in so that Apco's June, 1970, sulfuric acid spill at Carbo could kill another 5,300 fish in the Clinch. Downstream of Dumps Creek and spaced around the north end of Kiser Bend, Apco has three other major wastewater discharges on the left bank of the Clinch.

Just below the plant and still alongside the plant fence, there is a long, straight run of prime mussel habitat in a straight stretch of river running south. On river right, there is a healthy population of mussels that have reestablished themselves since the 1967 and 1970 spills. There are no mussels on river left, and attempts to import mussels here uniformly fail. Farther downstream, after the Apco discharges have a chance to mix across the stream, there are hardly any mussels for about 20 miles.

For over 3 miles downstream from the Apco plant, the Clinch meanders through small, wooded mountains, with only the N&W railroad on the left and the dirt road and Apco's fly ash landfill on the right to distract the paddler. This is the prettiest part of the run, and it should have the best fishing. Too soon, the river passes under the Route 614 bridge at Carterton and the paddler runs the only significant rapids of the trip, a small ledge (Class I if you run it on the inside of the turn where you belong), just before the take-out at the Virginia Game Commission landing on the left. (WARNING: Be alert for an occasional tree. Several years ago, the small channel on river right under the Route 614 bridge had a downed tree completely blocking it, making a terminal strainer for the unwary.)

Saint Paul to Dungannon

The last classic whitewater section of the Clinch is the 18-mile stretch from Saint Paul to Dungannon. This is a very scenic part of the Clinch with pretty mountain vistas and few intrusions. Indeed, the valley here is very remote and contains cliffs, woods, and numerous good campsites. Although there are strip mines in the area, very few are visible from the river. Fishing also continues to be great so break out your rod and be ready to challenge muskie, smallmouth bass, and redeye sunfish.

The Class I–II whitewater is mild but perhaps more constant than the section from Pucketts Hole to Nash Ford. The rapids are cobble bars, rock gardens, and ledges. At

high water some of these drops probably reach Class III. The average gradient for this section is 13 feet per mile. Although there are some slow moving pools, you mostly have a good current. The occasional ledges are generally 2 to 3 feet and one is even 4 feet. At higher water there are some good 2-to 3-foot standing waves. The Saint Paul put-in at the Virginia Game Commission landing at Memorial Park is quite good. This launching point is just upstream of US 58 on river right.

A mile or so below Saint Paul there is a solid 4-foot Class III ledge across the river. At low water you'll find some nice chutes, but at high water the hydraulic below this ledge could be dangerous.

The area around Carfax (over 8 miles below Saint Paul) has some of the best rapids. They are mostly chutes through 2-to 3-foot ledges and good standing waves as the river sweeps by the edge of high cliffs. None of these rapids require scouting from the bank at moderate levels.

Just over 2 miles below Carfax, the heavy duty Guest River (which drops 160 feet in an eye-popping 1-mile section, also described in this chapter) dumps into the Clinch. It would be nice if the Clinch had just a little of the Guest's gradient to add a little more spice to this trip.

The remaining 6 miles to Dungannon can be bypassed by using a take-out on the south side (river left) at Miller Yard. This take-out can be accessed by taking Route 716 about 3 miles east of Dungannon on Route 65. Route 716 crosses a very scenic high bluff and then plunges 700 vertical feet to the river just south of Miller Yard. You can also reach Miller Yard on the north side of the river. However, I don't recommend this because there is a steep bank here, and you will have to get permission to cross private property.

Another option for shortening the 18 miles between Saint Paul and Dungannon is to start at Burtons Ford, 5 miles downstream from Saint Paul. You can get to this put-in by turning north on Route 611 at Mew about 3 miles west of Castlewood High School on Route 65. Follow Route 611 to the river just after a railroad underpass. Use Burtons Ford only if you have no aversion to cans, bottles, and assorted litter. This trashy put-in is an exception to the general cleanliness of the Clinch. Also, Burtons Ford is on private property, so get permission first.

In the last 6 miles before you reach Dungannon you pass a nationally significant geological formation on river left about one-quarter mile away from the river. This is Polje Karst—a large limestone sinkhole area. You can see this as you drive along Route 65 several miles east of Dungannon by the aptly named Sinking Creek.

The take-out at Dungannon is on river left downstream of an abandoned bridge below Route 65.

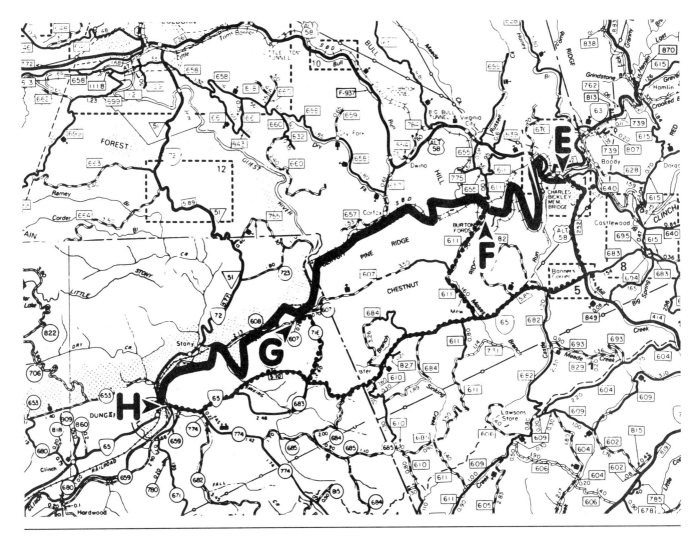

Section: Saint Paul (US 58) to Dungannon (near Rt. 65)

Counties: Wise, Russell, Scott

USGS Quads: St. Paul, Coeburn, Dungannon

Suitable for: Day cruising

Skill Level: Novices

Months Runnable: Winter, spring, and early summer

Interest Highlights: Pretty mountain vistas, fishing

Scenery: Pretty to beautiful in spots

Difficulty: Class I–II at moderate levels with 1 Class III

Average Width: 60 to 90 feet

Velocity: Moderate

Gradient: 13 feet per mile

Runnable Water Levels:
  Minimum: No gauge; if runnable at put-in, should be runnable for entire trip

Maximum: Flood stage

Hazards: Maybe an occasional tree

Scouting: None

Portages: None

Rescue Index: Accessible to remote

Source of Additional Information: None

Access Points	River Miles	Shuttle Miles
E–F	5	8
F–G	7	10
G–H	6	6

Access Point Ratings:
E—at St. Paul (US 58), excellent
F—at Burtons Ford (Rt. 611), good
G—at Millers Yard (Rt. 716), good
H—at Dungannon (near Rt. 65), good

Dungannon (near Route 65) to Kyles Ford (Route 70)

All sections of the Clinch below Cleveland are suitable for canoe camping. This is particularly true for the 47 miles between Dungannon and Kyles Ford, Tennessee, since the rapids are Class I or less. Many areas are bounded by national forest, and there are many small islands that can be camped on when there are no threats of heavy rain or flooding. Drinking water is uncertain, but there are occasionally nice springs to be found, if one looks for them. You should treat all water first to be safe.

In addition to the major access points listed for this long section, there are other roads on banks of the Clinch in Virginia and Tennessee. These roads will allow you to fine tune your put-ins/take-outs to fit the length of your trip. The map of this section shows these other access points.

The few rapids between Dungannon and Kyles Ford are mostly Class I cobble bars with an occasional ledge. However, this area is rich in scenic beauty and wildlife. For example, it is not unusual to see deer drinking from the river or to spot an osprey or unusual looking crane overhead. Also, just below Fort Blackmore (10 miles downstream from Dungannon) the Nature Conservancy has established a preserve at Pendleton Island. On and around this island are nine species of globally endangered and federally protected mussels (including the green-blossom pearl mussel) and 36 other mollusk species.

The access point at Fort Blackmore is on the south side (river left) of the highway (Route 619/72) to Gate City; you have a 100-yard carry across the floodplain. After you leave Fort Blackmore, the river continues its pastoral journey through an open valley with occasional cliffs. The fishing is good, and eventually you reach the next take-out at Clinchport, which is 14 miles below Fort Blackmore. You have two choices here: you can take out at the Virginia Game Commission public landing on river right or 1.5 miles downstream on river left at the mouth of Copper Creek (Route 627) under a spectacular, high railroad trestle.

Incidentally, do not worry if you notice two dams on the topo maps for this stretch (one 6 miles above and the other 2 miles below Clinchport). These are now gone, so breathe easy.

In the 23 miles between Clinchport and Kyles Ford the Clinch continues its placid pace. Perhaps the most interesting place on this stretch is The Rounds, about 5.5 miles after you cross the Virginia-Tennessee state line and 6.5 miles above Kyles Ford. The Rounds is a flask-shaped parcel of land that rises 300 feet but is only 100 yards wide at the neck of a 1.5 mile loop in the Clinch. There are rather steep cliffs around this parcel, thus creating 75 acres of well-protected land. The owner of The Rounds many years ago turned this naturally protected area into a game preserve by stocking a variety of game animals here. Just below The Rounds is a long, easy cobble rapid.

Another scenic aspect of this last section of the Clinch is Copper Ridge, which bounds most of the river's south side. Copper Ridge is a steep, tree-covered ridge rising up to 1,000 feet above the river. In the autumn, this ridge sports brilliant colors, making this an excellent stretch for a fall colors canoeing trip. What could be finer than a lovely river with blue skies and white, fluffy clouds above, and a continuous ridge ablaze with brilliant reds and yellows at your side. And then, there are the fallen, curled up leaves floating like little boats next to your canoe. This is the Clinch at its best!

After such an experience, it is almost a shame to continue down to Kyles Ford. The take-out here is at Kyles Ford Bridge on river right, or on roads on both sides of the river upstream at Wallens Bend.

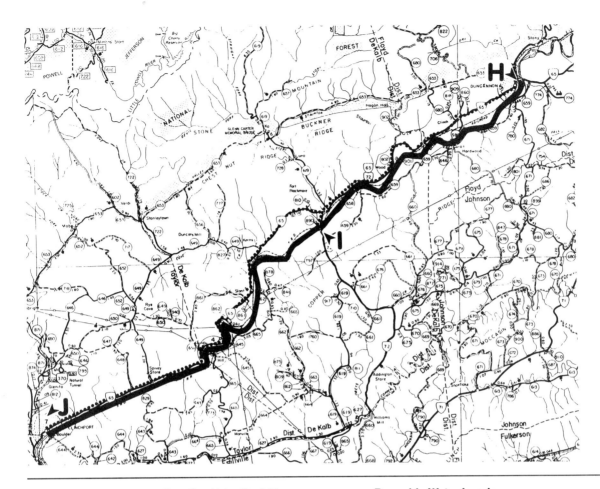

Section: Dungannon (near Rt. 65) to Kyles Ford, Tennessee (Rt. 70)

Counties: Scott and Lee (VA), and Hancock (TN)

USGS Quads: Dungannon, Fort Blackmore, Clinchport, Gate City, Duffield, Plumb Grove, Looneys Gap, Kyles Ford

Suitable for: Day cruising and especially camping

Skill Level: Novices and families

Months Runnable: Virtually the entire year, except after an extended drought

Interest Highlights: Pendelton Island Nature Preserve (rare mussels), The Rounds, wildlife, fishing

Scenery: Pretty to beautiful in spots

Difficulty: Class A–I

Average Width: 200 to 300 feet

Velocity: Slow to moderate

Gradient: 3 feet per mile

Runnable Water Levels:
Minimum: By inspection at access points
Maximum: Flood stage

Hazards: Maybe an occasional tree in river

Scouting: None

Portages: None

Rescue Index: Generally accessible

Source of Additional Information: None

Access Points	River Miles	Shuttle Miles
H–I	10	9
I–J	14	14
I–K	15.5	16
J–L	23	23

Access Point Ratings:
H–Dungannon (near Rt. 65), good
I–Fort Blackmore (Rt. 619/72), fair to good
J–Clinchport (Rt. 65), excellent
K–Copper Creek (Rt. 627), excellent
L–Kyles Ford (Rt. 70), very good

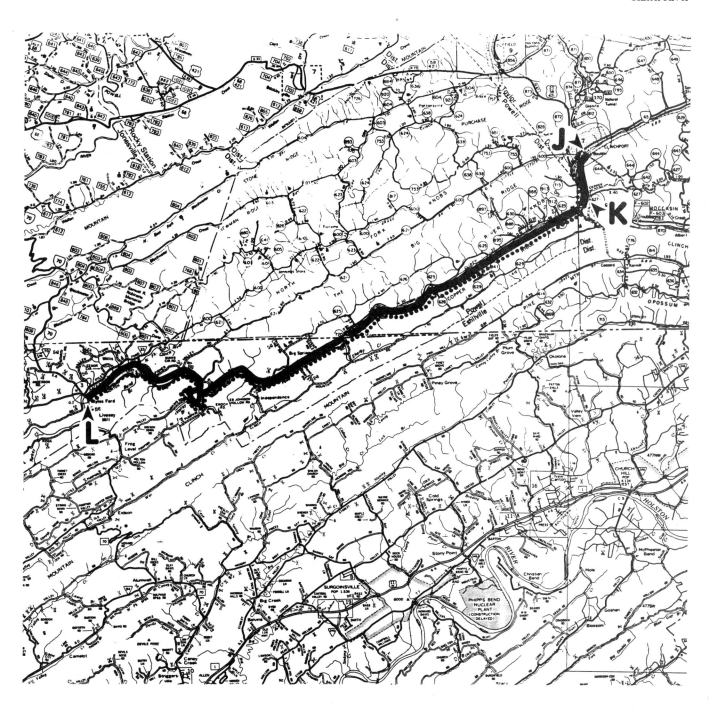

Copper Creek

Copper Creek lies in southwest Virginia and is a great trip for novices and relaxed intermediates. For the most part, this creek runs between the steep, knobby hills of Copper Ridge and Moccasin Ridge and flows west out of Russell County, through the length of Scott County, to its confluence with the Clinch River near Clinchport. This Class I–II creek is fairly narrow (25 to 30 feet) and is as crooked as a black snake as it twists along. Its classic meander typically produces 3 miles or more of creek for each mile of straight-line distance. Copper Creek flows through rocky woodlands and rocky farms. Often there are high bluffs and rocky ridges of Ordovician limestone on one or both sides of the creek. In some places the cliffs are over 500 feet high and quite colorful. The water quality is good. The only hazards are occasional trees in the river, an occasional barbed wire fence, and a 10-foot dam at Manville.

In 40 miles from Thompsons Ford to the Clinch River, the gradient of Copper Creek gradually decreases from 20 feet per mile to 5 feet per mile. The roughly first 20 miles of this stretch are characterized by 1-to 2-foot ledges spanning the entire creek. These create harmless hydraulics that offer playful challenges for paddlers who want to park in them sideways. In the remaining 20 miles Copper Creek flattens out and tends to be much deeper than the upper part.

There is very little canoe activity on Copper Creek. Consequently, reliable information about minimum and maximum water levels is not available. You probably need a third of a bankful for a minimum run, with a good half bankful for a comfortable trip. Nevertheless, Copper Creek is runnable fairly often—in the winter, spring, and after good rainy periods other times of the year.

The 40 miles of Copper Creek can be broken into five sections. The 6 miles beginning at Thompsons Ford (the junction of Routes 611 and 612) have numerous Class I–II ledges that can be boat scouted. The first section ends at Kilgore Fort on Route 71. The fort (also known as Dortens Fort) was built in 1789 by Robert Kilgore, an early settler in this area. Kilgore Fort was one of 12 forts between Castlewood and Cumberland Gap providing ready refuge for settlers from Indian attacks in the late eighteenth century.

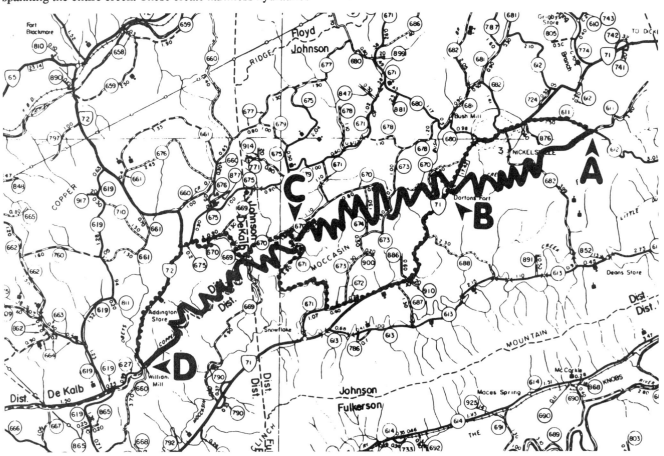

Section: Thompsons Ford (Jct. Rts. 611 and 612) to Clinch River (Rt. 627)

Counties: Scott

USGS Quads: Dungannon, Hilton, Gate City, Clinchport

Suitable for: Day cruising or overnight

Skill Level: Novices or laid-back intermediates

Months Runnable: Winter, spring, and rainy periods

Interest Highlights: Beautiful, high, sheer rocky cliffs, disappearing creek, tree-climbing turtles

Scenery: Pretty to beautiful in spots

Difficulty: Class I–II in first 28 miles; Class A–I in last 12 miles

Average Width: 25 to 30 feet

Velocity: Moderate to slow

Gradient: 20 feet per mile for first 6 miles; 15 feet per mile for next 10 miles; 10 feet per mile for next 12 miles; and 6 feet per mile for last 12 miles

Runnable Water Levels:
Minimum: No gauge; inspect from road; perhaps one-third bankful

Maximum: Flood stage

Hazards: Occasional trees in river, occasional barbed wire fence, low-head dam at Manville

Scouting: None

Portages: Low-head dam at Manville

Rescue Index: Accessible to remote

Source of Additional Information: None

Access Points	River Miles	Shuttle Miles
A–B	6.0	3.5
B–C	9.5	8.0
C–D	12.0	8.0
D–E	6.0	6.0
E–F	6.0	7.0

Access Point Ratings:
A–at Thompsons Ford (Jct. Rts. 611 and 612), good
B–at Kilgore Fort (Rt. 71), excellent
C–at Rt. 671, good
D–at Obeys Creek (Old Rt. 660/New Rt. 72), good
E–at Manville (Rt. 665), good
F–at Clinch River (Rt. 627), excellent

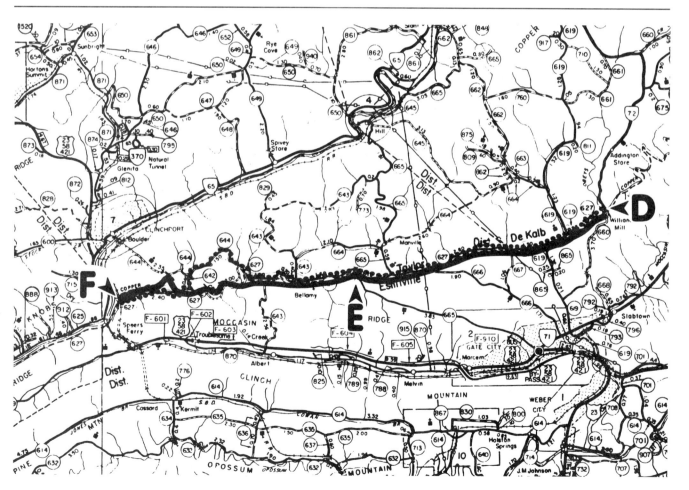

From Kilgore Fort to Snowflake Road, Copper Creek continues to wind its way through the limestone-dotted farms of Scott County, and the numerous small ledges continue. In this 9.5-mile second section there are a series of 180-degree turns at the base of high rocky bluffs.

The 12-mile third section from Route 671 to Obeys Creek is perhaps the most interesting. It starts out similarly to the upper two sections, but changes character just below the confluence with Valley Creek, about 3 miles below Route 671. Here there is a 100-yard Class II rock garden with some small ledges, which can be lots of fun at high water when it becomes a Class II–III drop.

After this rapid, a strange thing happens: the water in the creek decreases substantially! As you travel south for almost a half mile, over half of the creek flow disappears. What happens is that as Copper Creek makes a very narrow horseshoe bend, several underground caves pirate the water. After this half mile, Copper Creek regains its full flow, and just below Hale Spring Branch there is another good Class II rapid.

About 2 miles farther the creek flattens somewhat, and it is in this stretch that the famous tree-climbing Copper Creek turtles hang out. Here, many trees overhang the creek at low angles; this enables the turtles to climb well out and above the creek. Consequently, on a warm, sunny spring day, the paddler is likely to be welcomed by a domino line of turtles leaping 6 to 10 feet into the water, one by one, as the boat approaches. Some of these acrobatic turtles have even been known to bounce off flotation in canoes. Obviously, the remainder of this section is anticlimactic after such a display of terrapin daring.

The 12 miles from Obeys Creek to the Clinch River are basically flat and pastoral. This stretch is split into two equal 6-mile sections at Manville. You need to exercise care just above Manville where there is an old mill pond and low-head dam across the creek. This is just before you reach the Route 665 bridge. Portage the dam and its lethal hydraulic on the left. For the last 6 miles to the Clinch River the valley narrows, and Copper Creek moves along at a pleasant pace. The last take-out is on river left at the Clinch River and Route 627.

Chris Hipgrave running the last drop of the Streamers during the Sixth Annual Great Falls Race on the Potomac River in 1995. Photo by Emmy Truckenmiller.

Guest River

There is an old-timer's story of two "timber bucks" working in the Coeburn area who thought they would save time by floating their flat bottom boat down the Guest River into the Clinch River to get home. Unfortunately, neither they nor their boat made it.

Driving from Norton to Coeburn, Virginia, on Route 58, you would probably form the same opinion of the Guest—just a Class I–II stream flowing through pastures as it meanders along. But, when the Guest disappears from sight and begins its descent from Coeburn toward the Clinch River, it changes its whole personality. "Out of sight, out of mind" takes on a whole new definition: the river goes out of sight and you'll go out of your mind! You better have plenty of rocker in your boat and plenty of control in your paddling "stick" because you're going to need them both on this Class IV–V river.

The Guest River is a textbook example of how sandstone can make superlative whitewater rivers. Massive layers of hard Pennsylvanian sandstone are sandwiched between layers of coal, shale, and more sandstone to form the bulk of the rugged plateau country of Wise County, the land from which the Guest is born. After twisting through this plateau, the Guest leaves the high country to plunge

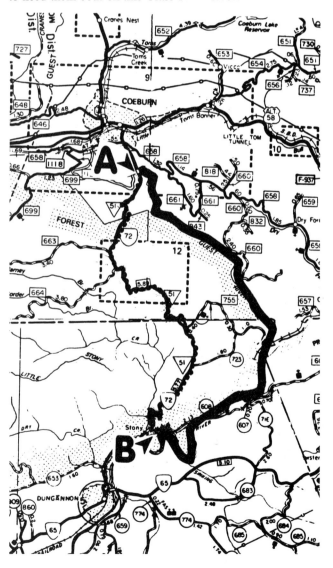

Section: Coeburn (Rt. 72) to Clinch River (Rt. 608 off Rt. 72)

Counties: Wise, Scott

USGS Quads: Coeburn, Dungannon

Suitable for: Day cruising

Skill Level: Experts only

Months Runnable: Winter and spring within a day of a moderate rain

Interest Highlights: Beautiful sandstone/rhododendron gorge, heavy duty rapids

Scenery: Generally beautiful to spectacular in spots

Difficulty: Class IV–V with 1 Class VI rapid

Average Width: 30 to 50 feet

Velocity: Fast

Gradient: 6 miles at 87 feet per mile, with 1 mile at 160 feet per mile

Runnable Water Levels:
  Minimum: 6 inches on the put-in (Rt. 72) gauge
  Maximum: 2 feet on the put-in gauge

Hazards: Trees in river; limited visibility; sharp, undercut rocks; hydraulics; tough rapids; high water

Scouting: Many rapids and blind drops

Portages: 1 Class VI rapid about a third of the way into the trip after slide drop on the left; maybe several lesser rapids; strainers

Rescue Index: Remote

Source of Additional Information: Run this river with someone who knows it: you'll be glad you did! Call Ron Arney (540) 395-6489

Access Points	River Miles	Shuttle Miles
A–B	8	12

Access Point Ratings:
  A—Coeburn (Rt. 72), very good
  B—at Clinch River (Rt. 608), very good

550 feet at a rate of nearly 90 feet per mile to the Clinch River upstream of Dungannon. It is this rugged decent through all that sandstone that is responsible for one of the most challenging and intense whitewater runs in Virginia.

The scenery is excellent as you paddle through a deep, colorful sandstone gorge, complete with waterfalls, thick forest, and rhododendron. You will have sufficient time to admire it with all the scouting that is necessary. Be sure to allow yourself plenty of time to get down this difficult run. There is also a railroad on river left, which can be very useful in terms of safety.

From the Route 72 bridge at the put-in the river is flat. However, about 1.5 miles downstream the river quickly picks up gradient. Huge, angular, and often undercut sandstone boulders suddenly clog the bed creating long, amazingly complex rapids with terrible downstream visibility. Three-foot slots, 4-to 8-foot ledges, blind drops (many blind drops), and undercut rocks soon become the order of the day. This creek is very technical; 1 mile of this section drops at 160 feet per mile and a half mile of it even reaches 200 feet per mile!

At one point, at least at low water, the boulders literally choke the channel forcing the entire flow to filter under them. Speaking of filters, the narrow rock channels easily snag trees and other debris, resulting in some nasty strainer situations. In addition to these deadfalls, there is at least one Class VI rapid roughly a third of the way down—after a slide drop on river left. Also, several other rapids are split by islands or boulders (or both), which can make scouting difficult if you don't know where to go. The rocks in this river are unusually ugly, many being undercut and many exhibiting sharp upstream facets commonly referred to in paddling jargon as "meat cleavers."

In addition to plunging over boulders, the Guest also drops over fascinating ledges, some sharp, some sloping—the latter with powerful hydraulics at the bottom.

The gradient is the steepest in the first few miles, but the remaining miles are still difficult and technical, with continuous rapids formed by rounded boulders and giant cobble bars until you near the Clinch.

Unlike many difficult rivers, the bare minimum is not the easiest level at which to tackle the Guest. Low water requires incredibly quick decisions in narrow channels with poor eddies. Despite the additional power, 6 inches of water does much to open up passages, pad boulders, and create more spacious and catchable eddies.

Due to the fast runoff in this region, it is best to catch the Guest within a day of moderate rain during winter or spring. Given this fact and the difficulty of this run, you really should get in touch with one of the local paddlers to ensure sufficient water and an "easier" trip down this challenging creek. Actually, local paddlers will probably get in touch with you, considering the speed at which this creek rises and falls.

There is a gauge painted on the river right bridge abutment where Route 72 crosses the river at the put-in. Comfortable runnable levels vary from 6 inches (scrapy and technical) to 2 feet (pushy but full). About 1.5 feet is an ideal level for expert paddlers making a first run.

A description of the rapids is useless because there are too many coming at you too fast and scouting of many is mandatory. Besides, there's nothing like being there! So, if you persist, and are ready to take a day off from work at the drop of a hat, you may get to run one of the best (if not the best) heavy duty creeks in The Old Dominion.

There are two possible take-outs which are both off Route 72. The first is along Route 608 on the Clinch. The second is a couple of miles upstream on Route 755 at the confluence of the Guest and the Clinch. However, Roger Corbett points out that you need to negotiate this Route 755 take-out with a landowner who has a couple of large, vicious dogs guarding his property.

North Fork of the Holston

The prime part of the North Fork of the Holston is the 8-mile stretch between aptly named Tumbling Creek and Hayters Gap. This is a Class I–II trip at moderate levels with a couple of Class IIIs thrown in for added interest. The fact that Route 611 parallels the right side of the river makes for a convenient shuttle and easy scouting of the two Class III drops. This section of the North Fork goes through a very narrow valley of Mississippian limestone. Consequently, Route 611 is your only real access to the river. On your right is Little Mountain, which is 1,000 feet above you, while on your left are lesser hills 500 feet high.

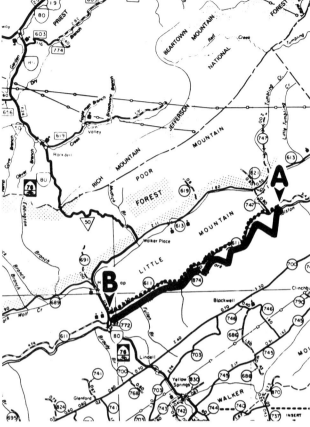

Section: Tumbling Creek (Jct. Rts. 611 and 747) to Hayters Gap (Rt. 611 or 80)

Counties: Washington

USGS Quads: Hayters Gap, Glade Spring

Suitable for: Day cruising

Skill Level: Carefully shepherded novices at moderate levels; intermediates

Months Runnable: Winter, spring, and early summer

Interest Highlights: Pretty, narrow valley

Scenery: Pretty to beautiful in spots

Difficulty: Class I–II with 2 Class III rapids

Average Width: 75 to 100 feet

Velocity: Generally moderate

Gradient: 11 feet per mile

Runnable Water Levels:
 Minimum: By inspection along Rt. 611
 Maximum: Maybe 2 to 3 feet of water in the river

Hazards: Occasional tree in river, Falls Hill Rapid

Scouting: Class III rapids on loop just below Tumbling Creek, Falls Hill Rapid (Class III), on river right/left

Portages: None, except perhaps Falls Hill Rapid

Rescue Index: Accessible

Source of Additional Information: None

Access Points	River Miles	Shuttle Miles
A–B	8	6.5

Access Point Ratings:
 A–at Tumbling Creek (Jct. Rts. 611 and 747), very good
 B–Hayters Gap, on Rt. 611 or 80, very good

Incidentally, the valley of the North Fork is between two valleys with very interesting names—Rich Valley to the north and Poor Valley to the south. Also noteworthy are several swinging bridges and fords that cross the river on this trip.

You probably could put in on Route 611 just above where Tumbling Creek enters the river, next to Route 747 on river right. If you do, you will have a mile long loop and will get to run a long, pleasant Class III, which you can see from Route 611. This long rock garden rapid is a right turn at the base of a rocky bluff and requires some technical moves.

Below that hopefully invigorating warm-up, the rapids are nicely spaced Class I–II drops for 5 miles or so until you reach Falls Hill Rapid. This tough Class III is the biggest drop of the trip and comes just below a trio of footbridges. Paddlers should first scout it from Route 611 on river right while running the shuttle; it is about 2.5 miles upstream of Route 80. Once on the river, you can scout this ledgy drop of 5 feet from river left, too. The toughest route over this bumpy stair-step is close to the right bank where most of the water flows. Set throw ropes below on river right.

For the last 3 miles to Route 80, the North Fork of the Holston resumes its easy Class I–II pace. You can take out on river right along either Route 611 or Route 80.

South Fork of the Holston

As mentioned earlier, one part of the tenderloin of the upper Tennessee drainage is the South Fork of the Holston. The best small section of the South Fork is the 6-mile stretch from the US 58 bridge near Damascus to well below Route 710 at the TVA campground on South Holston Lake.

Near the Drowning Ford Bridge (what a name for paddlers!) on US 58 is a put-in road to the river that also goes to the county dump on the river left side, upstream of the bridge. Just don't look too carefully at the stuff coming down a cement trough from the local sewage treatment plant as you carry your boat over the cobbles down to the river. If you don't like the smell and want 1.5 miles more of paddling with some Class I-II drops, you can put in upstream on Laurel Creek between Roetown and Vails Mill next to an abandoned mill dam.

The scenery on this short stretch immediately gets much better below US 58, with some very impressive bluffs both above the put-in and for the 3.5 miles down to Route 710. The rapids are Class I-II limestone cobble bars, rock gardens, and tiny ledges at moderate levels.

With a gradient of 20 feet per mile in the first 3 miles, this river moves right along.

You can take out at Route 710 in Alvarado, but you will miss a good Class II rock garden 300 yards downstream. Hard core paddlers can run this drop and carry back up to Route 710. Or, alternatively, you can continue downstream another 2.5 miles to Holston Lake Campground on river/lake left off Route 664. Although you have to paddle 2 miles on a lake, you will see pretty, 300-foot-high hills on your left below Alvarado. A mile before you reach the campground, the Middle Fork of the Holston enters on the right.

Incidentally, before South Holston Lake was created, the South Fork entered a gorge. This gorge and its impressive rapids are now covered during normal water levels.

The South Fork is also full of fish, primarily largemouth bass and sunfish. Because of the plentiful fish, there are numerous osprey as well as many wild ducks. As the weather warms up and the river drops, tubers also are active on this short section.

Santa takes a break before Christmas by running the Back Canyon of Fish Ladder channel down Great Falls on the Potomac River. Photo by Emmy Truckenmiller.

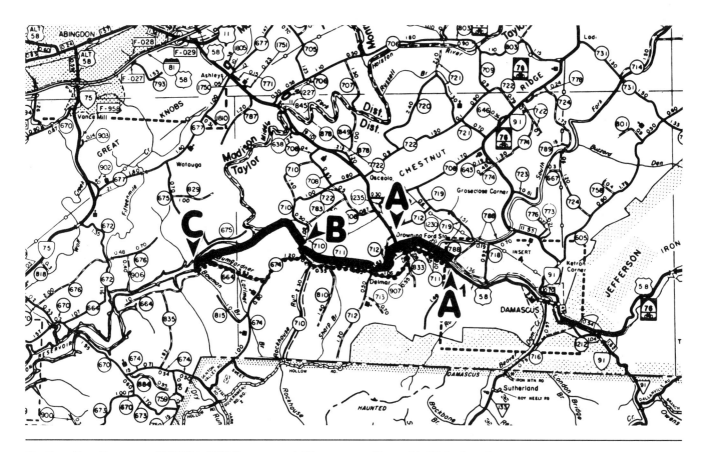

Section: Near Damascus (US 58) to TVA Campground (Rt. 664) on South Holston Lake

Counties: Washington

USGS Quads: Abington, Damascus

Suitable for: Day cruising

Skill Level: Novices

Months Runnable: Winter, spring, and early summer

Interest Highlights: Beautiful high bluffs, fishing

Scenery: Pretty to beautiful in spots

Difficulty: Class I–II

Average Width: 30 to 50 feet

Velocity: Moderate

Gradient: 20 feet per mile for first 3 miles below US 58; little gradient below Rt. 710 because of lake

Runnable Water Levels:

Minimum: No gauge; if runnable at put-in, should be runnable for entire trip

Maximum: Flood stage

Hazards: Maybe an occasional tree

Scouting: None

Portages: None

Rescue Index: Accessible to remote

Source of Additional Information: None

Access Points	River Miles	Shuttle Miles
A^1–B	5.0	5.0
A–B	3.5	3.5
A–C	6	5.5

Access Point Ratings:
A^1—on Laurel Creek (US 58) at Roetown, very good
A—near Damascus (US 58), good
B—at Rt. 710, good
C—at TVA Campground (Rt. 664), South Holston Lake, very good

Powell River

Norton to Big Stone Gap

The Powell River begins near Norton, Virginia, and drains the heavily mined area of southern Wise County. As it leaves Norton and begins winding its way toward Appalachia, Virginia, it becomes a beautiful little trout stream secluded by many fir trees and mountain laurel. Currently I know of no one who has ventured to paddle the 11-mile section of the Powell between Norton and Appalachia. However, anglers talk of some pretty 2-to 3-foot drops and rapids. On the other hand, there is reason to believe that there are downed trees across the river. This section is generally only 10 to 20 feet wide, and a heavy dose of rain or snowmelt is needed to raise it to paddling levels.

For the 3-mile stretch from Appalachia to the town of Big Stone Gap, the Powell widens for about a half mile when it leaves Appalachia and then narrows greatly as the bottom drops out and it flushes through the gap in the mountains between these two towns. As you drive south along US 23, which parallels the river, you will notice impressive ledges, a boulder-choked river, and (if there

has been a heavy rain) intense whitewater. Actually it's brownwater because the river here carries a heavy sediment load. Depending on nerve and water levels, you can put in at several places on this stretch. However, the best put-in is across from a coal preparation plant on the right side of US 23 for a 2-mile run to the "Town Bridge" (US 23/Alt. US 58) in Big Stone Gap. This short section is a favorite of local expert kayakers, and part of it reaches highly technical Class IV–V difficulty.

The heavy duty part of this 2-mile stretch can and should be scouted from US 23. The river changes character quickly as levels change and there can be deadfalls in the river. From the alternate coal plant put-in, the river runs through a Class II+ section with playful waves and holes. It then turns left and The Rapid begins. The Rapid is a three-quarter mile stretch of western-style whitewater, complete with large holes, fast chutes, and small eddies. Pick your landmarks when you scout, you'll need them on the river. At the end of The Rapid, the river splits into three channels that move left. The first channel has a strong river-wide hole, which can be run at moderate levels (up to 3.5 feet) on the Big Stone Gap bridge gauge. The second

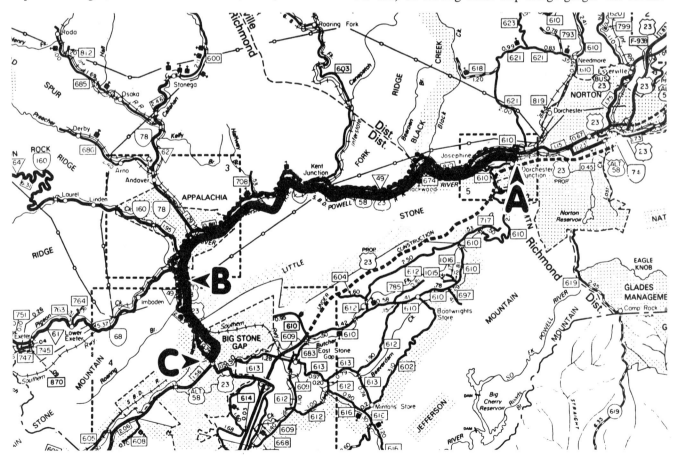

channel is usually trashy and should be avoided. The third channel is also trashy, but can usually be run. Scout these three channels carefully and pick your route before putting in. Then, boat scout from the river to be sure of your route.

Once through this section, the river rejoins and continues with low Class III rapids to the "Town Bridge" take-out in Big Stone Gap. The entire 2-mile run can be completed easily in 45 minutes. This includes a warm-up before The Rapid. So while you're here, you might as well do it at least twice: you might have fun the second time around.

Nearby terrain announces the severity of this section. A stream called Roaring Branch enters on the right, and the left bank is called Dark Hollow. Also, the gradient here is over 130 feet per mile, and the river is really pushy. Because The Rapid is so continuous and rocky, it is not the place for a swim.

As with the section above, you can paddle from Appalachia to Big Stone Gap only during snowmelt or following a few days of rain. There is a gauge on the river right side of "Town Bridge" in Big Stone Gap. This section is roughly runnable from 2.5 feet (moderately low) to 4.5 feet (jamming!). A good level is 3.5 feet.

This is generally decked boater territory. Bill Reynolds, a paddler who lives in Big Stone Gap, has only seen a canoe try it once. Two local fools ventured on this section during the flood of 1977. The flood did considerable damage to the towns as well as to their canoe. However, expert open boaters can scout from the road and make up their own minds.

Big Stone Gap to Dryden

If you put in at the "Town Bridge" in Big Stone Gap, you will have a mile of Class I–II paddling on the Powell before the South Fork joins it. Until you reach the confluence, however, the river is still not comfortably navigable except following a lengthy rain or period of snowmelt.

Consequently, in most cases it is better to put in below the confluence or at other urban spots at the west end of Big Stone Gap near the confluence. Here the river is 30 to 50 feet wide and the South Fork provides enough water so the trip downstream can be made almost any time during the year.

In the 12 miles from Big Stone Gap to Dryden the Powell River winds its way through picturesque farmland with scenic views of distant mountains on both sides. The

Section: Norton (US 23/Alt. US 58) to Big Stone Gap (US 23/Alt. US 58)

Counties: Wise

USGS Quads: Norton, Appalachia, Big Stone Gap

Suitable for: Day cruising

Skill Level: Intermediates first 11 miles; advanced/expert last 3 miles

Months Runnable: Winter and spring after heavy rain or snowmelt

Interest Highlights: Upper part, trout stream; lower part, Big Stone Gap through mountains

Scenery: Fair to beautiful in spots

Difficulty: Class II–III in upper 11 miles; up to Class IV–V last 3 miles

Average Width: 10 to 40 feet

Velocity: Generally fast

Gradient: 35 feet per mile first 11 miles; 47 feet per mile last 3 miles, with three-quarters of a mile at up to 130 feet per mile

Runnable Water Levels:
  Minimum: 2.5 feet on "Town Bridge" (US 23/Alt. US 58) gauge in Big Stone Gap

Maximum: 4.5 feet on "Town Bridge" gauge in Big Stone Gap

Hazards: Occasional trees in river from Norton to Appalachia, hydraulics, pinning rocks and strainers between towns of Appalachia and Big Stone Gap; three-quarter-mile Class IV–V just before town of Big Stone Gap

Scouting: All of river from Norton to Big Stone Gap should be scouted, particularly the three-quarter-mile Class IV–V just before the town of Big Stone Gap

Portages: Occasional trees; maybe three-quarter mile Class IV–V stretch

Rescue Index: Accessible

Source of Additional Information: Town of Big Stone Gap (540) 523-0115

Access Points	River Miles	Shuttle Miles
A–B	11	10
B–C	3*	3

Access Point Ratings:
  A–at Norton (US 23/Alt. US 58), very good
  B–at Appalachia (US 23/Alt. US 58), very good
  C–at Big Stone Gap ("Town Bridge"—US 23/Alt. US 58), very good

*For a shorter 2-mile trip of just The Rapid, put in by a coal preparation plant on US 23

Section: Big Stone Gap (Alt. US 58 near confluence) to Dryden (Alt. US 58)

Counties: Wise, Lee

USGS Quads: Big Stone Gap, Keokee

Suitable for: Day cruising

Skill Level: Novices

Months Runnable: Most of year, except after extended dry spell

Interest Highlights: Picturesque farmland, scenic mountain views

Scenery: Fair to beautiful in spots

Difficulty: Class I–II

Average Width: 30 to 50 feet

Velocity: Moderate

Gradient: 5 feet per mile

Runnable Water Levels:
  Minimum: No gauge; check by inspection
  Maximum: No gauge; check by inspection

Hazards: Maybe an occasional tree in river

Scouting: None

Portages: None

Rescue Index: Generally accessible

Source of Additional Information: Town of Big Stone Gap (540) 523-0115

Access Points	River Miles	Shuttle Miles
D–E	12	11

Access Point Ratings:
  D–at Big Stone Gap (near confluence, Alt. US 58), good
  E–near Dryden (Alt. US 58), very good

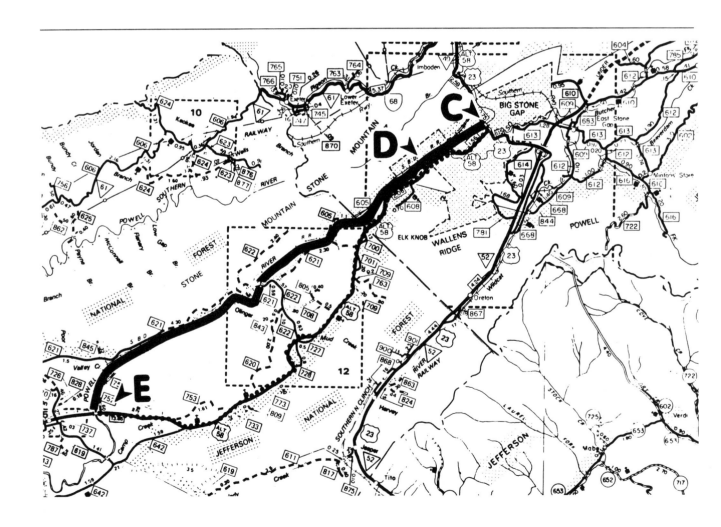

rapids are periodic Class I riffles. Water quality from Appalachia/Big Stone Gap to Dryden is poor, but your nose will become anesthetized if you concentrate on the scenery.

From Norton through Appalachia to Big Stone Gap, the Powell flows near US 23/Alt. US 58. After the "Town Bridge" in Big Stone Gap and several other access points, the major road following the Powell west to Dryden is Alt. US 58. Interestingly, this road is also known as The Trail of the Lonesome Pine. Once past the corporate limits on the western end of Big Stone Gap, one can access the river at the Route 605 bridge at Litton's Fabric Shop, at the Olinger Bridge on Route 622, and at the Dryden Bridge on Alt. US 58, just east of Dryden.

We are unfamiliar with the Powell west of Dryden, but believe it is similar to the stretch from Big Stone Gap to Dryden. The Powell eventually enters Norris Lake in Tennessee, so one probably could take a nice multi-day float camping trip down to the lake from Dryden.

Bill Hay with an exciting run of The Slot on Whitetop Laurel. Photo by Mayo Gravatt.

Whitetop Laurel Creek

Born at the confluence of Big and Little Laurel Creeks, Whitetop Laurel cascades down Whitetop Mountain (near Damascus, Virginia) in what can best be described as whitewater ecstasy. Characterized by some paddlers as the premier whitewater stream in southwest Virginia, its only drawbacks are a relatively short season and its distance from most paddlers (3.5 hours south of Roanoke). With an average gradient of about 72 feet per mile, Whitetop Laurel flows through intimate gorges of magnificent scenery, excellent water quality, and continuous rapids. Basically a Class III–IV run of 12 miles, Whitetop displays a broad spectrum of treats for the advanced boater: big ledges; steep, tricky rock and boulder gardens; some uncharacteristically big holes; and eddies and other play spots galore.

Another special treat for the boater as well as spectator is the Virginia Creeper. Although it winds around quite a bit, the Creeper is not the vine known to gardeners but is the remains of an old narrow gauge logging railroad that runs the entire length of Whitetop Laurel. The Forest Service maintains the area as a hiking and cross country ski trail, providing recreation for the nonboating crowd. The Creeper is also quite significant to boaters—not only as an

access route, but also because of the numerous railroad trestles crossing the stream, some at unusual angles to the river flow. These can provide some heart-stopping moments at higher levels.

Most trips on Whitetop Laurel begin at Creek Junction, just downstream of its confluence with Green Cove Creek and near the Appalachian Trail. Creek Junction is 1.5 miles from Route 58 on Route 728, a dirt road made from the old logging railroad. As you follow Route 728 for a mile to the Green Cove confluence, notice the beginning of Whitetop Laurel's first gorge. Not recommended for boating, this gorge contains falls of over 15 feet; tight, boulder-choked rapids; and strainers. The preferred Creek Junction put-in is a half mile further at the end of Route 728, where you'll also find suitable sites for primitive camping.

Soon after you put in here, the river goes under the first railroad trestle. About 150 yards downstream, the river bends slightly left. Before venturing farther, the boater should eddy out on river left, walk downstream, and scout The Slot, an 8-foot (Class IV+) drop. In low water it can be run center through the Class IV slot. Higher water allows a more difficult run over a turbulent S-turn (Class IV–V) on

Glenn Rose enjoying a typical drop on Whitetop Laurel. Photo by Doug Howell.

Section: Creek Junction (off Rt. 728) to east of Damascus (US 58)

Counties: Washington

USGS Quads: Whitetop Mountain, Grayson, Konnarock, Laurel Bloomery, Damascus

Suitable for: Day cruising

Skill Level: Advanced paddlers

Months Runnable: Winter and spring after heavy rains

Interest Highlights: 2 beautiful, intimate gorges; Virginia Creeper Trail; Mount Rogers National Recreation Area; Appalachian Trail

Scenery: Exceptionally beautiful to spectacular

Difficulty: Class III–IV with 3 Class IV and 1 Class V–VI rapids

Average Width: 20 to 40 feet

Velocity: Fast

Gradient: 72 feet per mile

Runnable Water Levels:
Minimum: See gauge at the railroad bridge at the take-out; also if the river is barely runnable at the take-out; South Fork of Holston gauge should be over 1200 cfs

Maximum: Maybe 1 or 2 feet on gauge; another indicator is if the river is easily runnable at the take-out

Hazards: The Slot (Class IV+), Big Rock Falls (Class V–VI), occasional fallen trees (particularly one place in second gorge where river braids)

Scouting: The Slot (Class IV+); the rapids below railroad trestle No. 8 (Class III+); Taylors Valley (Class IV); a high ledge (Class IV) and braided area somewhat below in second gorge; Big Rock Falls (Class V–VI)

Portages: Possibly The Slot (on left), definitely Big Rock Falls (on right)

Rescue Index: Remote

Source of Additional Information: Call Marc Raskin of the Coastal Canoeists (540) 947-5576; South Fork of Holston gauge at 1-800-238-2264 and then press 3 on touch tone phone

Access Points	River Miles	Shuttle Miles
A–B	12	15

Access Point Ratings:
A–at Creek Junction, a dirt road 2 miles off Rt. 728, good
B–at US 58 east of Damascus, very good

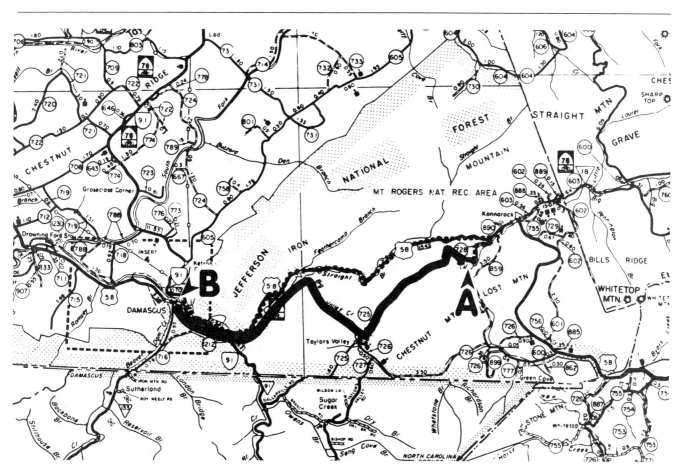

river left. For those not wishing to attempt this rapid, an easy carry and put-in below The Slot are available on river left.

For the next mile, the river is fairly narrow and creates some interesting holes. Good rapids continue, providing great fun. Not far below trestle number 8, the river picks up with a series of bigger rapids culminating in a 4-to 5-foot drop into an intimidating but benign hole. Just run this Class III+ drop down the center.

In a few more miles, the paddler will notice the gorge opening up and, as the river bends hard right, will see signs of civilization. This is Taylors Valley, and you are about to encounter the rapid of the same name (Class IV). You can't really see all of this rapid until you are in it, so be ready to scramble for an eddy, preferably on river right. At most levels, the best route is also along the right bank. Higher water opens up a left side run over a sloping diagonal ledge. On a recent trip someone had installed a log bridge across this rapid, so it would be wise to look before committing a group to run it. There are two road bridges in this valley. Immediately below the second one, on river right, is a pretty community wayside, perfect for a lunch stop. This marks the halfway point of the trip.

Leaving Taylors Valley, Whitetop enters its second gorge. The rapids are much like those before, only a little steeper. Another high ledge (Class IV) awaits a few miles downstream. Easily spotted, it can be run on river right in low water and left of center as the level gets higher. At low water this center route has nasty rocks at the bottom.

Somewhat below here, the river briefly braids around several islands, with some channels blocked by fallen trees. Look before you leap here! These islands are a significant landmark for the paddler: less than a mile beyond them, the river again is crossed by a railroad trestle. As you go underneath, quickly move to river right and catch an eddy above Big Rock Falls. Big Rock (Class V–VI) is a two-step drop of 10 to 12 feet. It has been run tight left by demented experts, but is better left alone. A mistake here could be costly. A fairly easy carry can be made on river right, where you'll find a piece of narrow gauge rail track to use as a ladder.

Just downstream, after about 10 miles, Whitetop finally comes back to the US 58 highway. The water in the remaining 2-mile stretch to the take-out is very deceptive, especially when viewed from the highway. It is turbulent with some very rambunctious holes that are best avoided at higher levels. The take-out is just below the third railroad trestle after the river comes to the road.

Below the recommended take-out, the river eases up considerably. It joins with the Tennessee Laurel at the US

58 intersection with Route 91, and becomes Laurel Creek. (Notice anything strange about all the creek names in this area?) Laurel Creek then travels through the town of Damascus on to its confluence with the South Fork of the Holston.

There is a gauge on the railroad bridge at the Whitetop Laurel take-out. However, its distance from most boaters still requires a long drive to ascertain whether there is sufficient water to run this stream. If there's been heavy rain or snowmelt in the spring, it's a good bet Whitetop will have water. It comes up easily but, unfortunately, goes down fast. Also, since it is one of the most popular trout streams in southwestern Virginia, late March and early April runs are to be avoided. Find out when fishing season opens to avoid an unfortunate experience. Call coastal canoeist Marc Raskin at (540) 947-5576 if you are planning a trip.

If the lucky boater comes to the area and finds water in Whitetop, there are several nearby streams to paddle as well. Head up Route 91 from its junction with US 58 and you immediately find Tennessee Laurel on your right. More difficult to catch with water than Whitetop, it is also steeper with a gradient of over 80 feet per mile. Scout from the road as you do; and put in as high up this Class III stream as you feel comfortable. However, just in Virginia near the state line be alert for Triple Drop (Class IV+).

For an easier trip, drive into Damascus and find your way to Backbone Rock State Park. The stream running along your right is Beaverdam Creek. Dropping 55 feet per mile, it is a fun Class III run. Just put in as far up this stream as your nerve and the water will allow. It has a few surprises to keep the boater awake. (For example, by Backbone Rock State Park the river runs underneath the highway—which you can scout on the shuttle.) Also available are numerous Class I–II runs on the Holston and its forks.

With some time, water, and topographic maps, the exploratory boater could spend several days exploring the creeks running out of the mountains around this area. However, if you can't wait for water, wait for winter, grab your cross country skis, and hit the Virginia Creeper Trail or the many other trails around Mount Rogers and Grayson Highlands State Park. In early spring there is a Maple Syrup Festival similar to that held near Back Creek and the Jackson River in Highland County to the north. This is a great place for hiking and backpacking, too.

Finally, the geology of Whitetop Laurel is quite interesting. From the put-in to Taylor Valley the bedrock is a purple pebbly glacial mudstone of the late Precambrian age. From Taylor Valley to Damascus the river rocks are younger Cambrian sandstone, siltstone and basalt.

Index of Virginia Rivers

Little	York	I-II (IV-V)	Cruising	42
Mattaponi	York	A	Cruising	44
Maury (upper)	James	III (IV)	Whitewater cruising	246
Maury (lower)	James	I-II (II-III)	Whitewater cruising	251
Merchants Millpond	Atlantic	A	Camping	25
Mill Creek	James	II-III	Whitewater cruising	254
Moormans	James	II-III	Whitewater cruising	256
New	New	I-II (III)	Cruising, camping, fishing	301
North	Shenandoah	II-III (III-IV)	Whitewater cruising	150
North Anna	York	I-II (III-IV)	Cruising	46
Northwest	Atlantic	A	Cruising	28
Nottoway	Chowan	I-II (II-III)	Camping	38
Ogle Creek	James	II (III)	Whitewater cruising	259
Pamunkey	York	A	Camping, fishing	48
Passage Creek (upper)	Shenandoah	I-II	Cruising, fishing	153
Passage Creek (lower)	Shenandoah	II-III	Whitewater cruising, fishing	156
Piney (upper)	James	III-V	Whitewater cruising	260
Piney (lower)	James	II-III	Whitewater cruising	261
Potomac (upper)	Potomac	I-II (II-III)	Camping, fishing	106
Potomac (middle)	Potomac	A-II (II-III)	Camping, fishing	113
Potomac (lower)	Potomac	II-III (VI) (III-IV)	Whitewater cruising	118
Potts Creek	James	I-II (III-IV)	Cruising, fishing	263
Powell (upper)	Tennessee	II-III (IV-V)	Whitewater cruising	340
Powell (lower)	Tennessee	I-II	Cruising	341
Rapidan (upper)	Rappahannock	I-II+ (III-IV)	Whitewater cruising	62
Rapidan (middle)	Rappahannock	A-I	Cruising, fishing	64
Rapidan (lower)	Rappahannock	I-II (II-III)	Cruising, fishing	66
Rappahannock (upper)	Rappahannock	I-III	Whitewater cruising	69
Rappahannock (middle)	Rappahannock	I-II (II-III)	Camping, fishing	76
Rappahannock (lower)	Rappahannock	I-III	Whitewater cruising	78
Rivanna	James	I-II	Camping, fishing	267
Roanoke/Staunton	Roanoke	I-II	Cruising, fishing	282
Robinson	Rappahannock	II (II-III)	Whitewater cruising	82
Rock Creek	Potomac	I-II (III)	Whitewater cruising	132
Rucker Run	James	II-III (III)	Whitewater cruising	271
Russell Fork	Big Sandy	IV-V++	Whitewater cruising	312
Shenandoah (upper)	Shenandoah	I-II	Camping, fishing	159
Shenandoah (lower)	Shenandoah	II-III	Whitewater cruising	162
Shenandoah North Fk.	Shenandoah	I-II (III)	Camping, fishing	168
Shenandoah South Fk.	Shenandoah	I-II	Camping, fishing	176
Slate	James	I-II	Cruising, fishing	273
Smith	Roanoke	I-II (III)	Whitewater cruising	285
South	Shenandoah	I-II (II-III)	Cruising	182
South Anna	York	I-II+	Whitewater cruising	51
Stony Creek	Shenandoah	II (II-III)	Whitewater cruising, fishing	185
Tearcoat Creek	Potomac	II-III	Whitewater cruising	135
Thornton	Rappahannock	II (III)	Whitewater cruising	85
Trout Run	Potomac	II-IV	Whitewater cruising	138
Tye (upper)	James	III-IV	Whitewater cruising	276
Tye (lower)	James	I-III	Whitewater cruising	278
West Neck Creek	Atlantic	A	Cruising	30
Whitetop Laurel	Tennessee	III-IV (V-VI)	Whitewater cruising	344

*Parentheses indicate a short section or individual rapids of higher difficulty on these stretches. See the river write-up for specifics.

Glossary

Blackwater Stream. A river with waters dyed a very dark reddish color by tannic acid from tree roots and rotting vegetation.

Bow. The front of a boat.

Broaching. A boat that is sideways to the current and usually out of control or pinned to an obstacle in the stream.

By-pass. A channel cut across a meander that creates an island or oxbow lake.

cfs. Cubic feet per second; an accurate method of expressing river flow in terms of flow and volume.

C-1. One-person, decked canoe equipped with a spray skirt, frequently mistaken for a kayak. The canoeist kneels in the boat and uses a single-bladed paddle.

C-2. A two-person, decked canoe, frequently mistaken for a two-person kayak.

Chute. A clear channel between obstructions that has faster current than the surrounding water.

Curler. A wave that curls or falls back on itself (up-stream).

Deadfalls. Trees that have fallen into the stream totally or partially obstructing it.

Decked boat. A completely enclosed canoe or kayak fitted with a spray skirt. When the boater is properly in place, this forms a nearly waterproof unit.

Downstream ferry. A technique for moving sideways in the current while facing downstream. Can also be done by "surfing" on a wave.

Downward erosion. The wearing away of the bottom of a stream by the current.

Drainage area. Officially defined as an area measured in a horizontal plane, enclosed by a topographic divide, from which direct surface runoff from precipitation normally drains by gravity into a stream above a specified point. In other words, this is an area that has provided the water on which you are paddling at any given time. Accordingly, the drainage area increases as you go downstream. The drainage basin of a river is expressed in square miles. (Also known as the "watershed.")

Drop. Paddler's term for gradient.

Eddy. The water behind an obstruction in the current or behind a river bend. The water may be relatively calm or boiling and will flow upstream.

Eddy line. The boundary at the edge of an eddy between two currents of different velocity and direction.

Eddy out. See Eddy turn.

Eddy turn. Maneuver used to move into an eddy from the downstream current.

Eskimo roll. The technique used to upright an overturned canoe or kayak by the occupant while remaining in the craft. This is done by coordinated body motion and made easier by proper use of the paddle.

Expert boater. A person with extensive experience and good judgment who is familiar with up-to-date boating techniques, practical hydrology, and proper safety practices. An expert boater never paddles alone and always uses the proper equipment.

Fall line. The line between the Piedmont and Coastal Plain where the land slopes sharply.

Falls. A portion of river where the water falls freely over a drop. This designation has nothing to do with hazard rating or difficulty. See Rapids.

Ferry. Moving sideways to the current facing either up- or downstream.

Flotation. Additional buoyant materials (air bags, styrofoam, inner tubes, etc.) placed in a boat to provide displacement of water and extra buoyancy in case of upset.

Grab loops. Loops (about 6 inches in diameter) of nylon rope or similar material attached to the bow and stern of a boat to facilitate rescue.

Gradient. The geographical drop of the river expressed in feet per mile.

Hair. Very difficult whitewater.

Haystack. A pyramid-shaped standing wave caused by deceleration of current from underwater resistance.

Headward erosion. The wearing away of the rock strata forming the base of ledges or waterfalls by the current.

Heavy water. Fast current and large waves usually associated with holes and boulders.

Hydraulic. General term for souse holes and backrollers where there is a hydraulic jump (powerful current differential) and strong reversal current.

K-1. One-person, decked kayak equipped with spray skirt. In this book, this category does not include nondecked kayaks. The kayaker sits in the boat with both feet extended forward. A double-bladed paddle is used.

Keeper. A souse hole or hydraulic with sufficient vacuum in its trough to hold an object (paddler, boat, log, etc.) that floats into it for an undetermined time. Extremely dangerous and to be avoided.

Lateral erosion. The wearing away of the sides or banks of a stream by the current.

Lead. The first boat in a group.

Ledge. The exposed edge of a rock stratum that acts as a low, natural dam or as a series of such dams.

Left bank. Left bank of river when facing downstream.

Lining. A compromise between portaging and running a rapids. By the use of a rope (line), a boat can be worked downstream from the shore.

Logjam. A jumbled tangle of fallen trees, branches, and sometimes debris that totally or partially obstructs a stream.

Low-water bridge. A bridge across the river that barely clears the surface of the water or may even be awash; very dangerous for the paddler if there is a fast current.

Meander. A large loop in a river's path through a wide floodplain.

PFD. Personal floatation device; e.g., life jacket.

Painter. A rope attached to the end of a craft.

Pillow. Bulge on surface created by underwater obstruction, usually a rock. Remember, these pillows are stuffed with rocks.

Pool. A section of water that is usually deep and quiet, frequently found below rapids and falls.

Rapids. Portion of a river where there is appreciable turbulence usually accompanied by obstacles. See Falls.

Riffles. Slight turbulence with or without a few rocks tossed in, usually Class I on the International Scale of River Difficulty.

Right bank. Right bank of river when facing downstream.

Rock garden. Rapids that have many exposed or partially submerged rocks necessitating intricate maneuvering or an occasional carry over shallow places.

Roller. Also curler or backroller; a wave that falls back on itself.

Scout. To look at rapids from the shore to decide whether or not to run them, or to facilitate selection of a suitable route through the rapids.

Section. A portion of river located between two points.

Shuttle. Movement of at least two vehicles, one to the take-out and one back to the put-in points. Used to avoid having to paddle back upstream at the end of a run.

Slide rapids. An elongated ledge that descends or slopes gently rather than abruptly, and is covered usually with only shallow water.

Souse hole. A wave at the bottom of a ledge that curls back on itself forming a hydraulic.

Spray skirt. A hemmed piece of waterproof material resembling a short skirt having an elastic hem fitting around the boater's waist and an elastic hem fitting around the cockpit rim of a decked boat.

Standing wave. A regular wave downstream of submerged rocks that does not move in relation to the riverbed (as opposed to a moving wave such as an ocean wave).

Stern. The back end of a boat.

Stopper. Any very heavy wave or turbulence that quickly impedes the downriver progress of a rapidly paddled boat.

Stretch. A portion of river located between two points.

Surfing wave. A very wide wave that is fairly steep. A good paddler can slide into it and either stay balanced on its upstream face or else travel back and forth across it much in the same manner as a surfer in the ocean.

Sweep. The last boat in a group.

Technical whitewater. Whitewater where the route is often not obvious and where maneuvering in the rapids is frequently required.

Thwart. Transverse braces from gunwale to gunwale.

Trim. The balance of a boat in the water. Paddler and duffel should be positioned so the waterline is even from bow to stern and the boat does not list to either side.

Undercut rock. A potentially dangerous situation where a large boulder has been eroded or undercut by water flow and could trap a paddler accidentally swept under it.

Upstream ferry. Similar to Downstream ferry except the paddler faces upstream. See also Surfing wave.

Appendices

Commercial Raft Trips and Expeditions

Several commercial raft outfitters operate in Virginia. All operate on whitewater streams of varying difficulty and most are reputable, safety conscious, and professional. There are, however, several companies that will rent rafts or other inflatables for use on rated whitewater to individuals who are totally ignorant and naive about the dangers involved. These companies normally do not run guided trips but rather send unsuspecting clients down the river on their own to cope with whatever problems or hazards materialize. Safe enjoyment of whitewater requres education and experience, and attempting to paddle whitewater in any type of craft, privately owned or rented, without the prerequisite skills or without on-river professional guidance is dangerous. That various companies will rent boats or rafts to the unknowing only proves that some people are unscrupulous, not that whitewater paddling is safe for the unaccompanied beginner.

All of the reputable raft companies throughout Virginia operate guided raft excursions only, where professional guides accompany and assist their clients throughout the run. This type of experience has an unparalleled safety record in the United States and represents an enjoyable and educational way of exposing the newcomer to this whitewater sport. Through professional outfitters, thousands of people every year are turned on to the exhilaration of paddling. Spouses and friends of paddlers, who are normally relegated to enjoying our beautiful rivers vicariously through the stories of their companions, are made welcome and provided the thrill of experiencing the tumbling cascades firsthand.

Choosing a commercial outfitter is made somewhat easier by America Outdoors, the professional organization for commercial river runners in the United States and Canada. Through its devotion to safety and its strict membership admission requirements, America Outdoors ensures that its member companies epitomize the highest standards in professional river outfitting. A directory of those outfitters can be obtained by writing to America Outdoors, P.O. Box 1348, Knoxville, TN 37901.

Where to Buy Maps

As indicated in the introductory material, maps used in this book are U.S. Geological Survey topographical quadrangle and county road maps. These maps can be purchased from the following locations:

United States

USGS Information Services
Box 25286
Denver, CO 80225

County Road Maps:

Virginia

Virginia Department of Transportation
Attn: Information Services
1221 East Broad Street
Richmond, VA 23219

Maryland

Map Distribution Sales
Maryland State Highway Administration
2323 West Joppa Road
Room 222
Brooklandville, MD 21022

North Carolina

North Carolina Department of Transportation
Division of Highways
Attn: Poe Cox
P.O. Box 25201
Raleigh, NC 27611

West Virginia

West Virginia Department of Highways
Planning Division, Map Sales
1900 Washington Street East
Charleston, WV 25305

About the Author

Ed Grove has enjoyed canoeing for over 40 years. In 1976 he became a hard-core whitewater buff after taking a course from Louis Matacia, a legendary Virginia paddler. Having graduated from Stanford University in the dark ages with two degrees in International Relations, Ed spent most of his career working for the Department of State in Washington, D.C. A fortuitous job change in 1984 allowed him to spend more time with his family and to write this book. Ed lives with his wife Carol in Arlington, Virginia, and has two sons (Greg and Grant).

Paddling is only one facet of his deep and abiding love for the outdoors. Those who look carefully may find Ed wandering the hills of Virginia in an aging van with a beat-up red canoe on top—looking for yet another classic Virginia river to savor. He is the principal co-author of *Appalachian Whitewater, Volume II, The Central Mountains*, published by Menasha Ridge Press, and the author of numerous articles in *Canoe* and *Paddler* magazines.

An American Gothic portrait of the author—Solo Canoeing Version.
Photo by Grant Grove.